The Mark J. Millard Architectural Collection

Volume II

British Books, Seventeenth through Nineteenth Centuries

Nº IV.
Pl. V.
Cornice & Base of the
Attic over the Columns.
Corniche et Base de
l'Attique au dessus
des Colonnes.
Ionic Order of the Anti-room
with the Profile of the Capital.
Ordre Ionique de l'Antichambre
avec le profil du Chapiteau.
pital for the Pilasters behind the Columns.
apiteau pour les Pilastres derrière les Colonnes.
Part of one of the Doors of the Anti-room.
Partie d'une des Portes de l'Antichambre.
Profile of the Truss.
Profil de la Console.
Base & Surbase of
the Anti-room.
Surbase et Base
de l'Antichambre.
Scale of
3 Feet.
Eques J. B. Piranesi incidit Romæ

The Mark J. Millard Architectural Collection

Volume II

British Books

Seventeenth through Nineteenth Centuries

Catalogue entries
Robin Middleton
Gerald Beasley
Nicholas Savage
with
Jonathan Franklin
Eileen Harris
Paul W. Nash
Alison Shell

Bibliographic descriptions
Claire Baines
Gerald Beasley

National Gallery of Art • Washington
George Braziller • New York

Editor-in-chief, Frances P. Smyth
Senior editor and manager of the Millard project, Mary Yakush
Production manager, Chris Vogel
Editor, Millard project, Katherine Whann

Edited by Susan Higman, with Nancy Eickel
Index by Edward Tingley and Gerald Beasley
Typeset in Adobe Caslon by G & S Typesetting, Austin, Texas
Printed by Hull Printing, Meriden, Connecticut, on Mohawk Superfine text
Designed by Roland Hoover and Tom Suzuki
Layout and Production by Kristin Bernhart

Library of Congress Cataloging-in-Publication Data
Middleton, Robin; Beasley, Gerald; Savage, Nicholas
The Mark J. Millard architectural collection
p. cm
ISBN 0-8076-1432-7
Includes bibliographical references and index.
Contents: v. 1. British books, seventeenth through nineteenth centuries.
1. Architecture–Britain–Bibliography–Catalogs. 2. Architecture, Modern–Britain–Bibliography–Catalogs. 3. Millard, Mark J. – Library–Catalogs 4. National Gallery of Art (U.S.) Library–Catalogs. I. Beasley, Gerald.
II. Title.
Z5944.F7W54 1993
[NA1044]
016.72'094–dc20 93-4308
CIP

The entry for cat. 3, William Adam's *Vitruvius Scoticus*, was first published in volume 1, Royal Institute of British Architects, *Early Printed Books 1478-1840: Catalogue of British Architectural Library Early Imprints Collection* (London, 1994). It is published here, with minor alterations, by kind permission of Bowker-Saur.

The entry for cat. 81, James Stuart and Nicholas Revett, *The Antiquities of Athens*, was first published in Eileen Harris and Nicholas Savage, *British Architectural Books and Writers 1556-1785* (Cambridge, 1990), no. 857, 439–449. It is published here by kind permission of the authors.

COVER: Cat. 22. James Gibbs. *A Book of Architecture, Containing Designs of Buildings.* "A perspective view of St. Martins' Church." 1985.61.582

FRONTISPIECE: Cat. 2. Robert and James Adam. *The Works in Architecture of Robert and James Adam, Esquires.* "Ionic order of the anti-room with the profile of the capital." 1985.61.142

FRONT ENDPAPER : Cat. 66. Humphry Repton. *Designs for the Pavillon at Brighton.* "West-front of the pavillon." 1985.61.2643
BACK ENDPAPER : Cat. 96. Christopher Wren. *A Catalogue of the Churches of the City of London.* "View of the wooden model of St. Paul's Cathedral, 'according to the first design of the architect'." 1985.61.2769

Contents

Foreword

To its expanding list of scholarly books on the collection, the National Gallery is delighted to add this second volume in the Mark J. Millard architectural series, cataloguing almost one hundred books published in Britain from the seventeenth through nineteenth centuries.

Robin Middleton and Nicholas Savage contributed more than half of the catalogue entries, writing on the big books recording the archaeological investigations of antiquity, topographical surveys and views, and especially upon the great folio volumes of the eighteenth century in which the architecture of Britain was recorded. These are among the many strengths of the Millard Collection. In the catalogue entries as well as the bibliographical descriptions, our authors have not only documented the structure and editions of the books, but also identified the artists, designers, and engravers, and discussed the historical and artistic contexts as well as the theoretical and practical contributions of these books, extraordinary works of art in their own right. Claire Baines accomplished the bibliographical research for much of this volume. Gerald Beasley completed the task, writing approximately one-fourth of the bibliographical descriptions and editing all of them in the final form in which they are published here. He also wrote catalogue entries, as did Jonathan Franklin, Eileen Harris, Paul W. Nash, and Alison Shell. We thank all of these scholars for the enlightening contributions each has made.

The authors would like to acknowledge their debt to the research published in 1990 in *British Architectural Books and Writers 1556–1785*, by Eileen Harris and Nicholas Savage, a comprehensive study that has provided both a source of inspiration and a high standard of scholarship. In addition, thanks are owed to: Elizabeth Fairman, Yale Center for British Art, New Haven; Hugh Pagan; Susan Palmer and Margaret Richardson of Sir John Soane's Museum, London; Helen Powell, assistant librarian at Queen's College, Oxford; Henry Raine, Folger Library, Washington; Carl Vuncannon of the Furniture Library, High Point, North Carolina; the Canadian Centre for Architecture, Montreal; and the Royal Institute of British Architects, London.

Many individuals at the National Gallery contributed time and expertise to this catalogue. We are especially grateful to Andrew Robison, whose association with the Millard Collection began in 1981, and also Virginia Clayton, in the department of prints, drawings, and photographs; in the library, Neal Turtell and Marsha Spieth; in the department of visual services, Dean Beasom, Lee Ewing, and the late Barbara Chabrowe; and in the editors office, Frances Smyth, Mary Yakush, Chris Vogel, Susan Higman, Katherine Whann, and Nancy Eickel. We are grateful to Roland Hoover and Tom Suzuki for the elegant design.

Our greatest thanks are owed to the late Mark Millard for his connoisseurship and energy in building this collection, and for his generosity in ensuring that it would come to the National Gallery. Our gratitude is offered also to Mark's widow, Liselotte, who continues to support the purchase of additional volumes for the collection. These include—just in the British field—one of the finest surviving copies of the great mid–nineteenth-century lithographic tour de force, Owen Jones' *Grammar of Ornament*, 1856, in an original Jones-designed binding. Thus, Mark Millard's collection is a major resource for visitors to the National Gallery, one that continues to live through exhibitions, study, and publications as well as through further acquisitions.

Earl A. Powell III
Director

Introduction

Among the almost one hundred British books in the Mark J. Millard Architectural Collection are several titles from the seventeenth century, about three-quarters from the eighteenth century, and one quarter from the nineteenth century. The collection is not focused on aesthetic theory, practical handbooks and "cottage books," or gardening, but upon the great folio volumes in which the architecture of Britain was recorded in the eighteenth century—the works of William and of Robert and James Adam, of Matthew Brettingham, Colen Campbell, James Gibbs, William Kent, James Paine, George Richardson, John Soane, John Vardy, and John Woolfe and James Gandon. This is a noble array, and to reenforce it is a group of significant topographical surveys—David Loggan's views of both Oxford (1675; cat. 39) and Cambridge (1688; cat. 40), both William Watts and William Angus' *Seats of the Nobility and Gentry* (c. 1779 and 1787; cats. 89 and 7), and John Neale's *Views of the Seats of Noblemen and Gentlemen* (1818–1829; cat. 45). The views by Leonard Knyff and Johannes Kip are not represented here. Imaginatively, though, architecture has been considered in relation to its internal adornment and use. All the large folios of the furniture makers of the eighteenth century are included—those of Thomas Johnson (1761; cat. 33), Thomas Chippendale (1762; cat. 15), William Ince and John Mayhew (1762; cat. 32), Thomas Sheraton (1793; cat. 75), and Alice Hepplewhite (1794; cat. 30). To further enhance understanding of the form of late eighteenth- and early nineteenth-century architecture are almost all the big books recording archaeological investigations of the architecture of antiquity, to serve as the basis for a refinement of the classical style. Here are the ruins of Palmyra (1753; cat. 92) and of Balbec (1757; cat. 93), the antiquities of Athens (from 1762 onward; cat. 81), the palace at Spalatro (1764; cat. 1), the temples of Paestum (1768; cat. 41), the antiquities of Ionia (in the second edition of volume one, of 1821, and the first edition of volume two, of 1798; cat. 80) and of Attica (1817; cat. 79). These works represent a significantly British contribution to the interpretation of the past. It is notable that Eileen Harris' entry on James Stuart and Nicholas Revett's *Antiquities of Athens* lays emphasis on British notions of proper procedure in the celebrated quarrel that arose with Julien-David Leroy as to archaeological aims. The British, as Robert Adam was the first to observe, sharply, valued above all else precision of observation and measurement—the Palmyra plates, he noted, were "as hard as iron and as false as hell"—the aim being to provide models and exemplars for imitation. Leroy, who certainly intended to win the honors of Athens for France when (two years before the appearance of the first volume of the *Antiquities of Athens*) he rushed *Les ruines des plus beaux monuments de la Grèce* into print in 1758 (Millard, vol. I, cat. 101), and who was indeed guilty of mistakes and misrepresentation, has nonetheless been judged far too harshly by British commentators. When he responded to Stuart's taunts in the second edition of *Les ruines*, of 1770, he indicated something of the French interest in the investigation of the remains of the past—"je n'aurois sûrement pas eté dans la Grèce, simplement pour observer le rapport des édifices et de leurs parties avec les divisions de notre pied" (preface, p. vi). Mere measurement was of secondary concern. There was no thought, whatsoever, of copying the forms and the details of classical architecture, no revivalist aim, rather a deep desire to attain to something of the essential spirit of the classical past. This is at once in evidence if one turns to those great monuments of archaeological exegesis to appear in France in the late eighteenth century—Jean Claude Richard de Saint-Non's *Voyage pittoresque; ou description des royaumes de Naples et de la Sicile* (Millard, vol. I, cat. 148), issued between 1778 and 1786, Jean Houel's *Voyage pittoresque des isles de Sicile, de Malte et de Lipari* (Millard, vol. I, cat. 80), of 1782 to 1787, and the comte de Choiseul-Gouffier's *Voyage pittoresque de la Grèce* (Millard, vol. I, cat. 51) of 1782 and 1809. These, like Leroy's work, are invariably condescended to by British critics, as mere scenic surveys, jumbling together the past and the present, architecture and costumes, agriculture and customs, whereas they represent, in fact, a very serious effort to investigate history through a survival of the past in the present. Their authors hoped thereby to discern something of the quality and distinction of antiquity, and its architecture in particular. They sought the spirit, not the form.

Big books—that is, books intended for the gentleman-amateur's library rather than the architect's office or builder's workshop—are the distinguishing feature of the Millard Collection. Although they comprise only one part of eighteenth-century architectural literature as a whole, they do reveal, in England especially, a sensitivity concerning properly *architectural* representation of buildings. This is not merely a reflection of, but rather an active determinant within, that complex expression of architectural taste through printed media that is so characteristic of the period.

The intellectual recovery of the theory and practice of classical architecture in the sixteenth century had been pursued, like that of other lost arts and sciences, primarily through the medium of written treatises that were supported but not propelled by illustration. This pursuit took place in countries at some remove from the epicenters of the Renaissance. Yet it was the representation of real and imagined architecture in printed images, typically of the classical orders and their application, that transmitted the new style further afield, in a way that tended to "leave behind" the humanist texts that these images were originally intended to illustrate. Untrammeled by the need to refer to classical precedent or theoretical argument, architectural imagery acquired an independent life, first in Dutch, Flemish, and German engraved pattern books, full of wild mannerist and baroque distortions of classical motifs, and later in pompous folios of engravings produced for the monarchs and princes of Europe, that showed buildings not as they really were but as artists were paid to imagine them to be.

The birth and development in eighteenth-century England of an indigenous architectural literature was marked above all else by efforts to counter what were perceived as the negative aspects of the continental influence. At the risk of gross over-simplification, these efforts can be categorized as three distinct but related projects. First, by purging from the representation of architecture all traces of the local and contingent—that is, setting, staffage, weather and lighting conditions, materials, visual effects—it would be possible to form judgments concerning architectural designs that were undistracted by considerations of the actual state, locality, or historical or current associations of particular buildings. Second, by memorializing the designs of Inigo Jones, the founding father of classical architecture in Britain, a national antidote could be found to cauterize the corruption of antique simplicity found in books promulgating the characteristic forms of the Italian Baroque (such as G. G. de Rossi's *Insignium Romae Templorum Prospectus* [1684] and Domenico de Rossi's *Studio d'Architettura Civile* [1702; both Millard Collection]). Third, by publishing highly detailed, measured reconstructions of antique remains, based on in-situ surveys rather than reinterpretations of second-hand sources, British artists would gain the advantage over their continental rivals of being able to approach nearer to the clear wellsprings of classical example.

It is thus no coincidence that the first book to proclaim the complete naturalization of classical architecture in Britain—Colen Campbell's *Vitruvius Britannicus* (1715–1725; cat. 10)—was also the first to segregate orthogonal representations from other depictions of buildings. In this way, their relative architectural merits and faults could be compared in purely graphic terms, without recourse to theoretical reasoning or justification. Campbell's decision to banish perspectives, bird's-eye views, and garden plans reveals a precise awareness of their respective functions and associations, and how these would have distracted from the force of the visual argument he wished to sustain. By artificially restricting the graphic means at his disposal he also, paradoxically, heightened their impact and thereby promoted among a lay British public an architect's, as opposed to an artist's or topographer's, vision of architectural reality. As the first book published by a professional architect in Britain, *Vitruvius Britannicus* laid the foundations of an entirely new genre, drawing for the first time a clear line between architectural and topographical/antiquarian concerns. That distinction was made immediately apparent not only through differing modes of representation, but also through the skillful juxtaposition and selection of designs. In the process, the humble, discredited pattern book was elevated to a kind of visual treatise that could proclaim the architectural credit due to the English nation, in much the same way as successive architectural treatises proclaimed the intellectual debt owed throughout Europe to France and Italy.

The lead given by *Vitruvius Britannicus* and its highly effective promotion of Inigo Jones as Britain's own Palladio, was by no means lost on other British architects, including, most notably, James Gibbs, who had been quite unjustly excluded by Campbell. Thus in spite of his training in Italy under Carlo Fontana, Gibbs was careful to publish his designs in the spare English manner of presentation, allowing himself no more than three perspectives among the 150 plates in *A Book of Architecture* (1728; cat. 22). Much the same is true of Kent's *Designs of Inigo Jones* (1727; cat. 34), which includes not a single perspective. Although Henry Hulsbergh had for the most part engraved the coldly orthogonal plates, they had first been painstakingly redrawn by Henry Flitcroft, Lord Burlington's favorite draftsman, from Jones' infinitely more subtle and feeling originals. Such narrow concentration on the formal qualities of architectural designs had its price. Above all, it imposed an artificial restriction upon an architect's ability to draw attention to other qualities in buildings relating to site, use, optical effects, lighting, space and volume, constructional techniques, and materials. All this is evident in a work such as Isaac Ware's *Plans... of Houghton* (1735; cat. 88)—incidentally the first English monograph devoted to a single classical building. Although loosely modeled on earlier French examples of the genre, such as Jean Marot's *Le magnifique chasteau de Richelieu* (c. 1660; Millard, vol. I, cat. 115) and J. Hardouin Mansart's *Livre...du chasteau de Clagny* (1680), we are given very much less visual information than Lepautre, Marot, or Silvestre had included in their engravings of the "maisons royales" for the "Cabinet du Roi." Ware does include a perspective view of the west front of the house, but it is noticeable how idealized this is when compared to the realistic countryside in which the elevations and sections of Clagny are set. Ware's inclusion of decorative architectural fragments in the foreground of the view hints at this idealization as does, even more remarkably, the unusual representation of Houghton's ground plan in corresponding perspective in the lower half of the sheet. (The clear implication here is that the view has been accurately set up and developed from the architect's plan, rather than drawn from nature.) It is instructive also to find that, for all their handsome detail and larger scale, the sections of Houghton contain less information about the house's construction, the materials used, or the nature of the site than Michel Hardouin's quite modest engraving of the "Coupe du Grand Sallon" at Clagny. Another telling difference between these two books is that, while the plans of Clagny record the use of every apartment, down to the smallest office on every floor, those of Houghton identify not a single room by name or function. Even as late as the mid-1760s, the potency of the *Vitruvius Britannicus* model, with its tight architectural focus, seems to have lost little force. For example, neither John Woolfe and James Gandon's continuation of Campbell's work (1765–1771; cat. 94), nor Matthew Brettingham's *Plans, Elevations and Sections of Holkham* (1761; cat. 8) included a single perspective of the houses and other buildings that they celebrated.

It is very remarkable indeed that we are given so little idea from their depiction in these books about where, how, or for what purpose these buildings were actually built. As early as the 1740s, printsellers such as John Boydell and artists such as Thomas Smith of Derby had been busy exploiting an ever growing market for naturalistic views of British topography, including of course the gentlemen's seats, parks, gardens, and great aristocratic houses of a particular region. The first real indication in English architectural engraving of a new susceptibility to the particular qualities of a place seems to occur in Sir William Chambers' *Designs of Chinese Buildings* (1757; cat. 12). Chambers' book was an effort to locate the principles of landscape gardening in Chinese practice. The subject was perhaps sufficiently *outré* to permit its author a more innovative approach to the traditional problems of architectural representation. The evidence for this claim resides in the two plates of a typical Cantonese merchant's house contributed by Edward Rooker, who was to become the leading architectural engraver of his generation, namely a section "thrown into perspective" (pl. IX), and two interior wall elevations showing the arrangement of furniture, fittings, and utensils (pl. X, figs. 1 and 2). Not only do both these plates employ techniques of presentation that are without precedent in any earlier English publication, but they were etched by Rooker in an entirely new manner, quite different from that used by Paul Fourdrinier for the other architectural subjects in the same book. The distinctive feature of Rooker's new style is its capacity to bathe orthogonal drawings of architecture in an airy, naturalistic light. The effect achieved through subtle and potentially infinite variations in the thickness and spacing of horizontal or vertical etched lines does not interfere with the clarity or precision with which architectural forms are depicted.

This technique represented a significant advance on the system of graphic notation first perfected by Henry Hulsbergh and Paul Fourdrinier more than thirty years earlier. In their engravings the architect's stylized use of monochrome washes, to register correctly the relative advance and recession of architectural elements shown in elevation or section, is translated into a fixed number of tonal values by means of cross- and/or diagonal hatching, flecking, or some other method of shading derived from the line engraver's repertoire.

How Rooker hit upon his new manner is not known. His earlier work in Abraham Swan's *The British Architect* (1745) and James Paine's *Plans...of the Mansion-House...of Doncaster* (1751) had conformed to the Hulsbergh/ Fourdrinier system. The view of the Parthenon that Rooker etched in a freehand style for Richard Dalton's poorly received series of "Twenty-one Prints of the Antiquities of Athens," which was published without a title in April 1751, may however have set him thinking about a way of combining accuracy of architectural draftsmanship with pictorial effect. It is also probably not coincidental that the architectural plates etched at around this time by the architects Pierre Patte and J. F. de Neufforge for Le Roy's *Les ruines des plus beaux monuments de la Grèce* (1758) show a very similar development in technique. Much more significant, however, than where or how Rooker derived his new technique—which was very quickly adopted as more or less standard for orthogonal engravings from the mid-1760s—is the way it clearly met a new pressure for such representations to act as something more than diagrams. Through a careful depiction of shadows and shading, in particular, it expressed not only the conceptual form but also the perceptual impact of an architectural design. It is misleading therefore to think of this development simply in terms of Rooker's personal graphic style, just as it is wrong to see the limitations of Hulsbergh and Fourdrinier's method simply as a corollary of their particular abilities as engravers. Fourdrinier, for instance, was perfectly capable of etching architecture in a much looser, impressionistic manner, as can be seen from the topographical views of classical ruins that he engraved for the continuation of John Breval's *Remarks on Several Parts of Europe* (1738).

The plates by Fourdrinier in Breval's volume show the ruins of temples at Agrigentum and Selinunte apparently dissolving before one's eyes in the powerful Sicilian sun. They are a salutary reminder, before one turns to the cold precision of the architectural details that he engraved for Robert Wood's *Ruins of Palmyra* (1753; cat.

92) and *Les Ruines de Balbec* (1757; cat. 93), that an essentially pictorial tradition of architectural engraving continued to flourish in English antiquarian and topographical literature—alongside the purely orthogonal subspecies that had evolved from *Vitruvius Britannicus*. Wood's achievement was remarkable not simply because he reintroduced into classical archaeology the high standards of architectural draftsmanship pioneered by Antoine Desgodetz in *Les Edifices Antiques de Rome* (1682; Millard, vol. I, cat. 62). Unlike Desgodetz, he combined this in the same work with impressive topographical views of the sites he described. As a result Borra's on-the-spot panoramas of the ruins of the cities of Palmyra and Balbec have a contradictory ambiguous function, offering in the same image both crucial archaeological evidence for their present state, and an artist's evocation of the ruined splendors of classical antiquity. Two diametrically opposed ways of trying to resolve this contradiction lie at the heart of the great English archaeological books produced in the 1750s and 1760s by Robert Wood, Stuart and Revett, Robert Adam, Thomas Major, and under the auspices of the Society of Dilettanti. One way was to lay ever greater stress on the accuracy of the engraved and written account of an author's first-hand experience of the sites and buildings he had surveyed—hence Wood's insistence that "the principal merit of works of this kind is truth." The other way, however, was to derive the necessary authenticity of the records given of this experience from the unique sensations that it aroused in the artist/observer, whose particular and unmediated response could become therefore a means of infusing the spirit of antiquity into the present, rather than a mere tool for recording and copying its physical remains. If the first route corresponds to that adopted by Robert Wood, the second was most assuredly the terrain of Robert Adam. It formed the ground for that genuine mutual regard that sprang up between Adam and Gimabattista Piranesi, the greatest living exponent of what might be called the art of passionate archaeology.

The influence of Piranesi's unique manner of depicting architecture is manifest throughout the Adams' *Works in Architecture* (2 volumes, 1778–1786; cat. 2)—so much so that the four plates that he contributed to the fourth number of volume II do not appear at all out of place. Yet this fact does not in any way diminish the extraordinary originality with which Adam exploded at a stroke virtually all the unsubconsciously accepted restraints that had hitherto governed the representation of architectural designs in English books. For the first time one is given the unmistakable impression that here is an architectural book that has been *designed* by its author with all the thought and creativity that would have brought to bear on the creation of a building. Both Adam and James Stuart had already designed appropriately neo-classical buildings for their own books, but never before had an architect been so careful to publish his oeuvre in a manner completely consonant with its unique character. As a result the representation of architecture and ornament in the *Works* is precisely that of the Adams' own highly imaginative response to the antique world, so that we see the designs as if they had been excavated and "recovered" from antiquity itself.

Although the Adams' *Works in Architecture* represents in many ways the apogee of the architectural book in Britain, there was still one more step to take before English architects could use the entire armory of graphic means available to the topographical artist for representing their designs. Since, for reasons probably connected with the protection of their reputation as architects, the Adam brothers consistently abstained from publishing unsolicited projects, the perspectives that they included in the Works were all of executed designs. It was not therefore until John Plaw published the first part of his *Rural Architecture* (cat. 57) in 1785, that architecture was presented in the abstract form of a series of designs for cottages and villas set within naturalistic scenery. This crucial development is often seen as simply a consequence of the availability, since the mid-1770s, of aquatint for engraving picturesque landscape watercolors. The first use of aquatint in an architectural book, however, occurs in George Richardson's *A New Collection of Chimney Pieces* (1778–1781; cat. 67), where it was employed as a convenient method of rendering textures and shadow in what were otherwise conventionally drawn elevations. A more likely impetus for Plaw's revolutionary step was the gradual general acceptance of architectural perspectives in the Royal Academy exhibition, a development that can be traced quite precisely to the early 1780s.

Nicholas Savage

Abbreviations for Frequently Cited References

Abbey, *Life*	*Life in England in Aquatint and Lithography, 1770–1860, From the Library of J. R. Abbey: A Bibliographical Catalogue.* London, 1953
Abbey, *Scenery*	*Scenery of Great Britain and Ireland in Aquatint and Lithography, 1770–1860, From the Library of J. R. Abbey: A Bibliographical Catalogue.* London, 1952
Abbey, *Travel*	*Travel in Aquatint and Lithography, 1770–1860, From the Library of J. R. Abbey: A Bibliographical Catalogue.* 2 vols. London, 1956
Archer	Archer, John. *The Literature of British Domestic Architecture, 1715–1842.* Cambridge, Mass., 1985
Belcher	Belcher, Margaret. *A. W. N. Pugin: An Annotated Critical Bibliography.* London, 1987
Berlin Cat.	Berlin, Staatliche Kunstbibliothek. *Katalog der ornamentstichsammlung der Staatlichen Kunstbibliothek Berlin.* Berlin and Leipzig, 1939
Berlin (1977)	Berlin, Kunstbibliothek. *Katalog der Architektur- und Ornamentstichsammlung. Teil I: Baukunst England.* Compiled by Marianne Fischer. Berlin, 1977
Brunet	Brunet, Jacques-Charles. *Manuel du libraire et de l'amateur de livres.* 6 vols. Paris, 1860–1865. Reprint. Berlin, 1922
Christie's (London)	London sale catalogues of the auction house Christie, Manson & Woods Ltd.
Cicognar	Cicognara, Leopoldo, conte. *Catalogo ragionato dei libri d'arte e d'antichità posseduti dal conte Cicognara.* Pisa, 1821. Reprint. Leipzig, 1931
Colvin	Colvin, H. A *Biographical Dictionary of British Architects 1600–1840.* 3d ed. New Haven and London, 1995
Colvin (1978)	Colvin, Howard. *A Biographical Dictionary of British Architects 1660–1840.* 2d ed. London, 1978
DNB	*Dictionary of National Biography.* Eds. Sir Leslie Stephen and Sir Sidney Lee. 22 vols. London, 1885–1901. Reprint. London, 1963–1964.
ESTC	*The English Short Title Catalogue* [Online]. London: British Library; Riverside, Ca.: ESTC/NA; New York: American Antiquarian Society (Producers). Available: Research Libraries Information Network (RLIN) File: ESTC
Fowler	Fowler, Laurence Hall, and Elizabeth Baer. *The Fowler Architectural Collection of the Johns Hopkins University.* Baltimore, 1961
Harris and Savage	Harris, E., and N. Savage. *British Architectural Books and Writers 1556–1785.* Cambridge, 1990
Madan	Madan, Falconer. *Oxford Books: A Bibliography of Printed Works Relating to the University of Oxford, or Printed and Published There.* 3 vols. Oxford, 1895–1931
Marlborough Rare Books cat.	Catalogues of the London booksellers Marlborough Rare Books, Ltd
Millard, vol. 1	*The Mark J. Millard Architectural Collection. Vol. 1. French Books, Sixteenth through Nineteenth Centuries.* Introduction and catalogue, Dora Wiebenson. Bibliographic descriptions, Claire Baines. Washington and New York, 1993
RIBA, *Early Printed Books*	British Architectural Library, Royal Institute of British Architects. *Early Printed Books 1478–1840: Catalogue of the British Architectural Library Early Imprints Collection.* Vols. 1–2. London, 1994–1995
STC	*A Short-Title Catalogue of Books Printed in England, Scotland and Ireland, and of the English Books Printed Abroad, 1475–1640.* Compiled by A. W. Pollard and G. R. Redgrave. 2d ed., begun by W. A. Jackson and F. S. Ferguson, and completed by Katherine Pantzer. 3 vols. London, 1986–1991

Thieme-Becker — Thieme, Ulrich, and Felix Becker. *Allgemeines Lexikon der bildenden Künstler von der Antike bis zur Gegenwart....* 37 vols. Leipzig, 1908–1950

Upcott — Upcott, William. *A Bibliographical Account of the Principal Works Relating to English Topography.* 3 vols. London, 1818. Reprint. New York, 1968

Weinreb cat. — Catalogues of the London bookseller Ben Weinreb

Wing — *Short-Title Catalogue of Books Printed in England, Scotland, Ireland, Wales and British America, and of English Books Printed in Other Countries, 1641–1700.* Compiled by Donald Wing. 2d ed., rev. and enl. 3 vols. New York, 1972–1988

Notes to the Reader

The entries are listed alphabetically by author. Multiple titles by a single author are presented chronologically, by date of publication, with reissues following the first copy in the collection.

At the head of each entry, the author's name is transcribed from the title page or title plate.

The title of the book has been transcribed from the title page. Original spelling and punctuation have been maintained, but line breaks, ornaments, and typographic conventions such as the letter i for j, v for u, and vv for w have been ignored. The first letter of words appearing in upper case has been capitalized.

Place of publication, the publisher, and date follow the title.

The accession number (for example, 1981.70.1) indicates the date of acquisition (1981), the donor number of that year (70), and the object number (1). The greater part of the Mark J. Millard Architectural Collection is held in the department of prints and drawings. A few titles are in the National Gallery library and are identified by call number (for example, NGA Lib. Rare Book: NA2840L2).

The fold of the sheet is followed by the measurement of the page size in millimeters, height preceding width. Inch equivalents follow in parentheses.

"Edition" indicates whether the book is a first edition, a reissue, a translation, and so forth.

Each entry has two sections: a bibliographic description and a catalogue text. Under "Pagination" or "Foliation," the total count of leaves and the numbering of the pages are given. Brackets enclose aggregate numbers or sequential numbers that are not printed in the text. The plate count refers to the number of illustrated leaves printed outside the text gatherings. All plates have blank versos. The "Text" section provides a summary description of all parts and singularities of the book.

In the "Illustration" section, all illustrative and decorative matter is described, including intaglio or planographic text but excluding printer's stock ornaments. In addition to the number and types of illustrations, the section notes significant prints and suites and their artistic designers as well as their engravers, whose names are directly transcribed from the print. As in the titles, the intention in the bibliographic descriptions has been to follow closely the original text and to limit the use of *[sic]* to areas of possible confusion. Quotation marks are used to indicate words and passages taken directly from the original.

The discussion under "Binding" describes the material and decoration of each volume or set.

Information on previous owners, bookplates, or inscriptions is given under "Provenance."

Two books that fall slightly outside the main subject areas covered by the Millard collection have been catalogued here without accompanying entries: (cat. 25), Thomas Girtin, *A Selection of Twenty of the most picturesque Views in Paris,* and (cat. 46), John Nichols and George Steevens, *The Genuine Works of William Hogarth.*

Catalogue

I

Robert Adam (1728–1792)

Ruins Of The Palace Of The Emperor Dio-cletian At Spalatro In Dalmatia By R. Adam F. R. S F. S. A. Architect To The King And To The Queen

[London]: printed for the author, 1764

1985.61.144

Folio: 515 × 343 (20¼ × 13½)

Pagination iv, [v–xii], 33, [1] pp., engraved frontispiece, [53] engraved plates (8 double-page, 6 folding)

Edition First edition

Text pp. [i] title page (verso blank); [iii]–iv Adam's dedication to the king; [v–xi] list of subscribers; [xii] blank; [1]–4 introduction; [5]–17 text; [18] blank; [19]–33 explanation of the plates; [34] blank

Illustrations Engraved frontispiece numbered I, plus 60 engraved plates numbered II–LXI printed on 53 leaves (2 leaves have 3 plates each; 3 leaves have 2 plates each). The frontispiece and 20 of the plates are signed as engraved by Francesco Bartolozzi; 21 are signed by [Francesco, Antonio Pietro, or Giuseppe Carlo] Zucchi; and most of the remainder by either Francis Patton, Paolo Santini, Edward Rooker, Anthony Walker, Domenico Cunego, Peter Mazell, or James Basire senior

Binding Contemporary full straight-grained red morocco, gilt edges

Provenance Donor's inscription on title page "Donné par Mr. le Dr. Butini père"; canceled library stamp of the Société de Lecture; bookplate of Charles Frederic Mewes

References Berlin Cat. 1893; Cicognara 3567; ESTC t46923; Fowler 2; Harris and Savage 4; RIBA, *Early Printed Books* 27

ANOTHER COPY

1981.70.1

Folio: 545 × 370 (21½ × 14½)

Binding Recent three-quarter calf, marbled-paper boards

Robert Adam was consumed from the first with a wild ambition; he was conscious also of his high ability, yet in 1754, at the age of twenty-six, having trained with his father, William Adam, the leading architect in Scotland, and having succeeded to his practice with his brothers John and James, he was sufficiently aware of his failings in architectural understanding to decide upon a Grand Tour. He had amassed the considerable capital of five thousand pounds through the demanding work of contracting to the Board of Ordnance; he thought to spend the money traveling in gentlemanly fashion to Italy, to see for himself the monuments of classical antiquity. He aimed to acquire a proper manner and taste, and an elegant style of drawing. Conceived as a preliminary to launching himself in London, the enterprise seems to have involved, even at this stage, the idea of a publication that would advertise his scholarship and sensibility. Lord Burlington had published Palladio's drawings of the Roman baths in the *Fabbriche antiche* of 1730 (issued some years later); the three volumes of Richard Pococke's *A Description of the East and Other Countries* had appeared between 1743 and 1745, with illustrations of buildings in Greece, Asia Minor, and Egypt (mostly execrable); and the first sheaves of engravings and the lengthy prospectus of Richard Dalton's *Antiquities and Views in Greece and Egypt* had appeared in 1751 and 1752 (though the book achieved its final form only in 1792); but an entirely new kind of work on classical remains had recently appeared in the form of Robert Wood's *The Ruins of Palmyra*, of 1753, though this was indebted to Antoine Desgodetz's *Les edifices antiques de Rome* of 1682. Wood offered a short historical introduction, a record of inscriptions, and a brief account of the journey, followed by fifty plates recording a measured survey of the buildings with large-scaled details of the orders and ornamental moldings, all of unprecedented accuracy, providing a repertoire of elements for imitation. There were, in addition, interspersed, seven plates of views. The acclaim that greeted Wood's book was quite extraordinary. His reputation was at once established. Proposals for the sequel, *The Ruins of Balbec*, were advertised in 1754. The initial proposals for James Stuart and Nicholas Revett's even more ambitious undertaking, *The Antiquities of Athens*, had appeared in 1751, though the first engraved views were not to be made public before the beginning of 1755, when a new proposal was published. These works presented a challenge to Adam, who intended to do something of the kind himself. Soon after arriving in Paris in November 1754, he called on the engraver John Ingram, and there met the famous engraver C.-N. Cochin, whose devastating attack on the rococo style was to be published in the *Mercure de France* in the following month. Adam noted in his diary that the two men had recommended Babile (Pierre-Edmé Babel) "as a good man to do any ornaments for our books etc. as having a genteel taste in that way" (SRO GD 18/4753, p. 6 verso).

But for the moment all such enterprise was set aside. In Florence, which he reached at the end of January 1755, he was introduced to the young French architect Charles-Louis Clérisseau, staying at the house of the painter Ignazio Hugford. Clérisseau had recently been employed as guide and drawing instructor to William

Chambers, another Scotsman on the Grand Tour, whom Adam recognized even then as an arch rival.

"I found out Clerisseau," Adam wrote to his brother James on 19 February, "A Nathaniel in whom tho' there is no guile, Yet there is the utmost knowledge of Architecture, of perspective, and of Designing and Colouring I ever Saw, or had any conception of; He rais'd my Ideas, He created emulation and fire in my Breast. I wish'd above all to learn his manner, to have him with me at Rome, to Study close with him and to purchase of his works. What I wish'd for I obtain'd; He took a liking to me . . ." (SRO GD 18/4764). Clérisseau was to act as Adam's instructor for the next two years, and later, in 1760, when James traveled to Italy, was to act as his cicerone too. He was to do even more. He was to do most of the drawings for the *Ruins of Spalatro* and to supervise much of the engraving, and he understood the challenge of that work; at Sir Horace Mann's in Florence, in 1754, he had seen a copy of Wood's book on Palmyra.

In Rome Adam thought first to play the gentleman, but under Clérisseau's tutelage became more and more dedicated to artistic pursuits. He gossiped and dined with his old friend Allan Ramsay, Wood, and even Giovanni Battista Piranesi, with whom he often went sketching. By the middle of 1755 he was beginning to think seriously of his publication. In conversation with Ramsay and Wood he conceived the idea of a revised edition of Desgodetz's survey of the monuments of Rome, *Les edifices antiques de Rome*, first issued in 1682, again in 1695, and long out of print. "Where any of my measures differed from Desgodets," he explained to James on 4 July, "these I show by a red line, which lets them know the error and this with a Smart preface, a Clever print of the Author's head, an Allegorical print in the way of palladio, and Some remarks added to those of Desgodets in different Characters could not faill to be of great authority and introduce me into England with an uncommon splendour" (SRO GD 18/4777).

He began at once on this undertaking and continued at it for more than a year. At one time he had six draftsmen at work, but by September 1756 he had given it up—at least, for the moment. It was far too demanding. By then he had thought to revise Burlington's *Fabbriche antiche* and was measuring up the baths of Diocletian and Caracalla. He also had Hadrian's Villa in mind. Then, in October, he mentioned for the first time his intention to visit Dalmatia. He was thinking at first of Pola in Istria (where Stuart and Revett had been at work in 1750) and some months later of Spalato in Dalmatia (he called it Spalatro; today it is known as Split) still unsurveyed. The following year he took advice on this from Sir James Gray, the British envoy in Naples, brother of Colonel George Gray, secretary to the Society of Dilettanti, himself a founder member, who had helped arrange Stuart and Revett's expedition to Athens in 1751, and also from Count Gazzola, who had first introduced the ruins of Paestum to the cognoscenti of Europe; they recommended to him Daniel Farlato's *Illyricum sacrum*, the printing of which began in Venice in 1751. Robert obtained a copy of the early volumes in Italy, which were to prove invaluable.

But nothing was settled. Adam left Rome to travel north toward Venice in May 1757; in his last letter before leaving, dated 24 April, he informed his sister Betty that he would "put over my trip into Dalmatia with all expedition" (SRO GD 18/4835) when he reached Venice. Had he the time and the money he would have traveled rather to Greece, even to Egypt, but Spalato was not too far distant and it was the most important unexplored classical site to hand, though it had been illustrated in Johann Fischer von Erlach's *Entwurff einer historischen Architectur*, the English edition of which was issued in 1730. It had the distinction, moreover, of consisting not in a public building, but a private residence: the emperor Diocletian's palace. This might serve as a fitting inspiration for future country houses. In Venice, on 1 July, he visited Consul Smith (to whom he had a letter of introduction from Francesco Algarotti) to obtain the letters of permission to survey and excavate at Spalato. He found out then that General William Graeme, whom he had met at Tournai at the beginning of his tour, was commander in chief of the Venetian land forces and was shortly to review his troops at Spalato; Adam thought he might be invited to stay. Within a few days he had chartered a boat and stocked it with provisions, and on 11 July set sail. With him were his manservant, Donald; Clérisseau, the linchpin of the expedition; and two of his draftsmen from Rome, the painter Agostino Brunias and a young Belgian architect, Laurent-Benoit Dewez, both of whom were to work for him later in England. "This jaunt to Dalmatia with my four people," he wrote home on 6 July, "makes a great puff even in Italy and cannot fail doing much more in England" (SRO GD 18/4840).

It is evident both from Adam's "Reasons and motives for undertaking the voyage to Spalatro in Dalmatia" (SRO GD 18/4953) and from surviving drawings by Clérisseau that they stopped first at Priam (now Poréc) and Pola (now Pula) before reaching Spalato on 22 July. The details of their stay are sketchy; only two letters relating to it survive. Adam did not stay long with Graeme; he was obliged instead to take a house and rent furniture, but he dined with him almost daily and they were entertained by a visiting Venetian theatrical troupe. When the local governor grew suspicious of Adam's activities and stopped all surveying—the letters of permission had not arrived from Venice—Graeme interposed firmly on Adam's behalf and the work continued. But digging was not allowed, and Adam was watched all the time. He managed to send a letter to James on 6 August, among Graeme's dispatches, and noted then that he hoped to leave in eight or ten days, a fortnight at most. He did not depart, however, until 28 August. He was at Spalato just more than five weeks, longer, he noted, than the fifteen days that Wood, with one draftsman, claimed to have spent in Palmyra (though Wood's diary indicates five days).

Returned to Venice on 11 September, Adam spent the next five weeks sightseeing, before turning north, accompanied by Donald, Brunias, and Dewez. Clérisseau remained in Venice to finish both the Desgodetz and Spalato drawings and to arrange for their engraving. He was to be paid one hundred pounds per annum and was to await the arrival of either John or James on their Grand Tour, which was expected the following year. Two complete sets of the Spalato drawings seem to have been prepared, one for London, one for Venice. The originals were probably all by Clérisseau, though only seven of the drawings used for the final engravings survive: six among the Clérisseau drawings in the Hermitage, for plates XVII, XX, XXIII, XXVII, XXXIII, and XLII, and one in the RIBA Drawings Collection, for plate XII, the Porta Aurea. Adam himself appears to have done almost no drawing. He clearly considered himself the leader of the expedition.

In Augsburg, from where he wrote home on 11 November, he inquired about the cost of engraving: "I have no notion of paying £20 in England for what will be done as well here for 20 shillings" (SRO GD 18/4844). In Amsterdam he stopped for two weeks, allowing Dewez to visit his family, but also to finalize all the drawings so that they might be ready for showing when he reached London. He arrived early in January 1758, elated that the custom's officer at Harwich had so admired the drawings that he had charged no duty. James came down from Edinburgh to welcome him back, and wrote home on 1 February, "Bob designs to make his first work the Ruins of Spalatro" (SRO 18/4847). There was, however, a difficulty. He needed someone to write the introduction, having neither the time nor the language abilities to do the necessary research. Most important, however, "he would not wish to let the world know that this was done by anybody but himself" (SRO 18/4847). His first thought was to ask John Drysdale, a divine married to his sister Mary, but he feared he was too dilatory. Instead, he persuaded his cousin William Robertson, who became famous with the publication of the *History of Scotland* in February 1759, and three years later was elected principal of Edinburgh University, to take on the task. Robertson wrote the proposal, the dedication, and the preface for the book.

"I cannot express my surprise and admiration for Willie's preface," Robert wrote on 1 November 1759, "it is beautifully said and in a few words contains the full sense of what would have taken many pages from any other historian of this age but himself. If anything can make me think more highly of his abilities than I did from his History, it is the masterly penning of my preface. I have made bold to mark on the margin of it some observations, which I think it will be necessary to consider. They are mostly in points of fact" (SRO GD 18/4843).

In September of the following year, Robertson stayed with Adam at Lower Grosvenor Street in London and

Robert Adam. *Ruins of the Palace of the Emperor Diocletian at Spalatro*. Plate VII. "View of the crypto-porticus or front towards the harbour." 1981.70.1

put the finishing strokes to the preface. This began with a summation of the whole eighteenth-century understanding of architecture: "The buildings of the ancients are in architecture what the works of nature are with respect to the other arts; they serve as models which we should imitate, and as standards by which we ought to judge" (p. 1).

But though Robertson had extracted the information required from Farlato's *Illyricum sacrum* (Adam's Latin was probably rudimentary, for though he had studied it at school from the age of six, it was omitted from the syllabus of Edinburgh University) and had added the appropriate flourishes from Virgil, Horace, Ovid, and Seneca, and composed the whole admirably and with a stern concern for accuracy, Adam himself had provided the first (unusable) outline in the form of "Reasons and Motives for Undertaking the Voyage to Spalatro in Dalmatia" (SRO GD 18/4953). It is clear, however, that Adam contributed not only the circumstantial details of the stay in Spalato and all direct architectural observations (such as the total absence of any antique fireplaces in the ruins), but also the whole approach to architectural analysis and understanding that conditioned the reconstruction.

The modern town of Spalato was built into the ruins of the palace precinct; though most of the encircling wall and the two temples and the peristyle within remained, little of the palace itself could be made out. The one area the party managed to survey in detail—which they took for the baths—was part of the undercroft. This they confidently assumed was repeated on the main floor, and on the main floor itself Adam imagined it was repeated yet again on the corresponding side of the central axis. The emperor's apartments, he thought, were on one side, the womens' on the other—"as there is an exact uniformity in these rooms on each side of the atrium," he writes in the preface, "as far as they remain, I thought it most eligible not to indulge my fancy in framing any new conjecture, but simply to repeat the same distribution on this as on the other side" (p. 13). The principle of axial symmetry guided the whole restoration. Clérisseau, it should be remarked, indicated the existing remains far more correctly and honestly in the plan of the palace he provided for L.-F. Cassas and J. Lavallée's *Voyage pittoresque et historique de l'Istrie* of 1802.

Adam must also have contributed the analysis of the plan of the palace, and in particular that of the sequence of central spaces, beginning with the *porticus*, followed by the circular *vestibulum*, on to the atrium, opening finally into the great *cryptoporticus*, which extended across the whole front of the palace (517 feet): "If from the center of the Crypto Porticus, we look back to those parts of the Palace which we have already passed through, we may observe a striking instance of that gradation from less to greater, of which some connoisseurs are so fond, and which they distinguish by the name of Climax in Architecture" (p. 9). He was clearly referring here to Henry Home, Lord Kames' notion of climax in architecture (taken, as he noted, from literature) outlined in the chapter "Gardening and Architecture" in the third volume of his *Elements of Criticism*, of 1762 (pp. 341–342). Like Kames, Adam was concerned not only with the progressively increasing size of the spaces, but with their variety of form, for this was a particular feature of his own designing during these years.

"We may likewise observe," he continues

> a remarkable diversity of form, as well as dimensions, in these apartments, which we have already viewed, and the same thing is conspicuous in the other parts of the Palace. This was a circumstance to which the Ancients were extremely attentive, and it seems to have had an happy effect, as it introduced into their buildings a variety, which, if it doth not constitute Beauty, at least greatly heightens it. Whereas Modern Architects, by paying too little regard to the example of the Ancients in this point, are apt to fatigue us with a dull succession of similar apartments (p. 9).

He referred here, no doubt, to the French practice of stringing rooms out along an enfilade; for though he greatly admired French planning, it was the intricate arrangements of the intimate apartments, with their provision for discreet servicing, that stirred him, rather than the more old-fashioned and straightforward procession of like rectangular rooms.

When he began the preface Adam turned his attention also to the engravings. The decision to have most of these, and in particular the views, done in Venice under Clérisseau's supervision, must have been made early. Adam intended thereby to add to the distinction of his work. Wood had relied on P. Fourdrinier, from Amsterdam, most of whose active career was spent in London, and Thomas Major, who had also lived abroad, in Paris, who, like Fourdrinier, was associated with the St. Martin's Lane Academy, to make his plates; as Adam remarked to James in his letter of 1 November 1759, "They are as hard as iron and as false as hell" (SRO GD 18/4843). Stuart and Revett were known to be employing Fourdrinier too, together with James Basire, Edward Rooker, Anthony Walker, Robert Strange, and Charles Grignion, all at work in London. Adam was after something more sophisticated, certainly more Italianate, for his views. Francesco Bartolozzi, commissioned before Adam left Venice, was paid fifty *zecchini* in advance. Bartolozzi had studied painting with Hugford in Florence and engraving with Joseph Wagner in Venice (for whom Piranesi had worked and for whom he acted as agent in Rome), and had opened his own workshop there in 1754. He scored his first real success only in 1761 with a series of scenes of the twelve months based on paintings by Giuseppe Zocchi, and a year after with a set of four atmospheric landscapes (on sale from Smith), derived from paintings by Marco Ricci. Bartolozzi was an excellent and prescient choice. He was technically

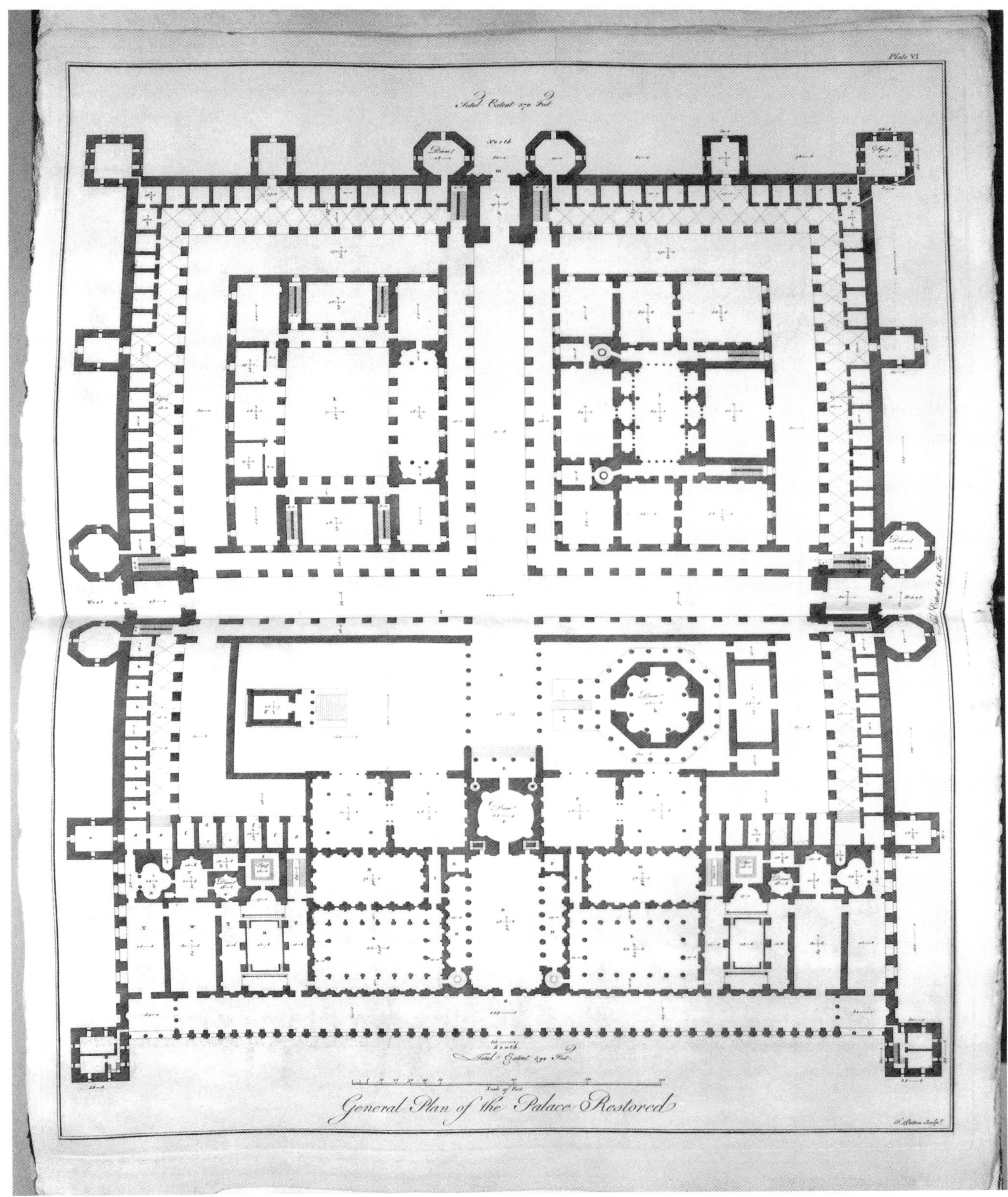

Robert Adam. *Ruins of the Palace of the Emperor Diocletian at Spalatro.* Plate VI. "General plan of the palace restored." 1981.70.1

very adept. Soon after, in 1763, he achieved something of fame when he engraved twelve drawings by Guercino—he was to dispose of these plates to Piranesi—and was invited in 1764 to London, by Dalton, George III's librarian, and there engraved the Guercino drawings in the Royal Collection, thus establishing himself in London. He was among the founder members of the Royal Academy of Arts (engraving its diploma) and became rich under contract to John Boydell—by 1773 he had fifty assistants in his employ, many of them Italian—and he left for Lisbon in 1801 only after his sons' disastrous speculations had ruined him. His forte during these years was the stipple and crayon engraving technique that he took over from William Ryland and Gilles Demarteau, who had introduced it first into England. He was to do twenty-one plates of the *Ruins of Spalatro*, just more than one-third; the frontispiece; and most of the views for which the folio is famous, but not all. Paolo Santini, a priest at Santa Maria Formosa in Venice, referred to in the Adam letters as "Clérisseau's abbé," did three of the best known: the view of the *cryptoporticus* from the harbor front (pl. VII); the views of the Porta Aurea, the main gate from the north (pl. XII); and the perspective of the main court, the peristyle (pl. XX). Curiously, Santini is today otherwise almost unremarked, other than as an engraver of maps. Two other Venetian engravers were also employed: Domenico Cunego, once again for views, that of the inside of the "Temple of Jupiter" (pl. XXXIII)—in fact the mausoleum, then the town cathedral, from which, Clérisseau's original drawing reveals, the later additions and adornments had to be carefully edited and the figure of the artist at work and others added—and the view of the aqueduct from Salona (pl. LXI), which was to cause Adam much vexation as Clérisseau, following Fischer von Erlach, thought it a viaduct; and Francesco Zucchi, who might have been assisted by his sons, Giuseppe Carlo and Antonio Pietro Zucchi (it was the latter who was to be taken later to Rome by James Adam) who contributed twenty-one plates, all, with the exception of the two long sections through the precinct (pls. XVIII, XIX) and the elevation to the *vestibulum* (pl. XXI), fine finished details of ornaments and moldings. Altogether the Venetians were responsible for forty-seven of the sixty-one plates. With the exception of the magnificent site plan (pl. II) by Rooker, engravers in England were commissioned only for plans, sections, and elevations, fourteen plates in all (if the unsigned plates are to be regarded as English contributions).

Early in 1758 Rooker was first approached, together with Paul Sandby, who was to add the "Rusticks"—presumably the staffage that would render the plates less hard than those of Wood. The arrangement did not work too well. In September Sandby complained that Rooker, who played harlequin at the Drury Lane Theatre in the evenings, was not able to devote more than an hour in a fortnight to his engravings during the theater season. Three months later Sandby was working with Francis Patton—"the front," Robert reported to James on 11 December, "is near finished by Paton and the figures by P. Sandby. The inside of the Temple of Bacchus (sic) is done by Paton and the front to the sea in ruins entire near finished by Walker" (SRO GD 18/4854). The engravings by Patton and Sandby were evidently rejected. They are not included in the finished work. Patton contributed only the ground plans of the precinct, before and after restoration (pls. V, VI), and the plans of the "Temple of Jupiter" (the mausoleum) (pl. XXVI) and the "Temple of Aesculapius" (Jupiter) (pl. XL). Walker, trained at the St. Martin's Lane Academy, working like Edward, the elder Rooker, for Stuart and Revett, did not only the ruined and restored elevations of the sea front (pl. VIII), but also the elevation of the Porta Aurea (pl. XIII), from which all "Rusticks" are notably absent. Rooker, in the event, finally produced four plates, the site map mentioned already (pl. II), the north elevation of the precinct, in ruin and restored (pl. XI)—this corresponding to Walker's elevation of the sea front—and the "Temple of Jupiter" (the mausoleum) (pl. XXIX), quite harsh, and the section through "Temple of Jupiter" (Aesculapius) (pl. XXXIV). The only other English engravers involved were Peter Mazell, who, like Bartolozzi and Walker, worked for Boydell, who did the eastern elevation of the precinct, in ruin and restored (pl. X), and Basire, who had traveled to Italy with Dalton and later became Stuart's preferred engraver, who did the side elevation of the "Temple of Aesculapius" (Jupiter) (pl. XLIII). This plate stirred Adam to rage. On 11 August 1758 he complained to James "That insignificant trifling ignorant puppyish Wretch Basire has spoilt me a plate entirely. It is the outside of the little sqr Temple, which is hard, ill-drawn, of a Bad Colour . . ." (SRO GD 18/4850). An early surviving proof is, indeed, irregular, but the final plate is, in fact, quite sharp and delicate. Adam, attuned to the more robust qualities of Piranesi's line, was thinking in pictorial rather than graphic terms.

Whatever the upsets in England, work there proceeded more evenly than in Italy. Clérisseau was forwarding proofs—on 5 September 1758 Adam sent James, in Edinburgh, "the last proof which Clérisseau sent me of Spalatro" (SRO GD 18/4852), with notes on the corrections required—but two months later Bartolozzi was demanding more money in advance and Clérisseau was threatening to move to Florence, where it would be cheaper to live. No seductive perspectives seem yet to have been done, for Adam made clear to James that he would not issue the proposal until a view could be put among the geometrical plates.

The work proceeded only intermittently until James finally embarked on his Grand Tour in 1760, traveling directly to Venice, from where he wrote Adam on 25 June that some copperplates were now dispatched to London and that the work might be completed, Clérisseau estimated, within three months, if they were to stay on in Venice to supervise. "Santini," he continued, "is turned out a capricious creature that must have a person over him to keep him to work" (SRO GD 18/4861). But both he and Zucchi, he added reassuringly, were now settled down and at work. James had decided, therefore, to have more plates engraved in Venice than originally intended. Zucchi was then awarded the two sections through the precinct (pls. XVIII, XIX) and the elevation of the entrance to the palace (pl. XXI)—his only large plates—for which he was to be paid thirty *zecchini* for each section and twenty for the elevation (SRO GD 18/4862, 2 July 1760). James also returned to Robert the proofs of the plates thus far engraved in London, with Clérisseau's comment that he considered them "better than expectation, but not near so well as his Abbe's" (SRO GD 18/4861).

On 24 July Adam sent James a summary of the state of the work: six plates of perspective views had been sent from Venice, thirty-one plates were still with the Venetian engravers, while ten others remained outstanding (forty-seven in all, the number eventually to be completed by the Italians). In England nine plates were finished, five half done. The whole, he calculated, might be complete by the following winter. But some proper advertisement was necessary to raise subscriptions, the time for which was altogether unpropitious, the Seven Years' War with France being in full spate. Wistfully, he concluded, "If the frontispiece could be done by Piranesi it would be showy and make a puff here" (SRO GD 18/4866). When Clérisseau was informed of this suggestion he promptly advised that Piranesi would refuse. James, meanwhile, issued a proposal in Italian, no doubt put out by Smith, who had published Stuart and Revett's in 1753. The *Ruins of Spalatro* was to have sixty plates and to cost six *zecchini*. James also made up the first dummy at this stage, and many discrepancies were revealed. The venetian window opening off Diocletian's bed chamber, corresponding to the colonnade of the *cryptoporticus*, suggested that the room was forty-six-feet high, higher than the main rooms along the palace front—the towers adjoining the bed chamber, he might also have noted, were shown at different heights on the south and east elevations. Changes were made. Some columns had to be inserted, fictitiously, into the elevation of the harbor front in its ruined state in order to match up with the perspective, which it would have been a shame to alter.

Adam's concern, however, was the crediting of Clérisseau's contribution. His alarm was raised on receiving a letter from Smith. In the same letter of 24 July, he wrote to James:

> I dont know if any of our people write to you that I had a letter from Mr. Smith in which he pays the highest flummery that you can imagine first of me then of Clerisseau and then of your great character and how he longs for you. I am sorry at several of his impressions which show how little precaution your messmate has taken to conceal his having drawn the view of Spalatro. As Smith terms them those very fine drawings done by Mr. C— under your eye. This he I mean C— has out of vanity I find told to all the English he coud lay his hands on, by which means they spread it in England and Mr. Chams [Chambers] and Mr. Milns [Robert Mylne, also from Scotland] and all of them may and I dont doubt but do give it out that all the drawings are Cl—'s and how can it be otherwise when he wishes it should be known. This only leads me to ask you a question, how can I put R.A. delint. at the bottom of the plates when Cl— has told the contrary, I really should be glad of your advice concerning this point (SRO GD 18/4866).

James replied in August that Robert might well put his name on the plates, as it was common practice for the architect initiating a work to sign it. The following month he changed his mind; why not be candid, he proposed, and put Clérisseau's name to the perspective views. In the end only engravers' names were retained. In his introduction, Adam—after trying to be more generous in a draft he included in his "Reasons and motives"—noted only that he had "prevailed on Mr. Clérisseau, the French artist, from whose taste and knowledge of antiquities I was certain of receiving great assistance in the execution of the scheme" (p. 2) to accompany him, together with two draftsmen. Clérisseau had a gentle revenge: on the tomb chest standing outside the entrance to the Mausoleum (pl. XXVIII) is engraved ICED IACET CORPUS CLERIƧƧI PICTOR, which Adam, surprisingly, seems to have missed. There might have been more of this kind. The inscription on the fountain in plate IV, which ends with "1759," had a thrust from Bartolozzi as well, though this Adam seems to have noticed and it has been hatched out.

James left Venice in November 1760, leaving instructions that the ten plates still in hand there be forwarded to him in Rome. He took with him Clérisseau. Cunego, whom he had found in Verona, followed soon after and there engraved his two views, still being occupied with them in May 1761. Antonio Zucchi joined James in this same year. When James departed in May 1763 he sought to take them with him, but Cunego was married and decided to settle in Rome. Zucchi returned to Venice, though in 1767 or even earlier he went to London, together with his brother Giuseppe Carlo, to work for the Adams, painting ruin scenes, such as those in the dining room at Osterley Park. In 1781 he married Angelica Kauffmann. Clérisseau moved to London in 1771, but stayed no more than two years.

The plates from Venice reached Rome in May 1761, when Cunego was still at work on his views. But by August all the plates were ready and a full dummy was made. This was forwarded to Adam in London, who received it on 4 February 1762. He was in an ill mood. Four days after he wrote irritably to James of the needless extravagances (a table of contents) and absurdities (captions both in English and French when no French edition was intended), but worst of all was the evidence of Clérisseau's inattention: there were fifteen steps in the plan and section of the "Temple of Aesculapius" (Jupiter), seven in the perspective; it was shown as faced with marble, whereas it was all stone; columns shown outside the "Temple of Jupiter" (the mausoleum) did not correspond with those marked as surviving on the plan; the "Rusticks" (that is the rustication) shown in the inside view of this temple did not appear in the section. And there was more. Were the hieroglyphics on the sphinx accurate?, he demanded angrily (they were). The second sphinx depicted he could not even recall. As a parting thrust he told James that his proposal of a portrait of the king for the frontispiece was very vulgar.

Problems relating to the book continued to emerge in

their correspondence until late in the year, but the work was, to all intents, done. Johann Winckelmann, to whom James showed a roughed up copy, tactfully asking him to check it, was enthusiastic: "Der Bericht darzu . . . ist mit vielem Verstande und Geschmacke entworfen," he wrote to his friend J. J. Volkmann on 18 June (*Briefe* 1954, 2: 238). To L. Usteri he wrote on 4 July, "ist geschrieben wie ich hatte zu schreiben gesuchte" (*Briefe* 1954, 2: 248). Winckelmann was to have no such kind words for the *Antiquities of Athens*, which he castigated in September 1764 as "monstrum horrendum ingens, cui lumen ademtum" (*Briefe* 1956, 3: 57).

When Adam heard of the imminent publication of this work in June 1762, he became apprehensive. The last copperplates arrived from Italy in August. Then in February 1763 the first volume of the *Antiquities of Athens* appeared to instant acclaim. Adam decided to delay publication until the excitement had subsided. The *Ruins of the Palace of the Emperor Diocletian at Spalatro in Dalmatia* was issued, finally, in 1764.

Betty Adam wrote to James, from London, on 21 December 1762: "Bob is perfectly sick of all publications, especially by subscription, as he has fully experienced by his own work that people look upon it as picking their pockets, which to be sure is not an agreeable way for a gentleman to make money" (SRO GD 18/4950). In fact, the Adams were astonishingly successful at soliciting subscriptions. No copy of their proposal has been found, but it must have been well considered. Their "List of subscribers" is headed by the king, to whom the work, like the *Antiquities of Athens*, was dedicated, followed by the queen, the dowager princess of Wales, the duke of York, Prince William, and Prince Henry. There were twenty-three more dukes and duchesses, six marquesses and marchionesses, fifty-five earls and countesses, almost as many other lords and ladies, together with a host of connoisseurs, scholars, and artists—Dalton, James Dawkins, George Dempster, Adam Ferguson, David Garrick,

Robert Adam. *Ruins of the Palace of the Emperor Diocletian at Spalatro.* Plate XX. "View of the peristylium of the palace." 1981.70.1

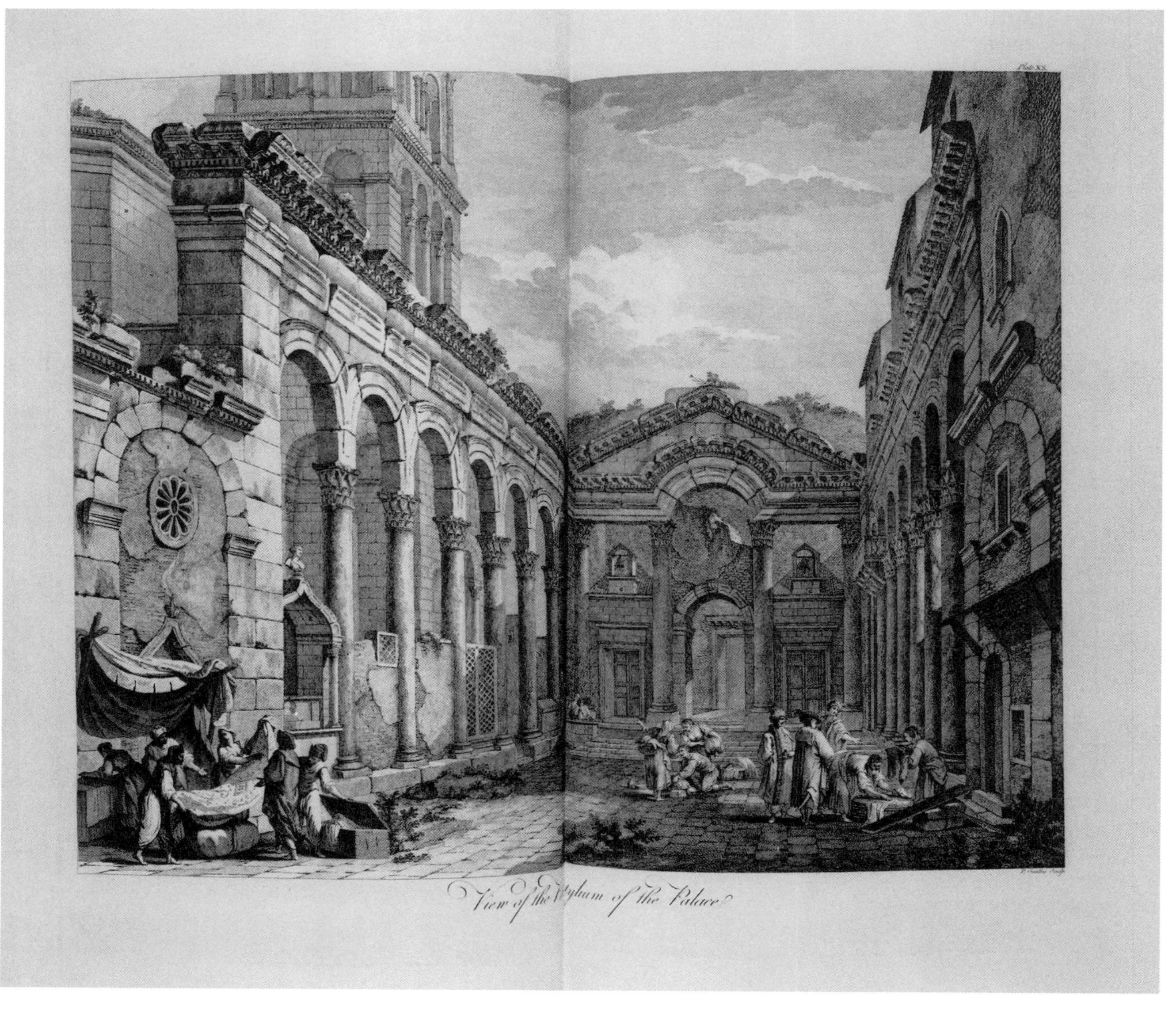

David Hume, Mrs. Montagu, Uvedale Price, Ramsay, Joshua Reynolds, William Robertson, Michael Rysbrack, Horace Walpole, William Warburton, Thomas Whately, Wood, and Samuel Wyatt among them. Five hundred and forty-four copies were sold in England by subscription alone. James' Venetian enterprise attracted twenty-six subscribers, headed by the doge of Venice, to include Algarotti, Filippo Farsetti, Piranesi, and Giandomenico Tiepolo. There was one celebrated subscriber from France, C.-G.-B. Le Normant, administrateur général des postes, brother-in-law to the marquis de Marigny.

The first volume of Stuart and Revett's *Antiquities of Athens* was splendidly bound, the presentation copies in red morocco embossed with motifs taken direct from ancient Greek monuments. Adam used the delay in the publication of his own work to ensure that he equaled in richness, if not in classical correctness, the splendor of the Stuart and Revett bindings. And he devised a code, both of elaboration of motif and color, to relate to the rank of his subscribers. The richest of the presentation copies, for members of the royal family and royal institutions, were bound in red morocco; Knights of the Garter were presented with blue bindings; Knights of the Thistle with green; and the simplest of the presentation copies were of mottled calf with an embossed border.

In the *Critical Review* for October 1764, *The Ruins of Spalatro* was lavishly praised, with the engravings upheld as done "with a taste and execution that has never been equalled in this country." Edward Gibbon, in *The Decline and Fall*. . . , was more reserved: "There is reason to suspect," he wrote, "that the elegance of his designs and engravings has somewhat flattered the objects which it was their purpose to represent" (chap. 12). He was, of course, altogether correct, and Adam himself was aware of the dilemma. Wood and Stuart and Revett had aimed at a dispassionate survey of the classical remains, sustained by an unprecedented reliance on precision and accuracy, hence Adam's comment on Wood's *Palmyra* "as hard as Iron, and as false as Hell." No more than seven of Wood's fifty-seven plates were views. He had stressed in his notes to the plates that "everything else may be understood by the measures, without further explication, which we shall always avoid where it is not absolutely necessary, and leave it entirely to the reader to make his own remarks upon the architecture" (p. 42). But Adam was unable to maintain such reserve; though he might inveigh against Clérisseau's artistic flourishes, he himself felt inevitably inclined to render the architecture as attractive as may be. He had a picturesque vision. He was a natural artist.

Though the format of his book is modeled directly on Wood's, he offers a far greater proportion of views; almost one-quarter of his plates are views, while Wood had only one view in eight.

Adam felt bound also to represent himself as a man of taste. Thus to the "Explanation of the plates," he added what he termed "occasional remarks on the style of the architecture." Much of the detail and ornamental molding, he saw at once, was richer and more florid than that found in Rome—though not, as he noted, than that at Palmyra and Baalbek—but this, though uncommon, he could accept as having a "bold and pleasing effect" (pl. XXXII) or even, being "so finely executed, that they afforded me the highest satisfaction" (pl. XLVI). He went so far as to suggest that Diocletian had perhaps "brought his artificers from Greece to Spalatro" (pl. XLVII), but departures from the accepted classical canon could not be so easily explained away: the lack of a base to the columns of the second order inside the mausoleum, which he noted as "very remarkable" (pl. XXXIV), or the manner in which the arch over the doorway and the flanking niches of the Porta Aurea "incroach too much upon the superior Order, and do not seem to add to the Beauty of the Building, either by their Form or Situation. It is not my Part to enquire into the Reasons that might induce Dioclesian's Architect to make this Disposition, which appears to me much inferior to many other Parts of the Building" (pl. XIII).

The Ruins of Spalatro, despite Adam's emulation of Wood, is thus a paradoxical work. It does not quite belong within the category of objective archaeological studies that the English established as the norm in the second half of the eighteenth century, nor does it belong within that more comprehensive analysis of classical architecture in its relation to an ongoing tradition that the French aimed at, beginning with Julien-David Leroy's *Les ruines des plus beaux monuments de la Grèce*, of 1758—which Adam admired, despite its inaccuracies, and well he might, for its views engraved by Jacques-Philippe Lebas, with whom Ryland had trained, had an airy spatiality that his Italian engravers never attained—and culminating in the final decades of the century in the expansive *Voyages pittoresques* of the Abbé Richard de Saint-Non, Jean-Pierre Houel, and the comte de Choiseul-Gouffier. Leroy's folio was offered as an artistic and intellectual challenge; Adam provided an artistic survey with some cultivated comment. R. M.

Bibliography

Brown, I. G. *Monumental Reputation. Robert Adam and the Emperor's Palace*. Edinburgh, 1992

Brown, I. G. "'With an Uncommon Splendour.' The Bindings of Robert Adam's *Ruins at Spalatro*." *Apollo* (January 1993): 6–11

Fleming, J. "The Journey to Spalatro." *The Architectural Review* 123 (February 1958): 103–107

Fleming, J. *Robert Adam and His Circle in Edinburgh and Rome*. London, 1962

Harris, E., and N. Savage. *British Architectural Books and Writers 1556–1785*. Cambridge, 1990

McCormick, T. *Charles-Louis Clerisseau and the Genesis of Neo-Classicism*. Cambridge, Mass., 1990

2

Robert Adam (1728–1792) and James Adam (1732–1794)

The Works In Architecture Of Robert And James Adam, Esquires . . .

London: printed for the authors, and sold by Peter Elmsly, 1778–1786

1985.61.141–142

Folio: 660 × 484 (26 × 19)

Pagination Vol. 1: [ii], 12, 10, [16] pp., engraved frontispiece, [40] engraved plates

Vol. 2: [26] pp., [40] engraved plates

(*Note:* Each volume comprises 5 parts or "Numbers")

Edition First edition, second issue (i.e., 1st ed. of vol. 1 with the 2d ed. of vol. 2. The second edition of vol. 2 is most easily distinguished from the first by the title pages to each part, dated 1786 throughout instead of 1779)

Text (parallel English and French) *vol. 1*: p. [i] title page (verso blank); *no. 1* [1] title page ". . . Designs of Sion House . . . ," dated 1773 (verso blank); [3]–7 preface; [8] blank; [9]–12 text; *no. 2* [1] title page ". . . Designs of Lord Mansfield's Villa at Kenwood . . . ," dated 1774 (verso blank); [3]–7 preface; [8]–10 text; *no. 3* [1] title page ". . . Designs of Luton House in Bedfordshire . . . ," dated 1774 (verso blank); [3] preface; [4] text; *no. 4* [1] title page ". . . Some Public Buildings . . . ," dated 1776 (verso blank); [3–5] preface; [6] text; *no. 5* [1] title page ". . . Designs for The King and Queen . . . ," dated 1778 (verso blank); [3–4] preface; [5] text (verso blank); *vol. 2*: p. [1] title page (verso blank); [3–26] title pages, dated 1786, and texts to nos. 1–5 (i.e., designs for the earl of Derby's House in Grosvenor Square; the house of Sir Watkin Williams Wynn; Shelburne House, in Berkeley-Square; Syon House, continuation; and "various Designs of Public and Private Buildings")

Illustrations Frontispiece engraved by Francesco Bartolozzi after a design by Antonio Pietro Zucchi (misbound in Millard copy before title page to vol. 1, no. 5). In addition, 80 engraved plates numbered I–VIII in 10 groups correspond with each volume's 5 parts or "Numbers." Plates are signed as engraved after Robert Adam, architect, except in the last parts to each volume, which credit some plates to James Adam alone or jointly with his brother. The following engravers are credited: Patrick Begbie; Robert Blyth; James Caldwall (vol. 2 only); Domenico Cunego; Alexander Finnie; Edward Malpas (vol. 2 only); Peter Mazell; Tobias Miller (vol. 1 only); Thomas Morris (vol. 2 only); Newton (vol. 1 only); Norval (vol. 2 only); Benedetto Pastorini; Giovanni Battista Piranesi ("J. B. Piranesi," vol. 2 only); Joseph Record (vol. 2 only); John Roberts; Roe (vol. 2 only); Edward Rooker (vol. 1 only); Giovanni Vitalba (vol. 1 only); Thomas Vivares; Charles White; Thomas White (vol. 1 only); Giuseppe Carlo Zucchi ("J. Zucchi")

Binding Contemporary calf, rebacked

References Berlin Cat. 2341; Berlin (1977) OS 2341; ESTC t52730; Harris and Savage 6; RIBA, *Early Printed Books* 28

The Works In Architecture Of The Late Robert And James Adam, Esquires. Complete In Three Volumes. Containing Plans, Elevations, Sections, And Detail [sic], Of The Principal Buildings, Public And Private, Erected In Great Britain In The Reign Of George The Third With Designs of every Kind, Both For Interior And Exterior Decoration. One hundred and twenty-five plates. Engraved by Bartolozzi, Piranesi, Zucchi, Pastorini, Cunego, &c. &c.

London: Priestley and Weale, 1822

1985.61.143

Folio: 640 × 480 (25 3/16 × 18 7/8)

Pagination Vol. 1: [ii], 12, 10, [16] pp., engraved frontispiece, [40] engraved plates

Vol. 2: [10] pp., [40] engraved plates

Vol. 3: [6] pp., [25] engraved plates (1 double-page)

Edition First edition in 3 volumes (i.e., reissue of 1st ed. of vol. 1; 3d ed. of vol. 2; 1st ed. of vol. 3)

Text (parallel English and French) *vol. 1*: cancel title leaf, otherwise as 1778 edition; *vol. 2*: p. [1] title page, dated 1822 (verso blank); [3–10] prefaces and explanations of the plates; *vol. 3*: p. [1] title page ". . . Volume III. Containing the remainder of the Designs . . . ," dated 1822 (verso blank); [3] advertisement (verso blank); [5–6] explanation of the plates

Illustrations Vols. 1–2 have a frontispiece and 80 plates as in the first edition. Vol. 3 has 25 plates, of which 11 are unsigned and the remainder engraved by Patrick Begbie (1); James Caldwall (2, 1 with Charles Grignion); Harding (1); Francis Jukes (2); Benedetto Pastorini (1); Francis Patton (1); John Roberts (2); Thomas Vivares (2); and Giuseppe Carlo Zucchi ("J. Zucchi," 2)

Binding 3 vols. bound as 1. Nineteenth-century three-quarter morocco, pebbled boards

Provenance Bookplate of Charles Frederic Mewes

References Harris and Savage 7; RIBA, *Early Printed Books*, 29 (facsimile ed.)

ROBERT ADAM was chary of publishing either his discoveries or his designs; as early as 13 November 1756, while still in Rome, he wrote to his sister in response to his elder brother John's suggestion that some garden designs be published: "we think it would be vastly imprudent to publish them, as that would be throwing your most precious works in the public's hands and removing that desire of seeing and admiring them at your own house. It would enable them to execute without your advice; besides that the best drawing you can imagine, when engraved by Vivares, loses its spirit and appears a very ordinary work" (SRO GD 18 4825). Later he was to demonstrate his knowledge and sharp assessment of classical antiquity in publishing the *Ruins of the Palace of the Emperor Diocletian at Spalatro in Dalmatia*, issued in 1764, but there is no indication that he intended to reveal the refinements of his own designs to the world. Then, in the early 1770s, two events shattered his easy confidence in his own success. A rival, able to manipulate and extend the style for which the Adams were famous, appeared in the form of James Wyatt, who sprung to fame with his first work, the Pantheon, in Oxford Street, opened in 1772. Horace Walpole acclaimed it in the following year, in relation to the work of the Adams, "still the most beautiful edifice in England" (*Correspondence* 28 102). The second event was the failure of the banking house of Neale, James, Fordyce, and Downe in June 1772, which led to the collapse of ten London and nine Edinburgh banks within a few days and almost drew the Adams, who were then engaged in their great speculative venture at the Adelphi, in the Strand, into bankruptcy. In February 1773 they were forced to sell off a large part of their collection of antiquities, and were saved only by the expedient of holding a lottery for the Adelphi houses in March 1774.

The crisis occasioned by these events seems to have precipitated the decision to publish *The Works in Architecture of Robert and James Adam*, the first announcement of which appeared in the *Public Advertiser* on 16 January 1773. The book was to be published in parts—not altogether usual at the time—rather than by subscription, which was a more secure but necessarily protracted process. The aim, as became evident in the preface that accompanied each part, was to establish the primacy of the Adams in creating and establishing a new style of architecture and in publicizing their abilities—and availability—in this respect. But the book was by no means a survey of their built works. Robert aimed to indicate the quality of their connections—the empress of Russia; Queen Charlotte; the princess dowager of Wales; the dukes of Montagu and Northumberland; the earls of Bute, Derby, Mansfield, and Shelburne; and Sir Watkin Williams Wynn—and to present a tantalizing glimpse of the realms that he had created for such notabilities.

The book was highly selective. The first volume was made up of five parts (of eight plates each): the first three were largely devoted to country houses close to London, Syon House, Kenwood, and Luton Park; the fourth to public buildings; and the fifth to miscellaneous royal commissions. The method of presentation is most eloquently and successfully revealed in the first part, issued on 24 July 1773, devoted to Syon House. One of his early triumphs, beginning in 1762, this involved the remodeling of a four-square sixteenth-century house. Adam begins his presentation with a plan and elevation of the entrance gate, in the form of an archway flanked with open, colonnaded screens. The second plate (engraved by Thomas Vivares, son of François Vivares, of Montpellier, engraver of several of the prints put out in April 1751 by Richard Dalton as a foretaste of his *Antiquities and Views in Greece and Egypt*, who had presumably occasioned Adam's earlier misgivings) features details of this gateway, arranged in the manner of antique fragments. The third plate reveals the plan and elevation of an ornamental bridge; the fourth a perspective view. No elevation of the house is shown—it being far too humdrum—instead, plate V offers the plan of the house, both as refashioned (solid black) and in Adam's ideal state of completion (hatched). None of the rooms inside is illustrated complete; no more than the end elevations of the entrance hall on plate VI are shown, with a glimpse through an arched doorway to the first anteroom, in perspective, and then, on plate VII, details of entablatures and panels from the hall, once again assembled like antique elements. Plate VIII illustrates various items of furniture—a pier glass and table, tripods and lamp brackets, engraved with verve by Benedetto Pastorini, an artist from the Veneto, who had followed his master Francesco Bartolozzi to London, where he was to engrave many of the works of Angelica Kauffmann. The furnishings were not designed, as one might expect, for Syon House, but for "different persons." No doubt the plates of the furnishings for Syon House that were eventually published, in 1822, in the third, made-up volume of the *Works in Architecture* and incorrectly described there as furniture for the earl of Bute, was originally intended for this position. But it was far less intense and lively a composition. Adam composed his impressionistic surveys of his commissioned works with the greatest possible care and discretion. The array of plates provided for Kenwood, which took up the whole of part two, issued only ten months later, on 14 May 1774, and Luton Park, taking up part three, issued after an even longer interval, on 28 April 1775, is very much the same. Seductive fragments are offered, but never the whole. Part four, issued on 14 September 1776, was somewhat different, an assemblage rather of parts of public buildings: the Admiralty Screen in Whitehall, in perspective (dated January 1770); an elevation of the paymaster general's office in Whitehall; the plans and elevation of the Society of Arts; the plans, elevation, and section of the Register House in Edinburgh; and an assortment of furnishings. Part five, issued on 5 June 1778, was, once again, much the same, though the assemblage on this occasion was of minor royal commissions, including a harpsichord for Catherine the Great. Adam wanted to stimulate, but not to give too much away. He was nonetheless spurred to give away a little more than he had originally intended by the appearance of *A Book of Ceilings, Composed in the Style of the Antique Grotesque*, by one of his own draftsmen, George Richardson, issued in parts between March 1774 and July 1776, with hand-colored plates at an added cost. Adam had intended to maintain the exclusivity of his style by pricing his book beyond the range of the ordinary craftsman, at one guinea or more per part, while Richardson was selling this same style in a book priced at eight shillings a part, or double that price with the ceilings colored. Adam had already offered in his introduction to color some of his plates for an additional cost. He colored one of the ceiling plates in part two, another in part three, and yet another and the empress' harpsichord in part five. The fifth part, which brought the first volume to completion, included the title page to the whole, dated 1778, and a frontispiece, dated 1775, designed by Antonio Pietro Zucchi and engraved by Bartolozzi, who had worked on the *Ruins of Spalatro*, with Minerva demonstrating to a student a map of Italy and Greece, the fountainhead of excellence and taste in architecture.

The slow pace of publication of the first volume of *The Works in Architecture* might have been caused by a certain slackness in demand (a large number of copies of part one, together with letterpress from the subsequent parts, was listed in the catalogue of the Adam sale on 10 July 1821), but its appearance was greeted enthusiastically both in the *Critical Review* of September 1773 and the *Monthly Review* of December 1773, and the delay might have been due to Adam's reluctance to reveal too much as also to his concern that the presentation should strike just the right note. The sudden decision to publish and the scale of the operation meant that a vast range of engravers were commissioned at the start, most of them English, despite the marked preference for Italians—especially for the views—that Adam had shown when preparing the *Ruins of Spalatro*. Even so, more than a third of the plates for the first volume were prepared by Italian artists: the frontispiece, as we have seen, by Bartolozzi; two plates, including the section of the library at Kenwood, by Giuseppe Carlo Zucchi, brother of Antonio Pietro, who came with him to London in 1767 or thereabouts; five plates, two of them views, by Domenico Cunego; and seven plates, mainly details and furnishings, but including also the view of Kenwood done in conjunction with Giovanni Vitalba, by Pastorini. Bartolozzi, Francesco Zucchi, and Cunego had all contributed earlier to the *Ruins of Spalatro*. Vitalba, like Pastorini, was a pupil of Bartolozzi who had followed him to London when he began to work for John Boydell.

The only view by an English artist was that of the proposed bridge for Syon, by Edward Rooker, who had worked also on the *Ruins of Spalatro*. So, too, had Peter Mazell, another of the engravers employed by Boydell, who was responsible for the plan of Syon. The only untried artist to whom Adam entrusted plates of some circumstance and complexity was Patrick Begbie, who is known to have done no other architectural engravings (unless he be the Bigby later employed by Chambers). For Adam he engraved the composed furnishings from Kenwood, which concluded part two, and that "for different persons," which concluded part four, together with the perspectives of Queen Charlotte's sedan chair and Catherine the Great's harpsichord in part five. But despite all effort to take as few risks as possible, there were plates ordered that Adam felt bound to reject. These, it is safe to assume, were among the fifteen unpublished plates included in the Adam sale of 1821, later to be included in the so-called volume three of *The Works in Architecture*. Plates obviously set aside from volume one are the furnishings engraved by Begbie from Luton (mislabeled Syon) (vol. 3, pl. VIII) and the elevational details from this house by Giuseppe Carlo Zucchi (vol. 3, pl. X). Also intended for volume one was the unsigned plate of furnishings from Syon (mislabeled for the earl of Bute) (vol. 3, pl. XI). Six more plates relating to Syon, all unsigned, were included in volume three, but it is difficult to determine whether they were intended for volumes one or two, for Syon was to be illustrated in both.

The agent for the sale of the first four parts of the first volume was Thomas Becket, the sale of the fifth part was handled by Peter Elmsly, who was to be entrusted with the whole of volume two and who seems to have advised on a swift conclusion to the operation. All five parts of the second volume were issued in April 1779, at the slightly reduced price of five guineas plain, six guineas colored. The volume was planned as a close parallel to the first. In place of the country houses were three town houses—Derby House, Sir Watkin Williams Wynn's house, and Shelburne House—all in London, presented in the same impressionistic manner, with eight plates each (though Shelburne House included a view of a bridge designed for the earl of Shelburne's country seat at Bowood Park). The fourth part was devoted to Syon House, with the plate of furnishings rejected earlier rejected yet again in favor of a plate of "furniture for different persons." The fifth part was an assemblage of various buildings: the church at Mistley (three plates); the British Coffee House (one plate); the gateway to Ashburnham House, London (one plate); the Theatre Royal, Drury Lane, London (two plates); and a garden pavilion at Richmond (one plate).

The decision to illustrate Syon again was probably because four plates for it had been done by the most famous etcher in Europe, Giovanni Battista Piranesi, a friend of Adam from his Roman days, earlier considered for the frontispiece of the *Ruins of Spalatro*. There was no certainty with Piranesi; his plates were perhaps expected for volume one. To judge by the large number of unused plates for Syon that were to appear in the

Robert and James Adam. *The Works in Architecture of Robert and James Adam, Esquires.* Vol. 2, No. 1, plate v. "Inside view of the third drawing-room at the Earl of Derby's House in Grosvenor Square." 1985.61.142

Adam sale in 1821, the extent of Piranesi's contribution could not be relied upon. The extra plates seem to have been done as a precautionary measure. Piranesi eventually provided the longitudinal section or elevation of the hall (a notable absence from the first volume), the ceiling of the hall, and two elevations and a plate of details of the doorcase and the Ionic screen in the first anteroom. The quality of the plates, though fine, is not greatly in advance of that already achieved by such English engravers as Thomas Vivares or Joseph Record, who was responsible for three plates of interior elevations of Derby House. Adam, however, seems to have held firm to his belief that for any task involving complexity of design or finesse of perspective, a foreigner, preferably an Italian, was best. Giuseppe Carlo Zucchi did two plates for volume two, the chimneypieces for Derby House and decorative details from the Williams Wynn house; Cunego did three, the richly articulated screen wall in the court of the Williams Wynn house, the organ case for the music room there, and the chimneypiece in the Syon House anteroom; while Pastorini did six, three of them views—the bridge at Bowood Park, the interior of the Theatre Royal, and, the most celebrated plate of all, the diagonal view across the third drawing room into the countess of Derby's dressing room, illustrating Adam's new dynamic approach to planning. Pastorini was also entrusted with the ceiling of the countess of Derby's dressing room, in the Etruscan style, which Adam regarded as a discovery all his own; and the composite plates of furnishings from Derby House and that "for different persons" included in the sheaf of engravings of Syon House. Piranesi, as we have seen, engraved four plates for Syon. In total, the Italians produced fifteen of the forty plates. The only views not done by Pastorini were two by Vivares: a ruinous bridge for Syon and the church at Mistley from the southwest.

Four plates were offered colored in volume two, Pastorini's ceiling and furniture plates for Derby House, Roe's ceiling of the eating room in the Williams Wynn house, and Thomas Morris' ceiling of the music room there. These were the only plates to be signed by Roe (otherwise unknown) and Morris (who had contributed earlier to Brettingham's book on Holkham Hall but is better known for his work for Boydell).

The publication of the second volume of *The Works in Architecture* brought the venture to a close as far as the Adam brothers were concerned, though in 1786 the letterpress for volume two was reset and the work was again offered for sale. Eventually, in 1822, they were offered yet again to the public by Priestley and Weale, together with a third volume, already remarked. The price for all three was now seven and a half guineas. The third volume, which included no preface or text, only an advertisement written by the publishers, was a compilation of twenty-five plates (never intended to be issued together by the Adam brothers), consisting of the fifteen unpublished plates, all but two unsigned, that appeared at the sale of 1821—seven engravings for Syon (pls. ii, iii, iv, v, vi, vii, xi) and two for Luton (pls. viii, x), already discussed; two for Shelburne House (pls. xviii, xix); three for the Williams Wynn house (pls. xxiii, xxiv, xxv); and one of furnishings from Osterley Park and elsewhere (pl. ix, incorrectly labeled as from Syon), all rejected by Adam—and ten plates that had been published independently: Francis Patton's plan and elevation of the Admiralty Screen, February 1761; Pastorini's view of the Adelphi, of 1770; the three engravings by John Roberts, James Caldwall, and Charles Grignion of the earl of Derby's supper pavilion and ballroom at the Oaks in Surrey, probably of 1774; two engravings by Roberts and Vivares of the deputy ranger's lodge in Green Park, London, of 1775; and the three plates by one of the Hardings and Francis Jukes of Edinburgh University, issued in 1791 to raise money for building.

To each of the five parts of the first volume a preface was provided in which the Adams gave expression, if briefly, to their aims and ideas. The extent of their aspiration is evident in the fact that the texts were printed in parallel columns of English and French. Their most provocative and much quoted statement was their claim, made at the very beginning of the first preface, "to have brought about, in this country; a kind of revolution in the whole system of this useful and elegant art." The claim was, in itself, sufficiently bold, but prefaced with the statement "We have not trod in the path of others, nor derived aid from their labours," it became positively brash. Walpole, in a letter to William Mason of 17 September 1773, responded sharply to this preface "of modesty and diffidence." He rejected the Adam style as crisp and superficial. Even the reviewers in the *Critical Review* and the *Monthly Review* expressed something of amazement at the Adams' presumption. But the Adam brothers seem to have been little taken aback. In the preface to the fifth part they again laid claim to the role of innovators in architecture, albeit on this occasion with marginally less arrogance: "Without detracting from the talents and merit of other artists," they wrote, "we are encouraged, by the public approbation, to flatter ourselves, that our works have somewhat contributed to diffuse juster ideas and a better taste in architecture. It was with a view of rendering them more generally useful, that we first engaged in this publication." And whereas, in the first preface, they had described their revolution, in general terms, as the replacement of ponderous compartmented ceilings, massive entablatures and taberna-

Robert and James Adam. *The Works in Architecture of Robert and James Adam, Esquires.* Vol. 2, No. 4, plate 1. "Section of one side of the hall at Sion." 1985.61.142

cle frames by a beautiful variety of light moldings, grotesques, and painted ornaments, that demonstrated, they again flattered themselves, that they had "been able to seize, with some degree of success, the beautiful spirit of antiquity, and to transfuse it, with novelty and variety, through all our numerous works," they became more specific and also more demanding of recognition for their discoveries in their later prefaces. The segmental ceiling of the library at Kenwood was advanced in the preface to part two of volume one, as also the ornamented pilasters applied to the garden facade. The preface to volume two, which served for all five parts, was taken up almost entirely with their claim to have evolved the new Etruscan style first in the ornamenting and coloring of the countess of Derby's dressing room. Various authorities on Etruscan remains were referred to in establishing their priority—Bernard de Montfaucon, the comte de Caylus, G. B. Passeri, A. F. Gori, and others—but no mention was made of Piranesi's *Diverse maniere d'adornare i cammini*, of 1769, which would have required them to modify somewhat their stakeout. They described the great drawing room from which the dressing room opened as "undoubtedly one of the most elegant in Europe." The Adam brothers were not reticent in upholding their reputation. And they alluded quite openly to the architect they regarded as the usurper of their style. In a note to the plate illustrating details of the stair at Luton, in the third part of volume one, they wrote: "The capital to the screen of columns in the great stairs is also new. These having been very closely imitated in various places, particularly in the Pantheon in Oxford Street, show the approbation they have met with from the public."

But the two significant and rewarding themes broached by the Adams in their prefaces were "movement" in architectural composition and, even more stirring to contemporaries, artistic freedom. "*Movement*," one reads in the first preface,

> is meant to express, the rise and fall, the advance and recess, with other diversity of form, in the different parts of a building, so as to add greatly to the picturesque of the composition. For the rising and falling, advancing and receding, with the convexity and concavity, and other forms of the great parts, have the same effect in architecture, that hill and dale, foreground and distance, swelling and sinking have in landscape: That is, they serve to produce an agreeable and diversified contour, that groups and contrasts like a picture, and creates a variety of light and shade, which gives great spirit, beauty and effect to the composition.

Though the concept of "movement" had been discussed by Italian Renaissance theorists and was certainly part of the theoretical framework of English Palladians, such as William Kent, the natural assumption would be that the Adams' analogy to landscape gardening had been sparked by a reading of that pioneering study on picturesque gardening, Thomas Whately's *Observations on Modern Gardening* of 1770. Such, however, was not the case. Alexander Carlyle records in his *Autobiography* that in May 1758 James Adam passed comment on Blenheim Palace: "Though he did not say that Sir John Vanbrugh's design was faultless, yet he said it ill deserved the aspersions laid upon it, for he had seen few palaces where there was more movement, as he called it, than in Blenheim." James was then, of course, living with Robert in London. But James was to elaborate on the theme and to expand it considerably in an essay he wrote in Rome, dated 27 November 1762. Therein, as John Fleming has shown, he provided the first outline for the prefaces of *The Works in Architecture*, and in particular for those parts dealing with "movement":

> What is so material an excellence in landscape is not less requisite for composition in architecture, namely the variety of contour, a rise and fall of the different parts and likewise those great projections and recesses which produce a broad light and shade. (I have seen buildings which without anything to recommend them but merely a considerable degree of this sort of movement, have by that alone been rendered agreeable and even interesting, such is Blenheim and Heriot's Hospital at Edinburgh) (Fleming 1962, 315–316).

There are other passages in this essay that parallel the prefaces, and passages expressive of Robert's rather than James' architectural concerns, such as those describing the movement and picturesque effects that might be contrived internally with changes of level and the use of vaults and domes. James writes: "A proper mixture of domes, vaults and coved ceilings and flat soffits over rooms of various shapes and sizes are capable of forming such a beautiful variety as cannot fail to delight and charm the instructed spectator. A movement in the section is likewise derived from steps in a great circular or long room. . . ." Remarking on the variety of floor levels in the old house at Syon, the author of the introduction to the notes to the first preface writes: "The inequality of levels has been managed in such a manner as to increase the scenery and add to the movement, so that an apparent defect has been converted into a real beauty." The theme is taken up again in the notes to plate v. Here we have Robert's thoughts. For Syon was designed and largely built by Robert alone, when James was still in Italy. The truth is, as John Fleming himself has concluded, that whatever perception or sharpness of observation might be contained in James' essay, it was almost certainly owing to discussions with Robert. Robert, though he might have informed Lord Kames in his famous letter to him of 31 March 1763 that he had "but few moments to dedicate to theory and speculation" (Bolton 1922, 1: 50), thought hard and clearly about architecture. James, as his essay as a whole reveals, was a muddled thinker.

The matter of artistic freedom with which the Adams were concerned was, of course, that of antique precedent and the degree of conformity to this required. "Architecture," the second preface states, "has not, like some other arts, an immediate standard in nature, to which the artist can always refer, and which would enable the skilful instantly to decide with respect to the degree of excellence attained in any work." Adam was in no doubt that taste in architecture could be formed only by the profound study and observation of the masterpieces of the past, in particular the classical past, but he was equally convinced that the creative artist should be unfettered by slavish imitation. In his first preface he had written already:

We beg leave to observe that among architects destitute of genius and incapable of venturing into the great line of their art, the attention paid to those rules and proportions is frequently minute and frivolous. The great masters of antiquity were not so rigidly scrupulous, they varied the proportions as the general spirit of their composition required, clearly perceiving, that however necessary these rules may be to form taste and to correct the licentiousness of the scholar, they often cramp the genius and circumscribe the ideas of the master.

The second preface was devoted in large part to the orders. Adam acknowledged only three—the Doric, the Ionic, and the Corinthian. But he would accept no fixed system of proportions, no established patterns of design. Everything could be varied according to situation or propriety. And, as was his wont, he described many of the variations he had himself introduced into the design of columns and entablatures. Even the whimsical and the bizarre, he had suggested earlier in the notes to the first preface, need not be excluded in light and gay compositions. The springs of his liberation no doubt lie in Lord Kames' *Elements of Criticism* of 1762.

His point of reference in all this, as with "movement," was the architecture of Sir John Vanbrugh, whom his father before him admired and upon whom even so stolid a figure as Sir Joshua Reynolds was later to deliver an encomium in his thirteenth discourse, delivered to the students of the Royal Academy of Arts on 11 December 1786; yet Adam's inquisitive interest and enthusiasm was unusual at the period and altogether engaging. His remarks on Vanbrugh are worth quoting in full. In note (A), to the first preface, he writes:

Sir John Vanbrugh's genius was of the first class; and, in point of movement, novelty and ingenuity, his works have not been exceeded by any thing in modern times. We should certainly have quoted Blenheim and Castle Howard as great examples of these perfections, in preference to any work of our own, or of any other modern architect; but unluckily for the reputation of this excellent artist, his taste kept no pace with his genius, and his works are so crouded with barbarisms and absurdities, and so borne down by their own preposterous weight, that none but the discerning can separate their merits from their defects. In the hands of the ingenious artist, who knows how to polish and refine and bring them into use, we have always regarded his productions, as rough jewels of inestimable value.

In the fifth preface, in which a brief survey of architecture from the Renaissance in Italy to the present in Britain is offered, Vanbrugh again emerges as a hero, of sorts. Having suitably praised Inigo Jones and Christopher Wren, Adam writes: "Vanbrugh understood better than either the art of living among the great. A commodious arrangement of apartments was therefore his peculiar merit. But his lively imagination scorned the restraint of any rule in composition; and his passion for what was fancifully magnificent, prevented him from discerning what was truly simple, elegant, and sublime." This, of course, was Adam's ideal.

There is a great deal more that might be discussed in the prefaces of *The Works in Architecture*, in particular the Adams' lessons in planning, which are essential to any understanding of the architecture, but it was not as a theoretical work, nor for its liveliness of opinion that the book was valued, but rather as the most beautiful and innovative in representation in English architectural literature of the eighteenth century. R. M.

Bibliography

Bolton, A. T. *The Architecture of Robert and James Adam*. London, 1922. (1: 50–54, for Robert Adam's letter to Lord Kames)

Fleming, J. *Robert Adam and His Circle in Edinburgh and Rome*. London, 1962. (James Adam's essay on architecture is published as an appendix)

Harris, E., and N. Savage. *British Architectural Books and Writers 1556–1785*. Cambridge, 1990

3

William Adam (1689–1748)

Vitruvius Scoticus; Being A Collection of Plans, Elevations, And Sections Of Public Buildings, Noblemen's And Gentlemen's Houses In Scotland: Principally From the Designs Of The Late William Adam, Esq. Architect

Edinburgh: printed for Adam Black and J. & J. Robertson, Edinburgh; T. Underwood and J. Taylor, London [1811]

1985.61.145–234, 1985.61.235–326

Folio: 530 × 344 (21 × 13½)

Pagination 5, [1] pp., [179] engraved plates (18 double-page, 2 folding)

Edition First edition

Text p. [1] title page (verso blank); [3]–5 list of plates; [6] blank

Illustrations 179 engraved plates, numbered 1–160 with 2 plates each numbered 5, 13, 19–21, 30, 72–74, 83, 94, 107–108, 121, 123, 135–136, 139–140. The "List of the Plans, &c." also lists 2 plates numbered 51, but 1 of these is, in fact, plate 53. Most plates are signed by William Adam as designer/draftsman, but 13 are attributable to John (and James?) Adam and 1 each is signed by John G. Borlach ("Borlack," plate 62) and John Wyck (plate 5 bis). The engraver is usually Richard Cooper, with a small number credited to Andrew Bell, Peter Mazell, Francis Patton, W. Proud, and T. Smith. For a detailed list, see RIBA, *Early Printed Books*, 30

Binding Disbound. Text and plates mounted on blue paper sheets and preserved in 2 green morocco-backed boxes

References Berlin (1977) 2343°; ESTC n64622; Harris and Savage 8; RIBA, *Early Printed Books*, 30

IN A LETTER to Sir John Clerk of Penicuik, dated 5 May 1726, William Adam states that in preparation for his much postponed journey to London with Lord Stair at the end of the year, he was "in the meantime . . . getting doubles of all my Draughts to carry with me in order to put them in the Engravers hands" (SRO GD18/4729/2). In the end Adam traveled part of the way to London with Sir John, the "Scottish Burlington," leading to the suggestion that a "Vitruvius Scoticus" was conceived during their work together on Mavisbank and inspired to some degree by Clerk's interest in the new style of architecture promulgated so effectively in *Vitruvius Britannicus* (Adam 1980, 11). It is much more likely, however, that Adam carried engravings to London because Lord Stair and Sir John Anstruther, the Scottish master of work, were specifically seeking to revive for his benefit the post of surveyor of the king's works in Scotland. The idea of using the engravings for a book was, in fact, almost certainly conceived during Adam's stay in London, where, within days of his arrival, his compatriot James Gibbs began collecting subscriptions for *A Book of Architecture* (*Daily Post*, 31 March 1727). According to Gibbs' advertisement, "90 of the Plates [were] already engraved," so when Adam took out his subscription he had ample opportunity to study Gibbs' example—the first in England—of how the designs of a living architect could be presented in book form. No doubt eager to impress the new monarch (George I died on 11 June 1727), Adam plunged into a publishing project modeled after that of Gibbs—an architect whose work he greatly admired—and immediately began collecting subscriptions for his own "Designs for Buildings &c. in 150 Plates," even though, as far as is known, not a single drawing was yet engraved. By 17 September 1727 he had 28 subscribers, a month later 72, and by March 1728, 135 (Fleming 1962, 48; Harris and Savage 1990, 101 n. 12).

Undoubtedly Adam's ill-conceived project would have collapsed but for the fortunate arrival of Richard Cooper in Edinburgh sometime in the late 1720s. It would be difficult to overestimate the importance of Cooper's contribution to *Vitruvius Scoticus*. Although nothing is known for certain of the contractual arrangement between Cooper and Adam with regard to the costs of engraving and materials (a key that might unlock much of the mysterious history of the book), there is enough circumstantial evidence (Harris and Savage 1990, 96–97) to suggest that, under the influence of Cooper, the whole direction of the project changed. The pair attempted, in effect, to revive the dream of an illustrated survey of Scottish buildings that had been almost, but not quite, extinguished with the failure of John Slezer's proposed *Scotia illustrata* twenty years earlier—a failure very largely resulting from the absence in Edinburgh of an engraver like Cooper who was capable of investing sufficient skill, labor, and materials in the project as to give it commercial and artistic viability. The impetus Cooper's involvement gave to the work may be gauged by the dramatic increase in subscriptions that had been received by the time the earl of Pembroke subscribed for a copy on 9 May 1731 (Adam's subscription receipt of that date at Wilton House is numbered 635).

Given this level of support, why did the book fail to appear within the next two years or so, as would have been reasonable to expect? The simple answer is lack of material: the decision to change the book from a collection of Adam's own designs into one that surveyed—and celebrated—classical architecture north of the Tweed, in the manner of Colen Campbell's *Vitruvius Britannicus*, failed to take into account the difficulties of maintaining a proper flow of drawings for engraving on a reasonable publishing schedule. Rather than concentrate on building up a "reservoir" of drawings for the engraver to work on steadily, Adam gave Cooper drawings as they became available as a by-product of his architectural practice. (At an equivalent stage in the preparation of *Vitruvius Britannicus*, 160 drawings were advertised as ready for engraving—see *Post Boy*, 1 June 1714.) There is nothing to suggest the kind of concerted effort to produce drawings that had clearly underpinned the schedule of *Vitruvius Britannicus*, which was directed by commercial imperatives imposed by its publishers, Joseph Smith and his partners. Indeed, of the 161 *Vitruvius Scoticus* plates eventually engraved by Cooper over a period of about twelve to fifteen years (c. 1728–1743?), only 37 are of buildings drawn by Adam apparently independently of any known architectural involvement in their design, alteration, or repair. As for the acquisition or borrowing of existing drawings, it was probably little more than chance that produced John Borlach's drawings of Bruce's Kinross House (pls. 61–62), Gibbs' Balveny House (pls. 90–91), and the original drawings (redrawn by Adam) of the exiled earl of Mar's design for a royal palace (pls. 109–110).

It would probably be a mistake to interpret the sluggish progress of Adam's book as an indication of diminishing interest on his part; indeed, as all three of his sons began to show signs of considerable architectural ability, and he became increasingly conscious of having founded an architectural dynasty (a self-image nicely illustrated by his adoption, in about 1740, of a seal bearing the head of Inigo Jones, the patriarch of classical architecture as it had taken root in British soil—see Brown 1990, 92), there is every reason to suppose that William Adam came to identify himself ever more closely with the eponymous title of his book. As work progressed, and became more and more dependent upon each new Adam commission, the project took on an increasingly private, family heirloom character. Those subscribers who lost patience and asked for their money back could be reimbursed without imperiling the project, since it was driven not by normal publishing or marketing criteria, but by the steady advance of the Adam family's architectural and business fortunes. Cooper, as a presumed investor in the work—possibly even a half-shareholder—might have instilled greater urgency for a return on his investment had he not been, as Adam had become, a man of considerable private wealth and in no way dependent upon the practice of his profession to make a living (Harris and Savage 1990, 96, 102 n. 14–16). And insofar as the book became a record simply of Adam's commissioned work, so too did it start to acquire a fatally open-ended character, especially later in the eyes of his sons. This is evident as Cooper continued to add plates beyond the original target of 150—if one includes the 6 unsigned plates almost certainly from his hand (pls. 14, 22, 23, 41, 61, and 159) as well as the 4 that were probably subsequently "corrected" and re-signed by Andrew Bell or T. Smith (pl. 13 bis, 31, 83 bis, and 121 bis—traces of Cooper's original signature are still visible on pl. 121 bis in the BAL copy), this target was exceeded by at least fifteen plates.

To judge from the approximate dates of the latest William Adam commissions to be engraved, Cooper ceased work on the book in the early to mid-1740s, but not before he (or an assistant) had numbered and signed the copperplates in readiness for the press. Three factors probably intervened at this stage to delay matters: first, the paper and printing expenses were heavy and, unlike that of the engraving, had to be met in one installment; second, an explanatory text at least as informative as Campbell's for *Vitruvius Britannicus* had to be written—no easy matter for a very busy architect with no claims as a man of letters; and third, the arrival of Bonnie Prince Charlie and the outbreak of a bitter and very bloody civil war put the cause of Scottish nationalism well beyond the pale of civilized (i.e., Anglocentric) debate, and with it, of course, all such obvious expressions of national pride as a long-promised, half-forgotten "Vitruvius Scoticus." As an official government contractor Adam was in a sensitive enough position as it was; drawing attention to his work for leading figures on either side could be easily misconstrued as a political statement and have a damaging effect on his reputation. (It has been suggested, for instance, that Adam's two designs of houses "for a Person of Quality" [pls. 96–97 and 124] had, in fact, been commissioned by attainted Jacobites whom it would have been unwise to name—see Adam 1980, 33; similarly, the earl of Mar's design is tactfully captioned as a "Royal Palace invented by a Person of Quality"—see pls. 109–110.)

As the eldest son and new *paterfamilias*, it not unnaturally fell to John Adam's lot to revive the book after his father's death in 1748. And just as naturally, he continued where his father had left off by updating the collection with engravings of his own and his brother's architectural work on their native soil. His interest in resuscitating the project—apart from a sense of duty to his father's long-suffering subscribers—may well have been an indirect response to the opinions expressed by his brother Robert, in a letter from Rome to his mother dated 13 November 1756 (Clerk of Penicuik MSS, SRO, Edinburgh; quoted in Fleming 1962, 363), concerning the inadvisability of publishing any designs that had not already been executed and "approved of and admired by the world." The earliest of the fourteen new plates added by John Adam (not including the four interpolated plates of buildings designed by his father—Hamilton Church (pl. 13 bis), Mount Stuart (pl. 31), Gartmore (pl. 83 bis), and Hamilton (i.e., Fala) House (pl. 121 bis)—were almost certainly the four devoted to Roger Morris' Inveraray Castle (executed 1745–1758 under the supervision of William and subsequently John Adam for the 3d duke of Argyll—see pls. [71]–74). These show the castle and its associated buildings in such disproportionate detail

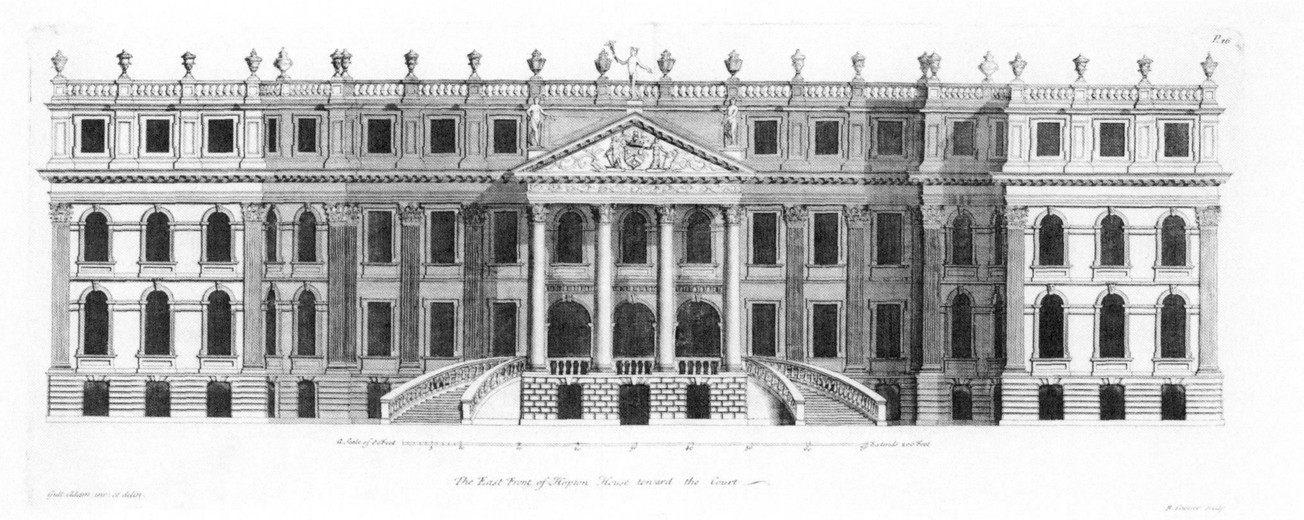

William Adam. *Vitruvius Scoticus.* Plate 16. "The East Front of Hopton House...." 1985.61.165

(including a plate of garden bridges out of keeping with the book's otherwise exclusive concentration on "principal regular building") that they may well have been originally intended to form part of a distinct suite of plates recording the Adam family's long connection with works undertaken there. (It is perhaps significant that an independent set of these plates is preserved at Inverary—see Adam 1980, 28). Although only two are signed, all four were almost certainly engraved by Andrew Bell who, following Cooper's retirement in the mid-1750s, had effectively succeeded him as Edinburgh's leading engraver. Indeed, having been apprenticed to Cooper, and no doubt involved in work on the *Vitruvius Scoticus* plates, Bell was an obvious choice for John Adam. And yet when it came to engraving more new plates, or "correcting" and completing existing ones, in only one instance was Bell used again (i.e., for the apparently corrected plate of Hamilton Church, pl. 13 bis). Instead, John distributed the work (no doubt on Robert's advice) among three well-known London-based engravers, namely Peter Mazell, Francis Patton, and W. Proud. Even allowing for the possibility that the shadowy "T. Smith" whose name appears on the other three "corrected" plates (pls. 31, 83 bis, and 121 bis), as well as on the "substitute" plates 45 and 63 and interpolated bis plate 135, might have been an Edinburgh-based engraver and possibly even associated with Bell, it is still very odd, to say the least, to read the following in the account given of *Vitruvius Scoticus* in the second, much enlarged edition of Richard Gough's *British Topography* (1780): "Most, if not the whole of Mr. Adam's designs were engraved, several reengraved upon a more elegant plan, some proof impressions whereof were taken by Andrew Bell, engraver in Edinburgh, who corrected many of the designs by the direction of John Adams, esq." (2: 605–606).

Gough's description of Adam's unpublished book in the first edition of his bibliography (1768) had been merely an edited version of the printed proposals issued in London on 20 March 1766, promising delivery of the work "in two large volumes in folio . . . on or before March 1767" (a copy of these proposals, marked up for the printer, is in the Gough Collection in the Bodleian Library, Oxford—MS Gough Gen. Top. 21). By 1780, however, some explanation for the continued nonappearance of Adam's book was clearly called for. The immediate source of Gough's new information was his "communicative friend Mr. George Paton, of the custom-house, Edinburgh," whom he acknowledges had enabled him "to nearly double the article of Scottish topography" (*British Topography* 1780, 2: 554). The collection of Paton's correspondence in the National Library of Scotland reveals him to have been not only extremely well informed but also, through a relation of his wife (a "Mr. J. Robertson," presumably a relation, in turn, of the Adam brothers' cousin William Robertson), to have derived the information he passed on to Gough concerning "Mr. Adams Book" not from some garbled bookshop gossip but from the horse's mouth, namely, John Adam himself.

Paton's first account of Adam's book, given in his letter to Gough of 18 April 1772, is clearly based on personal recollection only, and offered not in response to any specific inquiry but as a suggested ready-made source of plates for Gough's proposed idea for a collection of "Draughts & Views of the many Palaces, Castles, Seats of Gentlemen, Abbies &c. in Scotland"—in other words, a revival of the "Scotia Illustrata" that *Vitruvius Scoticus* might have been. Paton's excitement at Gough's idea becomes all the greater as he recollects past disappointments:

> A great many years ago Mr. William Adam Father to Messrs. Adamses who carry on presently such large Undertakings in London opened a subscription for publishing Views, Elevations, Plans, Sections &c. of the most remarkable Buildings in this Country to promote which Book he obtained many Subscribers, but for what Reasons is unknown to me the Book was never published in his Life, altho' a great many of

the Plates for it were engraved, & [I] remember when his son John Adam Esq sustained so great a Loss by Messrs. Fairholmes Bankers, that he revived the Scheme & gave the World hopes of the Book being soon to be usher'd into the public View, as many of the Old Plates were re-engraven, others corrected & many added, but soon after the Scheme was dropt, the Cause I shall endeavour to find out; Inquiry shall also be made of all that has been done & if agreeable to your proposed Plan, this you shall be informed of, likewise I will get notice if the Book is to be published; provided these Plates are engraved well, Proportion & Exactness observed (as undoubtedly its to be hoped is the case) several of these Views or Plans must supercede the taking of Draughts to engrave new Plates if Mr. Adams will publish his Father's Work with his more refined Improvements, or sell some or any of the Engraved Plates to complete the Collection you propose (G. Paton to R. Gough, 18 April 1772, NLS Adv. MSS 29.5.7[i], fol. 47).

Nine days later Paton reported the results of his inquiries as follows:

. . . Mr. Adams's Book is not yet publish'd owing to Mr. Bell Engraver here not having finished some Plates he was to cut for that Publication & Mr. Millar dying before the Bargain was concluded, so probably the Property is not transferred, but Mr. Robertson the Bearer hereof can introduce you to Mr. Adams of whom you can obtain more perfect Intelligence on this subject as well as about several other Matters in that style relating to this Country; I have told Mr. Robertson of my design of introducing you to Mr. Adams (G. Paton to R. Gough, 27 April 1772, NLS Adv. MSS 29.5.7[i], fol. 50r).

Even though there was some delay (see Paton's letter of 28 May 1772 advising Gough that "Mrs. Adams & Campbell's Vitruvius Britannicus are works on the same Plan, I shall write to Mr. Robertson to wait of you on your return to London that he may introduce you to Mr. Adams . . . ," fol. 56v)—Gough was not in London when Mr. Robertson called with Paton's letter—it is difficult to believe that Gough failed to take this opportunity to learn more about a book that, had it been published, would have provided the best source of illustrations of buildings in Scotland yet to appear. Although Gough's interest in *Vitruvius Scoticus* as a source of material for his own collection understandably lessened when he discovered that, like Campbell's work, it was devoted to "modern" and "regular" (i.e., classical) buildings only, one particular plate among those added by John Adam went on to become the subject of repeated inquiries, both by Paton in Edinburgh through the medium of Mr. Robertson, and by Gough in London through its engraver, Peter Mazell. The plate in question—Jan Wyck's perspective view of the "Inside of the Chappel Royal of Holyroodhouse"—was of prime antiquarian importance because it showed the interior of the Abbey Church as it had been briefly fitted out for James II in 1687 and before its destruction by a mob in December of the following year. The subsequent desecration of the ancient tombs of the kings of Scotland, and the collapse of the temporary roof (see Brewer 1810, 296), stood as a constant reproach to anyone with feeling for the pre-Union history of Scotland. (Archibald Constable was later to offer Sir Walter Scott an impression of Mazell's plate as worthy of the great Scotsman's antiquarian collection.) Repeated, but fruitless, attempts by both Gough and Paton to obtain impressions of this plate (related in their correspondence from 15 February 1773 until at least the same time the following year—see NLS Adv. MSS 29.5.6[i], fol. 29r; 29.5.7[i], fols. 88r, 100r, 101r, 104r, 138r) make it virtually certain that they not only contacted John Adam directly (either or both certainly did so through "Mr. Robertson") but that they also received from him the information that Gough subsequently incorporated in the second edition of his bibliography. Therefore the discrepancies noted in Gough's account—particularly the prominence given to Andrew Bell and the emphasis upon the degree of reengraving and correction of the old plates—take on a new significance if

William Adam. *Vitruvius Scoticus.* Plate 5 bis. "Section of the Royal Palace of Holy-rood House...." 1985.61.153

they are understood as elements of what was, in effect, a press release devised by John Adam to account for the nonappearance of his father's book.

Particularly after the issue of the March 1766 prospectus, there must have been many left wondering what had happened to the book—not only subscribers, both old and new, but also others interested perhaps in a specific building or plate—so it was obviously expedient for John Adam to publish an explanation of sorts through the medium of Gough's bibliography. The reason he did not do so directly—by issuing advertisements in the press, for instance—was quite simple: the situation required economy with the truth, a "story" that was true as far as it went but concealed the real reasons for the failure of the book to appear. The blame for this—laid squarely at Bell's door in Paton's letter of 27 April 1772—is softened in Gough's published account to merely an implication that the engraver had been, and might still be, working on a revision of the book for John Adam. Indeed, given the direct access he had to first-hand information, Gough's report appears extraordinarily circumspect and noncommittal: is the book to be published or not? Do the "proof impressions . . . taken by Andrew Bell" constitute an edition, available for purchase perhaps on application to him? This latter reference to the existence of proof copies of the book (almost certainly based on information derived directly from John Adam, since it is not mentioned by Paton) is at once the closest to the truth and the most misleading and ambiguous part of Gough/Adam's statement. For there can be little doubt that anyone who had subscribed to Adam's book would have been astounded to discover in 1780 that "some proof impressions" amounted in reality to an edition of 950 copies that had been printed and virtually ready for distribution at least fifteen years earlier.

It is possible to argue that the printing of this edition, as stated in the "Memorandum of Agreement" drawn up between John Adam and the publisher Andrew Millar on 10 August 1765 (Harris and Savage 1990, 99, 103 n. 36), was simply one of the conditions of its fulfillment (i.e., had not yet taken place), only if two major pieces of evidence to the contrary are ignored. First, it is extremely difficult to believe that John Adam, in the midst of a severe financial crisis brought about by the failure of the Fairholme bank, would have felt himself in a position to invest some £1,300 in printing an edition of 950 copies of his father's book in return for a mere £850 profit spread over three and a half years. It is virtually certain, therefore, that whatever edition the sheets of *Vitruvius Scoticus* were originally intended to form, the decision to go to press occurred before news broke in Edinburgh of the Fairholme debacle (26 March 1764). Second, as to the size of the edition printed, the offer of one hundred pounds made by a scrap-paper merchant in 1804 for the sheets stored in Cadell's London warehouse would have been excessively high for any amount significantly less than the 750 copies of the book that Millar's contract had stipulated.

This leads to the virtually inescapable conclusion that a decision to publish *Vitruvius Scoticus* was definitely made, almost certainly in the early 1760s; that this decision was modified after the Fairholme crash to the extent that a London publisher agreed to buy the unsubscribed portion of the edition; and finally that the entire edition was deliberately withheld under the pretense that the work was still undergoing revision by the engraver. Such an extraordinary fiasco might seem more far-fetched, were it not possible to detect, behind the scenes as it were, the influence of Robert and James Adam's rising star south of the border, where any publication connected with the family name might do more harm than good if it failed to evince the most advanced and novel taste of the day, especially in light of Robert's recent appearance as the learned author of *Ruins of the Palace of the Emperor Diocletian at Spalatro* (1764). N. S.

Bibliography

Adam, W. *Vitruvius Scoticus*. Facsimile. Ed. J. Simpson. Edinburgh, 1980

Brewer, J. N. *A Descriptive and Historical Account of the Various Palaces*. London, 1810.

Brown, I. G. "William Adam's Seal: Palladio, Inigo Jones and the Image of Vitruvius Scoticus." *Architectural Heritage* 1 (Edinburgh, 1990): 91–103

Fleming, J. *Robert Adam and His Circle in Edinburgh and Rome*. London, 1962

Harris, E., and N. Savage. *British Architectural Books and Writers 1556–1785*. Cambridge, 1990

4

Leon Battista Alberti (1404–1472)

The Architecture Of Leon Battista Alberti In Ten Books. Of Painting In Three Books And Of Statuary In One Book. Translated Into Italian By Cosimo Bartoli, And Now First Into English, And Divided Into Three Volumes By James Leoni, Venetian, Architect; To Which Are Added Several Designs Of His Own, For Buildings Both Public And Private

London: printed by Thomas Edlin, 1726 [i.e., 1726–1730]
1983.49.4

Folio: 448 × 285 (17 5/8 × 11 3/16)

Foliation Vol. 1: [xiii], 103 leaves, etched and engraved frontispiece, [9] engraved plates

Vol. 2: [ii], 130 leaves, [58] engraved plates (4 double-page)

Vol. 3: [ii], 34 leaves, [8] engraved plates; [viii], 6 leaves, 27 engraved plates (11 double-page, 8 folding)

(*Note:* This foliation does not include an unnumbered copyright privilege leaf, usually bound either in vol. 1 or 3, lacking in this copy)

Edition First edition

Text (parallel English and Italian) *vol. 1*: f. [i] title in Italian (verso blank); [ii] same in English (verso blank); [iii] dedication; [iv–v] list of subscribers; [vi–ix] Raphael du Fresne's biography of Alberti and list of Alberti's works; [x–xiii] preface; [1]–103 text of Architecture, books 1–5; *vol. 2*: f. [i] title of vol. 2 in Italian (verso blank); [ii] same in English "The Architecture Of Leon Battista Alberti Published By James Leoni . . ." (verso blank); [1]–130 text of Architecture, books 6–10 (f. 130 verso blank); *vol. 3*: f. [i] title in Italian (verso blank); [ii] same in English "The Painting Of Leon Battista Alberti In 3 Books. And Of Statuary In One Book. Published By James Leoni, To Which Are Added Several Designs Of His Own, &c. . . ." (verso blank); [1]–34 text of Alberti's treatises; *Supplement* f. [i] title in Italian (verso blank); [ii] same in English "Some Designs For Buildings Both Publick and Private By James Leoni . . ." (verso blank); [iii] dedication (verso blank); [iv–viii] note to the reader; 1–6 text, list of additional subscribers at end

Illustrations Etched and engraved allegorical frontispiece and 102 engraved plates, of which the 27 in the supplement are numbered I–XXVII and the remainder unnumbered but with folio directions for binding. 6 plates, including the frontispiece, are not credited to a draftsman. The remainder are signed by Leoni (sometimes also as *inventor*), except 3 plates by Bernard Picart in vol. 2. The engraver is unnamed or given as Picart (sometimes "direxit" only), John Harris, or J. Cole. For a fuller description, see RIBA, *Early Printed Books*

Binding 3 vols. bound as 1. Contemporary full calf, repaired, central panels tooled in blind, gilt borders, gilt arms of the marquess of Rockingham

Provenance Armorial bookplate of the marquess of Rockingham; ownership inscription "Abm. Welland, Feby. 13th 1829" on English title page; bookplate of Charles Frederic Mewes

References Berlin Cat. (2554) 2267; Cicognara 378; ESTC n65008; Fowler 11; Harris and Savage 12; RIBA, *Early Printed Books*, 48

On 15 January 1720 Giacomo Leoni published the last fascicle of his edition of Palladio's *Quattro Libri*. Its completion was a remarkable achievement by any standards. In 1715, with only 163 subscribers, he had undertaken an unprecedentedly lavish trilingual edition of a heavily illustrated work, on a subject hitherto associated in England more with builders' manuals than architects' treatises. Yet in the course of publication he had attracted so many new purchasers that he would soon be offering to buy back unwanted copies of volume one to resell; within a year, he had published a second edition. Leoni's Palladio, like Colen Campbell's *Vitruvius Britannicus*, was both a confirmation of renewed interest in the Palladian style and a significant element in its future domination of the national taste. The size and quality of the volume justified Leoni's boast, in his valedictory preface, that "As for what concerns the paper and letter, there has been no book hitherto so beautifully printed in England."

In thanking his subscribers, Leoni added a hope that "they will continue to honour me with the like encouragement in favour of another work, voluminous indeed, but most useful and curious, as by printed Proposals will shortly appear." No proposals have been found, but in the event he chose to capitalize on his success by providing the first English translation of another Renaissance architectural treatise, Alberti's *De Re Aedificatoria*. To this he added translations of Alberti's much shorter treatises on painting and statuary, and a separable section illustrating his own designs. After a long period gathering 264 subscribers, publication began in 1726 and continued until about March 1730, the date of the copyright privilege (probably the last leaf to be printed, usually inserted in either volume one or three, but missing from the Millard copy).

Similar in format and style to his Palladio, Leoni's Alberti was clearly intended as a companion piece. As a publishing venture, it cannot be understood in isolation from the earlier work. The two treatises were fundamentally different in origin and execution, but under Leoni's editorship these differences were minimized.

Palladio's was written in Italian and published in 1570 with numerous woodcuts from his own designs. Whatever liberties Leoni took with his source—and there were many—his starting point was unimpeachable, and the Italian text that appeared with French and English translations came direct from the master. Alberti's treatise, by contrast, was written in Latin, probably between 1443 and 1452, and no illustrations were provided either in manuscript or for the earliest printed versions of 1485, 1512, and 1541. There is no evidence that Leoni consulted this Latin text, or the first printed Italian translation by Pietro Lauro of 1546. Instead, Leoni and his unnamed translator, recently identified as John Ozell, took as their primary source Cosimo Bartoli's Italian translation of 1550, which was the first to be illustrated and certainly the version most widely available, having been reprinted twice in 1565 and translated into French by Jean Martin in 1553. The Italian text was reprinted with Ozell's English version in parallel columns, and Leoni's illustrations are mostly derived from Bartoli too. These mid-sixteenth-century woodcuts had been grafted onto a text that was addressed primarily to the nobility of the Florentine *quattrocento*. Inevitably, they not only clarified Alberti's treatise, but also interpreted it. Where the text suggested a range of harmonious proportions, Bartoli fixed the reader's eye on one in particular, and where Alberti stated what he knew of ancient Roman building types, Bartoli illustrated also what had been learned since. It is important to recognize, therefore, that although Leoni's editorial method was the same as for Palladio's *Quattro Libri*, the source that he used for his Alberti was already some distance removed from the original.

Another difference between the two projects stems from Leoni's enthusiastic Palladianism. As early as 1708 he had written a manuscript treatise in Düsseldorf on the five orders according to Palladio. Originally from Venice (by his own account), Leoni claimed to have made a personal study of Palladio's buildings, allowing him to correct the measurements of some of the woodcuts in *Quattro Libri*. He had also worked in Cologne for Count Matteo de' Alberti, an admirer of Palladio and Inigo Jones, before coming to England, perhaps at about the time of George I's accession in 1714. His own inclination, therefore, was toward an architectural style formed a century after *De Re Aedificatoria* was written—an inclination shared by most of his audience. Leoni had to decide whether to be faithful to Alberti's text, as mediated by Bartoli, or to the current notions of taste by which his efforts would be judged.

In the event, he attempted to do both. Leoni evidently read the text with some care, and emended Bartoli's woodcuts where he noticed an error. He was alert to the latter's incorrect illustration of an entablature when showing a column in full relief, and altered it to conform with the text ("In the whole relieve the entablature must not run all along the wall but be broke and project over the head of each column," book 6: 19). He also took considerable pains to provide more detail on his copperplate engravings than Bartoli could with woodcuts, and even filled a few obvious gaps in the sequence of illustrations (e.g., by providing a plate showing a Doric capital, book 7: 32, no. 1). There was scope for many more such illustrations, but Leoni did not stray as far from his source as he might have, and rejected most of the designs Martin had added to the French edition even though he must have consulted it (e.g., for his version of Caesar's bridge over the Rhine, book 4: 71). Equally, some of Bartoli's woodcuts are pedestrian to the point of redundancy, especially in the earlier books, but all are included. Some of these look preposterously oversized when transferred to Leoni's large folio page.

Instead of revising Bartoli's editorial program, Leoni invested all his creativity into revising the illustrations. The Palladian tendency of many of these revisions has been noted by Harris and Savage. Other alterations, however, seem to stem from carelessness or egotism. Perhaps the most glaring error is his addition of walls to the sides of the portico in his plan of an Etruscan temple. This is not only contrary to Bartoli's woodcut, based on Alberti's design for S. Andrea at Mantua, but also contradicts the text, which states simply enough that "The Portico, by its Nature, should have a continued Wall but of one Side, and all the other Sides should be full of large Apertures for Passage" (book 7: 27). Similarly, his engraving of a memorial column (book 8: 57) shows scant regard for Alberti's detailed recommendations for its proportions. No doubt Leoni saw all his alterations as straightforward improvements, and would have applied to them what he said of the designs in his Palladio, that is, that he had "made so many necessary Corrections with respect to Shading, dimensions, ornaments, &c. that this Work may in some sort be rather consider'd as an Original, than an Improvement" (preface to book 4, part 2). This proud claim—which Isaac Ware would use against him in his more correct edition of Palladio—gives the key to Leoni's editorial philosophy. It was neither in his nature to start anew, nor to leave alone. Rather, he engaged in a close dialogue with his material. His designs for Alberti's treatise are best appreciated as the visual equivalent of a well-established genre: the imitation, or studious adaptation of a canonical author to contemporary mores.

The appended translations of *De Pictura* and *De Statua* are also derived from Bartoli, who first published them as part of a collection of minor works, *Opuscoli Morali di Leon Batista Alberti* (1568). This was the source for Raphael Trichet du Fresne's versions, appended to his *Trattato della Pittura di Lionardo da Vinci* (1651), from which Leoni took his text and illustrations. The brief biography of Alberti also came from Du Fresne. This and the treatise on painting had not previously appeared in English, whereas Alberti's shorter work on statuary had been translated by John Evelyn and appended to his edition of Roland Fréart's *Parallèle de l'architecture antique et de la moderne*. Leoni does not seem to have used this earlier translation, first printed in 1664.

As a supplement to the works by Alberti, the third volume includes *Some Designs for Buildings both Publick and Private by James Leoni Architect*, which has an independent pagination and register and was available for separate purchase. Dated 1726 on the title page, it could not have appeared in either form until at least 1729, the date on two of the plates. In its separate issue, it was the second collection of designs published by a British architect and devoted to his own work, following James Gibbs' *Book of Architecture* (1728). As an appendix to Alberti, it follows a method of self-promotion successfully used by Campbell, who added his own designs to *Vitruvius Britannicus*, and by Lord Burlington, who (via William Kent) published designs for the Westminster Dormitory and Chiswick Villa in *Designs of Inigo Jones and Others* (1727). Since most of Leoni's designs are as Palladian, or rather as Jonesian, as he could manage, their association with Alberti was simply a marriage of convenience, providing a relatively easy way to get them into the homes of potential patrons. Ironically, he states in his address to the reader that "The English nation need [sic] no foreign examples of perfection in the way of Architecture. Inigo Jones, their illustrious Countryman, who flourished in the Reign of Charles I made in Italy so great a Progress in this Art, that he attained to the first rank in it."

This follows a scathing attack on various contemporary architectural practices and is succeeded by the sort of praise for Burlington that was soon to be a commonplace: "It is he that has revived and set in its true light, the Glory of that illustrious Architect [Jones], the Follower of our Andrea Palladio, that other great Light in this Art, whose Works thro' my means, were honoured by the generous Nobility of this Country with a magnificent Edition." Behind the praise, there may be a hint of resentment that he has to remind readers of his Palladio, published well before Burlington's adoption of the cause. On the other hand, four of Leoni's architectural projects were commissioned by kinsmen of Burlington, and a fifth patron was distantly related to him by marriage. It is possible, as Richard Hewlings has suggested, that Burlington regularly recommended Leoni to his cousins and that the relationship between the two architects was less strained than some historians suggest. Whatever Leoni thought, Burlington was by this time generally recognized as the national arbiter of architectural taste. Leoni acknowledges this again by dedicating to him a design for a country house with an Egyptian hall (in imitation of Palladio), and by relating an anecdote from when he was building Queensbury House on Burlington's London estate: "The portal on that side of the House which opens to the Court-yard, was designed by the Right Honourable the Earl of Burlington, who is the Owner of the Ground. When I laid this Design before him for his Approbation, his Lordship gave leave to the Person who executed it, to set the Front towards his own Garden; a Privilege denied to all the other Houses there."

Most of Leoni's designs were unexecuted, namely, the triumphal arch for Hyde Park (pls. 1–2), the country houses "in imitation of the stile of Inigo Jones" and of Palladio (pls. 16–19), the two town houses (pls. 23–26), and the stone bridge (pl. 27). Queensbury House and Argyll House in London (pls. 14–15, 20–22) had both been completed before 1724. Construction had begun

James Leoni. *The Architecture of Leon Battista Alberti in Ten Books*. Plate 6. "Elevation of the West front of Carshalton House." 1983.49.4

Leon Battista Alberti. *The Architecture of Leon Battista Alberti in Ten Books*. Frontispiece. 1983.49.4

Attributed to Sebastiano Galeotti. *Allegory of the Fine Arts*. Pen and ink with wash over chalk. [35.3 x 23.8 cm.] Art Gallery of Ontario, Toronto. Purchase, Walter C. Laidlaw Endowment, 1963

on Carshalton Park, Surrey (pls. 3–13), but the work was never finished due to the financial difficulties of its owner, the dedicatee of *Some Designs*, Thomas Scawen. In the pediments of the two main fronts to Carshalton, Leoni (or his engraver) introduced miniature versions of the allegorical frontispieces to his editions of Palladio and Alberti. There is no reason to take these pediment decorations as a serious part of Leoni's design. The frontispieces were probably being used as convenient but temporary fillers, especially as neither design originated with Leoni himself.

Interpreting the allegorical significance of these frontispieces requires caution. The design facing the title page to Leoni's Alberti shows Britannia on her throne directing the attention of a kneeling Architecture to a portrait of Alberti supported by Florence, his native city. The portrait is from a woodcut first used by Bartoli. Painting, seated in the foreground, gestures toward Architecture, while a putto behind her again points toward the portrait. A cherub displays a banner inscribed "Summo decore nitescat," in praise of Alberti's shining worth. There are also certain incongruous elements, however, such as the absence of Sculpture despite a treatise on the subject; the hinted presence of Drama (in the mask lying at Painting's feet); and the strangely rococo design of Britannia's throne. An examination of the original drawing, now in the Art Gallery of Ontario, shows that the engraving was actually an adaptation of a work not intended to be in praise of Alberti at all, but of an unidentified woman whose bust stands before the slab on which, in the engraving, the architect's portrait appears. As Walter Vitzthum noted, the drawing has traces of an oval paper slip, now lost, pasted over the bust. Presumably this slip depicted Alberti, and was added to guide the engraver Bernard Picart as he adapted this Allegory of the Arts for its new purpose. The drawing itself has been attributed to Sebastiano Galeotti, a Florentine pupil of Alessandro Gherardini and a painter whose most important commissions were frescoes executed in Genoa. (The attribution in a late hand to Pellegrini, given on the verso of the drawing, can be dismissed on stylistic grounds.) As Galeotti seems never to have visited England, Leoni's possession of the piece may have been through his contact with those Northern Italian artists who did, particularly Sebastiano Ricci. The drawing is dated "Anno del: 1724" on the cornice below the bust.

The retention of elements in the reversed copy represented by the engraving explains the incongruities mentioned above. In other respects the adaptation is skillfully managed. An enthroned Minerva becomes Britannia, by the addition of a chain with a pendant of St. George slaying the dragon. A Florentine fleur-de-lys replaces a cross on the figure holding the bust (now a portrait). One odd interpretation is visible on Britannia's helmet, where a half-length female crest has been added amid the plumes. In general, although the engraver's burin loses some of the drawing's grace, it preserves its spirit. Inevitably, therefore, the message of the Alberti frontispiece is far more diffuse than the sharply political allegory Sebastiano Ricci had provided for Leoni's Palladio. Neither it nor the letterpress dedication to the prince of Wales can be interpreted as an anticipation of royal favor. The dedication scarcely rises above the formulaic requirements of the period. These may be indications that Leoni no longer had the serious hopes of court patronage expressed in his earlier publication. The prince of Wales, elevated to the throne after the sudden death of George I in 1727, rewarded him with no more than a fourteen-year copyright privilege.

The frontispiece is signed "B. Picart sculpsit, 1726," and Picart's name appears on all the most highly finished plates illustrating the three volumes. Several of these, however, are signed "sculp. direxit" and were presumably engraved by others in his Amsterdam workshop. In most cases Leoni supplied him with drawings, but Picart signs five as draftsman (three in book ten and two for the treatise on statuary), and was clearly responsible for the style of several more, as they resemble his other work for a wide range of publications, most notably *Cérémonies et Coutumes Religieux*, 1721–1743. Although the *trompe-l'oeil* features of Leoni's edition of Palladio have gone, the baroque appearance of these plates reflects a taste that set him apart from the purists of the so-called Burlington circle. A few of the less elaborate plates are signed either by John Harris or James Cole, both standard London engravers for architectural subjects. At the close of the work, Leoni adds a personal recommendation of Thomas Heath, the mathematical instrument maker, whose name also appears on the same page as one of forty-one additional subscribers "after the publication of the first and second volume." G. B.

Bibliography

British Architectural Library, Royal Institute of British Architects. *Early Printed Books 1478–1840: Catalogue of the British Architectural Library Early Imprints Collection*. Vols. 1–2. London, 1994–1995

Colvin, H. *A Biographical Dictionary of British Architects 1600–1840*. 3d ed. New Haven and London, 1995: 608–611

Harris, E., and N. Savage. *British Architectural Books and Writers 1556–1785*. Cambridge, 1990

Hewlings, R. "James Leoni c. 1686–1746: An Anglicised Venetian." In *The Architectural Outsiders*. Ed. Roderick Brown. London, 1985

McTavish, D., et al. *The Arts of Italy in Toronto Collections*. Toronto, 1981

Vitzthum, W. *Drawings in the Collection of the Art Gallery of Ontario*. Toronto, 1970

5

Leon Battista Alberti (1404–1472)

The Architecture Of Leon Battista Alberti In Ten Books. Of Painting In Three Books And Of Statuary In One Book. Translated Into Italian By Cosimo Bartoli. The Second Edition And Divided Into Two Volumes By James Leoni, Venetian, Architect

London: printed by Thomas Edlin, 1739

1981.70.9–10

Folio: 429 × 275 (16 × 10¾)

Foliation Vol. 1: [xi], 103 leaves, etched and engraved frontispiece, [9] engraved plates

Vol. 2: [ii], 130 leaves, [58] engraved plates (4 double-page)

Vol. 3: [ii], 34 leaves, [8] engraved plates

Edition Reissue of the first edition

Text As first issue, but with a cancel title leaf and without the list of subscribers (2 leaves), the copyright privilege leaf, or the *Supplement* to vol. 3

Illustrations As first issue, without the *Supplement*

Binding 3 volumes bound as 2. Contemporary mottled calf, gilt spines, red morocco labels, sprinkled edges

Provenance Library stamps of the Royal Military Academy, Berlin ("K.K. Technische Militair Academie").

References ESTC n55084; Harris and Savage 14

When Giacomo Leoni committed his edition of Alberti's *De Re Aedificatoria* to the press he was not only interested in the British audience for whom he provided John Ozell's translation. His continental background and contacts would have made him more alert than most to the European market, as confirmed by his earlier publication of an edition of Palladio in three languages. Furthermore, in the same year that Thomas Edlin printed the text for the Alberti (1726), Leoni's Palladio was being published in a French language edition by Pierre Gosse at The Hague. Leoni did not add a French translation to the English and Italian texts of his Alberti, although one was available from the 1553 Paris edition. Instead, he seems to have prepared for demand outside Britain by publishing two versions of the work simultaneously. The most common of these is the bilingual edition, but immediately after printing it Edlin also ran off copies of a rare Italian-only edition, known at present from a single imperfect example in the Soane Museum library. It was printed with substantially the same setting of the Italian text as the bilingual edition, but the type was rearranged to cover both columns on each page. (At least one error in the bilingual edition was noted in the process: in the *Vita*, the date of construction of the tribuna of the Santissima Annunziata in Florence is corrected, or at least improved, from 1551 to 1451.) This rearrangement was made easier by the decision not to print illustrations and text on the same page. Combined with the narrowing of spaces between paragraphs, and minor deletions (such as the list of subscribers and the supplementary dedication to Thomas Scawen), much paper was saved. Leoni's supplement of his own designs was not included, and the whole was presented as a single volume. Overall, the aim seems to have been to provide a cheaper publication for the continental market—effectively a new edition of Cosimo Bartoli's translation of the ten books, with the addition of Alberti's two treatises on painting and statuary. Its existence helps to explain why relatively few Italians are named as subscribers to the bilingual version (a total of twenty-two names in the two lists). Through it, Leoni's plates may have gained a wider continental audience than the publication history of his bilingual edition would imply.

For although Leoni began with more subscribers than for his Palladio, his Alberti was probably not as

Leon Battista Alberti. *The Architecture of Leon Battista Alberti in Ten Books.* Pag. 11 N. 4 Lib. vi. Demonstration of a pulley. 1981.70.10

successful. It certainly had none of the impact of the former work. Nor could this be expected, given the hold Palladianism had on British taste. After the three hundred-odd subscribers' copies had been distributed, the rest of the edition sold slowly. This 1739 version is a reissue, with new title leaves, of unsold sheets nine years after completion. Like the Italian-only edition, it lacks the supplement of Leoni's own designs, perhaps because, having also been published separately, copies were no longer available. Alternatively, Leoni may have suppressed them because he was already hoping to produce a second collection. An engraved subscription receipt held at the RIBA is dated "174-" and offers a three-guinea "Treatise of Architecture, and ye Art of Building Publick and Private Edifices, in English and Italian, in two Columns in Folio, by J. Leoni, Architect, Containing Several Noblemens Houses & Country Seats already Built by him both in Town & Country, never Publish'd before" (reproduced in Harris and Savage 1990, 109). Leoni died in 1746 and these two volumes never appeared, but most of his executed architectural projects date from the 1730s, and he would probably not have wanted his new work to be in competition with the old. Evidence that he was hoping to publish his designs for 21 Arlington House, built for Richard Boyle, 2d (and last) Viscount Shannon, is provided by a volume recently acquired by the British Architectural Library Drawings Collection. *The Original Draughts, for a new House to be built in Arlington Street, St. James,* dated 25 May 1738, has the appearance of a manuscript prepared by Leoni with a view to publication, perhaps as part of the advertised treatise.

Another edition of *The Architecture of Leon Baptista Alberti* was advertised on 8 December 1753, and appeared in weekly sixpenny numbers until its completion in 1755, the date on its title page. The plates were unaltered from the first edition and accompany a text in English only. Thereafter the influence of Leoni on the history of Alberti's text may be traced through an Italian edition published by the Istituto delle Scienze in Bologna, 1782, which copied all of his illustrations on a slightly reduced scale, and another published in Milan in 1833, edited by Stefano Ticozzi, with simplified versions of the same designs further reduced onto thirty quarto leaves of plates. Facsimiles of the 1755 edition were published this century by Tiranti and Dover Publications, but there was no other English version of the text available until J. Rykwert, N. Leach, and R. Tavernor's recent translation, *On the Art of Building in Ten Books* (Cambridge, Mass., 1988). G. B.

Bibliography

Harris, E., and N. Savage. *British Architectural Books and Writers 1556–1785*. Cambridge, 1990

Hewlings, R. "Leoni's Drawings for 21 Arlington Street." *The Georgian Group Journal* 1992: 19–31

6

Henry Aldrich (1648–1710)

Elementa Architecturae Civilis Ad Vitruvii Veterumque Disciplinam, Et Recentiorum Praesertim A Palladii Exempla Probatiora Concinnata. Auctore Henrico Aldrich, S. T. P. Aedis Christi Olim Decano

Oxford: prostant apud D. Prince et J. Cooke; T. Payne et fil.; P. Elmsly, J. Robson et W. Clarke; R. Faulder, J. et T. Egerton, Londini, 1789

NGA Lib. Rare Book: NA 2515.A37

Octavo: 241 × 145 (9½ × 5¾)

Pagination [x], 54, [6], lxvi, 66 pp., engraved frontispiece portrait, 55 etched plates

Edition Second edition

Text p. [i] Latin title page (verso blank); [iii–x] list of subscribers; [1]–54 Latin text, in 2 parts; [55–56] blank; [i] English title page "The Elements Of Civil Architecture . . . Translated By The Rev. Philip Smyth, LL.B. Fellow Of New College" (verso blank); [iii–iv] advertisement; [i]–lxvi introduction; [1]–66 English translation, in 2 parts

Illustrations Stipple-engraved portrait of Aldrich by [James] Heath after Sir Gottfried Kneller; plus 55 unsigned etched plates of architectural elevations, sections, plans, details, and views numbered I–LV

Binding Nineteenth-century half morocco, gilt spine, marbled boards

Provenance Bookplate of the Surveyors Institution

References Berlin Cat. 2300; Berlin (1977) OS 2300; Cicognara 395; ESTC t154364; Fowler 18; Harris and Savage 17; RIBA, *Early Printed Books,* 67

THIS BOOK was published seventy-nine years after its author's death. Henry Aldrich, dean of Christ Church College, Oxford, died on 14 December 1710, reportedly of an ulcer in the bladder. In his will he bequeathed to his college his extensive library, including what was probably the finest collection of architectural books in private hands in England at the time. Duplicates from it were left to his nephew Charles Aldrich, also a member of Christ Church. His will also contained a controversial request that his papers be burned. Their value, however, was recognized by Canon William Stratford, one of Lord Harley's agents, who soon accused Charles of having stolen some of them; the new dean, Francis Atterbury, later accused Stratford of doing the same. Nevertheless, virtually all sources for a biography of Aldrich were destroyed.

Fortunately, Aldrich's friend Dr. George Clarke somehow acquired and preserved drawings that related to his unfinished architectural treatise, *Elementa Architecturae Civilis*, which clearly indicate that Aldrich was not only a learned academic but also a skilled draftsman. His achievements as an architect are harder to establish, although he certainly designed for his college one of the most important precursors of the Palladian revival in England, Peckwater Quadrangle (1706). He may also have had a hand in designs for several other buildings in Oxford, in particular Trinity College Chapel (1691–1694), All Saints' Church (1701–1710), and the Fellows' Building at Corpus Christi College (1706–1712). He was familiar with Nicholas Hawksmoor and Christopher Wren, and being outside the profession was a natural choice when impartial advice was sought by potential patrons. In 1710, when Sir Edward Hannes bequeathed one thousand pounds for a new dormitory at Westminster School, London, he named Wren and Aldrich as his preferred consultants. This provides a fortuitous link between Aldrich and Palladio's later champion Lord Burlington. After Aldrich's death, Atterbury intervened to ensure that the designs of Wren's protégé, William Dickenson, were rejected in favor of Burlington's radically astylar design, now regarded as a landmark in the progressive domination of the Palladian revival over the older, more eclectic school.

A renewed interest in Palladio appeared in England long before Lord Burlington adopted the cause. But until recently, 1715 was still seen as a watershed year, with publication of Colen Campbell's *Vitruvius Britannicus* and Leoni's edition of Palladio's *Quattro Libri.* Aldrich's design for Peckwater Quadrangle is one of the main arguments against the significance of this date; his *Elementa Architecturae Civilis* is another. For although the book was never finished, and never commercially published in his lifetime, a few incomplete copies (perhaps only ten) were printed and distributed to his friends in about 1708. These contain the first copies of designs by Palladio to be engraved and printed in England, and the first unequivocal recommendation of his superiority over all the other "Moderns." It is, therefore, a key source for the intellectual background to the Palladian revival.

Such a limited form of publication was fairly common at the time. It may have represented no more than Aldrich's desire to share with his colleagues a work in progress, to elicit advice or encouragement. Normally each copy would have been written out by a scribe. This was not necessary for Aldrich because he was a delegate of Oxford University's printing press, and could do for his architectural work what he had for his proposed volume of church music in 1696, namely, run off a part well before publication was properly in sight. His timing may have been one of practical convenience—perhaps the *Elementa* was typeset along with his *Institutionis*

Geometricae Pars Prima (1709). The section that he printed was all of book one (on civil architecture in general) and most of book two (on public and private buildings). According to his plan, this left a third section on civil architecture (ornament) and three more books on military architecture still to be undertaken. The printed version ends mid-sentence, although the remaining portion of book two was available to at least some of the recipients, as Clarke and others copied it out by hand at a later date. Nothing is known of the four last books, but Aldrich's proposal shows that he intended to cover all aspects of the discipline.

Unlike Palladio, his predilection was toward theory rather than practice. It is not known that he had any experience in military matters. The assumption must be that he was content to envisage his books on fortification, naval architecture, and weaponry as falling within the long tradition of European treatises that dealt with these subjects as branches of applied mathematics and geometry. This theoretical bias is also evident throughout the sections he did complete. There is not the slightest hint of the practical knowledge he possessed as an amateur architect, unless it influenced his judgment that one should not "restrain the architect by laws so rigid, as never to depart from the strictness of rules" (p. 24). Instead, his principles derived from a critical reading of the standard treatises available to him, notably those by Vitruvius, Juan Bautista Villalpandos, Claude Perrault, and, above all, Palladio. Aldrich adopted Palladio because he saw him as the best modern interpreter of ancient architecture, and ancient architecture, properly understood, could be shown to have its origins in primitive constructions close to natural formations, which together with Solomon's Temple offered the clue to architecture's divine origins. There was nothing new about this argument, but the bias toward Palladio's work implicitly contradicts the baroque style of many of Aldrich's contemporaries. Even as he wrote, for example, John Vanbrugh's Blenheim Palace was being erected just a few miles beyond Oxford.

It is quite possible Aldrich never intended to publish his treatise, even if he had finished it. Written in Latin, it was not in any case designed for the profession, any more than Charles Fairfax's Latin translation of Palladio's *Antichità di Roma* (1709), published by Oxford University with an acknowledgment of Aldrich's support. But when Clarke died he left his copy of the *Elementa* and the original drawings to Worcester College. As Aldrich's

Henry Aldrich. *Elementa architecturae civilis.* Plate XXXIV. Egyptian Hall. NGA Lib. Rare Book: NA2515A37

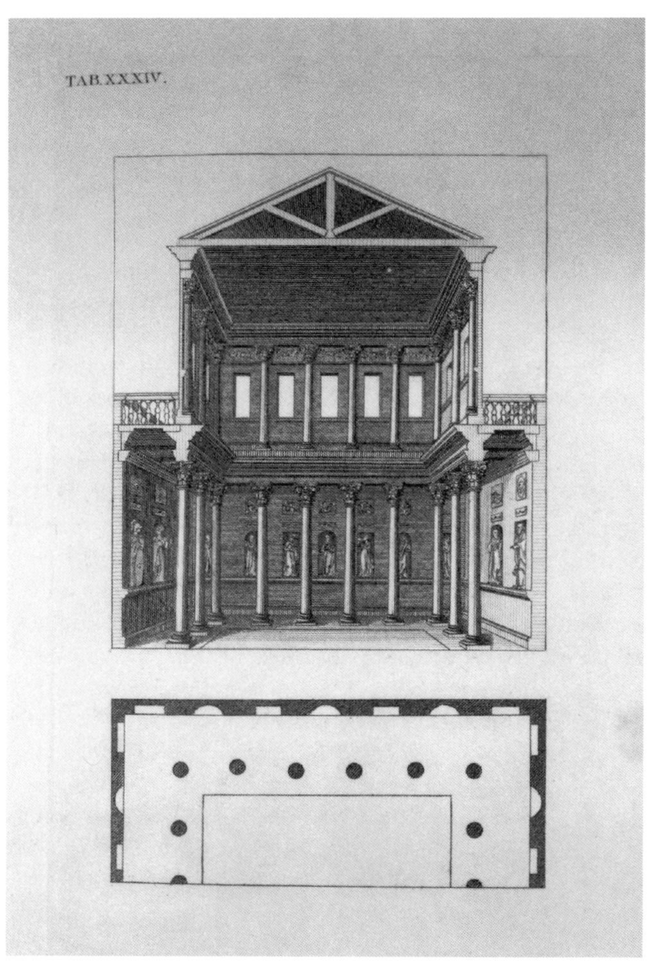

Henry Aldrich. *Elementa architecturae civilis.* Plate XXXV. Tuscan atrium. NGA Lib. Rare Book: NA2515A37

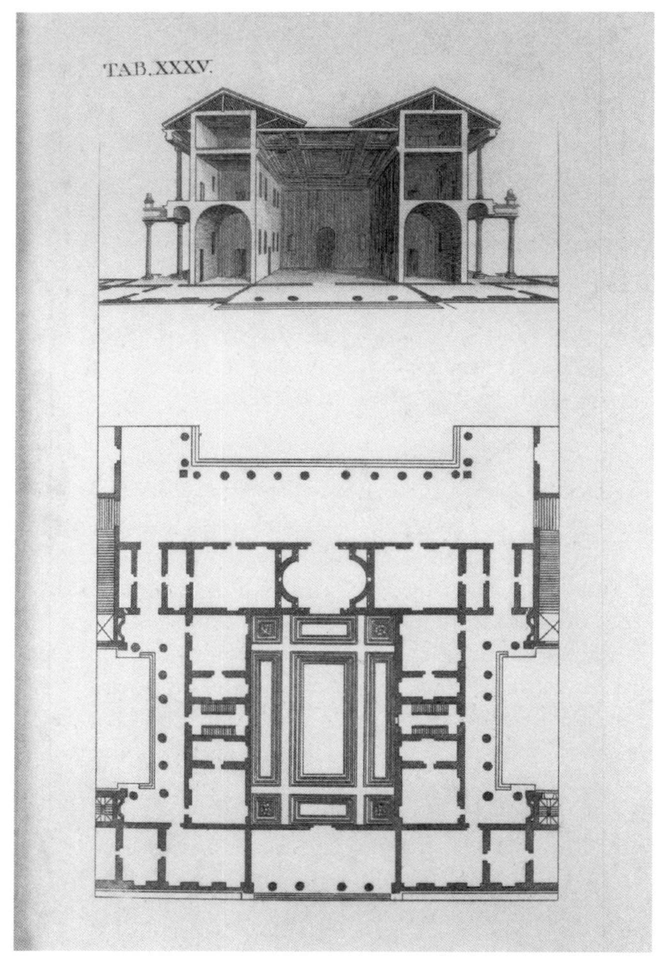

reputation as a model of learning grew in Oxford, it evidently became an act of piety to excavate the treatise and publish it by subscription. This project became the present 1789 edition. Of all the 242 subscribers only one, Thomas Whetten, is described as an architect. An English translation was provided by the Reverend Philip Smyth, a fellow of New College, Oxford, and brief and unoriginal biographies of the major Renaissance architects were added by a descendant of the dean, George Oakley Aldrich. These biographies are mostly derived from Francesco Milizia's *Memorie degli architetti antichi* (1785). James Heath provided the stipple-engraved frontispiece portrait of Aldrich, taken from Gottfried Kneller's original painting at Christ Church. An anonymous "Advertisement" and brief eulogy of the famous dean were added, both pieces too brief and circumlocutory to shed much light on the specific impulse behind publication.

Aldrich had assumed his readers had studied geometry and draftsmanship. The 1789 editor proposed instead that the work might be read by "The intire novice in that science [architecture]—the artist, whose attention the engagements of an early practice have withdrawn from the history of his profession—the traveller, who sets out unprepared for countries in which the wonders of ancient art, and the rival works of Masters, who from them have learned almost equal to them, are every where obvious." This use of his work as a tourist guide—let alone the clumsiness of its expression—was far from Aldrich's purpose. However, as a cheap and portable introduction to architecture by a highly respected name, the treatise did briefly take on a second life. The English translation was reprinted with the same biographical introduction in 1818 and 1824. "That it is not the light trumpery of the day, the name of ALDRICH, by whom the history was composed, will be held sufficient guarantee" (preface to the 1818 edition). Two years after the 1824 edition, Mrs. Edward Cresy (née Eliza Taylor) produced a full translation of Milizia's *Memorie*. This detracted from one of the earlier work's main selling points, and Aldrich's treatise has not been published since. G. B.

Bibliography

British Architectural Library, Royal Institute of British Architects. *Early Printed Books 1478–1840: Catalogue of the British Architectural Library Early Imprints Collection*. Vols. 1–2. London, 1994–1995

Colvin, H. *A Biographical Dictionary of British Architects 1600–1840*. 3d ed. New Haven and London, 1995: 69–72

Harris, E., and N. Savage. *British Architectural Books and Writers 1556–1785*. Cambridge, 1990

Harris, J. *The Palladian Revival*. Montreal, 1994

Hiscock, W. G. *Henry Aldrich of Christ Church*. Oxford, 1960

7

William Angus (1751 or 1752–1821)

The Seats Of The Nobility and Gentry, In Great Britain and Wales In a Collection of Select Views, Engraved by W. Angus. From Pictures and Drawings by the most Eminent Artists. With Descriptions of each View

[London]: published by W. Angus, 1787–1815

1985.61.375

Oblong quarto: 210 × 265 (8¼ × 10½)

Pagination [128] pp., engraved title plate, 63 engraved plates

Edition First edition. An earlier issue of 1797 consisted of the text and plates for 48 subjects only (see notes below)

Text pp. [1–126] single leaf of descriptive text for each interleaved plate, all versos blank; [127] list of contents (verso blank)

Illustrations Engraved title page signed "Cary sculp." plus 63 engraved plates numbered I–XLI, 42, XLIII–IV, 45–63. All of the views are signed "W. Angus sculp^t." or similar, the subjects and artists being as follows:

I "Broadlands in Hampshire" by Frederick Ponsonby, Lord Duncannon, later 3d earl of Bessborough (bound in this copy as a frontispiece); II "Brocket Hall in Hertfordshire" by Paul Sandby; III "Castle Howard in Yorkshire" by [William] Marlow; IV "Comb Bank in Kent" by Francis Wheatley; V "Blenheim in Oxfordshire" by Frederick Ponsonby, Lord Duncannon; VI "Busbridge in Surry" by William Beilby; VII "Dudmaster in Shropshire" by Claude Nattes; VIII "Flixton Hall in Suffolk" by Thomas Sandby; IX (bound as XI) "Dalkeith Palace in Scotland" by J. Barrett; X "Longford in Wiltshire" by Claude Nattes; XI (bound as IX) "Coghill Hall in Yorkshire" by N. T. Dall; XII "Armston in Herefordshire" by John Handy; XIII "Milton in Northamptonshire" by Frederick Ponsonby, Lord Duncannon; XIV "Oxenford in Scotland" by Robert Adam; XV "Lleweny Hall in Denbighshire" by John Bird; XVI "Cusworth in Yorkshire" by Thomas Malton, Jr.; XVII "Holland House in Middlesex" by George Samuel; XVIII "Broome in Kent" by Francis Wheatley; XIX "Moccas Court in Herefordshire" by James Wathen; XX "Tong Castle in Shropshire" by Evans; XXI "Saltram in Devonshire" by Frederick Ponsonby, Lord Duncannon; XXII "Brough Hall in Yorkshire" by Cuit, of Richmond [i.e., George Cuitt]; XXIII "Lartington in Yorkshire" by Howit, of Richmond [i.e., George Cuitt?]; XXIV "Clints in Yorkshire" by Howit, of Richmond [i.e., George Cuitt?]; XXV "Raby Castle in the County of Durham" by Edward Dayes; XXVI "Sheffield Place in Sussex" by Humphry Repton; XXVII "Barskimming, in Scotland" by Alexander Nasmyth; XXVIII "Hare Hall in Essex" by Thomas Day; XXIX "Melville Castle in Mid-Lothian" by J. Meheux; XXX "Panton House in Lincolnshire" by Claude Nattes; XXXI "Theobalds in Hertfordshire" by J. C. Barrow, F. S. A.; XXXII "Grove House in Middlesex" by William Watts; XXXIII "Nettlecombe Court in Somersetshire" by Smith; XXXIV "Chalfont House in Buckinghamshire" by [Charles?] Tomkins; XXXV "Bradwell Lodge in Essex" by Thomas Malton, Jr., with staffage by Thomas Rowlandson; XXXVI "Lacy House in Middlesex" by William Angus; XXXVII "Lumley Castle in the County of Durham" by Edward Dayes; XXXVIII "Newnham Court in Oxfordshire" by William Angus; XXXIX "Belton House in Lincolnshire" by Claude Nattes; XL "Twickenham Park House in Middlesex" by William Angus; XLI "Cirencester House in Gloucestershire" by George Samuel; 42 "Deanery in Somersetshire" by J. [i.e., John?] Carter, F. A. S.; XLIII "Lee in Kent" by Claude Nattes; XLIV "North Court House in the Isle of Wight" by J. C. Barrow; 45 "Lambeth Palace in Surrey" by Cooke; 46 "Bradbourn in Kent" by Claude Nattes; 47 "Gunnersbury House in Middlesex" by Edward Dayes; 48 "Duffryn-Alled in Denbigh-shire" by John Bird; 49 "Basildon House in Berkshire" by Rouviere; 50 "Fonthill House in Wiltshire" by W. [i.e., William?] Turner, A. R. A.; 51 "Pelling Place in Berkshire" by Cooke; 52 "Attingham in Shropshire" by Edward Dayes; 53 "Wanstead House in Essex" by Cooke; 54 "Blickling in Norfolk" by William Watts; 55 "Merton Place in Surry" by Edward Hawke Locker; 56 "Sundridge Park in Kent" by Humphry Repton; 57 "Kingsgate in the Isle of Thanet, Kent" by [Charles?] Tomkins; 58 "Addescombe Place in Surry" by William Angus; 59 "Whitley Court in Worcestershire" by Edward Dayes; 60 "West Hill in Surry" by Humphry Repton; 61 "Sion House in Middlesex" by William Angus; 62 "Chillingham Castle in Northumberland" by Arnold; 63 "Burley in Rutlandshire" by Humphry Repton

Binding Early nineteenth-century morocco, blind- and gilt-tooled

Provenance Bookplate of Charles Scott Murray of Hambledon

References ESTC t145837 (first issue); RIBA, *Early Printed Books*, III

THIS BOOK was published in parts between 1787 and 1815 as a continuation of William Watts' *The Seats of the Nobility and Gentry* (1779–1786), which it matches in size, format, style, and subject (see entry under Watts). The first number appeared in February 1787, about the time subscribers to Watts' views would have expected their next installment had Watts not sold out and left for Italy. Angus presumably advertised himself as Watts' successor and offered similar terms, but he did not, it

William Angus. *The Seats of the Nobility and Gentry.* Plate XXII. "Brough Hall in Yorkshire, the Seat of Sir John Lawson." 1985.61.375

seems, take over ownership of the earlier work, which passed either immediately or later on to the Boydell firm. Angus, therefore, presented his continuation as a new venture even though he adopted the old title, commissioning the engraver Cary to give it the same calligraphic flourishes as Shepherd had for Watts.

It is clear from the imprint lines to the first forty-eight plates that they were issued in groups of four, each view with its single leaf of text, at a rate that matched Watts' pace for the first three years, before declining to one installment about every fifteen months (i.e., February 1787; August/September 1787; April 1788; December 1788/January 1789; August/September 1789; July 1790; April/August 1791; July 1792; June/November 1793; November 1794/January 1795; April/September 1796; September/November 1797). At this point a letterpress half-title was issued reading "Angus's Select Views of Seats. Vol. 1" (British Library copy, shelfmark 1322.m.83). However, only fifteen plates were engraved toward volume two and these took so long to appear that it seems likely Angus gave up the whole idea of publication in regular parts long before he admitted defeat and allowed the work to stand as complete with sixty-three views, as in the Millard copy. After Angus' death in 1821, the work became devalued by frequent reprintings. Lowndes priced it at two guineas, or five guineas with proof plates, adding that it was "in little estimation except the impressions be good" and that "the copper plates of this work were lately in existence, and many copies have been struck off under the old date" (Lowndes 1864, 47).

Little is known of William Angus beyond the information supplied by Redgrave, supplemented by the entry for him in the *Allgemeines Künstler-Lexicon* (4: 110–111). Born in late 1751 or 1752, he was a pupil of William Walker (1729–1793), an engraver who, toward the end of his long career, worked on at least one of the many rivals to Watts' and Angus' *Seats*, Harrison and Co.'s *Picturesque Views of the Principal Seats of the Nobility and Gentry* (1786–1788). Angus earned his living as a reproductive engraver for periodicals such as the *European Magazine*, *Literary Magazine*, and *British Review*. He specialized in portraits and landscapes, and also worked on Josiah Boydell's *Collection of Prints . . . illustrating the Dramatic Works of Shakespeare* (1803) and at least two early bibliographical treatises, Thomas Dibdin's

William Angus. *The Seats of the Nobility and Gentry.* Plate xxvii. "Barskimming, in Scotland, the Seat of Sir William Millar Bart." 1985.61.375

Bibliographical Decameron (1817) and William Clarke's poetical *Repertorium bibliographicum* (1819). He is known to have painted, and credits himself as draftsman for five views in the present work (Lacy House, pl. xxxvi; Newnham Court, pl. xxxviii; Twickenham Park House, pl. xl; Addescombe Place, pl. 58; Syon House, pl. 61). His address while publishing the *Seats* is always given as 4, Gwynne's Buildings, Islington. He is not listed as exhibiting at the Royal Academy or the Society of Artists, and Redgrave's only comment on his character is that "he was improvident and died poor, after two years' painful illness, October 12, 1821, aged 69, leaving a widow without any provision" (Redgrave 1878, 11).

Many of Angus' artists are better known. Some, such as Paul and Thomas Sandby, Claude Nattes, Lord Duncannon, Humphry Repton, and Thomas Malton, Jr., had contributed to Watts' series. New names include Robert Adam, providing a distant view of Oxenfoord Castle that presumably dates from his remodeling of the interior, 1780–1782 (pl. xiv); Thomas Rowlandson, whose staffage enlivens a dull drawing of Bradwell Lodge by Malton, Jr. (pl. xxxv); Edward Dayes, a well-known watercolor artist until his suicide in 1804 (pls. xxv, xxxvii, 47, 52, 59); and George Cuitt, described by John Harris as having "unrivalled distinction as perhaps the finest provincial landscape painter of his generation" (Harris 1985, 255). Angus only credits Cuitt with one view, of Brough Hall (pl. xxii), immediately followed by two other houses in Yorkshire, Lartington Hall and Clints, supposedly by "Howit, of Richmond." Since Cuitt lived in Richmond and on his death left Yorkshire with "scarcely a park or a residence which he had not been commissioned to paint" (Redgrave 1878, 110), these too may tentatively be assigned to him. There is no evidence to suggest that Angus was personally acquainted with any of the artists who provided his views. In some cases he may have been exploiting material acquired from Watts' collection, including the latter's own drawings of Grove House (pl. xxxii) and Blickling Hall (pl. 54). In others, the text notes the owner of the original drawing from which Angus has made his copy—more often than not, also the owner of the house.

The series opens with a view of Broadlands, showing Lancelot "Capability" Brown's remodeling but not Henry Holland's work on the entrance portico that began the following year, in 1788. This is followed by Paul Sandby's drawing of James Paine's Brocket Hall (interesting also for its view of Lord Melbourne's Chinese boat) and then William Marlow's painting of the south front of Castle Howard. Marlow's view is one of four he painted c. 1771 and exhibited at the Royal Academy in 1772. Sir John Vanbrugh's other great country house, Blenheim Palace, opens the second installment (pl. v), and the text to both strikes a suitably patriotic note. Such famous seats are, however, the exception rather than the rule, and greater value now lies in Angus' smaller, less well-documented subjects. In a note on one of these, Aramstone House in Herefordshire (pl. xii), professional jealousy inspires a lengthy list of mansions omitted from William Gilpin's *Observations on the River Wye* (1782). Angus also allows himself an occasional criticism of the houses portrayed: Dalkeith Palace is "not elegant . . . the architect having been destitute of all the knowledge of his art, necessary to form a true judgement of what is really beautiful, without a profusion of unnecessary decorations" (pl. ix); Blickling Hall is "unfortunately situated" (pl. liv); the view of Addescombe "much confined, as it can only be seen in a kind of visto" (pl. lviii); and West Hill shows "such departures from the established rules of proportions of architecture, as must naturally be expected where the builder or surveyor is consulted instead of the regular architect" (pl. lx).

These strictures all tend toward a confirmation of the "modern" taste for classically proportioned houses open to picturesque landscapes, although there is considerably more variety here than in Watts' *Seats*. In fact, the subjects do not appear to have been chosen to fit any strong editorial program beyond the obvious idealization of rural British scenery. Old provincial castles such as Raby (pl. xxv), Lumley (pl. xxxvii), and Chillingham (pl. 62) are complacently ranged next to suburban country houses strung along the Thames (Grove House, pl. xxxii; Lacy House, pl. xxxvi; Twickenham Park House, pl. xl; Gunnersbury House, pl. xlvii; Syon House, pl. 61); and an old-fashioned Deanery in Somerset (pl. xlii) is flanked by views of Cirencester Park (Queen Anne style) and Lee Priory (James Wyatt's Gothic revival). There is even a prototypically romantic view of Barskimming in Ayrshire, an early work by the Scottish landscape artist Alexander Nasmyth that focuses on the natural rock formations of the river bank and leaves the house itself concealed behind trees (pl. xxvii).

Whether or not such variety reflected the heterogenous tastes of subscribers, it also highlights the inevitable tendency of a series like the *Seats* to grow into an incoherent miscellany. It is significant that, from 1801 onward, Angus began neglecting his own publication and devoting time instead to engraving views for *The Beauties of England and Wales* (1801–1815), a twenty-six-volume national survey begun with a far more disciplined and demanding schedule by John Britton and E. W. Brayley. The *Beauties* was the most successful of a new species of topographical publication that rapidly undercut the popular vogue for quarto picture books such as *The Seats of the Nobility and Gentry*. When Watts began publishing in 1775, the *Seats* occupied one corner at the lower end of a newly discovered market. But being a product of fashion, it inevitably became its victim, and by the turn of the century, although its views were well above the artistic standard of most of its line-engraved rivals, it was too slight, too infrequent, too unfocused, and probably too expensive to compete with the mass-produced series of the major London publishers. The upper end of the market, on the other hand, was increasingly dominated by aquatint engravers and, later on, lithographers. Soon after its demise, the place of Angus' *Seats* was taken by another work represented in the Millard collection, J. P. Neale's *Views of the Seats of Noblemen and Gentlemen* (1818–1829). G. B.

Bibliography

Allgemeines Künstler-Lexicon. Munich and Leipzig, 1992–.

British Architectural Library, Royal Institute of British Architects. *Early Printed Books 1478–1840: Catalogue of the British Architectural Library Early Imprints Collection*. Vols. 1–2. London, 1994–1995

Harris, J. *The Artist and the Country House*. Rev. ed. London, 1985

Lowndes, W. T. *The Bibliographer's Manual of English Literature*. New ed. London, 1864. Reprint, 1967

Redgrave, S. *A Dictionary of Artists of the English School*. London, 1878. Reprint, Amsterdam, 1970

8

Matthew Brettingham (1699–1769)

The Plans, Elevations and Sections, Of Holkham In Norfolk, The Seat of the late Earl of Leicester. To which are added, The Cielings and Chimney-Pieces; And Also A Descriptive Account of the Statues, Pictures, and Drawings; Not in the former Edition. By Matthew Brettingham, Architect

London: printed by T. Spilsbury; and sold by B. White, and S. Leacroft, 1773

1985.61.428

Folio: 560 × 370 (22 × 14½)

Pagination x, 24 pp., [66] engravings on [65] leaves (7 double-page or folding) (*Note:* This copy does not include 4 plates usually present)

Edition Second edition

Text pp. [i] title page (verso blank); [iii–iv] dedication to Margaret, countess dowager of Leicester; v–x preface; 1–20 explanation of the plates; 21 note to the reader in Italian; 22–24 explanation of the plates in Italian

Illustrations Copies of this work usually contain 70 engravings printed on either 69 or 70 leaves (2 small plates, "Arch Gate to the Garden" and "Seat in the Orangery," are sometimes printed on 1 leaf, as in the Millard copy). The plates are numbered irregularly, and are not listed in the English "Explanation." In the Italian "Spiegazione," however, the plates are referred to as nos. 1–69, with 4 double-page plates being given 2 numbers each (i.e., 6–7, 10–11, 12–13, and 14–15) and the numbers "24" and "32" repeated once and "27" repeated twice. 20 plates show designs by Matthew Brettingham. Other designer, draftsman, or architect signatures or attributions include "From the Antique of [Antoine] Desgodetz & [Andrea] Palladio" (drawn by James Miller); "Inigo Jones & the Antique"; "Inigo Jones & Desgodetz"; "Inigo Jones"; "W. [i.e., William] Kent & Desgodetz"; "W. Kent"; "Earl of Burlington Arch.t"; and "Antique." The engravers are Robert Baldwin, Placido Columbani, Peter Mazell, Tobias Miller (most), Thomas Morris, John Roberts, Edward Rooker, Giovanni Vitalba, Anthony Walker, and C. White.

The final 4 plates, listed as nos. 66–69 and described as "non messo [-messi, -messe] in opera," are not present in the Millard copy, which may therefore represent an early version of the first edition, issued before these were added. They illustrate, respectively, a "Building intended on the Chalk Cliff Church Wood" (misnumbered 21); "Front of the East Lodges next the Road" (misnumbered 27); "East Lodges" (unnumbered); and "West Entrance to the Park" (misnumbered 28)

Binding Recent three-quarter calf, marbled boards, uncut

References Berlin Cat. 2336; Berlin (1977) os 2336; ESTC t85980; Harris and Savage 48; RIBA, *Early Printed Books*, 373

The building of Holkham Hall, Norfolk, Thomas Coke, the 1st earl of Leicester's great house, which had been designed by William Kent under the close supervision of the earl and his friend Lord Burlington, was entrusted, from 1734 onward, to Matthew Brettingham. Brettingham had been born in 1699, in Norwich, the son of a bricklayer, and this had been his first training; but he had gradually built up an architectural practice in East Anglia, and was later to be employed by the nobility to design major country houses and mansions in London. He emerged as a competent, if extremely dull, Palladian.

Before the death, in 1753, of the earl's only son and heir, the earl had begun, with Brettingham, preparation of a publication on the house, a counterpart, presumably, to the one produced by Isaac Ware, in 1735, to record the building of the nearby seat of the earl's patron,

Matthew Brettingham. *The Plans, Elevations and Sections, of Holkham in Norfolk.* Plate 4/5. "North front." 1985.61.428

Matthew Brettingham. *The Plans, Elevations and Sections, of Holkham in Norfolk.* Plates 12–13. "Transverse section of the Hall, Saloon, and Portico." 1985.61.428

Sir Robert Walpole, *The Plans, Elevations and Sections: Chimney-pieces and Ceilings of Houghton in Norfolk.* They also planned a book of designs of country houses. Brettingham wrote in 1761:

> This was our joint study and amusement in the country, and the drawings for this work have been made by me near twenty years; but they were not to appear in print, till after the publication of Holkham: if leisure permits they may possibly be engraved next year, together with the Earl of Leicester's intended plans for a new house in town.

Some of Brettingham's drawings for this house survive, but nothing came of the second project.

The death of the earl's son, followed late in the same year by that of Lord Burlington, seems to have dulled his enthusiasm, and the preparation of the publications lagged. Then, in April 1759, the earl of Leicester died suddenly. Brettingham took the publication of Holkham in hand, had further plates engraved, "at no small expence and trouble" to himself, as he claimed, but did not include the chimneypieces and ceilings as originally intended. *The Plans, Elevations and Sections, of Holkham in Norfolk* appeared in 1761, printed by J. Haberkorn of Soho. The twenty-seven plates were engraved by R. Baldwin, T. Miller, Edward Rooker, Anthony Walker, and Thomas Morris. Unusually, most of the copies were printed in sepia, as used by Lord Burlington for the *Fabbriche antiche designate da Andrea Palladio*, of 1730, in simulation of the ink of the original drawings, and also for the engravings of his own Chiswick House, which was the basis of Holkham Hall.

The cost of the book, whatever Brettingham may have claimed, was no doubt defrayed by the family, but it was not dedicated, as one might expect, to the dowager countess, rather to the duke of Cumberland, who had consistently supported the earl in his endeavors.

Brettingham, having devoted so many years of his life to the building of Holkham, considered it "the great work of his life," and thus "assum'd all the merit of it in his publication," adding his own name to the plates as "Architect" making no reference at all to Burlington and Kent. Horace Walpole was aghast: "How the designs of that house," he wrote in his *Anecdotes*, "which I have seen an hundred times in Kent's original drawings, came to be published under another name, and without the slightest mention of the real architect is beyond comprehension." In point of fact, much the same had occurred with Ware's publication of Walpole's brother's house, where the contributions of Colen Campbell and James Gibbs went unrecorded in the first edition.

Brettingham died in 1769. His eldest son, also named Matthew, thought to still the outrage and make amends.

He had trained with his father and, in 1747, at the age of twenty-two, had traveled to Italy and Greece, with James Stuart and Nicholas Revett, staying on in Rome until June 1754, studying architecture and supervising the purchase of paintings and sculpture for Lord Leicester. On his return he put forth a proposal for "an Academy of Design in England," and made attempts to build up a practice in architecture, but he seems to have been employed rather by his father to supervise the continuing work at Holkham, Brettingham senior having turned his attention to London in his last years. Holkham was completed in 1764. In 1773 Brettingham junior published a thoroughly revised and enlarged edition of *The Plans, Elevations and Sections, of Holkham in Norfolk.* Plates 1, 14, and 15 from the first edition were reengraved, forty-four plates were added, engraved by T. Miller, T. Morris, Peter Mazell, Placido Columbani, C. White, John Roberts, and Giovanni Vitalba, mostly illustrating the chimneypieces and ceilings omitted from the first publication. The plates were erratically numbered, some still bearing numbers from the first edition. The list of plates was printed in both English and Italian, a flourish of newly acquired sophistication. The printing was in the usual black ink. The dedication was now to Margaret, the countess dowager of Leicester. Brettingham junior's text included a detailed description of the house and its contents, but attribution was the nub of the matter. "The general ideas," he acknowledged, "were first struck out by the Earls of Burlington and Leicester, assisted by Mr. William Kent," but he felt bound nonetheless to defend the merit of his father's claims, for the designs "were," he insisted, "departed from in every shape and he that had conducted the laying of every Brick from the foundation of the Roof thought he had a better claim to the Reputation of the Fabrick than he who only gave the designs, but never once attended the execution of any part of the work."

The contributions of Burlington and Kent, though clearly acknowledged on the new plates of the chimneypieces and ceilings, were minimized by reference also to their sources, Palladio, Inigo Jones, and Antoine Desgodetz's *Les édifices antiques de Rome*, of 1682. R. M.

Bibliography

Colvin, H. *A Biographical Dictionary of British Architects 1660–1840*. 2d ed. London, 1978

Harris, E., and N. Savage. *British Architectural Books and Writers 1556–1785*. Cambridge, 1990

Matthew Brettingham. *The Plans, Elevations and Sections, of Holkham in Norfolk.* Plate 17. "Section of the gallery." 1985.61.428

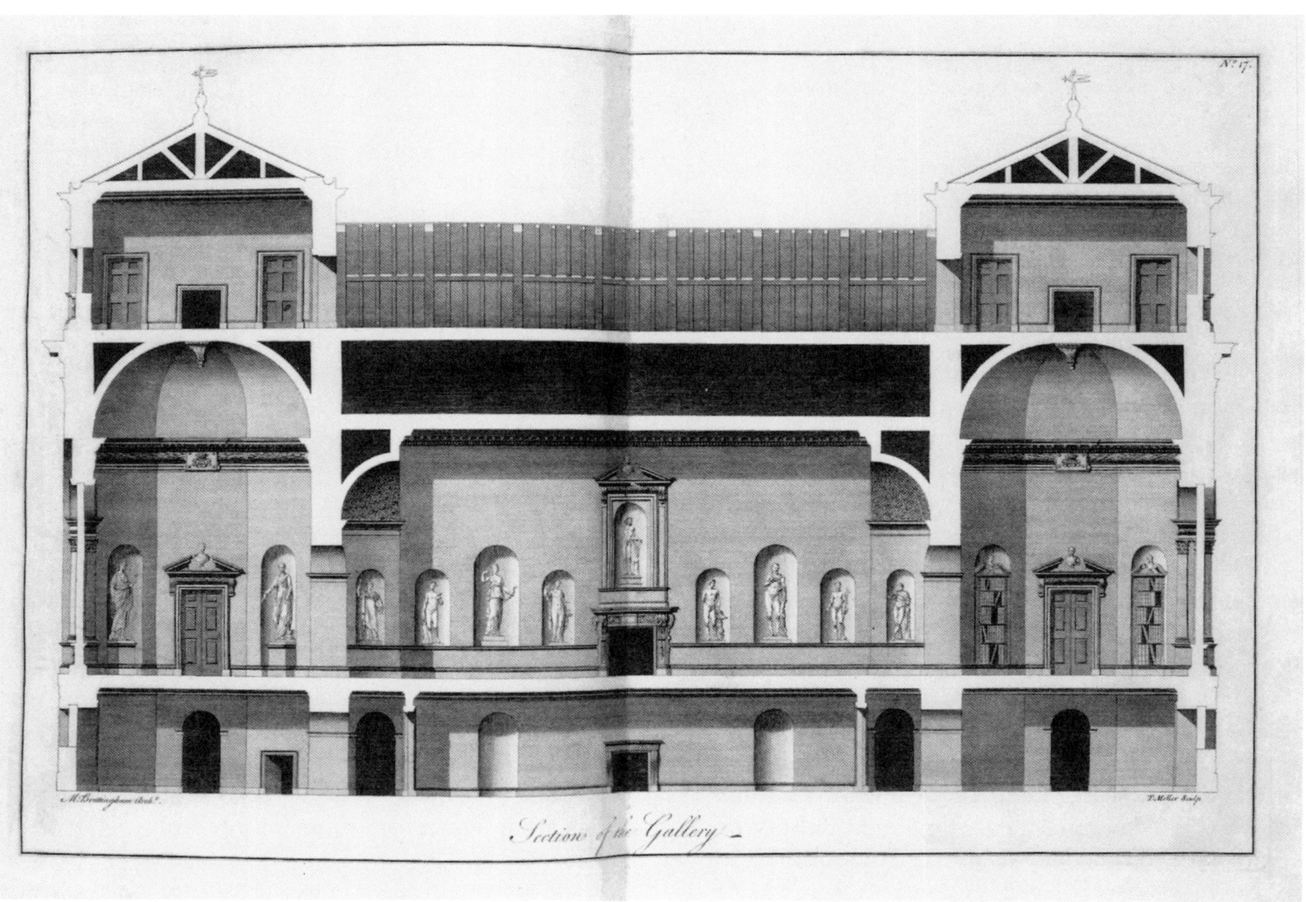

9

Charles Cameron (c. 1743–1812)

The Baths Of The Romans Explained And Illustrated. With The Restorations Of Palladio Corrected And Improved. To Which Is Prefixed, An Introductory Preface, Pointing Out The Nature Of The Work. And A Dissertation Upon The State Of The Arts During The Different Periods Of The Roman Empire. By Charles Cameron, Architect

London: printed by George Scott, and to be had of the author, 1772

1983.49.12

Folio: 530 × 360 (20⅞ × 14³⁄₁₆)

Pagination [2], iv, 65, [1]; [2], iv, 68 pp., engraved title plate, engraved dedication, [76] etched or engraved plates (38 double-page, 2 folding)

Edition First edition

Text (English and French) pp. [1] title in English; [2] blank, with pasted errata slip; [i]–iv introduction; [1]–21 text "State of the Arts . . ."; [22] plate I; [23]–65 text in English, chaps. 1–9; [66] blank; [1] title in French (verso blank); [i]–iv introduction in French; [1]–23 text "Etat des Arts . . ."; [24] plate I; [25]–68 text in French, chaps. 1–9

Illustrations Engraved title plate with bust of Palladio in rectangular frame flanked by male and female caryatids supporting pediment, English and French titles engraved on base below, engraved inscription beneath ("The Busto from a Painting in the Villa Capra, near Vicenza," and same in French). Dedication to the earl of Bute engraved by Charles Hall. 76 etched plates *hors texte* numbered II–LXXV, of which 2 are numbered XII and 2 XVI. 6 have extension flaps or overlays (VII, XIV, XV, XVII, XIX, XX). Plates XLVII, LXXI, and LXXII are signed by Cameron as draftsman; plates XXI and XXIII by him as etcher (the latter with Barnaby Mayor). Plate I appears on p. [22] of the English text, repeated on p. [24] of the French. Both English and French texts also include 19 etched head- or tailpieces, of which 4 in each are not repeated in the other series

Binding Contemporary marbled calf, gilt borders, gilt spine, hinges repaired

Provenance Large engraved armorial bookplate of the marquess of Donegall, signed "Yates Sculp."; small engaved armorial bookplate of "Clark" pasted over earlier armorial bookplate of "Arthur Hunt[?]. Newbold Revel"

References Berlin Cat. 1898; Cicognara 3640; ESTC t21409; Fowler 75; Harris and Savage 95; RIBA, *Early Printed Books*, 530 (reissue)

EMPRESS CATHERINE of Russia once confessed to Voltaire that "my Anglomania predominates over my plutomania," but Cameron's appointment in or about 1778 as her architect still remains one of the most spectacular promotions in British architectural history. It is not known who brought his name to Catherine's notice, but any recommendation must have been based largely on the merit of *The Baths of the Romans Explained and Illustrated.* Although he had been signing himself as an architect for some time, the only project before he left England with which he can be firmly associated is for a house in Hanover Square, built for Jervoise Clarke by, among others, his father Walter Cameron, a carpenter and builder. Even his involvement in that may have been minimal, the only evidence being his signature on an account for marble. He applied, but was not appointed, to a district surveyorship in Middlesex in 1774. Yet five years later the empress of Russia was writing that "A present je me suis emparée de Mister Cameron, écossais de nation, Jacobite de profession, grand dessinateur, nourri d'antiquités, connu par un livre sur les bains romains" (Loukomski 1943, 33). By the time he came to bind a copy of *The Baths* for himself, he was entitled to stamp the upper cover with the gilt initials C.C.A.M.I.R. (Charles Cameron Architecte à Sa Majesté Impériale Russe; see *Marlborough Rare Books*, cat. 160, no. 35). He also stamped it with the arms, crest, supporters, and motto of the Camerons of Lochiel, to which he had no right at all.

The book was probably planned while Cameron was a pupil of Isaac Ware. Cameron later claimed that Ware had intended to reprint Lord Burlington's *Fabbriche antiche*, but died without completing the project (*Proposals*, 20 March 1770). So few copies of the *Fabbriche* were printed that its scarcity alone would have commended this idea, particularly to one of Burlington's former assistants, reputedly in financial difficulties. Ware had worked on some of the original plates, and might well have given the task of copying them to his pupil. If the work on this more limited project had progressed far before Ware's death in January 1766, it would also explain certain features of the book as finally issued. But whether or not Ware's involvement was significant, Cameron soon took up the task, and in the spring of 1767 he exhibited six proof prints of the Roman baths "Intended for the work which is now publishing." Around the same time he printed subscription receipts for "Two Guineas being the first payment for a work entitled Ancient Thermae built in Rome which I promise to deliver agreeable to the printed proposals in payment of the remainder." Cameron, however, knew that his reputation as an architect would not be greatly enhanced by a straight reprint of Burlington's book. So in 1768 and 1769 he was in Rome to examine the baths firsthand. Soon after his return to England he renewed his efforts to acquire subscriptions and published *Proposals for Publishing by Subscription, in One Volume Folio, upon a fine Imperial Paper, elegantly engraved on Eighty Copper-plates; by Charles Cameron, Architect, the Thermae of the Roman Emperors.* It is in this broadsheet, dated 20 March 1770, that Cameron gives Ware credit for the initial plan.

He neglected to include a list of subscribers when the book finally appeared in 1772, so it is uncertain how successful his proposals were. The elaborately engraved dedication to John Stuart, 3d earl of Bute, may reflect actual or only hoped-for patronage. Bute was a natural target for Cameron's solicitations, being an architectural enthusiast as well as notoriously pro-Scottish during his years in power. It is hard to imagine how Cameron was able to sell enough copies of *The Baths* to cover his costs without some such aid, despite a well-timed exhibition of selected engravings from it at the Society of Artists in May 1772. The price for the complete work was high—four guineas—but copies were still unsold in 1775. By then Cameron had relinquished his publishing rights to the London booksellers Leacroft and Matthews, who reissued it with a new title leaf (RIBA copy). Another reissue dated 1774 is recorded by Talbot Rice, but no location has been traced.

Twenty-five of the plates are copied directly from Lord Burlington's *Fabbriche antiche disegnate da Andrea Palladio*; Cameron reproduces all of the plans, elevations, sections, and details (see pls. IV–VIII, X–XI, XII bis–XIII, XVI bis–XVIII, XXIV–XXXV). His black-ink line engravings are much cruder than the superbly toned plates of the original, but despite being reversed copies they transmit the information well enough, including the measurements often mistranscribed by Burlington's original draftsmen. These are always reprinted, but sometimes converted into English feet as well. Captions, where present, are in English and French. Cameron's identifications of the various baths, however, seem to be entirely dependent on the inadequate captions added to Burlington's plates, leaving a whole group not only without letters but completely ignored by the text. This might have been acceptable had Cameron's ambition been limited to reproducing the *Fabbriche antiche*, but as presented there was no way for the reader to know what he was looking at, or even whether it was by Palladio.

The additions Cameron made to his prime source are more interesting. Two improvements are due to the publication of Tommaso Temanza's *Vita di Andrea Palladio* (Venice, 1762). The frontispiece bust of Palladio is now taken from Temanza's engraving, based on the only known authentic portrait, instead of Sebastiano Ricci's forgery. More importantly, Cameron has added an engraving of Palladio's finished plan of the Baths of Agrippa (pl. III). This was a distinct omission from Lord Burlington's suite, as Temanza had pointed out

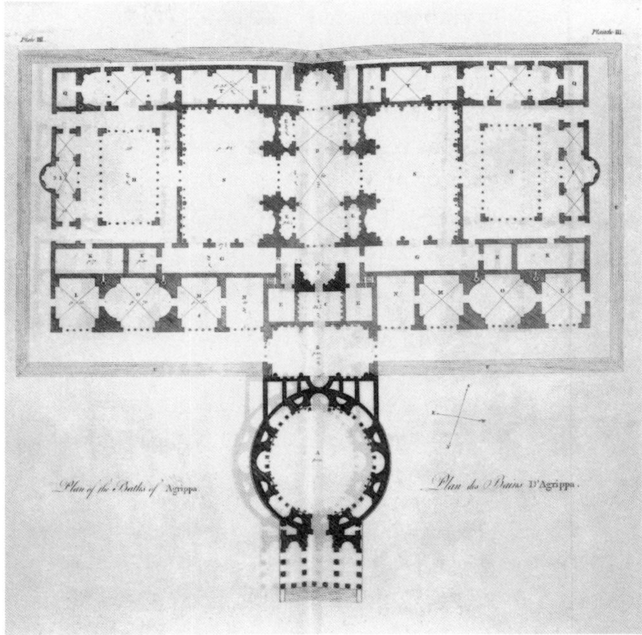

Charles Cameron. *The Baths of the Romans Explained and Illustrated.* Plate III. "Plan of the Baths of Agrippa." 1983.49.12

before declaring that he had the good fortune to possess the original drawing himself (pl. XLIV). No earlier reproduction has been traced; perhaps Cameron (or Ware) obtained a copy of it by applying directly to the owner. It was later included in Ottavio Bertotti-Scamozzi's Italian edition of the *Fabbriche antiche*, that is, *Le Terme dei Romani disegnate da A. Palladio* (Vicenza, 1785).

During his stay in Rome Cameron had visited several sites, including Pompeii, but concentrated most of his attention on the "Baths of Titus" (i.e., of Trajan), having obtained permission "to dig in such places as might assist me in my design of illustrating the Baths" (p. 54). At one point, he gives a rare but vivid impression of what this involved. Referring to the area marked A on one of the three overlays to plate VII, he notes that "It was with great difficulty I got into this room: I was obliged to cut a hole through the wall B. and to let myself down by a rope, and afterwards to creep through a hole in the wall O, upon my hands and knees. It was nearly full of earth to the ceiling" (p. 54). His efforts were rewarded by the discovery of parts of the Domus Aurea, or Golden House of Nero, which, lying beneath the baths, were not to be seen again until the early part of the twentieth century. Unfortunately, he was unaware of what he was describing, confounded it with the baths built on top of it, and added his "subterraneous" discoveries to the plate showing Palladio's earlier reconstruction. The use of overlays, repeated for one of the elevations of the Baths of Diocletian (pl. XVII), was not entirely novel by 1772, but it was still rare, mainly because this method of presentation, like the extension flaps on plates XIV–XV and XIX–XX, added to the cost and complexity of making up individual copies. The French translation was another extravagance, particularly because four of the illustrations printed around it were not in the English version and vice versa, so neither could be sold separately without loss.

Some of these illustrations are presented in a *trompe l'oeil* style, that is, as if incised on a tablet, or drawn on parchment scrolls or hide and then nailed to a board. There are other precedents, but Cameron was taking his cue from Piranesi's archaeological works. In other plates, too—notably of the capitals, cornices, and friezes from the Baths of Diocletian (pls. XXXI–XXXIII)—Cameron imitates Piranesi with large-scale, heavily etched details sharply defined against a plain white background. The elevations, sections, and views of the ruins in Rome, on the other hand, are stylistically distinctive but technically primitive. In the eyes of his contemporaries, Cameron's etchings must have suffered by comparison with similar works of the period, and he rarely achieves the magnificent effects of his closest British precursor, Robert Adam's *Ruins of the Palace of the Emperor Diocletian at Spalatro* (1764).

Of the illustrations not yet mentioned, plates XXXVI–LIII show Roman figures copied from the Baths of Trajan and Constantine. The remaining plates are of ceilings from the Palace of Augustus (pls. LIV–LVIII), the Baths of Trajan (pls. LIX–LXV), Hadrian's Villa (pls. LXVI–LXXII), and the Villa Madama (pls. LXXIII–LXXV). All such decorative details were obvious sources for neoclassical ornament, but without any proper description their presence is curious and difficult to justify. At least some derive from earlier publications. According to Frank Salmon, drawings reproduced in George Turnbull's *Curious Collection of Ancient Paintings* (1741) account for plates XXXVI–XL, XLIII–XLIV, and possibly XLVII, and engravings by Pietro Santi Bartoli for plates LIX and LXI. This is not surprising: Cameron was remarkably bookish for an eighteenth-century architect, and his text, too, is heavily dependent on his reading, notably of commentaries such as Bernard de Montfaucon's *L'Antiquité expliquée* (Paris, 1719–1724). By 1776 he had built up a considerable library—"ten book-cases, twenty busts, twenty pictures, twenty portrait pictures, five hundred printed books interwoven with prints taken from copper plates, five hundred other printed books, one thousand other prints of the value £1,500." At least, this was the

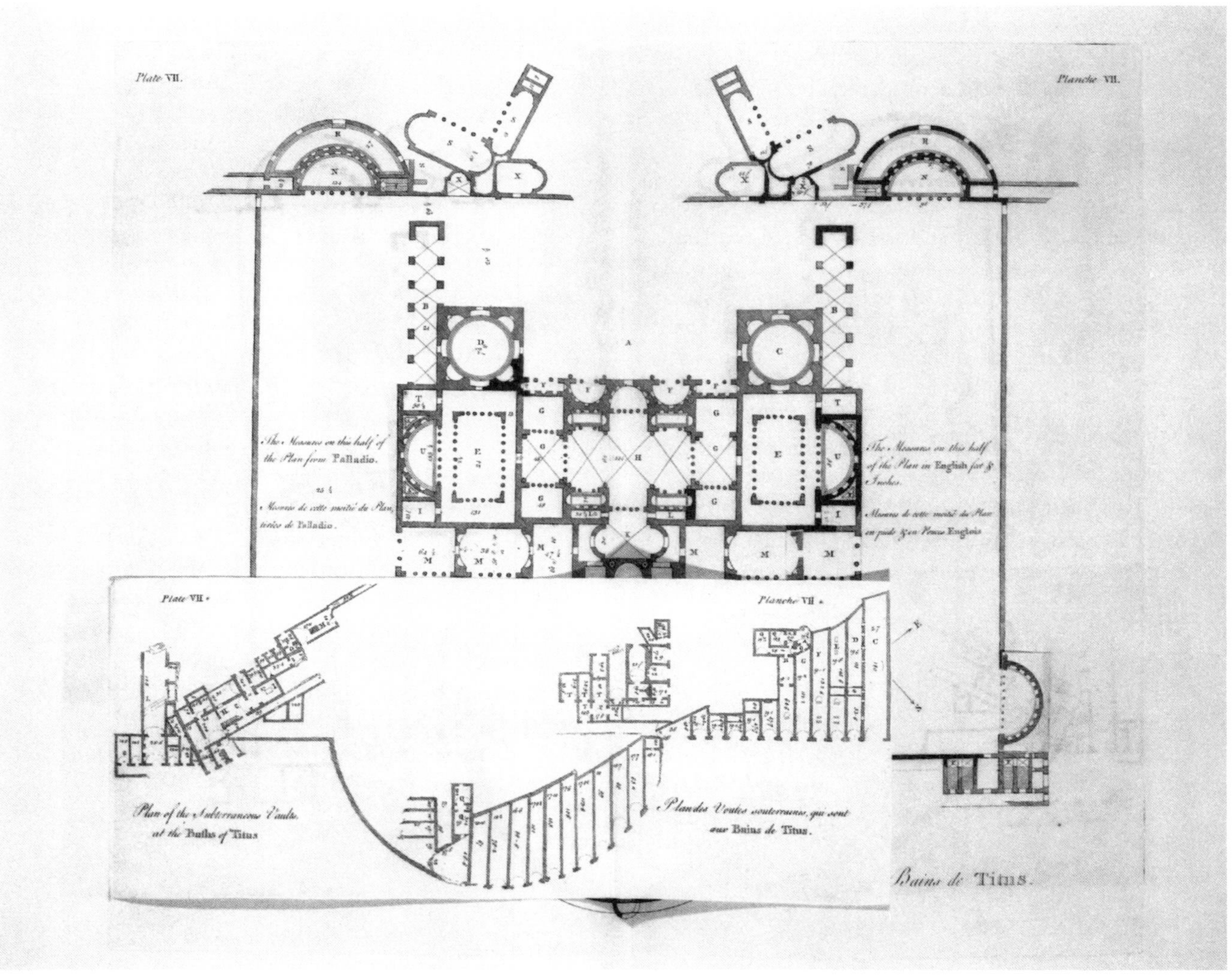

Charles Cameron. *The Baths of the Romans Explained and Illustrated.* Plate VII. "Baths of Titus" [i.e., Trajan], "Plan of the subterraneous vaults." 1983.49.12

description given when his father sold the lot in an attempt to pay off his own debts, causing his son to take legal action and send him to prison.

Family finances may be the chief reason why *The Baths of the Romans Explained*, although it developed beyond its original limits, probably fell short of its author's ambitions. Partly a Palladian reprint, partly an original work of scholarship, and partly a pattern book for neoclassical design, it may have satisfied none of its intended audiences as much as it did the empress of Russia. On the other hand, rapid changes in the intellectual climate in which Cameron was working may also have forced his hand. It is useful to compare the development of his project with the English edition of Antoine Desgodetz' *Les Edifices antiques de Rome* (Paris, 1682; see *French Books* 1993, no. 62). Like Lord Burlington's *Fabbriche antiche*, Desgodetz' book was in high demand and short supply from the mid-1750s, and a timely reprint of either would have had real commercial potential as British architects and others, enthused by the success of John Wood's *Ruins of Palmyra* (1753), scrambled to enhance their reputations by proving themselves students of Roman archaeology. As they did so, however, Palladio's and Desgodetz' inaccuracies were soon revealed. The Adam brothers, in particular, expended much time and money looking to revise first the one and then the other, although no publication came of either project. In 1762, meanwhile, George III commissioned an otherwise obscure self-styled "architect," George Marshall, to make exact copies of Desgodetz' plates. When Marshall's first volume was finally published in 1771, with text in English and French, it was recognizably outmoded—so much so that volume two was not published until I. and J. Taylor acquired the work in 1795. Cameron had long ago rejected the idea of reprinting the *Fabbriche antiche* precisely to avoid such a fate; but he may have felt that to delay his own, largely derivative, work any longer was unlikely to improve its chances of critical acclaim. He would surely have read, with a mixture of apprehension and excitement, the *Monthly Review*'s unfavorable comparison of Marshall's Desgodetz with the original work of Piranesi, Robert Wood, Thomas Major, James Stuart and Nicholas Revett, and others. It was, after all, published in the same month he suddenly announced his own work in the *Gazette*. G. B.

Charles Cameron. *The Baths of the Romans Explained and Illustrated.* Plate LXII. "Ceiling at the Baths of Titus" [i.e., Trajan]. 1983.49.12

Bibliography

British Architectural Library, Royal Institute of British Architects. *Early Printed Books 1478–1840: Catalogue of the British Architectural Library Early Imprints Collection.* Vols. 1–2. London, 1994–1995

Colvin, H. *A Biographical Dictionary of British Architects 1600–1840*. 3d ed. New Haven and London, 1995: 207–209

Harris, E., and N. Savage. *British Architectural Books and Writers 1556–1785*. Cambridge, 1990

Loukomski, G. *Charles Cameron*. London, 1943

Rae, I. *Charles Cameron: Architect to the Court of Russia*. London, 1971

Robinson, J. M. "A Dazzling Adventurer: Charles Cameron—The Lost Early Years." *Apollo* 135 (Jan. 1992): 31–35

Salmon, F. "Charles Cameron and Nero's Domus Aurea: 'una piccola esplorazione.'" *Architectural History: Journal of the Society of Architectural Historians of Great Britain* 36 (1993): 69–93

Shvidkovskii, D. *The Empress and the Architect: British Architecture and Gardens at the Court of Catherine the Great*. New Haven, 1996: 11–25

Talbot Rice, T. "Introduction." *Charles Cameron c. 1740–1812*. London, 1967

10

Colen Campbell (1676–1729)

Vitruvius Britannicus, or The British Architect, Containing The Plans, Elevations, and Sections of the Regular Buildings, both Publick and Private, In Great Britain, With Variety of New Designs; in 200 large Folio Plates, Engraven by the best Hands; and Drawn either from the Buildings themselves, or the Original Designs of the Architects; In II Volumes Vol. I. (Vol. II.) by Colen Campbell Esqr. . . . [same in French] . . . Cum Privilegio Regis

London: sold by the author, John Nicholson, Andrew Bell, W. Taylor, Henry Clements, and Jos. Smith, 1715–1717

The Third Volume Of Vitruvius Britannicus: Or, The British Architect. Containing The Geometrical Plans of the most Considerable Gardens and Plantations; also the Plans, Elevations, and Sections of the most Regular Buildings, not Published in the First and Second Volumes. With Large Views, in Perspective, of the most Remarkable Edifices in Great Britain. Engraven by the Best Hands in One Hundred large Folio Plates. By Colen Campbell, Esquire, Architect to His Royal Highness the Prince of Wales. . . . [same in French] . . . Cum Privilegio Regis

London: printed and sold by the author; and by Joseph Smith, 1725

1985.61.440–441

Folio: 480 × 320 (18 7/8 × 12 5/8)

Pagination Vol. 1: 10 pp., engraved title plate, engraved dedication, [84] engraved plates (14 double-page)

Vol. 2: 8 pp., engraved title plate, [74] engraved plates (13 double-page, 4 folding)

Vol. 3: 12 pp., [74] engraved plates (24 double-page)

Edition First editions

Text vol. 1: pp. [1–2] introduction; [3]–7 explanations of the plates; [8] privilege, dated 8 April 1715; [9]–10 list of subscribers; *vol. 2*: pp. [1]–6 explanations and list of plates; [7]–8 list of subscribers, ending with note "The Author has made a great Progress in a Third Volume, containing the Geometrical Plans of the most considerable Gardens and Plantations . . ."; *vol. 3*: pp. [1] title page, printed in red and black (verso blank); [3] printed dedication (verso blank); [5]–6 list of subscribers; [7]–12 explanations and list of plates

Illustrations Vol. 1: Calligraphic title plate engraved by John Sturt; calligraphic dedication engraved by R. [i.e., Ralph?] Snow for George Bickham; plus 84 engraved plates numbered 3–100 (14 double-page plates with 2 numbers each). Captions in French and English. 30 are signed by Colen Campbell as draftsman, 7 as draftsman and designer; and 1 each signed "Inigo Iones Inv:," "M^{r}. Hawksmoor Inv:" (both drafted by Campbell) and "Ex Autographo. D. I. Thornell." *Vol. 2*: Calligraphic title plate as vol. 1 but in second state, with volume number and date altered; plus 74 engraved plates numbered 2 to 100 (13 double-page plates given 2 numbers each; 4 folding plates, each consisting of 2 double-page plates pasted together, given 4 numbers each, i.e., 4–7, 8–11, 12–15, and 16–19). Campbell signed 44 plates as draftsman, including 9 as draftsman/designer. 7 are also signed "Inigo Jones Inv:" and 1 "Thom: Millner Esqr. Inv:." Henry Hulsbergh is the only credited engraver. *Vol. 3*: 74 engraved plates numbered 3 to 100 (24 double-page plates given 2 numbers each; Harris and Savage record 2 of the double-page plates pasted together as 1 quadruple plate, accounting for their total of 73). Nearly all are signed by Campbell as draftsman, draftsman/designer, or architect, and Henry Hulsbergh as engraver. 3 are also signed "Inigo Iones Inv^{t}."

Binding 3 vols. bound as 2 (vols. 1–2 bound together). Contemporary gray boards, new calf spines and corners, black leather labels. Uncut copy

References Berlin Cat. 2329 (vols. 1–5); Berlin (1977) OS 2329 (vols. 1–5); Cicognara 4116 (vols. 1–2); ESTC n24541; Fowler 76 (vols. 1–4); Harris and Savage 97 and 99 (vols. 1–3)

ANOTHER EDITION

Vitruvius Britannicus, or The British Architect . . . [as first ed.] . . . In II Volumes Vol. I. (Vol. II.) by Colen Campbell Esqr. . . . [same in French] . . .

[London, 1731?]

The Third Volume Of Vitruvius Britannicus: Or, The British Architect. Containing The Geometrical Plans . . . [as first ed.] . . . not publish'd in the First and Second Volumes. With large Views, in Perspective of the most Remarkable Edifices in Great Britain. . . . [same in French] . . .

London: printed in the year 1731

1981.70.6

Folio: 449 × 284 (17 11/16 × 11 3/16)

Pagination Vol. 1: 12 pp., engraved title plate, engraved dedication, [84] engraved plates (14 double-page)

Vol. 2: 12 pp., engraved title plate, [78] engraved plates (21 double-page)

Vol. 3: [ii], 12 pp., engraved dedication, [74] engraved plates (24 double-page)

(*Note:* The text of this edition calls for an additional plate in vol. 3, not present in the Millard copy)

Edition Third edition of vols. 1–2; second edition of vol. 3

Text (parallel English and French) *vol. 1*: pp. [1]–2 introduction; 3–10 explanation of the plates; 11–12 list of plates; *vol. 2*: pp. 1–10 explanation of the plates; 11–12 list of plates; *vol. 3*: pp. [i] title page printed in red and black (verso blank); 1–10 explanation of the plates; 11–12 list of plates

Illustrations As first edition, except that the imprint and Sturt's credit have been erased from the title plate and the engraved dedication is repeated in vol. 3. Although the explanation and list of the plates in vol. 3 now calls for an additional plate (pl. 101, a view of Umberslade), this is not present in the Millard copy

Binding 3 vols. bound as 1. Recent sheep, early gilt spine label, text edges sprinkled red

References ESTC t50966 and n56037; Harris and Savage 102

ANOTHER EDITION

Vitruvius Britannicus, or The British Architect . . . [as first ed.] . . . In III Volumes. Vol. I. (–Vol. III.) by Colen Campbell Esqr. . . . [same in French] . . .

[London, c. 1751?]

1985.61.444–446

Folio: 550 × 385 (21 5/8 × 15 3/16)

Pagination Vol. 1: 12 pp., engraved title plate, engraved dedication, [84] engraved plates (14 double-page)

Vol. 2: 12 pp., engraved title plate, [78] engraved plates (21 double-page)

Vol. 3: 12 pp., engraved title plate, engraved dedication, [74] engraved plates (24 double-page)

Edition Late edition, probably published c. 1751 (see Harris and Savage)

Text (parallel English and French) *vol. 1*: pp. [1]–2 introduction; 3–10 explanations of the plates; 11–12 list of plates; *vol. 2*: pp. 1–10 explanations of the plates; 11–12 list of plates; *vol. 3*: pp. 1–10 explanations of the plates; 11–12 list of plates

Illustrations As first edition, except that the title plate has been altered to read "III" volumes instead of "II," and its imprint and Sturt's credit line have been erased. The title plate and the engraved dedication are repeated in vol. 3. The additional plate of Umberslade present in some copies of the 1731 edition of vol. 3 is now neither called for nor present. In this copy, the 4 folding plates in the first edition of vol. 2 are bound as 8 double-page plates

Binding Late nineteenth-century three-quarter red morocco, dark green buckram boards, bound uniform as vols. 1–3 of S. D. Button's copy of *Vitruvius Britannicus* (for vols. 4–5, see under John Woolfe; for vols. 6–7, see under George Richardson)

Provenance Presented by S. D. Button to the Philadelphia Chapter of Architects, with inscription at upper right corner of titles. Each volume has MS date at bottom of title as follows: vol. 1, "1801"; vol. 2, "1802"; vol. 3, "1804."

References ESTC t50968; Harris and Savage 103

IN HER ACCOUNT of the genesis of *Vitruvius Britannicus*, probably the best known and most frequently consulted of all eighteenth-century English architectural books, Eileen Harris made a startling discovery. Colen Campbell, the author, was not publicly named as such until 9 April 1715, only ten days before copies were promised for delivery to the subscribers and more than ten months after the first known advertisement of subscription proposals appeared (*Post Boy*, 1–3 June 1714). Yet why did a book that didn't need an author to attract subscribers suddenly acquire one on the point of publication? How did it happen that the publishers, instead of buying a work from its author, seem to have sold it to him instead? And above all, what difference (if any) does this revision of Campbell's role make to the received view of *Vitruvius Britannicus* as the key pioneering manifesto of the rise of neo-Palladianism in early eighteenth-century Britain? Only tentative answers are possible here, but they may reveal something about the form and content of *Vitruvius Britannicus*, and perhaps suggest that certain classes of architectural books should be read according to models essentially different from those customarily employed for literary texts.

Campbell's authorship was made public at almost the same time that he bought into the project as an "undertaker," alongside the booksellers John Nicholson, Andrew Bell, William Taylor, and Henry Clements, and the map- and printseller Joseph Smith. If Campbell's new responsibilities, first made explicit in an advertisement in the *Post Boy* of 17–19 May 1715, represent a genuine shift in the book's parentage—and the fact that his name clearly *was* inserted on the title plate as an afterthought is fairly irrefutable proof of such a shift—then it becomes important to understand how he could have been given what appears to be editorial control of a corporate venture unprecedented in English publishing to that date. One answer might be simply that he had purchased this control by acquiring a majority stake in its ownership. Of the ten booksellers named in the earliest known advertisements, Christopher Bateman and Benjamin Took were to drop out within three weeks or so and be replaced by the prominent London printseller Smith (see *Daily Courant*, no. 3954, 26 June 1714). By the time Campbell is first named publicly as "Author" (*Daily Courant*, no. 4199, 9 April 1715), only three of the original ten—Bell, Taylor, and Clements—had retained their stake. Such unstable ownership must have had a direct impact on the book's form and content at a critical stage, when binding decisions had to be made about design, composition, and structure. All that is certain about Campbell's financial investment is that his stake, when added to that of Smith, amounted to a half-share of volumes one and two, and full ownership of volume three, when this property was jointly auctioned in eight equal lots at Smith's retirement sale on 5 April 1731. Thus, between the two of them, their stake was probably sufficient to give them effective direction of the book's design and final form. Smith's contribution to the shaping of *Vitruvius Britannicus* into a vehicle for Campbell's architectural ambitions should therefore be examined, for it would not have happened without Smith's backing and may even have occurred at his instigation.

Both Harris and Tim Connor have stressed that the expense of engraving the two hundred large folio copperplates promised for volumes one and two, and of printing these on the heavy imported paper necessary to achieve high-quality intaglio impressions (which cost, one advertisement claims, "near 3d. a Sheet, paying 40s per Ream Duty"—see *Post Boy*, 17–19 May 1715), involved a very large capital outlay. Connor conservatively estimated the costs for an edition of four hundred copies at about £1,750, which subscription sales—still quite a novel method of money raising—were by no means certain of offsetting. Indeed, John Sturt, the engraver of the title plate (which no doubt served to advertise the proposals before being adapted for publication), had himself met much difficulty in attracting subscribers for his edition of Pozzo's *Perspectiva* (1707), the first architectural book to be published in England in this way. Exposed to such an extent over a book that was really a collection of prints, the booksellers among the original promoters must have been heartened when so experienced and successful a printseller as Smith joined their ranks. Not only would Smith's reputation have encouraged potential subscribers to believe that the proposed book would be delivered (hence the readvertisement in the *Daily Courant* on 26 June 1714 indicating his involvement), but on a purely practical level the nature of the enterprise clearly demanded the kind of organizational skills and marketing expertise that only wholesaling publishers and sellers of prints such as Smith and Peter Dunoyer could offer. It was probably through Dunoyer, the only printseller among the original ten promoters, that Smith first became involved in *Vitruvius Britannicus*. Further up the Strand from Smith's "Picture-Shop" at the west end of Exeter Exchange, Dunoyer ran another print shop "at the sign of Erasmus' Head" for the publisher David Mortier, who had moved to Amsterdam in 1711 to help manage the great map-, print-, and bookselling business built up by his late brother Pierre. Aside from

Colen Campbell. *Vitruvius Britannicus*. Vol. 1, plate 13. Inigo Jones. "The Banquetting House at Whitehall. . . ." 1985.61.440

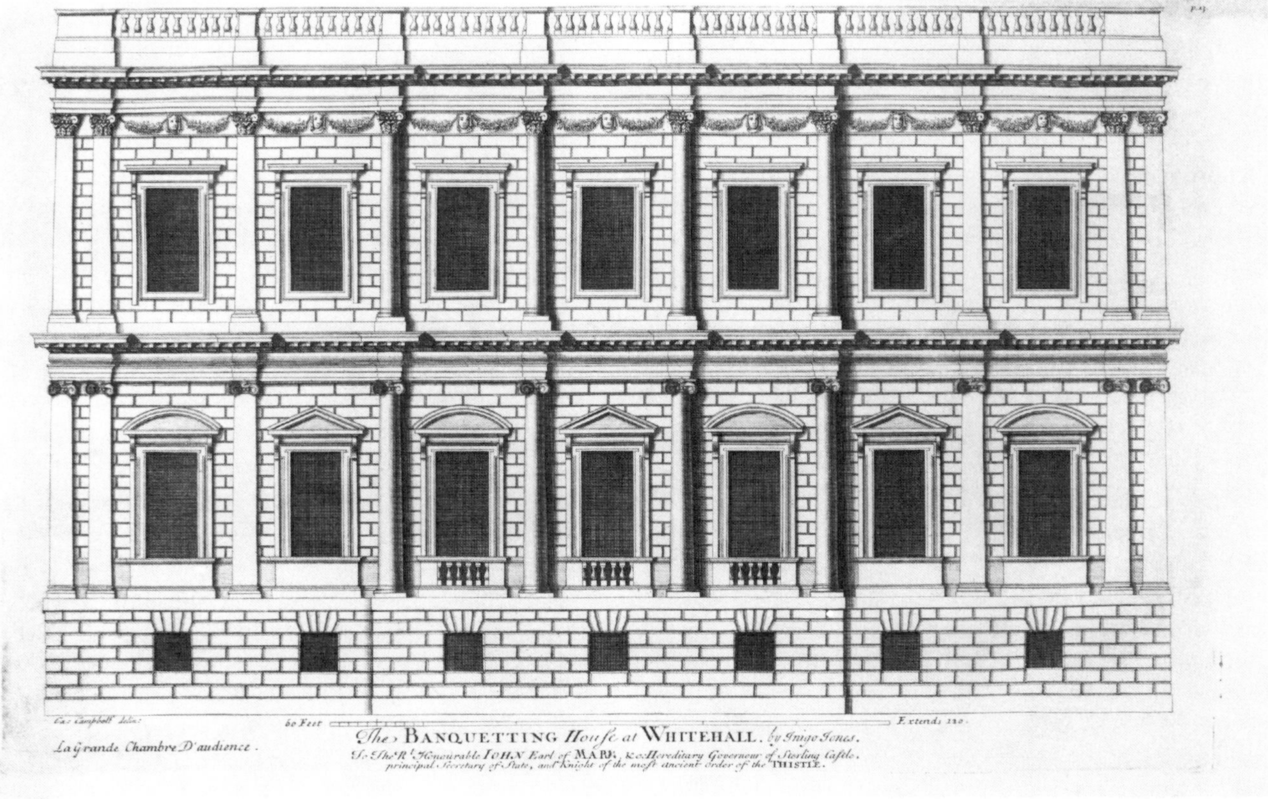

the routine trading links he is certain to have maintained with the London representative of an international supplier of maps and prints, Smith had another particular reason to be already associated with Mortier and Dunoyer. Within two years of the first appearance in book form of *Britannia Illustrata or Views of Several of the Queens Palaces As also of the Principal Seats of the Nobility and Gentry of Great Britain Curiously Engraven on 80 Copper Plates* (1707), the distribution of subsequent editions in London was being shared between its original publisher, David Mortier, and three other printsellers—Daniel Midwinter, Henry Overton, and Smith. By 1714, moreover, Smith had taken over sole rights to the home market for this work, and assembled from various sources a second volume of sixty-seven engraved views, mainly of London and provincial churches, Oxford and Cambridge colleges, the Royal Exchange and Royal Pensioners' Hospitals at Chelsea and Greenwich, and the important royal naval dockyard towns of Rochester, Chatham, Portsmouth, and Plymouth.

At the very moment Smith bought a stake in *Vitruvius Britannicus* he had either just published, or was about to publish, an expanded version of *Britannia Illustrata*, for the foreign sale of which, under the title *Nouveau Theatre de la Grande Bretagne*, he could rely on a partner in Amsterdam. This is a clear indication of the expectations he would have had of the book, of the sort of credibility he gave it in the eyes of subscribers, and also of the strength of the influence he would have been able to exert on its form and content. How far the effects of such influence are detectable in *Vitruvius Britannicus* as published is a matter of interpretation, but there is enough circumstantial evidence to suggest that the final form of the book was arrived at as much through Smith's need to reach a particular market as Campbell's determination to promote his architectural career. These two forces operated simultaneously to produce not only the first truly indigenous architectural book published in Britain, but one that demonstrated an important precedent: by abstracting architecture from the distractions of topography, on the one hand, and the responsibilities of theoretical argument, on the other, Campbell was free to present a surreptitious "battle of styles" through visual juxtaposition rather than reasoned debate.

The *Post Boy* advertisement of 1–3 June 1714 stating that "This Work is now in such Forwardness, that 160 of the Designs are ready for engraving, and several are engraved" needs to be treated with some caution. In particular, the admission that no more than "several" of the drawings had been engraved should be compared with James Gibbs' claim, at a similar moment in the production of his *A Book of Architecture*, that 90 (out of a total of 140) plates were "already engraved" (advertisement, *Daily Post*, 31 March 1727). In fact, the precise form and content of the first volume of *Vitruvius Britannicus* was, at this stage, probably still open to change. That volume three contains, among other things, bird's-eye views, perspectives, and/or garden plans of such front-rank buildings as Greenwich Hospital, Castle Howard, Wilton, Longleat, Chatsworth, and Blenheim—all major players in volumes one and two—has been seen as evidence of such a shift in the original conception of the book. Perspectives of such important subjects are certain to have been engraved early on, and were only displaced from their intended and more logical position to accommodate previously unplanned engravings of Campbell's "neo-Palladian" designs in volume one and the Whitehall Palace designs attributed to Inigo Jones in volume two. Attractive as this hypothesis is as evidence that helps to explain Campbell's "rise" to authorship, it is based on the assumption that, at the time the "displaced" views were engraved, *Vitruvius Britannicus* was either still being planned as, or had evolved into, a book modeled on those surveys of national architecture in which measured drawings of buildings are merely an accompaniment to a whole orchestra of visual and literary description designed to celebrate the history and culture of the nation or state in which they are found. Although "Britannicus" and "British" announce an obviously national (and nationalistic) bias, in the title of the book these adjectives qualify the noun "Architect" and its Latin eponym "Vitruvius," rather than buildings or architecture as such. This may seem a small point but it is an important one, for it implies that right from the start the proposed subject of *Vitruvius Britannicus, or the British Architect* was intended to be the practice of architectural design as exemplified in the "regular" (i.e., classical) buildings of Great Britain, rather than their topography and particularity as depicted in Knyff and Kip's bird's-eye views for *Britannia Illustrata* (1707). This implication, moreover, is reinforced by the emphasis in the *Post Boy* advertisement on "exact Plans, Elevations and Sections," and the omission of any mention of views. It is inconceivable that the inclusion of perspective views—at that date virtually the sole means employed in Britain to record the appearance of buildings in engravings—would not have been advertised had they been intended. Not only would potential subscribers have been reassured of the appeal of *Vitruvius Britannicus* beyond a narrow interest in the technicalities of architecture, but the promoters are certain to have drawn attention to such views because of the greater expense involved in their production as finished engravings when compared with ruler-drawn and etched geometrical subjects.

If no perspective views (or garden and estate plans) were intended at the time of the subscription proposals, when were they produced and why? Taking the two outside possibilities first, it is at least theoretically possible that these plates were engraved at some earlier phase in the project, before the idea of a book composed solely of measured drawings had taken hold. At the other extreme, it is also possible that they really were, in fact, engraved for volume three, as part of that "great Progress in a Third Volume" that the publishers announced in a note at the end of the list of subscribers in volume two. Neither of these possibilities can be discounted completely, however it seems unlikely that one of the book's most remarkable aspects—its use of orthogonal projection as a self-sufficient mode of representation for existing buildings—somehow evolved from an earlier plan to produce a straightforward topographical survey. Indeed, it is difficult to see how such an unusual, and for Britain at that time, unprecedented focus on architectural design could have come about except by adopting a specifically nontopographical model from the start. Nor is it easy to understand why Campbell and Smith, in planning volume three, should have abandoned the successful formula established in volumes one and two except to recoup on plates already engraved but not yet published. The announcement in volume two that the third volume will contain "Geometrical Plans of Gardens and Plantations, with large Perspectives of the most Regular Buildings, in a Method entirely new, and both instructive and pleasant" has, in fact, the authentic ring of a printseller's advertisement of stock in hand. And the hodgepodge character of volume three, when compared to the carefully modulated and coherent structure of the first two volumes, bears this out: had there been a genuine attempt to produce something "entirely new," the result would surely have been more coherent. As it is there are several distinct elements in the make-up of volume three that not only fail to cohere, but betray the marks of a "struggle" between two quite different conceptions of the original purpose of *Vitruvius Britannicus* that took place during a crucially formative period following Smith's advent in June 1714. To detect these marks it is necessary to examine more closely the so-called displaced views and garden plans in volume three, and to show how, in spite of their variety of form, they bear traces of the same conflicting intentions and attempted compromises.

To the standard formula of orthographic representation in volumes one and two, volume three adds not only the first published use of geometrically drawn "laid-out" wall elevations to reveal the interior design of a room (pls. 34, 50, and 100), but no less than five different ways of showing buildings in relation to their surroundings. The first of these is the large (i.e., double-page) "prospect," in which extensive and complex ranges of buildings are seen in single-point (i.e., parallel) perspective from an elevated viewpoint. Volume three opens in grand style with just such views of Greenwich Hospital (pls. 3–4) and Castle Howard (pls. 5–6), and seems to announce a book very different from the previous volumes, both of which begin with sober ground plans followed by the principal elevation of the buildings to which they refer. This opening flourish, however, is not quite what it appears: no other buildings are given this treatment in the volume, even though some, like Blenheim, were obvious candidates; and the rigorous omission of staffage or any other signs of life or activity to indicate scale give both views the appearance of having been drawn from models rather than on site. This is especially the case with Castle Howard, in which *repoussoir* allegorical figures lend the same air of unreality to the scene as landscape foregrounds often do to maps or plans (as, for example, in those engraved by Noël Cochin for Sébastien de Pontault and Étienne Desrocher's *Les Glorieuses Conquestes de Louis le Grand*, [1676]–1694).

The same lack of "reality," or of anything that might interfere with the essentially abstract nature of the building when viewed as architecture, is apparent in the barren foregrounds and empty skies that give a forlorn aspect to perspectives of even the most important houses. Whether, like Appuldurcombe House (pl. 61), High Meadow (pl. 62), Belton (pl. 70), and Althrop (pls. 83–84), only the main front is shown from near ground level in single-point perspective; or, like Longleat (pls. 65–66), Chatsworth (pls. 67–68), and Duncombe Park (pls. 87–88), an attempt is made at giving an oblique view of two fronts, the intended result is the same: to reveal the building's form in its true "naked" state, shorn of all associations pertaining to function or locality that might distract from an assessment of its essential quality as architecture. While it might be argued that the failure to employ more than one vanishing point in the oblique-view perspectives stemmed from incompetence, the effect, in which a straightforward elevation parallel to the picture plane is "attached" to its neighbor shown in recession, is the result of joining up drawings rather than recording what is seen, and betrays most clearly that the true origins (and intended destination) of these images lay in the architect's office, and not in the artist's sketchbook or printseller's "picture shop." The absence of figures, likewise, may be due to lack of expertise in their depiction—both Campbell and his engraver Henry Hulsbergh were probably less than competent in this area—but this is to ignore both how simple it would have been to employ another hand to introduce them (a common procedure), and how seriously their omission broke with the normal conventions of topographical engraving in which much of the meaning and history of a particular place or building was expressed through the visible evidence of people whose lives and activities came within the orbit of its influence. Such resistance to the "distractions" of topographical views was already implicit in the wording of the title of *Vitruvius Britannicus* announced at the beginning of June 1714, and the same motives can be seen at work in the way the other main attempt to extend the original focus of the book—through the inclusion of garden plans—was likewise modulated toward a more abstract, geometrical representation of the *design* of gardens, parkland, and plantations, and away from the essentially pictorial tradition of the estate map with its concern to record the particularities of a unique site. That this modulation or swing occurred during the course of selecting and engraving material for the book is apparent in the contrast between the more formal, "architectural" depiction of Charles Bridgeman's design for the gardens at Eastbury Park (pl. 15), echoed in that of the gardens and plantations at Belton (pl. 69), Boughton (pls. 73–74), Hampton Court, Herefordshire (pl. 75), and Lowther Hall (pls. 77–78), and the cartographic estate-map conventions employed for the representation of the gardens and surrounding terrain of Houghton (pls. 27–28), Goodwood (pls. 51–52), Longleat (pls. 63–64), Woodstock Park, Blenheim (pls. 71–72), Claremont (pls. 77–78—includes hachuring to indicate relief), Cholmondeley (pls. 79–80), Thoresby (pls. 81–82), Narford (pl. 95), and Caversham (pls. 96–97). The former are undoubtedly what are referred to in the notice in volume two as "Geometrical Plans of the most considerable Gardens and Plantations," and show an awareness of the architectural manner of representing the layout of the *planned* (as opposed to the given) surroundings of a house established in engravings of Versailles and other major gardens in France by Israel Silvestre and Michel Le Bouteux in the 1680s and given more recent currency in England in the plates (after Alexandre Le Blond) accompanying John James' translation of A. J. Dézallier D'Argenville's *La Théorie et la Pratique du Jardinage*, published in 1712. Even one of the more cartographic estate-plan engravings—that of the park and gardens at Narford (pl. 95)—signals an attempt to press into the service of architecture, as opposed to topography, the tradition of surrounding maps and plans with inset views of buildings, such as David Loggan had used to depict the entrance gateways in his plan of the Botanic Gardens at Oxford in *Oxonia Illustrata* (1675). Unlike John Rocque's later "surveys," in which garden plans are enlivened by inset perspectives of their main attractions, Campbell's Narford plan has inset elevations only of the "Portico" and "Deer house," each with a miniature scale bar as if to emphasize, once again, that these are products of the architect's measuring rod and compass, not the artist's flattering "pencil." Indeed, only one plate in *Vitruvius Britannicus*—the magnificent twin double-page bird's-eye view of Wilton showing Stonehenge in the distance (3: pls. 57–60)—completely escapes this determination to promote the architect's vision over that of the artist or cartographer; and for this reason, if for no other, there must be some doubt about the validity of Campbell's signature as the apparent draftsman of a perspective view worthy of the best works of Jan Kip and John Harris the Elder.

Returning to the partnership of interests between Campbell and Smith, it is clear that there are peculiarities about the perspective views and garden plans of the third volume that reveal signs of a "struggle" between opposing concepts of the book. However, although these opposing aims clearly express the ambitions of an aspiring architect, on the one hand, and the preconceptions of a topographical printseller, on the other, the eventual "victory" of the former over the latter—resulting in the banishment of perspectives and garden plans to a later volume and the elevation of Campbell to the status of "author"—was by no means a foregone conclusion. For one thing, Smith's ideas about what would sell would have carried immense weight with his co-proprietors, and for another, he would have undoubtedly pointed out to them (and to Campbell) that a collection of plans, elevations, and sections of buildings alone, however regular or exact, had never yet succeeded in appealing to the broad, nonspecialist, international market enjoyed by *Britannia Illustrata*. Smith would have been all too aware of the contrast between Campbell's dry, geometrical drawings and the rich variety of detailed maps, large bird's-eye views, dramatic "cut-away" sectional perspectives, and highly animated "prospects" that were the principal attraction in nearly all the previous surveys of national architecture, from the time of Jacques Androuet du Cerceau's *Les plus excellents Bastiments de France* (1576–1579) to the more recent engravings by Perelle, Leclerc, Silvestre, Le Pautre, and others for the magnificent "maisons royales" volumes of Louis XIV's "Cabinet du Roi" (available in the trade from about 1677); in the lavishly illustrated *Nouveau Théâtre d'Italie*, for instance (published by Pierre Mortier in 1704), and its companion, the *Nouveau Théâtre de Piemont et de la Savoye*, including previously published engravings by (or after) Jan Blaeu, Romeyn de Hooghe, and Innocente Guizzaro; or similarly in comparable surveys of the architecture of major cities, such as G. B. Falda and Alessandro Specchi's four-part *Il Nuovo Teatro delle Fabbriche et Edificii in prospettiva de Roma Moderna* (1665–1669; pt. 4, 1699) and Luca Carlevaris' *Le Fabbriche, e Vedute di Venetia* (1703–1704); or, closer to home and more prosaically, in the growing collection of engravings of gentlemen's seats and other buildings that attached itself to successive editions of J. Le Roy's *Notitia Marchionatus Sacri Romani Imperii hoc est Urbis et Agri Antverpiensis Oppidorum, Dominorum, Monasteriorum, Castellorumq. sub eo . . .* (Amsterdam 1678; revised editions as *Castella et Praetoria Nobilium Brabantiae*, Antwerp 1696 and Leiden 1699). Even the great assemblage of classical French buildings engraved by the specialist architectural draftsmen Jean Marot *père* and *fils*, known today as the "Grand Marot" and probably first published in volume form without title or text in 1683, did not fail to include numerous animated perspectives among its large-scale carefully measured plans, elevations, and sections. The pressure on *Vitruvius Britannicus* to follow suit was, therefore, very considerable. However, only one plate in the entire book—the large bird's-eye view of Wilton and its surroundings—can be said to acquiesce wholly to this pressure. Counterbalancing, and eventually prevailing against it, was a very different conception of the sort of book *Vitruvius Britannicus* should be. It would be easy, though incorrect, to suppose that Campbell somehow, through force of persuasion or influential friends, succeeded in imposing this different conception, thereby making *Vitruvius Britannicus* "his" book. But Smith and his bookseller partners in the enterprise stood to lose too much money to be persuaded into making changes against their commercial judgment. In other words, it was not enough for Campbell to simply demand what he wanted; there also had to be solid commercial reasons for undertaking the book in the form in which it eventually appeared. Campbell's buying into the project is more indicative of a shared conception—the resolution of the different pressures shaping the book—than of the imposition of his will over that of his colleagues in the enterprise. Indeed, it is quite possible that the germ of Campbell and Smith's agreed conception of *Vitruvius Britannicus* as a vehicle for the display of modern architecture lay in a shared realization that the comprehensive national historical and topographical survey could be separated out into its constituent elements (i.e., antiquities, topography, history, genealogy, customs, etc., as well as modern buildings) without necessarily losing its broad appeal. The example of Capt. John Slezer's failed attempt in the late 1690s to expand his commercially unsuccessful *Theatrum Scotiae* (1693), a collection of topographical "prospects" (i.e., views) of Scottish towns, ruined abbeys, and royal castles, into a semi-official, government-backed survey of "The Ancient and Present State of Scotland" or "Scotia Illustrata," is also particularly relevant. This was to have included not only views of noblemen and gentlemen's private houses but "the Plans of their Stories and Ground Plat of the Gardens" alongside a whole range of other literary and visual material on the geography, antiquities, ancient families, and constitution of the kingdom of Scotland—an enterprise whose overt nationalistic agenda was intended to guarantee it government finance but led in the end to its falling victim to political vicissitudes. Even without Campbell telling him, Smith knew full well the fate of Slezer's project, as nine *Theatrum Scotiae* plates and nine others intended for "Scotia Illustrata" but previously unpublished were included in the expanded 1715 edition of *Britannia Illustrata* (see RIBA, *Early Printed Books*, no. 389, p. 218).

So what then were commercially sound reasons for sticking with a more architectural type of book at this particular moment, in the summer of 1714? One arose from the unexpected death of Queen Anne on 1 August. A book that set out to impress the new Hanoverian king—especially one who would inevitably bring with him continental tastes and advisers—with the best efforts of living, British-born architects, was now more certain than ever to stir powerful feelings of patriotism and to assuage that sense of inferiority to foreigners in matters of artistic taste that Campbell alludes to in the first sentence of his "Introduction." Suddenly, therefore, it was necessary not merely to select the best modern buildings in Britain, but to point out their architectural merits as well. But the idea of introducing the element of judgment, of commenting on architectural taste, of subjecting the houses of the most powerful families in the country to invidious comparison could not be contemplated if it ran the least risk of causing offense. Clearly the author of a text on the theory and practice of architecture who referred to his own work or who criticized that of others still living always exposed himself to accusations of partiality. Such accusations could be fatal to the chances of reaching that broad market, across the whole spectrum of both landed and city interests, which had kept *Britannia Illustrata* in continuous demand for nearly seven years. However, what could not be expounded in words could perhaps be expressed visually so that, given a few well chosen pointers that in themselves were uncontroversial, the reader could not fail to find what pleased him, whatever his opinions or taste.

Although no work of this kind had yet appeared in Britain, in which actual buildings, or details of buildings, are uniformly presented as if they were designs in a pattern book, this was an approach to architectural publishing recently employed with great success by the De Rossi family of printsellers and publishers in Rome. The publications of Giovanni Giacomo de Rossi (1627–1691) and of his son and successor Domenico (1647–1729) would have been very familiar both to Smith, as a leading importer of Italian prints and stockist of "Books of Architecture, with the large Books of Prints, proper for Publick Libraries" (*Post Boy*, 17–19 Dec. 1713), and to Campbell, as an architect whose attack on Bernini, Fontana, and Borromini in the introduction to *Vitruvius Britannicus*, was almost certainly suggested by the prominence given to their work in Domenico de Rossi's *Studio d'Architettura Civile* (1702). This book, and earlier companion volumes devoted to the palaces, churches, and altarpieces of modern Rome published by G. G. de Rossi (i.e., Pietro Ferrerio's *Palazzi di Roma* [book 1, 1655; book 2, c. 1675] and De Rossi's *Insignium Romae Templorum Prospectus* [1684]; and *Disegni di vari Altari e Capelle nelle Chiese di Roma* [c. 1686?]), gave an important lead to Smith and Campbell by demonstrating the practical and commercial viability of a purely architectural representation of the principal elements of recent buildings in a particular city. A more precise model for the publication of actual buildings as designs rather than places had been set in Rubens' *Palazzi di Genova* (1622), but important as that book may have been as a model in its restriction to purely orthographic representation, Smith is unlikely to have wished to commit himself to the extravagant detail of the original "Palazzi Antichi" part of Rubens' book, with its mass of measurements, complicated "fliers," and as many as five plans or sections for each building. Indeed, one might be tempted to cite the *Palazzi di Genova* as the sort of book that Smith was least likely to judge as marketable (and therefore a model to be avoided), were it not for the fact that it had been reprinted in Antwerp as recently as 1708, and had therefore, presumably, continued to attract a certain kind of less sophisticated buyer long after it had ceased to represent that advance of classical architecture that Rubens saw in his time as still dispelling "la maniera . . . che si chiama Barbara, ò Gothica" from countries north of the Alps.

An aspect of both the De Rossi books and Rubens' *Palazzi di Genova* that is particularly relevant to the genesis of *Vitruvius Britannicus* is that as compilations of engravings after drawings commissioned (or collected) by publishers, generally it was the latter who took on the intellectual responsibility for their selection and production, and in that capacity were understood to be the real authors of the books they published, not the draftsmen and engravers customarily credited with such a role. Even an important and successful architect such as Alessandro Specchi, who had been entrusted by his mentor, Carlo Fontana, with engraving the plates for the latter's great monograph on St. Peter's, published in 1694, is credited for his work as the draftsman and engraver of De Rossi's *Studio d'Architettura Civile* merely in a footnote on the title page. Although Specchi almost certainly had a hand in the selection and presentation of the contents of the *Studio*, and it was he who supplied the all-important measurements that rendered it of practical use, its authorship belonged to its commissioner and publisher, Domenico de Rossi. In the case of Rubens' publication, where no architect, patron, draftsman, or engraver is named anywhere in the book, this attitude to nonliterary, visual compilations is even more pronounced, since it is clear that "author" is here synonymous with the owner or collector of the material being published.

Bearing this in mind, it is easier to understand why *Vitruvius Britannicus* did not "need" an author so long as it was conceived as a collection of drawings of important recent buildings in Britain, the selection and arrangement of which were understood to be the responsibility of its publishers. Only when the choice and ordering of the material in such a collection was the expression of a particular viewpoint would it become necessary or desirable to name anyone as its author in justification or recommendation of the judgments it contained. The difficulty in assessing Campbell's role in the genesis of *Vitruvius Britannicus* lies precisely in the fact that it is not known how far he was personally responsible for steering it away from the concept of a collection of the "best" buildings in the publishing sense (where the selection and arrangement is not of itself expected to carry a particular significance) and toward one where buildings are effectively "played off" against each other in a dialogue (or "parallel") between foreign and native, modern and antique, "licentious" and "regular." As with every other shift in the evolution of *Vitruvius Britannicus*, however, this did not come about just because it suited Campbell's personal agenda. The temptation to read this development, bound up as it is with the decision to include a "variety of New Designs" (not mentioned in any known advertisements of the book until the naming of Campbell as author on 9 April 1715), as evidence that Campbell had at this point wrested editorial control from Smith and the other proprietors in some sort of deal that enabled him to pursue his own goals unilaterally, must be resisted. Campbell's project—his "vision" of *Vitruvius Britannicus*—could be achieved only insofar as it coincided with the commercial goals of his partners: he was not free to call the tune, least of all over the incorporation of his own designs in the fabric of what, only at the last minute, he was able to call "his" book. Campbell's ambition to promote his particular brand of neo-Palladianism, which in hindsight seems to be ample explanation for the final form of the book, was secondary to broader considerations outside his control.

By far the most important of these considerations—the perception of the necessity of giving *Vitruvius Britannicus* a "Palladian" bias in order to provide a "true" account of the best British architecture of the day—has been pinpointed by Harris to a last-minute realization that Giacomo Leoni's forthcoming new edition of Palladio's *I quattro libri di architettura* (the first to include a complete translation into English) was certain to heighten interest in and awareness of Palladio, and that consequently failure to include unmistakably Palladian designs threatened to make *Vitruvius Britannicus* seem out-of-date and old-fashioned even before it had appeared. While such a concern is entirely likely, there is no need to date it precisely from the moment when Smith and his colleagues first learned of Leoni's intentions, and certainly no necessity to presume that it was only "towards the end of March" 1715 that they decided to recast the book in order to give it a "Palladian" slant. For one thing, the list of those who had subscribed by 25 March 1715 (published in vol. 1) was sufficiently large (303 names for 370 copies) as to remove any purely commercial imperative for last-minute changes. Although Campbell's potential influence on the shape of *Vitruvius Britannicus* might perhaps have grown after the book's subscription had succeeded in guaranteeing a return on the capital outlay required for its printing, the cost of engraving substitute plates would have been too high if the *only* motive was last-minute competition with Leoni. In purely publishing terms, Leoni's Palladio posed no real threat to *Vitruvius Britannicus*, because it was not concerned with British architecture. Indeed, Leoni's awareness of this fact, and also of the risk that *Vitruvius Britannicus* might poach his market by demonstrating Palladio's relevance to British needs in a way that an English edition of *I Quattro Libri* could not by itself achieve, was almost certainly what lay behind his rash promise to include the "several Notes and Observations" from Inigo Jones' annotated copy of the 1601 edition of Palladio's book belonging to Dr. George Clarke, Fellow of All Souls, Oxford—a promise clearly made in the heat of the moment without the owner's permission,

Colen Campbell. *Vitruvius Britannicus.* Colen Campbell. Vol. 1, plate 24/25. "The West Front of Wanstead in Essex...." 1985.61.440

which, as a result, was not forthcoming until well after Clarke's death in 1736. The fact that Leoni turned to Jones as the means to make his edition more attractive is an important indication of the true nature of the Palladian bias that the inclusion of Campbell's theoretical designs was intended to give to *Vitruvius Britannicus.* Because of the literal quotation of Palladian sources in Campbell's unsolicited "palazzo" proposals for the duke of Argyll (1: pls. 19–20), earl of Halifax (1: pls. 28–30), earl of Ilay (1: pls. 53–54), Lord Percival (1: pls. 95–97), Tobias Jenkyns (2: pls. 41–42), Sir Robert Walpole (2: pls. 83–84), Paul Methuen (2: pls. 89–90), and Lord Cadogan (2: pls. 98–100), it has been assumed that his intention was to spark a reform in taste based on the kind of close study of Palladio's works that Lord Burlington and his circle were to undertake and, in large measure, achieve in the 1720s. However, Campbell was clearly far less original in his approach than such pioneering intentions suggest: his study of Palladio at this early stage probably amounted to little more than unacknowledged borrowing of ideas, and even complete designs, directly from illustrations in the *Quattro Libri*, or from James Smith, a prominent Scottish architect whose interest in Palladio, though only theoretical, almost certainly predated Campbell's by several years. In addition, the market contingencies shaping *Vitruvius Britannicus*, as viewed by its proprietors and publishers, constantly tended to pull it in the opposite direction, that is, to meet known demands by proven means rather than *consciously* to set out to break new ground. Both of these considerations should alert us to look much more closely at the positioning of Campbell's theoretical designs within the sequencing of plates in volumes one and two; at why this structure differs in volume three but nonetheless continues the same basic themes of the earlier volumes; and finally at how Campbell's celebrated "Introduction" in the first volume, with its apparently barbed, self-serving anti-baroque comments, supports rather than subverts the celebration of British architecture apparent in the body of the book as a whole.

An analysis of the arrangement of the plates in *Vitruvius Britannicus*, volumes one and two, reveals an unusually clear pattern of tacit comparisons based on the serial nature of their sequence within a volume. Thus, volume one opens by juxtaposing Wren's St. Paul's Cathedral (pls. 3–4), Michelangelo and Carlo Maderno's St. Peter's in Rome (pls. 6–7), Campbell's proposed design of 1712 for a large, centrally planned church in Lincoln's Inn Fields (pls. 8–9), and Thomas Archer's Italianate baroque St. Philip's, Birmingham (pls. 10–11). The implication of this sequence is plain: just as St. Paul's "noble Fabrick" outshines St. Peter's in terms of the beauty and correctness of its design, so Campbell's proposed church, planned on "the most perfect Figures" of circle and square, and "dress'd very plain, as most proper for the Sulphurous Air of the City, and, indeed, most conformable to the Simplicity of the Ancients," is offered as an implicitly preferable alternative to the obviously modern and foreign sources employed by "the ingenious Mr. Archer." Now this isn't just Campbell blowing his own trumpet—it is the announcement of a leitmotif that is going to run through the whole of the book; which is, that Britain has her own native, uncorrupted, and infallible guide to the purity and "Simplicity of the Ancients" or, in a word, her own Palladio, in "the famous Inigo Jones." It is highly significant, therefore, that Jones, the "British Vitruvius," makes his first entrance at this point with two of his most celebrated works, the Banqueting House at Whitehall (pls. 12–13) and the Queen's House at Greenwich (pls. 14–15), backed up by two others (thought at the time to be his but now ascribed to his pupil John Webb), the "Great

Gallery" on the river front of Old Somerset House (pl. 16) and Gunnersbury House, Middlesex (pls. 17–18).

To highlight that these buildings contain invaluable lessons for the present-day architect, Campbell introduces at this point the first of his theoretical designs, a grand house for his distant kinsman, the duke of Argyll, which he describes quite specifically as "a New Design of my own Invention in the style of Inigo Jones" (pls. 19–20). This is immediately followed by both a rejected and a preferred design for Wanstead, Sir Richard Child's vast new mansion six miles outside London. As Campbell's most recent, most prestigious, indeed almost only commissioned work, it is hardly surprising that he gave its long west front, "adorned with a just Hexastyle, the first yet practised in this manner in the Kingdom," the benefit of a double-page spread (pls. 24–25)—the first such to appear in the book—or that he had its section shown fully shaded (pl. 26) and not like previous sections (of St. Peter's Rome and the Banqueting House, Whitehall) in outline only. However, it is wrong to think of Campbell "interpolating" his own work here simply to advertise his abilities. Much more to the point, Wanstead is sandwiched between Campbell's "Argyll" design (pls. 19–20) and another huge theoretical palace design (pls. 28–30) inscribed to the first lord of the treasury, Lord Halifax, to form a solid counterpoint to and reflection upon the preceding designs by Inigo Jones.

With this yardstick firmly in place Campbell proceeds with the full range of "regular" buildings by other architects. Starting with old Burlington House (pls. 31–32) and Thomas Archer's garden pavilion for the duke of Kent at Wrest Park, Bedfordshire (pls. 31, 33), he is able rather neatly to suggest by the former precisely those "inconveniences of a plan that interrupts the grand visto to the Garden" that he claimed to overcome in his "Halifax" design, and by the latter to imply a comparison with the magnificent Greenhouse at Wanstead (pl. 27), which, although "design'd by another Hand" (probably William Talman), either he admired enough or was encouraged by Child to include alongside his own designs for the new house. After old Burlington House comes Montague House (pls. 34–36) built "in the French manner," and instructive therefore, like the equally "foreign" style of Drumlanrig Castle, Dumfriesshire, Scotland (pls. 37–38), by its contrast with three much more recent and fashionable London houses: Marlborough House, St. James' (1709–1711) by Wren (pls. 39–40); Powis House, Ormond Street (1714), architect unknown (pls. 41–42); and Buckingham House, St. James' (1702–1705), "conducted" by Capt. William Winde probably to the design of Talman (pls. 43–44).

Next Campbell turns our attention to country houses, contrasting Stoke Edith, Herefordshire (1710), designed and built by its owner, "Mr. Auditor Foley" (pls. 45–46), with the "great and Masculine" architecture of Kings Weston, Gloucestershire (pls. 47–48), designed in 1710–1712 by the most successful establishment architect of

Colen Campbell. *Vitruvius Britannicus.* Vol. 1, plate 56. "Plan of the Principal Floor of Blenheim." 1985.61.440

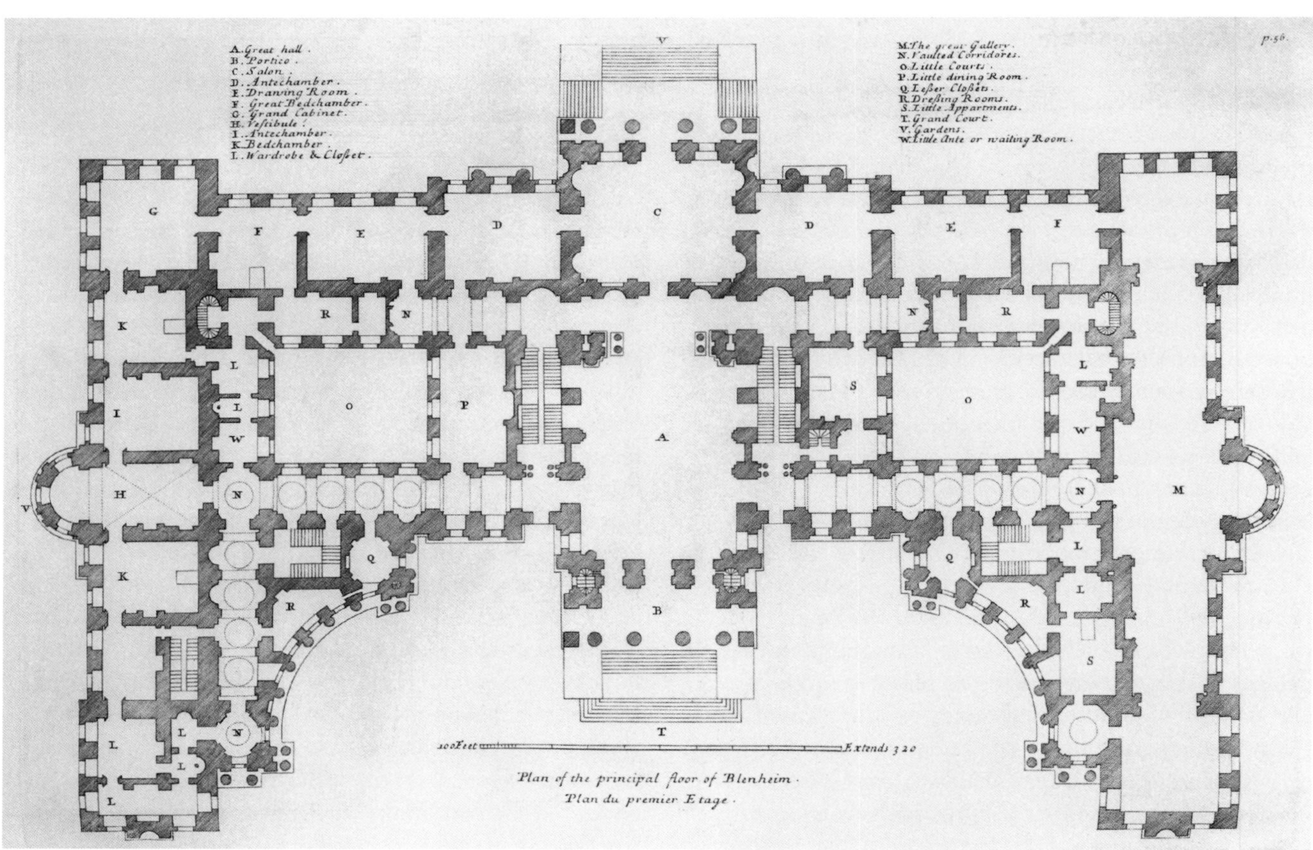

the day, Sir John Vanburgh, for Edward Southwell, "the Angaranno of our Age." (One of the points of this comparison was almost certainly the difference that enlightened patronage could make, though Campbell is careful to soften it by drawing attention to Thornhill's painted ceiling in the Great Hall at Stoke Edith.)

Logically, perhaps, one might expect Kings Weston to herald the great sequence of plates devoted to Vanbrugh's Blenheim (pls. 55–62) and Castle Howard (pls. 63–71), but Campbell is concerned to remind us once again of his yardstick, the works of the great Inigo Jones. It is immaterial that Lindsey House in Lincoln's Inn Fields (pls. 49–50), built c. 1640, is now attributed to Nicholas Stone: for Campbell, this was "another Piece of Inigo Jones" in which "the whole is conducted with that Harmony that shines in all the Productions of this great Master." What matters in the present context is that this serves to introduce William Benson's Wilbury House, Wiltshire (pls. 51–52)—a villa supposedly built in 1710 that pays both stylistic and nomenclative homage to nearby Amesbury Abbey and Wilton House (both thought to be by Jones)—and Campbell's third theoretical design—addressed to the earl of Ilay (pls. 53–54). To our eyes this latter design may be clearly composed of elements borrowed from Palladio's proposed town house for Count Angarano in Vicenza, and it is possible that subsequent recognition of this source by the youthful Lord Burlington may have prompted its selection as the basis of Campbell's eventual refronting of Burlington House in 1718–1719. However, in the context in which it is published in *Vitruvius Britannicus*, immediately following a town house supposed to have been designed by Jones and a villa consciously reviving his manner, it is surely more accurate to view Campbell's project as "Jonesian" rather than "Palladian" in intent. Thus the rusticated basement of the "Islay" design may be seen with equal justice as a quotation of that of the Queen's House, Greenwich, and the Ionic colonnade of its *piano nobile* (shown as a "pilastrade" in the plan) as intended not only to pick up on the example of Lindsey House just shown, but also to recall both the Ionic colonnade/pilastrade of the first story of the Banqueting House (pl. 13)—a source implied by Campbell's justification that he had "omitted to continue the Rusticks, to entertain the Eye with some repose"—and the window surrounds of the upper story of the Great Gallery at Old Somerset House (pl. 16).

The three most grandiose and richly adorned private palaces in the Kingdom—Blenheim (pls. 55–62), Castle Howard (pls. 63–71), and Chatsworth House (pls. 72–76)—now follow, each shown in greater than usual detail, suggesting an implied comparison not only with the Jonesian restraint (or "Antique simplicity") of the preceding designs, but also within themselves as varieties of a type. An obvious indication of this is the pointed juxtaposition of the "general" plans of Blenheim and Castle Howard in adjacent plates (pls. 62–63). The next trio of houses—a Thames-side villa at Twickenham (i.e., Orleans House; pl. 77) built to a design by John James in 1710 for the Hon. James Johnston, secretary of state for Scotland; a small country seat in Devonshire (i.e., Escot House; pls. 78–79) designed c. 1677–1678 for Sir Walter Yonge by Robert Hooke, founding member of the Royal Society and close associate of Wren; and the flamboyantly baroque Roehampton House, Wandsworth (pls. 80–81), "Invented by Thomas Archer Esq. 1712" for Thomas Cary, Esq.—act out a similar counterpoint, being comparable as fairly modest gentlemen's seats of equivalent status and situation, but clearly intended to reveal variety within their overall contrast to the aristocratic grandeur of the previous trio of "great houses." This series of private palaces and country seats forms, in turn, a balance to the undoubted climax of volume one—a magnificent sequence of four double-page plates devoted to Greenwich Hospital (pls. 82–89). It should come as no surprise that the design contributions of John Webb, Wren, and Nicholas Hawksmoor to the eventual form of this English "answer" to Les Invalides are ignored in Campbell's commentary, so that "this stupendous Structure," "for Magnificence, Extent, and Conveniency, the first Hospital in the World," can be presented as a *pièce de resistance*, "executed by Mr. Webb, from a Design of his great Master Inigo Jones" (1: p. 6). Criticism of the height of "the Attick over the great Corinthian Order" is justified as "probably . . . changed from the original Drawing," and enjoying in any case ample precedent "in the best Remains of Antiquity, [where] we find great Variety in their Proportions." The exceptional emphasis given to the Greenwich Hospital design is apparent not only in Campbell's eulogy ("Here the Rusticks are introduced with so much Art, the Ornaments with so much Grace, the whole Disposition is so Noble and Lofty, that, in the Opinion of many, it's one of the best Lines of Building in the World"), but also in the fact that it includes, for the first and only time in *Vitruvius Britannicus*, a plate that repeats part of a building in greater detail, namely, the elevation of the King Charles II Block (pls. 86–87). Indeed, the exceptionally careful and finished quality of this plate, in which the engraver Henry Hulsbergh employs no less than six different tonal differentiations (plain white for smooth masonry in full sunlight; flecked white for roughly dressed stone in sunlight; horizontal hatching for half-shading of ashlar; vertical hatching for half-shading of horizontal moldings such as plat-bandes, cornices, etc.; cross-hatching for window spaces; and diagonal cross-hatching for cast shadow), demonstrates for the first time the full capabilities of a systematization of graphic conventions that was to be arguably *Vitruvius Britannicus*' most significant influence upon the form and appearance of architectural books in England for the next three-quarters of a century.

After the excitement of Greenwich, volume one closes with a coda of four country houses that, in terms of social status, is pitched midway between the aristocratic palaces and modest gentlemen's seats that preceded it: Thoresby Hall, Nottinghamshire (pls. 90–91), the seat of the earl of Kingston, a Wren-style stone-coigned brick house with parapets, which, perhaps for the sake of his comparative schema, Campbell says was "built Anno 1671," an early date that must be wrong (see Colvin, pp. 804–805); Stainborough Hall (i.e., Wentworth Castle), Yorkshire (pls. 92–94), the seat of the earl of Strafford, where the emigré Johann von Bodt was from c. 1710 demonstrating another imported style, described by Campbell as "in the Venetian Manner" and by Howard Colvin as "a remarkable and almost unique example of Franco-Prussian architecture in Georgian England" (Colvin, p. 121); Easton Neston, Northants. (pls. 98–100), showing Hawksmoor's design for remodeling and enlarging the seat of Baron Leominster ("Lord Leimpster") which had been partially carried out by 1713; and finally, as should by now be no surprise, a parting shot from Campbell himself—a theoretical design (pls. 95–97) for a country house of equivalent importance inscribed to Lord Percival. Featuring projecting wings and forecourt and a double-hexastyle temple-front based on various Palladian villas, but leaving out "all manner of Rusticks and other Ornaments generally practised, purely to shew the Harmony of Proportion in the greatest Simplicity" (p. 7), Campbell's intention here was not merely to present his own alternative to the "foreign" or "outmoded" styles of other architects but to demonstrate once more those qualities of harmony, restraint, simplicity, and grandeur that are consistently associated everywhere in *Vitruvius Britannicus* with the achievements of its hero, Inigo Jones.

Volume two of *Vitruvius Britannicus*, which unlike volume three was intended from the start, continues the pattern established in volume one, where Jones' works are juxtaposed with Campbell's theoretical designs, and both are tacitly contrasted with those of other living architects. Although the double-page "General Plan" (pls. 2–3) and four quadruple-page engravings of Jones' supposed design for a new royal palace at Whitehall (pls. 4–7, 16–19) were clearly last-minute additions to the original scheme, and their inclusion contributed to the "displacement" of perspectives and garden plans to volume three, they are in no sense of the word interpolations. Given the essential role of Jones' work in *Vitruvius Britannicus* as the standard by which British architecture should be judged, it was an astonishing publishing coup to secure what were thought to be (or at least could be marketed as) the original drawings of Jones' fabled proposals for a magnificent new palace for Charles I at Whitehall, a huge project that, had it been built, would have outshone both the Louvre and the Escorial. Not only was the accession of a new monarch the obvious moment to publish such a scheme, but its inclusion was clearly perceived as essential to the success of *Vitruvius Britannicus* as a whole. Whereas the original announce-

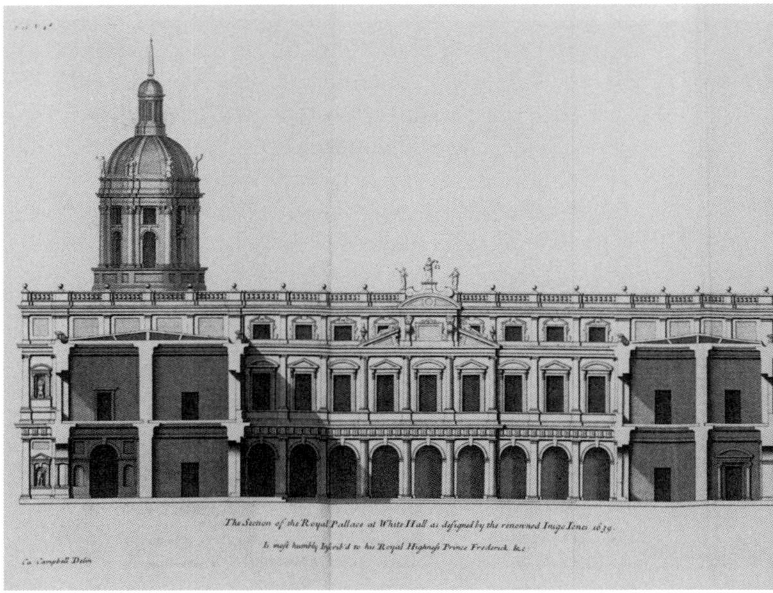

ments of subscription proposals had made no mention of Inigo Jones or any of his works, the Whitehall Palace designs were referred to without fail in every press advertisement once the printing of volume one was complete (i.e., from 9 April 1715 onward), by which time the importance of Jones' work both to the general appeal of *Vitruvius Britannicus* and to its compositional structure had become obvious.

It is worth noting, as an indication of the pressure on Campbell to publish Jones' Whitehall Palace designs, that he must have been aware that the five "original" drawings he had obtained from William Emmett (see Croft-Murray and Hulton 1960, 1: 378–379, nos. 11–15) could not possibly have been in Jones' hand, nor even prepared under his supervision, because it is inconceivable that the incorrectly drawn sequence of pediments on the windows of the Banqueting House (see Croft-Murray and Hulton 1960, 1: 378, no. 12) would have escaped their architect's notice. This egregious error, by confirming the uncertain status of Emmett's drawings, must have helped to ease Campbell's conscience when he came to "improve" on them by reducing the number of windows on the east front and replacing broken pediments with unbroken ones. A powerful commercial imperative to market *Vitruvius Britannicus* on the strength of Jones' fame makes it more than likely that it was through Smith's previous contact with Emmett as the artist responsible for the engravings of St. Paul's Cathedral included in the expanded version of *Britannia Illustrata* (1714) that Campbell was able "After much Labour and Expence" to track down "these excellent Designs of Inigo Jones, for Whitehall."

Although the Whitehall Palace engravings take up more of volume two than any other design or building in the book, they do form part of an opening sequence devoted to public buildings in London, followed by Jones' Covent Garden piazza and Church of St. Paul (pls. 20–22), the Royal Exchange (pls. 23–25), the steeple

Colen Campbell. *Vitruvius Britannicus.* Vol. 2, plate 16/19. "The Section of the Royal Pallace at Whitehall as designed by the renowned Inigo Jones 1639." 1985.61.440

of St. Mary-le-Bow, Cheapside (pl. 26), Campbell's design "for a Church in the Vitruvian Stile" (pl. 27), and the York Stairs river gate, said to be "Inv: by Inigo Jones 1626" (pl. 28), but in fact probably designed by Sir Balthasar Gerbier or Nicholas Stone. This may seem a somewhat random selection, but it is a tightly orchestrated sequence of implied contrasts and comparisons. The juxtaposition of Covent Garden and Royal Exchange enables Campbell to hold up the former as a model for avoiding "the Lanthorn way of Building so much in Practice of late Years," and point to the narrowness of the piers in the rustic arcade of the latter as an example of the ill effects of failing to do so. Similarly, the squeezing together of the plan, elevations, and section of Campbell's "Vitruvian" church project onto one single-page plate, despite the patent unsuitability of the shape to the placement on the page, is to be explained not just as space saving, but as a device also for implying an equivalence with the preceding single-page plate giving the plan, elevation, and section of Wren's Bow steeple (completed 1680). Of the latter, Campbell says in his commentary merely that "of this kind 'tis esteemed one of the best in the Kingdom," leaving it up to the reader to come to his or her own conclusions about its particular merits as compared with those of a very different kind exemplified in his own steepleless temple-church design. This, in turn, gives him the freedom to extol the virtue of having "abstained from any Ornaments between the Columns" on the side of his church, "which would only serve to enflame the Expence and clog the Building," *without* implying any criticism of Wren's steeple, the latter being obviously outside the scope of his strictures against "the trifling, licentious and insignificant Ornaments so much affected by some of our Moderns." Campbell rehearses at this point the ways in which the "moderns" have deviated from the example of antiquity by introducing unnecessary ornament; ignoring "the justness of the Intercolumnations, the precise proportions of the Orders and the greatness of Parts"; superimposing the orders "one over another in the same Temple in the Outside" for which there was no "Precedent either from the Greeks or Romans"; and instead of "one continued Pediment from the Portico to the Pastico," applying "no less than three in one Side where the Ancients never admitted any." Given Campbell's documented animosity against Gibbs (the only major living architect working in Britain unnamed in *Vitruvius Britannicus*), his thwarted ambition to obtain a post on the Commission for Building Fifty Churches (if necessary by ousting Gibbs from his surveyorship there), and his specific mention of superimposed orders on the outside, and three pediments along the flank, it is clear that his *private* target here was Gibbs' St. Mary-le-Strand, erection of which under the Fifty Churches Act had begun in 1714 and was still in progress in 1717. However, while there were no doubt some readers sufficiently in the know to recognize a particular target here, it is a mistake to interpret Campbell's remarks as nothing more than a self-serving personal attack on a professional rival, somehow "sneaked in" and without relevance to either the context of *Vitruvius Britannicus* or its market. First, Campbell is repeating one of the main themes of his "Introduction" to volume one, namely, that it was necessary to rediscover the virtues of "Antique Simplicity" in the works of faithful interpreters of the Ancients' example, such as Palladio and Inigo Jones, and to spurn the "capricious Ornaments" of the moderns, the "affected and licentious . . . works of Bernini and Fontana," and the "wildly Extravagant . . . Designs of Boromini, who has endeavoured to debauch Mankind with his odd and chimerical Beauties." Second, the message that Campbell is really concerned to establish with his Vitruvian church design is not just a private one of competition with Gibbs' "fair daughter in the Strand"; far more to the point is his obvious emulation of Jones' St. Paul, Covent Garden, "the only Piece the Moderns have yet produced, that can admit of a just Comparison with the Works of Antiquity, where a Majestick Simplicity commands the Approbation of the Judicious."

True to the pattern established in volume one, Campbell places examples of Jones' work either adjacent to his own designs, or as "markers" at the beginning and/or end of thematic "sections." Thus, following Campbell's Vitruvian church and concluding the public buildings' section, is York Stairs, thought to be by Jones, and the source of Campbell's design for the gateway to Burlington House (1718–1719) illustrated in volume three. The next two sequences, consisting of larger country houses (pls. 29–40) and smaller ones (pls. 44–50), are similarly provided with "anchor-points" at beginning and end, namely, Cobham Hall, in Kent (pls. 29–30)—another supposed Jones design but actually by Peter Mills; a theoretical project for a house inscribed to Tobias Jenkyns Esq. (pls. 41–42), designed in a so-called theatrical style, which according to Campbell "admits of more Gayety than is proper either for the Temple or Palatial Stile," and Campbell's own Shawfield Mansion, in Glasgow (pl. 51), his earliest executed commission, which is placed partly because of its location in Scotland, but also perhaps for private reasons, immediately after Smith's Melville House, Fife (pl. 50). After this comes Vanbrugh's "New Design for a Person of Quality in Dorsetshire" (pls. 52–55)—that is, Eastbury Park, for George Dodington—which is not only followed by (and therefore gains from comparison with) two quite ordinary, old-fashioned houses—Maiden Bradley, Wiltshire (pl. 56), and Shobdon Court, Herefordshire (pls. 59–60), seat of the then lord mayor of London, Sir James Bateman—but is also tacitly compared with the oldest, least regular, most castlelike building in the book, Henry IV's medieval palace at Hampton Court, Herefordshire (pls. 57–58). The placing of Shobdon here—a commonplace house almost certainly included for reasons other than architectural merit—also serves to dramatize the following sequence of magnificent plates devoted to those parts of Wilton supposed to have been designed by Inigo Jones (pls. 61–67). Just as Greenwich Hospital is the climax of volume one, so Wilton is the pinnacle of volume two; and just as the great twin double-page bird's-eye perspective of Wilton banished to volume three (pls. 57–60) exemplifies the virtues of its type, so also Campbell's perfectly judged rendition of its famous "Garden Front" (pls. 61–62) succeeds in translating into purely graphic terms all the qualities of restraint in ornament, harmony of proportions, "regularity," wide spacing between windows, and clearcut purity of forms that he admires in Jones' work and attempts to demonstrate, through his own designs, as the proper lead for British architects to follow. The placement of a long elevation above reduced-scale first- and second-floor plans is absolutely masterly, representing a huge advance in terms of clarity over its original source in Palladio's woodcuts, while its perfect balance of light and dark, solid and void, includes just enough cast shadow to suggest that the building is bathed in beneficent sunshine, but not so much as to disturb or detract from the geometrical purity of the architecture. These are the makings of a distinctly English manner of architectural representation, more precise than the looser-etched Dutch style from which it derives (cf., for example, Jacob Vennekool's engravings for Jacob van Campen's *Afbeeling van't Stadt Huys van Amsterdam*, 1664), but not as costly or difficult to achieve as the highly finished and detailed work perfected by a school of late seventeenth-century engravers in France working under the direct patronage of Colbert and the state (such as Louis Chastillon, Jean and Pierre Le Pautre, Nicolas Guérard, and Georges Tournier, who produced the majority of the plates for that tour-de-force of architectural precision and detail, Antoine Desgodetz's *Les Édifices antiques de Rome*, 1682).

As was the case with Greenwich, the special significance of Wilton is signaled by a departure from the standard scheme of plan and elevation to include, for the first time in the book, sections of specific rooms rather than of the building as a whole. The point to note is the imperative, once again, to present not so much the glories of Wilton as such—"this charming Place" as Campbell calls it, "a true Account of [which] would require an entire Volume"—but rather the glories of Inigo Jones' supposed work there: the "Garden Front 194 Foot long, which is justly esteemed one of the best Pieces of that great Architect" (pls. 61–62); "the grand Apartment . . . one of the noblest Architecture has yet produced, particularly the Sale and Salon," that is, the Double Cube and Cube Rooms, shown in detailed longitudinal and/or transverse section (pls. 63–64); the "Loggio in the Bowling-Green, with an Ionick Arcade," with "Pilasters . . . most beautifully rusticated"; the "Grotto, the front being curiously carved without, and all Marble within"; a "Rustick Ionick Door, in the Garden whereof there are 2 fronting each other two ways" (pl. 65); the "Stables disposed in a very handsome Manner" (pl. 66); and lastly "a Rustick Gate, which may serve for a Model to direct our Workmen on the like Ocasion" (pl. 67)—a suggestion that, as we have seen, underlies the deployment of Jones' work throughout *Vitruvius Britannicus*.

The sequence of great houses (pls. 68–80) that follows—Longleat, Wiltshire ("esteemed . . . the most regular Building in the Kingdom, being above 160 Years ago"); Cliveden, Buckinghamshire, notable, above all,

Colen Campbell. *Vitruvius Britannicus*. Vol. 3, plate 15. "Plan of the gardens and plantations of Eastbury in Dorsetshire..." 1985.61.441

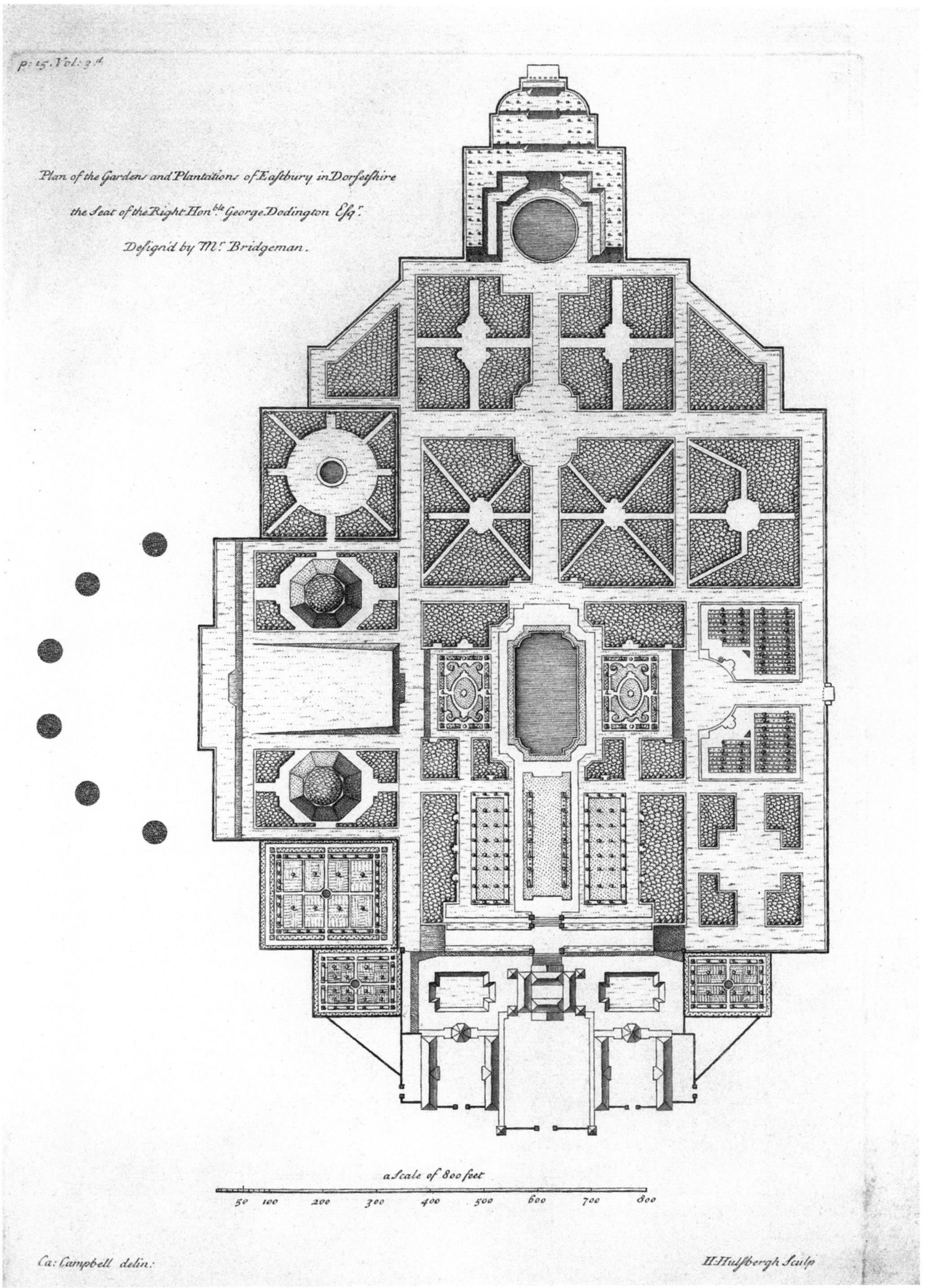
p: 15. Vol: 3d.
Plan of the Gardens and Plantations of Eastbury in Dorsetshire
the Seat of the Right Hon.ble George Dodington Esq.r
Design'd by M.r Bridgeman.
a Scale of 800 feet
50 100 200 300 400 500 600 700 800
Ca: Campbell delin:
H. Hulsbergh Sculp

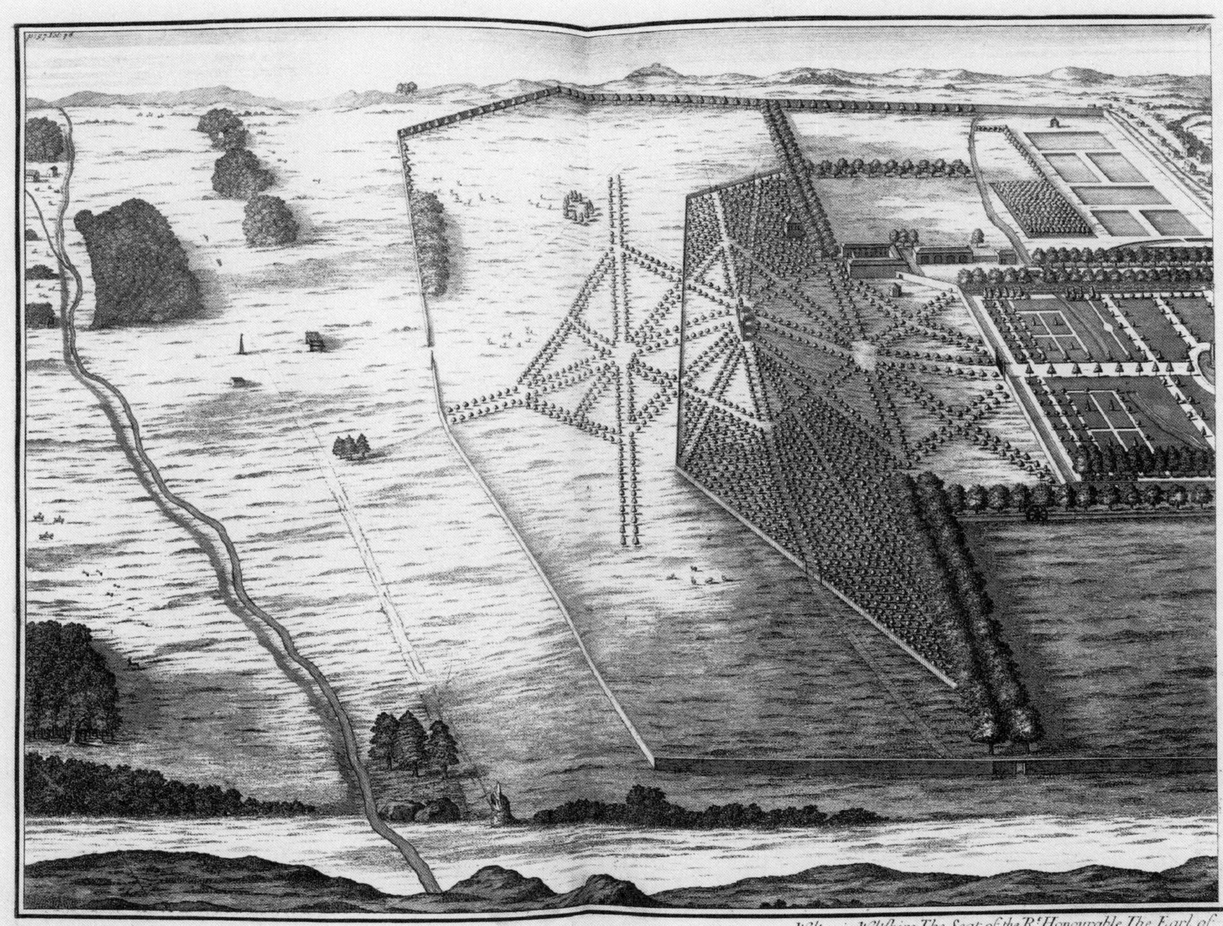

for the vast terrace on which it is built ("one of the most considerable . . . in the Kingdom"); Hopetoun House, West Lothian, of which the "Designs were given by Sir William Bruce, who was justly esteem'd the best Architect of his time in that Kingdom"; and Lowther Hall, Westmorland, built 1692–1695 with advice from Talman, the main front of which is praised by Campbell for the pedimented windows of its middle story and for having "a large Pediment at each End," while its principal idiosyncrasy, the oval library and chapel protruding at the end of each wing (possibly the work of James Gibbs), is passed over without comment—these form an obviously comparative group in relation both to Wilton, and to Bramham Park, Yorkshire (built c. 1705–1710, probably to the design of the owner, Lord Bingley) and Campbell's "new Design inscribed to Robert Walpole" (pls. 83–84). The latter design, based on an extraordinary re-use of the superstructure of Palladio's Rialto Bridge design, and about which Campbell says he has "endeavoured to introduce the Temple Beauties in a private Building," is clearly intended to demonstrate how pavilion "towers" (echoing those of Wilton in idea but not form) could allow for a better solution to the placing of a library and chapel in the wings than was achieved at Lowther Hall, and also, by an exact duplication of the visual arrangement of the plan elevations of Bramham Park (pls. 81–82), to offer his own design in "contest" with that as a better way of achieving the "Appearance of a large and magnificent Structure, when in Effect it is of a moderate Bigness, being no more than a Square of 100 Foot."

The next subject, inevitably, is another building "said to be designed by Inigo Jones." Chevening House, Kent (pl. 85), was clearly much admired by Campbell, and it is no accident that his designs for Sir Charles Hotham's house at Beverly, Yorkshire (pl. 87), and John Hedworth's house at Chester-le-Street, County Durham (pl. 88), both of which are stylistically indebted to this supposed work by Jones, should follow close by. What is surprising is to find a virtually unaltered copy of the street facade of Palladio's Palazzo Valmarana, Vicenza (pl. 86, inscribed to the owner of Chevening, "Mr Secretary Stanhope"), inserted between Chevening and its progeny. This is the first occasion in *Vitruvius Britannicus* that one of Campbell's "theoretical" designs bears absolutely no stylistic or thematic relation to its neighbors. Is it being overly subtle to suggest that this unprecedentedly direct quotation of a well-known Palladian building is placed here for no other reason than to flatter the owner of Chevening? Or that Campbell's disingenuous acknowledgment of his source for *only* that feature of his "new design" that the untutored would notice, was

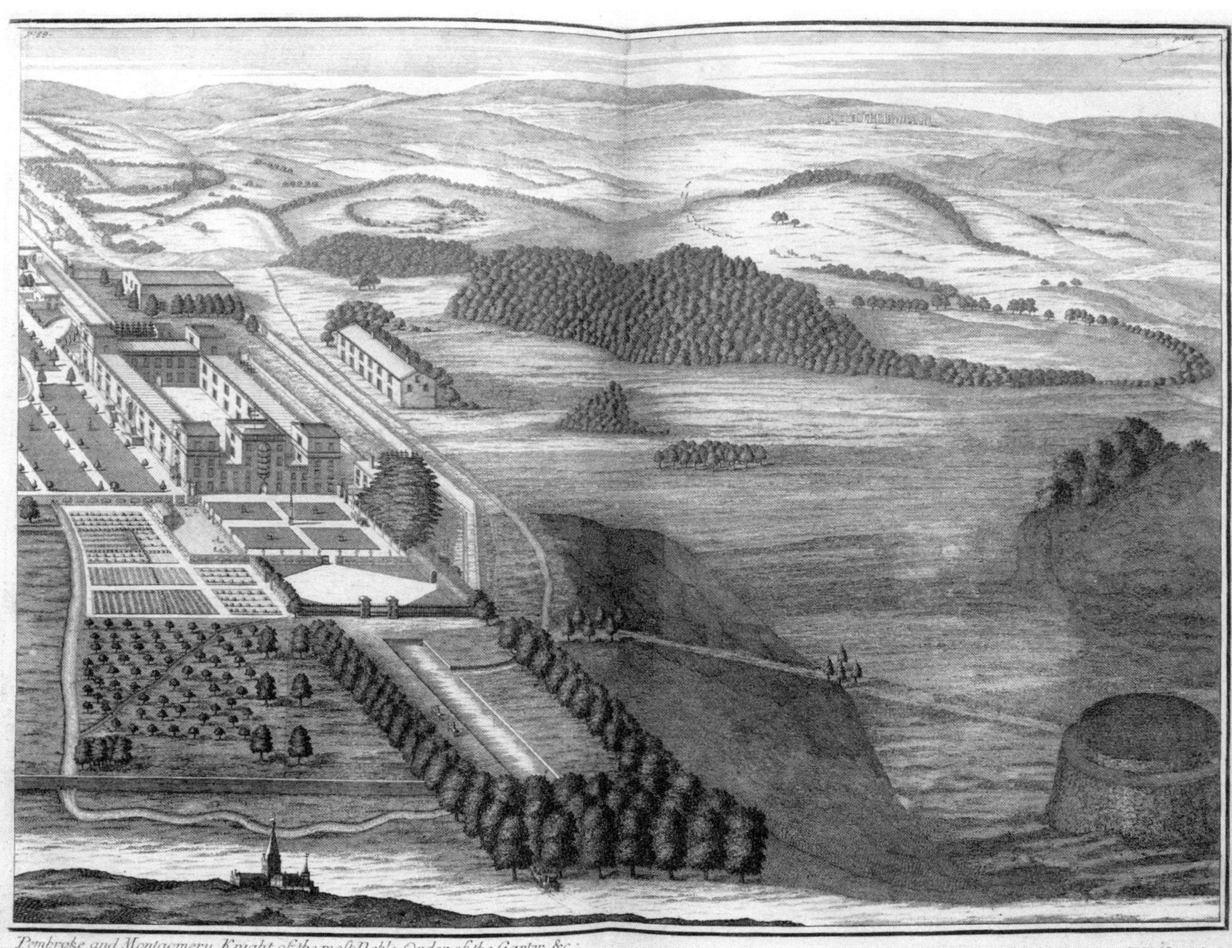

Colen Campbell. *Vitruvius Britannicus.* Vol. 3, plates 57/58 and 59/60. "Wilton in Wiltshire..." [with view of surrounding district including Stonehenge]. 1985.61.441

intended as a witty compliment to those cognoscenti, like Secretary Stanhope, for whom its entire dependence upon the Palazzo Valmarana facade was too obvious to need stating? This is the first time that Campbell makes a direct reference in his text to a specific building by Palladio. Even more interesting, in light of *Vitruvius Britannicus*' supposed status as a pioneering manifesto of neo-Palladianism, only two more such references occur in the book. And on all three occasions Campbell is concerned not so much to invoke Palladio's authority but rather either to improve upon him or to refer beyond him to the precedents in antiquity upon which this authority was based. Thus, of the "improvements" that Campbell made to the Valmarana facade—principally the straightening of the entablature of the main order, the elimination of pedestals in the basement, and the substitution of three-quarter applied columns in place of pilasters—only the last-mentioned can be put down to an ambiguity in Palladio's woodcut illustration of this design in the *Quattro Libri* (book 2, ch. 3). Similarly, although Campbell acknowledges a debt to Palladio's Rialto Bridge project when giving an account of his proposed design for Westminster Bridge (*Vitruvius Britannicus*, 3: pl. 56), it is only in respect of its proportions that he invokes Palladio's example, and then only after an excessively long and tedious parade of learning about the various forms and dimensions of bridges ancient and modern (*Vitruvius Britannicus*, 3: 10). The only other time Palladio is summoned directly to the reader's attention (apart from the "Introduction") is when Campbell sets out in the description of his design for Mereworth Castle, Kent (3: pls. 35–38) to enumerate the many ways in which he hopes his "learned Judges," the readers, will agree his design and its execution are "Improvements . . . from that of Palladio, for Signor Almerico"—the Villa Rotonda (ibid., p. 8).

The closing "section" of the second volume—a final series of grander houses bracketed, inevitably, by two of Campbell's own theoretical designs—recapitulates the comparative formula running throughout the book but without including a supposed work by Inigo Jones to act as "referee." Part of the reason for this was probably lack of space: there is a definite sense of squeezing material in at the closing stages of volume two, resulting, for instance, in the abandonment of the earlier principle of showing ground plans and elevations to the same scale (see pls. 85–88). Another factor was almost certainly Campbell's personal ambition to include as many of his own ideas as he possibly could. As we have seen, he was in no way free to do this to any extent that might interfere with the commercial appeal and universality of the book. Part of the price of being able to include a second house in his so-called theatrical style (inscribed to "Mr. Secretary Methuen," and very closely derived from a Palladian study by James Smith now in the RIBA Drawings Collection), and to sign off volume two with the final flourish of "a New Design of my Invention in the Palatial Stile" addressed to the earl of Cadogan (pls. 98–100), was the necessity of admitting, finally, a design by his enemy, James Gibbs. That Campbell toyed with the idea of not including Gibbs' project for Witham Friary, Somerset (pls. 91–92), is evident from the unpublished drawing he made of Talman's earlier "transparent portico" proposal for this house bound up in an album of his original drawings for *Vitruvius Britannicus*, volume two (RIBA Drawings Collection, Vitr. Brit. Album 2, fol. 92). In the end the choice was not his to make, but rather that of Witham's owner, Sir William Wyndham.

This capitulation on Campbell's part to external pressure is a reminder of the fact that he was working in partnership with a group of publishers, and most particularly with the printseller Smith. Paradoxically, when it came to composing volume three, a "sequel" in which Campbell and Smith were equal partners in terms of ownership and editorial control, the creative tension between nationalistic celebration and implied critical comparison evaporated. For one thing, Campbell chose to publish the fullest selection he could from his by now considerable portfolio of executed or approved designs (see 3: pls. 22–56), rather than continue the series of purely theoretical, unsolicited designs of the earlier volumes (only the very last subject in volume three [pls. 98–100] falls into this category, "a New Design" presented significantly without the buttress of a dedication to a potential patron). For his part, Smith was presumably equally keen to put to good use the perspectives and garden plans rejected from volumes one and two. And both partners would naturally have been concerned to maintain the Jonesian panegyric, especially in view of its importance to the success of the previous volumes, and possibly, also, out of an awareness of Lord Burlington's commissioning of William Kent in c. 1724 to prepare and publish the *Designs of Inigo Jones* (1727) from Flitcroft's careful copies of the Jones and Webb originals in Burlington's possession since 1720. Given the single-mindedness of their aims, it is perhaps not so surprising to find Smith and Campbell's divided ownership of the third volume of *Vitruvius Britannicus* reflected in distinct, unmodulated divisions that prevent it from achieving the thematic force or cohesion of its predecessors. The main symptom of the loss of cohesion is the abandonment of the comparative structure that dictated the arrangement of volumes one and two. Instead, the elements of this structure are, as it were, separated out into discrete units with nothing to say about each other. Thus the two grand prospects of Greenwich and Castle Howard that open the volume are an isolated fanfare; the three houses attributed to Jones—Ambresbury House, Wiltshire, Castle Ashby, Northants., and Stoke Park, Stoke Bruern, Northants.—are lumped together on plates 7 through 9 instead of being deployed strategically; Burlington's town house for General George Wade (pl. 10) is in no sense comparable to the great country house designs by Vanbrugh that follow it, Grimsthorpe Castle, Lincolnshire (pls. 11–14), Eastbury Park, Dorset (pls. 15–19, including the garden design by Charles Bridgeman), and Seaton Delaval, Northumberland (pls. 20–21); Campbell's own works are presented en masse on plates 22 to 56 inclusive; and the remainder of volume three, except for Campbell's "signing-off" with a theoretical design, is given over almost entirely to a random sequence of perspectives and garden plans displaced from the earlier volumes.

The preceding analysis of the structure and content of *Vitruvius Britannicus* opens the way to a clearer understanding of Campbell's "Introduction" than has hitherto been possible. The key here is the model that Fréart de Chambray's *Parallèle de l'Architecture antique et de la moderne* (1650) provided for the comparative structure that is the organizing principle in *Vitruvius Britannicus*. The indebtedness of Campbell's "Introduction" to the anti-baroque sentiments found in Fréart's *Parallèle* (Evelyn's English translation of which had been published in a new, enlarged edition as recently as 1707) was first noted by Connor, and has been recently reiterated both by John Harris (1994, 18 n. 36) and more fully by Giles Worsley (1995, 95–96). This indebtedness, however, goes deeper than a mere repetition of Fréart's complaint, in his peroration to the first part of the *Parallèle*, "that its now become as it were the Mode, I should say rather an universal Madness, to esteem nothing fine, but what is fill'd and surcharged with all sorts of Ornaments, without choice, without discretion or the least affinity to the Work or the Subject" (Fréart de Chambray 1707, ch. xxxvi). A crucial difference here is that whereas Fréart was free to blame "our small al a Mode Masters," the whole thrust of *Vitruvius Britannicus* is geared to identifying the source of any similar malaise in contemporary British architecture with a specifically foreign, that is, modern Italian "corruption" of antique simplicity. Far from being an attack on Wren and the English baroque, Campbell's "Introduction" deploys the classic chauvinist tactic of defining national virtue as the opposite of foreign vice, so that even if faults are to be found in the works of British architects (a question which is left for the reader to determine), these faults are imported and in no way a product of native genius. Part of the lesson to be learned in the light of Campbell's prescribed role as "author" is that it is a mistake to read his "Introduction" as simply a criticism of professional enemies such as Gibbs: it is far more importantly an expression of national pride.

Campbell's debt to Fréart is deeper also than is suggested by the simple fact of agreement about the preeminence of Palladio as the surest and most faithful interpreter of antique precedent. To dwell on Fréart's praise of Palladio as the best of the modern authorities is to obscure the fact that the originality of *Vitruvius Britannicus* in its final form lies precisely in what it borrowed from Fréart's book at a more fundamental level. Fréart's core idea was to weigh up, as in a balance, each of ten different modern authors' versions of the orders against the solid evidence of actual antique examples—a methodology that required, for the sake of fairness and objectivity, that the efforts of the moderns be shown to the same scale and in an exactly equivalent manner, which, in the original edition as copied in Evelyn's translation, was strictly diagrammatic, contrasting with the actuality of antique remains shown in fully finished, shaded etchings. Although Campbell did not go so far those of other architects, it is clear, both from his "Introduction"—where Jones is championed against all comers, even Palladio (adding to the latter's "Regularity" the qualities of "Beauty and Majesty in which our Architect is esteemed to have out done all that went before")—and from the strategic positioning of buildings thought to have been designed by Jones throughout volumes one and two, that Jones' achievements occupy the same position and serve the same function as antique exemplars had done in Fréart's *Parallèle*. The presentation of Jones' work as the yardstick by which to judge and compare the productions of all who have built after him, and as the lodestar to guide the future progress of the art in Britain, is the real driving force in *Vitruvius Britannicus*, rather than any personal ambition Campbell may have had of pioneering a neo-Palladian reform in taste through the publication of his own, mostly theoretical designs. Although the latter seem with hindsight prophetic of just such a reform, their task at the time was to proclaim Jones as Britain's own "Vitruvius," equal if not superior to Palladio himself. Was it not perhaps the central importance of this task to the success of the book that landed Campbell the "authorship" of *Vitruvius Britannicus*, and with it the first opportunity ever given to a British architect to show what he could do in print? It was certainly no idle fancy on Smith's part that led him to hang "the sign of Inigo Jones's Head" outside his shop in the Exeter Exchange. N. S.

Bibliography

Connor, T. P. "The Making of *Vitruvius Britannicus*." *Architectural History* 20 (1977): 14–30

Croft-Murray, E., and P. Hulton. *British Museum Catalogue of British Drawings*. London, 1960

Fréart de Chambray, R. *A Parallel of the Antient Architecture with the Modern*. 2d ed. London, 1707.

Harris, E. "*Vitruvius Britannicus* before Colen Campbell." *Burlington Magazine* (May 1986): 340–346

Harris, J. *The Palladian Revival: Lord Burlington, His Villa and Garden at Chiswick*. New Haven, 1994

Worsley, G. *Classical Architecture in Britain: The Heroic Age*. New Haven, 1995

II

Robert Castell (d. 1728)

The Villas Of The Ancients Illustrated.
By Robert Castell

London: printed for the author, 1728

1985.61.466

Folio: 491 × 357 (19 5/16 × 14 1/16)

Pagination [viii], 128, [2] pp., [13] engraved plates (6 double-page, 3 folding)

(*Note:* The title page is neither of the 2 variant, later settings listed by Harris and Savage)

Edition First edition

Text pp. [i] title page (verso blank); [III–IV] dedication to Lord Burlington; [V–VI] preface; [VII–VIII] list of subscribers; *part 1*: 1–16 "Pliny to Gallus" in parallel Latin (roman) and English (italic) with commentary in English at foot of pages; 17–54 "Remarks on Laurentinum"; *part 2*: 55–78 "The Villas of Varro Columella, &c."; *part 3*: 79–93 "Tuscum" in parallel Latin and English; 94 blank; 95–126 "Remarks on Tuscum"; 127–128 author's commentary (italic); [129–130] index, with errata at end

Illustrations 13 unnumbered engraved plates. The 4 single-page plates (lettered A to D) and the 3 folding plates (1 lettered E) were engraved by P. Fourdrinier, presumably Paul Fourdrinier, who is listed as a subscriber. According to manuscript attributions in the copy at the Canadian Centre for Architecture, other plates were drawn by T. Willson and P. Tuckey. The 6 double-page plans are unsigned. There are 5 engraved illustrations in the text, of which 2 are signed as engraved by George King. King also signed 4 of the 5 elaborate etched tailpieces, with landscape or figure vignettes and animal, floral, vegetable, and emblematic motifs (pp. 16, 54, 78, 93, 128). 2 etched pictorial headpieces are unsigned (pp. 55, 79)

Binding Contemporary calf, gilt spine, sprinkled edges

Provenance Contemporary ownership inscription on flyleaf (detached), "Rich[d]. Doidge"

References Berlin Cat. 1875; ESTC t50805; Fowler 81; Harris and Savage 108; RIBA, *Early Printed Books*, 581 (later ed.)

THE YOUNGER Pliny's letters to Gallus and Apollinaris, describing his country houses at Tuscum, near Lake Como, and Laurentinum, near Ostia, were well known to the architects of Renaissance Italy, and may well have inspired such buildings as the Villa Madama or Giuliano da San Gallo's Poggio a Caiano. So commonplace was the connection between Pliny and country-house architecture that Palladio made a specific point of rejecting his commentaries and reverting rather to Vitruvius. His disciple, Vincenzo Scamozzi, however, included a reconstruction of the Laurentinum in the twelfth chapter of the third book of his *Idea dell'architecttura universale*, of 1615. He offered one plate, a plan and section of the house alone, without any indication of the site or surrounds. This was not included in the excerpt of Scamozzi's work, published as *The Mirror of Architecture*, in London, in 1669. The next restoration of the Laurentinum and also the Tuscum villas to be published were those included in Claude Le Peletier's *Comes rusticus, ex optimis latinae linguae scriptoribus excerptus*, issued in Paris between 1692 and 1695. Le Peletier was Colbert's successor as Contrôleur général des finances, but he was also the author of a number of historical works. The restoration studies, six plates in all, all plans, were by Jean-François Félibien, son of André Félibien, and his successor as secretary to the *Académie d'architecture*. The members of the Académie were much intrigued, and began at once to discuss Scamozzi's and Félibien's restorations. In 1699 Félibien was incited to publish restorations of both the Laurentinum and the Tuscum villas, together with Pliny's letters, as *Les plans et les descriptions de deux des plus belles maisons de campagne de Pline le Consul, avec des remarques sur tous les bâtimens, et une disseration touchant l'architecture antique et l'architecture gothique*. This contained five plates, including a copy (handed) of Scamozzi's, illustrating a villa, formal in arrangement, surrounded by courts and parterres that were equally formal in layout. Félibien made clear that his reconstructions were based on the texts of the letters alone, no trace of the villas surviving. But in 1713 Marcello Sacchetti, owner of the supposed site of the Laurentinum villa at La Spinerba, near Ostia, began digging. He unearthed the remains of a villa, with courts and two towers, and many mosaics, and had plans drawn up to record his finds (now in the Vatican Library). But the plans did not correspond with Pliny's descriptions. Later researchers, in the closing years of the century, having failed to trace Sacchetti's drawings, explored the site yet again. Not much of the original villa remained, but they located six or seven more in the region, and became increasingly uncertain as to the identity of Pliny's villa.

Robert Castell, who, on the proposals for publishing *The Villas of the Ancients* identified himself as "R. C. architect" (though he is not known to have practiced as such), might have been stirred by gossip from France or Italy to take up his restorations, but he made no use at all of Félibien's study. What he really aimed at was a translation of Vitruvius. In the meantime, as a "necessary preparation to his entering on a Work of so much Labour and Difficulty" he determined upon "some inferior Performance in Architecture." On 1 February 1727

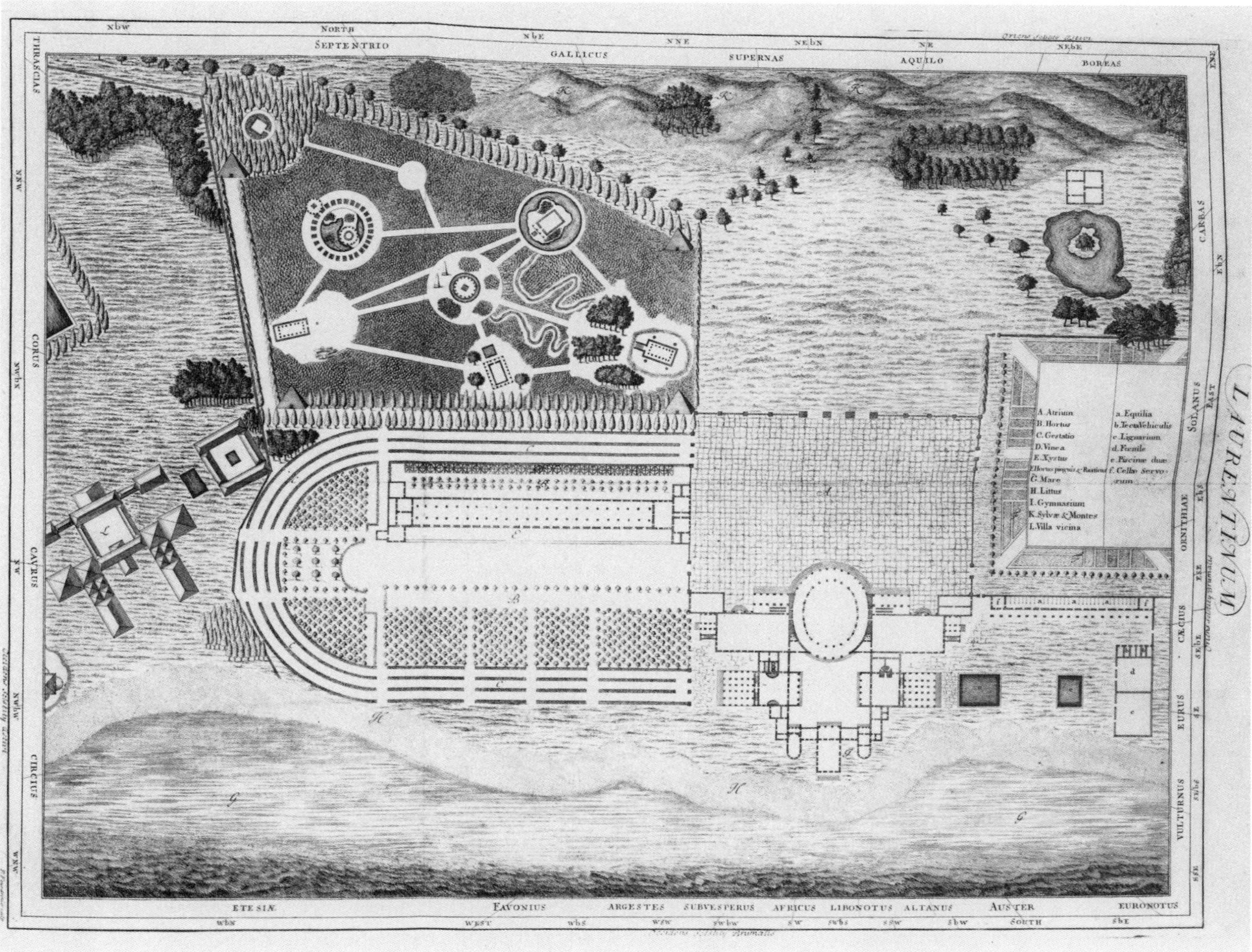

Robert Castell. *The Villas of the Ancients Illustrated.* "Laurentinum." 1985.61.466

proposals were printed for the publication of Pliny's two letters together with "large explanatory notes subjoin'd. To which are added, Remarks on these Two country houses and the Baths, Gardens & c of the Ancients: all illustrated in several large Drawings." Work must already have been far advanced, for the book was promised for the following month. Plates were exhibited at the shops of Woodman and Lyon and N. Prevost, where, after 15 March, the plates of Gibbs' *Book of Architecture* could also be seen. Gibbs was asking three guineas for his book, Castell two guineas. Castell's proposal was evidently not sufficiently attractive to rouse much interest, certainly not to raise the money for publication. This was put off. Some time later in the year Burlington came into contact with Castell and seems to have persuaded him that it would be more advantageous to proceed first with the translation of Vitruvius, to be followed by Pliny's villas, enlarged to include Varro's description of a country house. Both books might be dedicated to Burlington.

Proposals were announced on June 1728 for Castell's translation of Vitruvius, illustrated "with a great number of Engravings, from original drawings of Palladio and Pyrro Ligorio . . . from several Remains of old Roman buildings that were standing in their time, which inestemable Pieces were never published, and are now in the Library of the Rt. Honourable the Earl of Burlington, and by his Lordships special favour allowed to be copied for the benefit of this Undertaking, and the Encouragement of Architecture." To this were to be added "the Remarks of Mr. Inigo Jones, the Vitruvius of his Age, on the Italian version of the Author, by Daniel Barbaro," also in the library of Burlington.

Two weeks later, on 18 June, Castell was thrown into the Fleet Prison, for debt. He owed no more than four hundred pounds, but the warden, Thomas Bambridge, demanded bail security and payments totaling four thousand pounds. This Castell refused to pay. He was moved to a sponging house where he contracted smallpox and died on 12 December 1728. A group of parliamentarians, outraged by this and other cases of abuse, prepared a report, on the basis of which Bambridge was twice tried, and twice acquitted. Castell's only assets were the plates and texts for his books. The Vitruvius was abandoned. *The Villas of the Ancients* was published on 5 July 1729. Most of the money for the venture had come from 117 subscribers who offered to support the work, lawyers,

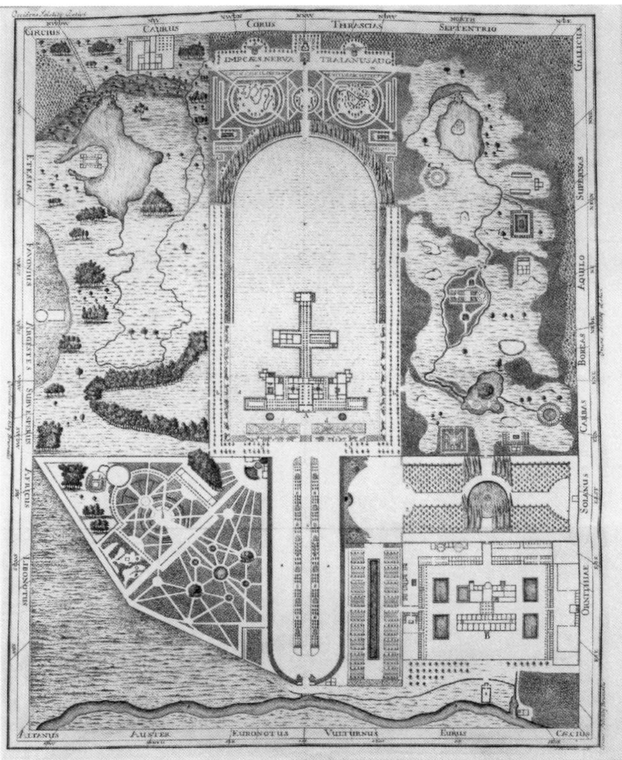

Robert Castell. *The Villas of the Ancients Illustrated.* "Tuscum." 1985.61.466

parliamentarians, and reformers for the most part. No architects were included, nor was Burlington, who might have been expected to lend his support. The book was, however, dedicated to him.

The Villas of the Ancients is arranged in three parts, that on the Laurentinum villa first, that on the villa at Tuscum last, with Varro's and Columella's descriptions of farming establishments set in between. In his commentary or "Remarks" on the villas Castell argues that the rules laid down for town houses by Vitruvius must be taken to apply also to the "villa urbana" or "villa rustica." Though Pliny's *cryptoporticum* and Varro's *tholos*—the only two buildings he reconstructed in elevation and section—Castell regarded as outside the canon. The villas themselves are illustrated only in plan.

The site plans, however, included wildernesses and irregular areas that indicate that Castell was familiar with the writings of Joseph Addison and that he had profited considerably from the plates of Stephen Switzer's *Ichnographia rustica*, of 1718. But by linking this new manner in gardening to antique precedents Castell provided an unexpected authority for further experimentation.

The plates were drawn by T. Willson (with the exception of one by P. Tuckey) and engraved by P. Fourdrinier. The head- and tailpieces are by George King, a pupil of Vertue.

Copies of the subscribers' edition exist with a variant of the title leaf and with a passage in the text reprinted in a shorter form. There is also a "trade" edition, which omits the subscribers' list and the whole of the Latin text. R. M.

Bibliography

Culot, M. and P. Pinon, eds. *La laurentine et l'invention de la villa romaine.* Paris, 1982

Harris, E., and N. Savage. *British Architectural Books and Writers 1556–1785.* Cambridge, 1990

12

Sir William Chambers (1723–1796)

Designs Of Chinese Buildings, Furniture, Dresses, Machines, and Utensils. Engraved by the Best Hands, From the Originals drawn in China By Mr. Chambers, Architect, Member of the Imperial Academy of Arts at Florence. To which is annexed, A Description of their Temples, Houses, Gardens, &c.

London: published for the author, and sold by him: also by Mess. Dodsley; Mess. Wilson and Durham; Mr. A. Millar, and Mr. R. Wilcock, 1757

Desseins Des Edifices, Meubles, Habits, Machines, Et Ustenciles Des Chinois. Gravés Sur les Originaux dessinés à la Chine Par Mr. Chambers, Architecte, Membre de l'Académie Impériale des Arts à Florence. Auxquels est ajoutée Une Description de leurs Temples, de leurs Maisons, de leurs Jardins, &c.

A Londres: de l'imprimerie de J. Haberkorn; se vend chez l'auteur; & chez A. Millar & J. Nourse, 1757

1983.49.16.a

Folio: 531 × 356 (20 7/8 × 14 1/16)

Pagination [x], 19, [1]; [viii], 19, [1] pp., 21 engraved plates

(*Note:* Text in English followed by text in French)

Edition First edition

Text English pp. [i] title page (verso blank); [iii] dedication to George, prince of Wales (verso blank); [v–vi] list of subscribers; [vii–x] preface; 1–19 text; [20] blank; *French* pp. [i] title page (verso blank); [iii] dedication (verso blank); [v–viii] preface; 1–19 text; [20] blank

Illustrations 21 engraved plates numbered I–XXI, of which I, III–VII, and XI–XVI are signed as engraved by P. Fourdrinier; II and VIII by Ignace Fougeron; IX–X by Edward Rooker; XVII by Paul Sandby; and XIX–XXI by Charles Grignion (plate XVIII unsigned)

Binding Contemporary marbled boards, rebacked, red sprinkled edges. Bound with a copy of the author's *Treatise on Civil Architecture*, 1759

Provenance Eighteenth-century engraved bookplate of Robert Shafto, Esq., Benwell. Early nineteenth-century engraved bookplate of William Adair, Esq., inside lower cover

References Berlin Cat. 2784 (French); Cicognara 1623 (misdated 1753); ESTC t31726 and n50196; Fowler 85 (French); Harris and Savage 113 and 114; RIBA, *Early Printed Books*, 595 (English)

ANOTHER COPY (plates and English text only)

1985.61.469

Folio: 550 × 368 (21 3/4 × 14 1/2)

Binding Bound after the author's *Plans, Elevations . . . at Kew*, 1763 (q.v.)

Provenance As for the author's *Plans, Elevations . . . at Kew*

WILLIAM CHAMBERS was not destined for architecture. He was born on 23 February 1723, in Gothenburg, Sweden, the first son of a well-connected Scots merchant. He was educated at Ripon, Yorkshire, under the eye of his father's cousin, Dr. William Chambers. But in 1739, at the age of sixteen, he was back in Gothenburg ready to embark on a mercantile career. He joined the Swedish East India Company, and in April 1740 set sail for Bengal, returning in October 1742. Six weeks later he was sent off on another voyage, on this occasion to Canton, where he spent several months. He was away for two and one-half years. After a two-year respite, during which he traveled to England, through the Low Countries, and France, he set off from Gothenburg on a third voyage, on 20 January 1748, once again bound for Canton. He returned to Gothenburg on 11 July 1749. By then he seems to have decided not to follow his father's occupation, but to take up architecture instead. Already he had established something of a reputation as a scholar of Chinese subjects

Later, during the same year, he was introduced to Frederick, prince of Wales, who was dallying then with chinoiserie and other exotic tastes, and perhaps sketched designs then for the House of Confucius (called the India House) at Kew, construction on which began in this year, though it was later resited. Chambers was responsible also for sending the prince a design for an "Alhambra," in 1750, by Johann Henry Muntz, who had traveled recently in Spain, and was to move himself to England in 1755. But despite such activity, Chambers clearly required hard training if he was to become an architect.

In the autumn of 1749 he enrolled in Jacques-François Blondel's school in Paris, but by the following autumn he was ready to begin exploring Italy. He was established in Rome for five years, making a brief trip to Paris in the summer of 1751, to escort his future wife to Rome, where he married and where his two daughters were born. He returned to England in March or April 1755.

Once again Chambers managed to establish a reputation for himself on the basis of his newly acquired knowledge and studies. Robert Adam recognized him at once as a potential rival. Writing to his brother John on 18 April 1755, after meeting Chambers in Florence, he noted:

All the English who have travelled for these five years are much prepossessed in his favour and imagine him a prodigy for Genius, for Sense and good taste . . . that he in great measure deserves their encomiums, though his taste is more architectonick than Picturesque, as for Grounds & gardens, Boutcher can't be more Gothick. But his taste for Bas relieves, Ornaments, & decorations of Buildings, he both knows well and draws exquisitely. His Sense is middling, but his appearance is genteel & his personage good, which are most material circumstances. . . . He despises others as much as he admires his own talents which he shows with a slow and dignified air, conveying an idea of great wisdom which is no less useful than all his other endowments and I find sways much with every Englishman. . . .

Chambers' first patron, Frederick, prince of Wales, died in March 1751. In this and the following year, while yet in Rome, Chambers prepared designs for a mausoleum, no doubt intended for Kew, but nothing was to be built. After his return, in 1756, Chambers proposed an ambitious scheme for the rebuilding of Harewood House, Yorkshire, for Edwin Lascelles, but this was at once rejected as too French. This was not an easy year for Chambers, as the Adam brothers once again noted, but Augusta, the dowager princess of Wales, was intent to explore further her late husband's tastes at Kew, and with her encouragement, it would seem, Chambers undertook to publish the first serious book of designs of Chinese architecture. There were, of course, a great many works illustrating rococo confections in the Chinese style, most notably William Halfpenny's *New Designs for Chinese Temples*, the first edition of 1750, and *Chinese and Gothic Architecture Properly Ornamented*, of 1752, but there was nothing that could be said to be based on firsthand experience and knowledge. Chambers himself had clearly never intended such a publication when he was in the East, though he must have made sketches and drawings in Canton. In June 1756 he wrote to his brother John in Gothenburg, asking where he might find information on Chinese houses. He certainly consulted Jean Baptiste Du Halde's *Description géographique, historique, chronologique et physique de l'Empire de la Chine*, published in Paris in 1735, and in London in 1738, which he was to quote often enough, and also Athanasius Kircher's *China monumentis qua sacris qua prophanis*, published first in 1667 in Amsterdam. But he was hard put to gather enough information of an authentic kind.

When his book was issued in May 1757, it comprised an odd medley of plates—twelve of them architectural, illustrating the plan of a temple precinct; elevations of a pagoda; assorted pavilions and a bridge; columns and

William Chambers. *Designs of Chinese Buildings.* Plate IX. Section of a Chinese House. 1983.49.16.a

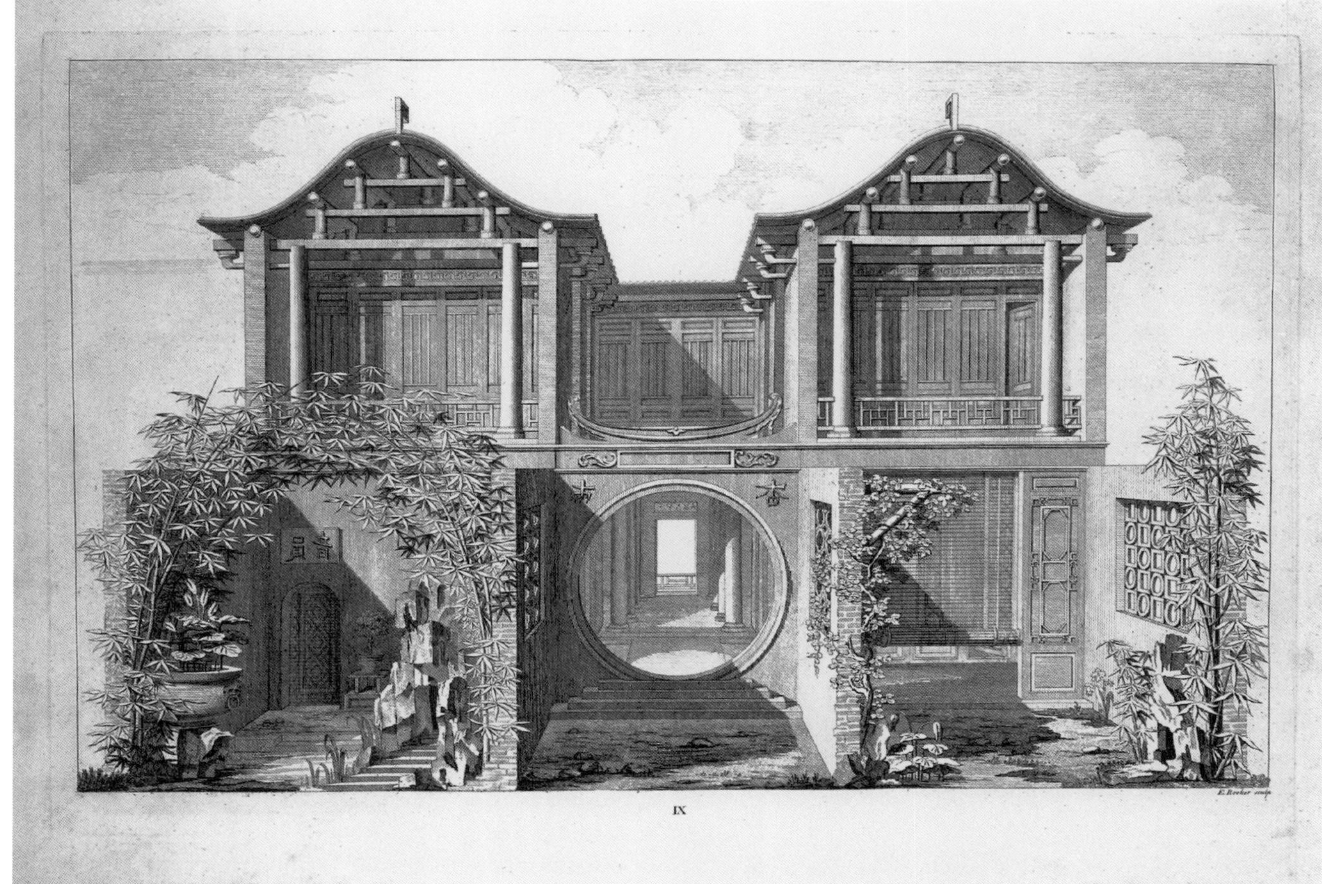

archways; and, most intriguingly, the plans, interior elevations, and a view of a merchant's house on a river. There were two plates of furniture; two of cups, teapots, and bowls; one of boats (derived, as Chambers admitted from a painting); one of farming machinery; and three of costumes. The best of the plates, thirteen in all, were engraved by P. Fourdrinier, possibly the same man who had worked for James Gibbs and most of the architects associated with Lord Burlington; two were by Edward Rooker, so much admired by Horace Walpole; two by Charles Grignion, who proposed Chambers for the Society of Artists in 1757; and one each by Ignace Fougeron and Paul Sandby, with whom Chambers was to be associated at the Royal Academy of Arts. Two plates were unsigned. Altogether Chambers had selected his engravers with care.

The proposals he had issued in 1756 had attracted 165 subscribers, who agreed to purchase 185 copies of the work; these were headed by George, prince of Wales, who agreed to accept the dedication, and his mother, Augusta. Among the artists and architects who subscribed were John and James Adam, William Kent, James Paine, Thomas and Paul Sandby, John Vardy, and Joseph Wilton.

But whatever the support offered, Chambers had misgivings about the whole enterprise; it did not strike quite the right note to usher in his career. His designs would not have been published, he wrote in his preface:

William Chambers. *Designs of Chinese Buildings.* Plate XIV. Tables, chairs, and stands. 1983.49.16.a

> were it not in compliance with the desire of several lovers of the arts, who thought them worthy of the perusal of the publick, and that they might be of use in putting a stop to the extravagancies that daily appear under the name of Chinese.
>
> Though I am publishing a work of Chinese architecture, let it not be suspected that my intention is to promote a taste so much inferior to the antique, and so very unfit for our climate: but a particular so interesting as the architecture of one of the most extraordinary nations in the universe cannot be a matter of indifference to a true lover of the arts.

His friends had warned him, he concluded, that the work would hurt his reputation—"yet I cannot conceive why it should be criminal in a traveller to give an account of what he had seen worthy of notice in China, any more than in Italy, France, or any other country."

Though Chambers illustrated no gardens in his book, the section that roused the most interest and response was the four and a half pages of text "Of the art of laying out gardens among the Chinese," set at the end. The taste for variety, and the sweet disorders of nature that underpins this, is adapted from Joseph Addison's famous essays "On the Pleasures of the Imagination," published forty-five years earlier in the *Spectator*. The actual descriptions of Chinese gardens—limited indeed—are taken from Frère Attiret's reports in the *Lettres édifiantes et curieuses, écrites des Missions Étrangères, par quelques Missionaires de la Compagnie de Jésus*, published in Paris in 1749, and in English, in 1752, in Joseph Spence's translation *A Particular Account of the Emperor of China's Gardens Near Pekin*, included, in part, in the *Monthly Review*, the *Scots Magazine*, and the *London Magazine*. Chambers seems to have been quite unaware of the thirty-six views of Emperor K'ang Hsi's palace and gardens at Jehol, engraved by Matteo Ripa, and bought from him in 1724 by Lord Burlington.

The Chinese aimed, Chambers reported, to imitate all the beautiful irregularities of nature in their gardens, contriving as much diversity as might be possible. Their gardens were made up of three species of scenes, the one succeeding the other, described as pleasing, horrid, and enchanted. The horrid scene was the one that concerned him most.

> In their scenes of horror, they introduce impending rocks, dark caverns and impetuous cataracts rushing down the mountains from all sides; the trees are ill-formed, and seemingly torn to pieces by the violence of tempests; some are thrown down, and interrupt the course of the torrents, appearing as if they had been brought down by the fury of the waters; others look as if shattered and blasted by the force of lightning; the buildings are some in ruins, others half-consumed by fire, and some miserable huts dispersed in the mountains serve, at once to indicate the existence and wretchedness of the inhabitants.

Chambers seems to have been describing no more than scenes from the paintings of Salvator Rosa, but he claimed to have been instructed in such knowledge by Lepqua, a Chinese painter—a figment, it seems, of his imagination. At any event, it was the frisson of delight evoked by such scenes that attracted the attention of the young Edmund Burke, who, in the same year published his *Enquiry into the Origin of Our Ideas of the Sublime and Beautiful*. Some critics had mocked Burke's notion that terror might be a source of the sublime, and thus of exalted pleasure. When Chambers' account of the laying out of Chinese gardens was reprinted in May 1757 in the *Gentleman's Magazine*, Burke proclaimed it "much the best that has been written on the subject," and himself published it in 1758 in the first volume of his *Annual Register*. It was reprinted again in 1762 in Bishop Thomas Percy's *Miscellaneous Pieces Relating to the Chinese*, and was taken up in the same year by Lord Kames as the basis for his remarks on gardens, inserted at the end of the second volume of his *Elements of Criticism*.

The publication of the *Designs of Chinese Buildings* brought calculated successes for Chambers. Within two months he was appointed architect to the dowager princess of Wales, and erected an array of extraordinary structures for her, in the years that followed, at Kew. Even more rewarding, he was appointed tutor in architecture to her son George, prince of Wales, the future king. His instruction was to form the basis of *A Treatise on Civil Architecture*.

But the *Designs of Chinese Buildings* also led to embarrassment and ridicule. At the end of the section on gardening he had inserted a jibe at Capability Brown's method of gardening:

> What we call clumps, the Chinese gardeners are not unacquainted with; but they use them somewhat more sparingly than we do. They never fill a whole piece of ground with clumps: they consider a plantation as painters do a picture, and groupe their trees in the same manner as those do their figures, having their principal and subservient masses.

In May 1772 Chambers published a *Dissertation on Oriental Gardening*, an even more overt and ironical attack on Brown (still unnamed), in which the descriptions of the horrors of Chinese gardens were exaggerated to absurdity. Unfortunately, just as the *Designs of Chinese Buildings* had been taken seriously, so was the later elaboration of the ideas contained therein. But now Chambers was mocked for his nonsense. He endeavored to set things straight by appending an *Explanatory Discourse* (said to have been written by Tan Chetqua, a Cantonese sculptor, who was real enough, but who had conveniently just left England) to the second edition of the *Dissertation*, issued in March 1773. Two weeks before its appearance however, an *Heroic Epistle*, later identified as the work of William Mason, was issued, in which Chambers was wittily mocked and traduced. The *Heroic Epistle* was an extraordinary success, running to ten editions in 1773 alone. Though it was a serious defense of the art of Capability Brown, its acclaim was equally owing to its political implications, as an attack on the Tory establishment, in which Chambers, as an intimate of the king, was by then a leading figure.

The *Designs of Chinese Buildings* does not appear to have had much practical influence on the design of garden structures in England—only two structures relate directly to it, Chambers' own design for a temple at Ansley, of 1769, and Robert Abraham's copy of the Canton pagoda erected at Alton Towers in 1827. Despite the acclaim of Burke and the notoriety that resulted from the *Heroic Epistle*, its impact on picturesque theory was slight, even in France, where it was circulated in translation as *Desseins des édifices, meubles, habits, machines et ustensiles des chinois*, first in 1757, and then in 1776, renamed *Traité des édifices, meubles, habits, machines et ustensiles des chinois*, issued as the fifth cahier of G. L. Le Rouge's *Jardins anglo-chinois*, the most compendiously illustrated survey of garden design to be published in the eighteenth century. Chambers' text was, indeed, the only theoretical excursus offered in that work. But though Charles de Wailly copied some of Chambers' urns for his suite of vases in 1760, and though some of Chambers' notions no doubt had their effect, serious theorists in France such as C.-H. Watelet and J.-M. Morel, who sustained the introduction of the picturesque landscaping in the 1770s, found nothing to stir them in Chambers' writings. They were interested neither in evoking horror, nor in achieving variety through the scattering of exotic architecture in the landscape. They preferred to compose with the elements of nature, unadulterated. R. M.

Bibliography

Harris, E. "Burke and Chambers on the Sublime and Beautiful." In *Essays in the History of Architecture Presented to Rudolf Wittkower*. Ed. D. Fraser, H. Hibbard, and M. J. Lewine. London, 1967: 207–213

Harris, E., and N. Savage. *British Architectural Books and Writers 1556–1785*. Cambridge, 1990

Harris, J. *Sir William Chambers. Knight of the Polar Star*, with contributions by J. Mordaunt Crook and E. Harris. London, 1970

13

Sir William Chambers (1723–1796)

A Treatise On Civil Architecture, In Which The Principles of that Art Are laid down, and Illustrated by A great Number of Plates, Accurately Designed, and Elegantly Engraved by the best Hands. By William Chambers . . .

London: printed for the author, by J. Haberkorn. To be had of the author's house; likewise of A. Millar, J. Nourse, Wilson and Durham, T. Osborne, J. and R. Dodsley, R. Sayer, Piers and Webley, and J. Gretton, 1759

1983.49.16.b

Folio: 531 × 356 (20 7/8 × 14 1/16)

Pagination [6], iv, 85, [1] pp., [50] engraved plates

Edition First edition

Text pp. [1] title page (verso blank); [3] dedication to the earl of Bute (verso blank); [5–6] list of subscribers; [i]–iv preface; [1]–85 text; [86] directions to the binder and errata

Illustrations 50 unnumbered engraved plates, 39 of which are signed by Chambers as architect/draftsman; 8 by James Gandon as draftsman; and 1 by G. B. Cipriani. The credited engravers are Francis Patton (16), P. Fourdrinier (12), Edward Rooker (7), Peter Mazell (5), Charles Grignion (4), T. Miller (4), and Ignace Fougeron (1). 1 plate unsigned

Binding Bound with the author's *Designs of Chinese Buildings*, 1757 (q.v.)

Provenance As for the author's *Designs*

References Berlin Cat. 2286 (1768 ed.); Berlin (1977) os 2285[2]; ESTC t51636; Fowler 86; Harris and Savage 122; RIBA, *Early Printed Books*, 598

ANOTHER COPY

1985.61.468

Folio: 534 × 360 (21 × 14 1/8)

Binding Contemporary sprinkled calf, rebacked, sprinkled edges

William Chambers was thirty-three, in the summer of 1756, when he failed to win the commission from Edwin Lascelles to rebuild Harewood House, in Yorkshire. This, he had hoped, would serve to inaugurate his career. Instead he was forced to rely on smaller commissions, of the following year, from the earl of Pembroke, who built a triumphal arch, a *cascina*, and a handful of bridges in the garden at Wilton, and the duke of Richmond, who erected a rather grand stable range at Goodwood. These commissions led to Richmond House in Whitehall, and works at Great Barton, Castletown, and Dublin for the duke's sisters and, also in Dublin, at the Casino at Marino, for the earl of Charlemont, which though begun in 1759, was still incomplete ten years later.

Chamber's initial success, however, was owing rather to royal patronage. In 1749, before he traveled to France and Italy, he had advised on some of the exotic buildings that Frederick, prince of Wales, was erecting at Kew. The prince died in March 1751, during Chambers' stay in Rome, but on his return to London in March or April 1755, Chambers was persuaded by the dowager princess Augusta to advance her late husband's tastes by composing the *Designs of Chinese Buildings*, proposals for which were issued in 1756. The book, published in May 1757, was dedicated to her son George, prince of Wales, who three years later ascended the throne. In the summer of 1757 Chambers was appointed both architect to the dowager princess, for whom he was to erect almost thirty garden structures at Kew during the next six years, and architectural tutor to the young prince.

He wrote:

> My hands are full of work, but my pockets are not full of money. The prince employs me three mornings in a week to teach him architecture; the building (and) other decorations at Kew fill up the remaining time. The princess has the rest of the week which is scarcely sufficient as she is forever adding new embellishments at Kew, all which I direct the execution (and) measure the work. I have also the care of the house there, Carlton House in London with three other habitations occupied in different parts of the town by her attendants, for all which I am rewarded with fifty pounds a year punctually paid by the prince and one hundred by the princess.

Whatever the small advantages of royal patronage, the public emphasis that it gave to his knowledge of Chinese architecture was clearly something of an embarrassment to Chambers, as his frequent remarks and disclaimers in the *Designs of Chinese Buildings* make evident. Exotic tastes did not offer the solid basis on which to found a serious career. Already, on 6 April 1757, a month before the appearance of *Chinese Buildings*, Chambers had issued

> Proposals For Publishing by Subscription, Designs of Villas, Temples, Gates, Doors, and chimney Pieces; Composed by W. Chambers, Architect Engraved by Fourdrinier and Rooker. Conditions The work consists of a least Sixty Large Folio-Plates, printed on the best Paper; with the necessary Descriptions and References. The Price to Subscribers to be two Guineas. One to be paid at the Time of subscribing, the other on Delivery of the Work; which is now in hand, and will be finished with all Expedition. . . .

His appointment as architectural tutor to the prince prompted a reappraisal of this book of designs. The course that he prepared for his young charge required that he look more seriously than otherwise at the textbooks of architecture, and analyze them with some care. Much later, when he was requesting permission to dedicate the third and revised edition of *A Treatise on Civil Architecture* to George III, he noted that it was "originally written for Your Majesties information. . . . Your Majesties indulgence and encouragement first prompted me to render publick what first was certainly not designed for publication."

The drawings that survive in the Royal Library, Windsor Castle, to give evidence of the nature of Chambers' instruction to the prince, indicate that his claims were not altogether correct—though the prince was required to draw out the orders, gateways, and arches, he was also instructed to copy designs by William Kent and Colen Campbell, and also the temples at Kew—but there is no need to doubt that it was the royal appointment that stirred Chambers to embark on a full-scale treatise on architecture.

A Treatise on Civil Architecture was published in April 1759, by John Haberkorn, who was soon after to print the *Antiquities of Athens*. The cost of the book was 2 guineas. It was dedicated to the earl of Bute, a favorite of both the prince and dowager princess, who seems to have first brought Chambers to royal attention and who was later, in November 1761, when he achieved power, to ensure his appointment, along with his rival Robert Adam, as architect to the Works, the beginnings of Chambers' career as a public architect. There were 264 subscribers to the book (headed by both the prince and dowager princess of Wales), who contracted to buy 336 copies of the work, among them the architects Robert Adam and James Paine, and the painters Thomas Gainsborough and Joshua Reynolds. There were also three notable subscribers from France: the sculptor Pajou; Jacques-François Blondel, by whom Chambers had been taught; and his successor Julien-David Leroy, who had the year before published *Les Ruines des plus beaux monuments de la Grèce*.

The organization of the treatise is surprisingly simple, even rudimentary. There is a short introduction on the origins of the orders, involving something by way of their subsequent history, but the real emphasis of the work is on an analysis of each of the five orders and their related parts, including pilasters and caryatids, followed by sections on the rules governing their spacing and superimposition; on basements and attics, with a guide to the design of balustrades, followed by sections on gates, doors, and piers; windows; niches and statues; chimneypieces; the proportion of rooms and, finally, a sheaf of sixteen plates illustrating small compositions such as garden temples, gateways, and doors. The compositions are all by Chambers, except for two doorways by Palladio. The range is scarcely more extensive than that offered in so elementary a work as Batty Langley's *Builder's Jewel*, issued first in 1741. Indeed, Langley's plates include far more by way of information on vaulting, trusses, and joists. Chambers was, clearly, not much interested in structural matters. Such material, he wrote, is "of little service to the generality of men of fortune who are desirous of being enabled to judge of the Beauties of a building," and it was to them that he addressed his book. He promised, however, "reserving for a future work those parts which relate to Convenience, Oeconomy and Strength." But the companion book was never forthcoming, nor was it ever embarked upon (though Chambers found time to revise, painstakingly, and to much rewarding effect, *A Treatise on Civil Architecture*), until it emerged, in 1791, in a third edition, as *A Treatise On the Decorative Part of Civil Architecture*. This is the work on which his authority as a theorist rests.

Though Chambers' work was commonplace in its organization and limited in scope, it was, even in its initial form, far more penetrating and subtle than any other treatise of architectural instruction written in England during the eighteenth century. Chambers adopted from Jacques-François Blondel that analytical method, associated as a rule with the French academies (though Blondel had not yet become professor of architecture to the Académie Royale d'Architecture when Chambers was his pupil, and the *Cours d'Architecture* itself was not to be published for two decades) that

William Chambers. *A Treatise on Civil Architecture.* "Regular mouldings with their proper ornaments." 1985.61.468

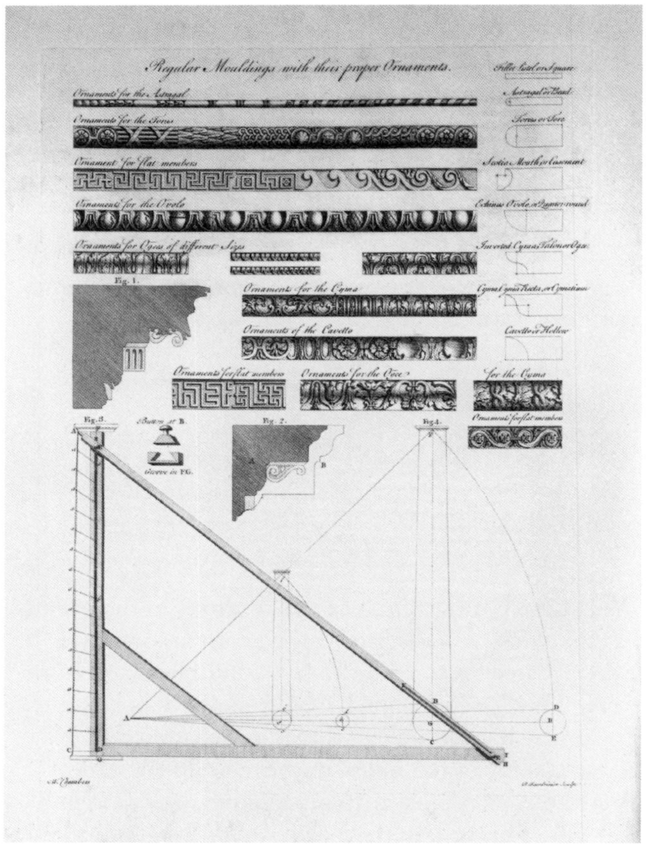

aimed to accept nothing as sacrosanct, nothing as absolute. Everything was open to question, but once assessed, it became part of a canon. Chambers sought to establish standards on the basis of precedent, whether ancient or modern. He referred to most of the well-known textbooks on architecture, both Italian and French, from Alberti to Leclerc. He was familiar even with such recondite authors as the Abbé de Cordemoy, to whom he referred more than once; Pierre Estève, author of *L'Esprit des Beaux–Arts*, of 1753, even Adrien Auzoult, the physicist, remembered, if at all, as the perfecter of Christian Huyghens' micrometer, but who also spent the last years of his life in Rome, exploring the ruins and aqueducts, and working on a translation of Vitruvius.

But Chambers relied, equally, on his own knowledge and experience of architecture. In Italy he had measured many antique and contemporary structures. He could dispute the measurements provided by Palladio and Antoine Desgodetz. He could refer with confidence to details not only in Palladio's works in Vicenza and Venice, but to such palaces as the Pandolfini and Rinuccini in Florence, the Mattei and Massimi in Rome, and to churches such as S. Carlo al Corso, likewise in Rome, and even to the design for the Caffé at Caserta. In Paris he knew not only the Louvre and the Tuileries, but a range of other buildings that included St. Gervais and the church of the Sorbonne. London, of course, provided him with myriad examples. Again and again he cites the Banqueting House, Whitehall, and Burlington House in Piccadilly (usually with reference to Gibbs' forecourt), but he finds details to note also in Bow Church; St. John's, Westminster; St. George's, Hanover Square; and even in the stables of the King's Mews, at Charing Cross, by Kent. Spencer House appears in 1759, to be removed in 1791. Throughout he gives evidence of an easy familiarity with the architecture of Italy, France, and England. He lays claim, moreover, to an untoward openness, tolerance even, in assessing such works. But one should not be misled. In the manner of his mentor Blondel, he was firm in his belief that though rules and rigid standards were difficult to justify, there were indeed standards, and these were to be ordained by himself, as representing a "generality of judicious spectators." Chambers was, in fact, inflexible in his tastes. He disliked all experiment, and his prejudices became even more entrenched as he grew older, though he did extend his understanding to include Gothic architecture in later years.

He prefaced the *Treatise* with an account of the civilizing influence of architecture:

> Thus it appears that architecture, by furnishing men with convenient habitations, procures them that ease of body, and vigour of mind, which are necessary for inventing and improving Arts; that when, by their industry or ingenuity, they have multiplied their productions so as to exceed domestick demands, she supplies the means of transporting them to foreign markets; and when, by Commerce, Individuals or Communities are enriched, she affords them a rational, noble, and benevolent method of enjoying their wealth, which will procure honour and pleasure to themselves and their descendants, dignity to the State, and profit both to their Contemporaries and to Posterity. She farther teaches them to defend their properties, and to secure their liberties, lives and fortunes, from the attempts of lawless rapine, and unbounded ambition.

There is no hint, in all this, of the corrupting influences of civilization invoked by Rousseau. Chambers was happily content with the state of society and the arts, with architecture in particular—"few things remain either to be discovered or improved, every branch of the Art having been maturely considered, and brought very near the utmost degree of certainty of which it is capable." Chambers' task, thus, was to select from the vast range of knowledge and opinion available and to assemble a series of sound precepts and perfect examples of design within the pages of a single volume. And this, to all intents, is what he, and many of his contemporaries, including even Horace Walpole, thought he had achieved—"the most sensible book," Walpole wrote, "and the most exempt from prejudice that ever was written in that science."

Chambers dealt summarily with the early development of architecture, with the building of the first crude shelter in the form of a conical hut, soon found inconvenient and thus transformed, first into the more convenient cubic hut and then into the pedimented hut, the basis not only of columns and beams, but of the whole of the decorative part of architecture. Though the Greeks might have been the first to give convincing form to the elements of architecture, there was no doubt in Chambers' mind, even at this stage, that it was the Romans who had brought the art to perfection. He jibbed more than once at Fréart de Chambray's preference for the Grecian orders, and in their original form—his "blind attachment," as Chambers put it, to the antique. Later, when the publications of James Stuart and Nicholas Revett stirred a greater interest in Greek architecture, Chambers was to greatly expand on his animadversions and to vilify what he called the "Gusto Greco." But that was, inevitably, not part of the *Treatise* of 1759, when he looked forward, he wrote, with interest, to the appearance of *The Antiquities of Athens*.

Immediately following his summary history of the development of architecture, Chambers offered a detailed analysis of the eight principal classical moldings—the ovolo, talon, cyma, cavetto, torus, astragal, scotia, and fillet—and the method of their assembly to form profiles. Surprising though this juxtaposition may seem, it is inherent to Chambers' understanding of architecture. The primitive hut, he explained, had produced the primary elements that were absolutely necessary to architecture, the column and the architrave; the secondary elements, the moldings, were those that had been evolved to give a more pleasing appearance to the basic elements. The primary and secondary elements together constituted the orders. Their exposition, as has been noted, constitutes the core of Chambers' treatise. He deals at length with each of the five orders—the Tuscan, Doric, Ionic, Composite, and Corinthian (in Scamozzi's sequence)—itemizing the parts and their proportional relationships. He measured the orders by a module, a half-diameter, divided into thirty minutes, instead of the newer method, derived from Claude Perrault and taken up by Gibbs, of division into equal parts. Rather than giving a common diameter, he illustrates them all at one height, the better to compare them. He derives their proportions, for the most part, from Giacomo da Vignola, though Palladio is referred to often enough, and parts are incorporated from other authors and also from extant buildings. Always, Chambers is ready to apply his own corrections.

Chambers is at his best when analyzing the visual effects not only of the larger elements of the orders, but also their smallest details. Given the enthusiastic response that Edmund Burke had given to Chambers' *Designs of Chinese Buildings*, it is not surprising to find that Chambers more than once takes up notions of beauty and optical transformations from Burke's *Enquiry into the Origin of Our Ideas of the Sublime and Beautiful*, of 1757, though Burke's name was to be included only in 1791. Not that Chambers was always in agreement with Burke; he thought, for instance, like Perrault, that there could be no absolute system for proportions, but he was unwilling, like Burke, to consider that proportions were not, therefore, necessary to beauty. There can be no doubt, however, that Burke provided an added dimension to his thought, and stirred him to seek to explain the niceties of architectural forms and detailing with more finesse than ever before—"there are delicacies," he wrote, "which, though they escape the vulgar, afford uncommon satisfactions to persons of more enlightened conceptions." He made bold to discuss the effect of the ovolo molding in the Doric cornice and the roses in soffit panels in their relation to the larger elements, at length, and entirely in Burkeian terms—and to greatly illuminating effect, one might note. Anyone wishing to grasp something of the eighteenth-century understanding of architecture should read these passages from Chambers. Though his use of Burke's concepts was equally, on occasion, quite specious; as in his justification of his desire to diminish pilasters at the top. This, however, was no more than an aspect of Chamber's distaste for the tenets of Cordemoy and Marc-Antoine Laugier. Their rejection of statues on parapets was, he thought, no more than a ridiculous affectation of propriety. He thought piers and pedestals acceptable, curved pediments, too. What irritated him beyond all measure was the criterion of judgment that Laugier, in particular, wished to impose on architecture.

William Chambers. *A Treatise on Civil Architecture.* "The primitive buildings &c." 1985.61.468

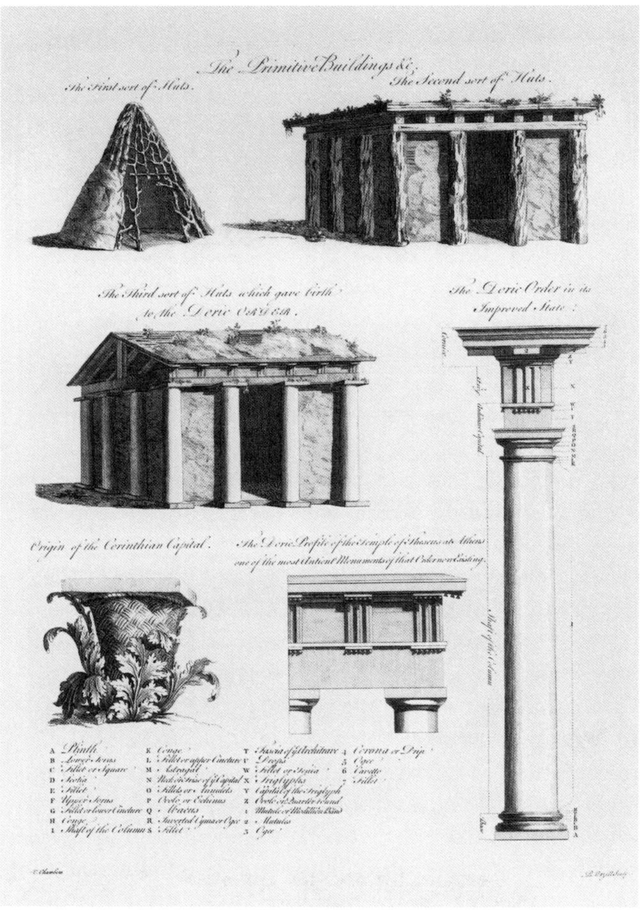

Father Laugier; who, having sagaciously found out that the first buildings consisted of nothing but four stumps of trees and a covering, considers almost every part of Architecture, excepting the Column, the Entablature, and the Pediment, as licentious or faulty and, in consequence, very cavalierly banishes at once all Pedestals, Pilasters, Niches, Arcades, Attiks, Domes, etc. and it is only by special favour, that he tolerates Doors, or Windows, or even Walls.

There are many savourer's of this writer's system, who, like him, concentrate all perfection in Propriety. It were, indeed to be wished that some invariable standard could be discovered, whereby to decide the merit of every production of Art: but, certainly, Father Laugier hath not, as yet, hit the right nail on the head and therefore must give himself the trouble to think again. Beauty and Fitness are qualities that have very little connection with each other: in Architecture they are sometimes incompatible; as may be easily demonstrated from some of the Father's own Compositions; with a detail of which he hath favoured the world in his book. And there are many things in that Art, which, though beautiful in the highest degree, yet, in their application, carry with them an evident absurdity: one instance whereof is the Corinthian Capital; a form composed of a slight basket surrounded with leaves and flowers. Can anything be more unfit to support a heavy load of Entablature, and such other weights as are usually placed upon it? Yet this has been approved and admired for some thousands of years, and will still continue to be, as long as men have eyes to see, and souls to feel. It is not, however, by any means, my intention entirely to lay aside a regard to Propriety: on all occasions it must be kept in view: in things intended for use, it is the primary consideration; and therefore should on no account whatever be trespassed upon, but in objects merely ornamental, which are designed to captivate the senses, rather than to satisfy the understanding. It seems unreasonable to sacrifice other qualities much more efficacious, to Fitness alone.

Chambers might have been incorrect in his summary assessment of Laugier's system, though it was of little consequence. He was opposed to the imposition of any system. Judgment in architecture was a matter of development and slow refinement, a matter of a cultivated vision. Even the authority of Vitruvius could be rejected without demur, as in the matter of the introduction of modillions and dentils in the profiling of the horizontal member of the pediment, which would, otherwise, Chambers thought, be extremely ugly. He was wary always of too much ornamentation, but equally, he disliked too much frugality. Time and again he balances the effects of complexity and confusion against those of sameness and simplicity. But always, judgment must be made by the informed eye.

"In general," he writes,

excessive Ornaments, though they encrease the Magnificence of a building, always destroy the Grandeur of its effect. The parts in themselves are large, and so formed and disposed as to receive broad masses and strong impressions of light and shade, will of course excite great ideas: but if they are broken into a number of small divisions, and their surface so varied as to catch a thousand impressions of light, demi–tint, and darkness, the whole will be confused, trifling, and incapable of causing any grand emotions.

Chambers summarized his notion of the evolving excellencies of architecture and their limits, quite clearly in his 1791 edition:

Amongst the restorers of the ancient Roman architecture, the stile of Palladio is correct and elegant; his general dispositions are often happy; his outlines distinct and regular; his forms graceful: little appears that could with propriety be spared, nothing seems wanting: and all his measures accord so well, that no part attracts the attention, in prejudice to any of the rest.

Scamozzi, in attempting to refine upon the stile of Palladio, has over-detailed, and rendered his own rather trifling; sometimes confused. Vignola's manner, though bolder, and more stately than that of Palladio; is yet correct, and curbed within due limits; particularly in his orders: but in Michael Angelo's, we see licence, majesty, grandeur, and fierce effect; extended to bounds, beyond which, it would be very dangerous to soar.

This statement, no more than a clarification of notions that had informed Chambers' thinking from the start, occurs in the section "Of Gates, Doors, and Piers," which, curiously, whether in 1759 or 1791, offers the most sustained theoretical expositions in the whole of the treatise. There Chambers explored ideas on the connections between use and proportional systems, on the relation between musical harmonies and proportional systems (siding with Perrault rather than François Blondel, though concluding that their argument scarcely mattered, as both established their notions of architectural excellence with reference to the same antique models), and also on the planning arrangements of rooms (much derived from French practices, though Chambers studiously avoids the use of the term "enfilade").

Chambers' comments on his immediate predecessors and contemporaries in England are always of interest. John Vanbrugh's use of strong horizontal joints in his basement stories, in emulation of the French, is rejected, as it resembles wooden boarding. Vanbrugh's chimneypieces are also put down, as he converted them into castles. Burlington and Kent are the focus of Chambers' attention, both in 1759 and in 1791. Kent is both blamed and praised. His house on Berkeley Square had too many varied window openings. His Horse Guards was acknowledged to be generally disliked and elsewhere singled out on account of the ill-considered window surrounds in the basement story. Holkham Hall, too, was subjected to this same criticism, but even less acceptable there were the seven venetian windows in the north front, which "keep the spectator's eye in a perpetual dance to discover the outlines." Chambers disliked the introduction of the venetian window at all times, considering them "an irregular breach of the wall." Kent and Burlington were both castigated for their interiors, which included so many large doors that there was no place left for pictures and furniture. But despite all this Chambers delivered one of his highest encomiums on the interiors at Holkham:

The Earl of Leicester's house at Holkham is a masterpiece in this respect, as well as in many others: the distribution of the Plan, in particular, is never enough to be admired; it being inimitably well contrived, both for state and conveniency: and with regard to the whole interiour decoration, it may certainly vie in point either of magnificence or taste, with any thing now subsisting.

This comment, with no more than marginal alterations, Chambers let stand in his edition of 1791, but he felt impelled then to make further comment and to use the occasion to attack the work of his despised rival, Robert Adam. Adam, in the first preface to *The Works in Architecture of Robert and James Adam*, of 1773, claimed to have replaced ponderous compartmented ceilings, massive entablatures, and tabernacle frames by a beautiful variety of light moldings, grotesques, and painted ornaments. Chambers wanted nothing of their revolution.

In 1791 he commented of Holkham:

That stile, though somewhat heavy, was great; calculated to strike at the instant; and although the ornaments were neither so varied, nor so numerous as now; they had a more powerful effect: because more boldly marked, less complicated in their forms, and less profusely applied. They were easily perceptible without a microscope, and could not be mistaken for filigrane toy work. Content with the stores, which the refined ages of antiquity had left them, the architects of that day; ransacked not the works of barbarous times; nor the port-folios of whimsical composers; for boyish conceits, and trifling complicated ornaments.

Chambers was intent then to uphold Kent at all costs. He was intent also to reduce Adam whenever possible. He returned to the attack, also in 1791, in dealing with ceilings, or rather with the absence of painted ceilings in England—"For one cannot suffer to go by so high a name," he wrote, "the trifling, gaudy, ceilings now in fashion: which, composed as they are of little rounds, squares, octagons, hexagons and ovals; excite no other idea, than that of a desert: upon the plates of which are dished out, bad copies of indifferent antiques. They certainly have neither fancy, taste, splendour, execution, nor any other striking quality to recommend them."

Two of the added plates of 1791 of composed ornaments, engraved by Bigby (possibly to be identified with the Patrick Begbie employed by Adam for some of the decorative plates in the *Works*) must be regarded as a further challenge directed to the Adam brothers. Chambers demonstrates, altogether effectively, that he can compose in their rich and intricate manner.

Chambers' more forceful exposition of his tastes in 1791 is an aspect of his notion of himself as doyen of the profession. He was elected a Fellow of the Society of Arts on 16 January 1757, proposed by the engraver Charles Grignion. Three years later he helped to form the rival Incorporated Society of Artists of Great Britain. But his real achievement in establishing something by way of a professional status for architecture was the founding, in December 1768, of the Royal Academy. Joshua Reynolds was president, Chambers was treasurer, though, as Reynolds complained "Sir Wm was Viceroy over him"; Chambers, in fact, had the ear of the king, and for the first twelve years of its existence the Academy depended on funds from the privy purse. Thomas Sandby was appointed professor of architecture. When, in 1770, Sandby was too ill to deliver his lectures, Chambers thought to prepare some of his own. He wished also to compose something equivalent to Reynolds' *Discourses*, which were delivered from 1769 onward biennially, on prize-giving days, and individually published. On 30 January 1771, he wrote to Lord Charlemont: "Sir Joshua Reynolds is now with me. . . . He purposes sending you a copy of his dissertations or discourses. . . . I have also an intention of making discourses on architecture. One I have finished, which I have shown to a

William Chambers. *A Treatise on Civil Architecture.* "To Henry Willoughby Esq...." 1985.61.468

friend or two who tell me it is very well and encourage me to go on; but I am going on so many ways at once that God knows when I shall get to the end of any of them." Sandby, in the end, delivered his own lectures. Chambers wrote out two of his lectures and collected notes over the following years for several more, but he was never to complete his discourses. His lectures and notes survive today, divided, in the libraries of the Royal Academy and the Royal Institute of British Architects, in London. Much of their content—what Chambers termed his "loose materials"—was to be incorporated into *A Treatise On the Decorative Part of Civil Architecture*, of 1791. It is in this late, thoughtfully rewritten, greatly revised work that Chambers' ideas find their fullest expression, and through which, in later editions of 1825, 1826, 1836, and 1862, they were to be transmitted, far into the nineteenth century. R. M.

Bibliography

Harris, E. "Burke and Chambers on the Sublime and Beautiful." In *Essays in the History of Architecture Presented to Rudolf Wittkower.* Ed. D. Fraser, H. Hibbard, and M. J. Lewine. London, 1967: 207–213

Harris, E., and N. Savage. *British Architectural Books and Writers 1556–1785.* Cambridge, 1990

Harris, J. *Sir William Chambers Knight of the Polar Star*, with contributions by J. M. Crook and E. Harris. London, 1970

14

Sir William Chambers (1723–1796)

Plans, Elevations, Sections, and Perspective Views Of The Gardens And Buildings At Kew in Surry, The Seat of Her Royal Highness The Princess Dowager of Wales. By William Chambers . . .

London: printed by J. Haberkorn; published for the author, and to be had at his house; likewise of A. Millar, D. Wilson, and T. Becket; of R. and J. Dodsley; R. Sayer, A. Webley, J. Walter, and Dorothy Mercier, 1763

1985.61.469

Folio: 550 × 368 (21¾ × 4½)

Pagination [iv], 8 pp., [43] etched and engraved plates (3 folding)

Edition First edition

Text pp. [i] title page (verso blank); [iii] dedication to Augusta, princess dowager of Wales (verso blank); [1]-8 description of the plates; directions to the binder

Illustrations 43 unnumbered etched and engraved plates (pls. [1], [3], and [25] folding), subjects and engravers as follows: [1] "General Plan of the Palace" by Francis Patton; [2] "Principal floor of the Palace" by Francis Patton; [3] "Elevations of the Palace" by J. Muller (i.e., Johann Sebastian Müller = John Miller); [4] "South Elevation of the Greenhouse. Plan of the Greenhouse" by Edward Rooker; [5] "The Temple of the Sun" by Edward Rooker; [6] "The Ceiling, and Other Ornaments in the Temple of the Sun" by Charles Grignion; [7] "Plans Elevation & Sections of the Great Stove" by Tobias Miller; [8] "The Principal Entrance to the Flower Garden. Garden Seat" by Edward Rooker; [9] "The Aviary" by Edward Rooker; [10] "Plan of the Pheasant Ground" by Edward Rooker; [11] "Chinese Pavilion in the Pheasant Ground" by Edward Rooker; [12] "The Temple of Bellona" by James Basire; [13] "The Temple of Pan" by Edward Rooker; [14] "The Temple of Solitude. The Temple of Eolus" by James Basire; [15] "The House of Confucius" by Tobias Miller; [16] "The Water Engine" by Francis Patton; [17] "The Theatre of Augusta" by Edward Rooker; [18] "The Temple of Victory" by Edward Rooker; [19] "Ceiling of the Temple of Victory" by Edward Rooker; [20] "The Alambra" by Edward Rooker; [21] "Ceiling in the Alambra. Plan of the Alambra" by Edward Rooker; [22] "Plans of the Great Pagoda" by Edward Rooker; [23] "Elevation of the Great Pagoda as first Intended" by Tobias Miller; [24] "Section of the Great Pagoda" by J. Muller = John Miller; [25] "The Great Pagoda" by Tobias Miller; [26] "The Mosque" by Edward Rooker; [27] "Sections of the Mosque" by Charles Grignion; [28] "Plan & Elevation of the Gothic Cathedral" by J[a]. [i.e., James] Noual; [29] & [30] "Section of the Gallery of Antiques" by Edward Rooker; [31] "The Temple of Arethusa" by James Basire; [32] "Plan & Elevation of the Bridge" by Tobias Miller; [33] "Garden Seats" by James Basire; [34] "Various Plans" by Tobias Miller; [35] "The Temple of Peace" by Edward Rooker; [36] "A View of the Palace at Kew, from the Lawn" by William Woollett; [37] "A View of the Lake and Island, with the Orangerie, the Temples of Eolus and Bellona, and the House of Confucius" by Thomas Major; [38] "A View of the Lake and Island at Kew, seen from the Lawn" by Paul Sandby; [39] "A View of the Aviary and Flower Garden, at Kew" by Charles Grignion; [40] "A View of the Menagerie, and its Pavillion, at Kew" by Charles Grignion; [41] "North Prospect of the Ruin in the Gardens of Kew" by William Woollett; [42] "A View of the South Side of the Ruins at Kew" by William Woollett; [43] "A View of the Wilderness, with the Alhambra, the Pagoda and the Mosque" by Edward Rooker. The following architects are also credited: William Kent, plate [3]; William Chambers, plates [4–8], [10–15], [17–27], [29–33], [35]; [John] Smeaton, plate [16]; and J. Henry Muntz, plate [28]. The views were drawn by Joshua Kirby, plates [36], [41–42]; Thomas Marlow, plate [37]; William Marlow, plates [38], [43]; and Thomas Sandby, plates [39–40], all with figures by G. B. Cipriani

Binding Nineteenth-century red half morocco, restored, gilt-tooled, recent red cloth boards. Bound with the author's *Designs of Chinese Buildings*, 1757

Provenance Label and stamp of White Allom, Ltd.

References Berlin Cat. 2337; Berlin (1977) OS 2337; ESTC n38634; Fowler 87; Harris and Savage 121; RIBA, *Early Printed Books*, 597

Chambers' great folio illustrating the buildings at Kew is, inevitably, linked with his publications on Chinese buildings and garden design, but it contains no hint of the polemic that informs these works. It was designed, it would seem, as no more than a record of his activities.

Kew was acquired by Frederick, prince of Wales, in 1731. The sixteenth-century house in the grounds was rebuilt, in the same year, by William Kent. But nothing much seems to have been done in the garden at that time. Only during the last two years of his life did Frederick take any real interest in Kew. In December 1749 he purchased additional ground to the south. During the following year there was much gardening activity there, with tree planting and the making of "contrivances," including, in George Vertue's account, a "new Chinesia summer hous. painted in their stile & ornaments The story of Confusius and his doctrines, etc." The House of Confucius is usually assigned to the prince's cabinet painter, George Goupy, and Chambers himself describes it in the folio as "built a good many years ago, I believe from the designs of Mr. Goupy" (p. 4). But the plate illustrating it is signed *W. Chambers architectus*—though not the original drawing. Chambers might have reformed the pavilion when it was moved in 1757, or he might, as John Harris suggests, have been involved from the start. He resigned from the Swedish East India Company in July 1749 and was in England for a short time that summer, before departing in the early autumn, via Paris, for Rome. In Rome he was in contact with Johann Heinrich Muntz, who was to design a Moorish pavilion for Kew in 1750. Muntz traveled to England only in 1755. His pavilion, the Alhambra, was erected in 1758. The drawing for this was sold, in 1950, from the Bute Collection, indicating that John Stuart, 3d earl of Bute, adviser to both the prince and princess of Wales, was closely involved in the refashioning of the garden. How much was done to Kew before Frederick's death, in March 1751, is difficult to determine. A lake was being dug and a mount was being formed, but both were incomplete. However, Augusta, the dowager princess, soon took up her late husband's interests, erecting a new greenhouse at Kew in 1752 and, in the following year, building a terrace and indulging in further tree planting. Bute remained her closest adviser during these years. After Frederick's death he had been appointed groom of the stole to the young Prince George and, in 1755, his tutor. Chambers, who sought Bute's patronage after his return from Rome in that year, seems to have composed the *Designs of Chinese Buildings* at his suggestion, aiming to advance himself in Augusta's favor. The proposals for this were issued in 1756, and the book was published in May 1757. In August of that year Chambers was appointed architect to the princess at Kew and, even more surprisingly, tutor in architecture to the young prince of Wales (to whom Chambers had dedicated the *Designs*). But it was not until April 1758 when John Haverfield—another of Bute's nominees—was appointed head gardener at Kew, that Bute took control. Chambers referred to him, in his folio, as the "director" of the gardens. Bute aimed to transform Kew into a national garden, and not just a national botanical garden (of the kind Carl Linnaeus, known to Bute and Chambers, had laid out at Uppsala, Sweden), but a radiant image of a national culture. Chambers created a wonderful array of pavilions for the garden, set in relation one to another on cross-axes around three great lawns and a lake. The whole was rapidly built. In 1757 work was taken up again on the greenhouse and a gallery of antiquities built. The House of Confucius was moved to a new site at the east end of the lake. The following year the temples of Pan and Arethusa were erected, together with stables, a lodge, and sundry garden seats. Muntz's Alhambra was begun, together with a Gothic cathedral to his design. In 1759 the Ruined Arch and the Temple of Victory were started. With the arrival of William Aiton from the Chelsea Physic Garden in this same year, the Physic Garden, or Exotic Garden, was laid out. The Flower Garden and Aviary, the Menagerie, the Temple of Bellona, and the Theatre of Augusta followed a year later. In 1761 the Mosque, the Temple of the Sun (modeled on that at Baalbek), the Great Stove, the water pumps by Smeaton, and the Great Pagoda were built. The Temples of Eolus and Solitude were finished in 1763—though not the Temple of Peace, which was abandoned. In this same year Chambers published his folio, dedicated to Augusta, and probably paid for by her. It was advertised in *The Gentleman's Magazine* of May 1765 at a price of 2 guineas. The *Gazetteer and London Daily Advertiser*, of 10 May, described the edition as limited to three hundred copies, with forty-six plates. Chambers was altogether proud of his achievement.

William Chambers. *Plans, Elevations, Sections…at Kew.* "A View of the Lake and Island at Kew seen from the Lawn." 1985.61.469

"The gardens of Kew," he wrote, "are not very large. Nor is their situation by any means advantageous; as it is low, and commands no prospects. Originally the ground was one continued dead flat: the soil was in general barren, and without either wood or water. With so many disadvantages it was not easy to produce any thing even tolerable in gardening: but princely munificence, guided by a director, equally skilled in cultivating the earth, and in the politer arts, overcame all difficulties. What was once a Desart is now an Eden" (p. 2).

Augusta was the dedicatee, but to Bute Chambers gave a manuscript copy of the complete folio (including a general plan of the gardens, not present in the published work) now in the Metropolitan Museum of Art, in New York, with the inscription—"These original designs of the Gardens and Buildings of Kew Plan'd by His Lordship, and executed under his Inspection, are most humbly dedicated."

Chambers was by then architect to the king, Bute first lord of the treasury. The short text Chambers provided by way of introduction to the plates describes the intended route through the garden, beginning at the palace, proceeding to the Greenhouse or Orangery, the Temple of the Sun, on to the enclosed Physic or Exotic Garden, then to the Flower Garden and Aviary (yet another enclosed precinct) and the Menagerie or Pheasant Garden with its Chinese pavilion (likewise within an enclosure), and so on. The forty-three plates were arranged roughly in this sequence, though there is by no means a direct correspondence, some plates including more than one of the garden features. The plates illustrating the plans, sections, and elevations are all by established architectural engravers—James Basire (4), Charles Grignion (2), John Miller (Müller) (2), Tobias Miller (6), Francis Patton (3), and Edward Rooker (17), four of whom Chambers had already employed for the *Treatise on Civil Architecture*, of 1759. The odd man out among engravers was James Noual (Noval), who was responsible for Muntz's cathedral (pl. 28). The eight views of the garden, all grouped at the end of the book, were drawn by Joshua Kirby (3), Thomas (1) and William Marlow (2), and Thomas Sandby (2), all with figures by G. B. Cipriani. These plates too were engraved by established practitioners—Charles Grignion (2), Thomas Major (1), Edward Rooker (1), Paul Sandby (1), and William Woolett (3).

Though Chambers offers no hint of the significance intended by the extraordinary array of pavilions and features, it is clear that he was leading his visitors through an image of the world, both past and present. The garden has been interpreted by Richard Quaintance, first, in 1978, in his introduction to the Augustan Reprint Society's edition of *An Explanatory Discourse by Tan Chet-Qua, of Quang-Chew Fu, Gent.*, and, more recently, and in more detail, in a symposium at Dumbarton Oaks "The Landscape of Theme Parks and Their Antecedents" (forthcoming). Quaintance interprets Kew as a theme park, inspired by earlier imperial landscapes such as that of Hadrian's Villa at Tivoli and also the Yven-Ming Yven, the garden of gardens, of the emperor of China, designed, according to J. D. Attiret, "to procure the Emperor the Pleasure of seeing all the Bustle and Hurry of a great City in little, whenever he might have a Mind for that sort of Diversion." Several themes are invoked—Frederick's exotic interests; the advance in husbandry, botany, and engineering in contemporary Britain; and, most significantly, its new imperial role. The building of Kew, Quaintance notes, coincides precisely with the waging of the Seven Years' War, the first truly global conflict. Britain's empire is commemorated again and again. Thus the ruined arch on one side of the great lawn is countered on the other by the Gothic cathedral—the Roman Empire, the Holy Roman Empire even, overtaken by an image of British faith. The Temple of Victory, intended to commemorate the Battle of Minden, of 1 August 1759—when the French were defeated by combined British and Hanoverian forces, under Augusta's brother—was set midway in the garden, on a mount, serving as a platform to view both the palace at one end and the Great Pagoda at the other. The building, however, became an embarrassment and was left incomplete. A close friend, who it was no doubt intended to honor, was condemned by court-martial for cowardice during the battle. Garlands and medallions in honor of the fighting regiments were hung in the Temple of Bellona, begun a year later. But there was no uncertainty as to the aims of the war. At the far end of the meadow three buildings were erected to mark the ends of the earth—the Turkish mosque and the Alhambra, facing one another on a cross-axis, denoting the eastern and western ends of the Mediterranean trading basin, and, at the farthest point, the Great Pagoda, rivaling in height Nanking's Porcelain Tower, an emblem of the civilization most remote from Britain, but nonetheless clearly open to mercantile endeavor. The Temple of Peace, which was intended to set the seal on this vision of expansion and opportunity, though designed by Chambers and described in 1763 as "now erecting" (p. 7), was never completed. Bute's Peace Treaty of 1763 was thought to have conceded too much to the French; it proved unpopular and his ministry fell.

Chambers remained as architect to the princess until her death in 1772, and worked intermittently at Kew even after, for George III, but little was done after Bute's departure to advance the initial vision. Much was altered and even destroyed before Chambers died in 1796. R. M.

Bibliography

British Architectural Library, Royal Institute of British Architects. *Early Printed Books 1478–1840: Catalogue of the British Architectural Library Early Imprints Collection.* Vols. 1–2. London, 1994–1995

Harris, J. "Sir William Chambers and Kew Gardens." In *Sir William Chambers, Architect to George III.* Ed. J. Harris and M. Snodin. London 1996, 55–67

Quaintance, R. "Distinguishable Publics for 18th c. Antecedents: Chambers' 'Chinese' Theory and His 'Kew Practice.'" In *The Landscape of Theme Parks and Their Antecedents.* Ed. R. Riley and T. Young (forthcoming)

15

Thomas Chippendale (1718–1779)

The Gentleman and Cabinet-Maker's Director: Being a large Collection of the Most Elegant and Useful Designs Of Household Furniture, In the Most Fashionable Taste. . . . To Which Is Prefixed, A Short Explanation Of The Five Orders Of Architecture. . . . The Whole comprehended in Two Hundred Copper-Plates, neatly engraved. . . . By Thomas Chippendale, Cabinet-Maker and Upholsterer, In St. Martin's Lane, London. The Third Edition

London: printed for the author, and sold at his house; also by T. Becket and P.A. de Hondt, 1762

1985.61.471

Folio: 445 × 288 (17½ × 11⅜)

Pagination [iv], 20 pp., engraved dedication, 200 etched and engraved plates

Edition Third edition

Text pp. [i] title page (verso blank); [iii–iv] preface, dated 27 Feb. 1762; [1]–20 explanations of the plates

Illustrations In addition to an engraved dedication to Prince William Henry, which has a large armorial vignette etched by Matthias Darly, there are 200 etched and engraved plates, all but 2 signed by Chippendale as designer and draftsman ("T. Chippendale inv^t. et delin."). The plates were executed by Matthias Darly, Johann Sebastian Müller (= John Miller), Tobias Müller (= Tobias Miller), Isaac Taylor, William Foster, Butler Clowes, James Hulett, Cornelius H. Hemmerich, Thomas Morris, and Edward Rooker

Binding Nineteenth-century? reversed calf, morocco label

References Berlin Cat. 1227 (French ed.); ESTC t102007; RIBA, *Early Printed Books*, 631 (2d ed.)

Surprisingly little is known of the early life and career of Thomas Chippendale. He was born in June 1718 at Otley, in Yorkshire, the son of a local joiner, by whom he was probably trained. Though there are hints that he trained and began his career rather in York, twenty miles distant. The first evidence as to his employment is a short entry in Lord Burlington's private account book, dated 13 October 1747, "to Chippendale in full £ 6 16 0." The first documentary evidence as to his move to London is the register of his marriage, in St. George's Chapel, Mayfair, on 19 May 1748. He was then twenty-nine.

Attempts have been made to link Chippendale to the proselytes of the rococo style at the St. Martin's Lane Academy, but these remain inconclusive. He was certainly not a leading member of that group. More likely, he was taught drawing by Matthew or Matthias Darly, an active and versatile engraver and printseller, who also styled himself "Professor of Ornament to the Academy of Great Britain." Darly and Chippendale were later to be closely associated, and Darly engraved two-thirds of the signed plates in the first edition of the *Director*.

Chippendale's first child was baptized at St. Paul's, Covent Garden, on 23 April 1749, indicating that he lived in the parish. At Christmas of the same year he took a house at Conduit Court, off Long Acre, near the junction with St. Martin's Lane, where several furniture makers lived. Then, in the summer of 1752, he moved further south, to the newly built Somerset Court, off the Strand, backing on to Northumberland House. Darly took over the lease of this house on 25 March 1753—the year in which the plates of the *Director* were being engraved—but Chippendale seems to have remained in residence for several months more, before acquiring leases in December 1753 to three houses, nos. 60, 61, and 62 St. Martin's Lane, directly opposite Slaughter's Coffee House, the haunt of the St. Martin's Lane Academy coterie. The sudden expansion of his premises and workshops required money. No early commissions by Chippendale (Burlington's note apart) are recorded. He cannot have been too active a maker of furniture. The implication is that the capital both for the publication of the *Director* and the expansion of activity related to it came from his business partner James Rannie, a cabinetmaker, but an investor also in shipping and other merchant enterprises. No partnership agreement between them has been found, but in August 1754 Chippendale and Rannie signed a new lease for the St. Martin's Lane houses. There they lived and established a flourishing business (interrupted by a disastrous fire in one of the workshops on 5 April 1755) until, on Rannie's death, in 1766, much of the stock had to be sold to settle his estate. This upset forced Chippendale to take Thomas Haig, Rannie's accountant, into partnership, with another Scotsman, Henry Ferguson, as an additional investor. The establishment was known as "The Cabinet and Upholstery Warehouse," with a chair as its sign.

The *Director* was clearly designed to publicize Chippendale's ability and to attract commissions. And in this it succeeded; all Chippendale's known commissions date from after its appearance, though the only fully accredited collection of Chippendale furniture dating from the *Director* period—fifty pieces—is that at Dumfries House, Ayrshire, ordered in January 1759, shipped to Scotland in May.

Publication of the *Director* was first announced in the *London Daily Advertiser* of 19 March 1753. Advertisements in other papers followed. Subscriptions were invited for "... a New Book of Designs of Household

Furniture in the GOTHIC, CHINESE and MODERN TASTE, as improved by the politest and most able Artists. Comprehending an elegant Variety of curious and original Drawings in the most useful, ingenious, and ornamental Branches of Chair, Cabinet and Upholstery Work. With the Five Orders and Principles of Perspective, explained in a more easy and concise Method than ever hitherto has been made publick. A Work long wished for, of universal Utility, and accommodated to the Fancy and Circumstances of Persons in every Degree of Life." There were to be 160 folio plates, costing one pound ten shillings in sheets or one pound fourteen shillings bound in calf. Subscriptions in London were to be taken at Chippendale's (still behind Northumberland House), and at the booksellers H. Piers in Holborn and J. Swan in the Strand, and at Darly's in Chandos Street. The Edinburgh agents were Messrs. Hamilton and Balfour; in Dublin, John Smith. Publication was due in July 1754, changed later to August, but the book was available already in April 1754, being sold—in addition to the agents and booksellers already named—by Thomas Osborne of Gray's Inn, Robert Sayer of Fleet Street, and Messrs. Stabler and Barstow of York.

Chippendale seems to have been himself largely responsible for the promotion of the book. Three-hundred and eight subscribers were listed, the majority, about two-thirds, being craftsmen in the furniture trade, mostly in London. No more than one in six of the subscribers were members of the nobility and gentry, though such notable patrons as the duke of Kingston, the earl of Northumberland, Lord Chesterfield, and Sir Thomas Robinson, were among them. The number of artists was limited: only one architect, James Paine, an avid collector of books, who lived opposite Chippendale's shop in St. Martin's Lane; one of the Cheere family of sculptors; Gerard Van der Gucht, a carver and engraver; and, not unexpectedly, Darly and his associate, George Edwards, the ornithologist, who together issued *A New Book of Chinese Designs*, in 1754, several of the plates of which have affinities with Chippendale's.

Chippendale employed three engravers for the first edition: Darly, who signed ninety-eight of the plates; Johann Sebastien Müller (or John Miller), who had come to England from Nuremberg in 1744 and had studied at the St. Martin's Lane Academy, and was later to become famous for *An Illustration of the Sexual System of the Genera Plantarum of Linnaeus* of 1777, did twenty-six; and Müller's brother Tobias, likewise from Nuremberg, who had engraved plates for William Halfpenny's *The Modern Builder's Assistant*, of 1747, and had been employed five years after on the plates for Robert Wood's *Ruins of Palmyra*, was responsible for twenty-three. Fourteen plates were unsigned. About one-half are dated, in each case 1753.

No new plates were added to the second edition of the *Director*, of 1755, similar in most respects to the first, though many minor corrections were made. This was

Thomas Chippendale. *The Gentleman and Cabinet-Maker's Director.* No. LVII. "Sideboard table." 1985.61.471

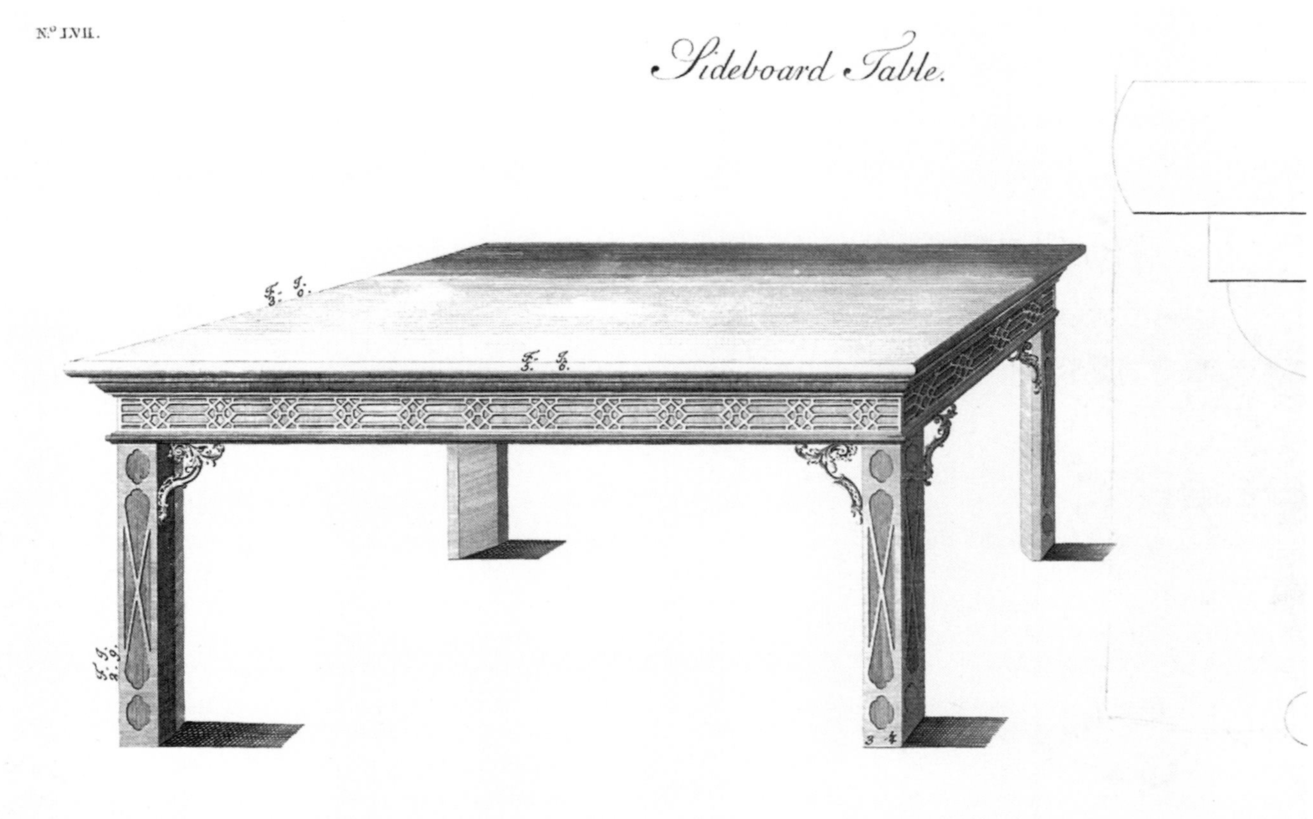

printed by John Haberkorn of Gerrard Street, Soho, and sold by Sayer, who appears to have taken over the distribution. The price was one pound sixteen shillings in sheets. The third edition was a more complex matter.

In 1756 Thomas Johnson launched a collection of designs, mainly for carvers, that was issued monthly, in parts, four sheets to a number, fifty-two plates in all. This was issued as a book, without a title page, in 1758. Sayer was to reissue it in 1761, with an extra plate, as *One Hundred and Fifty New Designs*. But there was a more significant rival to Chippendale's work. On 13 July 1759, the newly formed partnership of William Ince and John Mayhew, cabinetmakers and upholsterers, announced in the *Gentleman's Magazine* the proposed publication of "A General System of Useful and Ornamental Furniture," likewise to be issued in serial form, four folio sheets to a number, amounting to 160 plates in all. The plates were to be engraved by Darly, who was also to take subscriptions. Ince and Mayhew made no effort to conceal the fact that their publication was modeled directly on Chippendale's; indeed, they offered this as a guarantee to its success. Chippendale's response was sharp. On 6 October 1759, two months after the appearance of their first number, he announced in *The London Chronicle* the start of publication of a third edition of the *Director*, this time to be issued in weekly parts, costing one shilling, of four engravings each, to a total of one hundred plates. Some of the original plates were to be dropped, others revised, and fifty new ones added. Sayer was to be the principal agent. The weekly publication was maintained relentlessly, though not without interruption, through to the appearance of the twenty-fifth number, on 23 March 1760. By then it was clear from the irregularity of issue of the parts and a break in advertising that Ince and Mayhew's publication was not to be completed as planned. In the event, in 1762, Ince and Mayhew gathered their first eighty-four folio plates together with twelve small plates illustrating ironworks and issued the whole as a book, the *Universal System of Household Furniture*.

On 28 March 1760 a delay was announced in *The London Chronicle* in the appearance of the twenty-sixth number of the *Director*, the reason offered being the state of Chippendale's health, and also his intention to compose some new designs. He proposed now to offer subscribers a total of one hundred new designs instead of fifty. When the issue of the parts was resumed once again in August, it was under the auspices of a new agent, Thomas Becket, who had set up business in the Strand only eight months earlier, to be joined before the end of the year by Peter Abraham de Hond. Already, in *The London Chronicle* for 29–31 July, announcing the imminent appearance of number twenty-six, Becket offered new subscribers the option of buying the first twenty-five numbers as a batch and continuing to receive weekly the same issues as the original subscribers, or of beginning with the first number, to receive all succeeding numbers at weekly intervals. There were thus to be different dates of completion for the subscriptions. Becket's advertising campaign containing this offer continued for five weeks more, creating further disparities. The original subscribers should have received their final numbers in January 1761, but this is uncertain. The work was not published as a single volume until all the subscriptions were completed, on 3 April 1762. The full set of two hundred plates was offered then at two pounds twelve shillings and sixpence, the new plates, numbering 106, were also offered separately, for the benefit of owners of the first edition, at one pound ten shillings. The dedication was advertised then as to his Royal Highness Prince William.

Copies of the third edition vary greatly, some containing as many as twelve extra plates not keyed to the list of plates—XXV, XXXVI, XLV, XLIX, LXVII, LXVIII, CLIII, CLIX, CLXVII, CLXXI, CLXXIX, and CLXXXVII—all, one must assume, intended to be withdrawn. Four of these, even one dated 1759, were part of the first edition, seven were issued in 1760. Of the twelve twins to these plates, keyed to the prefatory notes, one is undated, two are dated 1761, nine 1762: these last must have been engraved very early in that year, for Chippendale's preface is dated 27 February 1762. Christopher Gilbert has deduced that these must have been distributed together with all the prefatory material in the first months of the year to the initial subscribers, who would already have received among their weekly numbers plates which were subsequently withdrawn and thus not keyed to the plate list. Copies of the book with twinned plates (other than double numbering as a result of obvious error, such as the plates numbered XXV in the first two editions) can thus be assumed to be the copies of subscribers who enrolled at an early date and retained the plates, which were subsequently withdrawn and replaced; whereas those copies with the "standard" 200 plates (94 from the first edition, 8 of them modified, and 106 new plates) must date from April 1762 or soon after. The note to plate CLXXIX, Gilbert further remarks, refers to a rejected plate, the mistake no doubt resulting from a last-minute substitution. Numerous minor anomalies relating to plate numbers and titles are to be found in copies of the third edition, corrected in some, left to stand in others.

Several new engravers were recruited for the third edition. Darly produced twenty-six new plates, the Millers three, while Isaac Taylor, a celebrated book illustrator, did twenty-five; William Foster, probably the painter, did seventeen; Butler Clowes, who had done most of the engraving for Thomas Johnson's collection, did nine; James Hulett, another book illustrator, did three; Cornelius H. Hemmerich, who like the Millers had come from Nuremberg, and like one of them, John, had worked on Halfpenny's *The Modern Builder's Assistant*, did two. Thomas Morris and Edward Rooker, each of whom contributed one plate, worked also for

Thomas Chippendale. *The Gentleman and Cabinet-Maker's Director.* No. LXXI. "A design for a commode table with two different designs for candle stands." 1985.61.471

Robert Adam. They were the only engravers of note, Rooker being named by Horace Walpole as "The Marc Antonio of Architecture" ("Catalogue of Engravers," in *Anecdotes of Painting in England*).

The number of plates attributed to the various engravers, it must be stressed, are those to be found in a "standard" third edition, as identified by Gilbert. But to judge by the remarkable variations in the reprints that have been reproduced on the basis of "standard editions," it is to be doubted that there is, indeed, an identifiable norm. The present copy, in which the plates are numbered through consistently in Roman numerals (plate 12 apart, and plates 147 and 148, which are misnumbered CXLVI and CXLVII, one of which might thus be a twin) must be considered as relatively sound. It has two hundred plates, as called for, corresponding to the list of plates, indicating that no withdrawn plates were included (with the possible exception of 147), but the number of newly engraved plates does not quite tally with Gilbert's formulations. There are twenty-six new plates by Darly and three by the Millers, but there are twenty-one rather than twenty-five new plates by Taylor, fourteen rather than seventeen by Foster, eleven rather than nine by Clowes. There are, however, three by Hulett, two by Hemmerich, and one each by Morris and Rooker, as required.

Some copies of the third edition are dedicated to the earl of Northumberland, to whom the first edition was dedicated, others to Prince William. As with other discrepancies in this work, there is no altogether satisfactory explanation for the variation. It is not unreasonable to suppose that early subscribers were given dedications to the earl of Northumberland, while the later ones, who took up subscriptions after Thomas Becket took over the publicity and distribution, received copies dedicated, in accord with his advertisements from 26 July 1760 and the weeks following, to Prince William. Becket described himself as "Bookseller to their Royal Highnesses the Prince of Wales, Prince William and Prince Henry." But this explanation is too simple, by far. Gilbert has suggested that as Prince William could not have been expected to allow his name to be used on reprinted material, the dedication must, strictly, have been accepted only with respect to the new plates in the third edition which, as has been noted, were offered for sale separately. In the event though, the prince's name was used at times for the whole volume. But once again this explanation is not altogether satisfactory. The alternate dedications appear on copies published at various times, both early and late, and no certain chronology can be determined. The present volume is dedicated to Prince William.

In the title to the third edition the words "HOUSEHOLD FURNITURE," by which the work was, for a time, known, were printed in bold capitals, and the description "In the Gothic, Chinese and Modern Taste" was replaced by "In the most Fashionable Taste." This indicates a recognition of new concerns. The preface too was altered. The engraved head- and tailpiece now included seated figures of Britannia, a response, perhaps, to Johnson's dedication of *One Hundred and Fifty New Designs* to Lord Blakeney, grand president of the Anti-Gallican Association. Though once the Seven Years' War was ended, a French edition of the *Director* was issued, in March 1763, *Guide Du Tapissier, De l'Ebéniste*. The preface itself was rewritten. Much of the pompous yet servile rhetoric remained, but allusions to Apelles and Phidias and knowing remarks on the Roman and Venetian schools of painting were removed, as were Latin quotations from Ovid and Horace. In the description of the plates Chippendale evinced more real confidence in his abilities and candid enthusiasm for his work, as also an easier command of practical matters—useful remarks on upholstery, timber, decorative finishes, glazing, and casting—is introduced.

All but twelve of the original drawings for the plates of the first edition of the *Director* survive, most of them in the print department of the Metropolitan Museum of Art, New York. Almost half the drawings for the new plates for the third edition have been traced, most of them, once again in the Metropolitan Museum, but also in the Victoria and Albert Museum and elsewhere. Gilbert has analyzed these in some detail, though even he has called for further research.

If any pattern can be discerned in the rejection and selection of new plates for the third edition, it is an emphasis on the artistic elevation of the art of furniture design. Most utilitarian pieces of furniture were removed and the number of technical diagrams reduced. The number of carvers' pieces was ruthlessly cut down. Some items of furniture, such as artists' tables and double chests of drawers, included in the first edition, do not appear in the third, but following the example of Ince and Mayhew, a far greater range of furniture is illustrated for the first time—hall chairs, garden seats, basin stands, shaving tables, teakettle stands, organs, chimneypieces and overmantles, wine cisterns, pedestals, lanterns and chandeliers, grates and escutcheons. And, as with Ince and Mayhew, more designs are set together on the plates.

The aim of the *Director* was to advertise Chippendale's skill, but the whole was intended also to set furniture alongside architecture as a notable art form. The very format of the book is an emulation of the great English architectural folios. The preface itself begins, "Of all the Arts which are either improved or ornamented by Architecture, that of CABINET-MAKING is not only the most useful and ornamental, but capable of receiving as great Assistance from it as any whatever," and to reinforce the connection Chippendale explained that he had introduced at the beginning of his work an explanation of the orders and the rules of perspective—"the very Soul and Basis" of his art—with eight plates illustrating the setting up of the five orders and their moldings. These Chippendale adapted, with little alteration, from James Gibbs' *Rules for Drawing the Several Parts of Architecture* of 1732, though he used modules and minutes to set them up. Chippendale even adapted Gibbs' text.

No review of the *Director* was published, and few enough contemporary references to it have been noted, though Ince and Mayhew's slavish imitation is evidence enough of its strong impact, no less than the printing of the new editions. Later, in 1793, in the preface to *The Cabinet-Maker and Upholsterer's Drawing-Book*, Thomas Sheraton singled out Chippendale's work, though with a certain sniffing: "as for the designs themselves, they are now wholly antiquated and laid aside, though possessed of great merit, according to the times in which they were executed." Though he evinced no more enthusiasm when he moved on to a consideration of Ince and Mayhew's *Universal System*: "In justice to the work, it may be said to have been a book of merit in its day, though inferior to Chippendale's, which was a real original, as well as more extensive and masterly in its designs."

There can be little doubt that the *Director* first served to establish Chippendale's name, and to maintain him in the public eye for many years, indeed, until the first revival of interest in his work, in the 1830s, when John Weale began to republish Johnson's plates under the name of Chippendale. By the middle of the nineteenth century the rococo furniture of the eighteenth century was all designated "Chippendale style." And the name of Chippendale has continued to eclipse those of all other English makers of furniture. The role of the *Director* in sustaining this reputation was paramount. R. M.

Bibliography

Gilbert, C. "The Early Furniture Designs of Matthias Darly." In *Furniture History* 11 (1975): 3–39

Gilbert, C. *The Life and Work of Thomas Chippendale*. London, 1978

16

John Crunden (c. 1741–1835)

Convenient And Ornamental Architecture, Consisting Of Original Designs, For Plans, Elevations, and Sections: Beginning With The Farm House, and regularly ascending to the most grand and magnificent Villa; Calculated Both for Town and Country, and to suit all Persons in every Station of Life. With a Reference and Explanation, in Letter-Press, of the Use of every Room in each separate Building, and the Dimensions accurately figured on the Plans, with exact Scales for Measurement. By John Crunden, Architect. The Whole Elegantly engraved on Seventy Copper-Plates, By Isaac Taylor

London: printed for the author, and A. Webley, 1770

NGA Lib. Rare Book: NA7328C78

Quarto: 265 × 178 (10 7/16 × 7)

Pagination viii, [4], 26 pp., 70 [i.e., 56] engraved plates (13 folding)

Edition Second edition (i.e., reissue of 1st ed.?)

Text pp. [i] title page (verso blank); [iii] dedication to the duke of Newcastle, dated 15 Aug. 1767 (verso blank); [v]–viii preface; [ix–xii] advertisements ("Books in Architecture Printed for and Sold by A. Webley, Bookseller, in Holborn, near Chancery-Lane"); [1]–26 explanation of the plates

Illustrations 56 unsigned engraved plates numbered 1–70 (14 plates given 2 numbers each, including 13 folding plates)

Binding Contemporary calf, rebacked preserving original gilt spine (alternating panels of floral and trellis designs separated by raised bands, contemporary morocco label)

Provenance Ownership inscription "W: E: 20th April 1773 Cost [£]1. 2[s.]"

References ESTC t139000; Harris and Savage 155; RIBA, *Early Printed Books,* 760

ANOTHER EDITION

Convenient And Ornamental Architecture . . . [as second edition] . . . to suit all Persons in every Station of Life. Engraved on Seventy Copper-Plates, with Reference and Explanation . . . By John Crunden, Architect. A New Edition

London: printed for I. Taylor, 1785

NGA Lib. Rare Book: NA.7328C781785

Quarto: 260 × 178 (10 1/4 × 7)

Pagination viii, 4, 26 pp., [56] engraved plates (13 folding)

Edition Third edition (i.e., reissue of the 2d ed.)

Text pp. [i] title page (verso blank); [iii] dedication (verso blank); [v]–viii preface; [1]–4 advertisements ("Books printed for I. Taylor, No. 56, High Holborn, London"); [1]–26 explanation of the plates

Illustrations 56 unsigned engraved plates numbered 1–70, as 1770 edition

Binding Contemporary calf, rebacked preserving spine, contemporary red morocco label

Provenance Early nineteenth-century? initials "R. H. C." neatly stenciled in sepia ink on front pastedown and at top of 3 plates. Verses penciled on verso of plate 3 ("In pensive silence o'er the Moor . . ."). More or less elaborate early nineteenth-century? architectural drawings (plans, elevations, views, calculations) in pencil or ink and pencil on versos of many plates and final endleaves

References Berlin Cat. 2288; Berlin (1977) OS 2288; ESTC t117640; Harris and Savage 161

Little is known of John Crunden. He was born, around 1741, in Sussex, and established something of a career for himself in the southern counties, beginning in 1767 with Brooklands, at Weybridge in Surrey, for George Payne, where he was first employed as a surveyor by Henry Holland. Crunden was responsible for at least six more buildings in this region—most notably Belfield, near Weymouth, in Dorset—dating from the 1770s. He also worked on Halton Place, near Hellifield, in Yorkshire. In 1774 he was appointed district surveyor to the parishes of Paddington, St. Pancras, and St. Luke, Chelsea, in London, and was busily occupied in that capacity until his death in 1835. In London he erected the most memorable and engaging of all his buildings, Boodle's Club, in St. James' Street, of 1775 to 1776. His architecture is of the derivative, charming kind, which is perhaps why he was so successful as a designer of architectural pattern books. Between 1765 and 1767 he was associated with five pattern books for the publisher Henry Webley (late A. Webley), two of which included the designs of J. H. Morris, Placido Columbani, and Thomas Milton, and two of which he designed and engraved himself, *Forty-eight Designs of Grand Corners for Stucco'd Ceilings* . . . and *The Joyner and Cabinet-maker's Darling*. The last of his pattern books, issued in 1767, was *Convenient and Ornamental Architecture*, in which he retained a proprietary interest, fortunately, for it was the most successful by far. Indeed it was the most successful pattern book to be published during the period. A second edition, identical with the first, though without the subscription list, was issued in 1770 by A. Webley, a new edition (with pls. 68–69 replaced by two new ones) was issued in 1785 by Isaac Taylor,

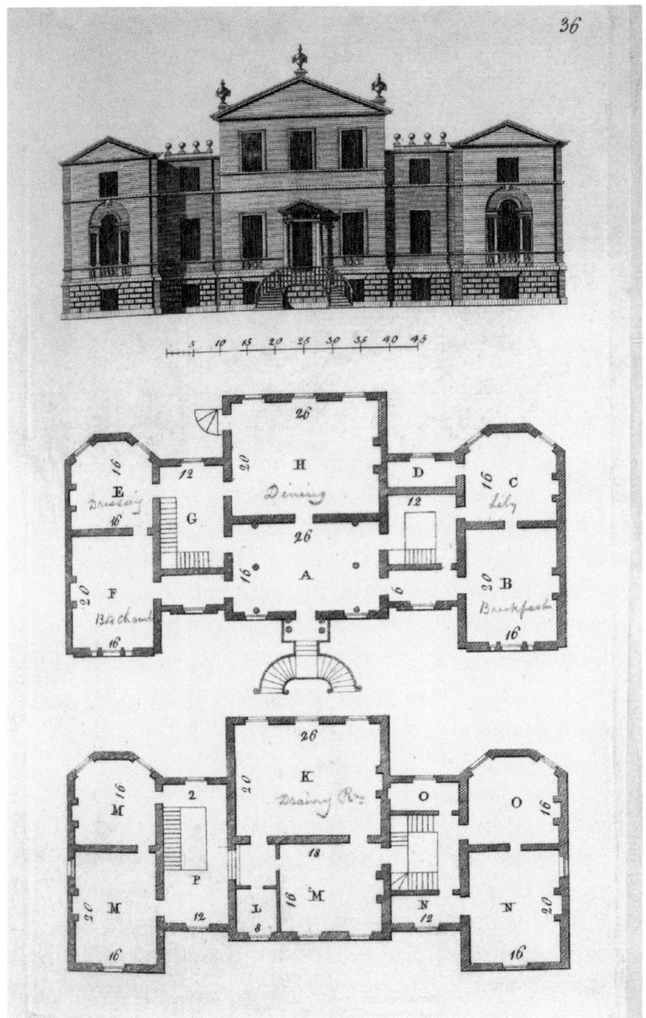

John Crunden. *Convenient and Ornamental Architecture.* Plate 36. NGA Lib. Rare Book: NA7328C78

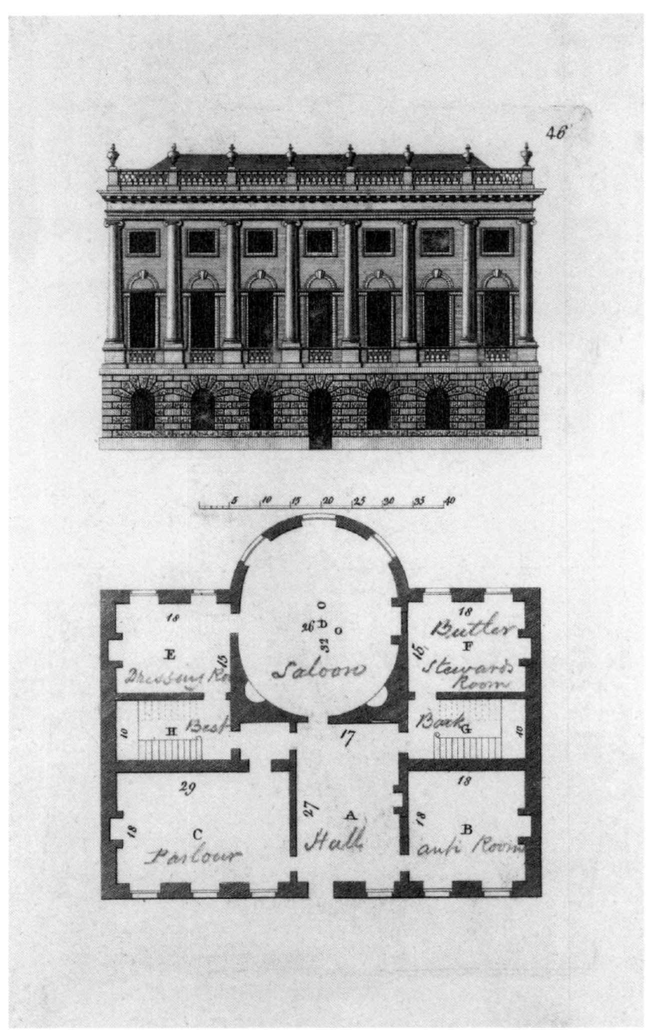

John Crunden. *Convenient and Ornamental Architecture.* Plate 46. NGA Lib. Rare Book: NA7328C78

who was the original engraver, to be repeated in 1788, 1791, and 1797 by I. and J. Taylor at the Architectural Library, and in 1805 and 1815 under J. Taylor's imprint alone. There were thus, over a period of fifty years, eight issues, almost unchanged.

What Crunden offered, as his title made clear, were "Plans, Elevations, and Sections: Beginning With The Farm House, and regularly ascending to the most grand and magnificent Villa; Calculated Both for Town and Country, and to suit all Persons in every Station of Life." There was thus a broad range of designs, mostly domestic, including his own Brooklands (pl. 36), though inns were illustrated also, all in an established Palladian manner, with rococo flourishes surviving still in the interiors. The only novelties offered were some Gothic details, pointed arches, pinnacles, and crenellations, in two of the designs. The most advanced of the plans (pl. 46) included an elliptical room, projecting to form a bow front.

Clearly Crunden provided an image of solid, respectable taste, with just enough liveliness, but no excess—"To be sparing of antique Ornaments, as they are termed," he wrote, "on the outside of a building, would shew a true taste in an Architect."

The book was dedicated to the duke of Newcastle, Thomas Pelham-Holles, to whose "constant patronage" Crunden was indebted. He was among the subscribers, seventy-seven in all, most of them in the building trade, but including Henry Banks, the painter, and Holland, who ordered six copies. R. M.

Bibliography

Colvin, H. *A Biographical Dictionary of British Architects 1660–1840.* 2d ed. London, 1978

Harris, E., and N. Savage. *British Architectural Books and Writers 1556–1785.* Cambridge, 1990

17

Sir William Dugdale (1605–1686)

The History Of St. Pauls Cathedral in London, From its Foundation untill these Times . . . By William Dugdale

London: printed by Tho. Warren, 1658

1985.61.550

Folio: 340 × 220 (13 3/8 × 8 3/4)

Pagination [vi], 113, [1], 117–136, 157–160, 171–178, 181–299, [7] pp., etched portrait, [14] etched plates (11 double-page, 1 folding)

(*Note:* 1 plate numbered as p. 115; 10 plates numbered as pp. 161–170. Pages 129, 174, and 293–297 misnumbered 126, 192, and 263–267, respectively)

Edition First edition

Text pp. [i] title page printed in red and black (verso blank); [iii–v] dedication to Christopher, Lord Hatton, dated 7 July 1657; [vi] blank; 1–"192" (i.e., 174) text; [175] divisional title page to appendix (verso blank); 177–288 appendix; 289–"266" (i.e., 296) "The Daunce Of Machabree . . ."; p. "267" (i.e., 297)–298 "The Kings Majesties proceeding to Paul's Church 26. Martii. 1620."; 299 list of dedicatees of the plates; [300] blank; [301–305] index, errata, addendum; [306] blank

Illustrations A total of 45 etched plates, etched by Wenceslaus Hollar and another, anonymous hand, after drawings by Hollar or William Sedgwick. Of these, the 15 *hors texte* plates are as follows: etched portrait of the author; interior view numbered 115 as part of the pagination; 10 plates (1 folding, 8 double-page, 1 single-page) numbered 161–170 as part of the pagination; and 3 double-page plates between pp. 40–41, 126–127, and 132–133, respectively. For detailed descriptions, see RIBA, *Early Printed Books*, 932, or the works by Pennington, Adams, Hind, or Parthey

Binding Seventeenth-century English paneled calf, sprinkled edges

Provenance Author presentation copy dated 1658, to Thomas Barlow, Queen's College, Oxford (title page inscribed "Lib. Th: Barlow è coll. Reg. Oxon ex dono Authoris. M. DC. LVIII."). Barlow was Bodley's librarian, 1642–1660; provost of Queen's College, 1658–1675; and bishop of Lincoln, 1675–1691. Eighteenth-century engraved Chippendale-style bookplate of George Kenyon, of Peel, Esq. Originally part of Barlow's collection in the library of Queen's College, Oxford, and probably discarded as a duplicate after the library of Sir Joseph Williamson, which contained another copy of *St. Paul's* (also *donum authoris*), was received by bequest in 1701. Eighteenth-century note on front pastedown "Collated & perfect"

References Bernard Adams, *London Illustrated 1604–1851* (London, 1983), 8; Berlin Cat. 2325; Berlin (1977) OS 2325; ESTC R16413; A. M. Hind, *Wenceslaus Hollar and his Views of London* (London, 1922); Gustav Parthey, *Wenzel Hollar* (Berlin, 1853); Richard Pennington, *A Descriptive Catalogue of the Works of Wenceslaus Hollar* (Cambridge, 1982); RIBA, *Early Printed Books* 932; Wing D2482

As THE MOST detailed study of a single building produced in seventeenth-century England, and the best evidence for how St. Paul's Cathedral looked before the 1666 Fire of London, William Dugdale's work hardly needs introduction. In compiling it, Dugdale was more concerned with recording inscriptions and establishing genealogies than describing architecture, but like many subsequent architectural historians, he used the occasion of the book's appearance to publicize the decay of a building and secure a record of its details. Given the non-architectural emphasis of the text, this was, of course, where the book's famously evocative etchings are most valuable; Wenceslas Hollar has usually been given the credit for these, though it has been pointed out that Daniel King had some input into the original drawings. The present copy is without the large folding plate with miniature etchings of the illustrations, surrounding verses by Edward Benlowes, "On St Paul's Cathedral represented by Mr. Daniel King." Hollar may have replaced King because of his superior technical skill; there are certainly two distinct ways that Hollar signs a plate, "W.H. del. et sculp." and "W.H. fecit," the latter perhaps indicating that he performed the engraving only. (Pennington assesses the extent of Hollar's contribution to each plate under the item number, and a summary of his findings is given in the RIBA catalogue. See also Parry 1995, 236–241; Jenkins 1952, 258–260.)

Written to exploit the vast archives that came into Dugdale's possession in 1656, following the death of their previous owner John Reading, the book is also a piece of polemic and an elegiac tribute to the past glories of English ecclesiastical architecture. As with Dugdale's earlier publication, *Monasticon Anglicanum* (vol. 1, 1655), the costs of the illustrations were defrayed by several well-wishers. In this context, the current copy's provenance is particularly interesting. Dugdale presented it to Thomas Barlow, a friend and correspondent, who also seems to have assisted him in his research. Bodleian MS Carte 255, a notebook of Dugdale's, includes a "Discourse of Mortuaryes" by Barlow, dated 1651 (Madan 1895, no. 10700). Previously, Dugdale had presented a copy of *Monasticon Anglicanum* to Barlow (Hamper 1827, 477–478).

Barlow also sponsored one of the plates. On 26 September 1656, replying to a letter in which Dugdale had asked for his sponsorship, he wrote, ". . . you tell me the Plate will stand me in 5li. I shall not question the price, soe it be well done. I know Mr. Hollar is an excellent person, and deserves all incouragement, nor shall I be wanteinge, or unwillinge to paye him liberally for his labour, onely be you the Judge, and what you say, I will send; and that when and whither you shall appoint." Barlow's monetary contribution is also recorded in a statement of costs incurred during the publication of the book (see Hamper 1827, 359).

At this period there tended to be a connection between interest in medieval remains and adherence to the Church of England, and so *St. Paul's* and volume one of *Monasticon Anglicanum*, both published in the 1650s, serve as, among other things, a directory of disaffected Anglicans. Barlow was Bodley's librarian from 1642 to 1660, and provost of Queen's College from 1658—when Dugdale penned his inscription—to 1675. As these dates indicate, he was able to accommodate his conscience to both royalist and republican authorities at Oxford; managing to escape ejection during the civil wars and interregnum, and again at the Restoration, he was rewarded with the bishopric of Lincoln in 1675. But though his life history reveals him as a trimmer, Barlow's Anglican sympathies come out strongly within the plate which he sponsored, the view of the south side at St. Paul's, showing the spire. In the letter quoted above, he continues, "I have sent this inclosed paper, if you like it. Armes I have none (nor deserve any) and therefore referr the whole to you, to have all these words, or as many of them as you shall thinke fitt, ingraven on the Plate, and with what devise you shall thinke fitt, onely I desire to see it, ere it be finished, soe as not to be altered."

The "inclosed paper" must have given a version of the captions that appear on the final plate, three in number. The first gives Barlow's name and titles, with the comment *Ne ingentes augustæ molis ruinæ etiam perirent* (In order that the huge masses of the august ruin may not also perish). The second falls into two parts: a description of the subject of the illustration, *Ecclesiæ Paulinæ Prospectvs, Qvalis Olim Erat, Priusquam Eius Pyramis, È*

William Dugdale. *The History of St. Pauls Cathedral.* View of St. Paul's, dedicated to Thomas Barlow. 1985.61.550

Coelo Tacta Conflagaverat (Prospect of St. Paul's Church, as it once was before its pyramid, touched from the sky, had burned), and a quotation from book ten of Lucan's *Pharsalia, Effigiem Templi, quod vix corruptior ætas / Extruat, ingratæ genti donavimus*. Lucan's epic took civil war as its topic, and so was an especially popular source for classical allusions during the 1640s and 1650s. The third comes from Horace's *Odes* 3: 6: *Delicta majorum et meritus lues / Britanne, donec Templa refeceris, / Ædesq[ue] labentes Deorum, et / Foeda nigro loca sacra fumo.*

This demure Latinity half conceals and half reveals a number of imprecations against the Cromwellian status quo. As cited by Barlow—and this may explain his anxiety about accurate transcription—the quotations from Lucan and Horace are both extensively altered. Imitation or rewriting of classical authors was, in early modern England, a very common means of commenting obliquely on current political woes; it deflected censorship, while lending classical gravity to contemporary matters. Lucan actually wrote *Ipse locus templi, quod vix corruptior ætas / Extruat, instar erat; laqueatque texta ferebant / Divitias . . .*, rendered by a seventeenth-century translator as "The house excell'd those temples, which men build / In wickedst times, the high-arch'd roofes were fill'd / With wealth . . ." (*Lucans Pharsalia*, trans. Thomas May, London, 1635, fol. S2a—book two, l. 111–113). A more literal translation is "The place itself was the size of a temple, such a temple as a corrupt age would hardly rear; the panels of the ceiling displayed wealth . . ." (Lucan, trans. J. D. Duff, Loeb Classical Translations, London, 1968). Barlow's adaptation can be translated "We have given to an ungrateful people the likeness of a temple which a more corrupt age would hardly rear," giving a contemporary spin to Lucan's comment that men spend less on building churches in evil times.

Similarly, the quotation from Horace should read *Delicta maiorum immeritus lues, / Romane, donec templa refeceris /aedesque labentes deorum et / foeda nigro simulacra fumo*, translated thus in Barton Holyday's 1652 version of the *Odes*:

> (Romane) resolve, thou shalt desertlesse tast,
> Sinn's scourge, for vice of Predecessor past,
> Vntill thou dost againe, repaire
> Decayed Temples and make fayre,
> The falling houses of the gods, disgrac'd,
> And cleanse their Images, with smoke defac'd (*Odes* 6: 3, l. 1–4, p. 30).

Barlow's version translates as: "O Briton, you will expiate your fathers' sins—and deservedly—till you restore the temples and crumbling shrines of the gods, and the holy places soiled with grimy smoke" (adapted from *Horace: the Odes and Epodes*, trans. J. D. Duff, Loeb Classical Translations, London, 1969). Like the other captions, this reprehends the ecclesiastical authorities at a time when St. Paul's and other church buildings around the country were falling into disrepair: though Barlow makes one impeccably Protestant emendation, *loca sacra* (holy places) for Horace's *simulacra* (images). Writing to Dugdale after the publication of the book, Barlow was even more explicit: "I reckon'd it amongst the cryinge sins of that City, yt they have profaned, and ruined, yt sacred place; and yet, *aliquisq' malo fuit usus in illo*, we have some benefit by their basenesse, and have gott by the ruines of Paul's, as haveing occasioned your excellent Booke, which will be a lasting monument of ye impiety of that place, and your industry" (Barlow to Dugdale, 3 May 1658, cited in Hamper 1827, 331–332).

Barlow's liberties with ancient texts are paralleled by the inscriptions on some of the other plates, such as the view of the choir screen donated by Henry Compton (p. 168). This gives four lines of Latin, and a fifth, *Dabit Deus his quoque finem* (God will grant an end to these things too). The source of this last line is given as the *Æneid*, book two (actually book one), and on a cursory glance, it looks as if the reference is meant to include all the Latin; but the epigraph to which it is attached occurs nowhere in Virgil and may be an original composition. A. S.

Bibliography

Hamper, W., ed. *The Life, Diary and Correspondence of Sir William Dugdale*. London, 1827

Jenkins, H. *Edward Benlowes*. Cambridge, Mass., 1952

Madan, F. *A Summary Catalogue of Western Manuscripts in the Bodleian Library at Oxford*. Oxford, 1895

Parry, G. *The Trophies of Time: English Antiquarians of the Seventeenth Century*. Oxford, 1995

Smith, N. *Literature and Revolution in England, 1640–1660*. New Haven, 1994: 204–207

18

Fra Francisco de los Santos (1617–1692)

A Description Of The Royal Palace, And Monastery Of St. Laurence, Called The Escurial; And Of The Chapel Royal Of The Pantheon. Translated From the Spanish of Frey Francisco De Los Santos, Chaplain to his Majesty Philip the Fourth. Illustrated With Copper-Plates. By George Thompson, of York, Esq.

London: printed by Dryden Leach, for S. Hooper, 1760

NGA Lib. Rare Book: NA7776E8X5613

Quarto: 282 × 216 (11 1/8 × 8 1/2)

Pagination [iii]–xxxvii, [1], 299, [1] pp.; xi, [1], 60 pp., 12 engraved plates (10 folding)

(*Note:* This copy lacks an initial half-title leaf)

Edition First edition of this translation

Text p. [iii] title page (verso blank); [v] errata; [vi] etched coat of arms; [vii] Thompson's dedication to Charles Watson Wentworth, marquis of Rockingham, &c. (verso blank); ix–xi translator's preface; [xii] blank; xiii–xviii list of subscribers; xix–xxxvii list of contents, book 1; [xxxviii] blank; [1]–9 introduction; [10] blank; [11]–299 text of book 1; [300] blank; [i] title page to book 2 "A Description Of The Chapel Royal, Called, The Pantheon . . ." (verso blank); [iii] Thompson's dedication to Sir George Saville (verso blank); v–xi list of contents, book 2; [xii] blank; [1]–50 text of book 2; 51–60 "A Catalogue Of All The Statues and Paintings, &c. Of which a Description is given in the foregoing Work; With an Account of the Famous Masters by whom they were executed, in alphabetical Order"

Illustrations 12 engraved plates, 10 of which require folding in the Millard copy, including 1 bound as a frontispiece. The plates are unnumbered, except for 2 numbered top right ("No. 11" in book 1 and "No. 12" in book 2). The credited draftsmen are Jacob Leroux (7), Samuel Wale (2), and "J. Gwyn" (1), the latter either John Gwynn or James Gwyn. The engravers are T. Miller, Francis Patton, A. Bannerman, Charles Grignion, Edward Rooker, and W. Charron (2 plates each). The arms of the marquis of Rockingham and Sir George Saville appear on p. [vi] of book 1 and p. [iii] of book 2, respectively

Binding Contemporary red morocco, gilt, rebacked

Provenance Etched and engraved bookplate of the earl of Donegall. A knight of the garter's etched monogram inscribed "Cirencester" has been cut round and pasted above the Donegall bookplate

References ESTC t31699; RIBA, *Early Printed Books,* 1129

This is the second English monograph on Philip II's royal palace outside Madrid. The first was a twenty-three-page quarto pamphlet entitled *The Escurial, or, A Description of that Wonder of the World for Architecture and Magnificence of Structure, built by K. Philip the IId of Spain* (1671). There were several reasons why curiosity about the Escorial had been aroused in England at the time. First, Francisco de los Santos had lately published the detailed study on which most subsequent descriptions have been based, the *Descripcion Breve del Monasterio de S. Lorenzo el Real del Escorial, unica Maravilla del Mundo* (Madrid, 1657). The English work describes itself as "Written in Spanish by Francisco de los Santos, a Frier of the Order of S. Hierome, and an Inhabitant there," and is generally taken to be abridged directly from the larger work. It is more probably a translation of Francisco's own abridgment, as it begins with the justification that "Although in a former discourse we have particularly shewed the principal parts of the prodigious piece of architecture, and the ornamentals belonging to it . . . there are some persons which love not such tedious discourses . . . that at once desire to know the greatness and distinct parts of it, and with this rest satisfied" (pp. 1–2). The translation was made by an unnamed servant of Edward Montagu, the 1st earl of Sandwich, who stayed in Madrid from May 1666 to September 1668 to arrange a treaty to end the long period of rivalry at sea between Spain and England. Peace, and the return of the ambassador's party, may have awakened interest in Spain's most famous building. But the immediate impulse behind the publication of *The Escurial* was to capitalize on news of the palace's destruction by the fire of 1671, which lasted for fifteen days and left only the church, part of the palace, and two towers uninjured. Coming just five years after the Great Fire of London, and descending on a monument to Roman Catholic devotion built for Queen Elizabeth's archenemy, this fire would have been a natural topic for discussion in London. As the "Epistle to the Reader" notes, it is "the usual fate of the greatest works, as well as of the most eminent persons, to be then most desired and talked of, when the world is deprived of them."

In the event, the world was not deprived of the Escorial, but the motivation behind the present translation of the whole of Francisco de Los Santos' book is less clear. By 1760, Spain still only rarely formed part of the customary Grand Tour of Europe undertaken by the young and affluent in Britain to finish their education. When the 2d duke of Richmond decided to visit in the 1720s, Lord Townsend could not imagine "what curiosity should lead his Grace so much out of the usual road of travellers," and although the country was regarded as safer and more accessible forty years later, it was not until the nineteenth century that the Escorial established itself as a tourist attraction. There is nothing in the book to suggest that the translator, George Thompson of York, had made the visit himself, although the sprinkling of Spanish names in the subscription list indicates he had contacts. Little is known about him, except that he is also credited with the authorship of a piece of political ephemera, *An Account of what Passed between Mr. George Thompson, of York and Doctor John Burton, of that city . . . at Mr. Sheriff Jubb's entertainment, and the consequences thereon* (1756). Dr. John Burton (1710–1770), satirized in Laurence Sterne's *Tristram Shandy* as "Doctor Slop," was an accomplished obstetrician and local antiquarian who wrote *Monasticon Eboracense, and Ecclesiastical History of Yorkshire* (1758). The pamphlet's existence at least indicates Thompson had some association with serious scholars. Despite the thoroughness of his translation, this might otherwise be doubted, as some of the other names associated with his work on the Escorial are either unknown for their interest in culture or famous for their lack of it. Book one is dedicated, "out of gratitude for the many favors received," to Charles Watson-Wentworth, 2d marquis of Rockingham (1730–1782), and book two to Sir George Savile (1726–1784), around the time both were embarking on their political careers. Each plate also carries a separate dedication, presumably reflecting a subvention toward the cost of producing it. As might be expected, the dedicatees are mostly Yorkshire dignitaries, often active in Parliament, such as the 1st Earl Grosvenor. Nevertheless, it is surprising to find among them the so-called bad earl of Lonsdale, Sir James Lowther (1736–1802)—"more detested than any man alive" (Alexander Carlyle)—and the poetaster John Hall-Stevenson, whose "sole aim in life was, he repeatedly declared, to amuse himself" (DNB 54: 239). At least two of the book's subscribers, the Rev. Robert Lascelles and Colonel Hall, were members of Hall-Stevenson's Club of Demoniacks, devoted to heavy drinking and obscene jests in Skelton. Sterne, a friend of Hall-Stevenson, also subscribed. There were 359 names for 465 copies in all, headed by the prince of Wales, soon to be George III. Whether or not the book was in part an attempt to direct the prince's attention to the state of the arts in Britain, by showing what royal patronage could achieve elsewhere, has yet to be confirmed.

Fra Francisco de los Santos. *A Description of the Royal Palace... called the Escurial.* Grand Altar. NGA Lib. Rare Book: NA7776E8X5613

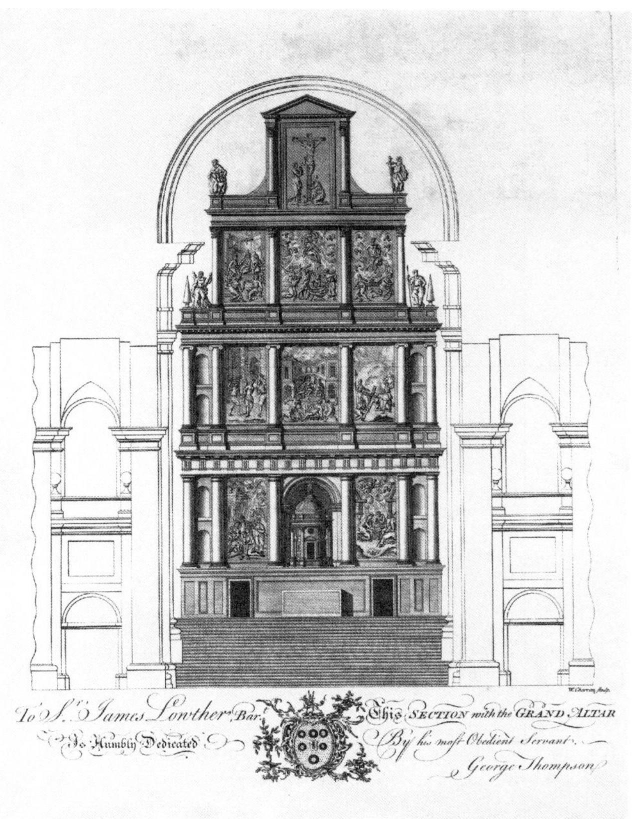

W. Cherron sculp.
To Sr. James Lowther, Bart.
This SECTION with the GRAND ALTAR
Is Humbly Dedicated
By his most Obedient Servant.
George Thompson

Only Robert Carr (1697–1760), his son John (1723–1807), and Jacob Leroux (fl. 1753–1788) are named as architect subscribers. The Carr family was already well established in the Yorkshire West Riding. Leroux, who is credited as draftsman on seven of Thompson's plates, was at the beginning of his career, having been articled to William Jones in 1753. His practice later included speculative building, and in 1788 he was accused by Charles Dibdin of possessing "a dastardly speciousness for which a hyena might envy him" (quoted in Colvin 1995, 611). Some authorities confuse him with the French architect Jean-Baptiste Leroux (c. 1676–1746). The other credited draftsmen are Samuel Wale on two plates and "J. Gwyn" on another. The latter is usually identified as James Gwyn, but it seems more likely to be John Gwynn, Wale's neighbor in Little Court at Castle Street, Leicester Fields. Wale and Gwynn cooperated on several projects and both began exhibiting at the Society of Artists of Great Britain in the same year that Thompson's book appeared. Gwynn (1713–1786) is now known for his friendship with Samuel Johnson; his campaign to establish a national academy of art; his books, especially *London and Westminster Improved* (1766); and his designs for bridges, several of which were executed. Wale (1721–1786) was a prolific book illustrator who thereby managed to support Gwynn as well as himself (see Harris and Savage 1990, 217). He was later the Royal Academy's first professor of perspective, until he was paralyzed, after which the Academy appointed him librarian.

Thompson is proud of the plates in his work, claiming at the end of his preface that the originals were "badly designed and worse engraved; and, at the same time, fewer in number than will be found in this performance." With the possible exception of one plate, however, his are not from original drawings. Leroux, Wale, and Gwynn seem to have been asked to copy their designs from previously published prints, for the engravers to copy in turn. All five plates illustrating the royal mausoleum, or pantheon, are from Francisco de los Santos' treatise (i.e., plan, section with altar, stairway, view of two lecterns, view of the chandelier). Six of the remaining illustrations derive from a much earlier suite of twelve designs on eleven plates engraved by Pieter (or Pedro) Perret after drawings commissioned by Juan de Herrera, and published with Herrera's explanation as *El Sumario y Breve Declaracion delos Diseños y Estampas de la Fabrica de San Lorencio el Real de el Escorial* (Madrid, 1589). Plates derived from Perret's were fairly common in Europe in the seventeenth century, and may have been used rather than the originals. The "Septimo Diseño" was especially popular, giving a magnificent bird's-eye perspective view of the principal front, showing in the background the surrounding countryside and, just below the horizon, Madrid itself. Francisco included a version of it in his *Descripcion Breve*. Leroux's engraving eliminates all of the scenographic elements to present the architectural design free from its context. He has also reversed the image, which would cause confusion for anyone comparing it with his unreversed plan and three sections, which are not in Francisco's treatise but derive from the first, third, fourth, and fifth engravings in Perret's suite.

The plate of the grand altar, engraved by W. Charron after an unnamed draftsman, has been described as a "composición medio fantasia, medio realidad" (Elena Santiago Páez and Juan Manuel Magariños, "El Escorial, historia de una imagen," in *El Escorial en la Biblioteca Nacional* 1985, 299). The altar is reproduced fairly faithfully, probably from Perret's eighth design, or a copy thereof. But the illustrations of the paintings in the *retablo* are inaccurate and in at least one case confusing. Eight were originally commissioned from Federico Zuccaro, and these are all discernible in Perret's engraving of about 1589. Five remain, but three were soon replaced with paintings by Pellegrino Tibaldi, including the central panel depicting the martyrdom of St. Lawrence. Zuccaro's version of this was thought to be so bad it was banished to a chapel built for workers in the village, and has since disappeared. In Charron's engraving, however, the central panel quite clearly shows a third martyrdom of St. Lawrence, very similar to the one attributed to Baccio Bandinelli and engraved by Marcantonio Raimondi. No other connection between this painting and the Escorial has been traced, so it must be assumed that its inclusion was simply a sleight of hand by the unidentified source for Thompson's design.

The one plate that may be wholly original is the elevation of the principal facade, signed by Francis Patton after Leroux and dedicated to the earl of Scarborough. Luis Cervera Vera is probably correct in suggesting that it was unskillfully derived from Perret's perspective elevation (*Las Estampas y el Sumario de el Escorial*, 1954). It is so inaccurate it could hardly have been drawn by someone who had seen the building. In particular, the dome rises far too high above the principal entrance,

Fra Francisco de los Santos. *A Description of the Royal Palace... called the Escurial.* Front elevation. NGA Lib. Rare Book: NA7776E8X5613

and the spires of the *colegio* and the *convento* have been brought forward to sit on top of the entrances to either side. That such an engraving should have been accepted by Thompson argues against any real knowledge of his subject. The most likely explanation is that by 1760 such elevations had become a standard feature of British architectural books, and Thompson felt he had to commission one from Leroux regardless of the young architect's ability to provide it. G. B.

Bibliography

British Architectural Library, Royal Institute of British Architects. *Early Printed Books 1478–1840: Catalogue of the British Architectural Library Early Imprints Collection*. Vols. 1–2. London, 1994–1995

Brown University (Dept. of Art). *Philip II and the Escorial*. Providence, 1990

Hibbert, C. *The Grand Tour*. London, 1987

Mulcahy, R. *The Decoration of the Royal Basilica of El Escorial*. Cambridge, 1994

Santiago Páez, E., and Manuel Magariños, J. "El Escorial, historia de una imagen." In *El Escorial en la Biblioteca Nacional*. Madrid [1985]: 223–366

Fra Francisco de los Santos. *A Description of the Royal Palace... called the Escurial*. Bird's-eye view. NGA Lib. Rare Book: NA7776E8X5613

19

Roland Fréart, sieur de Chambray (1606–1676)

A Parallel Of The Antient Architecture With The Modern, In a Collection of Ten Principal Authors who have Written upon the Five Orders, Viz. Palladio and Scamozzi, Serlio and Vignola, D. Barbaro and Cataneo, L. B. Alberti and Viola, Bullant and De Lorme, Compared with one another. The three Greek Orders, Dorick, Ionick and Corinthian, comprise the First Part of this Treatise. And the 2 Latin, Tuscan and Composita the Latter. Written in French by Roland Freart, Sieur de Chambray; Made English for the Benefit of Builders. To which is added an Account of Architects and Architecture, in an Historical and Etymological Explanation of certain Terms particularly affected by Architects. With Leon Baptista Alberti's Treatise of Statues. By John Evelyn Esq; Fellow of the Royal Society. The Second Edition with Large Additions

London: printed for D. Brown, J. Walthoe, B. Took, and D. Midwinter, 1707

1985.61.579

Folio: 349 × 228 ($13^{3}/_{4}$ × 9)

Pagination Part 1: [xx], 115, [1] pp.

Part 2: [vi], 75, [1] pp.

Edition Second edition of this translation

Text part 1: pp. [i] title page (verso blank); [iii–vii] dedication by Evelyn to Charles II, dated 20 August 1664; [viii] blank; [ix–xii] dedication by Evelyn to Sir John Denham; [xiii–xviii] letter by Fréart to his brothers Jean and Paul Fréart, sieurs de Chantelou, dated Paris, 22 May 1650; [xix] Latin verse addressed to Evelyn by John Beale (verso blank); 1–6 preface; 7–10 "Advertisement" to the present edition; 11–115 text and illustrations, "A Parallel . . ."; [116] blank; *part 2*: pp. [i] divisional title page "An Account Of Architects And Architecture . . . Much Inlarg'd and Improv'd, since the former Impression. By John Evelyn . . . Together, With Leon Baptist Alberti, Of Statues. London: Printed in the Year, 1706." (verso blank); [iii–iv] dedication by Evelyn to Sir Christopher Wren, dated 21 Feb. 1696/7; [v–vi] note to the reader; 1–57 text, "An Account . . ."; [58] blank; [59] note to the reader; [60] letter from Cosimo Bartoli to Bartolomeo Ammanati; 61–75 text, "Leon Baptista Alberti Of Statues"; [76] advertisement "Books Printed for Dan. Brown . . ."

Illustrations In part 1 there are 40 full-page engraved plates, all included in the signatures and pagination, plus an engraved title-page vignette; 4 engraved headpieces, p. [xiii], 1 (repeated 7), 9, 102; 4 engraved tailpieces, pp. 19, 68, 102, 105; and a woodcut headpiece, p. 11. Part 2 contains 2 small engraved plates in Alberti's treatise on statues, pp. 67 and 70—in this copy, the second of these printed upside down. The engravings are all reprinted from the first edition of Evelyn's translation, 1664, and all in part 1 are close copies of the plates and ornaments in the first edition of Fréart's work (Paris, 1650). Those in part 2 are close copies of the plates in Du Fresne's 1651 edition of Alberti's *Della Statua*, appended to Leonardo da Vinci's *Trattato della Pittura*. The small armorial shield on the wall in the second plate replaces a drawing in the original

Binding Contemporary paneled calf, rebacked, red morocco label, red sprinkled edges

References ESTC t118307; Fowler 130; Harris and Savage 232; RIBA, *Early Printed Books*, 1135

John Evelyn's most successful book, *Sylva*, was written in 1663, at the request of the Royal Society, of which he had been a founding member, and was published in 1664. In the same year he issued the first edition of his translation of Roland Fréart's *Parallèle de l'architecture antique avec la moderne*, of 1650—"I had," Evelyn wrote in his dedication, "(by the Commands of the Royal Society) endeavour'd the improvement of Timber, and the planting of Trees, I have advanced to that of Building as its proper and natural consequent." But Evelyn had contemplated the translation of Fréart's work many years earlier. He was in Paris when it was published, where his father-in-law, Sir Richard Browne, was English resident, and when he left in 1652 he brought a copy to England, the first, he thought, to be seen there.

"It is now some *ten* years since," he wrote in the second dedication in the *Parallel*, "that to gratifie a *friend* of mine in the *Country*, I began to interpret this *Parallel*; but other things intervening, it was lay'd aside, and had so continu'd without thoughts of reasumption, had not the passion of my worthy Friend Mr. *Hugh May* to oblige the *Publick*, and in commiseration of the few assistances which our *Workmen* have of this nature (compar'd to what are extant, in other Countries) found out an expedient, and by procuring a most accurate *Edition* of the *Plates*, encourag'd me to finish what I had begun; and to make a willing *Present* of my *labour* and of whatever else I was able to contribute to so generous a designe."

Eileen Harris has suggested that it was Hugh May also, who had been with the royal court in exile in Holland from 1656 to 1660, who arranged for the original

Roland Fréart. *A Parallel of the Antient Architecture with the Modern.* Page 23. "At the bath of Diocletian in Rome." 1985.61.579

plates by Charles Errard to be copied there for the English edition, no engraver in England being capable of producing plates of their quality.

Evelyn was a fervent supporter of the Restoration. His translation was dedicated to Charles II, upheld as a counterpart to "the Great Augustus" to whom Vitruvius had dedicated his work. The dedication was followed by an epistle to Sir John Denham, surveyor of the King's Works, who had begun the paving of the streets of Holborn, transforming London, Evelyn apotheosized, in the manner of Rome—"Nunc Roma es nuper magna taberna fuit" (Now Rome exists: of late it was a huge shop; Martial Epigrams book VII no. 61). There was yet another epistle, dated Paris, 22 May 1650, addressed by Roland to his brothers John and Paul Fréart, whom Evelyn knew, extolling the virtues of their cousin François Sublet de Noyers, who had been surintendant des batîments for five years before his dismissal in 1643. Together they had aimed to institute a policy of state-sponsored classicism. They even succeeded in luring Poussin from Rome to Paris 1640.

"Receive then," Roland concluded,

> (my dear *Brothers*) this *Fragment* of a *Book*, so much at least as remains of it, and if there occur any thing which may prove yet considerable in such clear and discerning eyes as yours are, and that my designs seem worthy of any place amongst your other *curiosities*, you owe the entire obligation of it to our common *Friend Monsieur Errard*, who was pleased to take a great deal of pains to see it perfected; and has not only perswaded me (as well as you) to publish it to the world, but has more than this contributed likewise to it, of his own labour and particular elucubrations.

Errard, it seems possible, might have been involved also in the making of Evelyn's plates.

The preface to the work strikes a new note in English architectural theory. The true model of architecture resides in antiquity, but not all examples of antique architecture are now considered worthy of imitation. The essential can be grasped only after painstaking study and analysis of the originals, and a firm rejection of all distortions and developments. This meant, in effect, that only the Greek models were to be upheld.

> . . . I willingly communicate the thoughts which I have had of separating in two branches the five *Orders of Architecture*, and forming a *body* a part of the *Three* which are deriv'd to us from the *Greeks*; to wit, the *Dorique*, *Ionique*, and the *Corinthian*, which one may with reason call the very flower and perfection of the *Orders*; since they not only contain whatever is excellent, but likewise all that is necessary of *Architecture*; there being but three manners of *Building*, the *Solid*, the *Mean* and the *Delicate*; all of them accurately express'd in these three *Orders here;* that have therefore no need of the other two (*Tuscan*, and *Composita*) which being purely of *Latine* extraction, and but forrainers in respect to *them*, seem as it were another species; so as being mingl'd, they do never well together.

The insistence on the merit of the Greek orders alone is repeated often enough, throughout the work. Fréart (and, one must assume Evelyn) was even prepared to accept the consequence of this search for original purity; the base to the Doric column was rejected as a later accretion. Vitruvius, of course, had recognized this, but he added a base without qualm. Fréart's stand evinces an unusual respect for antique precedent, and marks another distinctive feature of the *Parallel*.

Though the book is in essence an account of the setting up of the orders and their related parts—and the three Greek orders, as noted, rather than the Roman ones—they are considered only as a part of the whole:

> 'Tis not in the *detail* of the *minuter portions*, that the talent of an *Architect* appears; *this* is to by judg'd from the general distribution of the *Whole* work. These low and reptile *Souls*, who never arrive to the universal knowledge of the *Art*, and

embrace her in all her dimensions, are constrain'd to stop *there*, for want of abilities, incessantly crawling after these poor little things; and as their *studies* have no other objects, being already empty, and barren of themselves; their *Ideas* are so base and miserable, that they produce nothing save *Mascarons*, wretched *Cartouches*, and the like idle and impertinent *Grotesks*, with which they have even infected all our *Modern Architecture*. As for those others to whom Nature has been more propitious, and are indu'd with a clearer imagination, they very well perceive that the true and essential beauty of *Architecture* consists not simply in the minute separation of every member *apart*; but does rather principally result from the *Symmetry* and *Oeconomy* of the *whole*, which is the union and concourse of them all together, producing as 'twere a visible harmony and consent, which those eyes that are clear'd and enlightened by the real Intelligence of *Art*, contemplate and behold with excess of delectation.

It is notable that throughout the book Evelyn uses the term symmetry to contain something of its original Greek meaning, and not just an axial balance, as was to be accepted later in the century, in particular in the writings of Claude Perrault.

In the first part of the *Parallel* Fréart deals with the three Greek orders as illustrated by a range of theorists and commentators, Palladio and Scamozzi, Serlio and Vignola, Barbaro and Cataneo, Alberti and Viola, Bullant and De L'Orme ("the first of all is without any contest the famous Andrea Palladio"), though he also gives examples from antique buildings—the baseless "Doric" of the Theater of Marcellus and the Baths of Diocletian in Rome, and a tomb near Terracina (Fréart, of course, knew nothing of authentic Greek architecture); the Ionic again from the Theater of Marcellus and the Baths of Diocletian, and also that of the Temple of Fortuna Virilis; the Corinthian from the Baths of Diocletian, the Pantheon and Nero's palace in Rome, and also that of the "Temple of Jerusalem" as illustrated by Giovan Battista Villalpandus (". . . since it gave *Ornament* to that famous Temple of Jerusalem, which never yet had equal, we may with reason call it the *flower* of *Architecture*, and the *Order of Orders*"). Interleaved are chapters on caryatids and atlantes.

Roland Fréart. *A Parallel of the Antient Architecture with the Modern.* Page 39. "A very ancient sepulcher. . . ." 1985.61.579

The second part of the *Parallel* concerns the Tuscan and "Composita," dealt with in much the same way as before, but at less length. After a discussion of Serlio and Vignola's measures for the Tuscan, a note to the reader is inserted:

"'Twere altogether a fruitless *study*, and but labour lost to continue any longer in quest of this *Order* . . . I am therefore resolv'd to proceed no further." There is even less patience evinced in dealing with the "Composita" or compounded order:

"The Compounded Order which had hitherto obtain'd the first rank amongst the Moderns, will find itself extremely debas'd in this severe and exact review which I have made upon the five *Orders*."

But antique examples are nonetheless illustrated, such as the triumphal arch in Verona and the Arch of Titus in Rome.

At the end Evelyn made his own contribution; he expanded Fréart's one-page explanation of terms to a twenty-eight page "Account of Architects and Architecture, together with An Historical, and Etymological Explanation of certain *Tearms* particularly affected by *Architects*." He took his cue from Vitruvius, dealing, in an essay rather than in an alphabetical list, with the qualities requisite for a good architect, a good patron, and a good workman, and then with a detailed analysis of the various parts of the orders. There had been nothing like this before in English, and though Evelyn claimed to be addressing his work primarily to craftsmen, they would not have comprehended much of his meticulous analysis.

Appended to the *Parallel* was the first translation into English of Alberti's *Della Statua*—"There is no man pretending to this Art, or indeed to any other whatsoever, who does not greedily embrace all that bears the name of Leon Baptista Alberti."

The first edition of the *Parallel* was published by John Place, of Holborn, most of whose stock was made up of histories of legal works. He was unfamiliar with the niceties of architectural criticism. On 14 May 1696 he wrote to Evelyn to inform him that he intended to publish a second edition of the *Parallel* with "some additions, offer'd by Mr. Laybourn." Evelyn was no doubt taken aback. If William Leybourn, author of popular builder's books, was involved, he would have been offended in addition. He was certainly not averse to a second edition (a second printing of the first had been issued by J. P. Sold in 1680), and in no way opposed to additions and corrections, being only too well aware of the flow of major architectural publications that had occurred in France in recent years, books by Claude Perrault, Antoine Desgodetz, Jean-François Félibien, François Blondel, and Augustin-Charles d'Aviler, but he preferred to make all revisions himself. In particular

Roland Fréart. *A Parallel of the Antient Architecture with the Modern.* Page 69. "Of the Corinthian order." 1985.61.579

he wished some of the plates to be reengraved to take account of Desgodetz's careful measurement of the buildings of Rome, published in *Les Edifices Antiques de Rome* in 1682. "But he [Place] despairing to meet with any tolerable Graver among us (capable of Approaching those whom Monsieur Des Gaudetz employ'd) I could not impose it on him."

Evelyn rewrote the "Account of Architects and Architecture," doubling its length, softening his stance in relation to the Greek orders, and dedicating it to Sir Christopher Wren, but he made no haste to deliver the manuscript to Place, who wrote to him on 22 March 1698, suggesting that he bring it to London on his next visit. Evelyn died in February 1706. The new edition was published by D. Brown of Temple Bar only in November of that year.

The *Parallel* never enjoyed the success of Evelyn's other works, though it ran to a third edition in 1722 and was undoubtedly much respected, and strongly influential on at least one eighteenth-century follower, Robert Morris, who in *An Essay in Defence of Ancient Architecture* of 1728 took up Fréart's position concerning the sanctity and authority of the Greek orders, rejecting the Romans as imposters. But it was the Roman examples that were referred to rather by such solid authorities as Sir William Chambers in the middle years of the century. R. M.

Bibliography

Harris, E., and N. Savage. *British Architectural Books and Writers 1556–1785*. Cambridge, 1990

20

Joseph Michael Gandy (1771–1843)

Designs For Cottages, Cottage Farms, And Other Rural Buildings; Including Entrance Gates and Lodges. By Joseph Gandy, Architect, A. R. A.

London: printed for John Harding, 1805

1985.61.580

Quarto: 268 × 214 (10 9/16 × 8 7/16)

Pagination [2], x, 28, [2] pp., 43 aquatint plates

Edition First edition

Text pp. [1] title page (verso blank); [i] dedication to Thomas Hope (verso blank); [iii]–x introduction; [1]–28 explanation of the plates; [29–30] advertisements

Illustrations 43 aquatint plates, with etching, numbered upper right (some numbers cropped in Millard copy). See Abbey, *Life*, for a full list. Most are signed by Gandy as architect, and engraved by Charles Rosenberg or J. W. Harding

Binding Contemporary three-quarter calf, decorative glazed paper, gilt spine with floral ornaments and morocco label

Provenance Contemporary? ownership inscription on endpaper "Hon[ble] Mrs. Butler. Belvedere. Sandymount"

References Abbey, *Life*, 18; Berlin Cat. 2315; Berlin (1977) os 2315[c]; RIBA, *Early Printed Books*, 1171

No doubt with irony intended, John Summerson once suggested that Joseph-Michael Gandy be regarded as the English Piranesi. Gandy is indeed remembered chiefly for his great, obsessively detailed architectural visions, though he was rather more successful as the delineator of John Soane's extraordinary architecture, and in particular when Soane aspired to the sublime, as in his top-lit halls for the Bank of England or the Law Courts. Gandy's perspectives for Soane are his great achievement.

Gandy and Soane led curiously parallel lives, though Soane was the older, by far. Gandy was born in 1771, the son of an employee of White's, in London. The proprietor of the club, John Martindale, became his protector. He showed some of his drawings to James Wyatt, who took him into his office at the age of fifteen. Gandy also attended the schools of the Royal Academy, being awarded the gold medal in 1790. Four years later Martindale sent him to Italy, where he won a medal at the Accademia di San Luca. Back in London he started, in 1798, to make drawings for Soane. He started also to exhibit at the Royal Academy, being elected as associate in 1803. He seemed set, at this stage, for a reasonably successful career. His Phoenix Fire and Pelican Life Insurance Building, running from Spring Gardens to Charing Cross, in London, was completed in 1804; the following year he exhibited the most dramatic of all his architectural compositions, Pandemonium (inspired by Milton) at the Royal Academy.

It was at this period of expanding confidence and fulfillment that Gandy conceived his two books of designs for cottages and small farms, *Designs for Cottages, Cottage Farms, and Other Rural Buildings; Including Entrance Gates and Lodges* and *The Rural Architect; Consisting of Various Designs for Country Buildings*, both published in 1805. His designs are altogether unusual, strong and clear-cut, unlike anything he was to produce later in life.

A spate of books of cottage designs was issued in England during the last two decades of the eighteenth century and the first years of that following, quite unparalleled elsewhere. Interest in the subject was stirred first in 1775, with the repeal of an act prohibiting the erection of new cottages with less than four acres attached. In this same year Nathaniel Kent, a well-known agriculturist, published his *Hints to Gentlemen of Landed Property*, which included "Reflexions on the great importance of cottages" and four rude designs. His ideas were taken up and codified by John Wood the younger in *A Series of Plans, for Cottages or Habitations of the Landowner, Either in Husbandry, of the Mechanic Arts*, purportedly prepared and published in 1781, the year of Wood's death, but known only in "A new edition," of 1792. Wood's designs are bald, in the extreme, but his concern for the well-being of the laborer was genuine enough. The pattern books that followed, inspired rather by John Plaw's *Rural Architecture: Consisting of Designs, from the Simple Cottage, to the More Decorated Villa*, of 1785, were of a different ilk; buildings were considered rather as features in a picturesque landscape or as rustic retreats. Soane himself had produced a book of this kind, *Sketches in Architecture Containing Plans and Elevations of Cottages and Other Useful Buildings with Characteristic Scenery*, in 1793. Gandy's interests, however, were of the sterner sort. He was stirred, in particular, by two papers written by Soane's old employer, Henry Holland, "On cottages" and "Pisé, or the art of building strong and durable walls, to the height of several stories, with nothing but earth, or the most common materials," both published in 1797, in the first volume of the *Communications to the Board of Agriculture*. More than half the communications on farm buildings in this volume were devoted to cottages.

The Board of Agriculture was an anomalous body, set up in 1793 by William Pitt as a reward, as it were, to Sir John Sinclair, for having successfully launched a government loan in that year. Sinclair had long advocated a body of this sort to coordinate information on agricul-

Joseph Gandy. *Designs for Cottages.* Plate xv. "A Shepherd's Cottage and Conveniences." 1985.61.580

ture and to institute something by way of a policy. He had already begun to publish his *Statistical Account of Scotland* in 1791. Pitt wanted no policy. He was loath to use the board, even for information. Nonetheless, Sinclair commissioned and published a series of reports on the agriculture of each of the counties of England, beginning in 1793, largely complete by 1797, that he hoped to use as the basis of a general survey. Holland's memoranda were issued in the years of high activity and enthusiasm.

Holland outlined the chief practical considerations for cottage design, the siting, planning, and structural materials, and the supply of water and fuel. He illustrated a double cottage, "of the smallest size," and proposed a classification for four additional sizes. The most suitable building material, he suggested, was *pisé*, or rammed earth. This technique, employed in the Rhone Valley, had been revived in 1790 by François Cointeraux, who had opened a small school on the outskirts of Paris and had begun to publish a series of four cahiers on the subject from 1790 to 1806. These ran to several editions. Cointeraux had been invited to Scarisbrick Hall in Lancashire by Mr. Ecclestone even earlier, in 1789, to demonstrate the technique. But he had sent two workman instead. Plaw took up Cointeraux's ideas, in 1795, in his *Ferme ornée; or Rural Improvements*, one of the more popular of the picturesque cottage books; but Holland, leaning heavily on Cointeraux, was the first to describe *pisé* construction in detail, in English. He also appended an abstract of one of Cointeraux's papers.

"The idea of the following work," Gandy wrote in the introduction to the *Designs for Cottages*, "was suggested by the hints thrown out in the valuable Publication issued under the direction of the Board of Agriculture. We there find some very intelligent Communications on the subject of Cottages and Farm-buildings, replete with observations dictated by the soundest policy, and originating in the humane desire of increasing the comforts and improving the condition of the Labouring Poor."

Gandy illustrated a range of cottages and rural buildings, from the single-roomed cottage to the farmhouse, with outbuildings, and extending even to the design of grouped cottages, either in a range or in circular clusters that could be composed to form an ideal village, all of which are inevitably simple and rudimentary in plan, but which show, nonetheless, careful consideration of patterns of use. The single-roomed laborer's cottage, for instance, has wide-projecting eaves and a bench alongside the front door to provide some extended amenity. The buildings were all to be constructed with *pisé*, covered with thatch, stone, or slate, or other local material. Columns, when they occurred, were to "consist of young trees cut to size, and the bark left on."

This gives a hint of Gandy's aesthetic concerns. His work was dedicated to Thomas Hope, the most fastidious of connoisseurs, the arch-proselytizer of taste at the period. He had just opened up his house in Duchess Street for viewing by members of the Royal Academy. Gandy aimed, as he said, to "unite *convenience* and *taste* in a greater degree than has hitherto prevailed in this class of Buildings." Rural architecture might thus dispose the laboring class to neatness and cleanliness and at the same time be satisfying to the most refined eye.

Gandy's tastes were quite specific. Too much uniformity, he thought, was dull; but variety was extremely difficult to manage, requiring "the same sort of skill and genius as fine music." He approved of the picturesque, but he approached it with the classical eye.

"What can be more frightful," he wrote, "than the black and white daubings to successively projecting stories in some market towns, as if they wished to show all the deformities of the timbers, and exhibit the skeleton of a house? How strong is the contrast between the appearance of those and that of Bath and Oxford; the first all cheerfulness; the latter everything that is grand, and almost sublime, in Architecture?"

He stressed at once the importance in architecture of "simple mass of form" rather than surface ornamentation, and offered as exemplars both St. Paul's and Westminster Abbey. "Simplicity and variety in the great outline of buildings, should be considered, both in the greatest and the smallest works."

Such a notion certainly determined Gandy's designs for cottages and lodges; his built works relied rather for their effect on crisp ornamentation, his visionary paintings on the rich elaboration of extraordinary details.

Indeed the designs in his cottage books stand apart in his oeuvre, with a clarity and power and individual vitality that he was never again to achieve. His stark geometrical combinations, the horizontal stress—with far-projecting eaves and serried rows of windows—and the hard and odd punctuation of the forms that mark these designs do not appear in built works before the advent of Alexander Thompson. Gandy has even been noted, here, as a precursor of Frank Lloyd Wright. But there was to be nothing more of this kind.

What, one is bound to ask, stimulated this surge of creativity? Idealist notions of a humane kind clearly had their influence, but it is perhaps not fanciful to propose also the influence of the stunning geometrical representations in C.-N. Ledoux's *L'architecture considérée sous le rapport del'art, des moeurs et de la législation*, issued in 1804. Soane acquired his copy of this work in this year and one may safely assume that it was known to Gandy.

Gandy's two cottage books seem to have been prepared in rapid succession, both in the year 1805. Their publisher was John Harding, of 36 St. James' Street, London, who specialized in "books on agriculture and rural affairs," handling numerous practical works and also the *Communications to the Board of Agriculture* (though later, in 1807, after the board had been forced to set up in its own premises at 32 Sackville Street, nearby, these publications were sold instead by Phillips, who, by the end of 1810, was bankrupt). Harding also sold the works on rural architecture of Barber, John Crunden, Richard Elsam, Laing, Lugar, James Malton, Middleton, Miller, Plaw, Richard Pococke, Soane, and Wood.

The forty-three plates of the *Designs for Cottages* were aquatints, with backgrounds sketched in behind the elevations, as first introduced in works of this kind by Plaw. Nine of the plates were by J. W. Harding and twenty-five by C. Rosenberg; thirty-four are dated to March 1805. Gandy's preface is dated January 1805, but he must already have begun preparation of *The Rural Architect*, for its publication was announced for the following 10 May—though this was to prove optimistic.
R. M.

Bibliography

Lukacher, B. and D. Hill. *Joseph Michael Gandy (1771–1843)*. London, 1982

Mitchison, R. "The Old Board of Agriculture (1793–1822)." *TheEnglish Historical Review* 74 (1959): 41–69

Robinson, J. M. *Georgian Model Farms. A Study of Decorative and Model Farm Buildings in the Age of Improvement, 700–1846*. Oxford, 1983

Summerson, J. "The Vision of J. M. Gandy." In *Heavenly Mansions*. London, 1949: 111–134

Joseph Gandy. *Designs for Cottages*. Plate XXVII. "This Picturesque Building...." 1985.61.580

21

Joseph Michael Gandy (1771–1843)

The Rural Architect; Consisting Of Various Designs For Country Buildings, Accompanied With Ground Plans, Estimates, And Descriptions. By Joseph Gandy, Architect, A. R. A. . . .

London: printed for John Harding, 1805

1985.61.581

Quarto: 310 × 238 (12 ⅛ × 9 $^{5}/_{16}$)

Pagination [iv], 27, [1] pp., 42 aquatint plates

Edition First edition

Text pp. [i] title page; [ii] imprint "Printed by B. M^c^Millan, Bow Street, Covent Garden"; [iii] author's note, "Advertisement" (verso blank); [1]–27 explanation of the plates; [28] advertisement for the author's *Designs for Cottages*

Illustrations 42 aquatint plates, with etching, printed in umber and numbered I–XLII upper right. Nearly all of the plates are signed by Gandy as architect, engraved by J. W. Harding, Charles Rosenberg, or Samuel Alken

Binding Contemporary half red morocco, gilt with glazed paper boards, large ornamental paper roundel pasted on upper cover "Gandy's Rural Architect"

Provenance Ownership inscription on title page "Hugh Stuart Carlow"; bookplate of A. De Kluijs, and stamp on flyleaf "Boekeru A. P. M. de Kluijs Tilburg"

References Berlin Cat. 2315; Berlin (1977) OS 2315[d]; RIBA, *Early Printed Books*, 1172

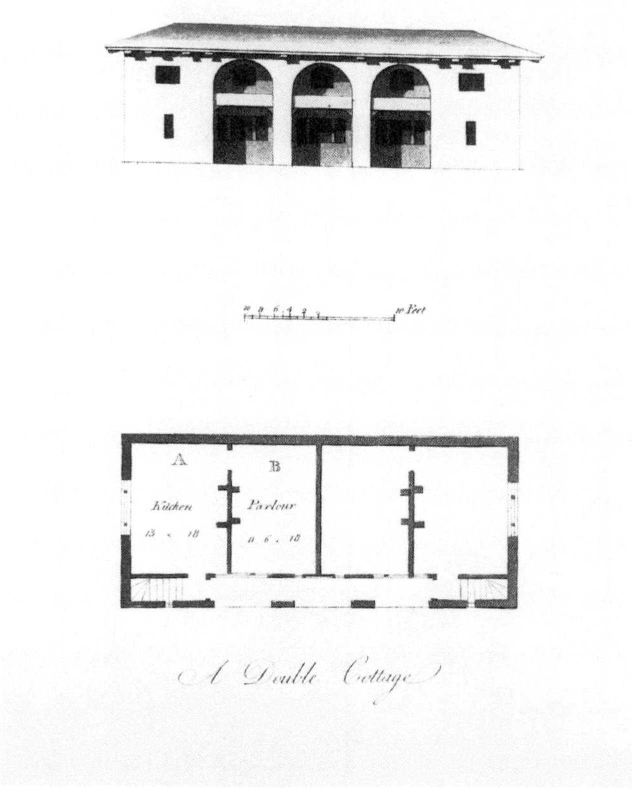

Joseph Gandy. *The Rural Architect.* Plate XII. "A double cottage." 1985.61.581

GANDY'S SECOND BOOK of designs for rural buildings stemmed from much the same concerns that inspired his first work, the *Designs for Cottages*, though he refers in this instance to William Marshall's *Treatise on the Purchase, Improvement, and Management of Landed Property*, rather than to the communications of the Board of Agriculture. Both works were prepared for the bookseller John Harding, and both were issued in the same year. Announced for May 1805, the second book cannot have been issued before the end of the year, as Gandy's short "advertisement" is dated August 1805. He offers no further introduction to the subject, only the terse note "The author, encouraged by the success which has attended his first Essay on Cottage Architecture, submits with more confidence the present Volume to Public Patronage."

The designs were much as before, though with less sharp emphasis on the laborer's cottage. A "picturesque dwelling" for a retired naval officer is illustrated, as is a small villa. There are three inns in this volume, as opposed to one in the first. The village or "rural institute" illustrated on two plates (nos. 35 and 36) has long, arcaded runs of buildings, reminiscent both of the designs of Claude-Nicolas Ledoux and the architecture of the *campagna* that Gandy must have seen during his years in Italy. One of his designs is, in fact, referred to as a dwelling "after the Italian manner" (pl. 33).

The aquatint plates, one less than previously, with landscapes sketched in around the elevations as before, were for the most part again prepared by J. W. Harding (twelve) and C. Rosenberg (eighteen). S. Alken was responsible for eight. The plates are all dated, mostly March and July 1805, indicating that work was in hand on both books at the same time.

Whatever twentieth-century opinion of Gandy's idiosyncratic designs, they were not much appreciated by contemporary reviewers. The *Annual Review and History of Literature for 1805* began the attack: "Cottage architecture, if it may be so called, is a subject in itself trivial and ungrateful, and has been exhausted by innumerable publications," and then continued, specifically,

> In a wild pursuit of novelty, he has adopted a style of frigid extravagance, disregarding the requisites of climate, manners, and convenience, and with a singular dereliction, or rather inversion, of usual proportions. Till very lately the designers of the smaller buildings of this country, villas, cottages, &c. considered uniformity as the first essential of architectural beauty; but at present what is called the picturesque style, that enemy of regularity and symmetry, is gaining ground. Now it is acknowledged on all hands, that the best examples in this

manner are the fortuitous result of circumstances, that have no connexion with the design of pleasing.

The picturesque architect, the critic concluded, might thus explore internal convenience unfettered, but even this, he thought, Gandy had neglected. "Full little would the farmer or labourer praise the taste that should lodge him in these picturesque hovels" (1806, 4: 891). R. M.

Bibliography

Lukacher, B. and D. Hill. *Joseph Michael Gandy (1771–1843)*. London, 1982

Summerson, J. "The Vision of J. M. Gandy." In *Heavenly Mansions*. London, 1949: 111–134

Joseph Gandy. *The Rural Architect.* Plate XXXII. "A picturesque dwelling." 1985.61.581

22

James Gibbs (1682–1754)

A Book Of Architecture, Containing Designs Of Buildings And Ornaments. By James Gibbs

London, 1728

1985.61.582

Folio: 540 × 367 (21 1/8 × 14 1/2)

Pagination [4], 28 pp., 150 engraved plates (4 double-page)

Edition First edition

Text pp. [1] title page (verso blank); [3–4] dedication; i–iii introduction; iv–xxv description of the plates; xxvi–xxviii list of subscribers

Illustrations 150 engraved plates (pls. 1, 7, 26, 111 double-page), all signed by Gibbs as architect or designer/draftsman. Credited engravers are Elisha Kirkall, Henry Hulsbergh, John Harris (senior), J. Mynde, George Vertue, and Bernard Baron

Binding Contemporary marbled boards, spine and corners renewed. Uncut

Provenance Engraved armorial bookplate with interlaced initials "AA"; ownership inscription of Reginald W. Cooper on flyleaf

References Berlin Cat. 2270; Berlin (1977) OS 2270; ESTC t22978; Fowler 138; Harris and Savage 257; RIBA, *Early Printed Books,* 1206

James Gibbs was born in the far north of Scotland, at Fittysmire in Aberdeen, on 23 December 1682. His father was a local merchant, his mother "a gentlewoman of a good family." Both died while he was young. Just before his eighteenth birthday he moved to Holland, where he had relatives, perhaps to study with a local architect. But before long he moved to Rome, where on 12 October 1703 he registered as a student at the Scots College. Though a Roman Catholic, he was unwilling to commit himself to the priesthood. A year later he began to study architecture under Carlo Fontana, no doubt at the Accademia di San Luca. He was thus the first British architect to be trained abroad. By November 1708 he was back in Britain, intent on establishing a career in London. This was by no means easy. But he had met John Erskine, 6th earl of Mar (of the creation of 1565), one of the secretaries of state for Scotland, who, in the following year offered him a post at Stirling Castle, a sinecure that was to provide him with a basic income, and soon after commissioned him to remodel his house in Whitehall. At this period Gibbs prepared designs for a neat, Italianate lodge for the earl's estate at Alloa, in Clackmanshire, near Stirling, and, for the earl's father-in-law, Thomas Hay, 6th earl of Kinnoull, an even more enterprising, altogether unexpected project for Dupplin Castle, in Perthshire, the plan in the form of St. Andrew's cross, inspired perhaps by Germain Boffrand's second design for the Château of Malgrange, of 1711. Neither of these was built, but engravings were made of both, the basis, perhaps, of Gibbs' first attempts to publicize himself. In 1713 Gibbs wrote to Robert Harley, earl of Oxford, lord high treasurer, father of Thomas Hay's son's wife, Abigail:

> I would willingly be doing something to establish my reputation here, by showing the world by demonstration that I know something of what I pretend I have learned while I was abroad, and by making this as advantageous as I can, till such a time as your Lordship shall think fit to provide for me. In order to [do] this I have a mind to publish a book of architecture, which indeed is a science that everybody criticises here, and in all the countries that ever I was in, never did I see worse performers. Be that as it will, this is my design, which I think to go about this summer if your Lordship will encourage me by accepting the dedication, and being at the expense of the plates, for I am so far from being able to pay the charge myself, that I am fifty pounds in debt. . . .

Nothing more is known of this scheme. With the firm support of Mar and Harley, Gibbs was appointed one of the surveyors to the Commissioners for Building Fifty New Churches on 18 November 1713, and his official career was initiated with the design and construction of St. Mary-le-Strand in London. This venture was almost brought to an abrupt halt with the death, in August 1714, of Queen Anne, followed by the Hanoverian succession and the defeat of the Tory government by the Whigs. Harley and Mar were stripped of their posts; Harley was sent to the Tower. By the summer of 1715 Mar was marching south with a Jacobite army, to be defeated in November by the troops of John Campbell, 2d duke of Argyll and Greenwich. Mar fled to exile on the Continent, from where he wrote secretly to Gibbs, inviting him to join him. But Gibbs, even before the Jacobite rising, had started to build a precocious, Palladian-inspired villa, Sudbrook House, at Petersham, Surrey, for the duke of Argyll, to whom he was to dedicate *A Book of Architecture.* In December 1715, after the replacement of Tories by Whigs on the church commission, Gibbs was deprived of his surveyorship. He petitioned, however, to be allowed to continue as architect to St. Mary-le-Strand, a request that was granted. The church was consecrated on 1 January 1724, the first of Gibbs' major works that served to publicize his abilities. Already, however, in September 1720, the vestry had selected his design for the new St. Martin-in-the-Fields, nearby, the most celebrated and the most often imitated of all his buildings. Construction was started two years later, to be completed at the end of 1726. Gibbs was then forty-three. Though his churches were at once criticized—St. Mary-le-Strand for the profusion of ornament both inside and out, St. Martin-in-the-Fields for the manner in which the steeple rode astride the classical pediment—he was even earlier esteemed one of the leading architects in the country, along with Christopher Wren, John Vanbrugh, Nicholas Hawksmoor, and Thomas Archer. He was not, however, to be ranked among the Palladians.

Colen Campbell, a fellow Scot, opposed him from the start. Indeed, Gibbs' loss of his surveyorship is thought to have been in part owing to a letter he sent to the church commissioners denouncing Gibbs as a papist. Gibbs denied this charge in a letter to the commissioners of 13 January 1716, though he was to remain a practicing Catholic to the end of his life. Campbell failed to win Gibbs' surveyorship, just as he failed to win the commission for the duke of Argyll's villa, a design for which he included in the first volume of *Vitruvius Britannicus*, published in 1715. In the introduction to this work he condemned the modern Italian taste, the "affected and licentious" works of Bernini and Carlo Fontana, and the "wildly extravagant" designs of Borromini, "who has endeavoured to debauch mankind with his odd and chimerical beauties, where the parts are without proportion, solids without their true bearing, heaps of materials without strength, excessive ornaments without grace, and the whole without symmetry." And though his spleen was probably directed in part at Giacomo Leoni, who was at just that moment making a bid as arbiter of the new Palladian taste, with the publication of the first complete edition in English of Palladio's *I Quattro Libri dell'architettura,* his rivalry with Gibbs was even more to the fore. Gibbs' designs for Burlington House in Piccadilly (1715–1716), Witham Friary in Somerset, and Lowther Hall in Westmorland, both of about 1717, were included in the subsequent volumes of *Vitruvius Britannicus*, but without acknowledgment (2: 22, 78, 79, 80, 91, 92; 3: 76). Gibbs was to be excluded from the Palladian rule of taste, though as is evident, soon after his return from his Grand Tour, in May 1715, Richard Boyle, 3d earl of Burlington, had turned to Gibbs to remodel his great London mansion, notably by building sweeping curved colonnades to form a forecourt. These were of French rather than Italian inspiration. But Colen Campbell was to supplant him soon enough, in 1717, and though Gibbs might, a year or two later, have been responsible for a pavilion in Burlington's garden at Chiswick, his architecture was too fantastical in its decoration for evolving Palladian tastes.

James Gibbs. *A Book of Architecture, Containing Designs of Buildings.* Plate 1. "A perspective view of St. Martins church." 1985.61.582

By February 1725 the third volume of *Vitruvius Britannicus* was published, with no mention of Gibbs. In the same year notice was given of the forthcoming publication of *The Designs of Inigo Jones,* issued eventually in May 1727. The drawings had been edited by William Kent and prepared for engraving by Henry Flitcroft, all under the aegis of Burlington. Burlington had already installed them in positions of authority; in May 1726 Kent was appointed to the Board of Works as master carpenter, though he had no knowledge of building, and Flitcroft enrolled as clerk of works at Whitehall, Westminster, and St. James'. Gibbs, himself a subscriber to *The Designs of Inigo Jones*, must have been all too aware of the new structure of taste. On 15 March 1727 he issued his "Proposals for printing by subscription, plans, uprights, sections and perspectives of buildings . . ." and he continued to list the churches, university buildings, garden pavilions, ornamental details, monuments, etc., for which he had been responsible. The book was to consist entirely of his own designs. The text was to be in English and French. There were to be 140 plates, some of which were already engraved, to be viewed at Gibbs' own house in Henrietta Street, Marylebone, or four London booksellers, one of whom, Woodman and Lyon, was the publisher of *The Designs of Inigo Jones*. Gibbs' book, *Designs of Buildings and Ornaments*, was to cost four guineas, half to be paid on subscription, and was to be published by Michaelmas 1727. Similar advertisements appeared in the *Daily Post* for 31 March 1727 and in the *Monthly Catalogue* for April 1727, when ninety plates, it was claimed, had already been engraved. But on 1 May 1727, two weeks before the final delivery of *The Designs of Inigo Jones*, Gibbs issued a greatly revised proposal. The text was no longer to be in French, his designs for Shipbourne church and the chapel at Cannons were not to be included, the number of plates, however, was to be increased to 150, at no extra cost, and were now to survey as well the country houses and villas he had designed. The whole was not to be ready before Christmas. On 31 May Gibbs placed the first of a series of advertisements for subscribers in the *Daily Post*. He attracted 481 in all, 100 more than Kent. There were no members of the royal family and fewer members of the nobility than might have been expected, but there was a string of dukes and titled men, many of great influence, and a surprising number of fellow artists and architects—including William Adam, Archer, Charles Bridgeman, James Essex, Flitcroft, Hawksmoor, Kent, Roger Morris, Michael Rysbrack, George Sampson, James Thornhill, George Vertue, and the younger Christopher Wren—together with many of the craftsmen who had been employed on Gibbs' buildings. On 22 March 1728 Gibbs announced in the *Daily Post* that the plates were finished and were being printed; on 9 May copies were ready for subscribers and available for collection at his house in Henrietta Street, between seven and eleven in the morning or four and seven in the afternoon.

This was the first book to be published in Britain devoted to the designs of a single architect, just preceding Leoni's *Designs for Buildings Publick and Private*, announced in 1726, but not published until 1730, and then as a supplement to his translation of Alberti. The type, which was to become common in the second half of the century, was already familiar in France, though Gibbs' source of inspiration was no doubt Palladio's *I Quattro libri dell'architettura*, a book he greatly admired and by which he was much influenced (whatever English Palladians might think).

Gibbs was clearly concerned to promote his own work, but he was also offering his designs for imitation, as he explained in his introduction, hoping that the book

> would be of use to such gentlemen as might be concerned in building, especially in the remote parts of the country, when little or no assistance for designs can be procured. Such may be here furnished with draughts of useful and convenient buildings and proper ornaments; which may be executed by any workman who understands lines, whether as here design'd, or with some alteration, which may be easily made by a person of judgment; without which a variation in draughts, once well digested, frequently proves a detriment to the building, as well as a disparagement to the person that gives them. I mention this to caution gentlemen from suffering any material change to be made in their designs, by the forwardness of unskillful workmen, or the caprice of ignorant, assuming pretenders.

But though he set himself up as a model, he was intent to reveal the source and the strength of his own inspiration. "I have taken the utmost care that these designs should be done in the best taste I could form upon the instructions of the greatest masters in Italy, as well as my own observations upon the antient buildings there, during many years application to these studies: for a cursory view of those august remains can no more qualify the spectator, or admirer, than the air of the country can inspire him with a knowledge of architecture"—a thrust at all those arbiters of taste who lacked his training in Rome.

A Book of Architecture begins, not altogether surprisingly, with a series of fifteen plates of the most attractive and prominent of all Gibbs' buildings, St. Martin-in-the-Fields, of 1720 to 1726, including two variants of the initial design for the church as a domed rotunda. This is followed by eight plates of St. Mary-le-Strand, of 1714 to 1724, including an early design for a more broadly proportioned project for the church. Next are two plates of the proprietary chapel commissioned in 1721 by Edward Harley, 2d earl of Oxford (son of Gibbs' earlier patron, Robert Harley) for Marylebone (now St. Peter, Vere Street, London), followed by two plates of All Saints, Derby, of 1723 to 1726, where the existing perpendicular tower was retained; then a single plate of the steeple Gibbs designed in 1719 to complete Wren's St. Clement Danes. The ecclesiastical section is finished off with three plates illustrating eleven designs for steeples, six prepared in connection with St. Martin-in-the-Fields, five for St. Mary-le-Strand. "Steeples," Gibbs noted, "are indeed of Gothick extraction; but they have their beauties."

Five plates are devoted to Gibbs' buildings for Cambridge, the University Building, the first draft of which dates from 1721, only a part of which, the Senate House, was to be built; and an even grander design for King's College, only the Fellows Buildings for which was erected, between 1724 and 1731.

Thirty plates, not envisaged in the first proposals, are given over to designs for villas and country houses. Though Gibbs had prepared ambitious plans for Cannon's House, Kedleston Hall, Lowther Hall, Wimpole Hall, and Witham Park by this date, these were not illustrated. Many of the designs were no more than projects intended to demonstrate his abilities. But more than half can be identified: plate 39, Ditchley House, Oxfordshire, probably designed in 1720, for George Henry Lee, 2d earl of Lichfield, the most important of Gibbs' early country houses; plate 40, an updated version of Sudbrook House, Petersham, Surrey, begun in 1715, for the duke of Argyll, Gibbs' first villa; plate 41, the second design for Kirkleatham Hall, Cleveland, for Cholmondley Turner, probably dating from 1728, for which Gibbs employed the motif of a giant temple portico for the central portion of the facade, a motif first introduced as such about ten years earlier by Colen Campbell. This was not built. Plates 46 and 47, Park Terrace, Greenwich, designed in 1720 for Sir Gregory Page, but abandoned in the panic caused by the collapse of the South Sea Company; plates 48, 49, 50, and 51, two versions of the design for Milton House, Northamptonshire, prepared in 1726 for the 2d earl of Fitzwilliam, given up when the earl died in 1728; plates 52 and 53, Sacombe Park, Hertfordshire, the first of Gibbs' temple fronted houses, dating from June 1719, for

Edward Rolt, who died in December 1722, before building was begun; plate 55, Down Hall, Essex, commissioned in 1720 by Matthew Prior, but abandoned on his death the following year; plate 57, Anthony House, Cornwall, for Sir William Carew, probably of 1720, with proposals for remodeling the house newly built by John Moyle; plates 59, 60, 61, and 62, three variants of a villa for Whitton Place, Middlesex, for Archibald Campbell, earl of Ilay, the duke of Argyll's younger brother, dating from 1725 to 1728. Colen Campbell had tried earlier to attract the earl's attention with a design of his own, included in the first volume of *Vitruvius Britannicus*. The earl eventually chose Roger Morris as his architect.

Gibbs' designs for villas and country houses are all strongly influenced by the works of Palladio, Vincenzo Scamozzi, and Giacoma da Vignola, and he was at pains to indicate his early contribution to this new fashion; three of the plates, 43, 44, and 54, are specifically dated to 1720. But though the basic form and organization of Gibbs' houses was of Italian inspiration, he had particular concerns of his own that marks their difference. He took up the Italian and French manner of composing plans with apartments, usually of three rooms, an anteroom, a chamber, and a closet, which he set for the most part at the four corners of the houses, the major public rooms in between—a chapel, a library or billiard room on the flanks, the entrance hall, the saloon or dining room on the main cross axis. The placing of the dining room, often the largest of the rooms, in the center of the garden front is a particularly English usage. In France the dining room was either separated from the main sequence of spaces or set up in one of the anterooms. Another current concern that distinguishes Gibbs is the thoughtful introduction of corridors and service stairs, thus relieving the main rooms of through traffic. Gibbs was particularly pleased with his achievements in this respect; of the most overtly Italian of his adaptations—plate 44, a foursquare villa, an octagonal hall in the center—he notes: "The Octagon Room may be private or publick at pleasure, because of the passages of Communication betwixt the Hall and Withdrawing-room. The Bedchambers over this Floor are also render'd very convenient by Passages, which are lighted by round Openings in the Freeze of the great Room."

Plates 67 to 84 illustrate garden buildings and pavilions, thirty-six in all, most of which are offered as exercises in design, though some were commissioned: plates 68 and 69 for Down Hall, Essex, for Edward Harley, who inherited the property after Matthew Prior's death; plate 70 for Lord Curzon at Kedleston Hall, of 1726; plate 71, James Johnston's celebrated octagon at Twickenham, of 1720; plates 72 and 73, pavilions for Charles Pawlett, 3d duke of Bolton, at Hackwood Park, Hampshire, of about 1728; plate 76, the great Boycot pavilions at Stowe, Buckinghamshire, of about 1727, shown with the original obelisk-shaped roofs, inspired by Johann Fischer von Erlach's reconstruction of the pyramid of

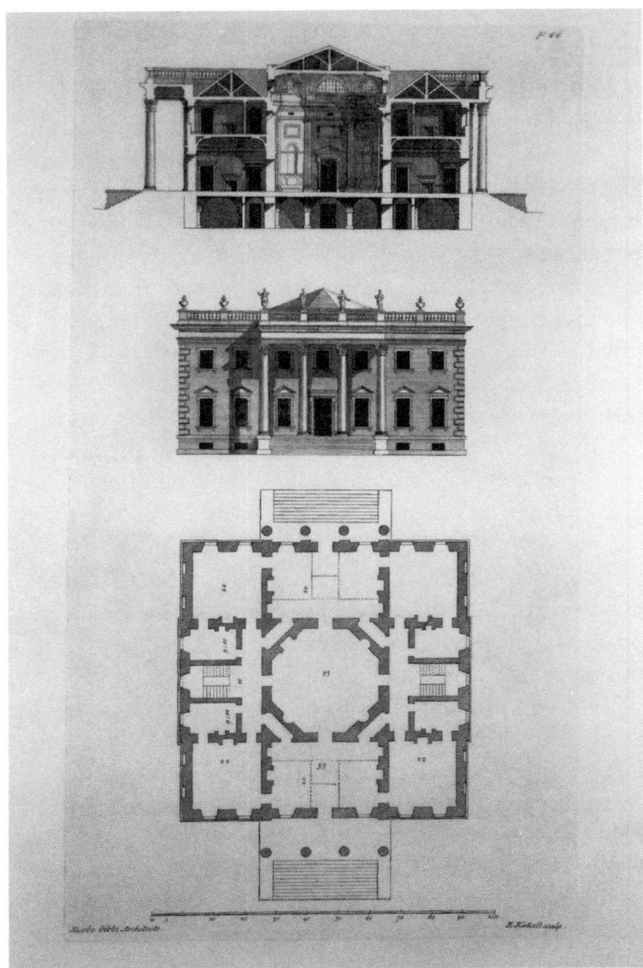

James Gibbs. *A Book of Architecture, Containing Designs of Buildings.* Plate 44. "The plan, Front and Section of a House made for a Gentleman...." 1985.61.582

Sostis of Heliopolis, replaced by domes in 1758; plates 79, 80, 81, and 82, for William Gore at Tring Park in Hertfordshire, from 1724 onward; plate 83 for Lord Burlington, perhaps, of Chiswick, around 1719.

The remaining sixty-six plates are devoted to separate architectural details or ornamental features—columns and obelisks, gateways, chimneypieces (forty-four designs), doorcases (twenty-four designs, some surprisingly, with the Borrominesque scrolls, sometimes designated as "ears," which are a common feature of Gibbs' interiors, but which one would not have expected him to publicize thus blatantly), window surrounds (eleven), niches (nine), church monuments (twenty-nine), cartouches (thirty-three), sarcophagi (sixteen), vases (fifty-seven), cisterns (eight), assorted pedestals and sundials (forty-seven in all).

The most notable of all these features were the church monuments, which Gibbs was to take up as a particular specialty. Though architects habitually designed tombs in Italy, the usual practice in England was to commission them from sculptors and master masons. However, beginning with the most ostentatious of all his monuments, for John Holles, 1st duke of Newcastle, erected in Westminster Abbey between 1721 and 1723, Gibbs made the form his own (pl. 111). There were to be eleven monuments designed for Westminster Abbey (pls. 115, 116, 120, 122), including three in Poet's Corner to John Dryden, Ben Johnson (pl. 124) and Matthew Prior (pl. 112). There were ambitious ones elsewhere, such as the memorial to the Cavendish family in St. Mary's, Bolsover, Derbyshire of 1727 (pl. 114); to Edward Colston in All Saints, Bristol, Avon, of 1728 (pl. 113); and others (pl. 121). Gibbs' success was in part owing to the fact that he had spotted and taken up Rysbrack, the sculptor, in 1720, soon after his arrival from Antwerp. Together they dominated the field for some years, though when Gibbs' great patron, the duke of Newcastle, died in 1743, his monument was to be commissioned from Louis François Roubiliac. Gibbs had made no great efforts after 1730.

The sheer number and variety of buildings and ornamental forms provided by Gibbs clearly appealed to amateur architects and craftsmen. His thirty-three cartouches were engraved in reduced format and issued independently in 1731 by John Clark, though he did credit Gibbs. Batty Langley simply plagiarized his designs for *The City and Country Builder's and Workman's Treasury of Designs*, first issued in 1740. Others followed suit.

The influence of *A Book of Architecture* was enormous. St. Martin-in-the-Fields served as a model for church-building throughout the English-speaking world, and in particular in the American colonies, where architects such as Peter Harrison drew heavily from his example. Thomas McBean and James Crommelin Laurence's St. Paul's Chapel, New York, of 1763 to 1794, is an obvious adaptation of St. Martin-in-the-Fields, as is Asher Benjamin and Ithiel Town's First Congregational Church, New Haven, Connecticut, of 1812. Even the rotunda design for the church was taken up, first, in 1771, in a project for St. Marlyebone parish by William Chambers, then by Andrew Frazer and William Sibbald for St. Andrew's, Edinburgh, of 1781 to 1787, for David Stephenson's All Saints, Newcastle-upon-Tyne, of 1786 to 1789, for George Steuart's St. Chad's, Shrewsbury, of 1790 to 1792, for S. P. Cockerell's church at Banbury of 1792 to 1797, and, in a particularly pure form, for Thomas De Havilland's St. Andrew's in Madras, India, of 1818 to 1820. The extraordinarily diverse and numerous borrowings from Gibbs through the eighteenth and nineteenth centuries, including those of Thomas Jefferson for Monticello, are carefully surveyed by Terry Friedman in *James Gibbs*, of 1984. They cannot be further considered here.

Most of Gibbs' plates, the drawings for which survive among the collections he bequeathed to the Ashmolean Museum in Oxford, were engraved by Elisha Kirkall and Hendrick Hulsberg (Henry Hulsburgh). Hulsberg, who had come to England from Holland, was one of the more accomplished engravers active in England in the early years of the century. He was responsible for most of the plates of *Vitruvius Britannicus* and *The Designs of Inigo Jones*. The plates he prepared for Gibbs must have been among his last works, for Vertue records that he was paralyzed, incapable of work for two years before his death in May 1729.

At least eight of the plates were prepared and issued independently and only later incorporated into *A Book of Architecture*: plate 1, a perspective of St. Martin-in-the-Fields, engraved by Hulsberg; plate 21, a perspective of St. Mary-le-Strand, of 1714, by Harris; plate 26, a plan and side elevation of All Saints, Derby, for which Hulsberg was paid £ 12–17–8 in 1723 for the copper-plates and three hundred pulls; plates 32 and 33, issued in 1724 to raise money for the building of King's College, Cambridge, engraved by Hulsberg; plate 36, the plan and perspective of Gibbs' final design for the Public Buildings at Cambridge engraved by Hulsberg, who had also engraved the first design, being paid eight guineas for his work on 2 July 1722, and in April of the following year had also engraved Gibbs' second project, though neither of these last two plates was to be included in *A Book of Architecture*; plate 111, the vast monument to the duke of Newcastle in Westminster Abbey, commissioned from Gibbs by his daughter, Henrietta, wife of Edward Harley, 2d earl of Oxford, engraved by Vertue in 1725; plate 112, the monument to Harley's protégé, Prior, probably of 1712, engraved by B. Baron. These independently commissioned plates are the finest in the book.

The plates for the book were sold by Gibbs to the publishers Innys and Manby, J. and P. Knapton, and C. Hitch, for four hundred pounds according to Vertue (who was told also by Gibbs that he had made fifteen hundred pounds, in addition, out of his books), and a second edition was issued by them in 1738, on subscription, for three guineas, one less than before. The book was completed in 1739. No subscription list was included in this edition. R. M.

Bibliography

Friedman, T. *James Gibbs*. New Haven and London, 1984

Harris, E., and N. Savage. *British Architectural Books and Writers 1556–1785*. Cambridge, 1990

Hudson, T. P. "James Gibbs's Designs for University Buildings at Cambridge." *Burlington Magazine* (December 1972): 842–848

23

James Gibbs (1682–1754)

Rules For Drawing The Several Parts of Architecture, In A More exact and easy manner than has been heretofore practised, by which all Fractions, in dividing the principal Members and their Parts, are avoided. By James Gibbs

London: printed by W. Bowyer for the author, 1732

NGA Lib. Rare Book: N44G4433A5 fol.

Folio: 466 × 281 (18 ¼ × 11 1/16)

Pagination [viii], 42 pp., 44 engraved plates

Edition First edition

Text pp. [i] blank; [ii] privilege, dated 19 May 1732; [iii] title page (verso blank); [v–vi] dedication; [vii–viii] table of contents; 1–2 note to the reader; 3–42 text, including explanation of the plates

Illustrations Sixty-four numbered engraved plates, all unsigned

Binding Contemporary mottled calf, rebacked. Large paper copy

Provenance Ownership inscription "Hen^y: Joynes Novr. 1732" on front pastedown; engraved armorial bookplate of his son, Samuel Joynes. Henry Joynes (c. 1684–1754) was Sir John Vanbrugh's clerk of the works at Blenheim Palace, 1705–1715, and held the same position at Kensington Palace thereafter

References Berlin (1977) OS 2272^d (2nd ed.); ESTC t46960; Harris and Savage 259; RIBA, *Early Printed Books,* 1207

HAVING PUBLICIZED his works in *A Book of Architecture*, Gibbs attempted a practical handbook for architects and craftsmen in his second book, *Rules for Drawing the Several Parts of Architecture*. This was issued in 1732, the privilege being dated 19 May. It was dedicated to Edward Harley, 2d earl of Oxford, son of one of Gibbs' first patrons.

The book appears as a conventional work on the five orders and their related features, but is in fact quite exceptional. "I thought," Gibbs wrote in his introduction, "there might be a method found out so to divide the principle Members and their Parts, both as to their heights and Projections, as to avoid Fractions."

Early commentators had determined to simplify the method of setting up the orders by employing a module—Hans Blum's *Quinque columnarum exacta descriptio atque delineatio* was printed first in Zurich in 1550, the first of many English editions, *The Booke of Five Collumnes of Architecture* appearing in 1601; *L'architecture de Julien Mauclerc* was issued in La Rochelle in 1600, the expanded English version, *A New Treatise of Architecture*, appearing in 1660; while Claude Perrault's *Ordonnance des cinq espèces de colonnes*, of 1683, was issued in English as *A Treatise of the Five Orders of Columns in Architecture*, first in 1708, again in 1722. In each of these books the practicalities of translating the proportions of the orders into timber and stone were greatly simplified through the use of a module. But though Gibbs might have been spurred by their example, his method was simpler yet, and quite different. He demonstrated that the proportions upheld by Palladio might be obtained—more or less—by "dividing the Orders mechanically into equal parts." He did not avoid the fraction entirely, but he did do away altogether with minutes. His method, moreover, had the great advantage that, given a particular height, one might determine the correct proportion for any of the orders.

Whatever the order, the height was to be divided into five parts, one of these parts serving as the pedestal. The remaining four parts were to be divided, in turn, into five parts for the Tuscan and Doric, and into six parts for the Ionic, Corinthian, and Composite orders. One of these parts served as the entablature, the remaining parts formed the column, including its capital and base. The column was, in turn, to be divided into parts—seven for the Tuscan, eight for the Doric, nine for the Ionic, ten for the Corinthian and Composite—and one of these parts was to serve as the diameter. All subdivisions, projections, and moldings were determined in a like manner. The diameter itself was used only to provide the proportions of arches, doors, and openings.

More than half the plates were devoted to the orders, intercolumnations and superimpositions, with and without arches; the remainder of the plates describe door cases and surrounds, niches, window surrounds—including a venetian window—cornices and brackets, chimneypieces, moldings, domes and ceiling coffers, balustrades and balconies. There is a single plate (LIV) illustrating general proportions for rooms, including those for a one hundred-foot gallery, a form Gibbs had used more than once in *A Book of Architecture*. The drawings for the plates are in the Gibbs Collection at the Ashmolean Museum, Oxford. All plates are unsigned.

The very real advantages of Gibbs' method were at once recognized and taken up by Batty Langley in *Ancient Masonry*, of 1733 to 1734, and Edward Hoppus in the *Gentleman and Builder's Repository* of 1737. There were other adaptations. Gibbs' publisher, W. Bowyer, issued a second edition in 1736, with a vignette by Bernard Baron, a portrait of Gibbs, on the title page, that served also as Gibbs' bookplate. Soon after Gibbs sold the plates for both *A Book of Architecture* and *Rules for Drawing the Several Parts of Architecture* for £400—according to George Vertue—to a group of book publishers, A. Bettesworth and C. Hitch, W. Innes and R. Manby, and J. and P. Knapton, who issued a second edition in twenty-one weekly parts, at a shilling each, from 27 May to 21 October 1738. A slightly altered consortium issued a third edition in 1753. In the following year Thomas Chippendale brazenly adapted Gibbs' illustrations for the eight plates on the orders that he included in the *Gentleman and Cabinet-Makers Director*. He copied Gibbs' text too, but he reverted to modules and minutes, all the same.

Gibbs' book seems to have been widely used, in particular by workmen, until well into the nineteenth century. In America it was especially popular. John Singleton Copley owned a copy, as did Thomas Jefferson; it was first advertised, in a Philadelphia bookseller's catalogue, in 1754, and parts were copied in 1786 in *The Town and Country Builder's Assistant*, published in Boston by J. Norman, and in the *Articles of the Carpenters Company of Philadelphia*. R. M.

Bibliography

Friedman, T. *James Gibbs*. New Haven and London, 1984

Harris, E., and N. Savage. *British Architectural Books and Writers 1556–1785*. Cambridge, 1990

James Gibbs. *Rules for Drawing the Several Parts of Architecture.* Plate LIV. NGA Lib. Rare Book: N44G4433A5 fol.

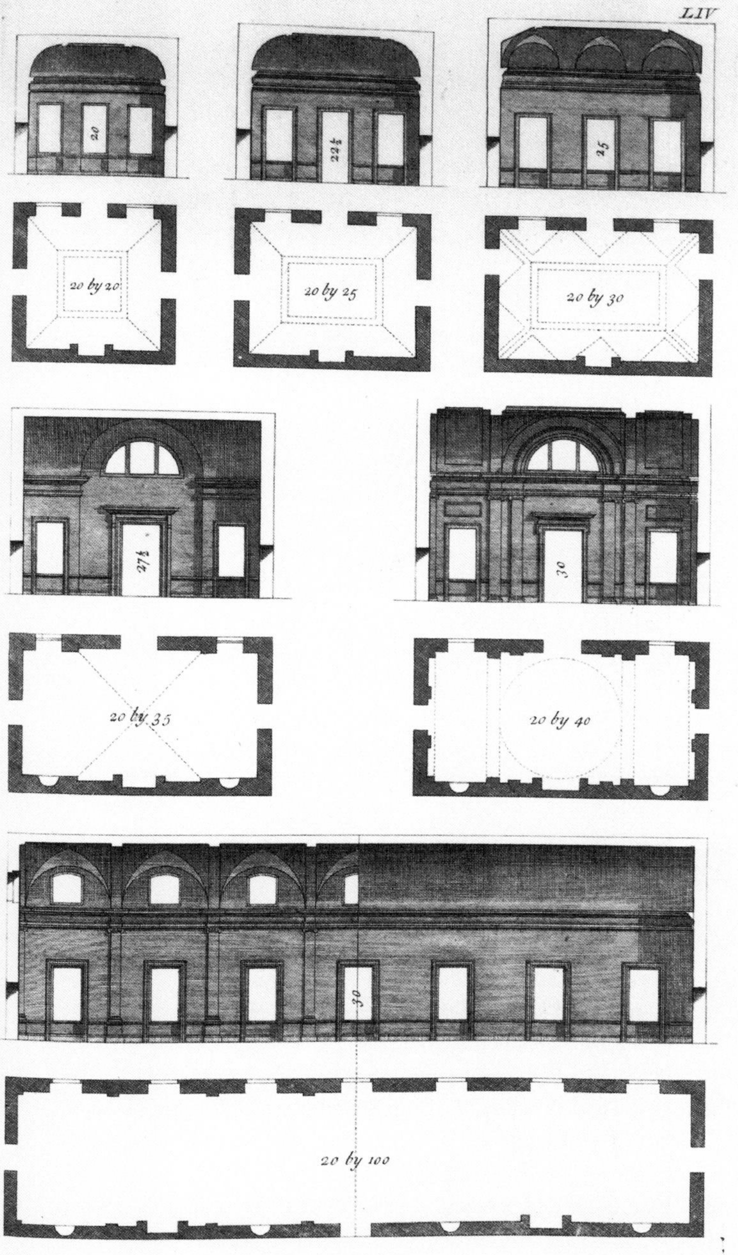

24

James Gibbs (1682–1754)

Bibliotheca Radcliviana: Or, A Short Description Of The Radcliffe Library, At Oxford. Containing Its Several Plans, Uprights, Sections, and Ornaments, On Twenty three Copper Plates, neatly engraved, With the Explanation of each Plate. By James Gibbs, Architect . . .

London: printed for the author, 1747

1985.61.583

Folio: 41 × 252 (16 1/8 × 9 7/8)

Pagination 12 pp., [2] engraved portraits, 21 engraved plates

Edition First edition

Text pp. [1] title page (verso blank); [3]–4 dedication to the Trustees of the Radcliffe Library; 5–6 preface; 7–12 description of the plates

Illustrations Frontispiece portrait of Gibbs engraved by Bernard Baron after William Hogarth; portrait of John Radcliffe engraved by P. Fourdrinier after Godfrey Kneller; and 21 plates, all signed by P. Fourdrinier after Gibbs

Binding Nineteenth-century half calf, rebacked

Provenance Engraved armorial bookplate of Audenham House, Hertfordshire, loosely inserted

References Berlin Cat. 2334; Berlin (1977) OS 2334; ESTC t21607; Fowler 139; Harris and Savage 256; RIBA, *Early Printed Books*, 1205

AT BOTH Cambridge and Oxford, Gibbs succeeded Nicholas Hawksmoor as architect, and was spurred to design the noblest of all his buildings. His designs for King's College and the University Building at Cambridge were published in *A Book of Architecture* in 1728, though the Fellows Building for King's, and the Senate House—the only part to be built—were yet unfinished. The Radcliffe Library in Oxford was a more protracted affair, and Gibbs took control there only after Hawksmoor's death in March 1736. By this stage Gibbs had already submitted four proposals to the Radcliffe Trustees, three variants for a rectangular library, not unlike Wren's Trinity College library in Cambridge, in 1720, and, in May 1735, a variant of the concept on which Hawksmoor had long been engaged, a great domed rotunda. By 1737 he had produced yet another variant of the rotunda design, articulated with pilasters rather than engaged columns. The estimate for the building with pilasters was cheaper. In May 1737 the trustees ordered five plates illustrating this scheme, engraved by George Vertue, to be distributed among themselves, heads of houses, and various noblemen, to canvas their views and, no doubt, to raise money. One hundred and twenty sets were distributed. The foundation stone was laid on 17 May 1737, but Gibbs continued to modify the design; by April of the following year the trustees had decided to revert to a design with engaged columns. Gibbs strengthened the design of the niches in the basement story by giving them projecting bases, he made the crowning balustrade continuous, rather than alternating between open and solid panels, and, most significantly, he reduced the height of the drum while increasing the height of the dome and the lantern above. Internally there were changes too: pilaster panels were introduced around the drum, and on the dome itself corresponding ribs, with hexagonal coffering between, in the manner of Bernini's S. Andrea al Quirinale. The dome of Borromini's S. Carlo alle Quattro Fontana was to be commemorated in the design of the vaults of the porch. The new design was again engraved on five plates, dated 1737 and 1740, by Vertue, who was paid £65–11–6 in February 1741. Two of the plates were new, three were merely revisions of the earlier ones. They were issued in 1740 under the title *Bibliotheca Radcliffiana MDCCXL.*

Much the same procedure, one may note, had been followed at Cambridge. A perspective of the "Publick Building" had been engraved by Henry Hulsbergh in 1722 and issued in one thousand prints in an attempt to attract benefactors; a second design was engraved in 1723 and promoted with 524 prints. A third design was issued independently. The plans for King's College had, likewise, been published thus, in 1724.

The trustees had hoped that there would be no further alterations to the design. By the end of 1740 the stone carcass was complete up to the level of the balustrade and estimates for the dome and lantern were being called for. There was some hesitation, for no dome of the size had been built in stone in England. In April 1741 Gibbs proposed a structure of oak, covered with metal, and this was agreed upon; the internal dome was thereby greatly reduced in height. By 1747 the building was complete.

Gibbs at once prepared a record of his own great achievement—twenty-one copperplates of plans, sections, elevations, and details of the library as finally built, all engraved by P. Fourdrinier. The frontispiece to the book, *Bibliotheca Radcliviana: or, a Short Description of the Radcliffe Library*, at Oxford, was a portrait of Gibbs, engraved by Bernard Baron (who in 1736 had engraved Gibbs' bookplate) after a drawing by William Hogarth, set in an elaborate frame to Gibbs' own design, dated 1747. This was a gesture of brazen self-confidence, almost unprecedented in British architectural publications (Gibbs had, in fact, included a portrait of himself on the title page of the 1736 edition of his *Rules for Drawing*). James Paine was to follow this lead in the elevation of the architect above the patron or client in the *Plans, Elevations, Sections and Other Ornaments of the Mansion-house . . . of Doncaster*, of 1751. Also included in Gibbs' work was a portrait of Dr. Radcliffe, set in a similar frame, based on Baron's copy of an original by Godfrey Kneller of 1710, engraved by Fourdrinier in 1741. The plates were ready for issue in May 1748. R. M.

Bibliography

Friedman, T. *James Gibbs*. New Haven and London, 1984

Harris, E., and N. Savage. *British Architectural Books and Writers 1556–1785*. Cambridge, 1990

James Gibbs. *Bibliotheca Radcliviana*. Plate IX. "A section shewing the inside of the library." 1985.61.583

25

Thomas Girtin (1775–1802)

A Selection Of Twenty of the most Picturesque Views in Paris, and its environs, Drawn and Etched In the Year 1802, by the late Thomas Girtin; Being the Only Etchings of that Celebrated Artist: And Aquatinted in exact Imitation of the Original Drawings, In the Collection of the Rt. Honble The Earl of Essex . . .

London: M. A. & John Girtin, 22 March, 1803

1985.61.594

Oblong folio: 623 × 470 (24 9/16 × 18 1/2)

Pagination Engraved title plate, engraved dedication, 20 aquatint plates

Edition First edition

Illustrations Engraved title plate; dedication with armorial headpiece engraved by John Girtin; and 20 etched and aquatint plates printed in various shades of sepia and umber, all with plain paper guards. Captions in English and French. The views are in a horizontal format ranging from 198 × 271 to 299 × 559, except some longer plates with plate marks trimmed. All signed as drawn and etched by Thomas Girtin, the aquatint work by F. C. Lewis (pls. 1, 3, 7–14, 17–18, 20), J. B. Harraden (pls. 2, 4, 15, 19), W. Pickett (pls. 5, 6), or J. C. Stadler (pl. 16). For a full list, see Abbey, *Travel*

Binding Contemporary marbled-paper boards, new calf back and corners

References Abbey, *Travel*, 1: 102; Fowler 140

Thomas Girtin. *A Selection of Twenty of the most Picturesque Views.* "View of the Louvre & Bridge of the Tuileries taken from Pont Neuf." 1985.61.594

26

Wilhelm Heinrich Ludwig Gruner (1801–1882)

Fresco Decorations And Stuccoes Of Churches & Palaces, In Italy, During the Fifteenth & Sixteenth Centuries With Descriptions By Lewis Gruner, And A Comparison between the Ancient Arabesques & those of the Sixteenth Century By Mr. A. [corrected in ink to J. J.] Hittorff. Architect

London: John Murray, P. D. Colnaghi, Hering & Remington, & at the authors [sic], 1844

1985.61.596

Folio: 568 × 459 (22 3/8 × 18 1/16)

Pagination [6] pp., zincograph title plate, 46 etched and engraved plates

(*Note*: Atlas only. This copy lacks the quarto text volume)

Edition First edition

Text pp. [1] dedication to Prince Albert and the Royal Commission on the Fine Arts (verso blank); [3] preface (verso blank); [5] "List Of Plates" (verso blank)

Illustrations Hand-colored zincograph title plate, with arabesques and grotesques after Baldassare Peruzzi surrounding the title, "Printed from Zinc by J. Aresti. . . ." 46 etched and engraved plates numbered 1–2, 2 bis, 3–17, 17 bis, 18–30, I–XIII, 46, as listed. Most are hand-colored. The initials of J. G. Gutensohn and Josef Thürmer frequently appear on the first 20 plates. Other plates are usually unsigned but include credits to Gruner, S. Pistrucci, G. Biaggi, Friedrich Lose, or A. Angelini as draftsmen, and/or Domenico Ascani or E. Salandri as engravers (see note below for details)

Binding Contemporary dark blue morocco, richly decorated in gilt with red and green onlays. Bound for the king of Hanover, with his coat of arms on the cover and the ticket of Wilhelm Ermold, his binder, on the flyleaf

References Brunet 2: 1769

Wilhelm Heinrich Ludwig Gruner (or Grüner), better known by his anglicized name Lewis Gruner, probably first met Prince Albert in Rome during the latter's postgraduate tour of Italy, shortly before the royal marriage in February 1841. He followed Albert to England in the same month, bearing a letter of introduction to the RIBA from the Italian archaeologist Luigi Canina (see RIBA, *Early Printed Books* 1994, no. 543). After studying interior decoration under E. G. Krüger at the Dresden Academy and under Giuseppe Longhi and Pietro Anderloni in Milan, Gruner was in the middle of a long sojourn in Rome, where he published his first book, *I mosaici della cupola nella Capella Chigiana di S. Maria del Popolo in Roma, inventati da Raffaelle Sanzio d'Urbino, incisi ed editi da Lodovico Gruner, illustrati da Antonio Grifi* (1839). The degree to which Gruner formed Albert's taste, rather than merely sharing it, is hard to determine, because no correspondence between the two has survived. But soon he was acting as the prince's chief artistic adviser, buying paintings for him and other wealthy clients at the continental auctions and engaging himself in numerous projects in England. One of these was the publication of all the Raphael holdings at Windsor, an undertaking only completed by Karl Ruland long after Albert's death (*The Works of Raphael Santi da Urbino as represented in the Raphael Collection in the Royal Library at Windsor Castle*, 1876). The present work, dedicated to Albert "by special command," joins to Raphael another of the prince's great enthusiasms: fresco painting.

Albert's views were an important element in the direction British art took in the 1840s and 1850s. Although Queen Victoria was willing to show her husband the occasional government paper, his previous lack of interest in politics made it advisable that in the months immediately following his marriage he should be diverted from the most pressing issues of the day. The prime minister, Robert Peel, therefore arranged for him to head the Royal Commission that was established in October 1841 by the "Select Committee to Take into Consideration the Promotion of the Fine Arts of this Country, in Connexion with the Rebuilding of the Houses of Parliament." In this position, Albert expounded the virtues of fresco painting, showing the influence on him of a group of German painters from the previous generation. Dressing themselves in biblical costumes, leading semimonastic lives, and promoting medieval and early Renaissance art, these earnest artists had formed a "Brotherhood of St. Luke" in 1809. They were better known by their nickname, the Nazarenes. The group's fresco decorations in Rome had been debated in England even before Albert's appearance, but at the time only two or three British artists had experience in the technique. To remedy this, the prince undertook a garden pavilion project in the grounds of Buckingham Palace, and Gruner published the results (see next entry). The commissioners also announced a competition for large-scale preliminary designs, to be submitted on paper, as candidates for the walls of Westminster.

Gruner's *Fresco Decorations and Stuccoes of Churches and Palaces in Italy* was published as part of the same educational program, and a royal contribution toward the cost seems more than likely:

> At a moment when the study of art in this country appears to be guided by a new spirit, and the erection of the Houses of Parliament upon a scale of unusual splendour gives additional interest to every kind of architectural embellishment, it cannot

be doubted that the access afforded to compositions of such skill and beauty, as are comprised in this work, will be gratefully acknowledged even by those painters whose efforts are directed to the higher branches of the profession. While striving to justify the confidence felt by the public that British art, in order to rival that of other nations, in the very noblest department, requires only to be honourably appealed to, and judiciously encouraged, the historical painter will surely be thankful for being furnished with the inferior but necessary accompaniments which these plates either suggest or supply, since he will thus be enabled to give his unbroken energies to the attainment of his principal object (preface).

The allusion to "inferior but necessary accompaniments" represents Gruner's attempt to throw off those critics (including the Nazarenes) who had argued that the frescoes of the Renaissance, no matter how beautiful, were frivolous and decadent. He thus carefully perpetuates the tradition that arabesques and other purely decorative motifs are below historical subjects in the artistic hierarchy, while at the same time offering his readers the most seductive set of plates to illustrate the former ever published. Albert's love of Raphael led him into the same dilemma, out of which came his official position that, as for beauty and morality, there was no need to sacrifice one for the other. As his first biographer wrote of the prince's work for the commission:

Himself a great admirer of fresco painting, the Prince threw himself with great zeal into the question of its applicability for the decoration of the Houses of Parliament, and the researches into the best methods of applying it, which occupied much of the attention of the Commission. The opinions of its members were not a little divided as to the subjects to be dealt with. Some considered that mere decoration by arabesques and otherwise was alone necessary; others condemned any attempt at a moral aim. The Prince took an opposite view, holding that the purposes of decoration might be combined with a patriotic and moral aim, and that, although many would give but a passing glance to the works, the painter was not therefore to forget that others might view them with more thoughtful eyes. This was the view which ultimately prevailed, and there can be no doubt it was the sound one. For the incidents embodied in the frescoes, which now decorate the walls of both Houses of Parliament, although the frescoes themselves have failed for the most part most pitiably in the durability that was hoped for, excite the liveliest curiosity in the crowds which may be constantly seen around them (Martin 1875, 1: 167).

With hindsight, *Fresco Decorations* might seem more relevant to Gruner and John Pennethorne's decoration of the Buckingham Palace ballroom, where frivolity was allowable, than to the Houses of Parliament. But the artists for Westminster were chosen in the same year Gruner's work appeared, and his main intention was surely not to contribute anything new to the scholarship that had already grown up around these famous paintings, but rather to provide accurate and imitable specimens of decorative elements that would win the prince's personal approval.

The first half of the work, on secular buildings, is largely derived from a book published some years earlier

Lewis Gruner. *Fresco Decorations and Stuccoes of Churches.* Plate 3. Third-story loggia, Cortile of San Damaso, Vatican. 1985.61.596

by two German architects, J. G. Gutensohn and Josef Thürmer's *Sammlung von Denkmalen und Verzierungen der Baukunst in Rom vom 16.ten Jahrhundert* (Rome, 1826). It has not been possible to compare a copy of this atlas with Gruner's, but the latter's preface mentions his adoption of both plates and original drawings, as if he had access to published and unpublished material. This is quite likely since Thürmer's estate was sold at auction in Dresden in April 1834. In any case, Gruner certainly obtained measured drawings and views of the Vatican's Cortile di San Damaso (pls. 1–5); the Villa Madama (pls. 6–12); ceilings in the Villa Poniatowski, Palazzo Montalto, and Palazzo Altieri (pls. 13–15); the Palazzo Farnesina (pls. 16–18); and the Villa Lanti (pls. 19–20). All of these plates are signed with either or both Gutensohn and Thürmer's initials, and two have been reproduced to show the extraordinary care with which they were hand-colored. The two bis plates in this series may have been added by Gruner: plate 2a is unsigned, and plate 17a is signed by Domenico Ascani. Gruner justifies inclusion of the latter, a view of the so-called Loggia of Psyche at the Palazzo Farnesina, by commenting that "The paintings of this hall, being purely historical, do not belong properly to a work on arabesque decoration; yet, as they are the greatest ornament of this palace, it was thought that a perspective view of the gallery would be a welcome addition." Most of the plates of the Palazzo del Tè and Palazzo Ducale in Mantua (pls. 21–23, 24–30) are uncredited, except two drawn by Gruner (pls. 28–29), one engraved by Ascani and E. Salandri (pl. 23), one engraved by Ascani after S. Pistrucci (pl. 24), and one engraved by G. Biaggi after a drawing by himself and Pistrucci (pl. 25).

The second sequence of plates is entitled "Decorations of Ecclesiastical Buildings." Ten etchings are devoted to the Certosa near Pavia (pls. I–X), and one each to the Monastero Maggiore in Milan, the libreria of Siena Cathedral, and the choir ceiling of S. Maria del Popolo in Rome (pls. XI–XIII). The final plate, numbered 46, is a collection of details intended to act as a key to coloring the other plates, although it is largely uncolored in the Millard copy. Gruner owed none of the ecclesiastical plates to Gutensohn and Thürmer's atlas, but the extent of his artistic responsibility remains to be established. The Certosa etchings are not, at least, derived from the similarly magnificent series that Gaetano and Francesco Durelli began publishing in Milan in 1823 (*La Certosa di Pavia descritta ed illustrata*). The credits are as follows: plate I is signed as engraved by Salandri and XII by Ascani and Salandri; plates II, IX, XI as drawn by Friedrich Lose; and plate XIII as engraved by Salandri after a drawing by A. Angelini.

Only a small number of copies of the first edition were published, as its present rarity testifies. The captions on the plates are in French and German, which might suggest a continental market, but the preface states this is an inheritance from Gutensohn and Thürmer, which Gruner merely chose to extend to his other material. According to D. D. Schneider, an octavo French edition of the complete work was published by Gratiot in the same year. Apart from the title plate, dedication, and preface, the text for the English edition was only available in a quarto pamphlet lacking from the Millard collection (but available in the Library of Congress), *Descriptions of the Plates of Fresco Decorations and Stuccoes of Churches and Palaces in Italy. . . .* It is important not only for Gruner's lucid explanation of each plate, but also for Jakob Hittorff's accompanying essay "On the Arabesques of the Ancients as Compared with those of Raphael and his School" (pp. [ix]–xvi). Gratiot's French version of this, "Parallèle entre les arabesques peintes des anciens et celles de Raphaël et de ses élèves," is apparently identical to the second part of Hittorff's memoir "Sur une collection de dessins relatifs à l'art de la décoration dans l'antiquité et aux plus belles époques de la Renaissance en Italie, par M. Denuelle," read to the Société libre des Beaux-Arts on 19 March 1844 and printed in the Society's *Annales*. Schneider (1977, I: 205–214) provides a detailed analysis, notes significant differences between the English and French versions, and relates Hittorff's interest in the subject to his attempt to persuade Ingres to decorate one of his own buildings, Saint-Vincent de Paul. In his essay, Hittorff declares that the Renaissance artists had more genius than the ancient Roman artists after whom they modeled their work. Gruner evidently saw how well the memoir would fit his purpose, elevating the status of his subject and allowing him to print the enthusiastic praise of a well-respected scholar. The pamphlet includes additional illustrations, and the errata note that the atlas plates 23 and XIII "have in the first impression a wrong scale for the foot measure, while the miles are throughout correct"; and that "in Plate 46 the number 5 has by mistake been engraved in several cases instead of letter S, particularly in the border of the Libreria of Siena" (p. [viii]).

In 1854 Thomas McLean published a second edition, sometimes found with the revised text printed to size but more often accompanied as before by a quarto pamphlet. A French language version of this edition appeared as *Décorations de palais et d'églises en Italie peintres à fresque ou exécutées en stuc* (Paris and London, 1854). In the meantime, Gruner had edited a small stream of similar publications, most notably *Specimens of Ornamental Art* (1850), an even larger pattern book with a wider

Lewis Gruner. *Fresco Decorations and Stuccoes of Churches.* Plate 9. Ceiling, Villa Madama. 1985.61.596

range of subject matter. For the new edition of *Fresco Decorations* he added nine new designs: a third ceiling from the Villa Lanti (plate 20a, described as a sketch Gruner had met with "among Prof. Thürmer's Roman studies, viz., that of the Seasons"); an additional loggia from the Palazzo Ducale in Mantua (27a); Pope Clement VII's bathroom in the Castel Sant'Angelo (31); further details of the Certosa di Pavia (va); the groined ceiling of Alby Cathedral (XIV); plan, elevation, and ceiling of the Villa Belcaro, near Siena (XV); twelve soffit decorations from the windows of S. Sigismondo near Cremona (XVI); elevation and plan of S. Bernardino, Perugia (XVII); and frescoes from the Eroli chapel in Spoleto Cathedral (XVIII). Two final plates (XIX–XX) provide a key to coloring the "Palaces, Villas etc." and "Ecclesiastical Buildings," respectively. They replace plate 46 of the present edition, making a new total of fifty-six excluding the title, and a second sequence of numbers was added to the plates accordingly. In some copies, plates XIV, XV, and XVII have English captions as well as French and German.

Although they thus broadened the scope of the work, Gruner and McLean economized for the second edition by leaving all of the plates uncolored except nine, and these are chromolithographs. Seven replace hand-colored etchings (1, 2a, 3, 12, 17a, 26, and X) and two are new (the final key plates). The so-called flat-tone style of chromolithography fully lives up to its name when contrasted with the plates of the Millard copy, but the views in particular are still impressive examples of the process. In some copies plate 17a has a new credit line: "Lith. v. C. Köpper. lith. Farbendruck v. Winckelmann u. Söhne in Berlin unt: Leit: v. J. Storch." Brunet claims that even this, relatively common, edition was advertised as a limited edition of 150 copies only, costing five pounds, ten shillings each.

In the 1870s Ruskin used plates from *Fresco Decorations* to teach art at Oxford (Cook and Wedderburn 1906, 21: 199, 203). This represents a high compliment to their accuracy—Ruskin even referred to plate IX as "very admirably representing, as far as stamped colour and engraving can, one of the compartments of the church at Milan"—and particularly surprising in view of Ruskin's notoriously anti-German sentiments. On the other hand, the very sumptuousness of some of the plates probably served his purposes well. Gruner produced his plates of the Villa Madama as possible sources for decorating the British Parliament; Ruskin adopted them to show "The arts devoted entirely to the pleasure of the eye and caprice of fancy, perfect in skill by the practice of ages, but now entirely destructive of morality, intellectual power, and national character." G. B.

Bibliography

Ames, W. *Prince Albert and Victorian Taste.* London, 1967

Martin, T. *The Life of His Royal Highness the Prince Consort.* Vol. 1. London, 1875

Ruskin, J. *Instructions in Practice of Elementary Drawing, arranged with Reference to the First Series of Examples in the Drawing Schools of the University of Oxford*, 1872. Reprinted in Cook, E. T., and A. Wedderburn. *The Works of John Ruskin*. Vol. 21. London, 1906

Schneider, D. D. *The Works and Doctrine of Jacques Ignace Hittorff, 1792–1867.* New York, 1977

Steegman, J. *Victorian Taste: A Study of the Arts and Architecture from 1830 to 1870.* Cambridge, Mass., 1970

Thieme-Becker 15: 147 et passim

27

Wilhelm Heinrich Ludwig Gruner (1801–1882)

The Decorations Of The Garden-Pavilion In The Grounds Of Buckingham Palace. Engraved Under The Superintendence Of L. Gruner . . . With An Introduction By Mrs. Jameson

London: published by John Murray; Longman & Co.; P. & D. Colnaghi; F. G. Moon; and L. Gruner, 1846

1985.61.2800

Folio: 446 × 338 (17½ × 13 5/16)

Pagination 11, [1] pp., 15 etched or chromolithographed plates

Edition First edition

Text pp. [1] half-title (verso blank); [3] title page; [4] note by Gruner, printer's imprint at foot; [5]–11 text by Mrs. Jameson; [12] list of plates

Illustrations Unsigned wood-engraved vignette on half-title, plus 15 unsigned plates (pls. 1–2, 13–15 etchings; 3–6, 11–12 chromolithographs; 7–10 etchings over-printed with woodblocks to give pale green background and white highlights). 1 copy of this work has recently been recorded with an extra plate, a chromolithograph of the Sir Walter Scott Room, with additional hand-coloring (Marlborough Rare Books cat. 166)

Binding Original red cloth, gilt, with printed ticket "Bound By Remnant & Edmonds London"

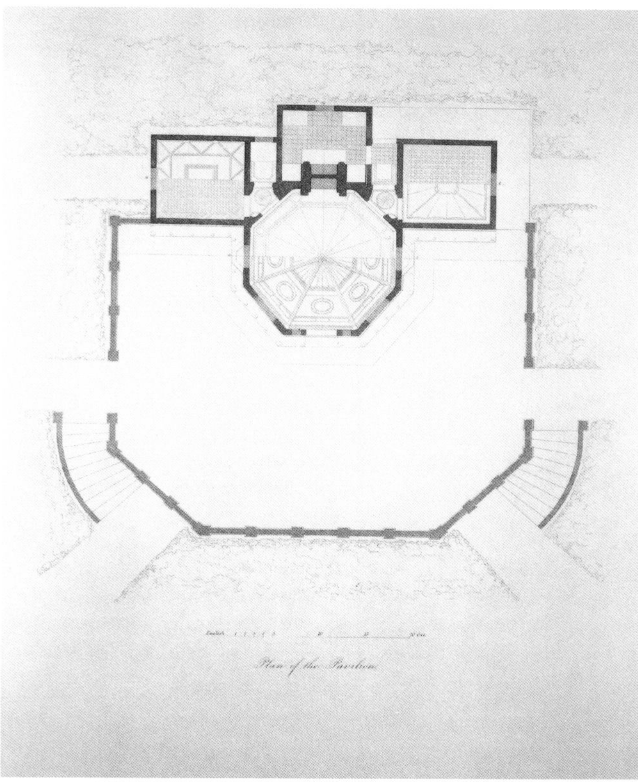

Lewis Gruner. *The Decorations of the Garden-Pavilion.* Plate 1. Plan of the pavilion. 1985.61.2800

As HEAD of a Royal Commission on the Fine Arts, Prince Albert looked at various ways in which he might introduce fresco painting into Britain, specifically for the decoration of the new Parliament buildings. One of his schemes was to use a garden pavilion recently erected on the grounds of Buckingham Palace as a test site. According to Mrs. [Anna Brownell] Jameson, this pavilion was "originally intended only for a simple cottage" (p. 6), an idea supported by its Swiss-style exterior. The commissioners of woods and works called it "a place of refuge" when authorizing the payment of two hundred and fifty pounds toward the cost in July 1842. The queen's special architect, Edward Blore, constructed the house on a mound formed during the excavation of the palace lake, and it seems that Prince Albert was involved in designing at least the terrace and balustrade that was built in front of it. Its main feature was a domed octagonal central room, which led to a kitchen at the back, and single square-shaped rooms either side. The building was destroyed in August 1928, after a long period of neglect, and the present book is the only substantial record of it.

The cottage could scarcely have been finished before it was pressed into its new role as a laboratory for the prince's artistic experiment. On 9 March 1842 Albert had seen a performance of *Comus* at Covent Garden, and Milton's masque was adopted as the theme for the fresco decorations in the octagonal room, for which eight royal academicians were chosen to paint one lunette each. The original list of artists could hardly have been less surprising: Charles Eastlake, William Etty, Edwin Landseer, C. R. Leslie, Daniel Maclise, Sir William Ross, Clarkson Stanfield, and Thomas Uwins. Each were to be paid forty pounds. In May 1843 painting began, but within a month they were having problems, and the sixty-six-year-old Agostino Aglio was brought in as technical adviser. Aglio's involvement must have been critical: he probably had more relevant experience than anyone else living in England, having over a long career received numerous commissions for wall decorations, including the London Opera House, Drury Lane Theatre, Woolley Hall, the Pantheon, Woburn Abbey, Manchester Town Hall, churches in Reading and Leeds, and a Roman Catholic chapel in Islington. He also entered the Houses of Parliament competition, and it is hard not to sympathize with the position of this Italian who was so much more experienced than any of the British artists but who, for political reasons, would never be chosen above them.

Work continued, and Albert managed to interest

his wife in the project. Uwins wrote in a letter dated 15 August 1843:

It has happened to me in life to see something of many royal personages, and I must say, with the single exception of the Duke of Kent, I have never met with any, either in England or on the Continent of Europe, who have impressed me so favourably as our reigning Sovereign, and her young and interesting husband. Coming to us twice a day unannounced, and without attendants, entirely stript of all state and ceremony, courting conversation, and desiring reason rather than obedience, they have gained our admiration and love. In many things they are an example to the age. They have breakfast, hear morning prayers with the household in the private chapel, and are out some distance from the Palace talking to us in the summerhouse, before half-past nine o'clock—sometimes earlier. After the public duties of the day, and before their dinner, they come out again, evidently delighted to get away from the bustle of the world to enjoy each other's society in the solitude of the garden. Our peaceful pursuits are in accordance with the scene; and the opportunity of watching our proceedings seems to give a zest to the enjoyment of these moments snatched from the state, parade, and ceremony. Here, too, the royal children are brought out by their nurses, and the whole arrangement seems like real domestic pleasure (Martin 1875, 1: 168–169).

Considerable progress must have been made by March 1844, when Eastlake's future wife, Elizabeth Rigby, visited. She thought the pavilion "a little Chinesey box" and the octagon room "overfinished," but liked Eastlake and Etty's work, and singled out the latter's as "the nearest to real fresco effect" (Ames 1967, 53). In the same year, the Reverend Henry Wellesley wrote about the pavilion for the *Quarterly Review*, commenting that "We look forward with much interest to the result of the experiment, as showing what can be done and thus defining the true starting-point of an English school of fresco-painting" (Steegman 1970, 204). There were further problems, however, and despite Rigby's praise it was Etty who became so dissatisfied that he proposed he should be allowed to provide a canvas painting instead. This, he suggested, could be white-leaded to the pavilion wall after completion in his studio. Given the purpose of the experiment, the proposal must have sounded like backsliding to the prince, and although Albert went out of his way to praise one of Etty's *Comus* designs, "Hesperus and His Daughters," at a Royal Academy dinner in May 1844, the artist was replaced on the project by William Dyce. In this publication, Dyce's work is therefore illustrated instead of Etty's—which may be one reason why the latter chose to exhibit a second subject from the same masque at the Academy in the year of its publication ("Circe with the Sirens Three"). By then the dispute was common knowledge. *The Builder* for 26 July 1845, in an interesting anonymous review of the pavilion, which also announced its completion, reported that "as many ill-natured comments have been made on the removal of the fresco executed by him [Mr. Etty], it is but just to say that the step was unavoidable. We are much pained that so distinguished an artist—the first colourist of our day,—should have his work superseded, but truth compels us to say, after careful examination of the removed panel, that the fame of Mr. Etty would have suffered materially if it had been allowed to remain" (*The Builder* 3: 350).

Another problem was caused by giving the *Comus* artists too free a rein, for as Jameson wittily points out in her introduction, "three of the subjects are nearly similar, yet presenting, even in their monotony, a sort of inconsistency, for we have three different Ladies on three different chairs: while two subjects [Ross and Landseer's] are absolutely identical" (p. 7). To Jameson, the result proved "the absolute necessity of a presiding mind" and this was eventually provided by Gruner. Reading his own account, dated December 1845, one suspects the academicians of leaving a mess for him to tidy up:

After the execution of most of the Fresco Lunettes in the Octagon Room of the Garden-Pavilion, I was honoured by the gracious commands of Her Majesty and His Royal Highness Prince Albert to present designs for the completion and decoration of the three rooms of which the Summer-house consists: and I was also directed to procure the execution of these designs by the different artists whose names appear in the list printed at the end of Mrs. Jameson's introduction (title page, verso).

Gruner's choice of decoration was consistent with the experimental nature of the project. The right-hand room was Pompeiian, with

all the ornaments, friezes, and panels being suggested by, or accurately copied from, existing remains, except the coved ceiling, which is invented by A. Aglio. This room may be considered a very perfect and genuine example of classical domestic decoration, such as we find in the buildings of Pompeii,—a style totally distinct from that of the Baths of Titus, which suggested to Raphael, and his school, the rich arabesques and ornaments in painting, and in relief, which prevailed in the sixteenth century, and which have been chiefly followed in the other two rooms (p. 9).

The room on the left, by contrast, was treated as another experiment in illustrating English literature. Here, Sir Walter Scott was the chosen theme, and a number of scenes from his novels were painted as lunette and frieze decorations, some from Gruner's own sketches. Gruner also supervised a small army of painters and decorators as they copied Raphaelesque decorations above the gray imitation marble walls—the perfection of which was apparently attained by varnishing ten times, and rubbing down after each coat. It is not easy to see how combining the pseudo-Gothic romance of Scott with the Italian Renaissance could have failed to be offensive. But the above-mentioned *Builder* review maintained that

The advantage of mingling in the interior decoration of a building isolated figures and historical subjects with arabesque ornaments, has been proved to be twofold. If the locality be small, the space appears to be enlarged to the eye by the invo-

Lewis Gruner. *The Decorations of the Garden-Pavilion.* Plate 3. "Perspective View of the Octagon or Milton Room." 1985.61.2800

lution and continuation of multiplied and varied forms and colours; while, if the dimensions be large, the interest is concentrated by the presence of a leading idea, connecting all these separate compartments and all this maze of variety into one harmonious whole. The wild and dream-like arabesques are like vague, delicious music; the historical subjects form resting-places for the fancy; and the two in combination are like the lyrical drama,—action, sentiment, and melody woven together.

Whether or not Gruner approved of the pavilion once the experiment was completed, he could not have avoided the queen's command to publish the results. The indefatigable Jameson had already written several popular books on art and art galleries, and was a natural choice for providing a neutral text that would neither offend royalty nor inflate the artistic value of the experiment. Her text is accompanied by a plan and two sections of the house (pls. 1–2); interior views and details of the octagonal room, including all eight lunettes (pls. 3–10); perspective views of the Pompeiian and Scott rooms, with the lunettes and bas reliefs of the latter (pls. 11–14); and lastly, an artistically grouped selection of the furniture from each room. Sadly, there is no mention of the furniture in the text, and its origin (and destiny) perhaps deserves further research. Although Gruner refers to the plates as engravings, only plates 1–2, 7–10, and 13–15 are intaglio designs, and these mostly etchings. The four plates of *Comus* lunettes have been overprinted with woodblocks to give a green tint and white highlighting. The other plates are chromolithographs, credited at the end of the text to Joseph Aresti and "Hanhard [i.e., Hanhart?], Newman-street." Most of them have hand-colored areas—consistently so for Victoria and Albert's ciphers, perhaps because these were late additions. G. B.

Bibliography

Ames, W. *Prince Albert and Victorian Taste.* London, 1967

The History of the King's Works. Ed. H. M. Colvin. Vol. 6. London, 1963–1982

Hobhouse, H. *Prince Albert: His Life and Work.* London, 1983

Martin, T. *The Life of His Royal Highness the Prince Consort.* Vol. 1. London, 1875

Steegman, J. *Victorian Taste: A Study of the Arts and Architecture from 1830 to 1870.* Cambridge, Mass., 1970

28

William Halfpenny (d. 1755)

Practical Architecture, or a Sure Guide to the true working according to the Rules of that Science: Representing the Five Orders, with their several Doors & Windows taken from Inigo Jones & other Celebrated Architects to each Plate Tables Containing the exact Proportions of the several Parts are likewise fitted Very usefull to all true Lovers of Architecture, but particularly so to those who are engag'd in y[e] Noble Art of Building By Will[m]. Halfpenny. The fifth Edition 1736

[London]: printed for & sold by Tho: Bowles, by Jer. Batley, & by J. Bowles, [1736 or later]

NGA Lib. Rare Book: NA2810H351736

Small octavo: 163 × 97 (6 7/16 × 3 1/16)

Pagination Engraved title plate, engraved dedication, engraved preface, 48 engraved plates

Edition "Fifth" edition

Illustrations 3 unnumbered plates (title, dedication to Thomas Frankland, preface), and 48 numbered plates (all versos blank). All the odd-numbered plates are tables of proportions, bound to face the even-numbered illustrations of the architectural elements to which they apply. Title plate signed "J. Clark sc. 1724," otherwise all unsigned with double-rule borders

Binding Contemporary calf, gilt borders, rebacked

Provenance Ownership inscription "Chas Greenwood" on endpaper

References Berlin (1977) OS 2265[8]; ESTC t78313; Harris and Savage 309; RIBA, *Early Printed Books*, 1447

Surprising little is known of William Halfpenny, one of the most prolific authors of practical handbooks and pattern books on architecture in the eighteenth century. He published at least eighteen books between 1724 and 1754, the year before he died. Some of the later works were in part by his son, John.

Halfpenny began his career as a carpenter, though he was later to describe himself as "architect and carpenter." He is first recorded, in 1723, in Leeds, Yorkshire, as the designer of Holy Trinity Church, but it was not built to his draft. He was active soon after in Surrey, in Richmond. Between 1731 and the late 1740s he was at work in Bristol and also Ireland, though only minor buildings seem to have been carried out there to his design. Only the Redland Chapel in Bristol, 1742, is thought to be his, though this was begun by another architect, probably John Strahan.

Halfpenny's publishing activity divides neatly into two parts—divided, it would seem, by his activities in Bristol. During the first phase he produced five books—*Practical Architecture* (1724); *The Art of Sound Building* (1725); *The Builder's Pocket Companion* (1728), under the alias Michael Hoare; *Magnum in parvo: or, the Marrow of Architecture* (1728); and *Perspective Made Easy* (1731)—all designed to enable builders and craftsmen to prepare drawings and to set up their buildings easily and to correct proportions. He prepared additional books like this later, but his second phase of publishing was dominated by pattern books for farms and small houses, pavilions and garden features, which became progressively more whimsical and fantastical: *A New and Compleat System of Architecture* (1749); *Twelve Beautiful Designs for Farmhouses* (1750); *Six New Designs for Convenient Farmhouses* (1751)

William Halfpenny. *Practical Architecture.* "A rustick door from Palladio." NGA Lib. Rare Book: NA2810H351736 (here enlarged)

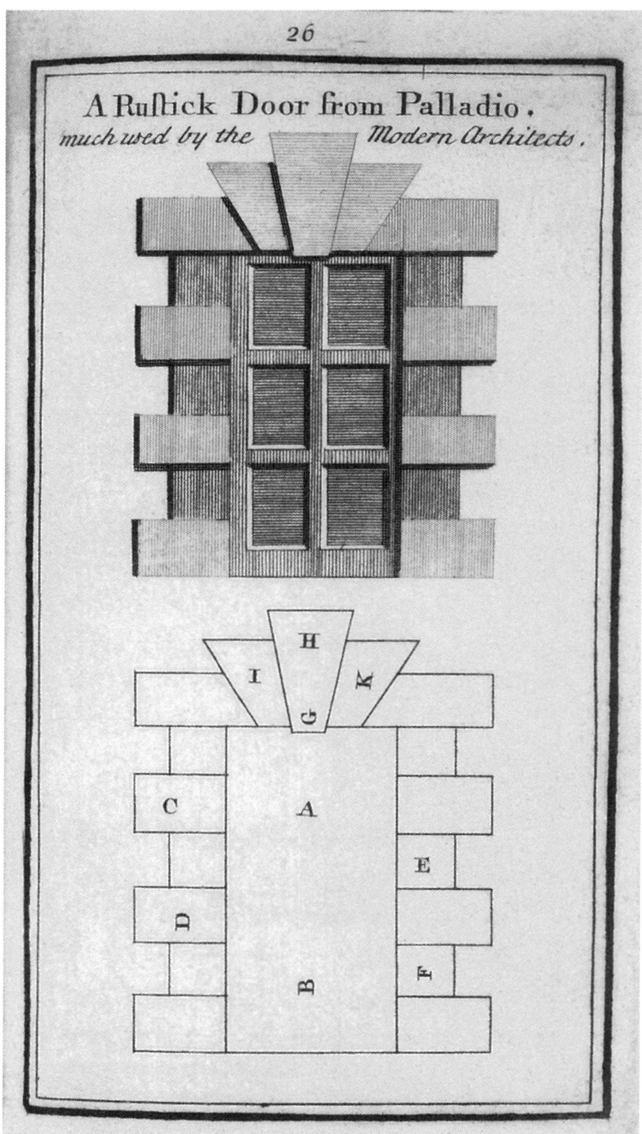

and *Thirteen New Designs for Small Convenient Parsonage and Farm Houses* (1752), which were issued together as *Useful Architecture in Twenty-one New Designs for Erecting Parsonage-houses, Farm-houses, and Inns* (1752); *Rural Architecture in the Chinese Taste* (1752); *Rural Architecture in the Gothick Taste* (1752); and *The Country Gentleman's Pocket Companion* (1753).

Halfpenny's *Practical Architecture*, dedicated to Thomas Frankland, eldest son of Sir Thomas Frankland of Thirsk, in Yorkshire, was, as the title makes clear, among his publications "Very usefull to all true Lovers of Architecture, but particularly so to those who are engag'd in ye Noble Art of Building." It was a builder's pocketbook. Adapting the method of Abraham Bosse's *Traité des manières de dessiner les ordres*, of 1664, he tabulated the dimensions of the parts of all five orders, and related doors and windows (a venetian window included), in feet and inches, so that the correct proportions outlined by Palladio would result. Bosse had converted the modular measurement to one size only; to provide more flexibility, Halfpenny offered dimensions for several sizes. Oddly, however, neither he nor Bosse provided the overall height for the order, the door, or the window, but the book was clearly useful and extremely successful. By 1730 five editions had been issued, though the edition of 1736, with the collation and contents still as for the first, of 1724, was also labeled "The fifth edition." The early editions were all printed and sold by Thomas Bowles; the last, undated edition, assumed to be of 1764 or later, was issued by his successor, Carrington Bowles. R. M.

Bibliography

Colvin, H. *A Biographical Dictionary of British Architects 1660–1840*. 2d ed. London, 1978

Harris, E., and N. Savage. *British Architectural Books and Writers 1556–1785*. Cambridge, 1990

29

William Halfpenny (d. 1755) and John Halfpenny

Rural Architecture in the Chinese Taste, Being Designs Entirely New for the Decoration of Gardens, Parks, Forrests, Insides of Houses, &c. on Sixty Copper Plates with full Instructions for Workmen Also A near Estimate of the Charge, and Hints where proper to be Erected. the Whole Invented & Drawn by Willm. & Jn^{n}. Halfpenny, Architects. The 3^{d}. Edition. With the Adition [sic] of 4 Plates in Quarto . . .

London: printed for Robt. Sayer, [1755 or later]

1985.61.599

Quarto: 225 × 143 (8⅞ × 5⅝)

Pagination Part 1: 8 pp., engraved title plate, 14 engraved plates

Part 2: 8 pp., [14] (i.e., 15–28) engraved plates (4 folding)

Part 3: 4 pp., [16] (i.e., 29–44) engraved plates (7 folding)

Part 4: 8 pp., [20] (i.e., 45–64) engraved plates (4 folding)

Edition Third edition (2d, undated, issue)

Text part 1: pp. [1–2] preface; 3–8 text; *part 2*: pp. [1] printed title page "New Designs For Chinese Bridges, Temples, Triumphal Arches, Garden-Seats, Palings, Obelisks, Termini, &c. . . ." (verso blank); [3] preface (verso blank); 5–8 text; *part 3*: pp. [1] printed title page "New Designs For Chinese Doors, Windows, Piers, Pilasters, Garden-Seats, Green-Houses, Summer-Houses, &c. . . ." (verso blank); 3–4 explanation of the plates; *part 4*: printed title page "New Designs For Chinese Gates, Palisades, Stair-Cases, Chimney-Pieces, Ceilings, Garden Seats, Chairs, Temples, &c. . . ." (verso blank); 3–8 explanation of the plates

Illustrations Engraved title plate as above, plus 64 numbered engraved plates of which the first is an engraved title to part 1, "New Designs For Chinese Temples Triumphal Arches, Garden Seats, Paling &c. . . ." Some plates are signed by William or John Halfpenny as designer or draftsman, and many by Parr as engraver. Benjamin Cole engraved the final 4, supplementary plates

Binding Contemporary Dutch gilt-paper wrappers. Untrimmed copy. Preserved in marbled paper-covered box, calf back

Provenance Early nineteenth-century ownership inscription of Lord Blantyre on title page

References Berlin Cat. 3415 (3d ed., 1st issue); Berlin (1977) OS 2280^{b} (3d ed., 1st issue); ESTC t126582; Harris and Savage 303; RIBA, *Early Printed Books*, 1444 (3rd ed., 1st issue)

William Halfpenny's *Rural Architecture in the Chinese Taste* belongs to his second phase of publishing activity, beginning, in 1749, with *A New and Complete System of Architecture*; which was first printed for John Brindley of New Bond Street. This was later to be taken over by Robert Sayer of Fleet Street, who was to issue all of Halfpenny's fanciful pattern books. *Rural Architecture* was the first work to exploit the Chinese fashion initiated in 1749 by Frederick, prince of Wales, who commissioned the House of Confucius at Kew from William Chambers and had a barge built in a Chinese style to be rowed on the Thames. The book was initially issued in four parts, no doubt to gauge the response. Sayer published the first fourteen plates in 1750 as *New Designs for Chinese Temples* . . . ; the second part, with plates 15 to 28, was issued in 1751 as *New Designs for Chinese Bridges* . . . ; the third, with plates 29 to 44, in 1751, as *New Designs for Chinese Doors* . . . ; and the last, with plates 45 to 60, in 1752, as *New Designs for Chinese Gates*. . . . Halfpenny's son John collaborated on the last three parts. Parts one and two were issued concurrently, with the imprint of Brindley as

William and John Halfpenny. *Rural Architecture in the Chinese Taste*. Plate 11. "A building in the Chinese tast." 1985.61.599

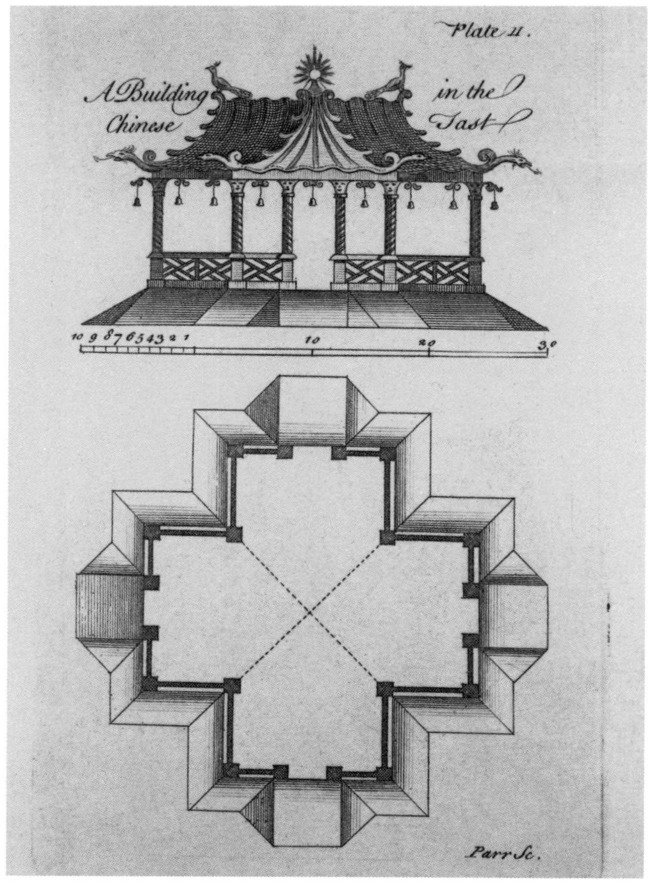

well as Sayer. The title *Rural Architecture in the Chinese Taste* was first used for the second edition, published by Sayer in 1752. He also published the third edition, of 1755, in which four plates of Chinese roofs, taken from Halfpenny's *Improvements in Architecture and Carpentry*, issued by Sayer in 1754, were added to the fourth part. The subsequent undated edition of *Rural Architecture*, also printed by Sayer, has the same collation and contents as that of 1755. The plates were engraved by Remigius Parr, with the additional plates by B. Cole.

The preface is explicit, short, and latitudinarian:

> The Art of designing Architecture is not confined to any particular Taste or Country, more than justly observing a graceful Symmetry, and an exact Proportion through the whole. And the *Chinese* Manner of Building being introduced here with Success, the few following Essays are an Attempt to rescue those agreeable Decorations from the many bad Consequences usually attending such slight Structures, when unskillfully erected: Which must often unavoidably happen at a Distance from this Metropolis, without such Helps as, I flatter myself, the Workmen will here find laid down by, Their Well-Wisher, Wil. Halfpenny.

Halfpenny's designs for temples, alcoves, garden seats, and other such features, for which he gave dimensions and costs, are all symmetrical in arrangement, with ground plans made up with clear-cut geometrical figures. They are adorned, however, with all manner of frets and scrolls, bells, and snakes adapted, as far as may be, from Jean Baptiste Du Haldes' *Description géographique . . . de la Chine*, of 1735, translated the following year into English. Motifs from Chinese prints and porcelain were imitated also. Some of the structures had an admixture of Gothic. Halfpenny set the fashion for books of this kind, and not only in the field of architecture. The engraver Matthias Darly issued *A New Book of Chinese, Gothic and Modern Chairs*, in 1751, and with George Edwards, *A New Book of Chinese Designs* in 1754. Thomas Chippendale's *The Gentleman and Cabinet-Makers Director* appeared, also in 1754, with designs in the Chinese taste (Sayer was to take over the issue for a period); and two years later the first issue of Thomas Johnson's more fanciful rococo confections for carvers, *One Hundred and Fifty New Designs*, was on sale (this too was to be taken over by Sayer).

William and John Halfpenny. *Rural Architecture in the Chinese Taste.* Plate 54. "The elevation of a temple partly in the Chinese taste." 1985.61.599

In a postscript to his *Architectural Remembrances*, published in April 1751, Robert Morris attacked the new fashion for the "improperly called" Chinese taste, which

> consists in mere *Whim* and *Chimera*, without *Rules* or *Order*, it requires no Fertility of Genius to put in Execution; the Principals are a good Choice of *Chains* and *Bells*, and different Colours of *Paint*. As to the *Serpents*, *Dragons*, and *Monkeys*, &c. they, like the rest of the Beauties, may be cut in Paper, and pasted on any where, or in any Manner: A few *Laths* nailed across each other, and made Black, Red, Blue, Yellow, or any other Colour, or mix'd with any sort of Chequer Work, or Impropriety of Ornament, completes the Whole.

Halfpenny, assuming that these strictures were aimed primarily at his works, defended himself in the preface to his *Chinese and Gothic Architecture Properly Ornamented...*, issued by Sayer in 1752, on the grounds of invention and variety, but he had a more effective revenge in taking over the title *Rural Architecture...* for his work, for it was a calculated thrust at Morris, whose own *Rural Architecture* of 1750 had as its subtitle "Consisting Of Regular Designs Of Plans and Elevations For Buildings in the Country. In Which The Purity and Simplicity of the Art of Designing are variously exemplified." In 1752 Halfpenny published a companion volume of rococo designs, *Rural Architecture in the Gothic Taste.* R. M.

Bibliography

Colvin, H. *A Biographical Dictionary of British Architects 1660–1840.* 2d ed. London, 1978

Harris, E., and N. Savage. *British Architectural Books and Writers 1556–1785.* Cambridge, 1990

Harris, J. "Exoticism at Kew." *Apollo* (August 1963): 103–108

30

Alice Hepplewhite and Co.

The Cabinet-Maker And Upholsterer's Guide; Or, Repository Of Designs For Every Article Of Household Furniture, In The Newest And Most Approved Taste . . . From Drawings By A. Hepplewhite and Co. Cabinet-Makers. The Third Edition, Improved

London: published by I. and J. Taylor, 1794

1985.61.600

Folio: 366 × 236 (14 3/8 × 9 1/2)

Pagination [vi], 24 pp., [127] engraved plates (1 double-page)

Edition Third edition

Text pp. [i] title page (verso blank); [iii–iv] preface; [v–vi] index; [1]–24 text

Illustrations 127 unsigned engraved plates as listed, numbered 1–125 (bis plates 9, 40*, 78*; final double-page plate numbered 124–125). Publisher's imprint on nearly all plates, dated 1 Sept. 1787; 2 July 1787; 1 Oct. 1787; or (pls. 12–13 only) 1 Jan. 1794

Binding Contemporary stained calf, rebacked

Provenance Royal Library stamp on title page "E. R. 63," with coronet

References Berlin Cat. 1233 (1789 ed.); ESTC t146852; RIBA, *Early Printed Books,* 1488 (1788 ed.)

Chippendale, Hepplewhite, and Sheraton are the great, representative names in the history of English furniture design. But Hepplewhite has left the barest trace of his activity. No item of furniture can be ascribed to him, and no commission is recorded. He is listed in only one trade directory as a cabinetmaker, as Kepplewhite and Son of 48 Redcross Street, in 1786, the year of his death. On 27 June 1786 his widow, Alice, was appointed executor of his estate, which amounted to no more than six hundred pounds. Six designs in *The Cabinet-Makers' London Book of Prices of 1788*, and later editions, are signed "Hepplewhite" and "Heppelwhite." But only in 1788 was the famous work *The Cabinet-Maker and Upholsterer's Guide* published by I. and J. Taylor, from drawings by A. Hepplewhite and Co., cabinetmakers, at a price of two guineas. The book was sold by subscription, though no subscriber list survives.

The drawings illustrated on the 125 plates, all unsigned, are assumed to be the work of George Hepplewhite, but there is no certainty on this matter. Many of the designs are close to those of such contemporary designers as Thomas Shearer and Thomas Sheraton. Some may be related to Robert Adam's designs for furniture. But there is a coherence and consistent elegance and style to the designs that indicate the hand of a single person, probably Hepplewhite.

The two-page preface to the book makes no large claims. It opens with the conventional aim "To unite elegance and utility, and blend the useful with the agreeable," and to be both "useful to the mechanic, and serviceable to the gentleman," offering examples of furniture that are in general use and that might be said to "convey a just idea of English taste in furniture for houses." It was addressed thus both to foreigners and to "our own Courtrymen [sic] and Artizans, whose distance from the metropolis makes even an imperfect knowledge of its improvements acquired with much trouble and expence."

Though there was some elaboration and contrivance in some of the designs offered, they are on the whole clear-cut and sharp, supremely elegant, and representative of a particular phase of English furniture design. French ideas are in evidence, but they have been carefully absorbed. The range of items offered is wide and comprehensive: chairs, stools, and sofas; sideboards, pedestals, and knife-cases; desks and library furniture; chests of drawers, tables, and tea stands; dressing tables, desks, wardrobes, screens, and beds; window cornices, candle stands, lamps, and girandoles; pier glasses, pedestals, and moldings. The final plate, a double one, illustrates a plan and four walls, showing an arrangement of furniture that can be modified to suit both a drawing or a dining room: "The proper furniture for a Drawing-room, and for a Dining-room or Parlour, being thus pointed out, it remains only to observe that the general appearance of the latter should be plain and neat, while the former, being considered as a State-room, should possess all the elegance embellishments can give." There was a hint of caution however, that the lavish use of looking glass was proper only to the "first nobility."

The Cabinet-Maker and Upholsterer's Guide was reprinted in 1789 with minor alterations and an additional plate. But in 1791, in the prospectus and in the general remarks included in *The Cabinet Maker and Upholsterer's Drawing-Book*, Sheraton reviewed Hepplewhite's work: "Some of these designs," he wrote, "are not without merit, though it is evident that the perspective is, in some instances, erroneous. But, notwithstanding the late date of Hepplewhite's book, if we compare some of the designs, particularly the chairs, with the newest taste, we shall find that this work has already caught the decline, and perhaps, in a little time, will suddenly die in the disorder."

When the third, "improved," edition of *The Cabinet-Maker and Upholsterer's Guide* was issued in 1794, one plate was added and plates 12 and 13, which had illustrated chairs with curved cabriole legs, were replaced by new ones showing stiff, squarely designed chair backs, not unlike those shown on plate 25 of Sheraton's *Appendix to the . . . Drawing-Book* of 1793. The cabriole leg was allowed to remain, however, on the stools of plates 16 and 17, and the pier table of plate 65. The term "cabriole chair"—still used in France at that date for a chair with a stuffed back, but unusual in England—was used as the label for the chairs on plates 10 and 11, one of which, it was claimed, had been "executed with good effect for his Royal Highness the Prince of Wales." No bills for this, however, have been traced. Nor is the claim that Hepplewhite worked for Gillows, in Lancashire, sustainable. R. M.

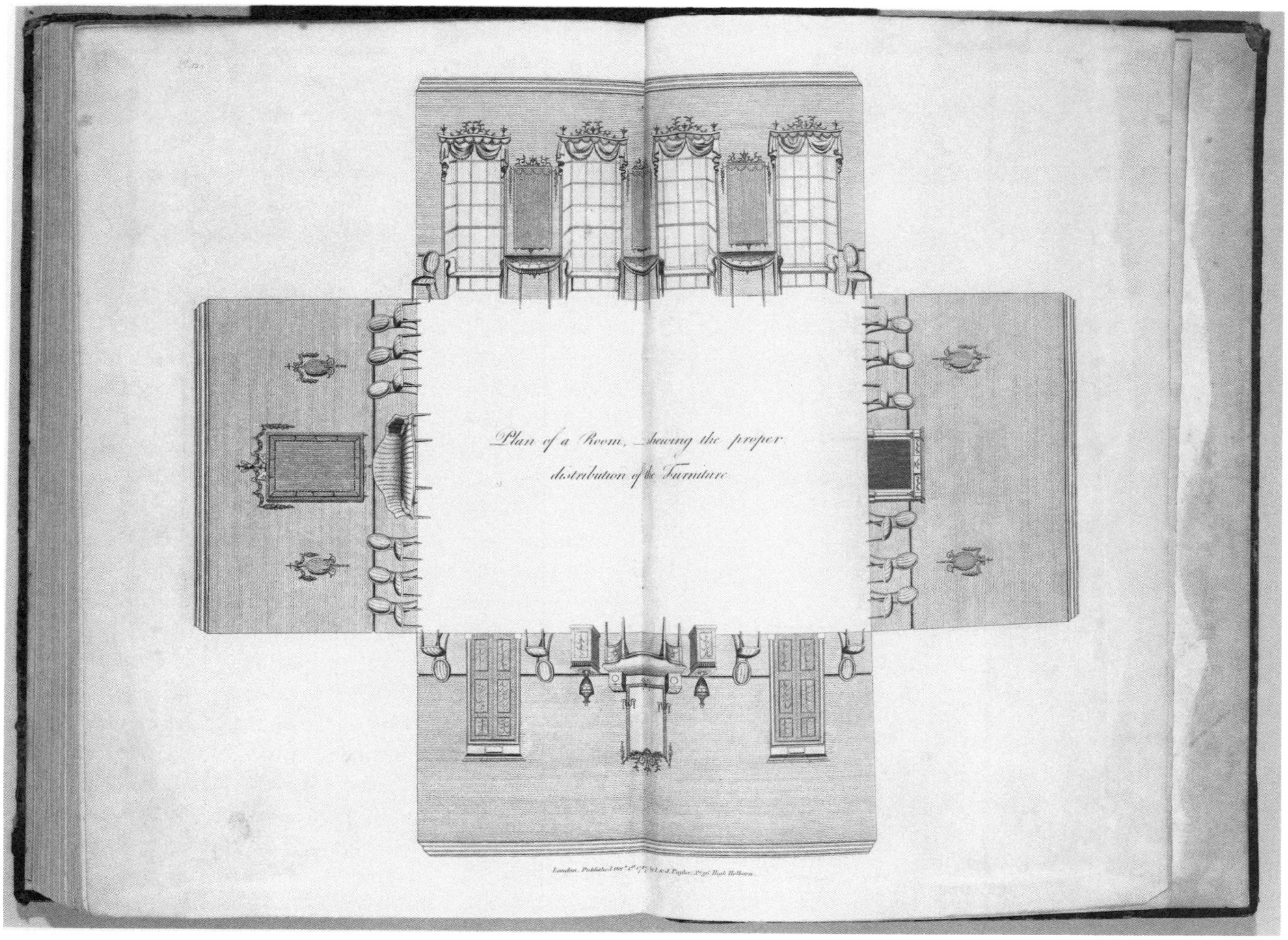

Bibliography

Beard, G. and C. Gilbert. *Dictionary of English Furniture Makers 1660–1840*. Leeds, 1986

Hepplewhite, G. *The Cabinet-Maker and Upholsterer's Guide*, introduction by J. Aronson. Reprint of the third edition of 1794. New York, 1969

A. Hepplewhite and Co. *The Cabinet-Maker and Upholsterer's Guide.* Plate 124/125. "Plan of a room, shewing the proper distribution of the furniture." 1985.61.600

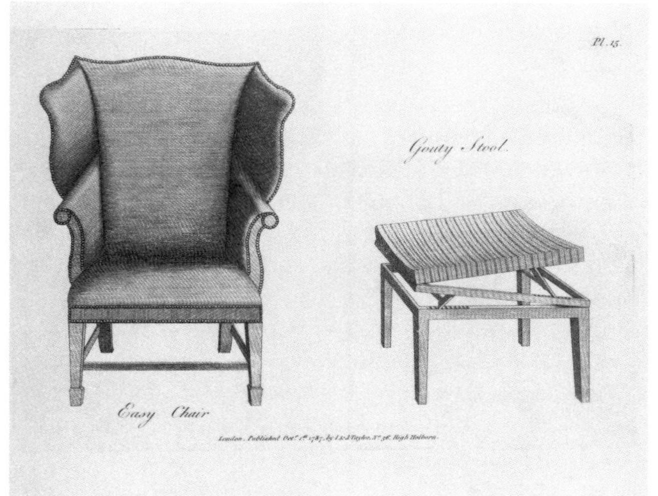

A. Hepplewhite and Co. *The Cabinet-Maker and Upholsterer's Guide.* Plate 15. "Easy chair and gouty stool." 1985.61.600

31

Thomas Frederick Hunt (c. 1791–1831)

Architettura Campestre: Displayed In Lodges, Gardeners' Houses, And Other Buildings, Composed Of Simple And Economical Forms In The Modern Or Italian Style; Introducing A Picturesque Method Of Roofing. By T. F. Hunt, Architect . . .

London: Longman, Rees, Orme, Brown, and Green, 1827

1985.61.612

Quarto: 283 × 231 (11 1/8 × 9 1/8)

Pagination xix, [1], 28 pp., 12 lithograph plates

Edition First edition

Text pp. [i] title page (verso blank); [iii] dedication to Lieut.-Col. Stephenson (verso blank); [v]–vi preface; [vii] contents (verso blank); [ix]–xix introduction; [xx] blank; [1]–25 text (i.e., literary quotation on rectos, description of facing plate on versos; text relating to pl. XII extended to pp. 24–25); [26] blank; [27]–28 index

Illustrations 12 lithographic plates numbered I–XII, printed by Charles Hullmandel after designs by Hunt, the elevations lithographed by James Duffield Harding

Binding Contemporary three-quarter calf, morocco boards, morocco label

References Berlin Cat. 2322; Berlin (1977) OS 2322; RIBA, *Early Printed Books*, 1573

THIS IS THE third of four quarto volumes published by T. F. Hunt, an employee of the Office of Works. He worked at St. James' Palace as laborer in trust from 1813 to 1829 and, after a promotion, at Kensington Palace from 1829 until his death, at forty, on 4 January 1831. His architectural career was launched in 1815, when he won the competition to design a mausoleum for the Burns family in Dumfries, Scotland. Various subsequent commissions were exhibited by him at the Royal Academy, and he also designed country houses at Danehill in Sussex and Patrixbourne in Kent. Howard Colvin records that he was respected but always in debt, only venturing out of St. James' on Sundays for fear of arrest and on one occasion hiding from bailiffs in the palace gatehouse.

His first book was *Half a Dozen Hints on Picturesque Domestic Architecture, in a Series of Designs for Gate Lodges, Gamekeepers' Cottages, and other Rural Residences* (1825). This collection of nine designs was a modest development of a theme successfully opened up by P. F. Robinson, whose first publication of many, *Rural Architecture, or Series of Designs for Ornamental Cottages*, had appeared two years earlier. This theme was the application of the picturesque aesthetic to what Hunt called the "Old English Domestic Style." It was intended to show that Tudor buildings for gardeners, lodge keepers, etc., were more appropriate on a country estate than either their classical equivalents or the "ruinous and useless hovels" with which the picturesque was more usually associated (see Hunt's preface). Given the ignorance at the time about what constituted Tudor architecture, it is not surprising that both Robinson and Hunt have been credited with, or rather accused of, being the originators of the "Tudor Parsonage style," which in turn led to the hugely popular mock-Tudor suburban dwellings of the twentieth century (see Wrightson 1977, 52). Hunt's second collection, *Designs for Parsonage Houses, Alms Houses, etc.* (1827), was certainly in this vein. His last and by far his most important work, however, was a significant contribution to the development of a better appreciation of the style. Entitled *Exemplars of Tudor Architecture, adapted to Modern Habitations* (1830), it is in large part a scholarly investigation of the rationale behind Tudor architecture and those decorative features that characterize it.

Knowledge of Hunt's preoccupation with his national heritage makes his choice of subject in *Architettura Campestre* seem oddly perverse. As the title makes plain, its twelve designs are far removed from Hunt's interests, and they are practically disowned by the author in his preface:

> In adopting a style of architecture different from that of my former publications, I yield rather to the suggestions and wishes of many patrons of those works than to any inclination of my own; persuaded that in the event of succeeding in my object of illustrating the character of Modern or Italian architecture, as applied to simple domestic structures, I shall do little more than render manifest its inferiority to that beautiful and appropriate style miscalled Gothic.

Hunt's "many patrons" were evidently not yet ready to prefer domestic vernacular over Italian Renaissance. One reason for this, as hinted toward the end of Hunt's introduction, may have been because many of them were already ensconced in a Palladian country house and wanted their estate buildings to conform. Hunt goes out of his way to contradict this, and so further compromise the book, by using Lord Farnborough's Bromley Hill as an example of "an Italian Villa . . . whilst the lodges are cottages in the picturesque style of our own architecture, blending admirably with the park scenery" (pp. xviii–xix). Hunt had dedicated *Designs for Parsonage Houses* to Lord Farnborough and it may be significant that Robinson also claimed a connection, stating Bromley Hill was "partially adopted" from a scheme in his *Designs for Ornamental Villas* of 1827 (quoted from 3d ed., 1836, 43). The precise relationship between Hunt and Robinson has yet to be explored, but given Hunt's impecunious circumstances, it is possible that he pushed himself (or his publishers did) to produce *Architettura Campestre* as a response to Robinson's cheerful eclecticism.

The result was a curious and unhappy volume. Further evidence that Hunt produced it under protest is provided by the poor quota of Italian features in the designs themselves. The first he confesses to be "a neutral object where the mansion or other buildings differing in style might appear in the same view"; the second is "not strictly Italian"; and similar retractions, notwithstanding the Italian roof tiles Hunt was keen to promote, could also be applied to designs IV–VIII. The third plate is a gate lodge design that looks more genuinely Mediterranean, but it has been given a rugged setting where no such lodge could actually function. According to Archer, pl. IX, a prospect tower was later executed on the Alton estate in Staffordshire, but it is followed by a bridge design that seems less than serious, with corner fountains and a "summer-house or billiard-room" that effectively blocks the way. The final two plates show more fully developed designs for a small villa and a casino.

Each design is introduced by a quotation from an English author followed by a cursory description. The

Thomas Frederick Hunt. *Architettura Campestre.* "A casino." 1985.61.612

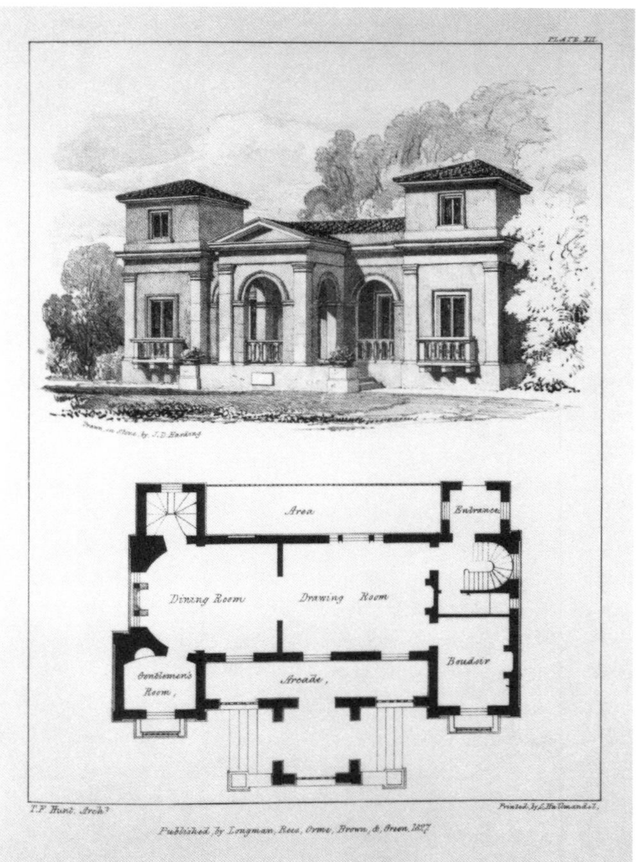

plates are typical of many pattern books in the nineteenth century, J. D. Harding's lithographs combining a sketched view and a ground plan on the same plate. But no measurements or prices are given, and coming just three months after *Designs for Parsonage Houses,* according to their dated prefaces, it is hard not to conclude that Hunt was eager to dispose of his Italian excursion as quickly as possible. G. B.

Bibliography

Archer, J. *The Literature of British Domestic Architecture, 1715–1842.* Cambridge, Mass., 1985

British Architectural Library, Royal Institute of British Architects. *Early Printed Books 1478–1840: Catalogue of the British Architectural Library Early Imprints Collection.* Vols. 1–2. London, 1994–1995

Wrightson, P. *The Small English House.* London, 1977 (Weinreb cat. 35)

32

William Ince (d. 1804) and John Mayhew (1736–1811)

The Universal System of Household Furniture. Consisting of above 300 Designs in the most elegant taste, both useful & Ornamental Finely Engraved, in which the nature of Ornament & Perspective, is accurately exemplified. The Whole made convenient to the Nobility and Gentry, in their choice, & comprehensive to the Workman, by directions for executing the several Designs, with Specimens of Ornament for Young Practitioners in Drawing. By Ince & Mayhew Cabinet-Makers & Upholders . . .

[London]: sold by Rob[t]. Sayer, [1765?]

1985.61.613

Folio: 444 × 269 (17½ × 10⁹⁄₁₆)

Pagination iv [i.e., 2], 11, [1] pp., [2] engraved title plates, engraved dedication, 95 etched and engraved plates

Edition First edition, third issue?

Text pp. iii–iv preface; [1]–11 explanation of the plates in English and French; [12] blank

Illustrations A total of 101 impressions on 95 leaves. The total includes 3 preliminary plates, namely, an etched and engraved title plate in English (elaborate triple cartouche with figures, foliage, and emblems of art and design, signed "W. Ince inv[t]. et delin."); the same in French (cartouche and emblems, printed in bister); and an engraved dedication to George Spencer, duke of Marlborough, with large etched armorial headpiece. There are 89 full-page plates numbered I–LXXXIX and 12 half-page plates printed 2 to a page, including 6 numbered 90–95. The full-page plates are all signed by Matthias Darly as engraver and Ince as designer and draftsman, except plates XXVIII–XXIX, XXXI, XXXV, XLVI, LVII, LX–LXII, and LXIV (signed by Mayhew instead of Ince) and plate LXV (dedication to Lady Fludyer, signed by both Ince and Mayhew). The half-page plates are unsigned. In the Millard copy, plate LXXXIX is bound after 4 unnumbered half-page plates and before plates 90–95, with the 2 remaining unnumbered plates bound last. Plates I–III and LXVI are printed in different shades of sanguine or sepia

Binding Recent full green morocco, gilt ornamental borders, gilt spine, red morocco label, gilt edges

References Berlin Cat. 1229 (1st issue); ESTC t128516; Christie's (London), 30 Oct. 1996, lot 76 (2d issue)

DEFEND
DIEU ET MON DROIT
To the most NOBLE
George Spencer,
DUKE of MARLBOROUGH, MARQUIS of BLANDFORD,
Earl of Sunderland and Marlborough,
Baron Spencer of Wormleighton, & Baron Churchill of Sandridge;
Lord Lieutenant, & CUSTOS ROTULORUM of the County of Oxford & Lord Chamberl
Majesties Hous

May it please Your Grace,
Being sensible of Your Grace's exte
Knowledge, in the Arts & Sciences, but more particularly in Drawing and Your b
ever willing to promote, and encourage Industry & Ingenuity, will justly account fo
presumption in claiming the protection of so worthy a Patron to this Work, which if so for
nate as to merit Your GRACE'S approbation will be esteem'd as the greatest Honour
ever conferred on
Your Graces
most Respectful,
most Obedient,
and very faithful Ser
Mayhew & Inc

William Ince and John Mayhew. *The Universal System of Household Furniture.* Dedication plate. 1985.61.613

THE PARTNERSHIP of William Ince and John Mayhew, of London, was one of the longest lasting in the eighteenth-century English furnituremaking trade and one of the most active, but relatively few examples of furniture can be ascribed to them with certainty, though their documented commissions, listed only in 1986 in the *Dictionary of English Furniture Makers 1660–1840*, are quite considerable. Evidence of their design abilities has, for far too long, been judged with reference to the plates of *The Universal System of Household Furniture*, a work that marks no more than the earliest phase of their activity.

Ince, son of a glass grinder, was bound in July 1752 to John West, a cabinetmaker of Covent Garden, who died in May 1758, before Ince could complete his apprenticeship. Mayhew, the son of a builder, was apprenticed to an upholsterer named Bradshaw (probably William Bradshaw of Soho Square). Mayhew took over West's premises in November 1758, together with Samuel Norman and James Whittle. However, by 25 December of this same year he had entered into a partnership with Ince, and together they bought the cabinetmaking and upholstery firm of Charles Smith, in Carnaby Market, opposite Broad Street. They agreed to live together in the house in which they worked until either should marry. In February 1762 they married sisters and continued to live on the premises for another year, when Mayhew's wife died and he moved to another house on the site. Their partnership continued long after the initial agreement of twenty-one years, to 1804, when Ince died. The firm continued to trade under the name of Ince and Mayhew until 1808, Ince's son Charles, having, it seems, joined his uncle.

The Universal System of Household Furniture was an early promotional exercise. A flurry of books or sheaves of plates of ornamental design, chiefly for carvers, had been published in the 1740s and 1750s, but few were concerned with furniture as such. As early as 1736 Gaetano Brunetti had issued *Sixty Different Sorts of Ornaments.* This was followed by William De la Cour's eight *Books of Ornament*, of 1741 to 1747. Matthias Lock issued *Six Sconces* in 1744 and *Six Tables* in 1746, and, with Henry Copland, *A New Book of Ornaments* in 1752. Copland had already published ten plates with this same title in 1746. Matthias Darly, an active engraver and printseller, rather than a designer, had offered *A New Book of Chinese, Gothic and Modern Chairs*, on eight leaves, in 1751, and, with the ornithologist George Edwards, *A New Book of Chinese Designs*, in 1754, with 120 plates, twenty-two of which were categorized as "furniture." Thomas Johnson, himself a carver, had produced *Twelve Gerandoles* in 1755, but then attempted something more comprehensive and ambitious than usual, issuing fifty-two plates, in groups of four, between 1756 and 1757, illustrating "Glass, Picture, and Table Frames, Chimney Pieces, Gerandoles, Candle-Stands, Clock-Cases, Brackets, and other Ornaments in the Chinese, Gothick and Rural Taste." This first appeared in the form of a book, without a title, in 1758. The whole was to be issued again, with an additional plate, in 1761, by Robert Sayer, one of the most enterprising publishers of pattern and architectural books in London, as *One Hundred and Fifty New Designs.*

Ince and Mayhew were evidently inspired by the rococo fantasy of Johnson's designs, and some of Johnson's motifs were to be taken over by them. But more influential by far was the only really significant work on furniture design to have appeared in England, Thomas Chippendale's *The Gentleman and Cabinet-Maker's Director: Containing Great Variety of Designs of Household Furniture in the Gothic, Chinese and Modern Taste*, which served in almost every respect as their model. Ince, while still an apprentice, subscribed to the first edition of this work.

Chippendale's *Director* was first announced on 19 March 1753 in the *London Daily Advertiser*; it was to consist of 160 plates, to be issued to subscribers at one pound ten shillings in sheets, or one pound fourteen shillings bound in calf. The whole was due for release in August 1754, but had in fact been issued already by April of that year. Ninety-eight of the 147 signed plates were engraved by Darly, who was also a drawing master, possibly Chippendale's, certainly his friend. Darly was the only agent, other than booksellers, to take orders for the work. Despite the fact that Chippendale seems to have been responsible for commissioning and promoting the book, it was an early success. The second edition, issued in 1755, was printed by John Haberkorn of Gerrard Street and sold by Sayer for one pound sixteen shillings in sheets.

This was the spur to Ince and Mayhew. In the *Gentleman's Magazine* of 13 July 1759 they announced "A General System of Useful and Ornamental Furniture. By Mess. *Ince* and *Mayhew*, publishing in numbers. 1s each, *Piers.*" (H. Piers was a Holborn bookseller.) Each part, as with Johnson's work, was to consist of four plates. The first part was due the next day. An advertisement on the part wrapper (and on those of the thirteen following, all bound into a unique copy of the book in the print department of the Metropolitan Museum of Art, New York) details their aim to produce 160 folio plates. The number, size, and format was to be that of Chippendale's *Director*. Their imitation of Chippendale was even more overt. Their advertisement states:

> As the Authors, who have separately spent their Times in the most distinguished Houses of the Cabinet and Upholstery Branch, have had great Opportunity of making their Remarks on an infinite Variety of well chosen Furniture, they are now engaged in Business for themselves, wishing to gain Recommendation for their Industry: And as a Work of this Kind was delivered to the Public some few Years since, by a very ingenious Artificer, and met its deserved Applause; they being instigated by so good an Example, hope the Candid and Ingenious will be kind enough to receive this their Attempt; and if it should be so fortunate to meet their Approbation, will be a Matter of the greatest Encouragement, and esteemed as a particular Favour.

Subscriptions were to be taken by none other than Darly, who, whatever his relation with Chippendale, had been persuaded to engrave the plates. The book was to be distributed also from the eighth part onward by A. Webley, off Chancery Lane, Holborn. The first sixteen parts had appeared by February 1760—about one a fortnight—but the eighteenth was announced in *The British Chronicle*, only in the issue for August 15–18. Three more parts were issued, for a total of eighty-four plates. In the subscriber's copy in the Metropolitan Museum these are sporadically numbered to 155. Five more plates in folio format were issued, bringing the total to eighty-nine. These were renumbered consecutively from I to LXXXIX, and were issued together with engraved title pages in English and French, a dedication to the duke of Marlborough (his office of lord chamberlain appearing as a late addition to the plate), a preface, eleven pages of explanations of the plates, once again in both English and French, and twelve additional plates, set in pairs on six sheets, numbered 90 to 95. The additional plates, illustrating stove grates, fire dogs, and other ironwork, were clearly not a part of the original enterprise, though they were being advertised as a part of it in *The British Chronicle* as early as 15–18 August 1760. The resulting book thus had ninety-five numbered plates, at least in the copies sold by the authors and at A. Webley's (held in the Avery Library, Columbia University, New York, and formerly in the Kunstbibliothek, Berlin). In the copies sold by Sayer, who seems to have taken over the work, the arrangement of the smaller plates is irregular. The copy in the Victoria and Albert Museum, London, has the six copperplates numbered 90 to 95, printed in pairs on three leaves, and the other six associated, unnumbered copperplates, on the following three leaves. The present copy, also with a Sayer imprint, has a varying sequence, as detailed in the bibliographic description above. The title pages are all undated, but the date of publication is assumed to be 1762, when George Spencer, the 4th duke of Marlborough, was appointed lord chamberlain.

It is clear from the advertisement of August 1760 that Ince and Mayhew were fully resigned to the fact that their book was not to be completed as planned. In that year they were involved in another of Sayer's ventures, *Household Furniture in Genteel Taste for the Year 1760*, an octavo volume of sixty unsigned plates, ascribed to Darly, based, it is thought, on designs by Robert Manwaring, Johnson, and Chippendale, in addition to Ince and Mayhew. Fiske Kimball and Edna Donnell have assigned as many as twenty of the plates included in the final edition of this work (which by 1764 had 120 plates) to Ince and Mayhew. The plates of ironwork added to their *Universal System* might also have been intended for this work. Whatever their contribution, it cannot be considered the cause for their abandonment of the *Universal System* as planned. Lack of funds is a more plausible reason. Pat Kirkham, in her article on the business matters of the firm, has shown that despite a very considerable trade, there was a constant shortage of cash. But the real reason for the retrenchment was Chippendale's response to their enterprise.

On 6 October 1759, two months after the first appearance of the *Universal System*, Chippendale announced in *The London Chronicle* the publication of the third edition of his *Director*. This was to be made up of 150 of the original plates (some improved) and fifty new plates, two hundred in all, to be issued weekly in fifty numbers at a shilling each. Sayer was the principal agent. Publishing momentum was maintained until 23 March 1760, when number twenty-five was issued. Then

William Ince and John Mayhew. *The Universal System of Household Furniture.* Plate LXV. "Side section of the dressing room." 1985.61.613

Chippendale paused. By then, it seems, Ince and Mayhew were ready to withdraw from the race. The removal of their advertisement for the *Universal System* from the wrappers of the fifteenth part, issued in January 1760, and from those of the sixteenth also, announced in *The Public Ledger* for 13 February, made evident their decision. On 28 March Chippendale announced a delay in the publication of his twenty-sixth suite in *The London Chronicle*. In the issue for 29–31 July he set forth an entirely new proposal for the contents and organization of his book. Though the total number of plates was to remain the same, there were to be one hundred rather than fifty new designs. There was also to be a new agent, the bookseller Thomas Becket, in the Strand. When the book was finally issued as a single volume in the spring of 1762, 106 of the 200 plates were new, in the standard edition, though many of the early subscribers, recruited before Becket's publicity campaign was launched, received a slightly more varied series of plates. When a new impression was launched in March 1763 (after the end of the Seven Years' War) the description of Chippendale's plates was made available for the first time in French, in this, at least, owing something to the example of Ince and Mayhew. But it is clear that Chippendale had in all ways outstripped them; indeed, he had routed them.

The designs for furniture offered in the *Universal System* (about three hundred in all) are wide-ranging; indeed, many are not to be found even in the *Director*, such as "Claw" tables or tripods, library steps, "Ecoineurs" or corner shelves, and "Voiders" or trays. And there is a certain distinction of motif in the form of a Gothic or chinoiserie lattice panel, pierced or laid on a ground, that appears again and again. But the style remains an amalgam of that of Johnson and Chippendale—less insistently spiky or curvilinear than Johnson in the rococo elements, more exaggerated and coarser than Chippendale in the geometric compositions. The style of the whole, however, is very much that of the mid-century; although, already in September 1764, Ince and Mayhew had made and supplied a pair of inlaid satinwood commodes to the earl of Coventry, in the manner of Adam. These represented a considerable advance in neoclassical taste. And the firm was to undertake more of this kind in the years that followed, for Lord Derby and others. Ince and Mayhew adapted quickly to changes of fashion.

The tone of the *Universal System* was set from the start, in the first three plates, illustrating foliated ornaments, the second plate inscribed "A systematical Order of Raffle leaf, from the Line of Beauty," a clear reference to Hogarth's *Analysis of Beauty* of 1753. Chippendale had introduced his work with the five orders.

The designs on ten of the eighty-nine signed folio plates are by Mayhew and the rest are by Ince, with the exception of plate LXV, an elevation to a dressing room, an alcove in the middle, which is signed by both partners. This was dedicated to "The Honorable Lady Fludyer," probably Caroline, wife of Sir Samuel Fludyer, lord mayor of London in 1761. This single interior elevation finds a parallel in the solitary elevation, for a paneled room, illustrated in Johnson's *Collection of Designs* of 1758 (pl. 25). Only one original drawing relating to the plates has survived, Ince's design for a state bed (pl. XXXII), in the Victoria and Albert Museum.

Mayhew's designs are noticeably clumsier than those of Ince, which confirms the evidence adduced by Pat Kirkham that Mayhew was responsible mainly for the management and business matters, while Ince concentrated on the design and supervision in the workshops, though both seem to have dealt quite independently with clients.

The *Universal System*, though ambitious and large, was evidently not of much influence or effect. Many of Ince and Mayhew's clients possessed copies, but very few examples of furniture can be related to its plates. Its publication was curtailed and it was not reprinted. Chippendale's work might have superseded it in the first instance, but it was soon enough overtaken by the change in sensibility from the rococo to the neoclassical, in which Ince and Mayhew themselves partook. Sheraton perhaps assessed the book most finely in pronouncing it "to have been a book of merit in its day, though much inferior to Chippendale's, which was a real original, as well as more extensive and masterly in its designs" (*The Cabinet-Maker and Upholsterer's Drawing-Book*, 1793).
R. M.

Bibliography

Beard, G. and C. Gilbert, eds. *Dictionary of English Furniture Makers 1660–1840*. Leeds, 1986

Gilbert, C. "The Early Furniture Designs of Matthias Darly." *Furniture History* 11 (1975): 33–39

Gilbert, C. *The Life and Work of Thomas Chippendale*. London, 1978

Hayward, H. *Thomas Johnson and English Rococo*. London, 1964

Hayward, H. "Newly Discovered Designs by Thomas Johnson." *Furniture History* 11 (1975): 40–42

Heckscher, M. "Ince and Mayhew: Bibliographical Notes from New York." *Furniture History* 10 (1974): 61–67

Ince, W. and J. Mayhew. *The Universal System of Household Furniture*. Reprinted with a preface by R. Edwards. London, 1960

Kirkham, P. "The Partnership of William Ince and John Mayhew 1759–1804." *Furniture History* 10 (1974): 56–60

Snodin, M., et al. *Rococo Art and Design in Hogarth's England*. London, 1984

33

Thomas Johnson (1714–c. 1779)

One Hundred & Fifty, New Designs, By Thos. Johnson Carver. Consisting of Cielings, Chimney Pieces, Slab, Glass & Picture Frames, Stands for China &c. Clock, & Watch Cases, Girondoles, Brackets, Grates, Lanthorns, &c. &c. The whole well adapted for Decorating all kinds of Ornamental Furniture, in the Present Taste. Engrav'd on 56 Copper Plates. N.B. This Work is regularly divided into 4 Parts. Part 1st. (–4th.)

London: sold by Robert Sayer, 1761

1985.61.615

Quarto: 289 × 232 (11 3/8 × 9 1/8)

Pagination 56 etched plates

Edition Third edition

Illustrations 56 plates, including 4 title plates, 1 for each part (pls. [1], 15, 29, 43). All but 1 of the plates are signed by Johnson as designer and draftsman; 5 by James Kirk as engraver (pls. 22, 24, 26, 34, and 37); and the remainder by Butler Clowes or unsigned. William Austin engraved the unsigned plate 17 and contributed to plate 2 (see notes)

Binding Recent three-quarter straight-grain green morocco, marbled boards, gilt spine

References Berlin Cat. 1228; RIBA, *Early Printed Books*, 1616 (later ed.)

A BOOK has been written on Thomas Johnson, but he remains a shadowy figure. He was baptized at the church of St. Giles-in-the-Fields, London, on 13 January 1714. His family was poor. Nothing is known of his early life or training. Later, in 1763, in Mortimer's *Universal Director*, he was described as a "Carver, Teacher of Drawing and Modelling and Author of a Book of Designs for Chimney-pieces and other ornaments and of several other pieces." His activities as a teacher are unrecorded. Several chimneypieces, mirrors, candlesticks, girandoles, and console tables exist that relate closely to his designs—notably at Corsham Court in Wiltshire and the duke of Atholl's country seats, Dunkeld House and Blair Castle—but not one is documented as the work of Johnson. He is thus to be judged on the basis of his designs. His first set of designs, *Twelve Gerandoles*, engraved by William Austin, was issued in September 1755 from Queen Street, Seven Dials, London. This was a house rented eight years earlier by his mother, with which he maintained a connection, though not as a rate-payer. The designs were on four sheets, sold at two shillings; they are wildly asymmetrical, spiky and jagged, with Chinese and rustic figures and animals that appear to have been copied both from wallpapers and Francis Barlow's illustrations to Aesop's *Fables*, of 1666.

These were not the first examples of rococo furnishings to be published in England. Gaetano Brunetti had published *Sixty Different Sorts of Ornaments* as early as 1736. Batty Langley's *The City and Country Builder's and Workman's Treasury of Designs*, of 1740, included six console tables copied without acknowledgment from Nicolas Pineau. In the same year the carver, Matthias Lock, issued the first of his books showing an evident knowledge of the new French style: *A New Drawing Book of Ornaments, Shields, Compartments, Masks, etc.* This was followed in 1744 by his *Six Sconces* and, in 1746, by *Six Tables*, in which something of an English rococo style for furnishings was established. Lock went even further, in 1752, when, with Henry Copland, he produced *A New Book of Ornaments with Twelve Leaves Consisting of Chimneys, Sconces, Tables, Spandle Pannels, Spring Clock Cases, and Stands, a Chandelier and Gerandole etc.* Between 1741 and 1747 William De la Cour issued eight *Books of Ornament*. Matthias Darly, the printseller and engraver, offered *A New Book of Chinese, Gothic and Modern Chairs*, on eight leaves, in 1751, and, together with his friend George Edwards, the ornithologist, *A New Book of Chinese Designs*, in 1754. This had 120 plates, twenty-two of which were categorized as "furniture." But the real stimulus came from Thomas Chippendale's *The Gentleman and Cabinet-Makers Director* (almost two-thirds of the plates for which were engraved by Darly), which was available by April 1754. Publication of this was first announced in March 1753, when subscriptions were invited for ". . . a New Book of Designs of Household Furniture in the GOTHIC, CHINESE and MODERN TASTE as improved by the politest and most able Artists."

This was a challenge Johnson could not resist. In 1755 he produced a flyer announcing his intention of issuing fifty-two plates illustrating "Glass, Picture, and Table Frames; Chimney Pieces, Gerandoles, Candle-Stands, Clock-Cases, Brackets, and other Ornaments in the Chinese, Gothick, and Rural Taste." There were to be thirteen parts, consisting of four sheets each, issued monthly to be obtained by subscription from "Thomas Johnson, Carver, at the corner of Queen Street near the Seven Dials, London." Subscribers were to pay 1/6 a part, plus an overall fee of 1/6. For those who did not subscribe, the book was to cost £1–5–0. The first part appears to have been issued in February 1756, and continuing through to the following February, as planned. But no title page was issued at this time.

The flyer, which was headed with a fantastical landscape, was engraved by Austin. He also engraved one of the plates (1758, pl. 52; 1761, pl. 17 unsigned). James Kirk engraved five, while Butler Clowes (who was later to be employed by Chippendale for the third edition of his *Director*) did forty-one—one of which incorporated Austin's landscape from the flyer (1758, pl. 16; 1761, pl. 2).

In 1758 the plates were issued again, as a collection, from "The Golden Boy," Grafton Street, Soho, the workshop to which Johnson had moved early in 1757. There was, as before, no title page, but a contents page engraved by Clowes and a framed dedication to Lord Blakeney, grand president of the Anti-Gallican Association, and to the Brethren of the Order, together with an epistle, a contents page, a four-page text and fifty-three plates (the additional plate that made-up with the flyer). William Blakeney was something of a British hero. He had first achieved fame as lieutenant governor of Stirling Castle, defeating the Highlanders in the Rising of 1745. Then, in 1756, as lieutenant governor of Minorca, abandoned by Admiral Byng, he had withstood a French attack for seventy days and had surrendered only on condition that the garrison was transported to Gibraltar. He was an obvious enemy of France. The Anti-Gallican Association, founded in 1745, was intended "to oppose the arts of the French Nation"—not the rococo style as such, it would seem, rather the "French Paper Machee," which is opposed to "Genius" on the ribbons at the head of the dedication plate, clearly a threat to the carvers' trade. Johnson, like so many other staunch defenders of British artistic independence in these years—Langley, William Hogarth, James Thornhill, and others—was a Freemason, clerk of the Charlotte St. Chapel, and janitor to several other masonic lodges.

On 13 July 1759 a far more serious and comprehensive imitation of Chippendale's *Director* was announced in the *Gentleman's Magazine* by William Ince and Charles Mayhew, *The Universal System of Household Furniture.* This, like Johnson's work, was to be issued in parts, each consisting of four plates, for a total of 160, like Chippendale's. In the event, the final book had ninety-five numbered plates. The date of publication is assumed to have been 1762. The book was sold at first by the authors and at A. Webley's, off Chancery Lane, Holborn, but the work was soon enough taken over by the more active and enterprising Robert Sayer, of Fleet Street. Sayer was also the principal agent for the subscriptions for the much-enlarged third edition of the *Director*, which Chippendale announced on 6 October 1759, in direct response to the threat of Ince and Mayhew's work. Before the completion of Chippendale's book, in the spring of 1762, it was taken over, however, by the bookseller, Thomas Becket, in the Strand, who issued a revised proposal at the end of July 1760. But Sayer clearly aimed, as far as he might, to control the market in books of this sort. He issued *Household Furniture in Genteel Taste for the Year 1760*, an octavo volume of sixty unsigned plates, ascribed to Darly,

Thomas Johnson. *One Hundred & Fifty, New Designs.* Plate 10. 1985.61.615

based, it is thought, on designs by Robert Manwaring, Thomas Johnson, Ince and Mayhew, and Chippendale. This was published in four variant editions in the ensuing years. More important, in 1761 Sayer published Johnson's fifty-two plates of designs, rearranged, with one in addition (pl. 48, dated 1753). The framed dedication to Blakeney was now adapted to serve as a title page, and three other title pages, dividing the work into four parts, were contrived, the first from the "Contents" plate of 1758, the other two from plates 33 and 12 of the 1758 edition. The total number of plates was now fifty-six. The epistle to Blakeney and the four-page preface of 1758 were no longer needed. The title of the book was now *One Hundred and Fifty New Designs.*

Other sheaves of designs were issued by Johnson, four sheets of girandoles representing the elements, in December 1760, *A New Book of Ornament*, consisting of a title page and seven sheets in the same year; another *New Book of Ornaments*, "Designe'd for Tablets and Frizes for Chimney-Pieces Useful for Youth to draw after," in August 1762, and a further set, only one sheet of which survives, dated August 1775, illustrating three mirrors or sconces in a firmer classical style. Johnson died about three years later.

Johnson's real claim to fame is *One Hundred and Fifty New Designs*, rococo confections for carvers, some wonderfully exuberant and fanciful, all intricate, curved, and spiky. All the designs are presented as independent, isolated objects; only one plate, for the "Side of a Room" (pl. 25, 1758; pl. 10, 1761), attempts something of an ensemble in the French manner. Even by the date of publication the book was slightly old-fashioned, and as tastes hardened further in the closing years of the century, it was dismissed as outlandish. Johnson was forgotten. John Weale, the publisher, who had obtained possession of the plates, published eleven of them around 1833 under the title *Chippendale's Designs for Sconces, Chimney and Looking Glass Frames, In the Old French Style.* No one seems to have noticed that the designs were by Johnson. In 1834 Weale issued an even larger set of Johnson's plates, *Chippendale's One Hundred and Thirty-three Designs for Interior Decoration in the Old French and Antique Styles.* Johnson's name had been removed from all the plates, and Chippendale's substituted. Johnson's title page was reused, with Weale's name in the cartouche. And so the misrepresentation continued, until 1903, when it was noticed by R. S. Clouston. Since then Johnson has slowly come into his own, a contemporary, but not a rival to Chippendale.
R. M.

Bibliography

Beard, G. and C. Gilbert. *Dictionary of English Furniture Makers 1660–1840.* Leeds, 1986

Hayward, H. *Thomas Johnson and English Rococo.* London, 1964

Hayward, H. "Newly-Discovered Designs by Thomas Johnson."*Furniture History* 2 (1975): 40–42

Thomas Johnson. *One Hundred & Fifty, New Designs.* Plate 13. 1985.61.615

34

William Kent (1685–1748)

The Designs Of Inigo Jones, Consisting of Plans and Elevations For Publick and Private Buildings. Publish'd by William Kent, With some Additional Designs. The First (–Second) Volume

[London], 1727

1983.49.33

Folio: 505 × 348 ($19\frac{7}{8} \times 13\frac{3}{4}$)

Pagination Vol. 1: [14] pp., engraved frontispiece, 73 [i.e., 51] engraved plates (7 double-page, 5 folding)

Vol. 2: [8] pp., 63 [i.e., 46] plates (17 double-page)

(*Note*: This copy lacks the half-title to vol. 1)

Edition First edition

Text vol. 1: pp. [1] title page (verso blank); [3] dedication to George I (verso blank); [5–6] "Advertisement"; [7–12] list of plates in vol. 1; [13–14] list of subscribers; *vol. 2*: pp. [1] title page (verso blank); [3–8] list of plates in vol. 2

Illustrations Vol. 1: engraved allegorical frontispiece, including portrait of Jones, engraved by Bernard Baron after a design by Kent; 51 engraved plates numbered 1–73 (7 double-page plates with 2 numbers each; 5 folding plates with 4 numbers each); engraved vignette medallion portrait of Jones on title page by P. Fourdrinier after Kent; 6 engraved head- or tailpieces by Fourdrinier after Kent; and 2 engraved initials. Designs are credited to the architects Inigo Jones (pls. 1–62), William Kent (pls. 63–65, 67–69), and Lord Burlington (pls. 70–73), all drawn by Henry Flitcroft except for 3 unsigned and 2 by Kent (pls. 49, 72). Engravers are P. Fourdrinier, Henry Hulsbergh, James Cole, and Antoine Herisset. *Vol. 2*: 46 engraved plates numbered 1–63 (17 double-page plates with 2 numbers each); engraved title page vignette (as vol. 1); head- and tailpiece by Fourdrinier after Kent; engraved initial. All numbered plates signed by Flitcroft as draftsman and Hulsbergh as engraver, except 2 engraved by James Cole. Designs are credited to Inigo Jones (pls. 1–9, 13–50, 54–56), Burlington (pls. 10–12, 51–53), and Palladio (pls. 57–63)

Binding 2 volumes bound as 1. Recent half calf, marbled boards

References Berlin Cat. 2268 (1770 ed.); Berlin (1977) OS 2268 (1770 ed.); Cicognara 533 (1770 ed.); ESTC t31727; Fowler 162; Harris and Savage 385; RIBA, *Early Printed Books*, 1624

William Kent began his career as a coach painter in Hull, but his talents were spotted and he was sent to Italy in 1709 by a group of young landowners—Sir

William Kent. *The Designs of Inigo Jones, Consisting of Plans and Elevations.* Volume II, plates 44/45. "The Plan of the First Floor of a Palace..." 1983.49.33

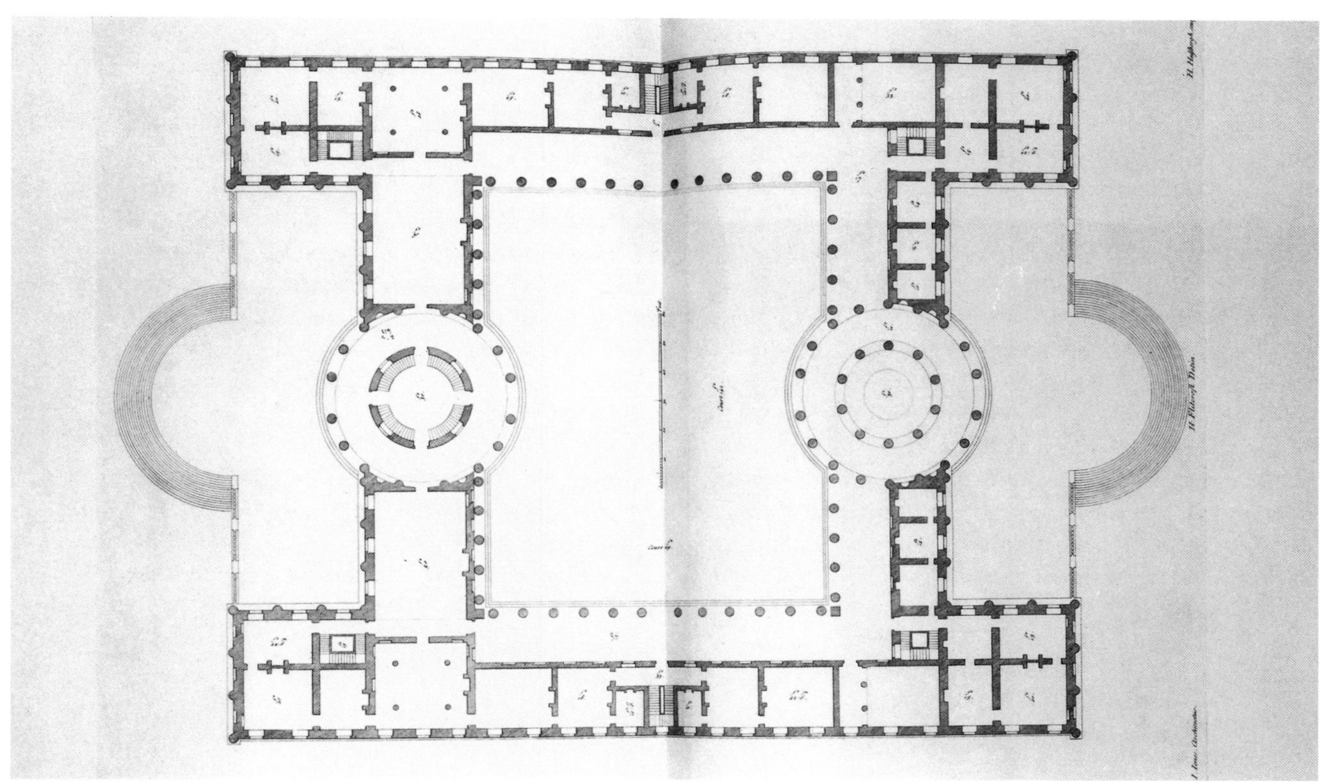

William Wentworth, Burrell Massingberd, and Sir John Chester—for whom he acted as agent in the purchase of paintings and artworks. He studied painting with the same master as Panini, Benedetto Luti. Lord Burlington met him in Rome in the winter of 1714 and became forthwith his patron, bringing him back to England in 1719 and seeing to it that he was commissioned to paint the state rooms at Kensington Palace, rather than James Thornhill. Neither Thornhill nor his son-in-law, William Hogarth, ever forgave Kent. But though he was promoted as a painter, Kent was indifferent in this art. He evolved under Burlington's guidance, first as a designer of interiors and then as an architect and landscape architect. He began on the interiors of Houghton Hall and Chiswick House in the late 1720s. But even before this Burlington had involved him in architecture.

In May 1720 Burlington had bought a collection of drawings of designs by Inigo Jones from William Talman, and at once commissioned Henry Flitcroft, a joiner who had fallen from a scaffold at Burlington House, to redraw some of the designs in preparation for publication. Flitcroft's drawings are now in the RIBA Drawings Collection. Burlington also commissioned Henry Hulsbergh to begin with the engraving. But it was not until a few years later, about 1724, that Kent was asked to edit and publish *The Designs of Inigo Jones.*

Subscriptions were invited—Nicholas Hawksmoor was one of the 380 subscribers—the king was persuaded to accept the dedication, and the book was published, in two parts, by 17 May 1727. By then Kent had begun his official career in the Office of Works, being appointed master carpenter in May 1726. Flitcroft was at the same time appointed clerk of works at Whitehall, Westminster, and St. James'. Kent and Burlington were clearly intent to promote public works, in particular the building of a royal palace. More than two-thirds of the plates in the first volume are devoted to designs for a palace at Whitehall—a palace designed, it would seem, by John Webb rather than Jones, and even then an assemblage based on drawings in both Burlington's collection and that of Dr. George Clarke at Oxford, rather than a finished scheme. Kent admitted in his perfunctory "Advertisement" that the designs were based on drawings by Jones and Webb, but he offered them all as the creations of Jones. Only in the twentieth century have scholars such as J. A. Gotch, from 1912, and Margaret Whinney, in 1946, unraveled some of the complexities of the designs, assigning all the surviving drawings to Webb, some of different periods of time.

The remaining plates in this volume include details of doors and windows by Jones (or Webb), "With some Additional Designs" by Burlington and Kent, namely, a plan, elevation, and section of Chiswick House by Burlington, with chimneypieces by Kent, including one also for Houghton Hall.

William Kent. *The Designs of Inigo Jones, Consisting of Plans and Elevations.* Volume II, plate 46. "A principal front of the foregoing palace." 1983.49.33

The second volume comprises domestic buildings for the most part, including the Queen's House at Greenwich, and a remarkable design for a palace on the Thames, at Richmond, with great colonnaded courts and an open, circular feature, that has affinities with Robert Castell's reconstruction of Pliny's villa at Laurentinum, of 1727, and that must have been a stimulus later to architects in the last years of the century. Nothing by Kent is illustrated in this volume; Burlington, however, is well represented, in particular by the extraordinary dormitory of Westminster School, a design he prepared without the support of Kent. At the end of the folio, Jones' designs for the portico of Old St. Paul's are included, as are seven plates of Palladio's S. Giorgio Maggiore, in Venice.

The Designs of Inigo Jones was a significant feature in Burlington's campaign to establish a new standard of taste in England: the first, as it were, in a series of visual exemplars, followed in 1731 by Isaac Ware's *Designs of Inigo Jones and Others* (reissued in 1743) and in 1744 by John Vardy's *Some Designs of Mr. Inigo Jones and Mr. Wm. Kent.* It was published again as late as 1770, with an additional perspective view of the Whitehall Palace. R. M.

Bibliography

Colvin, H. *Biographical Dictionary of British Architects 1660–1840.* London, 1978

Harris, E., and N. Savage. *British Architectural Books and Writers 1556–1785.* Cambridge, 1990

35

John Joshua Kirby (1716–1774)

The Perspective Of Architecture. In Two Parts. A Work Entirely New; Deduced from the Principles of Dr. Brook Taylor; And performed by Two Rules only of Universal Application. Part The First, Contains The Description and Use of a new Instrument called the Architectonic Sector. Part The Second, A New Method of Drawing the Five Orders, Elegant Structures, &c. in Perspective. Begun By Command of His Present Majesty, When Prince Of Wales. By Joshua Kirby, Designer in Perspective to His Majesty

London: printed for the author, by R. Francklin; and sold by T. Payne; Messieurs Knapton and Horsfield; Messieurs Dodsley; T. Longman; T. Davies; and J. Gretton, 1761

1985.61.618–619

Folio: 535 × 365 (21 1/16 × 14 3/8)

Pagination Vol. 1: [vi], 82 pp., engraved frontispiece, engraved dedication, 25 engraved plates; *Vol. 2*: [2], ii, 60, [2] pp., 73 engraved plates

Edition First edition

Text vol. 1: pp. [i] title page (verso blank); [iii–v] preface; [vi] blank; [1]–82 text; *vol. 2*: [1] title page (verso blank); [i]–ii introduction; 1–60 text; [61–2] index, errata, and directions for placing the plates (". . . But the best method by far, is to bind the letter-press and plates in separate volumes," i.e., as present copy)

Illustrations Allegorical frontispiece engraved by William Woollett after William Hogarth (Paulson 242); calligraphic dedication to the king engraved by John Ryland; and 98 numbered engraved plates (25 in vol. 1; 73 in vol. 2). In vol. 1, 5 of the plates are signed as engraved by Peter Mazell after [John?] Gwynn and 6 as engraved by Ignace Fougeron. In vol. 2, the credited engravers are Anthony Walker, Francis Patton, Ignace Fougeron, [William?] Kirby ("Kirby Jun."), Samuel Boyce, Peter Mazell, James Basire (senior), and John Ryland. 1 plate bears the name of Inigo Jones as architect and many have Joshua Kirby's imprint dated 21 February 1761. The text to vol. 1 begins with an unsigned engraved headpiece showing putti engaged in the various arts, and ends with a tailpiece engraved by Isaac Taylor. Similar pieces in vol. 2 are by Charles Grignion and Thomas Chambers ("Chambars"), both after Samuel Wale

Binding Text and plates bound separately. Contemporary calf, rebacked, leather labels

Provenance Early nineteenth-century stenciled ownership inscription of J. J. Davies, builder, Leominster, on prelims (and faintly visible on upper covers)

References Berlin Cat. 4738; ESTC t133638; Harris and Savage 397; Ronald Paulson, *Hogarth's Graphic Works* (New Haven, 1965), 242; RIBA, *Early Printed Books*, 1674 and 1675

John Joshua Kirby, born in Wickham Market, Suffolk, was apprenticed to a coach- and house painter in Ipswich. His father, John Kirby, was a local topographer and author of the first monograph devoted to the county, *The Suffolk Traveller* (1735). Joshua might have followed suit: his first publication was a small collection of drawings, intended for a county history that never materialized, called *Twelve Prints of Monasteries, Castles, An-tient Churches, and Monuments in the County of Suffolk* [26 March 1748]. The plates were engraved by John Wood. In a separate pamphlet describing them Kirby etched and drew some additional views (*An Historical Account of the Twelve Prints* . . . [1748]). None of these drawings hints at his future success, but Kirby was already a friend of Thomas Gainsborough (who painted his and his father's portrait), and by 1751 had another influential ally in William Hogarth. In May of that year he advertised "Proposals for printing by subscription, in one volume quarto, with a frontispiece design'd by Mr. Hogarth," a work to be called *Dr. Brook Taylor's Method of Perspective Made Easy* (*London Evening Post*, 25–28 May 1751). Although it did not appear until 1754, this work established his reputation as a perspectivist. In the same year Kirby delivered a series of lectures on the subject at the St. Martin's Lane Academy, and published *A Syllabus to Four Lectures on Perspective. With Remarks for Assisting the Memory*.

The man whose method Kirby borrowed, Brook Taylor (1685–1731), was a brilliant mathematician of the previous generation whose principal achievements were the development of the calculus of finite differences and the basic principle of differential calculus (now called Taylor's theorem). Even fellow mathematicians found his writings obscure, however, and although he was an accomplished artist himself, his treatise on perspective was little noticed when first published as *Linear Perspective, or A New Method of Representing Justly All Manner of Objects as they Appear to the Eye in All Situations* (1715; 2d ed., 1719). It contained the first general treatment of the principle of vanishing points, but Taylor's rival Johann Bernoulli described it as "abstruse to all and unintelligible to artists for whom it was more especially written," and this seems to have remained true despite Professor John Colson's editorship of a third edition in 1749, called (like the second of 1719) *New Principles of Linear Perspective*. The case for some more accessible version was therefore a strong one. According to the preface to *Dr. Brook Taylor's Method*, it was Hogarth who encouraged Kirby to take the work on. Its success allowed a second edition to appear in 1755; a third in 1765; and another, also describing itself as the third, in 1768.

Despite its popularity, Kirby's work was not universally welcomed. The painter Joseph Highmore (1692–1780), an older and better-known student of Taylor, accused him, quite rightly, of departing from the latter's principles by introducing exceptions to rules whenever those rules seemed to produce the wrong result. Kirby believed that in cases where the experience of perspective tells us something different from its mathematics, the former could be preferred. The most famous dispute concerned whether columns in a colonnade parallel to the picture plane ought to be painted broader as they recede from the center, which would fit the rules of perspective but would not conform to ordinary perception Highmore attacked Kirby's position in *A Critical Examination of Those Two Paintings On the Cieling of the Banqueting-House at Whitehall in which Architecture is Introduced, so far as Relates to the Perspective* (1754). Another, less menacing attack, came from Isaac Ware, who in 1756 published a translation of book one of a relatively obscure Italian Renaissance treatise on perspective, Lorenzo Sirigatti's *La Pratica di Prospettiva* (Venice, 1596). Advertising its rules as "the simplest, and therefore the easier to be understood than any thing hitherto published in the English language," Ware was clearly trying to undermine sales of Kirby's treatise. The latter responded with *Dr. Brook Taylor's Method of Perspective, Compared with the Examples lately publish'd on this subject as Sirigatti's, by Isaac Ware, Esq. . . . in which the superior excellence of Taylor's is shewn by self-evident principles, or simple inspection* [1757]. According to a later writer on perspective, Thomas Malton, this pamphlet was suppressed, but it remains an indication of how vicious the rivalry between fellow members of the St. Martin's Lane Academy could be at this time. Ware is described, for example, as a "pert smatterer in the insufficient rules of Sirigatti" (p. 31).

Soon after publication of *Dr. Brook Taylor's Method* Kirby was appointed teacher of drawing and perspective to the prince of Wales, through the influence of the prince's main adviser John Stuart, 3d earl of Bute. Since Kirby was by now also a good friend of Sir Joshua Reynolds, his entrance into London society may be judged an extraordinary success, especially as his artistic output in this period seems to have been fairly meager. At this stage he began composing his treatise on perspective. In 1760 the prince was crowned George III and the following year two events confirmed Kirby's new status. First, he and his eighteen-year-old son William were appointed joint clerks of the works at Richmond and Kew palaces. Second, he published, in grand style, *The Perspective of Architecture*. Its two volumes were also available for separate purchase.

The treatise begins with a striking frontispiece designed by Hogarth (his signature is dated July 1760) and engraved by William Woollett. A dedication to the king is followed by a preface in which Kirby admits that he would not have attempted such a work without a royal subvention, and that all of it remains based on Taylor. He begs his readers to consider "whether the digesting theorems into regular order, deducing proper corollaries from them, and illustrating them by new schemes and examples, has not as just a claim to the title of original, as any thing that can be produced in an age like this, when almost every subject seems to be quite exhausted." The fact remains, however, that Kirby's treatise added little to what had been written earlier.

Volume one is devoted to a description of Kirby's architectonic sector (advertised as manufactured in silver, ivory, or wood by George III's mathematical instrument maker George Adams). Although the title page describes it as a new instrument, Kirby admits in the text that the real inventor of this type of sector was Ottavio Revesi Bruti, whose treatise was translated by Thomas Malie, under the patronage of Lord Burlington, in 1737 (*A New and Accurate Method of Delineating all the Parts of the Different Orders in Architecture, by means of a Well Contriv'd, and Most Easily Manag'd Instrument*). Kirby altered the divisions marked off on the sector to make the orders "chiefly from Palladio, corrected however by the purest examples of antiquity" (p. 2). This could not (or at least should not) have taken him too far away from his source, since Bruti also used Palladio, even if he generally preferred the work of Vincenzo Scamozzi. What unites Malie's translation of Revesi Bruti and Kirby's essay on the same instrument is that, both being expensive folios, neither were written for the trade. They both reflect the newly acquired dignity of the technical sciences when applied to the arts. This part of Kirby's treatise is indeed little more than an instruction manual writ large for royalty.

In volume two Kirby begins with a discussion of the correct distance and height the eye should be from its object—but characteristically admits almost immediately that these will vary to suit the occasion and cannot be fixed. It also emerges that the "two rules only of universal application," mentioned on the title page, are simply Taylor's rules for representing the square and the circle, as "An order of architecture (as to it's mouldings only) may be considered as a number of square or horizontal planes, of different diameters, laid in such a manner upon one another, as to give the peculiar shape or outline of each" (introduction). Readers expecting "A work entirely new" were therefore left to content themselves with the methodical application of these rules to the six orders (separating ancient from modern Ionic); to sciography; and to "buildings in general." The latter section is much the most interesting.

It begins with a recapitulation of the arguments surrounding the depiction of columns in a colonnade.

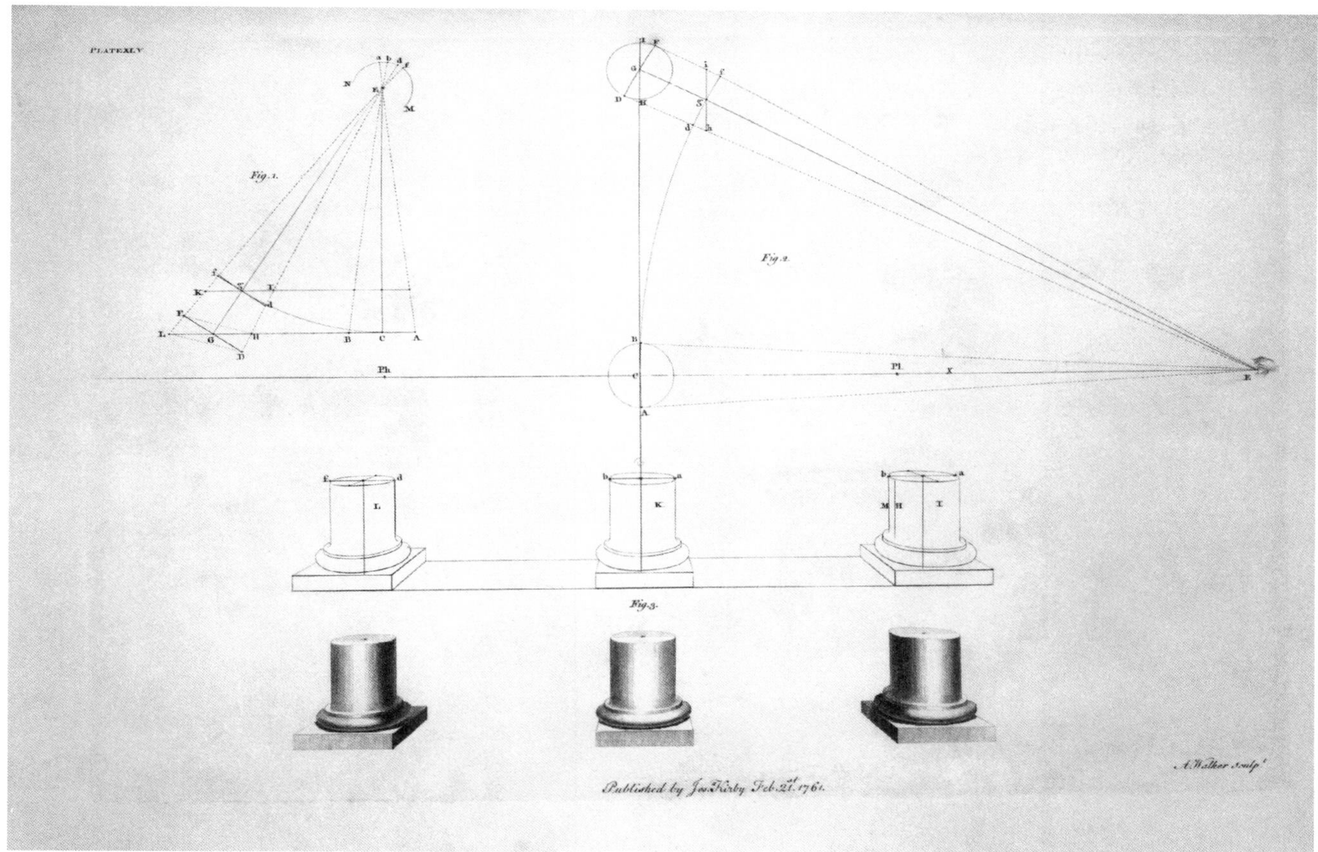

Joshua Kirby. *The Perspective of Architecture.* Plate XLV. Perspective representation of columns. 1985.61.619

Kirby retains his opinion that strict mathematical perspective fails to produce the correct result, but now offers a new formula that would ensure that "those who would draw columns thus situated, so as to make them all of the same size in perspective, have . . . a universal rule for doing it" (p. 45). In an attempt to prevent a revival of arguments arising from his first treatise, however, he gives the reader the choice of both systems, and adds that "the opinion of candid and sensible persons will be thankfully attended to; but the strictures of snarling and malevolent critics will be entirely disregarded" (p. 46). Defending himself against accusations of plagiarism, he further notes that only after his new scheme was engraved was he informed "that one of the same nature has been invented, some time ago, by Mr. Wright, an ingenious mathematician" (p. 44).

Kirby then applies his rules to various structures, including "An house from a design of Inigo Jones" and Jones' Banqueting House in Whitehall. The finished drawing of the latter (pl. LXII) is announced as "a small part of that most magnificent structure, which was designed by a native of this kingdom, as a palace for the kings and queens of Great Britain, and which, were it ever to be carried into execution would be a striking proof of the great abilities of the architect, and of the refined dignity of a British monarch" (p. 55). The idea of reviving Jones' (attributed) palace design must have been widely discussed when Colen Campbell and William Kent published the drawings for it in volume 2 of *Vitrivius Britannicus* (1717) and *The Designs of Inigo Jones* (1727), respectively. The pointed reference to it here, in a book by a clerk of the works intended for the eyes of a new king, indicates that in some circles the project had not yet been abandoned. And if building such a palace meant the destruction of Kent's Horse Guards this would only have delighted Kirby all the more, because he considered the latter a "lasting monument of the ill-taste and want of genius in the contrivers" (*Critical Review*, Nov. 1757, 427). It was left to Robert Dodsley to point out, in the same year Kirby's treatise was published, that the masks and swags on the exterior of the Banqueting House were by then "soe corroded as to be scarce intelligible" (*London and its Environs Described*). In the event George III's main intervention was to authorize its refacing in Portland stone, 1774.

The plates devoted to the Banqueting House are immediately followed by two giving, respectively, the perspective method and finished result of a drawing for "a house with a colonnade, etc." (pls. LXIII–IV). The original for the second of these, in pen and gray wash, is preserved at Windsor Castle. It is initialed "G[eorge]. P[rince of]. W[ales]. 1760" (changed from 1761) and inscribed on its verso "This Drawing was designed & executed for my book on perspective by His Majesty King George III" (remainder cropped). Kirby does not refer to the origin of the design in his text, but does state that "This, and the last finished print in the book,

are esteemed by me as the most valuable parts of it" (p. 55), surely a hint that both originated with his royal pupil. The original drawing for the last plate (pl. LXXIII), "a little more than one half of a most magnificent design, which was made and given me for this work; and which (if well executed) would make an excellent piece of scenery for a theatre" (p. 58), seems not to have survived.
G. B.

Joshua Kirby. *The Perspective of Architecture.* Plate LXIIII. Design for a house with a colonnade. 1985.61.619

Bibliography

Colvin, H. *A Biographical Dictionary of British Architects 1600–1840.* 3d ed. New Haven and London, 1995

DNB 31: 198–199

Harris, E., and N. Savage. *British Architectural Books and Writers 1556–1785.* Cambridge, 1990

The History of the King's Works. Ed. H. M. Colvin. Vol. 5. London, 1976

Oppé, A. P. *English Drawings, Stuart and Georgian Periods, in the Collection of His Majesty the King at Windsor Castle.* London, 1950

36

Isaac Landmann (1741–1826?)

A Course Of The Five Orders Of Civil Architecture; With A Plan, And Some Geometrical Elevations Of Town Gates of Fortified Places. By J. Landmann, Professor of Fortification and Artillery To The Royal Military Academy at Woolwich. The Five Orders are taken from Mr. Chambers's Elegant Treatise on Civil Architecture

London: printed for the author, by James Dixwell; and sold by T. and J. Egerton, at the Military Library, 1785

NGA Lib. Rare Book: NA2810L36 fol.

Folio: 410 × 258 (16 3/16 × 10 1/2)

Pagination [ii], 25, [1] pp., 14 aquatint plates

Edition First edition

Text pp. [i] title page (verso blank); [1]–25 text; [26] blank

Illustrations 14 plates numbered I–XIV, all aquatints with borders, only plate XIII signed by Landmann

Binding Recent half calf, marbled boards, red morocco label

Provenance Ownership inscription "James Havard Thomas 1873," p. [1]

References ESTC t135726; Harris and Savage 406

Isaac Landmann, German by birth, was born on 30 April 1741, on the same day that the Royal Military Academy in Woolwich was founded by Royal Warrant. Nothing is known about his early life except that he was attached to the École militaire in Paris before his appointment as professor of fortification and artillery at the above-mentioned academy in November 1777. A few further anecdotes are scattered throughout the first volume of his precocious son's amusing memoirs, *Adventures and Recollections of Colonel Landmann* (1852), from which all the following quotations are taken. The appointment was apparently engineered by George, Viscount (later Marquis) Townsend, and Landmann took up residence in the academy's so-called warren as a neighbor of Charles Hutton, the academy's professor of mathematics and author of, among other works, *A Treatise on Mensuration* (1770) and *The Principles of Bridges* (1772). He remained in the same post until his retirement in 1815, nicknamed Old Snout "in consequence of the extra dimensions of his nose," just as Hutton was Old Crump because of his "invariable roughness of manner." The Warren had in its garden Prince Rupert's Tower, whose origin and function was much debated until recently. Before its destruction, Landmann commissioned a model of it from the ordnance modeler, Mr. Short ("a man six feet four inches high"). This model was later presented by Isaac's son to the United Services Institution and is discussed by Brigadier Hogg (*The Royal Arsenal: Its Background, Origin, and Subsequent History* [London, 1963], 191 ff). In 1789 Landmann took a house in Blackheath for himself and his wife, son, and daughter.

George III was a frequent visitor to Woolwich. According to his son's memoirs, on 9 July 1785 Landmann was able to show the king a drawing of a cannon and its carriage that used flaps, or overlays, to provide views and sections on the same sheet—at which

> the King was so much delighted that he clapped my father on the shoulder and exclaimed, "This is the best thing I have seen to-day." Several other drawings on the same principle were then produced, amongst which were a thirteen-inch sea-mortar, in its house; the plan and elevation of a powder magazine, showing the outside, then, by lifting the drop-leaf, the inside was displayed with all the barrels of gunpowder neatly stacked, &c. &c. The King's delight was expressed in strong terms on each being explained, and he asked for copies. The originals were immediately placed at his disposal (*Adventures* 1852, 4).

Such flaps were hardly original—they had been used by anatomists for well over two hundred years—but they were fairly new to architectural draftsmanship. (For their use in other contexts, see the works by Cameron

Isaac Landmann. *A Course of the Five Orders of Civil Architecture.* Plate XIII. "Geometrical elevation of a Town Gate." NGA Lib. Rare Book: NA2810L36 fol.

and Repton in the Millard collection.)

A Course of the Five Orders was published in the same year. It is a competent abridgment of the first forty-two pages of *A Treatise on Civil Architecture* (1759), taking from Chambers' discussion of the orders just enough text to make sense of the illustrations. At no point does Landmann question the opinions of his author. The first ten plates are copies of those on each of the five orders plus "The Doric order in its improved state"; "The orders of the ancients"; "Regular mouldings with their proper ornaments"; "Goldman[n]'s volute described"; and "Plans and elevations of pilaster capitals [with] Pedestals for the orders." No text is added to describe the final four plates, which give original designs for the gates of fortified towns "in a distinctly French neo-classical style" (Harris and Savage 1990, 262), which it would be interesting to compare with others published by students of the École militaire.

This was only the first of a series of books Landmann published for the benefit of his pupils. The remainder were on more purely military subjects, namely, *Elements of Tacticks . . . By a celebrated Prussian General [Saltern] . . . Translated from the Original in German by I. Landmann* (1787); *The Attack and Defense of Fortified Places . . . By John Muller. The 4th edition, corrected and very much enlarged, by Isaac Landmann* (1791); *The Principles of Fortification, Reduced into Questions and Answers* [1796] (2d ed., 1801; 3d ed., 1806; 4th ed., 1812; 5th ed., 1821; 6th ed., 1831; 7th ed., 1853); *Practical Geometry* (1798; 2d ed., 1805); *The Field Engineer's-Vade Mecum* (1802); and *A Treatise on Mines* (1815). G. B.

Bibliography

Harris, E., and N. Savage. *British Architectural Books and Writers 1556–1785*. Cambridge, 1990

Landmann, G. *Adventures and Recollections*. London, 1852

Isaac Landmann. *A Course of the Five Orders of Civil Architecture*. Plate XI. "Geometrical elevation of a Town Gate." NGA Lib. Rare Book: NA2810L36 fol.

37

Batty Langley (1696–1751) and Thomas Langley (c. 1700–1751)

The Builder's Jewel: Or, The Youth's Instructor, And Workman's Remembrancer. Explaining Short and Easy Rules, Made familiar to the meanest Capacity, For Drawing and Working . . . The Whole illustrated by upwards of 200 Examples, engraved on 100 Copper-Plates. By B. and T. Langley

London: printed for R. Ware, 1757

NGA Lib. Rare Book: NA2840L2

Sixteenmo: 139 × 110 (5 1/2 × 4 5/16)

Pagination 34, [2] pp., engraved frontispiece, 99 engraved plates

Edition Fifth edition

Text pp. [1] title page (verso blank); [3] introduction, signed by Thomas Langley, London, 2 Nov. 1746; 4–[36] text, with final advertisement "Books printed for R. Ware"

Illustrations Engraved frontispiece and 99 numbered plates, most signed as engraved by Thomas after Batty Langley's designs, often dated 1741. Plates 41, 77–78 are signed by Thomas as both designer and engraver

Binding Contemporary calf, rebacked

Provenance Ownership inscription "C. Percival Walgate. 1908" on front endpaper

References Berlin (1977) OS 2276[h] (11th ed.); ESTC t77976; Harris and Savage 435; RIBA, *Early Printed Books*, 1738

BATTY LANGLEY was more prolific even than William Halfpenny as a producer of architectural books. He published both the largest to appear in the eighteenth century, *Ancient Masonry*, issued between 1733 and 1736, and the smallest, *The Builder's Jewel*, first printed in 1741. The range of subject was diverse and erratic, including the first handbook on the layout of gardens, *New Principles of Gardening*, of 1728, and the first, altogether idiosyncratic, pattern book of gimcrack "gothick" designs, *Ancient Architecture Restored*, of 1742, reprinted in 1747 as *Gothic Architecture, Improved by Rules and Proportions*, but his main concern was with the provision of basic information on the setting up of the orders and their related parts. His books are on the whole derivative and slapdash—he and his brother Thomas owned an unusually large collection of books and prints, many of them from Europe, which he plundered for models.

Langley's name was long synonymous with bizarre and wayward design, but though he had little enough talent and gives no evidence of intellectual ability, he was a dogged and dedicated enthusiast. He was certainly motivated. He was at one with William Hogarth. He was fiercely opposed to foreign influences and fashions, in particular to Burlington's Rule of Taste. He was the champion of Nicholas Hawksmoor, though the Hawksmoor of Westminster Abbey rather than the architect of London churches. Langley was also a fervent Freemason. His name does not appear on surviving lists of masons, but there is no doubt that he was deeply involved in the fraternity, dedicating much of his energy to the support and instruction of craftsmen and builders. His odd and uninformed enthusiasm for Gothic was an aspect of both his xenophobia and his dedication to the masonic ideal, as indeed were all his handbooks of instruction.

Langley was not trained as an architect. He was born in 1696 at Twickenham, the son of Daniel Langley, a gardener, and this was his first career. Gardens were also the subject of his first books, in which he illustrated layouts in what he termed the "arti–natural" style, meanders and wiggles, derived from Stephen Switzer's *Ichnographica Rustica* of 1718, that marked the emergence of something of a rococo fashion in English gardening. By 1731 Langley was living in London, near Smith Square, with a yard in Lambeth where he sold columns, statues, and busts of "a new invention of casting in stone," in the description of George Vertue. Soon after, if one is to judge by the naming of the sixth of his children, Euclid, in August 1733, Langley began his masonic connection. Later sons were christened Vitruvius, Archimedes, and Hiram. In all he had fourteen children from his two marriages. By 1737 the Langleys had moved to 24 Meards Court, off Dean Street, in Soho, and there he set up a school or academy, as he termed it, with his brother Thomas. This was advertised in *Ancient Masonry* and elsewhere:

> Young Nobleman and Gentlemen taught to draw the Five Orders of Columns in Architecture. To design Geometrical Plans and Elevations for Temples, Hermitages, Caves, Grotto's, Cascades, Theaters and other Ornamental Buildings of Delight, to lay out, Plans and improve Parks and Gardens, by the author, by whom Buildings in general are Designed, Surveyed and performed in the most masterly manner.

Much is bombast. James Elmes noted in his lectures that Langley's disciples were all carpenters. Langley himself, though he produced a design for the Mansion House in 1735 and one for Westminster Bridge in 1736 (where the commission was awarded to that "Insolent, Arrogating Swiss," Charles Labelye), is known to have erected only one building—"a curious grotesque temple *in a taste entirely new*, finely decorated within with busts of King William III, George I, and five gentlemen of the club of liberty; and without, with an eagle on the vertex of its dome, with sphynxes on its entablature, and with wolves at the extremes of its base . . ." erected in 1734 or 1735, for Nathaniel Blackerby, deputy grand master of The Grand Lodge of Freemasons, one of the commissioners of the Fifty New Churches, who was to marry Hawksmoor's daughter in 1735.

The *Builder's Jewel, or Youth's Instructor*, was evidently a part of Batty and Thomas Langley's teaching enterprise, reflecting masonic concerns. The frontispiece, drawn by Batty and engraved by Thomas, consists of three columns on pedestals with entablatures (Tuscan, Doric, and Corinthian), marked W, S, and B—Wisdom, Strength, and Beauty—surmounted by a sun, a moon, and the bust of a mason, bedecked with drafting and surveying instruments and geometrical figures, and the plan of a lodge in the center.

Batty and Thomas Langley. *The Builder's Jewel.* Frontispiece. NGA Lib. Rare Book: NA2840L2

The introduction sets forth the intent:

> Notwithstanding there are many Volumes already extant on the Subject of Architecture; yet, as not one of them is made of a fit Size for the Pocket; and it being an Impossibility for the general Part of Workmen to retain and carry in their Minds all useful Rules and Proportions, by which Works in general are performed : I have therefore, at the Request of many good Workmen, and for the Sake of young Students, compiled this Work.

The book consists of ninety-nine plates illustrating the five orders and their parts, pedestals and plinths, dados and moldings, door and window surrounds, with arrangements for arcades, porticoes, pediments, and copings. Plates 79 to 81 illustrate proportions for coved ceilings, plate 82 the centering for the groins of vaults. Plates 83 to 95 are devoted to joists and roof trusses, some of them effected over highly irregular ground plans.

The first edition of the book, of 1741, was published by Richard Ware, as were all editions up to the tenth, of 1763, all with the collation and contents as for the second edition, of 1746, when the text was somewhat enlarged. But the popularity of the book was sustained for many years more. There were twelve further editions, the last printed in Edinburgh in 1808. An American edition was issued around the turn of the century in Charlestown, printed by S. Etheridge for Samuel Hill, engraver, of Boston. R. M.

Bibliography

Harris, E., and N. Savage. *British Architectural Books and Writers 1556–1785*. Cambridge, 1990

Harris, J. "The Arti-natural Style." In *The Rococo in England: A Symposium*. Ed. C. Hind. London, 1986: 8–20

Rowan, A. "Batty Langley's Gothic." In *Studies in Memory of David Talbot Rice*. Ed. G. Robertson and G. Henderson. Edinburgh, 1975: 197–215

38

Sebastien Leclerc (1637–1714)

A Treatise Of Architecture, With Remarks and Observations. By that Excellent Master thereof Sebastien Le Clerc . . . Necessary For Young People who would apply to that Noble Art. Engraven in CLXXXI. Copper Plates By John Sturt. Translated By Mr. Chambers

London: sold by Mr. Bateman and Mr. Taylor, Will. and John Innys, Mr. Osbourn, Mr. Senex, Mr. Sam. Tooke & Mr. Ben. Motte, and John Sturt, 1724

1985.61.652

Octavo: 194 × 122 ($7\frac{5}{8} \times 4\frac{1}{16}$)

Pagination Engraved portrait, engraved title plate, [2] engraved dedication plates, [2] list of subscribers plates, [180] engraved plates

(*Note*: Atlas only. This copy lacks the text volume. The atlas includes 2 plates usually bound in the text volume, listing the subscribers, but lacks plate 120 and 2 of 4 dedication plates, i.e., those to the masons and bricklayers companies)

Edition First edition

Illustrations Engraved title with vignette; portrait of Le Clerc engraved by John Sturt; dedication plates to the master and wardens of the Carpenters' Guild and of the Joiners' Guild; 180 engraved plates numbered 1–60, 61A, 61B, 62–78, 80–119, 121–181; and 2 plates with a list of subscribers (all versos blank). No plate 79 was published; this copy lacks 2 dedication plates and plate 120

Binding Contemporary paneled calf, rebacked

References ESTC t194549; Fowler 173 (later ed.); Harris and Savage 482 (variant: title plate in earlier state calling for "Two Hundred Copper Plates"); RIBA, *Early Printed Books,* 1803 (variant)

SEBASTIEN LECLERC is known to architects for the twenty-nine memorable plates that he engraved for Claude Perrault's *Les dix livres d'architecture de Vitruve*, of 1673. He prepared other plates of an architectural kind, including two stunning sections of the Pantheon for Antoine Desgodetz's *Les édifices antiques de Rome*, of 1682. But he was not an architect, nor was he trained as such. Born in Metz, in 1637, he was the son of a goldsmith who taught him the art of engraving. He also studied mathematics, geometry, and perspective drawing, and by 1660 was employed as a surveyor. His career, however, was to be that of an engraver. By 1665 he was working in Paris, and within a few years he was engraving plates for the publications of the *Académie des sciences*. He was also working for Charles Lebrun, at the Gobelins, where he was given an apartment and where he lived with his family until his death in October 1714. His first triumph was a rich and complex study of Lebrun's funeral decorations for Pierre Séguier, done in 1672. In August of this year he was admitted to the *Académie royale de peinture et sculpture*, to which he was to serve as professor of geometry and perspective drawing from 1680 to 1699. On 20 January 1693 he was appointed *graveur ordinaire du roi*. He became one of the most famous and active engravers of the period; more than three thousand plates are assigned to him. But he aspired also to produce books of instruction. In 1669 he published the *Pratique de la géométrie*, to which he began a sequel, then in 1679 a *Discours touchant le point de veue*, to which he did issue a sequel, the *Système de la vision*, of 1712. In 1690 he published a *Traité de géométrie*. Only toward the end of his life did he plan the *Traité d'architecture*, but he grew blind and it was published, incomplete, about six months before his death, in two volumes, one of text and one of plates. There were 184 plates in all, though seven more, illustrating a French order, survive, and were clearly intended for the *Traité*. According to the *Eloge* by the abbé de Vallemont,

A TREATISE OF
ARCHITECTURE,
With REMARKS and
OBSERVATIONS.
By that Excellent Master *thereof*
SEBASTIAN LE CLERC,
KNIGHT of the EMPIRE
Designer *and* Engraver *to the* Cabinet
Of the late FRENCH KING &: *Member*
Of the ACADEMY *of* ARTS & SCIENCES. *Necessary*
For Young People who would apply to that
NOBLE ART.
Engraven in CLXXXI. Copper Plates
By JOHN STURT.
TRANSLATED BY Mr CHAMBERS

SOLD by Mr. Bateman *and* Mr. Taylor *in* Pater-Noster-Row. Will. *and* John Innys *at the West end of* St. Pauls. Mr. Osbourn *in Lombard Street*. Mr. Senex *at ye Globe in Fleetstreet*. Mr. Sam. Tooke & Mr. Ben. Motte *at the Temple gate* Booksellers. *And* John Sturt *Engraver in Golden Lion Court in Aldersgate Street*
LONDON. MDCCXXIV.

Sebastien Leclerc. *A Treatise of Architecture.* Title page. 1985.61.652

published in 1715, there were to have been even more plates, plans, sections, and elevations of buildings, for a total of two hundred.

The English edition of the *Traité d'architecture* was promoted by the engraver John Sturt together with a group of London booksellers, William Taylor and John Innys, John Senex, and John Osborne. The translator was Ephraim Chambers. The work was to be published monthly, in parts, at two shillings each. One of these, issued in March 1723, had an engraved title page describing the contents as "Exercises for Free and accepted Masons." By the end of the year the first volume, the text, was complete and had been issued with a portrait of Leclerc, copied by Sturt from the abbé de Vallemont's *Eloge*, as a frontispiece, and an engraved title page. Only in the following year, on 23 April, was the volume of plates advertised, in the *Daily Journal*, to be sold by subscription. The initial booksellers were now joined by Christopher Bateman, Sam Tooke, and Ben Motte. There were 135 subscribers, craftsmen for the most part, but including the architects James Gibbs, Nicholas Hawksmoor, and John James. This volume seems to have been published late in 1724; its engraved title page records a contents of two hundred plates (as mentioned in the *Eloge*), but only 181 were issued. The cost of the two volumes was fifteen shillings.

In October 1724, presumably after the completion of the subscription volume, a trade issue of the book, at seventeen shillings, was advertised by Osbourne, William and John Innys, and Thomas Innys and Thomas Longman, who had taken over the share of Taylor, who had died in May 1724. No copy survives with this imprint, but a trade issue of volume two is known, sold by Richard Ware, William and John Innys, Osbourne, Senex, and Tooke and Motte. The plates of this are printed on both sides of the sheets. The title page, dated 1724, has the number of plates corrected to 181, and the name Richard Ware inserted in place of Bateman and Taylor. The two volumes were reissued by Ware in 1727, 1732, and around 1747. The volume of plates in the Millard collection is clearly the subscription issue, with particular variations, of 1724.

Leclerc's treatise is a humdrum work, the text offering no sharpness of comment or illumination. It is essentially a handbook for workmen describing and illustrating the orders and their related parts and the mode of their assembly. Leclerc's preferred authorities are Palladio and Giacomo da Vignola, but he is more eclectic than either of these, including a Spanish order and, right at the end, a French order of his own design. Many years earlier, when a competition for a French order was held to raise and complete the *Cour Carré* at the Louvre, Leclerc had engraved Lebrun's design, and also one of his own, but he suppressed his composition then lest it upset his former patron. Only in the final plate of the *Traité d'architecture* did he make public his design. R. M.

Bibliography

Harris, E., and N. Savage. *British Architectural Books and Writers 1556–1785*. Cambridge, 1990

Meaume, E. *Sébastien Le Clerc et son oeuvre*. Paris, 1877

Préaud, M. *Bibliothéque Nationale. Département de Estampes. Inventaire du fonds français. Graveurs du XVIIe siècle. 8,9 Sébastien Leclerc*. Paris, 1980

39

David Loggan (1635–1700?)

Oxonia Illustrata, sive Omnium Celeberrimæ istius Universitatis Collegiorum, Aularum, Bibliothecæ Bodleianæ, Scholarum Publicarum, Theatri Sheldoniani; nec non Urbis Totius Scenographia. Delineavit & Sculpsit Dav: Loggan Univ. Oxon. Chalcographus

Oxford: E Theatro Sheldoniano, 1675

1985.61.2505

Folio: 442 × 295 ($17\frac{3}{8} \times 11\frac{7}{8}$)

Pagination Engraved title plate, engraved dedication, [45] engraved plates (43 double-page, 2 folding)

(*Note*: Total includes 2 additional plates bound in with this copy)

Edition First edition

Illustrations Standard copies of this work contain a total of 45 unnumbered etched and engraved plates. There are 5 unnumbered preliminary plates as follows: unsigned title plate (title engraved on draped cloth supported by 3 putti, with Minerva below, seated before a view of Oxford and surrounded by emblems of learning); dedication to Charles II; preface; privilege; and numbered list of plates. The latter also gives page references to Anthony à Wood's *Historia et Antiquitates Universitatis Oxoniensis* (1674). It is followed by 40 views, as listed, each with Latin captions and a dedication signed by Loggan. Plate XXVIII is a large folding plate (here added from a later printing, with Henry Overton's *excudit*; crudely repaired). Most plates are also signed by Loggan as draftsman and engraver, and 2 are dated 1673.

The Millard copy is extra-illustrated with (1) a double-page engraved view of the east front of the Ashmolean Museum, with a dedication to Timothy Halton by Michael Burghers, signed "M. Burghers deline. sculp et excudit" and "T. Wood Archit." [i.e., Thomas Wood, d. 1695] (bound after plate [IX]); and (2) an eighteenth-century folding engraved plate of Tom Tower, Christ Church, cropped, no credit or caption remaining (bound after plate [XXIX])

Binding Contemporary mottled calf, rebacked

Provenance Engraved armorial bookplate of the Hon. Arthur Dillon

References Berlin Cat. 2327; Berlin (1977) OS 2327; ESTC r5725; Madan 3035; RIBA, *Early Printed Books*, 1914; Upcott, pp. 1105–1107; Wing L2838

David Loggan. *Oxonia Illustrata.* Sheldonian Theatre. 1985.61.2505

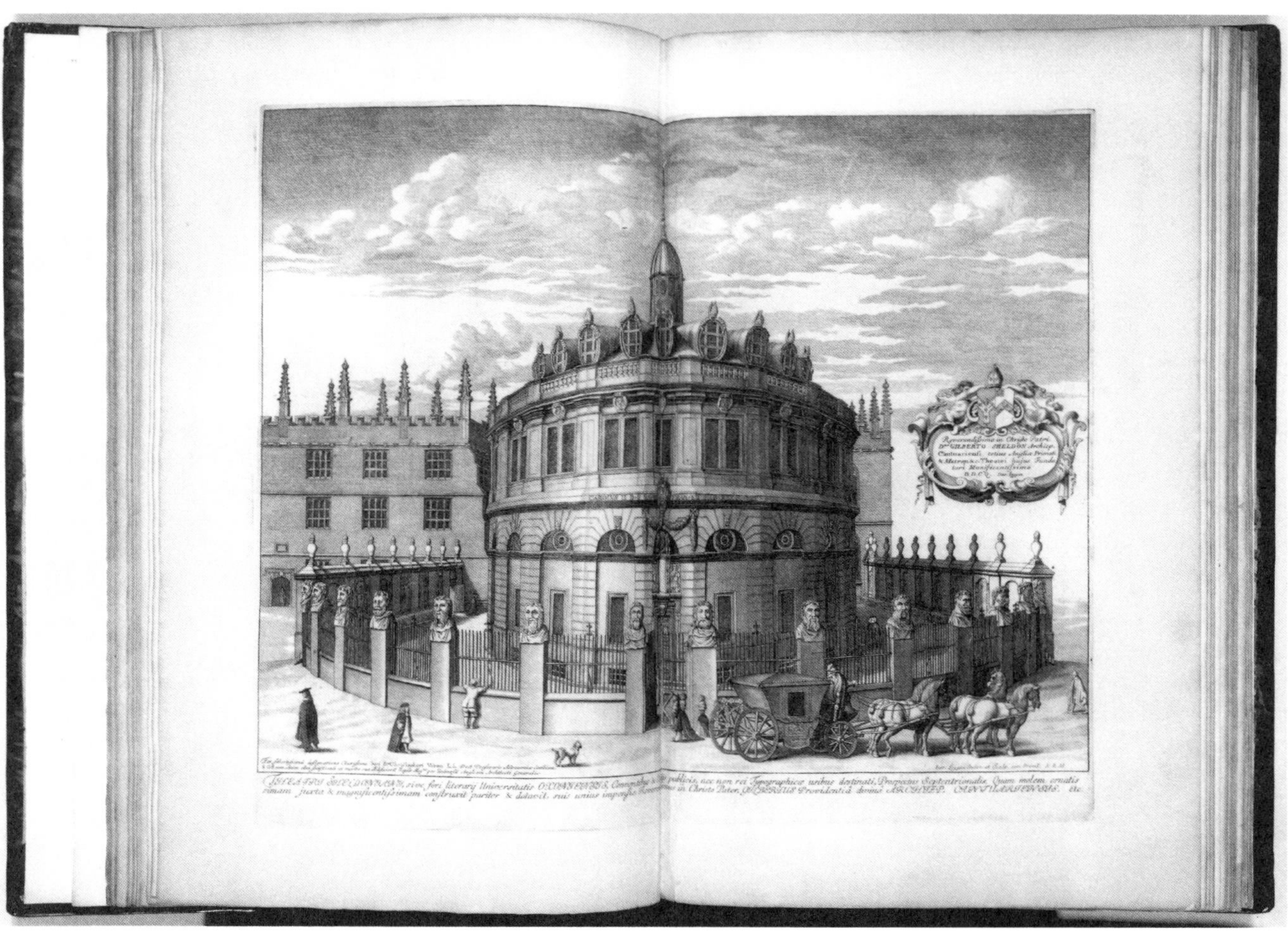

40

David Loggan (1635–1700?)

Cantabrigia Illustrata Sive Omnium Celeberrimæ istius Universitatis Collegiorum, Aularum, Bibliothecæ Academicæ Scholarum Publicarum Sacelli Coll: Regalis nec non Totius Oppidi Ichnographia Delineatore & Sculptore Dav: Loggan Utriusque Academiæ Calcographo

Cambridge: the author, [1690?]

1985.61.2504

Folio: 440 × 292 (17 5/16 × 11 1/2)

Pagination [34] etched and engraved plates (25 double-page, 5 folding)

Edition First edition

Illustrations The 34 etched and engraved plates, numbered I–XXXIV in the table of contents, consist of a title plate (title engraved on draped cloth supported by 2 angels above a broad landscape including distant view of Cambridge and hill of Parnassus); an engraved dedication to William and Mary; a preface; a table of contents (with etched university seal); east and west views of Cambridge engraved on 1 plate; a city plan; a plate showing varieties of academic dress; and 27 views of college buildings. All after plate [IV] are double-page size except plates [XXVII] and [XXIX], which require folding. A further 3 plates are bound as folding in the Millard copy. The views each have Latin captions and a dedication signed by Loggan, who also signs most as draftsman and engraver, although according to George Vertue, some of the drawings were contributed by "Kickers" (i.e., Everhardus Kickius) and Robert White. Plate [VI], a map of Cambridge, is dated 1688. The complete work was published in 1690 or later. For details, and further references, see RIBA, *Early Printed Books*

Binding Contemporary paneled calf, sprinkled, rebacked

References ESTC R19256; RIBA, *Early Printed Books*, 1913; Upcott, pp. 36–39; Wing L2837

"OF THE APPEARANCE of the exteriors of the colleges and the public buildings of the university between 1675 and 1690 we have the superbly accurate record of David Loggan," writes Elisabeth Leedham-Green in *A Concise History of the University of Cambridge* (1996, 106):

> In his pages, at first glance, each floats tidily on its own island, a few decorous academics pacing thoughtfully by. Closer inspection is rewarded by a more intimate view of the Cambridge of his time: the horses grazing outside King's College chapel, the burial party and the barrow outside Great St Mary's, the waggon creaking reluctantly past Pembroke, the coach passing Sidney Sussex, pack horses outside Queen's, a chimney-sweep and, as ever, an impending traffic jam outside Christ's, provisions being carried into St John's and the boats, here and in the view of Magdalene where, also, we see the exercise of the university's ancient right to expel prostitutes; and everywhere there are dogs, even fighting in King's College Chapel.

Her description makes it plain why Loggan's engravings have been prized not only as a valuable source of evidence for the contemporary appearance of buildings, but also as the work of an acute social commentator. In the preface to *Cantabrigia illustrata*, Loggan gives testimony to his own accuracy:

> To pay repeated visits to the University, and when there, to submit everything to the closest examination of the mind, as well as of the eye; to observe the limitations imposed by Optics as well as by Geometry; to examine, from some distant point, the roofs of all the buildings which came within my field of vision, all the objects which the subtle and varied art of architecture brought under my notice in the different materials which it employs; to draw them first from paper, then to engrave them properly on copper, and, lastly, to print them skilfully—are tasks which few know how to perform, and I must confess that I learnt by experience.

What Leedham-Green and Loggan say of *Cantabrigia illustrata* is also true of *Oxonia illustrata*, the first to be undertaken. Loggan was appointed Oxford's engraver to the university on 30 March 1669, the year that the Sheldonian Theatre was opened, giving Oxford printing a confident new start (Madan 1931, xxxv). It was originally intended that Loggan's plates should be ready at the same time as Anthony Wood's *Historia et antiquitates Universitatis Oxoniensis* (1674), but they did not appear until the following year; Wood desired the reader to note that he was not responsible for the descriptions on a number of plates (Madan 1931, 289). Loggan's "Index Tabularum" gives details of where descriptions of each building are to be found in Wood, and the two books were often bound together.

In the year after *Oxonia illustrata* was published, Loggan moved to Cambridge. The immediate occasion of this was to work on Wren's designs for Trinity College (see *Wren Society* 5: 42, for a note of payment to Loggan), but he probably began work on *Cantabrigia illustrata* the same year. There are designs of Trinity in the volume, so the two assignments would have overlapped. He would certainly have begun by 1678 or 1679 (Clark 1904, [vii]). The date of the work's completion—which should not be confused with the completion dates given on individual plates—is less easy to establish, but was probably between 1690 and 1700. Clark's estimation of 1690 rests on the fact that he

David Loggan. *Cantabrigia Illustrata.* View of the Nave of King's College Chapel. 1985.61.2504

SACELLI REGALIS apud Cantabrigienses Prospectus Interior ab Occidentali.
Reverendo admodum in Christo Patri ac Domino Dno THOMÆ BARLOW Lincolniensi Episcopo. Collegii Regalis in Acad. CANTAB. juxta vim statutorum
HENRICI 6ti Regis et Fundatoris Illustrissimi (Ratione Episcopatus) pleno Jure Visitori Annum Octogessimum secundum, vitæ integritate, morumq suavitate, agenti,
Ecclesiæ Anglicanæ Theologo nondum defatigato Fidei Orthodoxæ Patrono Summo, hanc Sacelli Delineationem a parte interiori accuratissimam tanquam Pietatis verè Regiæ monumentum, ad Futuram Tanti Viri, et Operis adeò augusti memoriam debitâ Reverentiâ
D. D. C. Q.
Dav. Loggan

interpreted payments in college account books as relating to completed copies of the book, rather than Loggan's original drawings for the plates.

The fact of these two colleges, King's and Trinity, paying for Loggan's drawings is testimony, with much else, to the official nature of the engravings. They were the universities' approved self-portraits, inspected by distinguished visitors and presented to them: on his trip to Oxford in 1669, Cosimo de Medici was shown a number of these engravings—a private view of work in progress, in essence, as the work had not yet been completed—and on 3 June 1675 a copy was presented to the prince of Neuberg. This continued well after the initial publication: the duke of York, for instance, was presented with a copy of Wood's *Historia* bound with Loggan's engravings in 1683 (Clark 1891–1900, 3: 54; 4: 71, 74, 75, 77). From the vice chancellor's accounts quoted in Wood's *Life and Times*, it appears that Loggan himself retained the engravings after publication.

Loggan signs nearly all the plates in both books, and no other draftsman or engraver is named. In his introduction he writes, "I discovered that [these tasks] are far beyond the capacity of a servant, nay more, that they cannot be wholly entrusted to any hired assistant, however skilful," but continues, "For this reason I have either worked out everything as accurately as I possibly could with my own hand; or, I have felt bound to delay my work until I could find artists sufficiently capable to relieve me to a certain extent of my labour." George Vertue (see Clark 1904, [vii]) stated that he was assisted by Everhardus Kickius and Robert White, and Madan adds that Michael Burghers and Woodfield (perhaps Charles Woodfield) also assisted with work on *Oxonia illustrata*. Though the Millard copy of *Cantabrigia illustrata* seems to be an early issue, many later copies were issued with a mezzotint portrait frontispiece engraved by J. Smith after a painting by J. Riley, depicting the chancellor of the University, Charles, duke of Somerset. Similarly, some copies of *Oxonia illustrata* are prefixed by a portrait of James, duke of Ormond, which was also engraved by J. Smith, and both may be associated with an early 18th-century issue of the plates by Smith. Some copies of *Cantabrigia illustrata* also have a double-page plate of the college coat of arms, dedicated to the duke of Somerset; a copy in the University Library, Cambridge (Cam. bb 690 1), preserves a hand-colored example. Large-paper copies of both books were issued.

Both volumes were reprinted in London by Henry Overton, *Oxonia illustrata* around 1715 and *Cantabrigia illustrata* around 1720, both with letterpress additions. The plates of both works were copied for James Beeverell's eight-volume *Les delices de la Grand Bretagne* (1st edition 1707: see also Bowes 1894, 728, 2833, 2982; Madan 1931, 472; Clark 1904, [ix]; RIBA, *Early Printed Books*). A. S.

Bibliography

Bowes, R. *A Catalogue of Books Printed at or Relating to the University Town and County of Cambridge.* Cambridge, 1894

British Architectural Library, Royal Institute of British Architects. *Early Printed Books 1478–1840: Catalogue of the British Architectural Library Early Imprints* Vols. 1–2. London, 1994–1995

Clark, A., ed. *Wood, Life and Times.* 5 vols. Oxford, 1891–1900

Clark, J. W. *Cantabrigia illustrata.* Cambridge, 1904

Madan, F. *Oxford Books.* Oxford, 1931

Wren Society. Oxford, 1924–1943: vol. 5

41

Thomas Major (1720–1799)

The Ruins Of Paestum, Otherwise Posidonia, In Magna Graecia. By Thomas Major, Engraver to His Majesty

London: published by T. Major. Printed by James Dixwell, 1768

1985.61.2516

Folio: 565 × 390 (22 1/8 × 15 1/4)

Pagination [4], 45, [1] pp., 24 [i.e., 25] etched and engraved plates

Edition First edition

Text pp. [1] title page (verso blank); [3] dedication (verso blank); [i–ii] list of subscribers; [iii]–iv note to the reader; [5]–39 text (including pls. XXV–XXIX); [40] blank; 41–42 table of Posidonian and Paestan coins (including pl. XXX); 43–45 explanation of the plates, ending with 4-line errata; [46] list of engravings by Thomas Major included in his *Works*

Illustrations 25 *hors texte* plates numbered I–XXIIII (2 plates numbered XIX), all signed as engraved by Major, and plates II–III are also signed Antonio Jolli (Joli) "pinxt." Most are dated as published January 1768, one April 1768. In addition, there are 6 small plates by Major printed as head- or tailpieces to the letterpress and numbered XXV–XXX (published January or May 1768); and a large etched armorial vignette on the dedication engraved by Major after Samuel Wale, published 1 June 1768

Binding Contemporary marbled boards, calf spine, uncut

Provenance Etched bookplate of Beilby Porteus (1731–1808). Early MS note at bottom of p. [iii] with 6-line quotation from Patrick Brydone's *Tour through Sicily to Malta* (1773, etc.)

References Berlin Cat. 1894; Cicognara 2680; ESTC t100079; Fowler 187; Harris and Savage 538

Paestum was for long abandoned and unvisited, but not altogether forgotten. It was mentioned in histories and guidebooks—Mazella (1597), Zapullo (1602), Ens (1609), Beltrano (1644), and Gatta (1723)—but there was nothing in these to stir an inquisitive interest in the ruins themselves, nothing by way of a picture. Even John Breval, who had traveled to Sicily in 1725 and had recorded and illustrated the Doric temples of Agrigentum and Selinunte in five plates, engraved by P. Fourdrinier, made no effort to venture to Paestum when be reached Salerno; though he noted in his *Remarks on Several Parts of Europe*, of 1738, "below *Agripoli*, is the ancient *Paestum* (now *Pesti*) so famous for its roses. *Biserque Rosario Paesti* Virg. Georg IV. Near it are some Tracks of an old Seaport, supposed to be the *Posidonia*, of Strabo, Solinus & c" (1: 51 n.p.).

The first crude representation of the walled site of Paestum and its three temples was published in Naples in 1732 in the second of Costantino Gatta's studies of the region—*Memorie topographiche-storiche della provincia di Lucania*. The following year, an Englishman, Robert Smith, wrote two letters from Rome to the Neapolitan scholar Matteo Egizio, encouraging him to make a study of Paestum with a view to publication. He had himself clearly visited the site, for he likened the architecture to that of the Egyptians. But it was only after 1734, when the Bourbons assumed control in Naples, that anything of an enlightened interest was taken in Paestum. The leading spirit was Count Felice Gazzola, originally from Piacenza, who had led the king's army to victory at Velletri and who remained his faithful aide, eventually accompanying him to Madrid, in 1759, when he was crowned as Charles III. Gazzola came to know the site of Paestum well, for the king had a hunting lodge at Persano, nearby, even before he built a country house there. The court, though, was not much in awe of the ruins at Paestum. In 1740, the architect Ferdinando Sanfelice suggested that the temples be quarried for the new palace at Capo di Monte; to judge from his report, he regarded the remains as Roman. But Gazzola commissioned measurements and drawings of the temples from Gaetano Magri and Gian Battista Natali and stirred a new interest in the ruins. He even planned a publication. Indeed, Gazzola's well-known dedication to this project inhibited most of the visitors he took to the site from venturing on anything of the sort. Even after Gazzola had moved to Madrid the constraint remained.

In 1745 Guiseppe Antonini had described the three temples—he called them "portici"—in *La Lucania Discorsi de Giuseppe Antonini, Barone di San Biase*, in 1758 Berardo Galiani included a plate of the "Pseudodiptero" temple of Paestum in *L'architettura di M. Vitruvio Pollione*, and in 1768 Mario Gioffredo used the temples as evidence of the development of architecture from the Etruscans to the Greeks in *Dell'architettura di Mario Gioffredo architetto Napoletano: Parte prima nella quale si tratta degli Ordini dell'Architettura de'Greci e degl'Italiani e si danno le regole più spedite per diseguarli*; all three books were published in Naples. But only in 1784 was the full range and extent of Gazzola's research made known in Paolo Antonio Paoli's *Rovine della città di Pesto detta ancora Posidonia*, issued in Rome. This was, even then, the first study to deal with the whole site and all its related remains.

The visitors who were to spread the fame of Paestum throughout Europe came only in the second half of the century, beginning with Jacques-Germain Soufflot, in

1750, who, in June, while the Marquis de Marigny was in Turin and C. N. Cochin in Frascati, inspected the site under the guidance of Gazzola and took detailed measurements with his compatriot G.-P.-M. Dumont. Soufflot described his impressions in lectures in Lyons and Paris, but he made no immediate move to publish anything. When it was rumored that he might, the Abbé Barthelemy wrote from Naples, on 20 December 1755, to the Comte de Caylus to dissuade him. Gazzola's prior claim, it was felt, must be respected. Soufflot's findings were published only in 1764 as *Suitte de plans, coupes, profils, élévations, géometrales et perspectives de trois temples antiques . . . mesurés et dessinés par les soins de G.-M. Dumont.* Though late in date, this was hastily compiled and none too authoritative, without a text, intended perhaps to forestall publications by both Filippo Morghen and James Bruce. Caylus seems to have been the instigator. He hastened the publication of J.-D. Leroy's *Les ruines des plus beaux monuments de la Grèce* in 1758 to ensure French priority over James Stuart and Nicholas Revett's *Antiquities of Athens*, the first volume of which was delayed until 1762. He seems to have been repeating this action again, but more intemperately. Caylus himself wrote to the antiquarian Paolo Maria Paciaudi, in Naples, on 24 December 1764, suggesting that a short account he had written on Paestum be used as an introduction to any future edition of Soufflot's work. Nothing came of this, however, as Caylus died the following year.

The most active and enthusiastic visitors to succeed Soufflot were British. Lascelles Raymond Iremonger wrote to Sir Roger Newdigate from Naples, on 22 July 1752, to describe the temples at Paestum—"these are," he noted, "all now engraving at Paris by order of Gazzola, Gen.t of Artll. here." Frederick, Lord North, traveling on the Continent with Lord Dartmouth in 1753, wrote a tantalizing letter to Charles Dampier, who had been his tutor at Eton, dated Lyons, 1 September, and Bern, 9 September, describing the temples at Paestum at considerable length, with sketch plans attached, though he was not much admiring—"The meanness of their materials & ye badness of their Architecture has been one principal cause of their preservation. Nobody has thought it worth his while to destroy them." He was in no doubt though, that the temples were Greek, and related both to those in Agrigentum and Athens. Both North and Dartmouth had spent time studying in Paris, where the young John Brudenell received his education between 1751 and 1754 (he also studied engraving there with Hubert Gravelot), and it was almost certainly on their advice that he, too, visited the site in 1756. A letter from his bear-leader, Henry Lyte, to his father, Lord Cardigan, dated 15 June 1756 from Naples, records their first visit:

> We returned yesterday from Pesti, an ancient colony of the Greeks. The curiosities there are well worth going to see. They consist of three temples of the Doric order, the most ancient that are anywhere to be found so entire. As they were built in the infancy of architecture, the proportion between height and breadth of the pillar is not well preserved, they being too short for their thickness, but the solidity of them is surprising. They appear to be built for eternity. A gentleman of this place has had drawings made of them which are now engraving and will soon be published, so that your Lordship will by means of them have a better idea of them than I am able to furnish you with by letter.

Brudenell's draftsman was Antonio Joli (or Jolli), then fifty-six years old. Brudenell might first have encountered Joli in London, where he was at work from 1744 to 1749. But it was in Naples that he took him up, commissioning thirty-eight view paintings of the places he had visited. Brudenell might also have been assisted in his inspection by the young Scots architect Robert Mylne, who was in Naples at this time and no doubt visited the ruins and took measurements, though his detailed inspection might have been of the following year, when he traveled to Sicily to inspect the Greek temples there. Brudenell got to know Paestum well; he insisted on staying in Naples and continuing his explorations, venturing to Sicily in November 1756 and to Taranto in the summer of 1757, returning to Rome only in 1758. Joli produced two views of Agrigento for Brudenell, also one of Paestum—the three temples viewed from the southeast, today in the collection of the duke of Buccleuch at Bowhill. But all these early explorers were outshone in enthusiasm by James Bruce of Kinnaird (famous later as "Abyssinian" Bruce). He arrived in Italy in July 1762, in preparation for an extraordinary mission to search for Roman ruins in North Africa, secured through the influence of Lord Halifax and his secretary, Robert Wood (of Palmyra fame). That autumn, in Florence, Bruce bought drawings of Paestum "made in the kingdom of Naples by a Spanish officer" (Murray 1808, 34), but whether direct from Gazzola or not, one cannot be sure. When Bruce reached Naples in January 1763 he consulted with James Gray, the British envoy stationed there from 1753 to 1763. Gray recommended that Bruce check the drawings for accuracy on the spot, before doing anything with them. Bruce visited Paestum with Magri, Gazzola's draftsman, who seems to have been selling copies of his drawings to all and sundry. By February 1763 Bruce was back in Florence, where he commissioned Giuseppe Zocchi to compose a frontispiece for an intended publication and Robert Strange to see to the engraving of the plates. Strange himself, one might note, had been to Naples and Paestum in October 1762. Soon after, Bruce embarked at Leghorn for Algiers, which he reached on 20 March 1763. He served there as consul general for two years, moving in August 1765 to Tunis to begin the exploration of the antique remains of the African coast. By then, not only had Soufflot's or Dumont's *Suitte de plans* appeared, but also the "Vedute della città de Pestum" issued in Naples soon after 25 February 1765 (the date of the dedication of one of the plates, dedicated to Frederick Calvert, Lord Baltimore). This consisted of seven views, on six plates, engraved by Morghen, based on drawings by Joli. Later Morghen was to add a note, a "spiegazione," on Paestum to this series, taken from Antonini's *La Lucania*. Morghen also did four more engravings of the temples at Paestum, three views and a plate of three plans. In 1769 he published forty more plates as *Le antichità di Pozzuoli, Baja, e Cuma*, which indicates something of his method of operation, each plate being dedicated to a foreign visitor, usually English. At least two of the six views of Paestum engraved by Morghen had been rendered by Joli in oils, one of them dated 1759. Four such paintings of Paestum by Joli are known, three dated to 1759—*Veduta laterale dei templi di Paestum*, exhibited at Colnaghi's, London, in 1978; *Intorno del tempio di Poseidone a Paestum*, in the Palazzo Reale, Caserta; and *La piana dei templi a Paestum*, a view from the west, in the Norton Simon Museum, Pasadena. There are three known variants of yet another view of the three temples from the southeast, an oblique rather than a frontal view, with a lower viewpoint (Duke of Buccleuch Collection, Bowhill; Sotheby's sale of 9 December 1987 and 19 April 1989), with still another version (Sotheby's, New York, 7 October 1994) possibly painted by Pietro Fabris rather than Joli.

Andrew Lumisden, brother-in-law of Strange, wrote to Bruce from Rome on 13 July 1765, to inform him of both Dumont's and Merghen's (sic) publications on Paestum—"These publications will be no disadvantage to you; they will only whet the appetite of the public to see something more complete and satisfactory" (Murray 1808, 181). Strange himself wrote to Bruce from London much later, on 25 July 1766, concerning the project: "Your work of Pesto has been long executed even to the very time you limited me when we last parted at Florence. I never doubted but your friends in England, who were to be charged with the remainder of the work, had all in readiness at my return to London, January was a twelve month but, on my conversing with Mr. Hamilton, I found it otherwise. The plates before that time were consigned to Mr. Ballantyne at Boulogne, as you may remember we concerted. They are yet in his possession, and, I presume, will remain so till you return to England. I make no doubt of their giving you that satisfaction you could wish for; be assured, that in the executing of them they were equally interesting to me with my other engagements" (Murray 1808, 183).

William Hamilton, Bruce's uncle, formerly his guardian, had already written to Bruce from London a year earlier, on 5 April 1765, about these same plates;

Mr Richardson [?] has been confined to his house for several months. I consulted him about your plates, but he said that he could not assist one in getting them home free from duty. Mr. Strange who came to London about three weeks ago has conveyed six or Eight to Mr. Hay's house in Boulogne, and expects that the other two will soon be there, & then he and I will concert some method of Importing them free from the Customhouse Impositions.

Hamilton noted in his same letter that he had been for several months past in daily expectation of Bruce's return. But Bruce was not to return to England until 1774, and contact with him in the intervening years was intermittent and altogether haphazard. He and his draftsman Luigi Balugani, who was found for him by Lumisden after George Dance and then J. F. T. Chalgrin had refused the offer, left Tunis to explore the cities along the coast in September 1765. They moved then to Crete and to Syria, and thence to Egypt and up the Nile. Balugani was to die at Gandar in February 1771.

Bruce did not receive Strange's letter of 25 July 1766 until 18 April 1768, and his reply to it was written from Sidon on 16 May 1768—

I hear with the utmost concern that the engraving of my prints of Paesto at Paris has produced an edition there by M. Soufflot, which neither has nor deserves to have had any success. I still am more vex'd to hear that, notwithstanding this, he is printing by subscription a work perfectly on my plan, I suppose during your absence he has seen my prints and probably copied them. Pray let me know how this is, and whether I have no friend that, in some review or periodical paper, will advertise the public of the matter, and engage them to wait for mine (Dennistoun 1855, 2: 48).

By this date *The Ruins of Paestum*, as engraved by Thomas Major, had been published in England. Bruce's letter suggests that he had some knowledge of this, relating to the proposals though, rather than the folio itself. Proposals for the work had been announced in the *Gazetteer* on 1 October 1767 (and again in the *Public Advertiser* for 30 October 1767):

Proposals for Engraving by subscription, in one Volume Folio . . . The Ruins of Paestum, otherwise Posidonia, in Magna Graecia. This work is comprised in twenty-four Copperplates elegantly engraved, and printed on Fine Paper (the size of Balbec and Palmyra) . . . from high finished drawings, some of the views from paintings done for his Excellency Sir James Gray. . . . The plans, elevations and measures, taken on the spot by Mons. Soufflot.

Publication was precipitated, it is safe to assume, by knowledge of the imminent appearance of yet another work on Paestum, THE RUINS OF POESTUM *or Posidonia. A City of Magna Graecia in The Kingdom of Naples. Containing A Description and Views of the remaining Antiquities, With The Ancient and Modern History, Inscriptions, &c. and Some Observations On The Ancient Dorick Order.* Publication of this was announced in both the *Gazetteer* and the *Public Advertiser* on 7 October 1767. This consisted of a title page, a two-page preface, seventeen pages of text, and four views of the temples, three of them similar to ones offered by Morghen, but all, probably, based directly on drawings or paintings by Joli. The engraver of the views was J. S. Miller (Johann Sebastian Muller) who had come to England from Nuremberg in 1744, soon establishing an excellent reputation. He engraved all the plates for Richard Chandler's *Marmora Oxoniensia*, of 1763. The author, for whom the book was printed, has for long been identified, incorrectly, as John Berkenhout; but Berkenhout himself named him as Dr. John Longfield. Longfield was of Irish extraction, educated at Trinity College, Dublin, and later Edinburgh University, where he took a degree in medicine in 1759. Berkenhout, reviewing the book in the *Monthly Review* of November 1767, noted that "our learned author . . . has certainly been on the spot." If so, it was presumably after his graduation. The information contained in his text was taken for the most part from Antonini's discourse in *La Lucania* of 1745, but the false account of the rediscovery of Paestum, dated to 1755, he took from P. J. Grosely's *Nouveaux mémoires, ou observations sur l'Italie* of 1764. Longfield, though of scholarly interests, was not greatly concerned with the architecture itself; he thought the study of this might await Gazzola's publication. He questioned, moreover, whether "that great degree of accuracy which has been used in measuring the remains of ancient Greece and Rome" had served to improve architecture. He himself was clearly convinced that it had not: "It prevents the mind from taking in the whole together, and from attaining to that sublimity and grandeur of stile which the ancients possessed in so eminent a degree."

Though Longfield's book, like Morghen's, was of limited interest to architects, it clearly posed a threat to others involved in the publication of the *Ruins of Paestum*, serving thus, as indicated, to precipitate the publication of *The Ruins of Paestum*, engraved by Major. There were 212 subscribers for this, twenty-five from abroad, including Barthelemy, Dumont, Le Blanc, Leroy, Mariette, and Soufflot. The book was published on 1 June 1768. When it was noted in the *Monthly Review* of July–December 1768, it was at once recognized as superior to all its predecessors—"a much more *elaborate* and *mature*, as well as more *expensive* performance."

Suzanne Lang, Michael McCarthy, and Nicholas Savage have all labored hard and admirably to unravel the history of this book. Their accounts are the basis of that offered here, and should be read for all confirmation of detail. There are divergences, however, in their interpretations, some inconsistencies even of fact; Lang was unaware of the Bruce project, but McCarthy and Savage have both taken as axiomatic that the book Bruce embarked on and that was produced under the name of Major are to be regarded as separate undertakings. Whereas the very evidence they adduce suggests, to the contrary, that they are one and the same. Bruce's friends, I would suggest, concerted to produce the work as best they could in his absence. No one, Bruce least of all, could be credited with it when complete; it was thus published anonymously. Major was credited only as the engraver.

In the note "To the READER," Major writes:

> . . . within these few Years, this Place has been visited by the Curious; and among others, by an *English* Gentleman, to whom the following Work owes its Birth; and who procured at *Naples* several fine Drawings of these Temples. The other Views were taken in Presence of his Excellency Sir JAMES GRAY, whilst His Majesty's Envoy Extraordinary and Plenipotentiary at the Court of *Naples*. The Plans, Elevations, and Measures, the Public owe to that eminent Artist, Mons. J. G. SOUFFLOT: They were by him accurately taken on the Spot, and he has generously assisted the Engraver in this Undertaking.
>
> Thus furnished with Materials, and not knowing that only Attempts of this Kind, in several detached Pieces, had been made by others, the Engraver was induced to believe that this Performance, from the singular Construction of the Edifices, would prove acceptable to the Public. These Temples are esteemed by the learned as some of the most curious Remains of *Grecian* Antiquity, the most entire of any now existing, and are noble monuments of the Magnificence of that ancient City.

In the paragraph following Major again singles out his role as engraver: "As no attention or Expense have been spared to render this Work as complete as possible, the Engraver hopes this Performance will be received with indulgence. For the Illustrations of the Prints, and Historical Account, he has availed himself of whatever could be gathered from various Authors who have treated on this Subject. . . ." This note is signed, London, June 1767 (July 1768 in the French edition).

Though the title page and the twenty-five plates bear Major's name, it is clear that the work was not his alone. Nor, indeed, would one expect it to be. Major had never been to Paestum, he was not a scholar, nor did he exhibit any interest in scholarship or in architecture as such. He put his name to no other book. He was trained as an engraver, with Hubert Gravelot, who advised him to move to Paris, to study with J. P. Le Bas, an artist of considerable skill and fame (responsible, on Caylus' persuading, for the engraving of the views in Leroy's *Les ruines des plus beaux monuments de la Grèce*, of 1758). Both Major and Le Bas, though they might have contributed on occasion to architectural works, were reputed rather as landscape engravers.

The person to whom prime responsibility for *The Ruins of Paestum* should, perhaps, be accorded, is Wood; though there is not a shred of evidence that he was directly involved. However, he was the one who arranged for Bruce to be appointed explorer at large. And it was to Robert Wood that Bruce intended from the start to dedicate his book on Paestum. Wood demurred. He wrote to Bruce, in Algiers, on 26 October 1764:

> I beg leave to return my thanks for the honour you intended me in the dedication of your work, and that you will be assured, I am thoroughly sensible of the value of that compliment, which I shall willingly accept of, if I cannot persuade you, when we meet, of the propriety of a different choice; but of this more when I shall have the pleasure of seeing you. Strange told me, that he thought it would satisfy public curiosity, and do you credit, though Count Gazzoli should publish his account of the same place, which I am told is very doubtful (Murray 1808, 163).

In hesitating to accept the dedication Wood might well, as Nicholas Savage has suggested, have been considering the greater advantages of having the king's name at the front. The book Bruce eventually wrote on his travels in Africa was presented to George III, as also was the *Ionian Antiquities* of 1769, the product of the best organized and conducted archaeological expedition of the century, led by Chandler, sponsored by the Society of Dilettanti. The leading spirit in the organization of this venture was Wood, who was to write the preface to the book. It was precisely in the early months of 1764 that Wood was most actively involved in the preparations for the expedition (Chandler and his friends left England on 9 June 1764). Wood was an obvious choice for Bruce as dedicatee, and he was an even more obvious choice as editor of his proposed publication, chief, one might hazard, among the "friends in England, who were to be charged with the remainder of the work," mentioned in Strange's letter to Bruce of 25 July 1766. Wood was a noted classical scholar and explorer; he had written and supervised the publication of two of the most successful archaeological publications to have appeared at that date, *The Ruins of Palmyra*, of 1753, and *The Ruins of Balbec*, of 1757. In 1756 he had been appointed undersecretary of state in the Pitt administration, and remained to his death, in September 1771, an administrator and politician of some influence. Even more important though was his active role in the Society of Dilettanti, of which he became a member on 1 May 1763, nominated by Richard Phelps, who had traveled in Italy around 1745 with Wood's patrons, James Dawkins and John Bouverie, and in 1757 had taken the architect Robert Mylne with him to Sicily with a view to publishing the Doric temples there. It is notable that two at least of the names that can definitely be connected with the plates of *The Ruins of Paestum*, those of Sir James Gray and his brother Major General George Gray, were members of the Society of Dilettanti. An unusually high proportion of the subscribers, moreover, were members, fourteen out of fifty-four, more than a quarter of the membership. Mylne, too, was a subscriber. So, even, was William Chambers. Another singularity of the list of subscribers was the number in Holland—a country in which Wood had stayed for some months, leading the negotiations for the Treaty of Paris that ended the Seven Years' War with France in 1763. Wood himself, one might note, subscribed for six copies of the book, more than anyone else. He still owned three of these at his death.

The Ruins of Paestum was evidently conceived as a sequel to the works on Palmyra and Baalbek; it was associated with them in the proposals for publication, it was conceived in the same image (the title page being a direct imitation) and organized, as far as may be, in exactly the same manner, with a short preface (two pages), a history of the site based almost entirely on classical authors (thirteen pages), a description of the temples (ten pages), in which any influence from Egypt was firmly rejected; an analysis of medals and coins found on the site (thirteen pages); and a list of plates

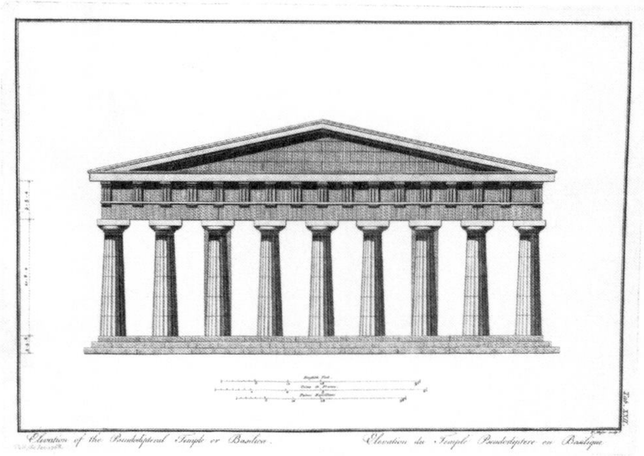

Thomas Major. *The Ruins of Paestum*. Tab. XXII. "Elevation of the pseudodipteral temple or basilica." 1985.61.2516

(four pages). This was followed by twenty-five plates (plate XIXB seems to have been a last-minute addition), the first five offering general views of the site and the gateway, followed by surveys of each of the three temples, beginning in each case with a plan, showing existing and conjectural elements, followed by three and, in one instance, four views, both outside and in, followed by a restored elevation and, in the case of the "Hexastyle Ipeteral temple," a restored section and a sheet of details, in the case of the "Pseudodipteral Temple or Basilica," a sheet of details alone. The last plate was devoted to coins. The presentation was as dispassionate as possible, with no conjectural dedications offered for the temples, and no judgments made on their architecture (exactly as in the Palmyra and Baalbek volumes). The author of the historical text might well have been Wood.

A folder of drawings in the Soane Museum labeled "The original Drawings for a Work Intituled The Ruins of Paestum of Posidonia Engraved by T. Major 1768," as also an assorted collection of engravings of the temples at Paestum and variant proofs of the plates for Major's volume, in particular plates II, VI, VII, XIII, XIV, and XVIII (Drawer 60, set 1), allow a more circumstantial analysis of the production of the plates. The first five views (I–V)—two general views of the temples and the three views of the gateway—all derive from drawings or paintings by Joli. Three (I, IV, and V) are very close to views included in Morghen's sheaf of engravings, but they seem to have been based directly on drawings by Joli, or copies of them, two of which are included in the portfolio (pls. I and IV). The figures added to IV and V are by Major. The remaining two engravings of this group (II and III) derive from paintings in the possession of Major General George Gray and his brother Sir James Gray, the first from a painting dated 1759, of which a squared-up drawing is in the Soane portfolio, the second from a painting done in 1758, a drawing of which is likewise in the Soane portfolio.

The sources for the plates of the individual temples can, likewise, be identified. The ten views (vii, ix, xiv, xv, xvi, xixa, xixb, xx, xxi) are all based on drawings by Magri, with figures in each instance added by Major. The drawings for all the plates are credited to Magri in the Soane portfolio, with the exception of that for xixa, which seems to have been a late addition. But the engraving is, exceptionally, signed with his name. The orientation of the views, as noted on the drawings, is in most instances incorrect, indicating that the author of the notes was unfamiliar with the site. The engraving of the restored elevations and sections (x, xi, xvii, xxii) are all based on drawings that can be assigned to Mylne, though only one of these (x) bears his initials. The three plans (vi, xiii, xviii) and the two sheets of details (xii, xxiii), though engraved it seems from drawings that may also be credited to Mylne (only that for xviii is noted in the index as "restored according to Mr. Robert Mylne"), have more complex origins.

The plan of the "Hexastyle Ipeteral Temple" (vi) was based on a drawing by Magri borrowed from a Mr. Horne (the Edward Horne who subscribed for three copies of the book, one assumes) and on a copy of another by Soufflot, done by Stephen Riou, an amateur-architect of Huguenot origin, who had traveled widely in Italy and the Levant in the early 1750s, and had himself published a work of propaganda on Greek architecture, *The Grecian Orders of Architecture*, early in 1768. The plan of the "Hexastyle Peripteral Temple" (xiii) was based, once again, on an Italian drawing borrowed from Mr. Horne, probably by Magri; a restoration copied from Leroy (not adopted); and a finished drawing by Mylne. The plan of the "Pseudodipteral Temple or Basilica" (xviii) was based, as before, on a drawing bought in Naples by Mr. Horne, off "Maugre"; a copy by Riou of a Soufflot drawing; and a finished restoration derived from it by Mylne. The engraved details of the "Hexastyle Ipeteral Temple" (xii) are derived in part from one of Dumont's engravings but redrawn and restored, perhaps by Mylne; the plate of details from the "Peripteral and Pseudodipteral Temples" (xxiii) is based on a drawing by Magri, lent by George Gray; a drawing by Soufflot; and a final drawing, also probably by Mylne.

To summarize, the five general views of the site derive from paintings or drawings by Joli and the ten views of the individual temples derive from drawings by Magri, with figures added by Major. The plans, sections, elevations, and detail plates of the temples appear to be engraved from drawings by Mylne, based on plans and sketches by Soufflot, Magri, and perhaps others. All the folio plates are signed "T. Major."

What, in all this, of the six or eight plates consigned by Strange, in May 1765, to Mr. Hay's house in Boulogne, with two more to follow? The simple answer would be that they were rendered redundant by the publication of *The Ruins of Paestum* by Major. But if this book is the one initiated by Bruce, then a further explanation is called for. They may have been impounded by customs,

Thomas Major. *The Ruins of Paestum.* Tab. ii. "A view of the three temples, taken from the East." 1985.61.2516

damaged, or lost—certainly no trace of their existence has ever come to light—but this is unlikely. What I propose, rather more speculatively, is that these plates, representing the nine or ten views by Magri (nine if XIXA is to be regarded as a later addition), were engraved in Paris in 1764 and early 1765 not by Strange, as is generally thought, but by Major, working under his supervision, and that they became part of the finished folio.

Strange had strong French connections. He and his brother-in-law Lumisden, were, like Bruce, Jacobites.

Strange left Edinburgh to study drawing in Rouen under J.-B. Descamps in September 1748, and moved in the following year to Paris to study engraving with Le Bas. Lumisden became secretary to the Pretender at this time, later serving his son. He was forced to live on the Continent, moving between Paris and Rome, until he was allowed to return to England in 1773. Strange left Paris for London in October 1750, setting himself up as a picture dealer and print seller. His first important commission as an engraver was the plates for William Hunter's work on the uterus, begun at this time, but not published until 1774. Strange did only two plates himself; the remainder were done in France under his direction. Likewise, of the three plates in the *Antiquities of Athens* for which he was given responsibility (Lips, chap. 3 pl. 17; Zephyr, chap. 3 pl. 18; Kaikos, chap. 3 pl. 13, of the Tower of the Winds), only two were signed by him; the third was done by his engraver. These, like the Paestum plates, fell outside his usual range of activity. He liked best the engraving of paintings, in particular Italian painting, details from Raphael and Titian, and especially the Bolognese School. He employed for these a specific technique of drypoint etching that had been developed and perfected by Le Bas. Strange despised the stipple technique that Francesco Bartolozzi had introduced to England (he despised Bartolozzi also for his and Richard Dalton's underhand dealings in a matter of the engraving of Guercinos in Bologna, and he was even more incensed when Bartolozzi, though an engraver, was received into the membership of the Royal Academy as a painter). Strange was to be accounted one of the greatest engravers in England, by Horace Walpole and Leigh Hunt, among others. His constant use of assistants was thus not owing to any inability or incompetence, but rather to his mode of operation. His method of engraving was more than unusually time-consuming; he rarely produced more than two plates a year, working extremely long hours, and with assistance. He resorted again and again to France to find this assistance (spending far more time there than in London, where his wife and family were based). In 1754 he asked Lumisden to find him an assistant in Rome, but failing in this he traveled himself to Paris to look out "for one bred an history engraver" (Dennistoun 1855, 1: 251).

"I am glad," Lumisden wrote to him in August of that year, "that you have at last got a fit person to assist you in those parts of your work that only consumed your time" (Dennistoun 1855, 1: 251).

Strange published his engravings from the Golden Head, Henrietta Street, Covent Garden, until 1762. But some years before he had left in pursuit of paintings in Italy. He had determined early on this venture. Already, in 1758, when he was asked to engrave Allan Ramsay's portraits of the prince of Wales and Lord Bute, he had refused, incurring their displeasure. He felt the payment offered was insufficient, but was chiefly concerned at the time that would be taken up. From June 1760 to June 1764 he was abroad, mainly in Italy, and mainly in Parma, Bologna, and Florence, though he ventured north to Venice and south to Rome (where he was elected a member of the Accademia di San Luca, Piranesi reading the oration), and also to Naples. By May 1764 he was returned to Paris, where he began preparation for the engraving of "Justice" and "Meekness" from Raphael's paintings in the Camera di Constantino in the Vatican. He dashed across to London in July to see his wife and family, but by September was back in Paris, at work—"with the assistance of an artist qualified to perform the merely mechanical portions of the plates" (Dennistoun 1855, 2: 29). At this time he was elected a member of the Académie Royale de Peinture et Sculpture, where he exhibited his drawings. When he carried his two finished plates to London in February 1765 his reception was less fulsome. He inserted a notice in the *Public Advertiser* of 18 May, and again in that of 20 May, announcing the closing of his exhibition on the 25th, he himself preparing to set out for Paris, to procure the "necessary assistance towards executing the inferior parts of his work." Some of his drawings were rejected for exhibition at the Society of Artists on the grounds that they were colored. Strange was enraged. He returned to Paris in July to prepare engravings of works by Guido Reni and Guercino. He was in London again, briefly, in midsummer 1766, but returned soon enough to Paris with his eldest daughter, Mary Bruce. The two Guercinos were finished only on 12 February 1767. Strange took his first proofs then, but the titles still remained to be engraved. These he intended to complete, print, and publish in London. "I find now, by experience," he wrote then to Lumisden, "that I am obliged with my own hands to execute above two-third of every plate I do. Nay, I often consume more time in correcting the work of others than had I done the whole myself" (Dennistoun 1855, 2: 57). He reached London in April. Finding his printer indisposed, he had to do the printing himself. He thought then to settle in London, but not before returning to Paris to find "a qualified assistant, willing to accompany him to Lon-don" (Dennistoun 1855, 2: 69). In the following years he launched plates by Guido Reni, Guercino, Titian, Raphael, and others, altogether successfully, and also had rewarding sales of the pictures and drawings he had collected in Italy. He was knighted in 1787 and died in London in 1792. But, as might be imagined, almost to the last, in 1789 and again in 1790, he traveled whenever he could, to Paris.

Major was an obvious choice as amanuensis for the Paestum plates, and might well have been determined upon by Strange and Bruce in Florence, in February 1763, when they planned the book. Major was established as an engraver of landscapes—of landscapes by Wouwermans, Teniers, and others—but he had contributed to architectural works, notably to Wood's *Ruins of Palmyra*, of 1753, for which he engraved the great panoramic view, on three plates, and also *The Ruins of Balbec*, of 1757, for which he engraved five views. More important, perhaps, like Strange, he had been trained in the studio of Le Bas. He was familiar with Paris; he even liked the French, shrugging off the short time he had spent, unjustly, in the Bastille in 1746, in a footnote in *The Ruins of Paestum*. Strange, as already indicated, reached Paris on his return from Italy in May 1764. Major is recorded as being in Paris in June 1764, when he delivered a group of Egyptian antiquities from an anonymous English collector to Caylus. It is perhaps not so fanciful to propose that he had come to Paris to work with Strange on the Paestum plates. He might also, at that time, have made contact with Soufflot and Leroy, in this same connection. The letters of Strange and Hamilton quoted much earlier indicate that eight to ten plates for the book were done in the second half of 1764 and the early months of 1765. These plates, as already noted, one can assume to be the views by Magri, which were ready for immediate engraving. In a portfolio labeled "The ruins and antiquities of Posidonia or Paesto in the kingdom of Naples," among the Bruce papers at the Yale Center for British Art, are seven views of the temples in an accomplished Italian hand, probably Magri's. There are seven more drawings in this collection, three ground plans, an unfinished elevation and three sheets of architectural details, all of which can be related to the drawings in the Soane portfolio, though there is nothing of the survey of the town wall of Paestum that Bruce's biographer records him as undertaking. Even if copies of these drawings had been forwarded by Bruce to the "friends in England," mentioned by Strange in his letter of 25 July 1766, they would have proved inadequate for the production of plates. Neapolitan and English feet had to be reconciled. A professional draftsman was required to do some drawing. The obvious choice would have been the young Mylne, a close friend of the whole Strange family, and of Bruce, who had explored Paestum himself in 1756 and had been employed in 1758 and 1759 for just such a task, namely, the drawing of the Doric temples of Sicily in preparation for their engraving by Mr. Phelps, the erstwhile companion of Woods' patrons, Dawkins and Bouverie. Mylne might have accepted the task from Bruce. Certainly, he was involved in the redrawing of the plans, sections, elevations, and details for the engravings of *The Ruins of Paestum*. But equally, like Strange, he might have delegated the work to assistants. When he returned from Italy to England, he won a competition for the building of Blackfriars Bridge, in February 1760, and was actively involved in that daunting undertaking from 1762 to 1770. He was also establishing a private practice. His diaries from 1762 onward give no hint of his involvement in the Paestum project. The magnificent engraving of Blackfriars Bridge under construction that he commissioned in 1765 was, moreover, commissioned from Piranesi (at a cost of fifty-four pounds).

The careers of Strange and Mylne drew them away from the Paestum affair. In his letter of 25 July 1766, in which Strange informed Bruce of the Paestum plates, he noted "Our friend, Mylne, is advancing in his great work with that security and honor which his most sanguine friends would wish him. He is now about the sixth arch . . ." (Murray 1808, 184). By 1767, Mylne was a respected architect; in October 1766 he had been appointed surveyor to St. Paul's. By 1767 Strange was established as a particularly fine engraver of great Italian paintings; he might then have preferred that Major put his name to the Paestum views. Major himself probably engraved the plans, sections, elevations, and details for the book with reluctance. He engraved a view of Kew gardens for Chambers' book of 1763, but did no work of a strictly architectural kind. Bruce, however, continued to view both Strange and Mylne in an archaeological role. On 16 September 1767 he had set out from Sidon to Baalbek, arriving three days after. A month later, to the day, he reached Palmyra. At both sites he made a number of drawings, in particular views, which he produced with a "camera obscura," recommended to him by Lumisden. In replying to Strange's letter, on 16 May 1768, he wrote,

> I thank you for your kind promise of assisting me in my works. I have nearly finished twelve drawings of Palmyra and four of Balbec [these were later presented to the king]; their size is 24 1/2 inches by 16 1/5. It is but to you I say it, they will be the most magnificent prints of the kind ever published. I have not meddled with the regular architecture or description (except notes for my own instruction), out of regard to Mr. Wood. I have collected all the dresses of the different nations of Asia for figures for them. What do you say? Will you go halves in the publication? I desire but your superintending and correcting the engraving (Dennistoun 1855, 1: 147).

Here, perhaps, is a parallel to the arrangement concerted in Florence.

There is also in this letter a reference to Mylne:

> I do recollect I think to have heard you say in Italy that Mr. Mylne had some intention to publish a work upon Sicily. I pray you to write me if it is so: I would not willingly interfere with anybody, and least of all with him. I am very sure what he offers to the public will be very much as it ought to be, and if his intention continues, I will willingly relinquish the journey, or, if the drawings I may make do any ways serve him, he shall be entirely master of them (Dennistoun 1855, 1: 147).

Though the plates for *The Ruins of Pasteum* were, I believe, initiated by Bruce, the published texts owe nothing to him. He began to write a text in January or February 1763, immediately after his return from Paestum to Naples (when he could enjoy the advice and library of Sir James Gray), but most of this must have been written in Algiers, which he reached (after concerting with Strange in Florence) on 20 March 1763. Lumisden wrote to Bruce from Rome, on 9 June 1764—"With infinite pleasure I received, my dear sir, your letter of April 21st, and heartily congratulate with you, that your account of Paesto is so far advanced" (Murray 1808, 177). Bruce completed a fair copy of this text. But it was lost, together with a great many other papers and his astronomical instruments, in a shipwreck in 1766, off Benghazi when he was embarked for Crete. He swam ashore. He had, however, taken the precaution of sending some of his baggage ahead, and this he recovered when he reached Rhodes in April 1767. His manuscript notes were safe. "After receiving no answer or account of my letters," he wrote to Strange in the oft-quoted letter of 16 May 1768 from Sidon, "I did not dare risque my manuscript, as no direct opportunity ever offer'd for England, and last winter the fair copy was lost in a bark in the Gulf of Sidra, together with many of my books and designs, and all my mathematical instruments. . . . I have made a fair copy anew, and it is now ready, but I have some thoughts to join it to the Antiquities of Sicily and make two volumes of the Antiquities of Magna Grecia" (Dennistoun 1855, 2: 48). It was in this connection that he made mention of Mylne.

Two copies of Bruce's manuscript were later among his papers, but they were not seen by the "friends in London." The obvious candidate as author of the historical text in *The Ruins of Paestum* is Wood, who might also have collaborated with Mylne and the Gray brothers to write the description of the temples. All men had been to Paestum. Sir James Gray I would propose as the author of the analysis of the local coins. Bruce had, in fact, invited him, in Naples, in February 1763, to undertake the task. Gray was particularly interested in the decipherment of history through coins, and himself had a large collection. However, he declined, ". . . promising at the same time all his influence and assistance in promoting the projected work" (Murray 1808, 35). He might, in the event, have been persuaded by Wood to write the piece. Certainly both he and his brother provided paintings and drawings for the plates of *The Ruins of Paestum*—all five views by Joli, one might hazard, and the additional view by Magri, perhaps Magri's plans as well.

The circumstantial evidence offered here as to the making of the book is, clearly, no more than partial, but it does suggest that the accepted histories are themselves incomplete. It is unthinkable that Mylne and the Gray brothers, together with a large proportion of the membership of the Society of Dilettanti, led by Wood, would have supported a publication on Paestum that was a rival to Bruce's. Or that Lord Brudenell's father, as the duke of Montagu, would have accepted the dedication. The duke, his wife, and his son, as marquis of Monthermer, were all subscribers. Brudenell was an early enthusiast of Paestum, perhaps the initiator of Bruce's own interest. One would imagine him as the provider of funds perhaps for the production of the book.

These men would have been spurred to advance publication in Bruce's absence, before the field was overtaken by rivals, and, in particular, by the work of Dr. Longfield, who deliberately eschewed the notion of accuracy of measurement. Wood had established his reputation on archaeological accuracy. Adam had poked fun at him for this. It must, indeed, have been something of an embarrassment to him to be forwarding a book on Paestum that was not based on the most accurate of measurement. Even Gray had warned Bruce as to the reliability of Magri in this respect. Hence, perhaps, the claim that the measures were supplied by Soufflot. Wood reverted to the issue of accuracy in the preface he wrote for the first volume of the *Ionian Antiquities* of 1769: the account of an explorer, he explained, must in all things be truthful and sure; in a composition of genius, on the other hand, personal taste might be reflected.

However anomalous *The Ruins of Paestum*, whatever the vagaries of dimensioning (though several of the plates were furnished with scales in Neapolitan palmi, French toises, and English feet, they do not always correspond with the dimensions marked), the book was surprisingly well received by reviewers—whether in England, in the *Monthly Review* of July–December 1768 (pp. 132–135), or in Belgium and in France, where a French edition was distributed later in 1768. *The Bibliothèque des Sciences et Beaux-Arts* of October–December 1768 noted the help of Gray, Dumont, and Soufflot in the production, the *Mercure de France* of January 1769, that of Soufflot alone, but both reviews gave high praise to the engraver and commended the painstaking nature of the work. Even Dumont, in the preface to the 1769 edition of *Les ruines de Paestum*, though he thought Major had relied too heavily on his own plates, and also Longfield's text, approved the book—"Son texte est plus étendu que le nôtre, nous convenons qu'on ne trouve pas de dissertation sur les monnoìes et sur les médailles de *Paestum*; indépendamment de cet avantage, la partie typographique de son oeuvre laisse peu à désirer; très beau papier, caractères nets, cul-de-lampes & vignettes agréables, gravures soigneusement traitées; en un mot on n'a rien épargné de ce qui pouvoit rendre ce livre intéressant." Soufflot seems to have agreed with him; he had the copy of Major's book to which he had subscribed when he died, but no copy of Dumont's edition of his own survey. Other subscribers in France were the Abbé's Barthélemy and Leblanc, Leroy, P. J. Mariette, and of course, Dumont.

Major's study remained the standard reference to Paestum until *Les Ruines de Paestum ou Posidonia* by C.-M. Delagardette was issued in 1798 (and Major was exonerated there of Dumont's charges of plagiarism), but even this was to be revealed as failing in accuracy, in 1829, when Henri Labrouste sent in his fourth-year *envoi* of the restoration of the temples. The wonder of Paestum, however, was revealed to the eyes of Europe by none of these works, but rather by the sheaf of twenty-one etched views by Piranesi, assisted by his son, published in 1778, just after his death. The power and formal grandeur of the architecture was there laid bare. Mere accuracy of measurement had nothing to do with the representation. Plans, sections, and elevations were rendered irrelevant. R. M.

Bibliography

Dennistoun, J. *Memoirs of Sir Robert Strange . . . and of His Brother-in-Law Andrew Lumisden.* 2 vols. London, 1855

Fleming, J. "Lord Brudenell and His Bear-Leader." *In English Miscellany 1958.* London, 1959

Gotch, C. "The Missing Years of Robert Mylne." *Architectural Review* (September 1951): 179–182

Harris, E., and N. Savage. *British Architectural Books and Writers 1556–1785.* Cambridge, 1990

Lang, S. "The Early Publication of the Temples at Paestum." *Journal of the Warburg and Courtauld Institutes* 13 (1950): 48–64

McCarthy, M. "Documents on the Greek Revival in Architecture." *Burlington Magazine* (November 1972): 760–769

McCarthy, M. "Una nuova interpretazione del 'Paestum' di Thomas Major e di altri disegni inglesi di epoca successiva." In *La fortuna di Paestum e la memoria moderna del dorico 1750–1830.* Ed. J. Raspi Serra. Vol. 1. Florence, 1986: 40–52

Middione, R. *Antonio Joli.* Soncino, 1995

Murray, A. *Account of the Life and Writings of James Bruce, of Kinnaird.* Edinburgh, 1808

Mustili, D. "Prime memorie dell rovine di Paestum." In *Studi in onore di Riccardo Filangieri.* Vol. 3. Naples, 1952: 107–111

Richardson, A. E. *Robert Mylne, Architect and Engineer 1733 to 1811.* London, 1955

Wiebenson, D. *Sources of Greek Revival Architecture.* London, 1969

42

James Malton (1765–1803)

An Essay on British Cottage Architecture; being An Attempt to perpetuate on Principle, that peculiar mode of Building, which was originally the effect of Chance. Supported by Fourteen Designs, with Their Ichnography, or Plans, laid down to Scale; comprising Dwellings for the Peasant and Farmer, and Retreats for the Gentleman; with various Observations thereon: the whole extending to Twenty-one Plates, Designed and Executed in Aqua-Tinta

London: published by Hookham and Carpenter: and to be had at Taylor's Architectural Library; at Egerton's Military Library; of Mr. Wilkinson; and of the author, 1798

1985.61.2517

Large quarto: 337 × 270 (13 5/16 × 10 5/8)

Pagination [iv], 27, [1] pp., 21 aquatint plates

Edition First edition

Text pp. [i] half-title (verso blank); [iii] title page (verso blank); [1]–12 introduction; 13–27 text; [28] blank

Illustrations 21 aquatint plates numbered 1–21, printed in sepia, all signed by Malton as designer, draftsman, and engraver

Binding Contemporary three-quarter diced calf, marbled boards

References Abbey, *Life,* 34; Berlin Cat. 2309 (2d ed.); Berlin (1977) OS 2308[2]; ESTC t89368

James Malton's *An Essay on British Cottage Architecture* was by no means the first publication to offer designs for rustic cottages—John Plaw had long preceded him with *Rural Architecture or Designs, from the Simple Cottage to the Decorated Villa* of 1785, which also had aquatint plates. But Malton had succumbed, deeply, to the influence of Uvedale Price; he approached the matter with a new, picturesque sensibility and something of the painter's eye. He was also far more reverent in his concern.

He was altogether unwilling to accept Dr. Johnson's definition of the cottage as "a mean habitation," regarding it rather as a hallowed sanctuary, enshrining the oldest traditions of bucolic bliss and innocence. It was a symbol, moreover, of a particularly British tradition, to be upheld and preserved at all costs: "I am most forcibly influenced by a desire to perpetuate, with my share of ability, the peculiar beauty of the British, picturesque, rustic habitations; regarding them, with the country church, as the most pleasing, the most suitable ornaments of art that can be introduced to embellish rural nature."

These parochial concerns were even more clearly defined at the end of his essay with a plea, surprisingly early, for preservation: "To gentlemen, and persons of cultivated taste, I address this essay, and recommend them to take the Cottage under protection; which, unless speadily done, will be found to exist no where but on the canvas of the painter."

Malton was the younger son of Thomas Malton, an architectural draftsman who taught perspective drawing for a time at his house in Poland Street, Soho, but who was impelled by financial difficulties to move to Ireland, where James accompanied him. James worked in Dublin, in the office of James Gandon, but "he so frequently betrayed all official confidence; and was guilty of so many irregularities, that it became quite necessary to dismiss him from the employment." His father died in Dublin in 1801, but James had returned nine years earlier to London, where he made a living as an architectural perspectivist, exhibiting frequently at the Royal Academy. In 1797 he published *A Descriptive View of Dublin.* His elder brother Thomas was also an architectural perspectivist, trained as an architect at the school of the Royal Academy, where he was awarded the gold medal in 1782. He, too, exhibited regularly at the Royal Academy. One of the first to take up the newly developed technique of aquatint for bookplates, between 1792 to 1801 he published *A Picturesque Tour through the Cities of London and Westminster*, with a hundred aquatint plates, giving the liveliest image of the Georgian city. This was the inspiration for *The Microcosm of London.* He died in 1804, while engaged on a similar book of views of Oxford.

James Malton adopted the aquatint for both of his books on cottage and villa architecture, *An Essay on British Cottage Architecture*, of 1798, and *A Collection of Designs for Rural Retreats and Villas,* of 1802. The *Essay* consists of a twelve-page introduction, in which the merits of the cottage are extolled as never before, not only as a rustic retreat, but as a visual delight, redolent of the imagery of Salvator Rosa, Claude and Poussin, and Ruysdael—all painters, one might note, approved by Price. For Malton, the irregular—albeit the "well chosen irregular"—was one of the chief characteristics of the cottage (a point of view that was to be strongly contested by Richard Elsam in *An Essay on Rural Architecture Illustrated with Original and Economical Designs Being an Attempt also to Refute, by Analogy, the Principles of Mr. James Malton's Essay on British Cottage Architecture*, of 1803). Malton required not only a general lack of symmetry, but a succession of irregular breaks in the outline and form, and a variety of materials and surface textures—"A porch at the entrance; irregular breaks in the direction of the walls; one part higher than

another; various roofing of different materials, thatch particularly, boldly projecting; fronts partly built of walls of brick, partly weather boarded, and partly brick-noggin dashed; casement window lights, are all conducive, and constitute its features."

Malton's twenty-one plates illustrate fourteen designs for rustic retreats, some showing variations of window treatment and surface finishes with the same basic form. But the designs are not all peasant cottages, for some "a splendid equipage might be drawn up, and not appear an inappropriate appendage."

"I have endeavoured," he wrote, "in the progress of fourteen designs, to advance the subject in regular gradation, from a peasant's simple hut, to a habitation worthy of a gentleman of fortune."

Malton's designs, with their half-timbering and barge boarding, lattice windows and stable doors, all embowered in bushes and trees, set the tone, with remarkable prescience, for the image of the picturesque dwelling that was to survive as the popular ideal in England for a hundred years and more. Several of his cottages look little different from the semidetached houses that were

James Malton. *An Essay on British Cottage Architecture.* Plate 4. "Designs for Peasant Huts." 1985.61.2517

built on the outskirts of London in the 1920s and 1930s, epitomized by Osbert Lancaster as Wimbledon Transitional and Bypass Variegated.

The first edition of the *Essay* was published by Hookham and Carpenter (the publishers also of Elsam). It appeared in addition in a variant issue, with hand-colored line and aquatint plates: the five ground plans in sepia, the plate of windows in blue, and the fifteen perspective views in three or four colors, varying from copy to copy. The second edition, of 1804, with two additional plates, dated December 1803, was published by Thomas Malton. R. M.

Bibliography

Colvin, H. *Biographical Dictionary of British Architects, 1660–1840.* 2d ed. London, 1978

Wrightson, P. *The Small English House. A Catalogue of Books.* London, 1977

43

James Malton (1765–1803)

The Young Painter's Maulstick; Being A Practical Treatise On Perspective; Containing Rules And Principles For Delineation On Planes, Treated so as to render the Art of Drawing correctly, easy of Attainment even to common Capacities; and entertaining at the same Time, from its Truth and Facility. Founded on the clear mechanical Process of Vignola And Sirigatti; United With The Theoretic Principles Of The Celebrated Dr. Brook Taylor. Addressed To Students In Drawing. By James Malton, Architect And Draftsman

London: printed by V. Griffiths; and published for the author, by Carpenter and Co., 1800

1985.61.2518

Quarto: 285 × 221 (11 3/16 × 8 1/16)

Pagination [4], ii, xiv, 71, [1] pp., [23] aquatint plates (1 folding)

Edition First edition. A variant imprint, naming J. Barfield as printer instead of V. Griffiths, appears to represent a later issue (paper watermarked "1803" as well as "1798"; see Abbey, *Life*, 152)

Text pp. [1] title page (verso blank); [3] dedication to Benjamin West, president of the Royal Academy (verso blank); [i]–ii "Apology"; [i]–xiv preface; [1]–17 introduction; [18]–27 text, "Practical Geometry"; [28]–71 text, "Practical Perspective"; [72] blank

Illustrations 23 line and aquatint plates numbered 1–23 (pl. 6 with pasted overslip; pl. 10 folding; pl. 14 with extension flap; pl. 23 misnumbered 13, corrected in ink). 8 woodcut diagrams in the text

Binding Contemporary half calf, marbled boards and edges, red morocco label

Provenance Nineteenth-century armorial bookplate of General Robert Taylor, with his monogram and arms in gilt at head of spine

References Abbey, *Life*, 152 (variant imprint); ESTC t90226

James Malton's third book, *The Young Painter's Maulstick: Being a Practical Treatise on Perspective*, though altogether straightforward and unpretentious, intended as a manual for students, must be viewed in relation to a succession of books on perspective published in England during the eighteenth century. Malton's work was, as his subtitle makes clear, "founded on the mechanical process of Vignola and Sirigatti; united with the theoretic principles of the celebrated Dr. Brook Taylor."

Taylor's *Linear Perspective* was published first in 1715. It was characterized by an empirical approach to perspective drawing, with basic mechanical rules, but with a clear recognition that objects were not always seen in accord with mathematical rules and that these might be adjusted or dispensed with on occasion to allow things to be represented as they were seen in experience. The work was at once successful and was revised and reissued in 1719 and 1749, but most notably and most extensively in 1754, as *Dr. Brook Taylor's Method of Perspective Made Easy*. The author of this was Joshua Kirby, friend and supporter of William Hogarth, who drew the frontispiece. Hogarth and Kirby were engaged in these years in a bitter dispute with their fellow members in the St. Martin's Lane Academy as to the merits of a national academy, and these disputes strongly influenced the reception and reputation of Kirby's book. It was attacked, in 1754, by Joseph Highmore, because he thought Kirby had taken more liberties in the drawing of columns than Taylor had intended. Kirby was forced to reply to Highmore's strictures in an appendix to the second edition of *Brook Taylor's Method*, published in 1755. While this edition was being prepared, Isaac Ware, the architect, chief opponent to Hogarth on the matter of the new, public academy, announced in the *Public Advertiser* of March 1755 his intention to issue a translation of Lorenzo Sirigatti's sixteenth-century work *Prattica di prospettiva*. Kirby saw this as an affront and a direct challenge. He denounced Ware's proposal forthwith and ensured unfavorable reviews when the *Perspective* appeared in 1756. He published a rude pamphlet himself in 1757. Ware felt bound to reply, in the *Monthly Review* of January 1758, rejecting Kirby's strictures, but acknowledging that Sirigatti's method was perhaps overcomplex. There were other repercussions in these disputes, but they are not germane to the matter of techniques of perspective drawing.

When Malton's elder brother Thomas published *A Compleat Treatise on Perspective, in Theory and Practice* in 1755, he adopted "the principles of Dr. Brook Taylor." His frontispiece, moreover, was a domed pavilion, dedicated to Taylor. This book was reissued in 1776, 1778, and 1779. In 1783 he published *An Appendix, or Second Part, to the Compleat Treatise on Perspective*, which comprised a history of the subject, and in particular the history of its eighteenth-century practitioners. Malton admired Ware's gentlemanly restraint in presenting his defense, though he made it clear that he was himself no admirer of Sirigatti's methods. The second edition of *An Appendix* was issued in 1800, by a new publisher, Carpenter and Co. Carpenter and Co. also published *The Young Painter's Maulstick*, which if one is to judge by its subtitle, was intended as a final resolution of the eighteenth-century conflicts. The result was a compromise, with Taylor's theories being accepted, but the

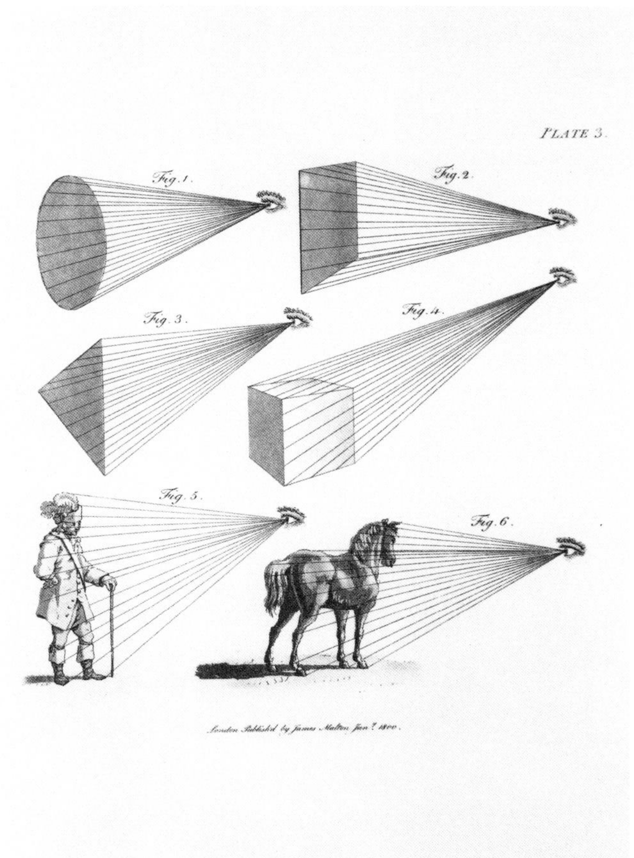

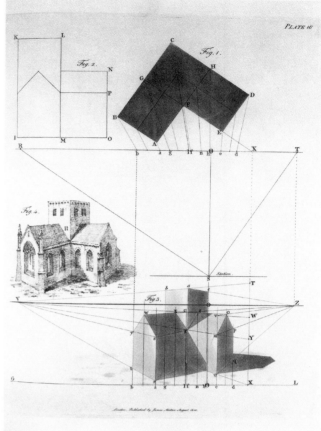

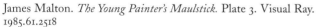

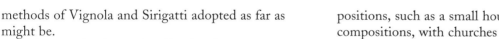

James Malton. *The Young Painter's Maulstick.* Plate 3. Visual Ray. 1985.61.2518

James Malton. *The Young Painter's Maulstick.* Plate 16. Representing a building in Perspective. 1985.61.2518

methods of Vignola and Sirigatti adopted as far as might be.

Malton made clear in his "Apology" that he aimed to provide "a practical treatise, which would exemplify the doctrine of delineation, in an easy, familiar, and engaging manner; and wherein its rules might be applied to pleasing and painter-like subjects."

The method of instruction involved the presentation of a series of practical examples of setting up perspectives, from a range of simple geometric forms such as cubes, cylinders, and cones, to formal architectural compositions, such as a small house, and thus to picturesque compositions, with churches and castles, barns and bridges, illustrated in twenty-three plates.

The book was issued in only one edition. R. M.

Bibliography

Colvin, H. *Biographical Dictionary of British Architects, 1660–1840*. London, 1978

Harris, E., and N. Savage. *British Architectural Books and Writers 1556–1785*. Cambridge, 1990

44

John Preston Neale (1780–1847) and Edward Wedlake Brayley (1773–1854)

The History And Antiquities Of The Abbey Church Of St. Peter, Westminster: Including Notices and Biographical Memoirs Of The Abbots And Deans Of That Foundation. Illustrated By John Preston Neale. The Whole of the Literary Department By Edward Wedlake Brayley. In Two Volumes. Vol. I. (II.)

[vol. 1] London: published by the proprietor, J. P. Neale; and sold by Longman, Hurst, Rees, Orme, and Brown, 1818

[vol. 2] London: printed for Hurst, Robinson, and Co., 1823

1985.61.2584–2585

Quarto: 365 × 262 (14 3/8 × 10 3/8); large paper copy

Pagination Vol. 1: [xviii], 227, [19] pp., etched frontispiece, etched title plate, [19] etched plates; 72, [10] pp., wood-engraved frontispiece, [10] etched plates

Vol. 2: [ii], 304, [40] pp., etched frontispiece, etched title plate, [47] etched plates

(*Note*: The first sequence of 19 etched plates in vol. 1 of this copy are extra illustrations)

Edition First edition

Text vol. 1 pp. [i] title; [ii] imprint of T. Davison, printer; [iii–iv] dedication to George IV; [v–x] list of subscribers; [xi–xvii] preface, dated 15 March 1823; [xviii] list of officers of Westminster School; [1] divisional title page (verso blank); [3]–227 text; [228–230] chronological table of dignitaries connected with the abbey; [231–246] index, errata; *Supplement* pp. [1] title "An Historical And Architectural Account Of King Henry The Seventh's Chapel . . ." (verso blank); [3]–72 text; [73–76] list of publications relating to Henry VII's chapel, general index; [77–81] "Index To The Monuments And Interments . . . ," "Index To The Arms," list of additional subscribers; [82] list of plates; *vol. 2* pp. [i] title; [ii] imprint of T. Davison, printer; [1] divisional title page (verso blank); [3]–304 text, additions and corrections; [305–331] indices; [332–340] list of publications relating to the Abbey; [341–344] list of plates

Illustrations Regular copies contain 3 frontispieces (2 etched, 1 wood-engraved), 2 etched title plates and 57 etched plates, numbered erratically but correctly listed at the end of each volume. For a detailed description of each, see Adams (1983). All of the plates were drawn by Neale except for 12 measured drawings by J. R. Thompson. The plates are signed as engraved by Cosmo Armstrong, Miss Elizabeth Byrne, John Byrne, James Carter, John Cleghorn, George Cooke, Henry Le Keux, John Le Keux, J. Lewis, T. Matthews, Henry Moses, William Radclyffe, John Roffe, Richard Roffe, Robert Sands, John Scott, W. R. Smith, James P. Stephanoff, W. D. Taylor, James Tingle, J. C. Varrall, and William Woolnoth. In addition, the dedication leaf in vol. 1 features the arms of the dedicatee, George IV, etched by John Byfield after Thomas Willement. In the Millard copy, most plates are marked "Proof," and vol. 1 is extra-illustrated with 19 portraits of the deans of Westminster etched by Robert Graves (8), James Stow (8), G. P. Harding (1), John Swaine (1), and J. Tuck (1), all after drawings by G. P. Harding

Binding Contemporary diced blue morocco, gilt borders, spine paneled in gilt with false raised bands, gilt edges

Provenance Engraved armorial bookplates of Thomas Parry

References Bernard Adams, *London Illustrated 1604–1851* (London, 1983), 123

J. P. Neale's first job was as a clerk at the general post office in Lombard Street, London. By the age of seventeen, however, he was exhibiting drawings of insects and fruit at the Royal Academy, and as early as 1801 he included a topographical subject (Bonner's Hall, Lambeth, shown alongside "Insects in their natural state, from Nature"). Although entomology continued to interest him—he contributed an article to the first volume of the *Transactions of the Entomological Society of London* in 1812—it was his skill as an architectural draftsman that eventually enabled him to leave the post office and become a full-time artist. According to Samuel Redgrave, he actually studied architecture, "to give greater truth to his buildings," but whether this was a formal education or one provided by his mentors is unclear. His lifelong friendship with the landscape painter John Varley had begun in 1796, and since Varley and John Britton knew each other by 1798 it is likely Neale too made this formative contact at an early age. In 1801 Britton and his companion, E. W. Brayley, began what turned into a twenty-five-volume topographical series, *The Beauties of England and Wales*. Neale was soon being employed to make drawings for it and, like many other young draftsmen, it was as a protégé of the authors that his career was launched.

Britton (in 1805) and Brayley (in 1811) resigned from the series long before it limped to its conclusion in 1815. Neale, on the other hand, continued working for the

John Preston Neale and Edward Wedlake Brayley. *The History and Antiquities of the Abbey Church of St. Peter, Westminster.* Plate XVIII. "Westminster Abbey. View in Poets Corner Looking South." 1985.61.2585

Drawn by J. P. Neale

Engraved by R. Sands.

WESTMINSTER ABBEY.

VIEW IN PORTS CORNER LOOKING SOUTH.

To THE MOST NOBLE the MARQUIS of BUCKINGHAM an admirer of Topographical Publications and a zealous Encourager of this work,

This Plate is gratefully inscribed by

J. P. Neale.

London, Published Nov.r 1 1817 by J. P. Neale 16 Bennett St. Blackfriars Road & Longman & Co. Paternoster Row

Proof.

Printed by Cox & Barnett

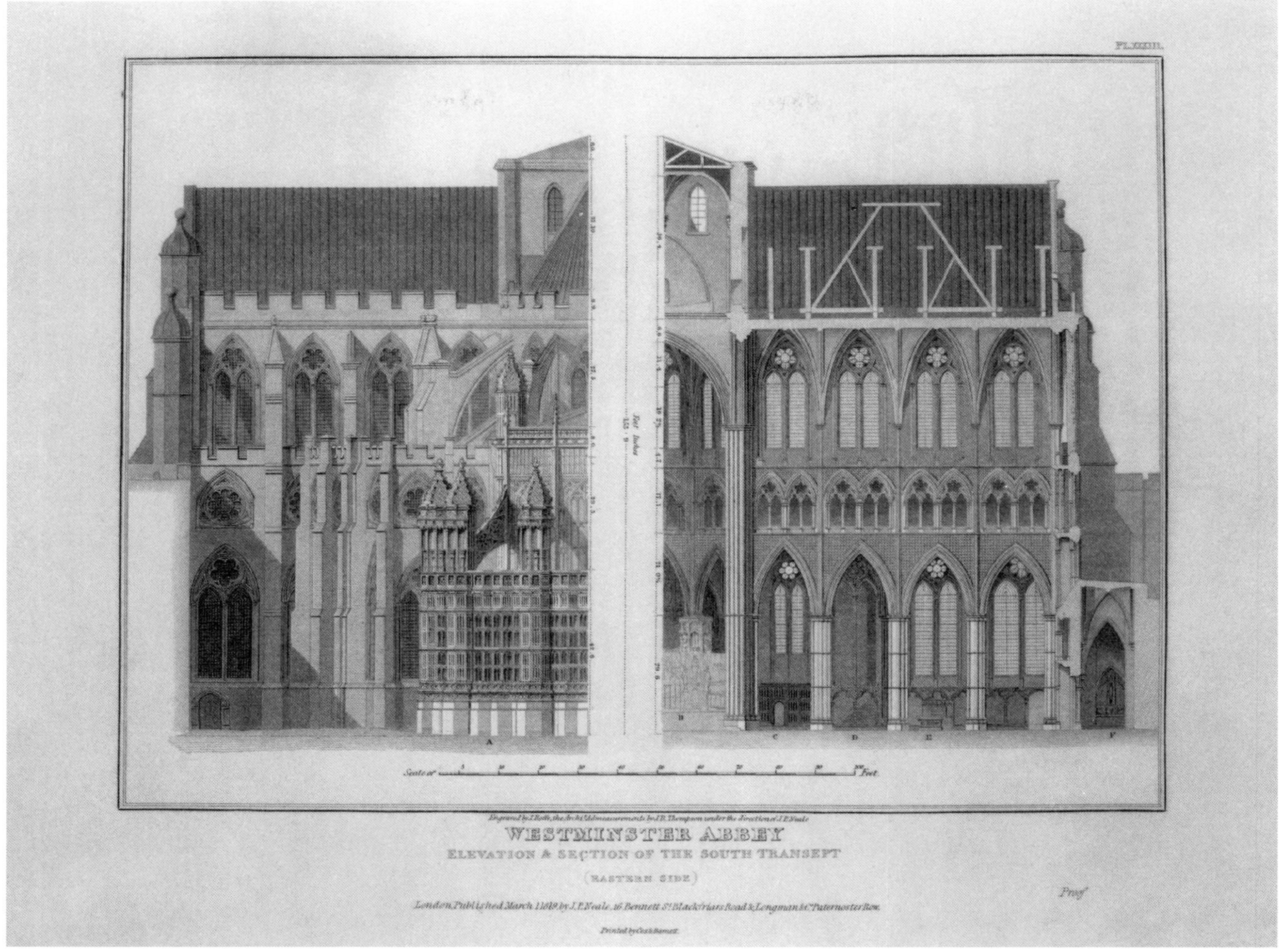

John Preston Neale and Edward Wedlake Brayley. *The History and Antiquities of the Abbey Church of St. Peter, Westminster.* Plate XXXIII. "Elevation and section of the south transept (eastern side)." 1985.61.2585

publishers to the end, becoming the principal supplier of views from 1811 onward, and playing no part in Britton's far more influential project, *The Architectural Antiquities of Great Britain* (1805–1814). When he renewed his partnership with Brayley for the present work it was under quite different circumstances. Neale's name is displayed on the title page more prominently than the author's, less, perhaps, because his reputation warranted it, than because he was not only the artist but also the book's proprietor and co-publisher with Longmans. In effect, he was employing Brayley to embellish his drawings with text, a reversal not at all uncommon at the time, but one against which Britton had consistently fought. Brayley not only fell in with the arrangement, but produced by far the best history and description of Westminster Abbey to date, still held in high esteem as one to which "all books on Westminster published since are but supplementary" (Francis Bond, quoted by Adams).

The pressure on the publishers to produce an outstanding work came from two main sources. First, Westminster Abbey had never been ignored by antiquarians, as Brayley's extensive bibliography shows. In particular, it had recently been the subject of one of Rudolf Ackermann's most elaborate monographs, *The History of the Abbey Church of St. Peter's Westminster* (1812). The hand-colored aquatints in this two-volume work were after Frederick Mackenzie, A. C. Pugin, François Huet-Villiers, and other notable artists. Ackermann was so proud of the results that he commissioned a binding designed by the architect J. B. Papworth to house the original watercolors. With this competitor in mind, little excuse can be made for Brayley's comment that "In the Architectural Illustration of this splendid Fabric, all preceding publications have been peculiarly deficient" (preface). For the text, however, Ackermann had used his malleable hack William Combe, and Brayley was on firmer ground when dismissing it with the comment that "scarcely any new fact is to be found in the whole Work" (bibliography). Although crushing comments about potential rivals were common enough among English antiquarians, Brayley was also well aware that he was part of a new and more rigorous school, the work of which largely justified the critical contempt it poured on its predecessors.

The leader of this new school was, of course, Britton, and he provided the second and more immediate pressure on Neale and his partners. The first volume of

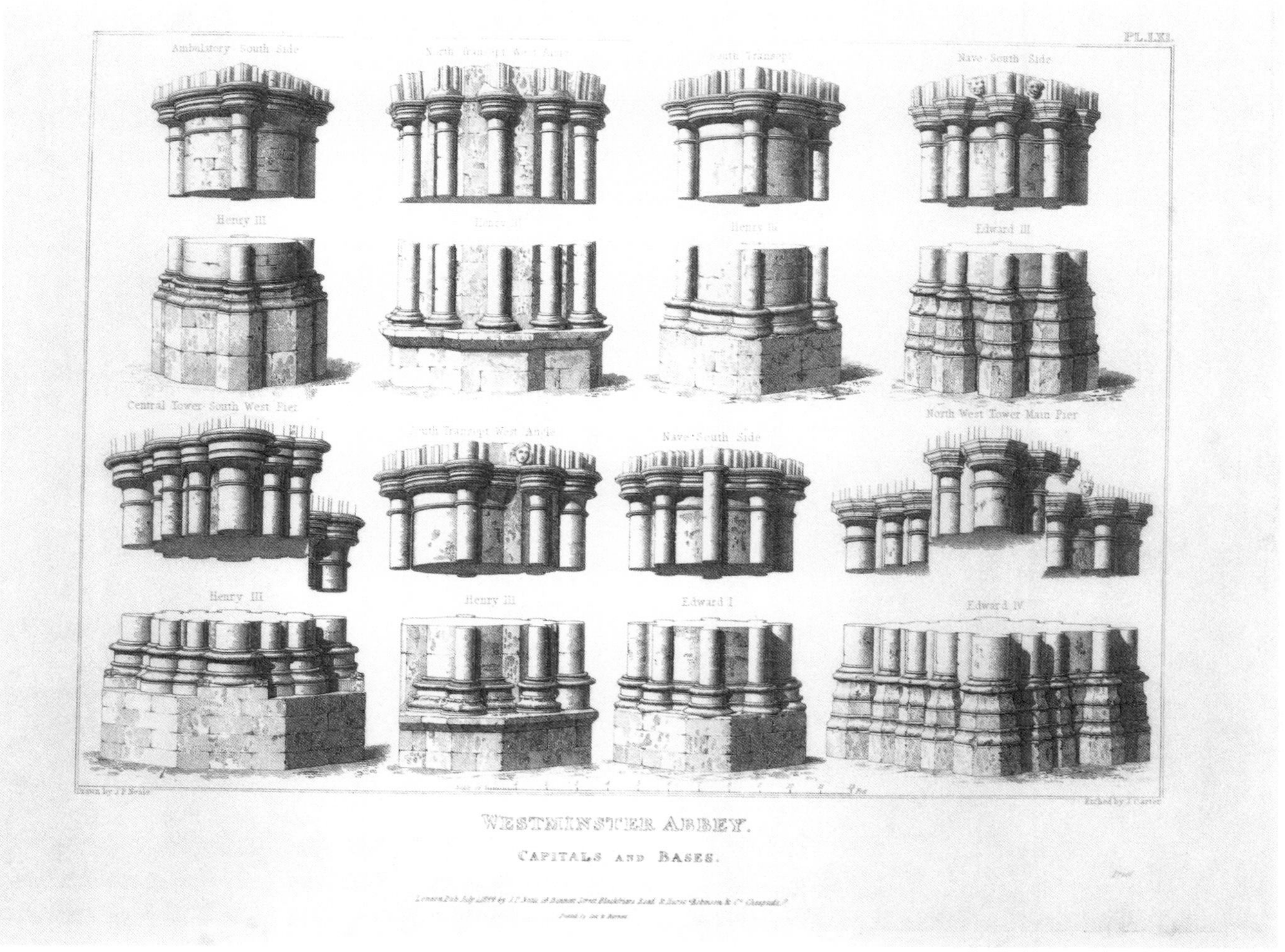

John Preston Neale and Edward Wedlake Brayley. *The History and Antiquities of the Abbey Church of St. Peter, Westminster.* Plate LXI. "Westminster Abbey. Capitals and bases." 1985.61.2585

Britton's *Cathedral Antiquities*, that is, *The History and Antiquities of the Cathedral Church of Salisbury*, was issued in parts between May 1814 and March 1815. Like Neale, Britton was a co-publisher with Longmans. Most of the plates illustrating Salisbury Cathedral were drawn by one of Ackermann's Westminster Abbey artists, Frederick Mackenzie, but their style and purpose was radically different. Under Britton's editorship, Mackenzie achieved new standards of architectural accuracy while retaining enough picturesque charm to attract the general reader. As he was writing about a subject on his favorite Wiltshire territory, Britton was able to add an informed and exhaustive text. The very favorable reviews the work received, and its immediate success, provided the commercial motivation behind the present work. The intellectual link was equally direct, and acknowledged by Brayley in the first sentence of volume two: "The Abbey Church of Westminster is one of the finest examples of the Pointed style of architecture that was ever erected in this country; and, with the single exception of Salisbury Cathedral, it is likewise the most complete and perfect that now remains."

Neale's Westminster Abbey borrowed its physical arrangement entirely from Britton's series. Textually, this involved the separation of biographical from architectural history, and the addition of lengthy bibliographies, indexes, and other critical apparatus. For the system of illustration it meant a complex combination of different types of drawing. Some are conventionally orthographic, offering measured plans, elevations, sections, and details, but usually with shading to add tone to outlines. For these plates, Neale used measured drawings prepared by J. R. Thompson. Another group masses examples of one or two details onto a single plate, for comparative purposes (e.g., capitals and bases, ancient shields, etc.). The third main group was the view, interior or exterior. These were the main selling points of the volume, and Neale's way of making them picturesque but still informative owes much to Mackenzie's influence. Staffage is minimal, and figures are used to enhance the abbey's architectural presence. Light is frequently cast more fully in the background of a plate, so that details remain equally visible regardless of distance. The surface of the stonework is etched with countless short irregular lines that give it a strong, pitted appearance. The credit for translating tone from Neale's original wash drawing to the plate rested with the engravers, many of whom had already achieved similar results for

John Preston Neale and Edward Wedlake Brayley. *The History and Antiquities of the Abbey Church of St. Peter, Westminster.* Plate L. "Henry the Seventh's Chapel, northeast view." 1985.61.2584

Britton. In 1817 Neale exhibited the original drawings for the north aisle and Lord Mansfield's monument at the Royal Academy.

Longman's, too, saw the project as complementary to Britton's, and accordingly issued it in the same array of formats: royal quarto (10 guineas), imperial quarto (15 guineas or £34 13s with proofs), crown folio (20 guineas), and large paper (£34 13s). It was first issued in parts between November 1816 and May 1823, enabling the publishers to see how successful it was before deciding to add a "Supplement," usually bound with volume one, on King Henry VII's Chapel. The latter had just been subject to a major restoration by Thomas Gayfere, and one of Neale's plates is accordingly inscribed to him. The supplement was a timely commemoration of his work, but in terms of architectural detail it cannot compete with Lewis Cottingham's nearly contemporary collection of *Plans, Elevations, Sections, Details, and Views, of the Magnificent Chapel of King Henry the Seventh* (1822–1829). At the same time, both Abbey and Chapel also formed part of an analysis of Gothic that was to help revolutionize architectural practice, namely, E. J. Willson and A. C. Pugin's *Specimens of Gothic Architecture* (1821–1823). However, its careful reproduction of measured details was a new path in which Neale was neither willing nor perhaps able to tread. In any case, he had already begun his series of *Views of the Seats of Noblemen and Gentlemen*, returning to the older, pre-*Beauties* tradition of small topographical views.

The Millard copy of this work is extra-illustrated with nineteen portraits after drawings by G. P. Harding. These formed what might be called a "satellite" suite. They represented an independent publishing venture by Harding, but they were intended mainly for sale with Neale and Brayley's work. In Brayley's bibliography, the suite is advertised as *Portraits of the Deans of Westminster*, "published in all the various sizes of this Work."

In 1856 Willis and Sotheran published another quarto edition of *The History and Antiquities of Westminster Abbey*, with a revised and abridged text. By then the book was generally known as *Neale's Westminster Abbey*, but the names given the highest profile on the title page were the engravers, "Le Keux, Woolnoth, Byrne, Scott, &c." This is no more than a reflection of the popular recognition these engravers deserved and subsequently achieved. Brayley, having died two years before, missed the disappointment of seeing his name entirely suppressed. G. B.

Bibliography

Adams, B. *London Illustrated 1604–1851*. London, 1983

Graves, A. *The Royal Academy of Arts: A Complete Dictionary of Contributors*. Reprint Wakefield, 1970

Redgrave, S. *A Dictionary of Artists of the English School.* Reprint, Amsterdam, 1970

45

John Preston Neale (1780–1847)

Views Of The Seats Of Noblemen And Gentlemen, In England, Wales, Scotland, And Ireland. From Drawings, By J. P. Neale. Vol. I. (–VI.)

[vol. 1] London: published for the proprietors, by W. H. Reid, 1818

[vols. 2–6] London: published by Sherwood, Neely, and Jones; and Thomas Moule, 1819–1823

NGA Lib. Rare Book: DA660N421818

Octavo: 233 × 140 (9 1/8 × 5 1/2)

Pagination Vol. 1: [4], xx, [144] pp., added etched title plate, [70] etched plates

Vol. 2: [152] pp., added etched title plate, [72] etched plates

Vol. 3: [168] pp., added etched title plate, [72] etched plates

Vol. 4: [150] pp., added etched title plate, [71] etched plates

Vol. 5: [150] pp., added etched title plate, [72] etched plates

Vol. 6: [5], 10–14, [148] pp., added etched title plate, [69] etched plates

(*Note*: This copy is without the unnumbered 8-page list of subscribers usually bound in vol. 1. Neale's 1824 "Address" to the reader, sometimes bound in vol. 1, is here bound in vol. 6)

Edition First edition

Text vol. 1: pp. [1] title page; [2] printer's imprint "J. McCreery, Printer, Black-Horse Court, London"; [3] dedication "To His Grace John Russell, Duke of Bedford . . ." (verso blank); [i]–xx introduction, signed "T. M. [i.e., Thomas Moule], January 31, 1823"; [1–142] descriptions of the houses; [143–144] "Index To The First Volume Of Noblemen's And Gentlemen's Seats"; *vol. 2*: pp. [1] title page; [2] McCreery's imprint; [3] dedication "To The Right Honourable William Wyndham Grenville, Lord Grenville . . ." (verso blank); [5–150] descriptions of the houses; [151–152] "Index To The Second Volume . . ."; *vol. 3*: pp. [1] title page; [2] McCreery's imprint; [3] dedication "To The Most Noble George Granville Leveson Gower, Marquess of Stafford . . ." (verso blank); [5–166] descriptions of the houses; [167–168] "Index To The Third Volume . . ."; *vol. 4*: pp. [1] title page; [2] McCreery's imprint; [3] dedication "To His Grace John Henry Manners, Duke of Rutland . . ." (verso blank); [5–148] description of the plates; [149–150] "Index To The Fourth Volume . . ."; *vol. 5*: pp. [1] title page; [2] McCreery's imprint; [3] dedication "To His Grace John Murray, Duke of Atholl . . ." (verso blank); [5–148] description of the plates; [149–150] "Index To The Fifth Volume . . ."; *vol. 6*: pp. [5] title page; [6] McCreery's imprint; [7] dedication "To The Right Honourable John Bligh, Earl of Darnley . . ." (verso blank); [9]–14 "Address" by Neale, dated 12 Jan., 1824; [1–146] description of the plates; [147–148] "Index To The Sixth Volume . . ."

Illustrations

Vol. 1: [71] etched plates including the illustrated title plate ("Neale's / Views / Of / Seats"). All of the plates are signed "Drawn by J. P. Neale" with the exception of plate [17], which is signed "Drawn by J. [i.e., John] Buckler." They are engraved by Robert Acon, Charles Askey (4), Thomas Barber (3), M. S. Barenger (2), John Bishop, Elizabeth Byrne (4), William Ensom, F. R. Hay (5), H. Hobson (7), Thomas Jeavons (3), Samuel Lacey (3), John Le Keux, James Lewis, T. Matthews (8), John Pye (2), William Radclyffe, Samuel Rawle, J. [i.e., James C.?] Redaway, E. [i.e., Edward John] Roberts, J. [i.e., John] Scott, J. Smith, W. R. Smith (2), H. S. Storer, William Tombleson, J. C. Varrall (8), J. Wallis, William Wallis (4), Henry Winkles, and William Woolnoth

Vol. 2: [73] etched plates including the illustrated title plate. All of the plates are signed "Drawn by J. P. Neale," engraved by Robert Acon (2), J. Barber, Thomas Barber (7), M. S. Barenger, John Bishop, William Cooke, Jun., William Ensom (4), F. R. Hay (3), J. Henshall, Thomas Higham (2), H. Hobson (6), Thomas Jeavons (2), Samuel Lacey (4), John Le Keux, Charles Pye, John Pye, William Radclyffe, J. A. Rolph, Robert Sands (2), W. R. Smith, T. Matthews (9), J. [i.e., John] Scott, William Tombleson, J. C. Varrall (10), T. C. [i.e., J. C.] Varrall (2), William Wallis (5), and Henry Winkles

Vol. 3: [73] etched plates including the illustrated title plate. All are signed "Drawn by J. P. Neale," with the exception of plate [43], which is signed "Drawn by Edw[ar]d Swinburne Esq.[r]," and plate [44], signed "Drawn by Miss E. Swinburne." The plates are engraved by Robert Acon (4), Thomas Barber (3), M. S. Barenger (2), Elizabeth Byrne, J. Godden, F. R. Hay (5), H. Hobson (8), Thomas Jeavons (2), Samuel Lacey (6), T. Matthews (9), H. Melville, William Radclyffe (2), J. [i.e., James C.?] Redaway, Robert Sands (2), John Shury, W. R. Smith (2), J. C. Varrall (11), Robert Wallis, William Wallis (7), Henry Winkles (3), and William Woolnoth

Vol. 4: [72] etched plates including the illustrated title plate. All are signed "Drawn by J. P. Neale," engraved by Robert Acon (3), Thomas Barber (2), J. Barnett, William Ensom (2), F. R. Hay (3), Thomas Higham (2), H. Hobson (4), Thomas Jeavons (4), Samuel Lacey (7),

James Lewis, T. Matthews (8), Thomas Milton, William Radclyffe (7), J. [i.e., James C.?] Redaway, H. F. Rose, Robert Sands (2), John Shury, William Tombleson (3), J. C. Varrall (6), William Wallis (12), and William Woolnoth

Vol. 5: [73] etched plates including the illustrated title plate. All are signed "Drawn by J. P. Neale," engraved by Charles Askey (3), J. Barber, Thomas Barber (5), John Byrne, William Ensom, F. R. Hay (3), Thomas Higham (3), H. Hobson (5), Thomas Jeavons, Samuel Lacey (2), James Lewis, T. Matthews (7), Charles Pye (2), William Radclyffe, Samuel Rawle (5), J. [i.e., James C.?] Redaway (5), Richard Roffe, J. A. Rolph, W. R. Smith, J. C. Varrall (11), Robert Wallis (2), William Wallis (9), Henry Winkles, and William Woolnoth

Vol. 6: [70] etched plates including the illustrated title plate. All are signed "Drawn by J. P. Neale," engraved by Robert Acon, Charles Askey (2), Thomas Barber (6), M. S. Barenger, John Bishop, John Byrne, J. Godden, F. R. Hay (9), Thomas Higham, H. Hobson (7), Thomas Hood, Thomas Jeavons, Samuel Lacey, T. Matthews (6), John Pye (2), William Radclyffe (4), Samuel Rawle (2), J. [i.e., James C.?] Redaway, Richard Roffe, Robert Sands, W. R. Smith, William Tombleson, J. C. Varrall (7), Robert Wallis (2), and William Wallis (10)

Binding Contemporary calf, blind-tooled

SECOND SERIES

Views Of The Seats Of Noblemen And Gentlemen, In England, Wales, Scotland, And Ireland. By J. P. Neale. Second Series. Vol. I. (–V.)

[vol. 1] London: published By Sherwood, Jones, and Co.; and Thomas Moule, 1824

[vol. 2] London: published by Sherwood, Jones, and Co., 1825

[vols. 3–5] London: published by Sherwood, Gilbert, and Piper, 1826–1829

Octavo: 233 × 143 (9 1/4 × 5 5/8)

Pagination Vol. 1: [136] pp., added etched title plate, [59] etched plates

Vol. 2: [122] pp., added etched title plate, [59] etched plates

Vol. 3: [128] pp., added etched title plate, [59] etched plates

Vol. 4: [126] pp., added etched title plate, [59] etched plates

Vol. 5: [126] pp., added etched title plate, [59] etched plates

Edition First edition

Text vol. 1: pp. [1] title page; [2] printer's imprint "J. Mc Creery, Printer, Tooks-Court, Chancery Lane"; [3] dedication "To The Most Noble Henry William Paget, Marquess of Anglesey, And Earl Of Uxbridge . . ." (verso blank); [5–6] "Second Series. Contents Of The First Volume Containing Sixty Engravings And Four Vignettes"; [7–136] description of the plates; *vol. 2*: pp. [1] title page; [2] McCreery's imprint; pp. [3] dedication "To The Most Noble Augustus Frederick Fitzgerald, Duke of Leinster . . ." (verso blank); [5–6] "Second Series. Contents Of The Second Volume, Containing Sixty Engravings And One Vignette"; [7–122] description of the plates; *vol. 3*: pp. [1] title page; [2] McCreery's imprint; [3] dedication "To The Right Honourable John Scott, Earl of Eldon . . ." (verso blank); [5–6] "Second Series. Contents Of The Third Volume, Containing Sixty Engravings And One Vignette"; [7–128] description of the plates; *vol. 4*: pp. [1] title page; [2] printer's imprint "Gunnell and Shearman, Salisbury Square"; [3] dedication "To The Right Honourable John Singleton Copley, Lord Lyndhurst . . ." (verso blank); [5–6] "Second Series. Contents Of The Fourth Volume, Containing Sixty Engravings And One Vignette"; [7–126] description of the plates; *vol. 5*: pp. [1] title page; [2] Gunnell and Shearman's imprint; [3] dedication "To The Right Honourable George Byng, Viscount Torrington . . ." (verso blank); [5–6] "Second Series. Contents Of The Fifth Volume, Containing Sixty Engravings"; [7–126] description of the plates

Illustrations

Vol. 1: [60] etched plates including the illustrated title plate ("Vol. I. Second Series / Neale's Views Of Seats"). All are signed "Drawn by J. P. Neale," engraved by J. C. Allen, Thomas Barber (11), William Deeble (3), J. Henshall, Thomas Jeavons (12), T. Matthews (6), Robert Sands (2), W. R. Smith, William Tombleson (5), J. C. Varrall (8), and William Wallis (10). 4 wood-engraved headpieces in the text (of Madingley Hall, Lyme Hall, Knebworth House, and Fonthill Abbey)

Vol. 2: [60] etched plates, including the illustrated title plate. All are signed "Drawn by J. P. Neale," engraved by J. B. Allen, Thomas Barber (14), H. [i.e., H. W.] Bond (9), Robert Brandard, William Cooke, Jun. (2), William Deeble, J. Henshall (4), Thomas Higham, Thomas Jeavons (12), J. H. Kernot, T. Matthews, E. J. Roberts (2), William Tombleson, and J. C. Varrall (10). 1 wood-engraved headpiece in the text (of Leeds Castle)

Vol. 3: [60] etched plates including the illustrated title plate. All are signed "Drawn by J. P. Neale," engraved by Thomas Barber (14), H. [i.e., H. W.] Bond (11), Thomas Jeavons (6), W. A. Le Petit (6), E. J. Roberts, G. I. [i.e., E. J.?] Roberts, William Tombleson (3), J. C. Varrall (7), Henry Wallis, and William Wallis (10). 1 wood-engraved headpiece in the text (of Deepdene)

Vol. 4: [60] etched plates including the illustrated title plate. All are signed "Drawn by J. P. Neale," engraved by Thomas Barber (8), H. [i.e., H. W.] Bond (8), A. Cruse (8), Thomas Jeavons (4), W. A. Le Petit (2), Robert Sands (2), William Taylor (2), William Tombleson (12), J. C. Varrall (8), William Wallis (5), and J. Westley. 1 wood-engraved headpiece in the text (of Melbury)

Vol. 5: [60] etched plates including the illustrated title plate. All are signed "Drawn by J. P. Neale," engraved by Thomas Barber (5), H. [i.e., H. W.] Bond (10), W. [i.e., H. W.?] Bond (2), A. Cruse (10), H. Hobson, W. A. Le Petit (2), William Tombleson (7), J. C. Varrall (11), William Wallis (7), and J. Westley (5)

Binding Recent half morocco, marbled boards, numbered on spine "VII–XI" in continuation of Neale's first series

THE FIRST SERIES of Neale's *Views of the Seats of Noblemen and Gentlemen* was issued in monthly parts between March 1818 and February 1824, each part consisting of six engraved views and accompanying letterpress, printed in royal octavo, price four shillings. A few copies were printed in quarto, with proof plates printed on India paper, and sold for eight shillings. After 432 plates had appeared in six annual accumulations, Neale closed this first series but immediately started a second. He reduced the number of views per part to five, promised more vignettes and interior views, but otherwise retained the same formula. The second series was completed in September 1829, by which time a further five volumes and three hundred plates had been added.

Referring to the location of any one view is difficult. Some copies apply to each volume the letterpress directions to bind them alphabetically by county, with Scotland and Ireland at the end. Others apply this rule to each series, thus grouping all the views outside England and Wales in the last volume. It should also be noted that the text, usually found without pagination or foliation, was partially or wholly reprinted at least once. All eleven volumes are indexed by John Harris and Michael Holmes (Harris 1979; Holmes 1986). The whole comprises the single most important early-nineteenth-century source for country-house architecture, and Colvin's biographical dictionary regularly cites views of buildings associated with particular architects (Colvin 1995).

The progress of Neale's *Views*, and the reasons for its commercial success, have been summarized by Nicholas Savage (see RIBA, *Early Printed Books*, nos. 2245–2246). Almost every aspect of it was an improvement over predecessors such as William Watts' *Seats of the Nobility and Gentry* (1779–1786) and William Angus' continuation of the same name (1787–1815). For less money, subscribers were guaranteed more views covering a wider geographical area, each with a longer and more informative text. The whole was published as regularly as a periodical rather than sporadically according to the time and energy of the editor. Furthermore, Neale's name carried weight with reviewers and a public already familiar with his work for *The Beauties of England and Wales* (1801–1815) and, more especially, the first few parts of *The History and Antiquities of the Abbey Church of St. Peter, Westminster* (1816–1823). Sales of the *Views* were large: some copies include an impressive list of 685 subscribers, and many who did not care for the whole series must have purchased selections. Credit for this lies in part with Neale's partners Sherwood, Neely, and Jones, who took over from W. H. Reid during the course of volume one and offered the sort of sophisticated advertising and distribution network that was unavailable to an artist working independently.

The other proprietor named on the title pages, Thomas Moule, was responsible for the text. Neale never had to return to post office employment after becoming a full-time artist, but Moule found he needed the steady income it offered, and for most of his life he worked as the clerk responsible for deciphering illegible addresses. Like other post office workers, notably Anthony Trollope, Moule still found himself able to write vast quantities in his spare time, as demonstrated even by the partial list of his works given in DNB (13: 1096–1097). His main interests beside topography were heraldry and numismatics.

Neale and Moule traveled extensively to gather the material required for their project, but they were also helped by a large number of contributing architects, artists, and local historians who are usually acknowledged in the text, though not often associated now with the finished work. In particular, Neale's signature on virtually every plate in both series conceals the fact that his role was often no more than that of an intermediary, supplying the engraver with a finished drawing worked up from someone else's sketch. In the same way, Moule was more often editing material than composing it. Cumulatively, these contributions by other hands greatly enriched the scope and value of the work, even though they also introduced an unevenness in subject matter for which Neale felt compelled to apologize in his address to the reader (". . . in some instances, indeed, private friendship, and a grateful remembrance of past favours, may have induced me to insert the view of a residence possessing no remarkable features either of locality or architectural arrangement," 1st series, 6: 10). Much of Neale's genius, in fact, consisted in his machinelike transformation of all kinds of source material into a single steady stream of homogenous images. The following survey of the principal contributing artists is a first effort to recover the nature of this source material, and thereby explain some idiosyncracies Neale attempted to smooth over for the finished work.

The further a seat was from London, the more likely its description was sent in by a local artist. Twenty-one of the thirty-six Irish views in the two series are of seats built or altered to the designs of Richard Morrison or his son, William Vitruvius Morrison, namely, Castlegar, Mount Bellew, St. Clerons (Galway); Castle Howard, Kilruddery Hall, Shelton Abbey (Wicklow); Ballyheigh Castle, Crotto, Miltown House (Kerry); Bear Forest, Castle Freke, Foaty Island House (Cork); Carton House and Lyons (Kildare); Thomastown House (Tipperary); Castle Richard (Waterford); Castle Coole (Fermanagh); Ballyfinn (Queen's County); Borris (Carlow); Moidrum Castle (Westmeath); and Glenarm Castle (Antrim). Frequent acknowledgments in the text show that the Morrisons supplied drawings for most if not all of these, usually executed by the son, and together they add up to an important contemporary record of a very productive practice (see the 1989 monograph cited below).

Another three Irish views are attributed to Frederick Ponsonby, 3d earl of Bessborough (1758–1844), namely, Kilkenny Castle and his own seat in Leinster, and the duke of Devonshire's Lismore Castle in Waterford. Ponsonby's pleasantly picturesque watercolor views had earlier been used by Watts and Angus, where they are signed Lord Duncannon, the courtesy title he held until succeeding to the earldom. He did not contribute to the art exhibitions in London and has been virtually ignored by later biographical dictionaries. Edward Deane Freeman and John Preston, Lord Tara, also loaned sketches of their seats, Castle Cor in County Cork and Bellinter in County Meath, respectively. The other ten Irish seats go uncredited, but it seems unlikely Neale traveled to see them himself.

For Scotland, Neale again had a principal source for his views, supplemented with occasional offerings by other hands. In his "Address" of 12 January 1824, published with the last volume of the first series, Neale thanks "J. Steuart, Esq., of Dalguise House, Perthshire . . . for many beautiful Scotch views" ("Address," 6: 11). John Steuart is not credited elsewhere in the text, but his house is illustrated and he was evidently the son of Charles Steuart, for whom James Paterson had designed a residence at Dalguise in 1794 (Colvin 1995, 739). This, however, was never executed, and the plate shows a very ordinary three-story house, built 1714–1716, which even Moule has to describe as "perfectly plain." Several other houses owned by the Steuarts or their relations are also featured, the family connections sometimes minutely described by Moule. But if John Steuart was responsible for many of these, it is all the more surprising that his

John Preston Neale. *Views of the Seats.* [1st series]. Vol. 6, plate 49. "Bessborough House, Kilkenny, Ireland." NGA Lib. Rare Book: DA660N421818

own house is credited to John A. Stewart of nearby Grandtully (presumably related to Sir George Stewart, whose seat at Grandtully is also illustrated). Stewart drew two more seats, Ochtertyre and Castle Menzies, for the second series. Other Scottish views were contributed by W. Hay, of Banff (Castle Forbes, Duff House, Gordon Castle), and one J. Bouet, of Durham, who made a tour of Scottish castles and drew those at Lumley, Raby, Airthrey, Inverary, and Kincardine. The Scottish painter Alexander Nasmyth provided two pencil sketches of Culzean Castle. A drawing of Lindertis was loaned by its owner, J. L. Meason; and of Barjarg Tower by its owner's wife, Mrs. William F. Hunter. G. L. A. Douglas drew Arbuthnott House and the landscape painter Hugh Irvine is represented by Drum Castle, where other paintings by him are still on display.

Carstairs is the only Scottish view explicitly credited to an architect. It was a Tudor Gothic residence built 1822–1824 by William Burn for Henry Monteith, and the drawing was supplied by Burns' pupil William Lambie Moffatt. However, one of the architects thanked for his contributions in Neale's "Address" is William Wilkins, and it seems likely the latter provided the views of two of his Scottish Tudor Gothic houses, Dalmeny and Dunmore. He may have helped with the text as well. Dalmeny House is described as "displaying a most curious example of the taste of former times, and forming a fine contrast to the regularity of Italian architecture, which has prevailed for the last two centuries, but is now rapidly on the decline, being superseded by works produced from the researches in Greece, or among the antiquities of our own country." This is surely an allusion to Wilkins' preference for the Greek Revival—one of his alternative proposals to the owner, Lord Rosebery, was for a house modeled on the Theseum at Athens. Being obliged to work in the more fashionable style, he produced a highly influential building, completed in 1817. Wilkins exhibited views of both Dalmeny and Dunmore at the Royal Academy. Other buildings by him that are featured in Neale's *Views* are Grange Park, Hampshire; Kingweston House, Somerset; Stourhead, Wiltshire; and Tregothnan, Cornwall. The emphatically unpicturesque perspective and shading of the Grange Park view in particular indicates that Neale worked from a drawing provided by Wilkins.

Like Wilkins, Robert Smirke, Jr., is thanked in the

John Preston Neale. *Views of the Seats.* [1st series]. Vol. 6, plate 22. "Dalmeny Park, Linlithgowshire, Scotland." NGA Lib. Rare Book: DA660N421818

"Address" for "similar favours" to those provided by Morrison and Steuart. Of at least nine houses built or enlarged by him and featured in the *Views*, two are Scottish. He may, therefore, have provided the distant view of Kinmount (or Kenmount), a residence he enlarged for the marquess of Queensbury in 1812. But the two views in the second series of his more famous work for Lord Gray at Kinfauns Castle are explicitly credited to "Gibb," probably identifiable as the Dundee landscape painter Robert Gibb (1801–1837). A little more about Gibb, whose drawing of the exterior of Kinfauns derives from a painting by John (or James) Francis Williams, is given in D. Morison's *Catalogue of the Collection of Pictures, Ancient and Modern, in Kinfauns Castle* (Kinfauns, 1833):

> This young artist was bred to the profession of house painting, but his zeal to excel as an artist induced him to leave this occupation, and commence his career in Edinburgh, as a landscape painter, without money, patronage, or knowledge. In this situation he was recommended to Lord Gray, who got him admitted into the Academy of the Royal Institution. His Lordship has since employed him to paint several pictures, the best of which is an interior of the Gallery at Kinfauns Castle, which is executed with much delicacy and truth. It has been engraved for Neal's Views. Mr. Gibb is at present (1827) following his profession at Edinburgh, and promises to arrive at considerable eminence as a faithful representer of Nature (caption to "No. III. Water Mill").

It is possible Neale also had an arrangement with the Scottish architect James Gillespie Graham, who is frequently mentioned in connection with individual seats, though not as the artist who supplied the drawings. Only a sense of obligation, one imagines, could have persuaded the perceptive Moule, in his text for Lee Place, Lanarkshire, to overpraise him as "an architect who has the merit of introducing the Gothic style into this country, in a greater degree of purity and perfection than had previously been exhibited." There are examples of Gillespie Graham's work in both series, namely, Duns Castle, Ross Priory, Culdees Castle (1st series);

John Preston Neale. *Views of the Seats.* [2d series]. Vol. 4, plate 57. "Kinfauns Castle, Scotland." NGA Lib. Rare Book: DA660N421818

and Armadale Castle, Mount Melville, Blytheswood, Lee Place, and Wishaw House (2d series). Of these, the two views of Lord Macdonald's castle at Armadale on the Isle of Skye are taken from paintings by William Daniell that had been exhibited at the Royal Academy in 1817. Moule was evidently unaware that they depicted a more ambitious building program than the one executed.

Neale probably toured parts of Wales himself, since he only acknowledges five views as deriving from other sources. Henry William Bayly Paget, marquis of Anglesey, provided the view of his seat at Plas-Newydd; Dunraven Castle was supplied by the owner's wife, Mrs. William Wyndham Quin; and two engravings of Gyrn in Flintshire were "copied from two large pictures, delightfully finished by Mr. Welchmann," perhaps J. W. Welchman (see Graves 1905 4: 203). Trevalyn Hall was drawn by John Hughes of Uffington, who also supplied Hagley (Worcestershire) and Warleigh House (Somerset).

Neale was certainly responsible for a large proportion of the views of English seats, although along with Wilkins and Smirke, Humphry Repton's eldest son John Adey Repton is thanked in the above-mentioned "Address" and presumably supplied occasional drawings of his or his father's work. Three views are explicitly credited elsewhere on the plates themselves, an early editorial practice soon dropped: a pair of Northumbrian houses, Capheaton and old Belsay Castle, are signed by Edward and Miss E. Swinburne, respectively, both children of the owner of Capheaton, Sir John Edward Swinburne; and Dropmore House, the residence of Baron Grenville, is signed by the architect and antiquarian John Buckler. Buckler knew Grenville well, having prepared drawings to extra-illustrate the Buckinghamshire section of the baron's copy of Daniel Lysons' *Magna Britannia*, 1806–1822 (see Colvin 1995, 177). His drawings were also used in the second series for Hornby Castle in Yorkshire.

Two views of Wilton Castle were copied from paintings by the royal academician George Arnald, but the list of other credited artists contains nobody notable. Bouet of Durham supplemented his Scottish views with Brancepath Castle, Oswald House, and Wilton Castle in his home county. The only other artist repeatedly acknowledged is Captain Edward Jones, who toured several counties to supply views of Beckford Hall, Slindon House, Wollashull Hall, Burton Park, and Standish Hall. The heraldry specialist Thomas Willement is thanked for Caerhays and Clumber; the topographer F. W. L. Stockdale for Ford House and Luscombe; G. Shepherd for Sheffield Place and Stanmer Park; "Mr. Hastings" for Alnwick Castle and Carham Hall; and James Everard Arundell, Lord Arundell, for Poxcote Hall and his own residence, Wardour Castle. Owners or their relations who may or may not have drawn the sketch they supplied include Cornelius Heathcote Rodes (Barlborough Hall, Derbyshire), James Pickering Ord (Langton Hall, Leicestershire), Mrs. Charles Calmady (Langdale Hall, Devon), "Miss Strickland" (Cokethorpe Park, Oxfordshire), W. G. M. Arundel, Viscount Galway (Serlby Hall, Nottinghamshire), Charles Bowyer Adderley (Hams Hall, Warwickshire), and Robert Berkeley (Spetchley, Worcestershire). Credits for a single view are also given to J. B. Watson (Collipriest House, Devon), "Lady Gordon" (North Court, Isle of Wight), the late Thomas Hearne (Cole Orton Hall, Leicestershire), "Mr. Burges" (Aynho, Northants.), Charles Tucker (Swinton Park, Yorkshire), J. Newton Lane (Blithfield, Staffordshire), and "Dr. Greville, of Edinburgh" (Eshton Hall, Yorkshire). Lastly, Moule provided his partner with a serviceable drawing of Ham House in Surrey.

The early demise of Neale's second series of *Views*, just one volume short of the six with which Neale triumphantly closed the first, has been accounted for by the widespread commercial exploitation of steel engraving (see RIBA, *Early Printed Books*, no. 2246). Neale's continued use of the traditional but more expensive copper for his engravings would have severely limited his competitiveness. Not only did his subscription price suddenly seem relatively high, but rival publishers were likely to be able to pay more than Neale for the loyalty of the large pool of engravers on whom the regular appearance of his work depended. As if to confirm the supremacy of the new process, the whole series was immediately transferred from copper to steel plates by the publishers Jones and Co. after they acquired the copyright from Neale around 1829. It was then reprinted as *Jones's Views of the Seats, Mansions, Castles, &c. of Noblemen and Gentlemen in England, Wales, Scotland and Ireland* [1829–1831].

There is no reason to doubt that the *Views* steadily lost its economic justification as the market adapted to this and other changes. However, a leaf bound in to the Canadian Centre for Architecture's copy shows that Neale preferred to offer another reason to his subscribers with the final number of volume five, in an announcement "To Subscribers" that is half-valedictory, half-promissory, and worth quoting in full:

> A very severe and protracted illness during the whole of the present summer has prevented me from fulfilling my engagements with many of my friends, having thereby been rendered incapable of visiting the mansions of which I intend to give views in my next and FINAL VOLUME. I regret this misfortune so much the more, as it compels me to suspend the publication of my work at the time when it was drawing towards its completion. I am besides more than usually anxious that the subjects introduced should exhibit all the talent in my power to bestow upon them, which gratitude towards those who have so long patronized my efforts, demands. It is now more than eleven years since I first undertook this publication—a length of time which would alone suggest the propriety of terminating my labours; for the extent to which they have reached, has rendered it the most voluminous work of the kind that has yet appeared. Of its merits in other respects it

would ill become me to speak; yet I may be allowed to say that, independently of the views themselves, the mass of topographical and historical information contained in the letter-press, gives this work a permanent interest; nor can I express myself sufficiently grateful to the respective proprietors for the kindness with which they have furnished communications, that must render my volumes not only amusing to the general reader, but also valuable to the topographer. In order therefore to render the LAST VOLUME superior to any of the preceding ones, I must inevitably postpone the publication of the next number till the FIRST OF JUNE, 1830, when the work will be regularly continued to the end.

J. P. NEALE

Bennet Street, Blackfriars Road,
August 29th, 1829.

P.S. Subscribers are respectfully requested not to have the second series of this work bound up, till the next volume is complete, as there will be a general index to the work, and a list of additional subscribers published in the last number.

Perhaps, therefore, the abrupt termination of the series can be explained simply by Neale's illness in the summer of 1829, resulting in a hiatus that would have lost him many of his subscribers and made any resumption of his greatest work a merely sentimental venture. G. B.

John Preston Neale. *Views of the Seats.* [2d series]. Vol. 1, plate 9. "Tessington Hall, Derbyshire." NGA Lib. Rare Book: DA660N421818

Bibliography

The Architecture of Richard Morrison (1767–1849) and William Vitruvius Morrison (1794–1838). Dublin, 1989

British Architectural Library, Royal Institute of British Architects. *Early Printed Books 1478–1840: Catalogue of the British Architectural Library Early Imprints Collection.* Vols. 1–2. London, 1994–1995

Colvin, H. *A Biographical Dictionary of British Architects 1600–1840.* 3d ed. New Haven and London, 1995

Graves, A. *The Royal Academy of Arts: A Complete Dictionary.* London, 1905. Reprint, 1970

Harris, J. *A Country House Index.* 2d ed. London, 1979

Holmes, M. *The Country House Described: An Index to the Country Houses of Great Britain and Ireland.* Winchester, 1986

46

John Nichols (1745–1826) and George Steevens (1736–1800)

The Genuine Works Of William Hogarth; Illustrated With Biographical Anecdotes, A Chronological Catalogue, And Commentary; By John Nichols . . . And The Late George Steevens . . . In Two Volumes. Volume 1. (11.)

London: printed for Longman, Hurst, Rees, and Orme, 1808–1810

Supplementary Volume To The Works Of William Hogarth; With Biographical Anecdotes, By John Nichols . . . And The Late George Steevens . . . Containing Clavis Hogarthiana, And Other Illustrative Essays: With Fifty Additional Plates

London: printed by and for Nichols, Son, and Bentley. Sold also by Longman, Hurst, Rees, Orme, and Brown, [1817]

NGA Lib. Rare Book: N44H715N48

Quarto: 262 × 210 (10$^{3}/_{8}$ × 8$^{1}/_{4}$)

Pagination Vol. 1: vii, [1], 524 pp., engraved frontispiece, [62] etched and engraved plates

Vol. 2: viii, 288, *287–*288, 289–444, [30] pp., [96] etched and engraved plates (1 folding)

Supplement: xxxii, 56, *57–*62, [57]–174, 171*–*176, 177–358 pp., [50] etched and engraved plates (13 folding)

Edition First edition

Text vol. 1: pp. [i] title page; [ii] imprint "Nichols and Son, Printers . . ."; [iii]–vii preface; [viii] blank; [1]–456 biographical anecdotes; 457–524 appendix; *vol. 2*: pp. [i] title page; [ii] printer's imprint; iii–iv advertisement; v–viii list of Hogarth's plates; [1]–18 biographical anecdotes; [19]–318 catalogue; 319–332 appendix to vol. 2; [333]–444 "The Analysis of Beauty . . . By William Hogarth"; [445–474] index, with corrigenda at end;

John Nichols and George Steevens. *The Genuine Works of William Hogarth.* "View at Chiswick." NGA Lib. Rare Book: N44H715N48

Supplement: pp. [i] title page, "Supplementary Volume To The Works Of William Hogarth . . ." (verso blank); iii–iv advertisement, dated 15 July 1817; v contents (verso blank); vii–viii "Plates In The Third Volume"; ix–xxxii "Memoir Of William Hogarth. By Thomas Phillips, Esq. R. A. Reprinted, by permission, from Dr. Rees's 'New Cyclopaedia'"; [1]–56, *57–*62 "Illustrations Of Hogarth, i.e., Hogarth Illustrated From Passages In Authors He Never Read, And Could Not Understand"; [57]–86 "Essay On The Genius And Character Of Hogarth . . . ," by Charles Lamb; 87–88 ". . . Critique on 1 of the plates in Marriage Alamode . . . ," by Thomas Street; 89–164 "Plates In The Third Volume"; 165–174 "Original Paintings And Sketches By Hogarth Exhibited In The British Gallery, 1814"; 171*–*176 same for 1817; 177–184 "Paintings By Hogarth Not Engraved"; 185–192 "Other Paintings Attributed To Hogarth"; 193–208 extracts from sales catalogues; 209–272 "Account Of The Variations In Hogarth's Plates"; 273–288 "Catalogue of Prints . . . In Addition To Those Described In Vol. II"; 289–350 additions and corrections; [351]–358 index, colophon "Printed by Nichols, Son, and Bentley . . ."

Illustrations *Vol. 1*: 63 etched and engraved plates including a frontispiece portrait of Hogarth, as numbered and described in the "List Of Hogarth's Plates" in vol. 2. All are signed "Hogarth pinx[t]. T. Cook sculp[t]." and variants. *Vol. 2*: 96 etched and engraved plates as numbered and described in the list. Most are again signed by Thomas Cook after paintings by Hogarth. An etched illustration appears on p. 272. *Supplement*: 51 etched or engraved on 50 leaves (pls. 38–39 on 1 leaf), as listed in the letterpress. The last plate, illustrating "Boors Drinking," is not numbered in the list because it is described as "probably not Hogarth's" (p. 285), although credited to him on the plate itself. Plate 1 is signed by T. Priscott after Thomas Worlidge; plates 2–4 by Thomas Cook after Hogarth; plates 16, 18–19, 21, 23–25, 32–34, 40–43, 49, and [51] by Richard Livesay after Hogarth; plates 17, 20, and 22 by Livesay after Scott (pl. 20 "the figures by Hogarth"); plate 30 etched by D. Smith after Hogarth; plate 35 "[Barak] Longmate sc."; plates 36–37 by Joseph Haynes after Hogarth; plate 38–39 by Francesco Bartolozzi after Hogarth; plates 44–45, 47 by [Barak] Longmate after Hogarth; and plate 48 "Copied from Hogarth's original Sketches, by I. [i.e., John] Mills." The text frequently adds useful glosses to these credit lines. Many of Livesay's etchings have aquatint shading and are printed in sepia

Binding Mixed set. *Vols. 1–2*: early nineteenth-century diced calf, blind- and gilt-tooled, rebacked. *Supplement*: early nineteenth-century straight-grained red morocco, blind- and gilt-tooled, false bands, all edges gilt, binder's ticket of J. Rowbotham

Provenance *Vols. 1–2*: engraved armorial bookplates of John Stephens

47

Thomas Collins Overton (b. 1734)

The Temple Builder's Most Useful Companion, Being Fifty Entire New Original Designs For Pleasure and Recreation; Consisting Of Plans, Elevations, and Sections, In The Greek, Roman, and Gothic Taste . . . By Thomas Collins Overton

FRONTISPIECE.
Palladio
Inigo Jones
Wale inv.t & delin.t
R. Pranker sculp.t
Jones and Palladio to themselves restore,
And be whate'er Vitruvius was before:
Pope.

London: printed for Henry Webley, 1766

1985.61.2599

Octavo: 232 × 144 ($9\frac{1}{8}$ × $5\frac{1}{8}$)

Pagination [3], 8–19, [1] pp., engraved frontispiece, 50 engraved plates (1 double-page)

Edition Second edition

Text pp. [1] title page; [2] advertisement (printed title page to a "companion volume," i.e., William Wrighte's *Grotesque Architecture*); [7]–19 explanation of the plates; [20] blank

Illustrations Frontispiece engraved by R. Pranker after a design and drawing by Samuel Wale, showing 2 gentlemen contemplating statues of Palladio and Inigo Jones in a landscape with classical temples and obelisk, Pope's verse inscribed below. 50 engraved plates (1 double-page) engraved by Pranker after Overton

Binding Contemporary sprinkled calf

References Berlin Cat. 2292 (3d ed.); Berlin (1977) os 2287[n] (3d ed.); ESTC t90195; Harris and Savage 610

Howard Colvin has suggested that Thomas Collins Overton was a member of a family of land surveyors practicing in Devizes, in the west country, during the eighteenth century. The parish records for St. John's at Devizes, as Hugh Pagan has found, confirm that a Thomas Overton was married there on 15 February 1729 and that the birth of his son, Thomas Collings, was recorded on 31 August 1734. Three of the plates in *The Temple Builders Most Useful Companion* illustrate buildings in that area: plate 30, a Gothic temple "built for Mr. Richards at Spittle Croft near Devizes"; plate 34, a rustic cottage "designed for Edward Goddard to be built near Cliffhill Copse, Wiltshire"; and plate 41, a triangular villa "built for Mr. Maynard near Devizes." None of these has survived, nor have any other buildings been identified as the work of Overton.

His only claim to recognition is *The Temple Builders Most Useful Companion*, a book of fifty plates, all engraved by R. Pranker, illustrating a range of designs for small houses, cottages, pavilions, and other garden structures in a Palladian mode, but including battlemented and "gothick" forms (some adapted from Batty Langley's *Ancient Architecture, Restored* . . . , issued first in 1742), printed first in 1766, for the author, under the title *Original Designs of Temples*. This was sold by Henry Webley, of Holborn, at twelve and fifteen shillings, depending on the paper size. This was retitled and republished in the same year by Webley, marginally reduced in size, greatly reduced in price, to seven shillings. Later, in 1774, the book was reissued, without the list of

Thomas Collins Overton. *The Temple Builder's Most Useful Companion.* Frontispiece. 1985.61.2599

5
10
15
20
25
30

subscribers, by I. Taylor, Webley's successor.

The book is without text, other than brief explanations to the plates. The frontispiece, designed by Samuel Wale, sets the tone for the undertaking. This has an arcadian landscape in the background, scattered with a temple and obelisk; in the foreground is a circular temple, Ionic, in front of which two figures gesture to statues of Palladio and Inigo Jones on pedestals. Underneath is a couplet from Alexander Pope:

"Jones and Palladio to themselves restore,
And be whate'er Vitruvius was before." R. M.

Bibliography

Colvin, H. *Biographical Dictionary of British Architects. 1660–1840*. London, 1978

Harris, E., and N. Savage. *British Architectural Books and Writers 1556–1785*. Cambridge, 1990

Thomas Collins Overton. *The Temple Builder's Most Useful Companion*. Plate 36. 1985.61.2599 (here enlarged)

48

William Pain (c. 1730–1794?)

The Builder's Companion, And Workman's General Assistant; Demonstrating, After the most easy and practical Method, All The Principal Rules of Architecture, From The Plan to the Ornamental Finish; Illustrated with a greater Number of useful and familiar Examples than any Work of that Kind hitherto published . . . The Whole correctly engraved on 92 Folio Copper-Plates . . . The Third Edition, With many Improvements and Additions by the Author

London: printed for Robert Sayer, 1769

1983.49.39

Folio: 385 × 240 ($15\frac{1}{8} \times 9\frac{1}{2}$)

Pagination [iv], 4, *1–*10 pp., [88] engraved plates (4 folding)

Edition "Third" (i.e., 4th ed.; earlier editions dated 1758, 1762, 1765)

Text pp. [i] title page (verso blank); [iii] table of contents; [iv] advertisement "Books of Architecture Printed for Robert Sayer . . ."; [1]–4 text "Concerning Foundations"; *1–*10 text (manual of labor prices for various workmen in the building trades)

Illustrations 88 unsigned engraved plates numbered to continue the pagination from "page 5" to "page 92" (4 folding)

Binding Contemporary calf, gilt borders, rebacked

Provenance Bookplate of John Henry Ware

References Berlin Cat. 2287 (1762 ed.); Berlin (1977) os 2285[n]; ESTC t132462; Harris and Savage 615

William Pain was one of the more successful authors of pattern books and manuals for builders and craftsmen in the second half of the eighteenth century. He published ten books, most of which went into several editions; four of his works were even reprinted in Philadelphia and Boston, one of them, *The Practical House Carpenter*, running to three editions. But nothing else is known of Pain's life and activities, other than that he was still alive in 1794, though three of his grandsons, James, George Richard, and Henry, became pupils of John Nash, the first two establishing practices in Ireland, the last in London.

The Builder's Companion, and Workman's General Assistant, the first of Pain's books, was published in 1758

William Pain. *The Builder's Companion, and Workman's General Assistant.* Page 22. "Trus roofs for churches temples pavilions or private buildings &c." 1983.49.39

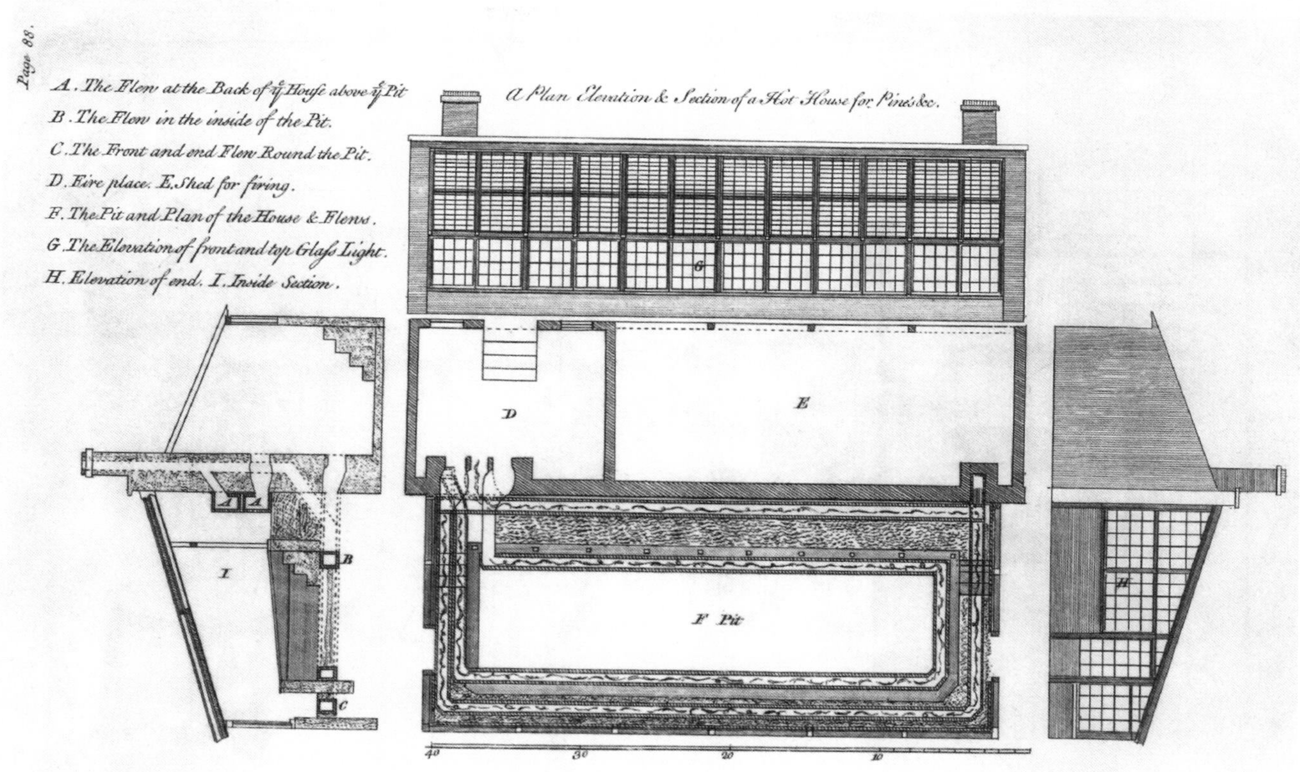

William Pain. *The Builder's Companion, and Workman's General Assistant.* Page 88. "A Plan & Section of a Hot House for Pine's &c." 1983.49.39

by Robert Sayer of Fleet Street. This included a single-page preface, a contents page, four pages of text—devoted for the most part to the building of foundations and chimneys—and seventy-seven plates, numbered as pages from 5 to 81. The book was designed as a ready reference for builders and craftsmen of all sorts (though it is evident from Pain's later publications that he was a carpenter or joiner). The plates, some with lengthy engraved texts, describe the range of operations from drawing and setting up, to the construction of all parts of buildings from foundations to ornamental details. Palladio is the preferred model for the orders. The second edition of 1762, likewise issued by Sayer, had twenty-five additional plates, interleaved. The editions of 1765 and 1769, still sold by Sayer, labeled second and third editions, have ten additional pages of text on rates and prices, and eighty-eight plates, labeled 5 to 92.

Though Pain was determinedly practical and conventional in his tastes—"in all things Order is to be observed"—he tempered the late Palladian mode that he offered with several plates of ornamental buildings and details in a Gothic style, culled, surprisingly, from Batty Langley. The last two editions also include a plate, no. 86, for two "Gentlemens houses." R. M.

Bibliography

Colvin, H. *Biographical Dictionary of British Architects, 1660–1840.* London, 1978

Harris, E., and N. Savage. *British Architectural Books and Writers 1556–1785.* Cambridge, 1990

Rowan, A. "Batty Langley's Gothic." In *Studies in Memory of David Talbot Rice.* Ed. G. Robertson and G. Henderson. Edinburgh, 1975: 197–21

49

William Pain (c. 1730–1794?) and James Pain

Pain's British Palladio: Or, The Builder's General Assistant. Demonstrating, In The Most Easy And Practical Method, All The Principal Rules Of Architecture, From The Ground Plan To The Ornamental Finish. Illustrated With Several New and Useful Designs of Houses, with their Plans, Elevations, and Sections. Also, Clear and Ample Instructions, annexed to each Subject, in Letter-Press; with a List of Prices for Materials and Labour, and Labour only. . . . The Whole correctly Engraved on Forty-two Folio Copper-Plates, from the Original Designs of William and James Pain

London: printed by H. D. Steel, for the authors, 1786

1983.49.38

Folio: 429 × 273 (16 7/8 × 10 3/4)

Pagination [ii], 14 pp., 42 engraved plates (1 double-page)

Edition First edition

Text pp. [i] title page; [ii] table of contents; 1–7 explanations of the plates; 8–14 "Estimate of Prices, for Materials and Labour, and Labour only . . ."

Illustrations 42 engraved plates (1 double-page) numbered I–XXXVI, 37–42, most signed "W. & J. Pain del." and "Woodman & Mutlow sc."

Binding Contemporary reversed calf, repaired, rebacked

Provenance Ownership stamp "C. L. Law, Architect, Northampton" inside front cover

References Berlin (1977) OS 2285[k]; ESTC t96023; Harris and Savage 634

British Palladio was one of William Pain's late books, done with the assistance of his son James. Though it was, like his earlier works, designed as a compendium of knowledge for builders and craftsmen, and was intended as a sternly practical guide, it was somewhat pretentious. The format was folio, and twenty-seven of the forty-two plates are devoted to the plans, sections, and elevations of five country houses, all conventionally Palladian throughout, all large in scale and extent. The remaining plates illustrate their structural and ornamental details, with particular emphasis on the staircases, and the layout of joists and trusses. Prices and estimates are dealt with in the preliminary pages.

The first edition was printed for the authors by H. D. Steel, of Lothbury, the plates being engraved by Woodman and Mutlow of Russel Court, and was sold at sixteen shillings in sheets. But the work was taken over by I. and J. Taylor, for their Architectural Library, and issued again, unchanged, pagination and minor corrections apart, in 1788, 1790, 1793, 1797, and 1804. The price remained at sixteen shillings though bound. R. M.

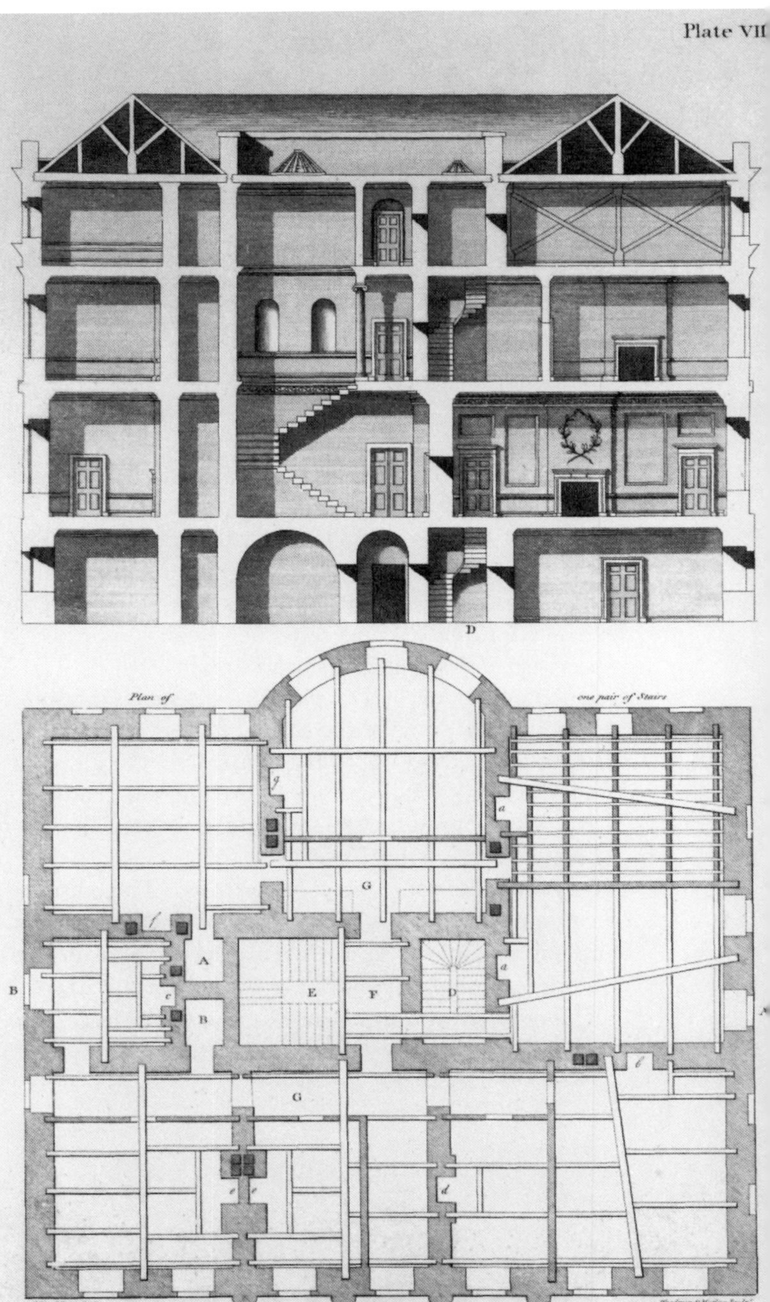

William and James Pain. *Pain's British Palladio: or, The Builder's General Assistant.* Plate VII. "The one-pair of stairs divided into nine bed-rooms." 1983.49.38

Bibliography

Colvin, H. *Biographical Dictionary of British Architects 1600–1840*. London, 1978

Harris, E., and N. Savage. *British Architectural Books and Writers 1556–1785*. Cambridge, 1990

William and James Pain. *Pain's British Palladio: or, The Builder's General Assistant.* Plate 41. Plans and elevations of stairs. 1983.49.38

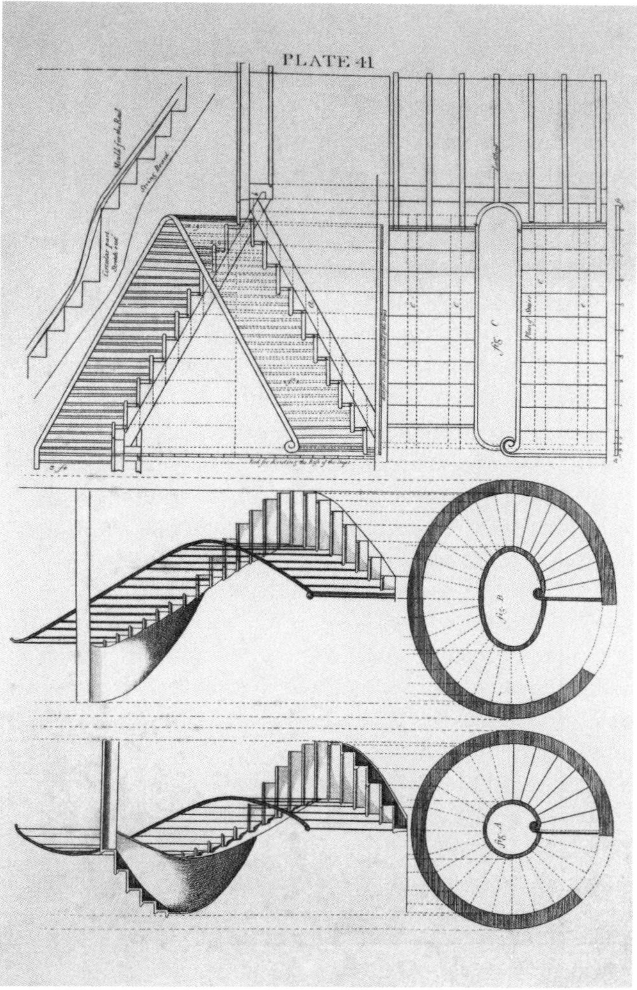

50

James Paine (1717–1789)

Plans, Elevations and Sections, Of Noblemen and Gentlemen's Houses, And Also Of Stabling, Bridges, Public and Private, Temples, and other Garden Buildings; Executed In The Counties Of Derby, Durham, Middlesex, Northumberland, Nottingham, and York. By James Paine, Architect . . . Part The First . . .

London: printed for the author, and sold by Mr. Davies; Mr. Dodsley; Mr. Brotherton; Mr. Webley; and at the author's house, 1767

Plans, Elevations, and Sections, Of Noblemen and Gentlemen's Houses, And Also Of Bridges, Public and Private, Temples, and other Garden Buildings; Executed In The Counties Of Nottingham, Essex, Wilts, Derby, Hertford, Suffolk, Salop, Middlesex, and Surrey. By James Paine, Architect. Part The Second . . .

London: printed for the author; and sold by Mess. Sayer and Bennett; Mr. Beckett; Mr. Robson, at Mr. Boydell's; and at the author's house, 1783

1983.49.40–41

Folio: 510 × 355 (20 × 14)

Pagination Vol. 1: [8], iv, [2], 16 [i.e., 17], [5] pp., 74 [i.e., 55] engraved plates (15 double-page, 4 folding)

(*Note*: Pagination irregular, omitting verso of p. 11)

Vol. 2: vi, 32 pp., 101 [i.e., 68] engraved plates (20 double-page, 14 folding)

Edition First edition

Text vol. 1: pp. [1] title page (verso blank); [3] dedication to the duke of Devonshire (verso blank); [5–6] list of subscribers; [7] list of plates (verso blank); [i]–iv preface; [v] history of Chatsworth (verso blank); [1–21] descriptions of the plates; [22] blank; *vol. 2*: pp. [i] title page (verso blank); [iii]–iv address to the king; v–vi list of plates; [1]–32 descriptions of the plates

Illustrations Vol. 1: 55 engraved plates numbered I–LXXIV, of which 19 are double-page or folding and therefore given 2 numbers each. The plates are signed as engraved after Paine by H. Mackworth (12), T. [or J.?] Miller (11), T. Morris (6), Francis Patton (6), T. White (5), John June (2), and Peter Mazell (2). *Vol. 2*: 68 engraved plates numbered I–CI (pls. XV–XVI misnumbered XIII–XIV), of which 33 double-page or folding plates are given 2 numbers each. The last plate, also double-page, has only 1 number. All are signed by Paine as architect, but only the last as "Executed by William Collins, and Engraved by Charles Grignion"

Binding Mixed set. Contemporary marbled boards (vol. 1) and contemporary reversed calf (vol. 2). Both volumes rebacked with matching reversed calf spines, red leather labels

Provenance Ownership inscription in eighteenth-century (?) hand on title page of vol. 1 "Wm Pears. Fenham Hall." Signature of Charles Brandling on plate XXXII and verso of plate LXIX

References Berlin Cat. 2339; Berlin (1977) OS 2339; ESTC t135969 and n23469; Fowler 207; Harris and Savage 664

Thomas Harwicke made a famous summary comment in 1825—"Sir Robert Taylor and Mr. James Paine nearly divided the practice of the profession between them, for they had few competitors till Mr. Robert Adam entered the lists. . . ." Paine's reputation as a solid, active mid-eighteenth-century practitioner has thus been epitomized. And it is amply confirmed by the first volume of the *Plans, Elevations and Sections, of Noblemen and Gentlemen's Houses*, published in 1767, the year of his fiftieth birthday. His view, he wrote in the preface, "is that of producing a collection of designs which have actually been put in execution; for of such as are merely ideal, he had no great opinion; he presumes, therefore, and hopes, that as he offers to the public, only such designs as have been approved by, and rendered useful to individuals of the greatest rank and taste, he may, in some degree, become serviceable to his country in general."

On fifty-five plates (the double ones numbered as two) he illustrated seventeen of his most important completed projects, including the magnificent stables of Chatsworth that he had built for the fourth duke of Devonshire, who died in 1764, and whose successor appointed Paine "Surveyor," and to whom he dedicated his book. All the projects, with the exception of Sir Matthew Featherstonhaugh's house in Whitehall, in London, were set in the north and north Midlands, where Paine had first established a practice. These included such striking works of his early maturity as Stockeld Park, Yorkshire; Bywell Hall, Northumberland; and Axwell Park, County Durham.

Paine had cause to be proud of his achievement. He had been born on 9 October 1717 in Andover, in Hampshire, the son of a carpenter, who died ten years later. He was introduced to the study of architecture, Paine claimed in his preface, by Thomas Jersey, an obscure figure who was later to become James Gibbs' clerk of works at the Radcliffe Camera. Paine seems to have learned drawing and something of architecture at the St. Martin's Lane Academy, where Isaac Ware was teaching in the late 1730s and early 1740s. Through Ware Paine might have made a connection with Lord Burlington and his circle, for his first significant employment was the supervision of the construction of

Nostell Priory in Yorkshire, from 1737 to 1747, to the design of Colonel James Moyser, a close friend of Burlington, another amateur architect. Paine seems to have contributed something to the interiors. By 1745 Paine had been appointed to the Office of Works. But his first important work was the Mansion House of Doncaster, Yorkshire, of 1745 to 1749, which he commemorated in 1751 with the publication of *Plans, Elevations, Sections and Other Ornaments of the Mansion House, belonging to the Corporation of Doncaster*. By then his career was established. Between 1745 and 1779 he designed or redesigned almost thirty country houses in south Yorkshire and the northeast. Surprisingly, in view of his late judgments, he broke off, between August 1755 and September 1756, to visit Italy. Little is known of his itinerary, but he seems to have visited the Villa Maser, for Palladio's chapel served as the basis for the one Paine built at Gibside between 1760 and 1769. In the preface to his *Plans, Elevations and Sections, of Noblemen and Gentlemen's Houses*, he wrote:

> It has been asserted, by a late author, that to have travelled, is to an architect the most essential of all qualifications: this may possibly be true in respect to the education of a fine gentleman, but with respect to an architect, it is a mistake. An artist who travels, and makes proper observations, undoubtedly may be the better for it; but if by travelling, he imbibes wrong principles in his art, and a blind veneration for inconsistent antiquated modes, and in the pursuit of such studies abroad, consequently neglects to make himself acquainted with the various necessary conveniences requisite for the country in which he is to exert his talents; such an artist may be said to be a man of taste, but he will hardly be considered as a man of judgement.

Paine's bugbear was the new fashion for archaeological exploration. Robert Wood's *Palmyra* had been published in 1753, his *Balbec*, in 1757; J.-D. Leroy's *Ruins of Athens* had appeared in English in 1759, James Stuart and Nicholas Revett's first volume of the *Antiquities of Athens* had followed in 1762, with Adam's *Ruins of the Palace of the Emperor Diocletian at Spalatro* in 1764.

Paine wrote:

> . . . in our time when all the finest examples of ancient architecture are faithfully given by numbers of ingenious persons, what more can be learned by going abroad, than that those very ruins are in a less perfect state now, than when they were drawn and measured a century or two ago. Desgodetz measured every thing *truly valuable* in the Roman state with the greatest accuracy. . . . If in consequence of the acquirement of modern travelling knowledge, convenience and propriety are to be sacrificed to the modes of the most despicable ruins of ancient Greece, it is greatly to be lamented. . . .

He thus dismissed Greek architecture at a stroke, setting himself alongside William Chambers. Palmyra and Baalbek, he conceded, might be curious, but they were valuable only for the ornaments. "It is beyond doubt," he wrote, "that the Romans carried this art to a greater height than any other people," but even they could not be taken as a model. Nor indeed could Palladio ". . . for although . . . we have received some real advantages from Palladio, and other Venetian masters, whose works were studied with great application by our countryman Inigo Jones; yet experience daily convinces us, that the houses built by that great master, are very ill adapted to our climate, still worse to our present mode of living, and consequently are not proper models for our imitation."

Paine was even less polite on the subject of his contemporaries; he did not mention Adam or Capability

James Paine. *Plans, Elevations and Sections*. Vol. 1, plate XL/XLI. "Section from South to North through the Centre of Wardour House, Wilts." 1983.49.41

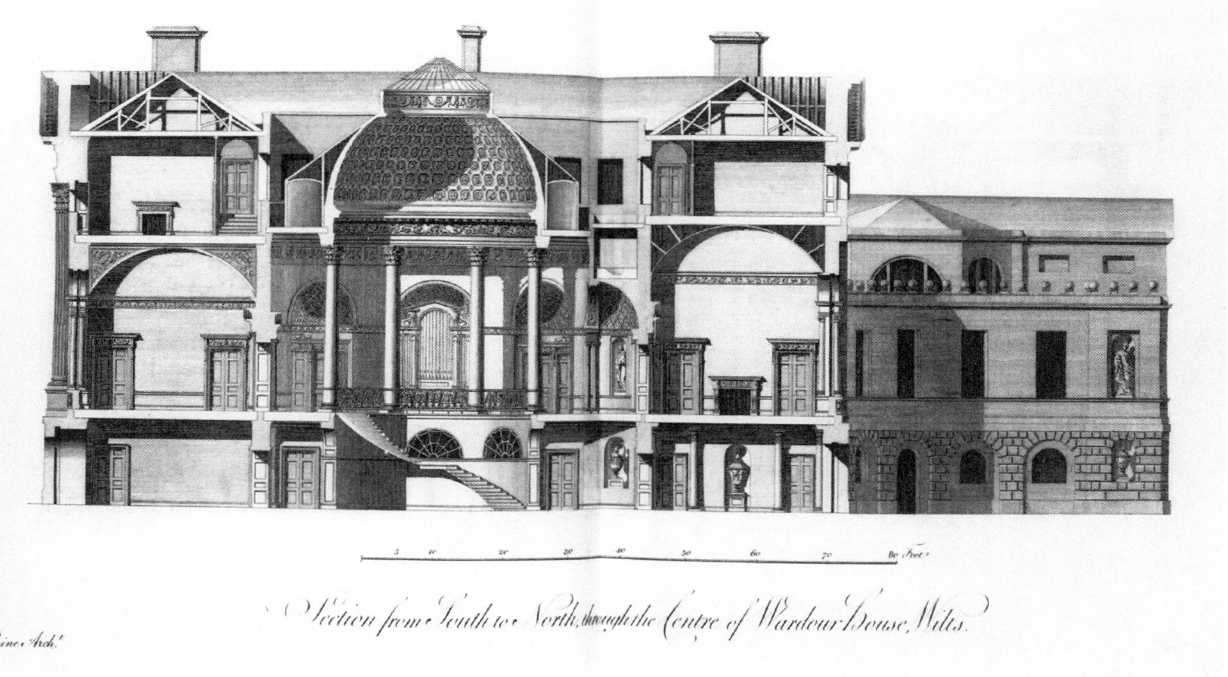

Brown by name, but he was clearly alluding to them when he poured scorn on architects who gave triumphal arch forms to dwelling houses (Paine had been replaced by Adam at Kedleston Hall), and those who emerged from "the serpentine walks of horticulture," to become the "*compleat architect*, and produce such things, as none but those who were *born* with such amazing *capability*, could possibly have done. . . ."

Eileen Harris has argued that Paine's decision to publish the *Plans, Elevations and Sections of Noblemen and Gentlemen's Houses*, somewhat precipitously, in 1767, must be seen as an aspect of the promotion of English causes fostered both by the St. Martin's Lane Academy and the Society of Artists of Great Britain, in which Paine played a very active role after its formation in 1760. Certainly, the date of publication is surprising. Paine was then engaged on such major works as Worksop Manor in Nottinghamshire for the duke of Norfolk and Thorndon Hall in Essex for Lord Petre, which could not be included if, as he sententiously announced, only executed works were to be published. The book was, moreover, produced with speed. Subscriptions, at two and a half guineas, were first invited in the *Public Advertiser* on 20 January 1767; more than two hundred subscriptions were collected, some from abroad; an array of eight engravers were commissioned, headed by H. Mackworth and T. Miller; by 13 January 1768 the book had appeared, according, once again, to the *Public Advertiser*. Paine's parochial sentiments set the tone for the whole publication, and are repeated more than once: "The rapid progress of architecture in Great Britain, within these last thirty years, is perhaps without example, in any age or country since the Romans. . . ."

Paine's subscription list was headed by the king and queen; the royal dukes of York, Gloucester, and Cumberland; followed by 212 names (there are variations in the lists published, some have only two royalty and 203 names, others 5 royalty and 215 names—the Millard copy has the king and queen and 203 names). The architects listed included Chambers, John Carr, James Essex, Henry Holland, Henry Keene, and Thomas Sandby. From abroad were the French sculptor Guillaume Coustou, and none other than Piranesi from Rome, who, Paine noted in a footnote, was an "excellent Artist."

The second volume of the *Plans, Elevations and Sections of Noblemen and Gentlemen's Houses* was published only after a break of sixteen years, in 1783, "for the author." This was larger than the first, with sixty-eight plates (thirty-three of them double, and numbered as two). Whereas the initial volume had illustrated fifteen different projects, the second surveyed only eleven, dominated by the major commissions for Roman Catholic patrons that occupied Paine in his later years—the palace, rather than house, of Worksop Manor in Nottinghamshire, for the duke of Norfolk; Wardour Castle in Wiltshire for Lord Arundell; Thordon Hall, Essex; and a residence in Park Lane, London for Lord Petre. It is notable that projects were now included that Paine could not have hoped to see fulfilled, including his remarkable design for Kedleston Hall, with a projecting, colonnaded circular feature on the garden front that was unprecedented in England. The strident tone of the first volume was entirely absent, the text is reduced to a minimum—Paine had withdrawn from the Society of Artists of Great Britain in 1773. The new volume was dedicated to the king, George III. The plates were mostly unsigned, other than "J. Paine, Architect," though plate 101 is signed C. Grignion. There was no subscription list to the second volume.

With the publication of the second volume, a second edition of the first was issued, with an additional plate, no. 75, illustrating the original design for the south front of Axwell Park, and without Paine's bitter diatribe against the owner, Sir Thomas Clavering, who had repeatedly altered the work during the course of construction. Even Adam and Brown were referred to now without complaint. Success had brought Paine ease and confidence. He was by then sixty-six. He died in 1789.
R. M.

Bibliography

Harris, E., and N. Savage. *British Architectural Books and Writers 1556–1785*. Cambridge, 1990

Leach, P. *James Paine*. London, 1988

James Paine. *Plans, Elevations and Sections*. Vol. 2, plate 50/51. "South front of Kedleston Derbyshire." 1983.49.41

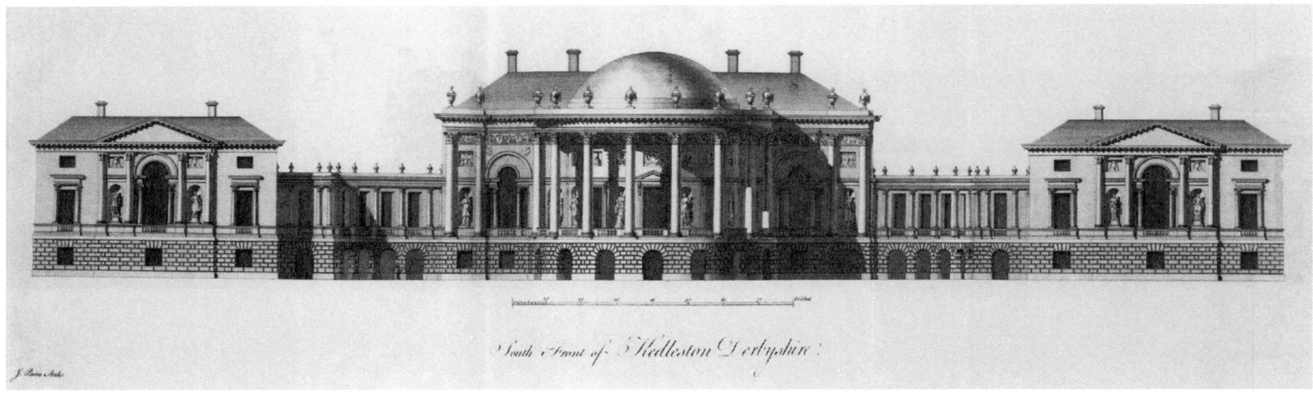

51

Andrea Palladio (1508–1580)

Andrea Palladio's Architecture, in Four Books Containing a Dissertation on the Five Orders & y^{e} most Necessary Observations relating to all kinds of Building. as also The Different Constructions of Public and Private-Houses, High-ways, Bridges, Market-Places, Xystes, & Temples, wth. their Plans, Sections, & Elevations. The Whole Containing 226 Folio Copper-Plates Carefully Revis'd and Redelineated By Edwd. Hoppus Surveyor . . . and Embellish'd wth. a Large Variety of Chimney Pieces Collected from the Works of Inigo Jones & others

London: printed for Benjn. Cole & John Wilcox, 1736

1983.49.49

Folio: 387 × 238 ($15\frac{1}{4} \times 9\frac{3}{8}$); large paper copy

Pagination 250, [12] pp., engraved title plate, engraved dedication, [210] engraved plates (13 folding)

Edition Second edition of this translation

Text pp. [i]–vi Palladio's preface; [7]–70 text of book 1; [71] printed title page to book 2 (verso blank); [73]–120 text of book 2; 121 "Remark" (verso blank); [123] printed title page to book 3 (verso blank); [125]–177 text of book 3; [178] blank; [179] printed title page to book 4 (verso blank); [181]–250 text of book 4; [251] "Remarks" (verso blank); [253–258] index; [259] note about Palladio (verso blank); [261–262] publisher's list

Illustrations Engraved title plate (as above); engraved title plate to book 1 (with bust of Palladio in architectural setting); engraved dedication to Lord Burlington (with coat of arms); and 4 series of plates, 1 for each book, numbered I–XXXV; I–LXI; I–XXII (i.e., 20 plates); and I–CIV (i.e., 93 plates). In the third series, numbers III–IV and V–VI are paired on 2 single-page plates and in the fourth series there are 13 folding plates, of which 7 have 2 numbers each and 2 have 3 numbers each. Nearly all the plates are signed by Cole as engraver after Edward Hoppus, although the latter only signed 1 in the first book.

In addition, book 1 contains a small engraved diagram in the text (p. 54) and 10 engraved head- and tailpiece illustrations, the first signed as "Design'd by Paladio" and 5 of the remainder after Inigo Jones. Book 2 has an engraved headpiece and 4 engraved tailpieces, 2 of the designs being credited to Jones as architect. Book 3 has 2 headpieces and 4 tailpieces, again credited to Jones

Andrea Palladio. *Andrea Palladio's Architecture.* Frontispiece to book one. 1983.49.49

(and the first credited to Hoppus as draftsman). Book 4 has 2 headpieces, the first signed as after "I. Neeld." Many of these in-text illustrations are signed as engraved by Cole

Binding Contemporary paneled calf, rebacked

References ESTC t114553; Fowler 228; Harris and Savage 689

THIS IS THE second edition of the second English version of Palladio's *I Quattro Libri dell'Architettura* (1570). The first edition was originally issued in parts between November 1732 and 1734 by the engraver Benjamin Cole. Cole began his career specializing in map engraving. He also worked on topographical subjects, collaborating, for example, with John Harris to publish a series of views of English and Welsh cathedrals in 1715, and at about the same time working on Henry Overton's *Prospects of the Most Remarkable Places in and about the Citty [sic] of London.* The first architectural treatise in which he is named is William Halfpenny's *The Art of Sound Building* (1725), where he is listed as one of nine publishers. In the 1730s he engraved plates for manuals by Halfpenny, Batty Langley, William Salmon, and Robert

Morris, and remained active until at least the mid-1750s. Clearly, he was part of the small pool of reproductive engravers on whom the London trade would routinely call when distributing work. Much of it was probably done anonymously.

A Freemason, Cole also engraved and published *The Ancient Constitutions of the Free and Accepted Masons* (1731), which contained the architect Edward Oakley's influential speech to the effect that it was "highly necessary for the improvement of the members of a lodge, that such instruments and books be provided, as be convenient and useful in the exercise, and for the advancement of this divine science of masonry." The present publication was probably a response to this call for affordable books on architecture, as well as a fine piece of commercial opportunism. Its presence in the Millard collection is important, because it is a piratical compilation of three other significant British architectural books that are otherwise unrepresented, and invites comparison with a fourth.

Three-quarters of Cole's edition of Palladio (i.e., books two to four) is a barely concealed copy of the first complete English translation published in Giacomo Leoni's trilingual edition *The Architecture of A. Palladio* (1715–1720). The English text has been reworded to avoid copyright but the plates are unaltered reduced copies by Cole's draftsman Edward Hoppus. They therefore retain all the baroque appearance of Leoni's original coppers. Sometimes presented in frames imitating unrolled sheets of paper, these interpretations of Palladio's sixteenth-century woodcuts were never intended to be mere faithful bearers of the master's meaning. As he declared in the preface to the second and final part of book four, Leoni had made them bigger, and with "so many necessary corrections with respect to shading, dimensions, ornaments, &c. that this work may in some sort be rather consider'd as an original than an improvement." The rapid success Leoni's version enjoyed—a second edition was required a year after completion of the first—was due partly to the impressive size, number, and quality of the engravings; and partly to the relative ignorance in which Palladio was being embraced by supporters of the new king (George I) and his new Whig government. However, once Lord Burlington returned from his second tour of Italy in 1720 with a cache of Palladio's original drawings, and then purchased others from William Talman, along with the bulk of the archive of England's first Palladian, Inigo Jones, the task of retrieving Palladio from Leoni's distortions was soon under way.

It is difficult to know how quickly, and how widely, Leoni's reworking of the *Quattro Libri* was known to be deficient. But the architect Edward Lovett Pearce certainly knew by 1724, when he visited the Convento della Carità in Venice and compared its atrium to Leoni's inaccurate version; and the influence of Lord Burlington's scholarly enthusiasm for Palladio was certainly being felt by May 1728, when the publisher Samuel Harding announced a new edition with plates "exactly copyed from the first Italian edition . . . anno 1570." Had Harding's intention to complete all four books been fulfilled, there is little doubt Cole would have passed over Leoni's outmoded illustrations entirely. In the event, Harding only managed to print book one. He had two collaborators: P. Fourdrinier, probably Paul Fourdrinier, an accomplished engraver highly regarded by Burlington and his circle, who used him for many of their major publications; and Colen Campbell, editor of *Vitruvius Britannicus* and by 1728 a well-established Palladian architect with a gift for self-promotion. Burlington himself may have sponsored the work, but there is no evidence for this. It is equally likely that Campbell was acting independently, using Harding to reassert his claim to be a true inheritor of the Palladian muse after having lost ground to the Burlington circle when the earldismissed him from his coterie in 1720, and after William Kent's *Designs of Inigo Jones* (1727) had established a new architectural lineage: Palladio-Jones-Burlington. Harding, for his part, needed Campbell's name to lend authority to his project even if the English text was no more than a careful correction of Leoni's earlier version, itself derived from the French of Dubois rather than Palladio's Italian. Harding exhibited book one to potential subscribers next to a copy of the 1570 first edition to show how accurate the engravings were, and advertised this section separately "for the use and benefit of workmen," thereby hoping to capture the place in the market long held by Godfrey Richards' version of book one.

In the event, the larger scheme failed. It is not known how many subscribed to the complete treatise, but Campbell fell ill soon after its announcement and died the following year. Instead of replacing him, Harding retitled book one *Andrea Palladio's Five Orders of Architecture*, added five plates of Campbell's own designs, and discontinued the project. When Benjamin Cole began to publish his edition in November 1732, he copied Harding's version for the whole of Palladio's book one, ignoring any inconsistency in combining it with Leoni's books two to four. Harding probably had a substantial number of copies still unsold, because as soon as Cole advertised his piracy in the *Daily Advertiser* he engaged in a minor war of words with his new rival, fully described by Harris and Savage. More practically, he also reduced the price of his version from ten to five shillings, thereby matching the total cost of Cole's book one, published in ten weekly numbers at sixpence each. However, Cole's more aggressive marketing won the day, because his subscribers were not only able to spread their payments over a long period, but were also offered extra plates of chimneypiece designs, and promised the other three books of Palladio's treatise at the same low price.

The chimneypiece designs added by Cole to book one—mainly to make the number of his illustrations

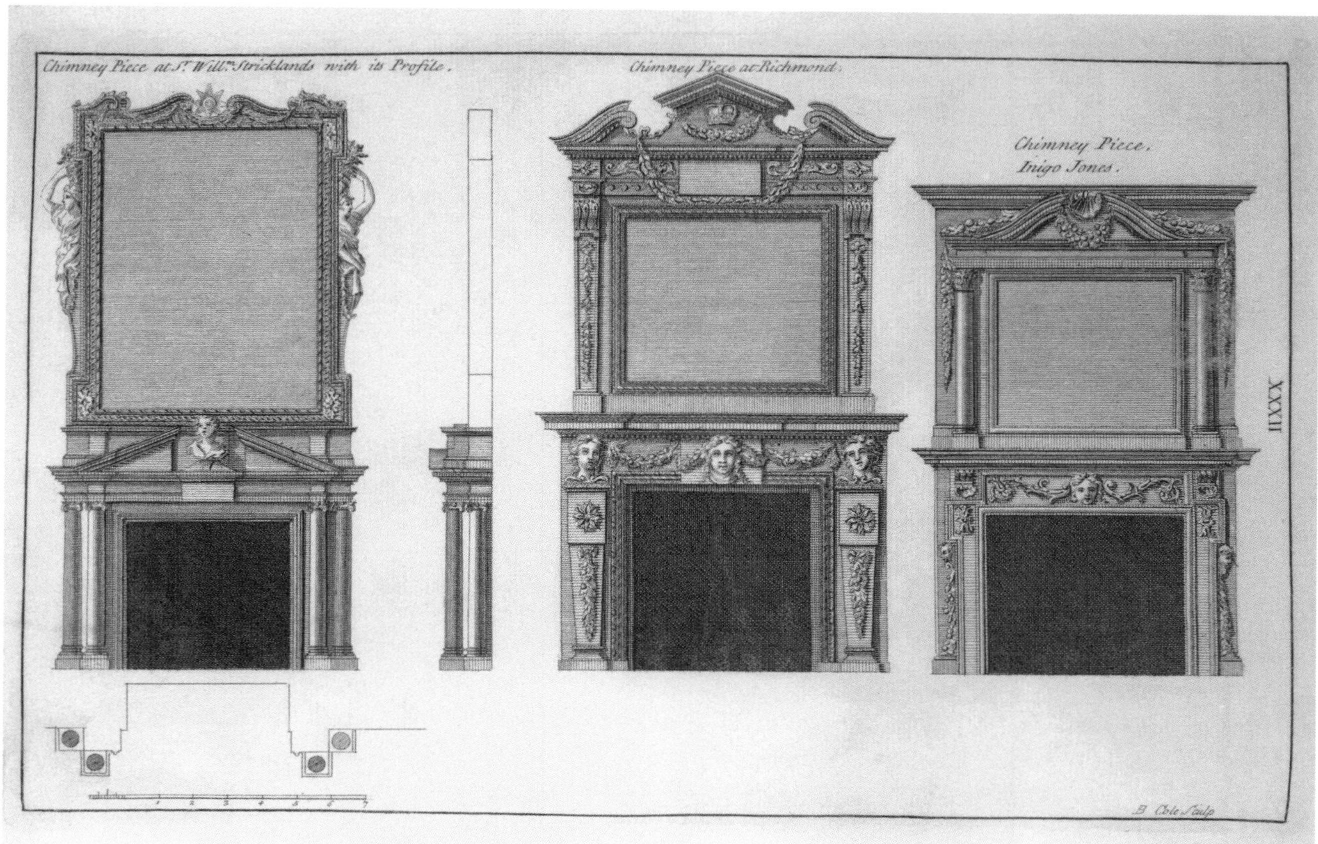

Andrea Palladio. *Andrea Palladio's Architecture*. Plate XXXII. Chimneypieces. 1983.49.49

match Harding's edition—were, like his engraved head- and tailpieces, copied from a third work, Isaac Ware's *Designs of Inigo Jones and Others* [1731]. This was an octavo suite of forty-eight plates (five double-page) published by one of Burlington's assistants and largely dependent on Burlington's collection of drawings. The relevance of these designs to an edition of Palladio is tenuous, to say the least, and copying them was pure piracy, but their presence does offer a key to understanding Cole's attitude toward his venture, which was rooted in a British tradition far older than the grand architectural folios that had begun to appear about twenty years earlier. This tradition had nothing to do with the scholarly reverence toward history evinced by Lord Burlington. It had two guiding principles: that craftsmen should have access to cheap and practical designs from which to copy, and that the more of these a book contained, the better. Cole's complete disregard for the intellectual integrity of his sources is matched in the many contemporaneous works by Langley, Halfpenny, and others, and another context for it is provided by Richards' earlier, partial translation.

The twelfth and last edition of this, *The First Book of Architecture, by Andrea Palladio*, was published in 1733. Since its first appearance as a small quarto in 1663, it had been one of the few affordable and comprehensible manuals available to British builders and carpenters. A large part of it was translated, with omissions and additions, from Pierre Le Muet's heavily reworked version of the section of book one dealing with the orders, *Traicté des Cinq Ordres* (1645). Palladio's name was displayed on the title page, but Richards was wholly intent on providing practical assistance to the profession, not on promoting any one style. He rejected the Italian's recommendations for rooms, windows, and doors in favor of Le Muet's designs, and added information on roof construction and timber framing. The resulting manual was popular, but never substantially updated, and to some extent its place in the market was by 1733 already being challenged. (Its appendix was definitively superseded in that year by Francis Price's *Treatise on Carpentry*.) Nevertheless, for seventy years this *portmanteau* of designs had kept the name of Palladio alive in the British trade. Leoni's edition was irrelevant in this respect, simply because its price was too high. Similarly, Campbell's more faithful version was, at its original price of ten shillings, much more expensive, and much less useful, than the older work. It was Cole's edition that finally signaled the end of its useful life, for although his Palladio would end up costing subscribers a guinea, this was payable in easy installments. Despite the size and superficial quality of *Andrea Palladio's Architecture*, it is actually within the more modest tradition of Richards' pocket manual that its first edition should be seen.

The present second edition is substantially the same as the first, and bears witness to its success, but a few minor differences are worth comment. First, Cole evidently did not retain sole rights to the book for long, because the professional publisher John Wilcox is now named with him on the title plate. Leoni's fourteen-year copyright privilege for his edition, dated 15 January 1720, had expired in the meantime. The new partners decided to reprint their piracy with a superior typeface and on better paper than before, and to offer special copies, such as that in the Millard collection, on large paper for two guineas instead of one. Having captured the bottom end of the market, this attempt to attract the top end was a natural step, and may have been rewarded with brief success. Ornaments were rearranged, and in order to provide extra decoration a few more chimneypiece designs were found. Almost all of these were again taken from Ware's *Designs*, but a few of the cruder engravings (i.e., pp. 34, 42, 48, 112, 114, 120) derive from some other source. Most of the captions to the designs copied from Ware were not present on the plates when they were printed for the first edition. Ware's attributions to Inigo Jones are not of course reliable, and in one instance Cole has compounded this problem by copying the wrong caption (i.e., book one, pl. XXXII, "Chimney piece at Sr. Willm. Stricklands with its profile"; actually a chimneypiece in the saloon at Houghton copied from Ware's *Designs*, pl. 51). This continued theft from his own work must have irritated Ware, just as the unsolicited dedication to Burlington would have his master. If Cole was naively hoping that Burlington, as a fellow Freemason, would approve of his project, he surely misjudged. Instead, Burlington and his wronged assistant set about producing the third complete English edition of Palladio's *Quattro Libri*, which would supersede Cole's as soon as it appeared in 1738. G. B.

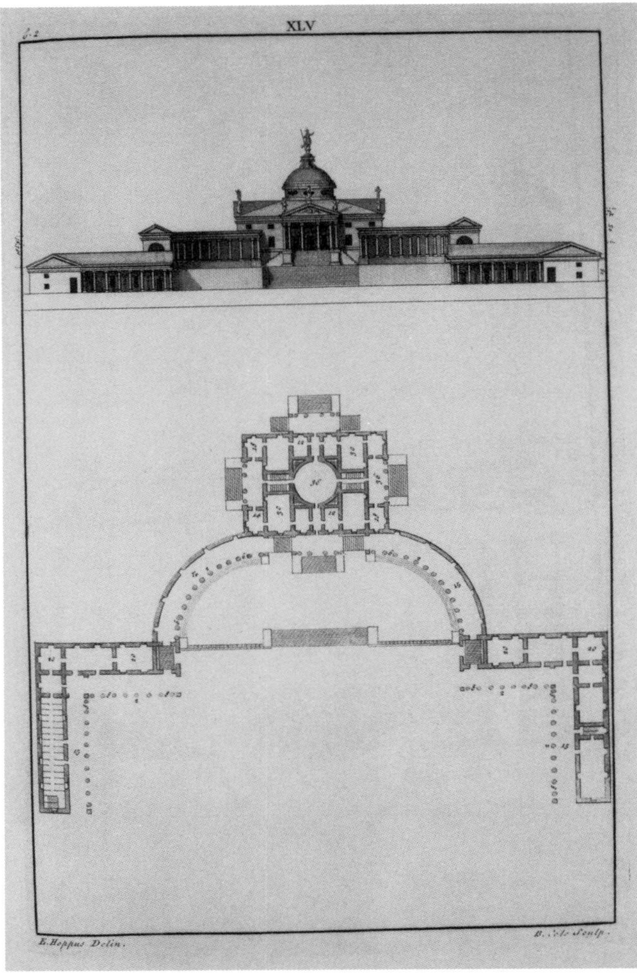

Andrea Palladio. *Andrea Palladio's Architecture.* Plate XLV. Villa Trissino. 1983.49.49

Bibliography

Adams, B. *London Illustrated 1604–1851.* London, 1983

Carré, J. *Lord Burlington (1694–1753): le connaisseur, le mécène, l'architecte.* Clermont-Ferrand, 1993

Harris, E., and N. Savage. *British Architectural Books and Writers 1556–1785.* Cambridge, 1990

52

Andrea Palladio (1508–1580)

Fabbriche Antiche Disegnate da Andrea Palladio Vicentino e Date in Luce da Riccardo Conte di Burlington Londra MDCCXXX

[London, between 1736 and 1740]

1983.49.48

Folio: 530 × 342 ($20\frac{7}{8} \times 13\frac{7}{16}$)

Pagination Etched and engraved title plate, [25] etched and engraved plates (16 double-page)

Edition First edition

Illustrations Etched and engraved title plate with bust of Palladio in niche, male and female terminal figures supporting pediment, signed at base of figures by Palladio's initials as designer and William Kent's as draftsman (usually bound facing the engraved preface, as in Millard copy). Etched and engraved preface with headpiece incorporating portrait of Palladio, signed as engraved by [George] Vertue after Kent's design. 24 etched or engraved plates, some with roulette work, of which 8 are single-page and 16 double-page. All are signed by P. Fourdrinier as engraver and 2 by Isaac Ware as draftsman. The plates are printed in a variety of brownish tones, including sanguine, sepia, and bister

Binding Late eighteenth or early nineteenth-century half straight-grain green morocco, rose and green marbled-paper boards, gilt title on spine, repaired

Provenance Ducal cipher of William, duke of Devonshire (Burlington's son-in-law and heir) on spine. Library stamp of the scientist Henry Cavendish (1731–1810) on dedication verso

References Berlin Cat. 1876; ESTC t35115; Fowler 227; Harris and Savage 669

RICHARD BOYLE, 3d earl of Burlington (1694–1753), was more responsible than anyone for the national and international influence of the Palladian revival in England. He achieved this partly by example, designing a number of critically important buildings including Tottenham Park (1720), Westminster Dormitory (1721), General Wade's House (1723), Richmond House (about 1730), the York Assembly Rooms (1730), and, above all, his own villa at Chiswick (1726). He was also keen to promote Palladianism in print, but in view of his social rank he felt obliged to keep his distance from the undignified world of commercial publishing. Some of the great architectural books published in the 1720s and 1730s were almost certainly suggested, financed, and even edited by him, but the degree of his involvement was more often hinted at than openly expressed. This, and the fact that little of his personal correspondence has survived, is why Burlington can best be known to us through a study of his buildings and the works of his friends, colleagues, and protégés. The present privately published suite of plates takes on particular significance because it is the only architectural book for which he claims responsibility on the title plate, and the only one to contain his words in the preface. Aside from its intrinsic value, it offers tantalizing hints as to the personality of the man who initiated it.

In 1719, Lord Burlington made a second journey to Italy. His first had been part of a more or less conventional Grand Tour, concluding his education before coming of age in 1715 and preceding any recognizable interest in architecture. The second visit, by contrast, had a specific purpose. His new-found friend William Kent expressed this when he wrote that Burlington was "agoing towards Vicenza and Venice to get architects to draw all the fine buildings of Palladio," and to find "a better gusto than the damd gusto that's been for this sixty years past." Kent's "sixty years," of course, is taken from the death of England's first Palladian, Inigo Jones, in 1652.

The plan to draw all Palladio's buildings proved impracticable—even visiting some of them was difficult, due to flooding in the Veneto. Burlington returned with nothing that could conclusively reform the "damd gusto" of Sir Christopher Wren and his followers. But while in Venice he did find, and purchase, what he casually referred to as "some drawings of Palladio" (letter to Sir Andrew Fountaine, 6 November 1719). These were the studies and reconstructions Palladio had made of ancient Roman buildings—especially baths and amphitheaters—during his visits to Rome between 1541 and 1554. The exact circumstances of the purchase remain a mystery. Bernardo Trevisan, a descendant of one of Palladio's friends and patrons, Daniele Barbaro, had brought them to Rome from his Villa Maser in 1710. Unfortunately, it is not known how they got from Rome to Venice or who Burlington bought them from—possibly John Talman, who was in Venice in 1719. (Colvin records a drawing of a font in St. Mark's Square, signed "I. Talman 1719," in Plymouth City Art Gallery.) Talman would certainly have been an interested and useful agent, because he was not only a great collector of prints and drawings himself, but his father, the architect William Talman, already possessed a group of designs by Palladio for private and public buildings.

Many of the drawings Burlington acquired have Palladio's autograph captions, but even so it must have taken him a considerable time to work out exactly what he had purchased. Some are clearly experimental, showing Palladio's thought processes as he reconstructed a building on the evidence of its sixteenth-century remains, in the light of Vitruvius and other classical authors. Others are more finished and could be directly

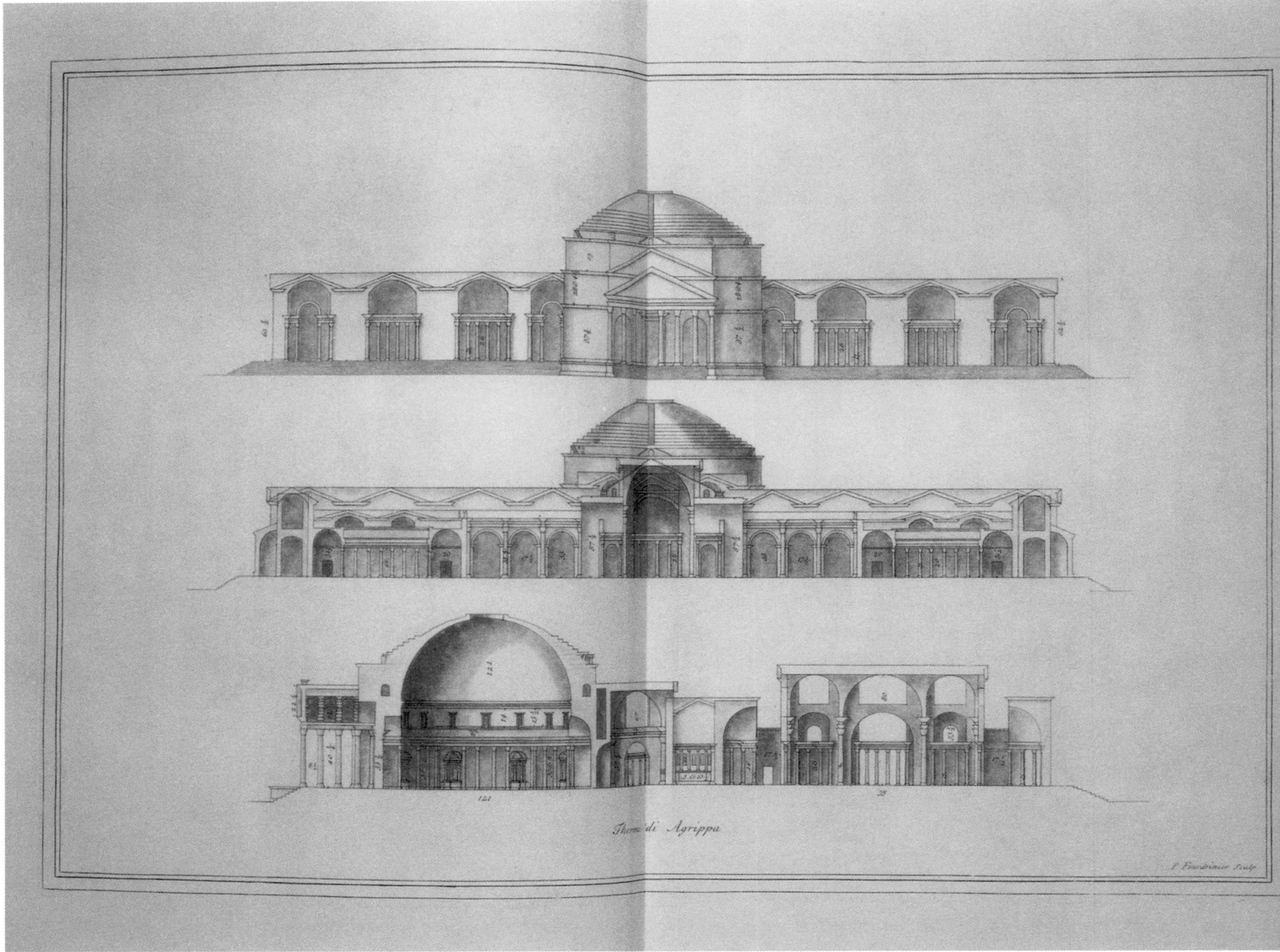

Andrea Palladio. *Fabbriche Antiche Disegnate da Andrea Palladio.* Baths of Agrippa. Elevation and sections. 1983.49.48

related to the books on ancient architecture promised by Palladio in his *Quattro Libri* (1570). None, however, would have seemed as self-explanatory as the drawings by Jones and John Webb that Burlington acquired from John Talman in 1720, or as relevant to the revival as the other Palladio designs that Talman relinquished the following year. Not surprisingly, Burlington decided that the Jones archive should be published first; only Palladio's designs for San Giorgio Maggiore were included in Kent's *Designs of Inigo Jones* (1727).

The project to publish *Fabbriche antiche* must have started soon after publication of the *Designs.* It is inconceivable that an elaborate title plate would be engraved with the date 1730 so boldly incorporated in the design if a considerable portion of the book was not ready. However, it is now known that it did not finally appear until sometime between 1736 and 1740, despite the publication in 1731 of Alexander Pope's celebratory poem, *An Epistle to the Right Honourable Richard, Earl of Burlington, occasion'd by his publishing Palladio's Designs of the Baths, Arches, Theatres, &c. of Ancient Rome.* This poem, generally known as Pope's *Epistle on Taste,* was evidently written when the projected work was grander than the final product. First, Pope mentions "Baths, Arches, Theatres, &c.," whereas only the Roman baths were printed (although his description should, of course, have been appropriate for a book entitled *Fabbriche antiche*). Second, the word "publishing" was scarcely appropriate for the twenty or so copies that were eventually printed and distributed to Burlington's friends. This would matter less if Pope's poem had not been sure of a circulation well into the thousands. It is hard to imagine what people were told if they tried to acquire a copy of "Palladio's Designs." Its title and provenance were sure to generate interest.

Pope was close enough to Burlington not to have unwittingly blundered when he advertised his friend's new book. The decision to delay or temporarily abandon the project must have come from Burlington and one can only speculate on the reason. It may have been because Pope's poem sparked off just the sort of controversy Burlington was anxious to avoid, drawing heavy fire from those outside (and, socially speaking, below) the so-called Burlington circle, such as James Ralph, Batty Langley, and the anonymous author of a satirical pamphlet, *The Miscellany on Taste* (1732). One of the few things certainly known about Burlington is his detestation of Grub Street controversy. He had no financial motive for publishing his collection; nor could his reputation rise much higher. It need not have taken much to put him off the whole idea. After all, when Burlington acquired the drawings the case for Palladianism was still unproven; by the early 1730s it was almost *de rigeur*. In his poem Pope refers to "Imitating Fools" who "random drawings from your sheets shall take, / And of one beauty many blunders make." His covering letter to Burlington, bound in with a manuscript of the poem now at Chatsworth, refers to these as lines added "on the common enemy, the bad imitators & pretenders." "Ignoranti Pretendori" occur again in Burlington's Italian preface to the *Fabbriche antiche*. These specters may have loomed sufficiently large in Burlington's mind for him to have laid the project aside.

Another possible reason for the delay is that text was being prepared, or hoped for, that would clarify some of the obscurities left by the drawings themselves. If so, it has never surfaced. Burlington's preface is not enough, although it helps by explaining his selection criteria (only finished drawings that could be copied to size were reproduced). The volume was finally made up, without text, sometime between May 1736, when Scipio Maffei visited Chiswick and began to look forward to its publication, and 1740, the receipt date inscribed in a copy now in Eton College library. Anybody fortunate enough to have received the book would have had to work even harder than Burlington had when faced with the original drawings, since many of Palladio's captions were not copied over, and measurements were often mistranscribed. These omissions and inaccuracies are all the more surprising given the effort the engraver, P. Fourdrinier, had taken to reproduce not just the lines but also the shading and tone of each drawing. This attempt to facsimilize Palladio's drawings was unprecedented in architectural publishing and shows how greatly Burlington revered his master: he used the same brown inks and sepia washes when making his own architectural designs. But it may also suggest that Burlington was unwilling or unable to interpret the drawings. A conscious effort clearly did go into the final selection and arrangement of plates, but no other help is provided, even though Burlington more than anyone would have known how much that help was needed.

The first plate after the title and preface is double-page size, and shows a reconstructed facade and two sections of the Baths of Agrippa ("Therme di Agrippa"; Zorzi 1959, no. 143; Lewis 1981, no. 76). These baths were built in Rome c. 25–12 B.C. and destroyed by fire in A.D. 80; Palladio incorporates Hadrian's Pantheon, behind which they were located. Burlington also possessed a sheet of several sketch plans by Palladio for these baths (Lewis 1981, no. 75; Zorzi 1959, no. 142), but they were too confused and preliminary to be satisfactorily reproduced. Another drawing giving a more finished plan did exist (Zorzi 1959, no. 136), but was not among those Burlington had acquired. He would have been delighted if it had been: not only does it complement the drawing he reproduces, but the room shapes and sequences shown in it are highly reminiscent of his own design for Chiswick Villa.

Following this impressive opening are four equally extraordinary pairs of double plates. The first of each pair gives elevations and/or sections, and the second a plan, of the Baths of Nero ("Therme di Nerone"; Zorzi 1959, nos. 98, 96), Titus (known to Palladio and Burlington as the "Therme di Vespasiano"; Zorzi 1959, nos. 91, 90), Trajan (known as the "Therme di Tito"; Zorzi 1959, nos. 107, 106; Lewis 1981, no. 74), and Caracalla ("Therme di Antonino"; Zorzi 1959, nos. 115, 110; Lewis 1981, nos. 79, 80). Thereafter, the rhythm of the sequence is interrupted by seven single-page plates of capitals, bases, and entablatures from the Baths of Caracalla (Zorzi 1959, nos. 119–121). Two of these are signed as drawn by Isaac Ware. The measurements given by Palladio in figures have not been copied over, although scale bars have been introduced on four of the seven. Two groups of three plates follow: elevations/sections, plan and etched view of the Baths of Diocletian ("Therme di Diocleziano"; Zorzi 1959, nos. 128, 126, 134), and elevations/sections, plan, and partial interior section of the Baths of Constantine ("Therme di Costantino"; Zorzi 1959, nos. 85, 84, 87). The final two plans, one a single and one a double-page plate, are unidentified. Zorzi attributes the first to the Baths of Helena; the last is a partial plan of the Baths of Titus (Zorzi 1959, nos. 144, 89).

Copies of two other drawings of Palladio's ancient Rome by one of Burlington's draftsmen, Henry Flitcroft, exist. One is of the Roman amphitheater at Verona (on which Scipio Maffei had published a book in 1728), and the other is of the Temple of Fortuna Primigenia at Palestrina. Both of these might have been intended for the *Fabbriche antiche*, but remained unpublished.

Palladio's drawings were, and still are, the single most valuable source for a reconstruction of the Roman baths. It must have been obvious to any student of the subject who gained a sight of the *Fabbriche antiche* that Burlington possessed enough material to reappraise the earlier archaeological studies of Rome that had culminated in Antoine Desgodetz' *Les Edifices Antiques de Rome* (1682). Robert Adam, writing to his brother James in September 1756, had an idea for just such a project, "to show the Baths [of Diocletian and Caracalla] in their present ruinous condition and from that to make other designs of them as they were entire in their glory, in which project Lord Burlington's book has been of unspeakable service as he is vastly exact in his measurements and in Palladio's time they were much more

entire so that I get great light from him." Although Adam eventually found the book less accurate than he hoped, and preferred in any case to study the ruins at Spalatro, his letter shows the value it had to the new generation of archaeologically minded architects that came after the Palladian revival. Since Burlington's own designs so often look forward to the neoclassical style that flourished after his death, it is entirely appropriate that *Fabbriche antiche* should be a bridge between the two periods. For what amounted to a second edition, see Charles Cameron, *The Baths of the Romans Explained and Illustrated* (1772). G. B.

Andrea Palladio. *Fabbriche Antiche Disegnate da Andrea Palladio.* Section of the Baths of Diocletian. 1983.49.48

Bibliography

Carré, J. *Lord Burlington (1694–1753): le connaisseur, le mécène, l'architecte.* Clermont-Ferrand, 1993

Harris, E., and N. Savage. *British Architectural Books and Writers 1556–1785.* Cambridge, 1990

Harris, J. *The Palladian Revival.* Montreal, 1994

Lewis, D. *The Drawings of Andrea Palladio.* Washington, 1981

Zorzi, G. G. *I Disegni delle Antichità di Andrea Palladio.* Venice, 1959

53

Andrea Palladio (1508–1580)

The Four Books Of Andrea Palladio's Architecture: Wherein, After a short Treatise of the Five Orders, Those Observations that are most necessary in Building, Private Houses, Streets, Bridges, Piazzas, Xisti, and Temples are treated of

London: published by Isaac Ware, 1738

1983.49.50

Folio: 530 × 342 (20 7/8 × 13 7/16)

Pagination [xii], 110 pp., etched and engraved title plate, [208] etched and engraved plates

Edition First edition of this translation

Text pp. [i] Ware's dedication to Lord Burlington (verso blank); [iii] "Advertisement" to the present edition; [iv–vi] Palladio's preface, ending with errata; [vii–ix] list of subscribers; [x] blank; [xi–xii] list of technical terms, with text references, ending with errata; [1]–36 text of book 1; [37]–56 text of book 2; [57]–78 text of book 3; [79]–110 text of book 4

Illustrations The etched and engraved title plate, with architectural border and allegorical figures, is reused with alterations for the divisional titles to books 2–4. In addition, there are 4 series of full-page plates, 1 for each book, numbered VIII–XXXIV, I–LVIII, I–XXI, and I–XCIX. The first series continues from 7 in-text engravings on 3 plates, numbered I–VII. Book 1 also contains 4 unnumbered engraved plates on pp. 12, 28, 29, and 30. In addition, there is an etched headpiece with putti and arabesques on the dedication leaf, signed by P. Fourdrinier after William Kent; an unsigned engraved initial on the same page; and a final tailpiece engraved by Ware after Kent. In book 1 of the Millard copy, the unnumbered engraving on page 28 and plates I–IIII, VIII–XX, and XXIII–XXXII are printed in sepia. Plate XVII is repeated

Binding Contemporary sprinkled calf, rebacked preserving original spine, red morocco label, text edges sprinkled red

Provenance Bookplate of the Rolle family; ownership inscription cut from title plate

References ESTC t40073; Fowler 229; Harris and Savage 691

ISAAC WARE's translation of Palladio's *Quattro Libri* was the third English version of the whole treatise to be published, following Leoni's trilingual *The Architecture of A. Palladio* (1715–1720) and Benjamin Cole's piratical *Andrea Palladio's Architecture, in Four Books* (1732–1734; see notes to the second edition of 1736). Dated 1738 on the title page, book one was actually published in June or July 1737 and the remainder sometime before 1743.

Ware's brief prefatory advertisement accurately criticizes both predecessors. Leoni, he writes

> . . . thought fit not only to vary from the scale of the originals, but also in many places to alter even the graceful proportions prescribed by this great master, by diminishing some of his measures, enlarging others, and putting in fanciful decorations of his own: and indeed his drawings are likewise very incorrect; which makes this performance, according to his own account in the preface, seem rather to be itself an original, than an improvement on Palladio.

Cole, on the other hand, does not deserve to be mentioned by name, and his edition is dismissed as "done with so little understanding, and so much negligence, that it cannot but give great offence to the judicious, and be of very bad consequence in misleading the unskilful, into whose hands it may happen to fall." Ware does not mention that Cole's edition also contained copies of virtually all the plates in Ware's own first publication, *Designs of Inigo Jones and Others* [1731]. If this theft gave a motive for Ware to embark on a rival translation, the active support of Lord Burlington provided him with the means. Cole had had the temerity to dedicate his piracy to Burlington. Ware's edition is also dedicated to Burlington, but this time with the dedicatee's agreement; and Burlington not only sanctioned the work, he allowed his assistant to state openly his direct involvement: "Your giving me free access to your study, wherein many of the original drawings of Palladio, besides those which compose this work, are preserved, and taking upon you the trouble of revising the translation, and correcting it with your own hands, are such instances of your love to arts, and of your friendship to me, that I cannot too publickly return your Lordship thanks for favours that surpass all acknowledgment" (dedication). Given Burlington's reputation, his endorsement would have been one of the main attractions of the new edition. It also seems unlikely Ware could have sold the work at the low price of one pound ten shillings (or two guineas bound) without a subvention from his patron.

Burlington's proximity to the project surely influenced Ware's editorial method. Although the earl's edition of Palladio's Roman bath drawings, *Fabbriche antiche,* is a very different work, both reveal the spirit of reverence that defined Burlington's attitude to Palladio and distinguished it from those outside his circle. As far as possible, Ware was attempting to produce an English language facsimile of his Italian original. Just as the *Fabbriche* plates were intended to be exact reproductions, so, as Ware carefully stresses in his preface, his

Palladio was to be the best edition by being the most faithful.

To do justice therefore to Palladio, and to perpetuate his most valuable remains amongst us, are the principal inducements to my undertaking so great and laborious a work; in executing of which, I have strictly kept to his proportions and measures, by exactly tracing all the plates from his originals, and engraved them with my own hands: so that the reader may depend upon having an exact copy of what our author published, without diminution or increase; nor have I taken upon me to alter, much less to correct, any thing that came from the hands of that excellent artist. From the same motive I have chosen to give a strict and literal translation, that the sense of our author might be delivered from his own words (advertisement).

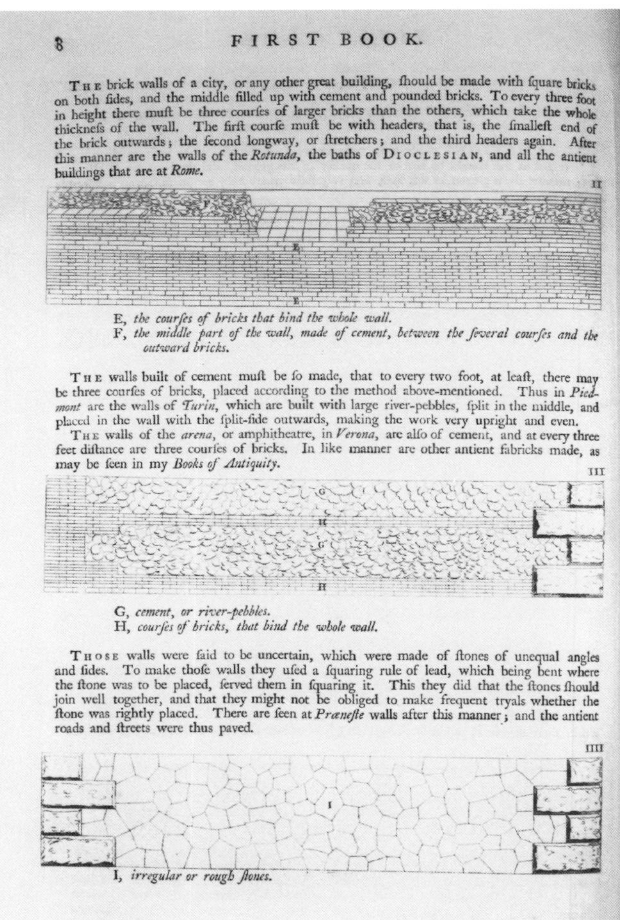

8 FIRST BOOK.

THE brick walls of a city, or any other great building, ſhould be made with ſquare bricks on both ſides, and the middle filled up with cement and pounded bricks. To every three foot in height there muſt be three courſes of larger bricks than the others, which take the whole thickneſs of the wall. The firſt courſe muſt be with headers, that is, the ſmalleſt end of the brick outwards; the ſecond longway, or ſtretchers; and the third headers again. After this manner are the walls of the *Rotunda*, the baths of DIOCLESIAN, and all the antient buildings that are at *Rome*.

II

E, *the courſes of bricks that bind the whole wall.*
F, *the middle part of the wall, made of cement, between the ſeveral courſes and the outward bricks.*

THE walls built of cement muſt be ſo made, that to every two foot, at leaſt, there may be three courſes of bricks, placed according to the method above-mentioned. Thus in *Piedmont* are the walls of *Turin*, which are built with large river-pebbles, ſplit in the middle, and placed in the wall with the ſplit-ſide outwards, making the work very upright and even.

THE walls of the *arena*, or amphitheatre, in *Verona*, are alſo of cement, and at every three feet diſtance are three courſes of bricks. In like manner are other antient fabricks made, as may be ſeen in my *Books of Antiquity*.

III

G, *cement, or river-pebbles.*
H, *courſes of bricks, that bind the whole wall.*

THOSE walls were ſaid to be uncertain, which were made of ſtones of unequal angles and ſides. To make thoſe walls they uſed a ſquaring rule of lead, which being bent where the ſtone was to be placed, ſerved them in ſquaring it. This they did that the ſtones ſhould join well together, and that they might not be obliged to make frequent tryals whether the ſtone was rightly placed. There are ſeen at *Prœneſte* walls after this manner; and the antient roads and ſtreets were thus paved.

IIII

I, *irregular or rough ſtones.*

Andrea Palladio. *The Four Books of Andrea Palladio's Architecture.* Of the several sorts of walls. 1983.49.50

Ware carefully suppresses any mention of Samuel Harding and Colen Campbell's 1728 edition of book one, which had similarly purported to carry Palladio's treatise unaltered to its English-speaking audience. Both versions may be seen as products of a new attempt to place Palladio among the select group of "Divine" Renaissance artists, headed by Michelangelo and Raphael, whose genius elevated them above all criticism. Or they may be seen as the continuation of a humanist tradition, the "scholarly, pedantic, bibliophilic" style of editing described by Dora Wiebenson in her notes on Roland Fréart's Palladio of 1650 (see Millard catalogue, *French Books* 1993, 379). Whatever the impetus, the first edition of Palladio's treatise was rapidly acquiring a status approaching that of a holy relic in England (Burlington bought three copies of it). Such an attitude was still rare in the first half of the eighteenth century, for even those who collected them did not generally value early printed books as original works of art. Yet Ware's preface is written as if *I Quattro Libri* revealed the hand of the master just as much as the Palladio drawings in Lord Burlington's study. It ignores the fact that, unlike the original drawings, it was a commercial reproduction already one important step away from its author. From a modern viewpoint, Ware's response to Leoni's heavy-handed editorial style was surely an overreaction. Only through eyes clouded by reverence could he have seen the original 1570 printing as perfect. Its woodcuts are frequently ill-drawn and badly printed. Lines sometimes contradict their numerical measurements, and the letterpress description of designs does not always match the illustrations, let alone the buildings themselves. However misguidedly, Leoni had recognized, as Ottavio Bertotti Scamozzi would later in the century, that editorial work was essential to retrieve Palladio's true intentions. Neither Campbell nor Ware acknowledged this. Campbell's project having failed after publication of book one, it was left to Ware to produce what for more than 250 years was regarded as the definitive English language edition of Palladio's treatise.

Ware's working method is clear from a study of the book he produced. For the illustrations, he provided himself with a copy of the Italian original, almost certainly disbound, and proceeded to trace each line first onto another sheet of paper, and then to the copperplate. He did not use a mirror for this second stage, as P. Fourdrinier had when working for Colen Campbell and Samuel Harding. Consequently all of the illustrations are printed in reverse. For nearly all of them, Ware used copperplates cut to a standard size (i.e., the size of the image area in Palladio's original folio). To use so much copper was probably considered a legitimate extravagance, since although many of the illustrations occupied half a page or less, having a standard plate size simplified the task of printing each under an even pressure. It did not, however, solve his biggest problem: how to register text and illustrations harmoniously on the same page. Palladio, of course, had the advantage of using woodcuts which, being a relief process like letterpress printing, could easily be inked and printed at the same time as his text. Ware's preference for the finer lines of copperplate engraving militated against this option. Because engraving is an intaglio process, two different printing presses were required to reproduce Palladio's arrangement.

In Harding and Campbell's edition of book one, the editors had decided how to treat each illustration individually. Sometimes Fourdrinier made one full-page plate out of a number of smaller illustrations; sometimes he required the printer to combine an engraving with letterpress; and for the simplest diagrams, woodcuts were still used. Ware, wanting his edition to consist only of engravings yet still to match Palladio's as closely as possible, went to considerable trouble to register type and image on the same page, notably on pages eight and nine of book one. On both pages, three illustrations have been engraved on a single full-page copper, at carefully calculated intervals to allow the text to appear in between. (Keeping faith with the original even led Ware to copy the exact shapes of the irregular stones and pebbles in Palladio's woodcut.) This would have been a painfully high compositorial standard to maintain throughout the treatise, especially since the original is by no means a model of perfect imposition. So in books two to four, Ware opted instead for the easier solution of printing plates and text on separate sheets, thus disrupting the order a little but saving a considerable amount of presswork. This slight compromise was probably a late decision, after all the plates had been engraved. Otherwise, Ware could have made further savings on paper by combining the smaller illustrations on one plate, whereas they are virtually all given a whole page even where they barely cover half of it. Significantly, though no longer surrounded by text, nearly all of them are in exactly the same position on the page as the 1570 woodcuts (see especially book four).

Ware also made some very minor alterations to a few of the designs, such as clearly separating the plan of the Palazzo Antonini from its elevation (book two, pl. 1), and occasionally adding his own shading. No attempt was made to imitate the typography or the historiated woodcut initials of the 1570 edition. Exceptionally, some of the plates in the Millard copy are printed in bister, an experiment that was discontinued after book one. The plainness of the overall presentation throws into relief the two architectural vignettes designed by William Kent, one set as a headpiece to the dedication (engraved by Fourdrinier) and the other as a tailpiece to book four. The latter is one of Kent's best efforts in this genre, engraved by Ware with a delicacy and tone otherwise absent.

The text was the first in English to be taken directly from the Italian. Leoni's had been derived by his translator Nicholas Dubois from Fréart's 1650 French edition. Harding and Campbell had only corrected Dubois' effort, and Benjamin Cole simply rephrased both earlier versions as a precaution against accusations of breach of copyright. It is generally assumed that Ware had sufficient Italian to perform the task himself, and there is no reason to doubt that Burlington revised it, as stated in the dedication. The result is certainly an improvement on the earlier versions and a reliable enough guide to the original text.

The Four Books of Andrea Palladio's Architecture effectively concluded the hectic attempt made in England between 1715 and 1738 to promote Palladianism by publishing the architect's own treatise. Partly inspired by this wave of foreign interest, Italian historians were the next to reexamine the *Quattro Libri*, mainly through two huge publishing projects, Francesco Muttoni's *Architettura di Andrea Palladio* (1740–1748) and Bertotti Scamozzi's *Le Fabbriche e i Disegni di Andrea Palladio* (1776–1783). Despite its superiority, however, Ware's Palladio did not put an absolute end to the English versions that preceded it. There was no further edition of Cole's piracy, but in 1742 a group of London booksellers reprinted Leoni's Palladio as the "Third edition, corrected" with considerable additions. Inigo Jones' notes on the treatise were transcribed (inaccurately) from his own copy at Worcester College, Oxford; and the first published English translation of Palladio's *Antichità di Roma* was appended along with a *Discorso sopra i fuochi de gli antichi* which, following tradition, was incorrectly ascribed to the same author. These additions may have extended the competitive life of the older work. When the present translation was reprinted and offered in weekly sixpenny numbers from September 1753 (or complete and bound for £1 11s 6d), it was still thought necessary to advertise it with a warning: "As there are several translations . . . be careful to ask for that translated by Isaac Ware Esq." G. B.

Bibliography

Harris, E., and N. Savage. *British Architectural Books and Writers 1556–1785*. Cambridge, 1990

Andrea Palladio. *The Four Books of Andrea Palladio's Architecture.* Tailpiece. 1983.49.50

54

Andrea Palladio (1508–1580)

The First Book Of Andrea Palladio's Architecture. Treating of the Five Orders; And What is most necessary in Building. Correctly drawn From his Original Work, publish'd by himself at Venice, Anno 1570. And Accurately engraved by I. Ware

[London?,] 1742

1983.49.55

Octavo: 202 × 123 (8 × 4 13/16)

Pagination [viii], 63, [1] pp., etched and engraved frontispiece, 34 [i.e., 29] engraved plates

Edition First edition of this abridgement

Text pp. [i] title page (verso blank); [iii]–viii explanation of technical terms; [1]–63 text; [64] "Advertisement" for Ware's edition of Palladio's Four Books, "Lately Published"

Illustrations Etched and engraved frontispiece with medallion portrait of Palladio by Ware after a design by William Kent, plus 29 engraved plates numbered I–XXXIV (nos. I–III and IIII–VII on 2 plates). In addition, there are 5 small vertical strips of engraved figures illustrating technical terms, pp. [iii]–vii

Binding Contemporary mottled calf, gilt borders, edges of text sprinkled red

Provenance Ownership inscription of Brent Gration-Maxfield

References ESTC n47296; Harris and Savage 690

Andrea Palladio. *The First Book of Andrea Palladio's Architecture.* Frontispiece. Portrait of Andrea Palladio. 1983.49.55 (here enlarged)

Isaac Ware's *Four Books of Andrea Palladio's Architecture* is advertised on the final page of the present work as "lately published . . . To be had of the Editor [i.e., Ware], at his house in Scotland-yard, Whitehall; of Mr. Osborne, bookseller, in Grey's-Inn; and J. Millan, bookseller, at Charing-Cross. Price bound two guineas." Having completed the larger work, this separate publication of book one in an octavo format represents an attempt to reenter the market at a lower level, providing for builders and their apprentices a cheaper and more portable version of the section in which Palladio deals with the five orders of architecture. Ever since 1663, when Godfrey Richards first printed his edition of Pierre Le Muet's French abridgment, Palladio's guidance on the subject had been recommended to British architects and craftsmen. But despite the natural conservatism of the trade, Richards' heavily edited version must have seemed increasingly out of date as the eighteenth century progressed, and as patrons vied with one another to commission town and country houses in the purest Palladian taste. Its twelfth and last edition appeared in 1733. *The First Book of Andrea Palladio's Architecture* continued the tradition established by Richards, but offered a more authoritative translation, corrected, as the dedication to the *Four Books* proudly declares, by Lord Burlington himself. As no publisher is mentioned on the title page, and the work is relatively scarce today, it is probable that Ware published it himself in a small edition, with the hope of subsequently selling the copyright to the London book trade. This was a common enough device for authors at the time, and Ware did just this with his folio Palladio and with an earlier collection, *Designs of Inigo Jones and others* [1731]. *The First Book*, however, was never reprinted.

In preparing the octavo edition, Ware chose to leaven the severe appearance of some of the plates by adding decorative shading. In other respects, the engravings appear to be straightforward copies of the folio plates, reduced and reversed but without significant alterations. (Ware was reversing the images from reversed copies of the original woodcuts, so they now have the correct orientation.) The text also appears to be a word-for-word resetting of the folio version. It is prefaced by a new section, "An explanation of the technical terms in this treatise." This contains forty definitions from astragal to zocco, though not arranged alphabetically beyond the first letter of each word. To the right of the very cursory textual definitions, twenty-five small illustrations, engraved on five narrow plates, give additional help. The whole work is prefixed by a frontispiece portrait of Palladio engraved by Ware after a design by William Kent. Like all of the portraits of Palladio current in Britain at the time, this is based on Sebastiano Ricci's fake portrait from Giacomo Leoni's edition of the *Quattro Libri*, there stated to be after an original painting by Paolo Veronese, and given wide currency by J. M. Rysbrack's use of it for his bust of Palladio at Chiswick Villa. G. B.

Bibliography

Harris, E., and N. Savage. *British Architectural Books and Writers 1556–1785*. Cambridge, 1990

55

Michel Angelo Pergolesi (d. 1801)

[A Great Variety Of Original Designs Of Vases, Figures, Medallions, Friezes, Pilasters, Pannels and other Ornaments, in the Etruscan and Grotesque Style; Executed In The Most Finished Manner. With several Pieces drawn by the late renowned J. B. Cipriani, Esq. R. A. and engraved by the celebrated F. Bartolozzi, Esq. R. A. . . . The Whole Designed And Etched By Michel Angelo Pergolesi . . .]

[London, 1777–1792]

1985.61.2611

Folio: 529 × 350 (20 3/4 × 13 3/4)

Pagination [2] pp., 66 [i.e., 67] etched plates

Edition First edition

Text pp. [1] publisher's printed subscription announcement, dated "London 178 [blank]," including description used as title above (verso blank)

(*Note*: Mounted on a blank leaf following pl. 55 is a smaller printed announcement "Mr. Pergolesi most respectfully begs leave to acquaint his Subscribers . . .")

Illustrations A total of 67 etched plates numbered 1–66 (2 plates numbered 56), with designs irregularly numbered 1–435. In the Millard copy, plates 20, 30, 40, and 55 are printed in sanguine, with a central medallion signed as engraved by Francesco Bartolozzi after G. B. Cipriani. The plates have credit lines as follows: plate 1 "Pergolesi Del^t. et Publish'd according to act of Parliament the 1st. May. 1777. Et. Scul:"; 2–5 "Pergolesi Del^t. Scul^t. et Publish'd, according to act of Parliament the 1. May. 1777"; 6–10 "Pergolesi Inue^t. Scul^t. and Publish'd according to act of Parliament the 1st. of September 1777"; 11–15 the same dated 30 May 1778; 16–20 the same dated 1 March 1779; 21–25 the same dated 1 February 1780; 26–30 the same dated 31 August 1780 (pl. 29 1 day earlier); 31–35 the same (but "Sucl^t.") dated 1st July 1781; 36–40 the same dated 29 February 1782; 41–45 the same dated 17 July 1782; 46–50 the same dated 27 February 1784; 51–55 the same dated 20 March 1785; 56 "To The Memory of the Late Most High And Puissant Prince Hugh Percy Duke of Northumberland . . ." signed "Pergolesi inv^t. sculp^t. & Publish'd July 26. 1791. according to act of Parliament, N°. 16 Broad Street, Golden Square"; 56 bis ". . . July 26, 1791"; 57, 59, 60, and 62 ". . . 1st April 1791"; 58 ". . . 29th April 1791"; 61, 63–65 ". . . Feby. 1792"; 66 "To Her Grace Elizabeth Duchess Of Buccleugh . . . August 30, 1792 . . ."

Binding Recent half calf, gilt-tooled spine, marbled boards. Plates mounted on linen

References Berlin Cat. 593; Harris and Savage 699

James Adam, in Rome and looking for Italian assistants to send back to England, reported to his brother Robert in February 1763 that he had failed to persuade either of his first two choices to accept the task. Antonio Zucchi, "a worthy honest lad, a most singular character in this degenerate country," was determined to go to Venice, and Domenico Cunego declared himself married and therefore "untransportable." Three other draftsmen were sent on the sea voyage instead. John Fleming suggests that one, described by James as "an arabesque painter, paints in oils and guazzo, a very sharp and mechanical man," was Michel Angelo Pergolesi (John Fleming, *Robert Adam and His Circle* [1962], 302). Eileen Harris, on the other hand, states he had arrived at Robert Adam's invitation in 1760. Either way, he would have been dependent initially on the Adam brothers for employment in England, although his only firmly documented work for them to date is at Syon House in Middlesex, where he was paid for painting the sixty-two pilasters in the Long Gallery when Robert Adam remodeled the interior for the 1st duke of Northumberland, 1762–1769. In the late sixties or early seventies he worked for William Chambers at Gower House in Whitehall, but no record of other commissions has been traced. His main income may have derived from the occupation of art teacher to the nobility and gentry.

The present work, his only publication, consists entirely of neoclassical designs for almost every type of ornament—ceilings, doors, wall panels, silverware, furniture, urns and vases, marquetry, etc.—interspersed with arabesques and grotesques. Because no title page or accompanying text was ever issued, the circumstances surrounding its appearance are obscure, although the imprint lines on the plates show that it was issued in parts, and that the first eleven suites of five plates each were published between May 1777 and March 1785. At this point the series seems to have stalled, since it had progressed no further when the "Proposals for Publishing," bound in with the Millard copy, were issued. This was sometime between June 1786, when the 1st duke of Northumberland had died, and the end of the decade. The proposals show Pergolesi attempting to relaunch the series, and giving himself more than enough scope for its continuation: two volumes each of twenty numbers would have required two hundred engravings in all. The promise that the last number would include an engraving of the late duke strongly suggests that the latter had supported its publication. His death is probably the reason why it was suspended, and why Pergolesi was compelled to solicit more subscriptions, having retained sole interest in the work—

"Subscriptions and Orders are received at the Author's, No. 16, Broad Street, Golden Square . . . and nowhere else." Golden Square was a notably cosmopolitan location in London, popular with many British and foreign artists. Pergolesi lived on its less fashionable, but still respectable, south side, which had better daylight for artists. Previous occupants of No. 16 included Angelica Kauffmann and Prince Hoare.

Pergolesi's proposals did not produce as many new subscriptions as hoped, and the series remained in abeyance for a further period. Although five plates are dated April 1791 (pls. 57–60, 62), his twelfth suite could not have appeared before 26 July of that year. That is the date on two plates, both numbered 56, commemorating the duke of Northumberland and dedicating the series to him. These were intended for the last of Pergolesi's twenty parts, so it might be thought he was completing the series, were it not for two additional announcements that propose, not only to continue it, but to make it

Michel Angelo Pergolesi. *A Great Variety of Original Designs of Vases, Figures, Medallions.* Proposals. 1985.61.2611

London, 178

PROPOSALS

For PUBLISHING by SUBSCRIPTION,

(Conſiſting of TWO VOLUMES, containing TWENTY NUMBERS each,)

DEDICATED, BY PERMISSION,

TO HIS GRACE

The late DUKE of NORTHUMBERLAND,

A GREAT VARIETY OF

ORIGINAL DESIGNS

OF

VASES, FIGURES, MEDALLIONS, FRIEZES, PILASTERS, PANNELS and other ORNAMENTS,

In the ETRUSCAN and GROTESQUE STYLE:

EXECUTED IN THE MOST FINISHED MANNER.

With ſeveral PIECES *drawn by the late renowned J. B. CIPRIANI, Eſq.* R. A. *and engraved by the celebrated F. BARTOLOZZI, Eſq.* R. A.

Every Number conſiſts of Five Plates; and on each Plate are ſeveral Deſigns, ready to be publiſhed, at the Price of SIX SHILLINGS to SUBSCRIBERS, printed on Superfine Imperial Paper, fit for Colouring.

☞ *TO BE PAID FOR ON DELIVERY.*

THE WHOLE DESIGNED AND ETCHED

by MICHEL ANGELO PERGOLESI,

Who has long applied his Attention to the Ornaments of the Ancients, and has had the Honour of deſigning and painting Rooms, Cielings, Staircaſes and Ornaments, for many of the NOBILITY and GENTRY in England, and other Countries.

To theſe Numbers are annexed ſeveral beautiful Drawings and Engravings, by the ſaid Meſſrs. CIPRIANI and BARTOLOZZI; and alſo, by the ſame Authors, two moſt rare and valuable Gems—one in No. 2, is the CUPID and SATYR, belonging to the Collection of his Grace the Duke of Marlborough; and in No. 4, is the SACRIFICE, in the Collection of his Eminence the Cardinal of York, at Rome. In No. 5, a fine Etching of APOLLO in his Chariot. In No. 6, the maſterly Engraving of SPRING. In No. 7, a fine Etching of DIANA on her Chariot. In No. 8, a fine Engraving of AUTUMN. And in No. 11, a ſuperior Engraving of WINTER.

ALL OF THEM MOST CAPITALLY EXECUTED.

The Publiſher flatters himſelf that theſe Deſigns will give Pleaſure to the Noblemen and Gentlemen, and be of great Utility to the Architect, Painter, Sculptor, Modeller, Carver, &c. or any Perſon concerned in thoſe Branches of the Polite Arts, were Taſte and Ornament are required.

*** SUBSCRIPTIONS and Orders are received at the AUTHOR'S, No. 16, BROAD STREET, Golden Square, where Specimens of his Works may be ſeen, and nowhere elſe.

Mr. PERGOLESI has Numbers out of Twenty ready to be delivered to any of the Subſcribers who wiſh to have them immediately.

Mr. PERGOLESI continues to teach Ladies and Gentlemen every Branch of ancient and modern Ornaments, Deſigns, Paintings, &c. on very reaſonable Terms, in a Manner, which for its Character and expeditious Method, and Novelty of Execution, has gained him the Patronage of many of the Nobility and Gentry of England.

Mr. PERGOLESI, if required, will wait on any Gentleman with a Specimen of his Work.

☞ A List of the SUBSCRIBERS' NAMES will be engraved and delivered with the laſt Number, with the Title, Dedication, and Index of the Work, in ENGLISH, FRENCH, ITALIAN, and GERMAN.

In the laſt Number will be publiſhed, an elegant Engraving of his Grace the late DUKE of NORTHUMBERLAND, deſigned and engraved by the ſaid Meſſ. CIPRIANI & BARTOLOZZI.

even bigger. One of these is bound in with the Millard copy, and was evidently issued with the twelfth number. It states that

> Mr. Pergolesi most respectfully begs Leave to acquaint his Subscribers, as well as the Public in general, that the next Number, being the 13th, as well as the succeeding Numbers to No. XXIV. the whole Numbers of the first Volume, will have one Plate each, additional; the Price will be 7s. 6d. each Number, including a Dedication (by Permission) and a Portrait of the Nobleman or Gentleman to whom the Number is dedicated. Mr. Pergolesi trusts, at the same Time, it will not be thought an Overcharge, if he is compelled, by new Duties being laid upon the principal Article of his Work, since the year 1777, when he began his Publication, to raise the Price of the above Numbers, which will just indemnify him for the new Duties he must now pay. No. XII. will be delivered to Subscribers at 6s.

A typewritten copy of proposals issued at around the same time, bound in with the National Art Library's copy and quoted in Harris and Savage, contains much the same information and confirms that Pergolesi now intended both volumes to contain twenty-four numbers each.

Had Pergolesi's *Great Variety of Original Designs* been a roaring success, and had he lined up at least a dozen patrons willing to sponsor the series in exchange for a portrait dedication, this shift in marketing technique might have been a shrewd and profitable way to counteract the effects of the new duties on paper to which he refers. In the event, however, it probably destroyed any chance the series had, and only one more suite appeared in Pergolesi's lifetime. In it Elizabeth, duchess of Buccleuch, was rewarded as an "Encourager of the Artists" with a dedication plate, dated 30 August 1792. She was the daughter of the duke of Montagu, and had brought the lion's share of her father's enormous wealth to the 3d duke of Buccleuch when they married in 1767. Hers is the last plate in the Millard copy.

After Pergolesi's death, in 1801, four more plates of designs were published by one M. Dulouchamp, describing himself as "Bookseller, Successor to the late Signor Pergolesi" (Canadian Centre for Architecture copy). Dulouchamp, spelled Dulonchamp on one plate, and Dulauchamp on another, had doubtless acquired the stock and copyright for the work and, finding unpublished designs, decided to add them to the sets he sold. Some of them may have been engraved after Pergolesi's death: plate 70 is apparently signed, very faintly, "N. Normand [?] sc." The publication history of the complete work therefore spans twenty-four years. It is not surprising that most sets are incomplete and only one, George III's copy in the British Library, has been found with the "maximum" number (i.e., 72: pls. 1–70 plus 56 bis, 66 bis; an additional plate called for by Harris and Savage is in fact an unnumbered printing of plate 9). It is also not surprising that plates exist in variant states: the imprint year in the CCA copy of plates 1–4 has been altered to 1788, and in plates 56 (bis)–60 to 1792, presumably to extend copyright. An attempt to correct the careless numbering of plates top right was also made at some stage, by hand or by alteration on the copper. Plates 56–65 in the Millard copy are part of a special issue printed on blue paper.

Apart from those published, Pergolesi had plenty more designs available to him. John Harris describes an album of his sepia pen, pencil, and wash drawings, held by the Pierpont Morgan Library, which contains the originals for most of the published designs, plus forty-three pages of other decorative motifs. Some relate to Lord Gower's house in Whitehall. There is a reasonable chance that others, published or unpublished, were originally commissioned for specific projects. Even so, Pergolesi's primary aim in publishing his designs was not to document his achievements, but rather to provide a pattern book for the fashionable Adam style of neoclassical ornament. In part, it was probably the critical success of the Adam brothers' *Works in Architecture* that inspired their former employee, just as it provided the motivation behind George Richardson's *Book of Ceilings*. Richardson hoped to promote his own career in print, and there is every likelihood Pergolesi intended the same. But unlike Richardson, Pergolesi was unwilling to enter into partnerships with publishers, and the limited circulation of his suite seems confirmed by its comparative scarcity today. It should probably be seen as much in the tradition of drawing books as architectural pattern books. The above-mentioned proposals advertise it as "fit for colouring."

An important selling point of the work was provided by Pergolesi's contacts with other Italian immigrant artists. Often printed in sanguine to emphasize their special value, Francesco Bartolozzi engraved six of the central vignettes after G. B. Cipriani. Only four are signed as theirs, but the Millard copy's "Proposals" credit them with:

> two most rare and valuable Gems—one in No. 2, is the Cupid and Satyr, belonging to the Collection of his Grace the Duke of Marlborough [i.e., pl. 10]; and in No. 4, is the Sacrifice, in the Collection of his Eminence the Cardinal of York, at Rome [pl. 20]. In No. 5, a fine etching of Apollo in his Chariot [pl. 21]. In No. 6, the masterly engraving of Spring [pl. 30, see illustration]. In No. 8, a fine engraving of Autumn [pl. 40]. And in No. 11, a superior Engraving of Winter [pl. 55].

Both Bartolozzi and Cipriani were much better known than Pergolesi, which is why he devotes so much space to itemizing their involvement; and why the second announcement bound in with the Millard copy concludes with the promise that "N.B. In No. 15 or 16, will be introduced a superior Engraving of Summer, designed by Cipriani, and engraved by Bartolozzi, R.A. Engraver to her Majesty." Sadly, this plate, which would have completed Cipriani's cycle of the seasons, was never part of the published series. Whether it, or others related to Pergolesi's suite, can be traced through the collections of Cipriani's designs published after his death, in December 1785, remains to be explored.

Michel Angelo Pergolesi. *A Great Variety of Original Designs of Vases, Figures, Medallions....* Designs for decorative panels, with a vignette of Spring. "G.B. Cipriani del." "F. Bartolozzi Sculp." 1985.61.2611

The tondo portrait of the 1st duke of Northumberland on plate 56 bis is signed, very faintly, "Drawn by P. Violet. Engraved by I. I. Van den Berge." Pierre Violet arrived in London in 1789 and became part of Bartolozzi's circle; Ignatius Joseph Van den Berghe was one of the latter's pupils. G. B.

Bibliography

Harris, E., and N. Savage. *British Architectural Books and Writers 1556–1785*. Cambridge, 1990

Harris, J. *A Catalogue of British Drawings for Architecture, Decoration, Sculpture and Landscape Gardening 1550–1900 in American Collections*. Upper Saddle River, N.J., 1971

Survey of London. Ed. F. H. W. Sheppard. Vol. 31 (The Parish of St. James Westminster). London, 1963

56

Claude Perrault (1613–1688)

A Treatise of the Five Orders of Columns In Architecture, Viz. Toscan, Doric, Ionic, Corinthian and Composite. Wherein The Proportions and Characters of the Members Of their several Pedestals, Columns and Entablatures, Are distinctly consider'd, with respect to the Practice of the Antients and Moderns. Also A most Natural, Easie and Practicable Method laid down, for determining the most minute Part in all the Orders, without a Fraction. To which is Annex'd, A Discourse concerning Pilasters: And Of Several Abuses introduc'd into Architecture. Engraven on Six Folio Plates of the several Orders, adorn'd with Twenty-Four Borders, as many Initial Letters, and a like number of Tail-Pieces, by John Sturt. Written in French by Claude Perrault, Of the Royal Academy of Paris, Author of ye Celebrated Comment On Vitruvius. Made English by John James of Greenwich

London: printed by Benj. Motte. Sold by John Sturt, 1708

1983.49.65

Folio: 355 × 223 (14 × 8 3/4)

Pagination [iv], XXI, [3], 42, 45–131, [5] pp., added engraved title plate, engraved title plate, engraved dedication, [9] engraved plates

Edition First English edition

Text pp. [I–IV] Perrault's dedication to Colbert; I–XXI preface; [XXII] table of chapters; [XXIII–XXIV] blank; I–42 text of Part I "Of Things common to all the Orders"; 45–131 text of Part II "Of Things appertaining to each Order"; [132] blank; [133] errata; [134–136] advertisement "Books and Plates engraven and sold by John Sturt . . ."

Illustrations 12 engraved plates, with occasional etching, as follows: [1] added title plate "A Treatise of the Five Orders Of Columns in Architecture . . ."; [2] title plate (with vignette); [3] John James' engraved dedication to Thomas, earl of Pembroke and Montgomery; [4–5] list of subscribers; [6] illustration of all 5 orders, with separately engraved tailpiece, "To Face Page. 92."; [7–12] illustrations of the orders numbered I–VI. In addition, the text includes unnumbered illustrations and etched and engraved initials, head- and tailpieces. All unsigned

Binding Recent half calf, gilt- and blind-tooled, marbled boards

Provenance Initials "E. R." on title

References ESTC t114390; Fowler 248; Harris and Savage 700

THERE WAS NOT much architectural literature available in England in the seventeenth century, and much that was available was of French origin: Roland Fréart's *A Parallel of the Antient Architecture with the Modern*, of 1664; Alexandre Francine's *A New Book of Architecture* and Julien Mauclerc's *A New Treatise of Architecture*, both of 1669; and Pierre Le Muet's *The Art of Fair Building*, of 1670 and 1675. Undoubtedly, the most challenging of these was the *Parallel*, a fourth edition of which was still being issued in 1733, translated by John Evelyn, who tried also to promote the translation of Claude Perrault's *Les dix livres d'architecture de Vitruve*, of 1673, and A. C. D'Aviler's *Cours d'architecture*, of 1691. Nothing came of Evelyn's efforts, though there was evidently a sustained interest in French ideas. *An Abridgement of the Architecture of Vitruvius*, by Perrault, was published in 1692 and, in 1708, another of his works, *A Treatise of the Five Orders of Columns in Architecture*, was issued. This was translated by John James (c. 1672–1746), remembered as the architect of St. George's, Hanover Square. James was a surprisingly competent linguist, already in his mid-thirties, but not much active as an architect at that time. Between 1707 and 1712 he produced translations not only of Perrault's *Treatise*, but also of Andrea Pozzo's *Rules and Examples of Perspective* (1707) and A. J. Dezallier d'Argenville's *The Theory and Practice of Gardening* (1717). Perrault's *Treatise* and Pozzo's *Perspective* were both promoted and sold by the engraver John Sturt, who was later to be responsible also for Sébastien Leclerc's *A Treatise of Architecture*, of 1723 and 1724 (with which the printer of the first two works, Benjamin Motte, was also involved). Pozzo's *Perspective* was by far the grandest architectural work to have been published in England and was regarded as a tour de force of engraving (if infinitely less impressive than the original). Perrault's *Treatise* was a book of an altogether different kind, provocative and controversial, replete with ideas, though it was probably as a handbook on the orders that Sturt took it up. The selection was no doubt made by James.

Perrault was already well known in England, both as the designer of the great east front of the Louvre and as the translator of Vitruvius. The reaction that his works stirred among the members of the *Académie d'Architecture* cannot have been unfamiliar to architects in England: Christopher Wren, a colleague of James, was certainly familiar with Perrault's ideas, if not entirely sympathetic to them.

Perrault, trained as a doctor and scientist, believed that the architecture of the seventeenth century should be superior to that of antiquity, though he saw clearly enough that it was not. He thought, therefore, to purify and reinvigorate the classical tradition, to lay bare its sources, and to construct a theory and practice of architecture on these foundations. His translation of Vitruvius, an enlarged edition of which was issued in 1684, together with his *Ordonnance des cinq espèces de colonnes selon la méthode des anciennes* of 1683, were intended to establish new rules and new norms in architecture, though many of the rules had been laid down already in his *Abrégé des dix livres d'architecture de Vitruve*, of 1674. There he demonstrated that architecture found its model in the primitive hut, passing thus "de l'imitation du naturel à celle de l'artificiel" (p. 23). And thus a system of design evolved. He thought that architects, working in conformity with the accepted rules, would develop and evolve new forms. He did not hesitate to introduce some rules of his own devising. Style was not static. At the end of the *Treatise* he devoted a section to abuses in architecture. Palladio, he noted, had listed four—brackets for supports, broken pediments, extended cornices, and engaged columns—he himself added ten more, all relating to the orders. But all could be sanctioned in time. Habit and custom made most things acceptable if they were introduced with tact. He argued for the sanctioning of the coupled columns used on the Louvre. He believed that such a process of change and evolution within the bounds of tradition was fully justified because the concept of beauty could not be fixed. He rejected—and he was probably the first to do so in a treatise—the Renaissance concept of an absolute, universal harmony, man in the image of God, with the parts of the body related by mathematical ratios to the proportions of architecture and the harmonies of music: the cosmos as one. Architectural proportions, Perrault insisted, were not analogous to musical harmonies, they could be changed without shocking the senses. His attack was directed, in particular, against René Ouvrard's *Architecture harmonique*, of 1679. Though there was, Perrault was prepared to concede, some foundation for beauty.

There were, he held, two types of beauty, positive and arbitrary—a notion widely upheld by French Cartesians. Positive beauty in architecture, Perrault wrote, was based on the quality of materials, precision and neatness of execution, size, magnificence, and symmetry. Arbitrary beauty relied on proportional relationships, form and shape. These were regulated by taste alone, fancy if you like. They might all be changed. Though it was precisely in his ability to control and order these particular aspects of architecture that the true architect was to be distinguished from his lesser brethren. The members of the *Académie d'Architecture* were shocked by these ideas. They did not grasp them entirely. They were confused, moreover, because though Perrault rejected the system of proportions sanctioned by Vitruvius, he proposed one of his own, based on a simple module, one-third the diameter of the column, rather than the usual half, and thus readily applicable to all parts of each of the five orders. His proposals smacked of an arbitrary authoritarianism at odds with his basic tenets. What he wanted though, was a practical working solution, something that would relate to existing standards of taste, but that could be used by even the humblest of builders. In a comparison of all the established systems of proportioning he tried to establish a working mean.

The intricate systems of proportioning evolved by the architects of the Renaissance were clearly Perrault's bugbear. "For 'tis hardly to be imagine'd," he wrote in the preface to the *Ordonnance*, "what a superstitious Reverence Architects have for those Work we call Antique, in which, they admire every thing, but principally the Mystery of their Proportions." Yet, like Fréart before him, who also upheld Greece as the "divine" source of architecture, he was deeply concerned to

Claude Perrault. *A Treatise of the Five Orders of Columns.* Plate 1. 1983.49.65

establish the authority of Greek architecture as established by Vitruvius. There were, he noted, three modes of architecture: the *Ancient*, as enshrined in Vitruvius; the *Antique*, which could be studied in Roman buildings; and the *Modern*, which had been propagated by architects and their publishers for 120 years. What he wished to see reestablished was the *Ancient*, the Greek style of Vitruvius. What he had in mind was an architecture that was clear-cut and pure, as in the paintings of Poussin.

The proposals for the *Treatise of the Five Orders* were published on 19 July 1702 in the *Post Boy*. The work was to be sold by subscription, 2s 6d down, 10s on delivery. Two hundred and sixty-nine subscribers are listed, many of them building craftsmen, but among them the architects Henry Aldrich, Nicholas Hawksmoor, James Smith (in Scotland), John Talman, and John Vanbrugh, and also Richard Boyle, the earl of Burlington, then no more than fourteen years old. The book was published at the end of March 1707. Perrault's dedication to Colbert was included, but there was a new dedication also to Thomas, earl of Pembroke and Montgomery, father of the architect earl. The frontispiece was adapted from plate 60 of Pozzo's *Perspective*. The title page included a vignette illustrating the story of Orpheus drawing the stones of Thebes into place with his lyre (a fiddle is shown). The six plates of the orders illustrated in Perrault's original were reproduced, as were the minor illustrations dealing with proportioning systems, but a whole range of vignettes was added, copied from the *Divers suites de figures, chevaux et paysages dessinées et gravées par le Clerc pour l'instruction de M. le Duc de Bourgogne*. There is a proof copy of the *Treatise* in the library of Worcester College, Oxford.

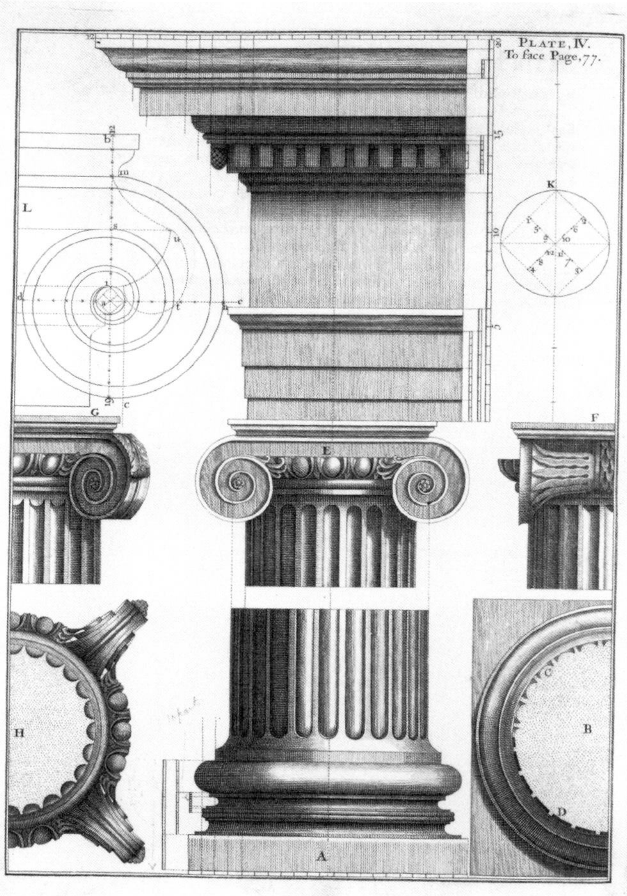

Claude Perrault. *A Treatise of the Five Orders of Columns*. Plate 4. 1983.49.65

Perrault's *Treatise* provided a solid ground for any thinking on architecture in the ensuing years. Roger North and Christopher Wren knew it already, in the French, but it was taken up by other theorists, in particular after the second edition was issued in 1722. Thomas Rowland quoted from Perrault in *A General Treatise of Architecture*, of 1732; Isaac Ware relied heavily upon him for ideas, even if he often traduced Perrault's intentions, in the *Complete Body of Architecture*, of 1756, while William Chambers adapted many of his notions for *A Treatise on Civil Architecture*, of 1759, even more perhaps, for the revised edition, *A Treatise on the Decorative Part of Civil Architecture*, of 1791. John Soane still thought it necessary to read Perrault when he was preparing his lectures for the Royal Academy in the early years of the nineteenth century. R. M.

Bibliography

Harris, E., and N. Savage. *British Architectural Books and Writers 1556–1785*. Cambridge, 1990

Herrmann, W. *The Theory of Claude Perrault*. London, 1973

Préaud, M. *Bibliothèque Nationale. Département des Estampes. Inventaire du fonds français. Graveurs de XVIIe siècle. T8 Sébastien Leclerc*. Paris, 1980

57

John Plaw (c. 1745–1820)

Rural Architecture; Or Designs, From The Simple Cottage To The Decorated Villa; Including Some Which Have Been Executed. By John Plaw, Architect and Surveyor. Etched And Shaded In Aqua-Tinta, On Sixty-Two Plates

London: published by J. and J. Taylors [i.e., Taylor], 1794

1985.61.2629

Quarto: 270 × 211 (10 5/8 × 8 3/8)

Pagination 8, viii pp., aquatint frontispiece, 60 [i.e., 61] aquatint plates

Edition Third edition

Text pp. [1] title page (verso blank); [3]–7 list of plates; 8 author's note; [i]–viii list of subscribers, ending with imprint "Printed by H. Reynell . . ."

Illustrations Aquatint frontispiece printed in sepia, signed by the author "J. P. Sc." and described in the "Contents" as "The Frontispiece, designed by the Author, the Figures drawn by Mr. Deare, Sculptor at Rome; the Landscape by Mr. Barrett. The Subject is Taste, accompanying Rural Simplicity, and pointing to . . . The Lake of Winandermere; on the largest Island in which, is built a circular Villa after a Design of the Author's; the Plan, Elevations, and Section, are in this Work." Another unnumbered plate, not called for in the letterpress list, shows the "Plan, Elevation and Sections, of a Hermitage, in the Garden of the Green-Park Lodge," drawn and engraved by Plaw. This is printed on laid paper of smaller dimensions, with Whatman's countermark, and is referred to by Archer as plate 1*. In addition there are 60 plates numbered I–LX, all printed in sepia. In this copy, the first has some hand-coloring and all have tissue guards. They are signed as engraved and designed by Plaw and 4 are additionally signed by Francis Jukes as aquatint artist (pls. XLVII, XLIX, LIII, LV)

Binding Contemporary marbled boards, morocco spine and corners renewed, red morocco label. Uncut. With a 4-page version of the Taylors' *A Catalogue of Modern Books on Architecture* bound in, folding

Provenance Later ownership inscription of J. A. Allan

References Berlin Cat. 2296; Berlin (1977) OS 2296; ESTC t102012

ALTOGETHER UNUSUAL and surprising books on rural architecture had been published earlier in the eighteenth century, notably Daniel Garrett's *Designs, and Estimates, of Farm Houses* of 1747 and William Halfpenny's *Twelve Beautiful Designs for Farm-houses* of 1750, but John Plaw's *Rural Architecture, Consisting of Designs, from the Simple Cottage, to the More Decorated Villa* initiated a new style and format for architectural publication when it first appeared in 1785. The earlier books were practical in intent. Plaw viewed the buildings he designed as part of a picturesque landscape. He was clearly influenced by the writings of Thomas Whately and other such theorists of picturesque landscape. He depicted his buildings in landscape settings, with the natural forms relating directly to those of the architecture. He was the first to do this consistently in an architectural publication. He was also the first to use aquatint for a publication of this sort, grading his lights and shadows with a freedom and variety hitherto unequaled. The buildings he illustrated—thirty designs in all—were mostly domestic and mostly modest. The villas, thirteen in all, were chastely classical, symmetrically composed (though some have projecting wings or bays); the cottages, five in all, include some of the thatched type, but nothing unruly. The very format of the book reflected his decorous aims; it was a thin quarto volume, quite unlike the grand folios that most architects of the period designed to advertise their abilities. Plaw set the model for villa and cottage pattern books that became a feature of architectural publishing in England for the next fifty years.

Not much is known of Plaw. He was born about 1745 and seems to have begun work as a bricklayer. In 1763, when he was awarded a prize by the Society of Arts for a drawing of the Banqueting House in Whitehall, he was described as "architect and master builder in Westminster." He later became a member of the Incorporated Society of Artists, and rose to its presidency, before its dissolution in 1791. He moved to Southampton a few years later, where he prepared some ambitious residential schemes, unexecuted, and erected

John Plaw. *Rural Architecture.* Plate 28. 1985.61.2629

John Plaw. *Rural Architecture.* Frontispiece. 1985.61.2629

barracks. Around 1819 he emigrated to Canada, settling in Charlottestown, Prince Edward Island, where he died, on 24 May 1820.

Several of the designs illustrated in *Rural Architecture* are described as commissions for specific sites and specific clients, though few seem to have been built. However, Belle Isle, a great domed circular house erected in 1774 and 1775 for Thomas English, on an island in Lake Windermere, Westmorland, illustrated by six plates (pls. 25–30), was a triumph of sorts, unparalleled in English architecture, imitated years later, in 1828, in Switzerland, in the country house of La Gordanne, near Perroy, on Lake Geneva, attributed to Giovanni Salucci. It is even possible that Belle Isle served as an inspiration for Thomas Jefferson's Rotunda, at the University of Virginia, of about 1822, though this was scarcely domestic.

To the third edition of *Rural Architecture*, described here, a plate was added illustrating another of Plaw's executed works, a hermitage in the grounds of the Green Park Lodge, in London. Howard Colvin has listed a handful of additional works by Plaw, mostly modest; St. Mary's in Paddington apart, he seems to have been none too active as an architect. As an author of pattern books, however, he was a great success. *Rural Architecture*, which was printed first for the author, with only thirty plates, in 1785, was enlarged to sixty-one plates in 1790, and sold by I. and J. Taylor, who published the third edition of 1794, with sixty-two plates (at two guineas), and also those of 1796, 1802, and 1804. Plaw was responsible also for two later books of the same kind, the *Ferme ornée, or Rural Improvements*, of 1795, and *Sketches for Country Houses, Villas and Rural Dwellings*, of 1800, both of which ran to five or more editions.

The text provided in *Rural Architecture* extends to no more than brief descriptions of the plates, but Plaw gave some hint of his aims in the frontispiece to the volume, an arcadian scene, including a domed rotunda on a lake, viewed by two figures, one fashionably attired, the other simply dressed: "The Subject is Taste, accompanying Rural Simplicity, and pointing to one of the most beautiful Scenes this Country can boast of viz. The Lake of Winandermere; on the largest Island in which, is built a circular Villa after a Design of the Author's; the Plan, Elevations, and Section are in this Work."

Plaw's subscribers, as might be expected, were for the most part surveyors and craftsmen, though the names of John Gandon, Henry Holland, James Playfair, and Thomas Sandby also appear. R. M.

Bibliography

Colvin, H. *Biographical Dictionary of British Architects 1660–1840*. London, 1978

Wrightson, P. *The Small English House. A Catalogue of Books.* London, 1977

58

Andrea Pozzo (1642–1709)

Rules and Examples of Perspective Proper For Painters and Architects, etc. In English and Latin: Containing a most easie and expeditious Method to Delineate in Perspective All Designs relating to Architecture, After A New Manner, Wholly free from the Confusion of Occult Lines: By That Great Master Thereof, Andrea Pozzo, Soc. Jes. Engraven in 105 ample folio Plates, and adorn'd with 200 Initial Letters to the Explanatory Discourses: Printed from Copper-Plates on ye best Paper By John Sturt. Done into English from the Original Printed at Rome 1693 in Lat. and Ital. By Mr John James of Greenwich.

London: printed by Benj. Motte. Sold by John Sturt, 1707

1983.49.80

Folio: 403 × 254 (16 × 10)

Pagination [122] pp., engraved frontispiece, [2] engraved title plates, [102] engraved plates

Edition First English edition

Text (parallel Latin and English) pp. [1–3] dedication to Queen Anne; [4] blank; [5–8] preface to this translation; [9] "Monita ad Tyrones," "Advice to Beginners"; [10] "Ad Lectorem Perspectivae studiosum," "To The Lovers of Perspective"; [11] approbation signed "Chr. Wren, J. Vanbrugh, N. Hawksmoor"; [12] engraved illustration of drawing instruments; [13] half-title "Pozzo's Architecture In Perspective"; [14–114] description of the plates; [115–118] further explanation of the first 12 figures; [119] "Respondetur objectioni factae circum punctum oculi opticum," "An Answer to the Objection made about the Point of Sight in Perspective"; [120–121] index; [122] blank

Illustrations Engraved frontispiece, 2 engraved titles in English (as above) and Latin ("Perspectiva Pictorum Et Architectorum, Andræ Putei . . ."), and an engraved list of subscribers (bound after approbation). There are also 101 engraved plates numbered I–C (including LIIIA and LIIIB)

Binding Recent calf, blind-tooled

References ESTC t114554; Fowler 252; Harris and Savage 703

PERSPECTIVA
PICTORUM
ET
ARCHITECTORUM,
ANDREÆ PUTEI,
E SOCIETATE JESU.
In quâ docetur Modus expeditissimus Delineandi
Opticè omnia quę pertinent ad Architecturam.

LONDINI:
Juxta Exemplar ROMÆ excusum, MDCXCIII.
Ex Sculpturâ Joannis Sturt, et ejusd. Curâ adornata:
TYPIS Benj. Motte, MDCCVII.

Andrea Pozzo. *Rules and Examples of Perspective Proper.* Latin title page. 1983.49.80

THE FIRST VOLUME of Andrea Pozzo's *Perspectiva pictorum et architectorum* was published in Rome in 1693. The work was a considerable success, but Pozzo's commissions to paint the ceiling of the church of San Ignazio in Rome and to design an altar to Ignatius of Loyola occupied him until the end of the century, so the second volume was not published until 1700. By this time the first volume had been widely disseminated throughout Europe and won considerable fame for its author. The text and illustrations of the two volumes form a complete manual of *quadratura* painting and its elements—perspective, scenography, fresco painting, architecture, and interior decoration. The popularity of the work, however, owes as much to the beauty of the etched and engraved illustrations as to the merits of Pozzo's method. (As a theorist Pozzo was not universally acclaimed; Thomas Malton had harsh words for him, and considered the second volume greatly superior to the first.) A second edition of *Perspectiva pictorum et architectorum* was published in 1702, with a revised description of the first twelve plates and an extra folded plate in volume one, showing the completed ceiling of San Ignazio, a stunning piece of work of which the author was rightly proud.

Although the work was relatively well known in England at the turn of the century, it seems that John Sturt (1658–1730) had only seen the first edition when he decided, around 1705, to publish his own edition of volume one, with an English translation of the original Latin text. Sturt had connections with the Office of Works and was among the most accomplished engravers of his period. As the *DNB* notes, he "engraved the Lord's Prayer within the space of a silver halfpenny, the Creed in that of a silver penny, and an elegy on Queen Mary on so small a scale that it could be inserted in a finger ring." He was responsible for engraving, and often publishing, a series of writing manuals from 1683, and designed the calligraphic title plate for *Vitruvius Britannicus*. In 1697, in collaboration with Bernard Lens, he founded one of the earliest drawing schools in London, where he taught, among others, the distinguished engraver George Bickham; the school was still in existence in 1710. However, Sturt's greatest achievement as an engraver is generally thought to be his edition of *The Book of Common Prayer*, engraved on 188 silver plates and published in 1717.

Sturt based his edition of Pozzo very closely on the 1693 volume, taking some two years to complete his copies of the original etchings. Pozzo's text was little more than a series of explanatory captions to the illustrations, and these were rendered into English by John James, who went on to produce more substantial translations of Claude Perrault's *Ordonnance* in 1708 and Dézallier d'Argenville's *Théorie et la pratique du Jardinage*

Andrea Pozzo. *Rules and Examples of Perspective Proper.* Plate XCI. 1983.49.80

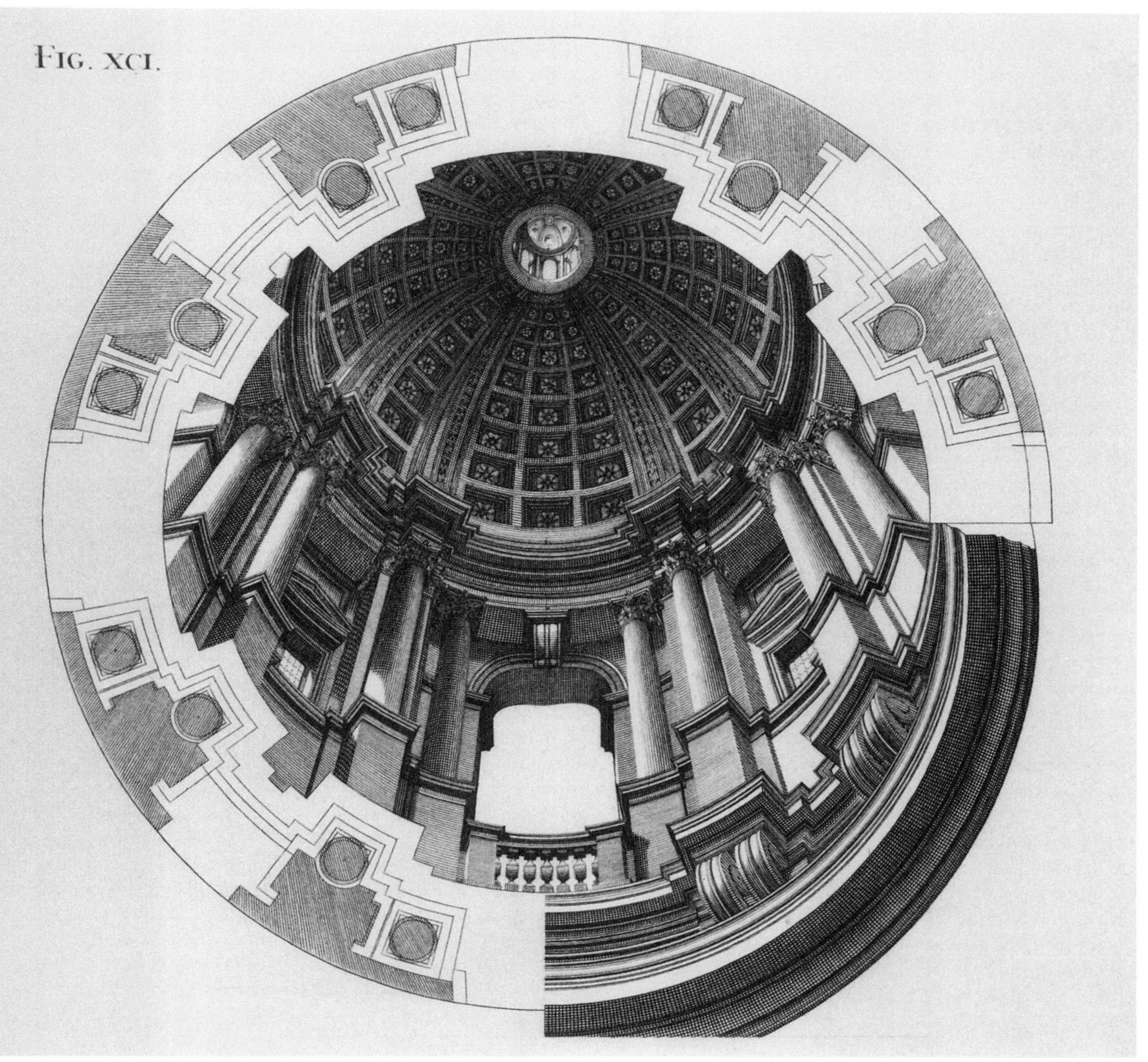

in 1712. In early 1706 the work on the plates was sufficiently advanced for Sturt to issue a single-sheet prospectus, in conjunction with the London bookseller John Nutt. This contained "Proposals for engraving and printing a large volume in folio of architecture and perspective, in English and Latin . . ." and for publishing the work by subscription, a method never before attempted for an architectural book. By mid-November 1706 Nutt had apparently dropped out, for an announcement in *The Post Boy* recorded that seventy plates were now ready for inspection at the offices of Sturt, Joseph Smart, and others in London, and at printsellers in Oxford and Cambridge. Sturt was painfully aware of the delay in publication, which had evidently been announced some months earlier, and felt constrained to present his subscribers with a complementary engraving in an attempt to retain their goodwill. The price of his Pozzo was to be thirty shillings "in sheets," with ten shillings to be paid in advance and the remainder on delivery. This was a staggering price in 1706, and the work was the most expensive architectural book to be published in Britain by this date. Notices continued to appear in the press in an attempt to attract additional subscribers and to keep interest alive while the copying of the plates continued. Complete copies were promised for 19 December 1706, with formal publication announced for January of the following year. The book still failed to appear, however, probably due to the continued failure to raise sufficient subscriptions to meet the substantial costs of copperplates and printing. Sturt struggled on through the first half of 1707 and seems to have made a final push in the autumn, when he invoked the magical names of his Office of Works comrades Christopher Wren, Nicholas Hawksmoor, and John Vanbrugh, who all signed an approbation for his edition of Pozzo. Notice of this prestigious recommendation is first found in the Stationers' Company Term Catalogue for November 1707, which appears to have been the date at which copies of the book were finally available (although the first advertisement omitted Wren's name, which was added to a corrected entry for Easter and Trinity 1708). Whether this approbation had any effect in promoting the work is uncertain, but that Sturt had managed to publish the work at all was testimony to his belief in the project and efforts to gather subscribers from among his friends at the Office of Works and in the book trade; indeed, it is likely that without these two groups, who make up a good proportion of the list of subscribers, the work would never have been completed. As it was, it seems improbable that Sturt covered his costs, which must have been considerable. He had hopes of publishing an English edition of the second volume, but the problems he had experienced with volume one led him to abandon this enterprise. (He did go on to publish the English editions of Perrault's *Ordonnance*, in 1708, and Sébastien Leclerc's *Traité d'architecture*, in 1723–1724.)

When it finally appeared, *Rules and Examples of Perspective* was a triumph of the engraver's art. Sturt's copies of Pozzo's etchings had all the illusionistic brilliance of the originals, but with the added refinement of plates produced more consistently with the burin than with the etcher's needle. In addition to the engraved copies of Pozzo's etchings, the work is notable for a series of large engraved or etched initials specially designed by Sturt. He produced a total of 103 different initials, all historiated with allegorical, mythological, or topographical scenes; by repeating some of them, and by reworking others after printing to contain different initial letters, he used them in 210 different positions in the work (21 of the initials reappeared in 1708 in Sturt's edition of Perrault, along with one of the plates). Despite the brilliance of the engravings, it was Sturt's great misfortune, or misjudgment, to publish the work at a time when the high baroque of Pozzo's designs was in the last pale glimmer of its vogue. However, there was sufficient interest in the book for Sturt to attempt to publish a second edition of his Pozzo, through the London booksellers John Senex, Robert Gosling, William Innys, John Osborn, and Thomas Longman. This new edition is undated, but can be fixed with some certainty no earlier than 1724, when Longman first began trading in Paternoster Row, and to before 1732, when Innys died. The most likely date seems to be 1725, since Longman was Osborn's apprentice and the two are only recorded as publishing together in this year. This date is further suggested by the probability that the work was launched on the back of Sturt's edition of Leclerc, issued in 1723 and 1724. Many of Sturt's initials were included in the new edition, with a series of small numbers etched onto the coppers, suggesting that they had appeared in the interim in some kind of catalogue or specimen of his work. The second edition appears not to have been a great success, however, and few copies have survived, suggesting a limited circulation. P. W. N.

Bibliography

Carboneri, N. *Andrea Pozzo architetto 1642–1709*. Trento, 1961

De Feo, V. *Andrea Pozzo: architettura e illusione*. Rome, 1988

De Feo, V., and V. Martinelli, eds. *Andrea Pozzo*. Milan, 1996

Kerber, B. *Andrea Pozzo*. Berlin and New York, 1971

Marini, R. *Andrea Pozzo pittore 1642–1709*. Trento, 1959

Russo, M. *Andrea Pozzo a Montepulciano*. Montepulciano, 1979

Wittkower, R. *Art and Architecture in Italy 1600 to 1750*. 3d ed. Harmondsworth, 1973

59

Augustus Charles Pugin (1768–1832)

Historical And Descriptive Essays Accompanying A Series Of Engraved Specimens Of The Architectural Antiquities Of Normandy. Edited By John Britton . . . The Subjects Measured And Drawn By Augustus Pugin, Architect . . . And Engraved By John And Henry Le Keux

London: printed for M. A. Nattali, 1833

NGA Lib. Rare Book: N44P9788A351833

Quarto: 310 × 245 (12 1/4 × 9 3/4)

Pagination viii, 64 pp., added etched title plate, [73] etched plates (6 double-page)

(*Note*: This copy is extra-illustrated with hand-colored duplicates of the final 2 plates)

Edition Second edition

Text pp. [i] title page; [ii] printer's imprint "Leicester: Printed By T. Combe, Junior, Gallowtree-Gate"; pp. [iii] dedication to Jeffry Wyatville, dated 20 June 1828 (verso blank); [v]–viii "The Editor's Preface"; [1]–4 list of plates; [5]–24 "Introduction: Embracing A Brief Review Of The Characteristics Of Christian Architecture In Normandy"; [25]–47 "An Essay On The Architectural Antiquities of Caen . . ."; [48]–59 "An Essay On The Architectural Antiquities of Rouen . . . ," "The Church At Caudbeck"; 60–64 "Account Of The Cathedral Of Bayeux," "Tower Of The Church Of St. Loup," printer's colophon

Illustrations Added etched title plate by John Le Keux after A. C. Pugin reading "Pugin and Le Keux's Specimens of the Architectural Antiquities of Normandy," with an imprint unaltered from the first edition (London, J. Britton, 1827); plus 73 etched plates including in this copy 2 hand-colored duplicates of the final 2 plates. Plates [1–3], [8], [15], [18–21], [30], [34–36], [39–40], [43], [45], [48–51], [54–55], [58], [60], [62–63], [65–66], [68], [72–73] are signed as etched by John Le Keux after A. C. Pugin; plates [4–6], [9], [13], [28], [31], [37–38], [41], [44], [52–53], [56], [59], [61], [69–71] by Henry Le Keux after Pugin; plates [7] and [32] by John Le Keux after G. B. Moore under Pugin's direction; plates [10], [14], [22], [33] by Henry Le Keux after Francis Arundale under Pugin's direction; plates [11–12] by John Le Keux after G. W. Shaw under Pugin's direction; plates [16–17] by John Le Keux after Pugin and John Willis; plate [23] by John Le Keux after T. T. Bury under Pugin's direction; plates [24–25], [46], [64] by John Le Keux after Francis Arundale under Pugin's direction; plate [26] by Henry Le Keux after G. B. Moore; plates [27], [47] by Henry Le Keux after T. T. Bury under Pugin's direction; plate [29] by Henry Le Keux after G. B. Moore under Pugin's direction; plate [42] by John Le Keux after John Willis under Pugin's direction; plate [57] by Henry Le Keux after Benjamin Ferrey under Pugin's direction; and plate [67] by John Le Keux, "Drawn by J. Kearnan, from measurements by A. Pugin"

Binding Nineteenth-century brown half morocco, marbled boards

References Fowler 257 (1827–1828 ed.); RIBA, *Early Printed Books*, 421

The reputation of Augustus Charles Pugin is overshadowed by that of his son, Augustus Welby Pugin, the most zealous advocate of a Gothic revival in the early nineteenth century. But though A. C. Pugin is often identified with the Gothic movement, he was not at first much concerned with that style. Nor did he first establish his reputation as a propagandist of Gothic.

The family was of Swiss origin, but he came to England from France, as an émigré, sometime before 27 March 1792 when, at the age of twenty-four, he entered the schools of the Royal Academy as a student of painting. He was involved at this time with John Nash, in Wales, engaged in theatrical work. But on 27 January 1802 he married Catherine Welby, the daughter of a barrister, of Lincolnshire, and in the same year moved into a house in Edwards Street, near Portman Square, London. He continued to be involved with Nash, though they were busy then on the Isle of Wight. However, Pugin was intent to establish himself as an illustrator and was beginning to experiment with aquatint. In 1805 a book of views by J. C. Nattes of Bath, Bristol, and other West Country towns was announced, with Pugin named as the etcher. The book was never published. But in the same year he and Nattes provided drawings for the sixteen plates of *A Tour of Oxford*, engraved by a handful of artists, some of them French. During the following years he prepared prints of public events—Lord Nelson's funeral, Lord Melville's trial, etc.—for Rudolph Ackermann, another immigrant, from Prussia on this occasion, who had opened a print shop in the Strand in 1796. This collaboration marked the beginning of Pugin's success, but he sprang to fame as the artist responsible, together with Thomas Rowlandson, for the watercolors reproduced in aquatint for another of Ackermann's ventures, the *Microcosm of London*, which began to appear in 1808. In January of the following year Ackermann initiated *The Repository of Arts, Literature, Commerce, Manufactures, Fashions and Politics*, a monthly publication of four aquatint plates, that was to continue until 1829. Pugin did most of the plates of furniture. For Ackermann he prepared plates also for *A History of the University of Oxford* (1813–1814) and *A History of the University of Cambridge* (1815–1816). There was more to follow. Some of the plates of *The Repository of Arts* were later gathered together and issued as independent volumes, nine in all, two of these consisting of plates by Pugin: J. B. Papworth's *Select Views of London*, of 1816, and Pugin's *Gothic Furniture*, of 1828. These confirmed Pugin's reputation.

But already, in 1818, Pugin had established himself as an independent dealer in prints and books. He had also begun to work for John Britton, the foremost publisher of English topographical works, contributing in this same year some of the views of York Cathedral for Britton's series, *Cathedral Antiquities*. These plates were perhaps commissioned as a result of Pugin's first endeavor to promote Gothic architecture, the *Specimens of Gothic Architecture consisting of Doors, Windows, Buttresses, Pinnacles, etc. with the Measurements Selected From Ancient Buildings at Oxford*, a sheaf of sixty-one plates drawn by himself and Frederick Mackenzie, another artist employed by both Britton and Ackermann, all of the plates, Phoebe Stanton has argued, etched by Pugin. This book was issued in 1816 by Josiah Taylor, the leading publisher of architectural books. Pugin was later to discount the work as the drawings, many of them in perspective, did not provide information sufficiently precise to serve for imitation. His first attempt to provide a practical handbook for designers and architects was the *Specimens of Gothic Architecture*—an altogether separate work—announced in 1821. This consisted of sixty plates, all but one, by Mackenzie, drawn by Pugin, engraved by E. Turrell, J. Cleghorn, G. Gladwin, and others. The examples illustrated, in measured drawings, were all English, with twelve plates devoted to Lincoln. Pugin's preface, "Remarks on Gothic Architecture; and on Modern Imitations," and the plates, issued in three parts, appeared as announced, in 1821, but the commentaries to the plates and, in particular, the "Glossary of Terms," written by the Lincoln architect and antiquary E. J. Willson, whom Pugin must have encountered during visits to his wife's family in Lincolnshire, were delayed.

The "Glossary of Terms" was distributed to subscribers only in 1822. Willson's contribution, however, based on a depth of scholarship and an unusual judiciousness of observation, was worth waiting for, as it represented a major contribution to Gothic studies. In particular, Willson, a Roman Catholic, first gave vent to the notion that the Reformation was the prime cause for the corruption of Gothic. He aimed at a revival of the style, but not at thoughtless imitation; "the architect," he noted, "must endeavour to *think* in the manner of the original inventors."

The book, somewhat surprisingly, was dedicated to Nash. The publishers were Taylor, A. C. Pugin, and John Britton. Even before its completion it was acclaimed, in *The Quarterly Review* of April–July 1821, in a notable survey of publications on Gothic by Francis Palgrave (ex Cohen), who had recently married the daughter of Dawson Turner, one of the pioneers of Norman studies. Pugin was stirred to announce a second volume in his preface. This volume, dedicated to Robert Smirke, with a preface by Pugin and commentaries by Willson as before, with fifty-four plates of measured examples of Gothic architecture, all but two of them (the Hôtel de Guise, at Calais) English, was complete by December 1822. Taylor's premises and all his stock were destroyed in a fire on the night of 23 November 1822, but the Pugin plates were, luckily, not there at the time. Some of the texts for the two volumes were lost, but these were soon reprinted and a second edition issued in 1823.

Despite his evident involvement with the Gothic cause, Pugin was busy on other fronts. He was doing perspective and other drawings for Nash in these years. And already, in 1822, he was preparing drawings and plates for *Illustrations of the Public Buildings of London*, another joint publishing venture with Taylor and Britton, the first volume of which was complete by April 1825, the second in 1828. But, as in all his dealings with Britton, he felt frustrated and cheated. Writing in the *Civil Engineer and Architect's Journal* in August 1840, long after Pugin's death, the critic William Henry Leeds (himself no friend to Britton) expressed something of amazement to find Britton's name linked firmly to Pugin's: "an association that is almost enough to make the latter start from his grave, for in his life-time the association between them was of the most cat-and-dog kind; nor was P. at all sparing of most highly flavoured epithets towards his quondam partner." Their discord erupted first with the publication of the *Specimens of the Architectural Antiquities of Normandy*.

With the ending of the Napoleonic Wars travel in France became once again possible. In September 1817 Pugin went to Paris with his wife and their five-year-old son, A. W. Pugin. They returned again in 1819, 1821, and 1824, when they stayed for the first time in Rouen. They might have traveled to France in the intervening years too. For Pugin had even earlier formed the habit of undertaking late summer expeditions, whether in England or France, to sketch and measure medieval antiquities, with his assistants and students. Thomas Kearnan and Christopher Moore are to be numbered among the first of these, being associated with him from 1816, at least, though it was not until 1819 that Pugin formed something of a school for draftsmen and engravers. Their expeditions were rambunctious affairs and were a formative influence in the development of the tastes and abilities of his son.

The drawings for the *Specimens of the Architectural Antiquities of Normandy* were begun in Rouen, in the autumn of 1824. Others were done in 1825, 1826, and 1827. The book was published in two parts, the first a sheaf of seventy-four plates (numbered 1 to 80), *Pugin and Le Keux's Specimens of the Architectural Antiquities of Normandy*, the initial twenty numbers of which were

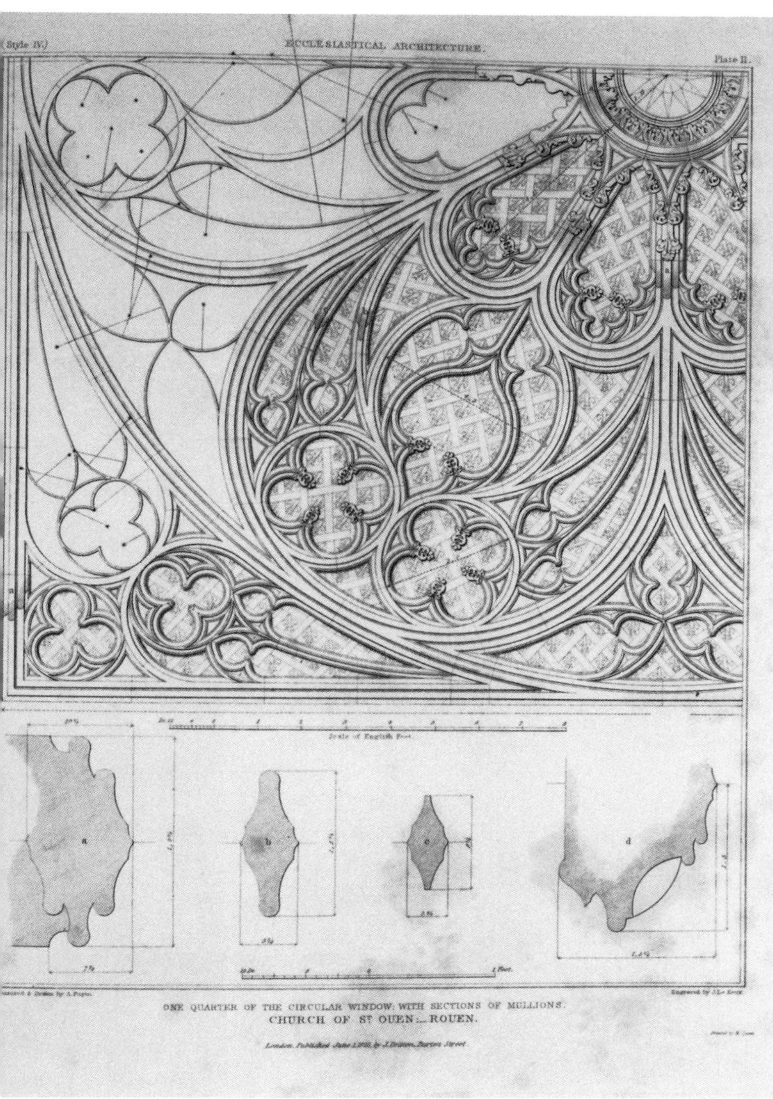

Augustus Charles Pugin. *Historical and Descriptive Essays.* Plate II. Detail of window in the Church of St. Ouen, Rouen. NGA Lib. Rare Book: N44P9788A351833

issued in July 1825, the last in October 1827. The text, quite separate, *Historical and Descriptive Essays Accompanying a Series of Engraved Specimens of the Architectural Antiquities of Normandy*, was written by Britton. This, dedicated to Jeffry Wyatville, was "given," in January 1828, to the subscribers to the plates, in order, as Britton explained in his preface, to circumvent the legal requirement that eleven copies of published books be deposited in specified "copyright" libraries. Britton was not willing to hand out free copies, even to ensure copyright.

Britton had intended in his text to resolve the matter of the origin of the Gothic style and to provide a comprehensive history of the medieval architecture of Normandy: "His views and wishes at the commencement," he wrote, "were to investigate the history, and definitively characterize the ancient architecture, of Normandy,—to ascertain and point out what is really indigenous and what is exotic,—to shew when and by whom its various changes of style were effected, and how these were progressively improved,—to seek diligently and scrupulously to ascertain the origin of the pointed style, and to compare and contrast the correspondencies and varieties of the architecture of Normandy with the contemporary architecture of England."

His serious investigations were thwarted, however, in part by a lack of response to his inquiries in France—though, like Pugin, he was by then an honorary member of the Society of Antiquaries of Normandy—in part by a fall in 1827, while measuring Gloucester Cathedral, that resulted in a compound fracture to his right leg. He was still on crutches in January 1828. Unable to visit Normandy, it must have been during this period of inactivity that he wrote his text. He consulted with John Coles, Samuel Tymms, and Turner, and he read Palgrave's review article, among other published works, but he provided nothing by way of a definitive account of the history of Norman architecture. When it came to determining the origins of Gothic, he acknowledged that the publication, in 1809, of the Reverend G. D. Whittington's unequivocal claim that the style had been fully developed first in France, and in particular in Normandy, and James Milner's firm rebuttal of this thesis in the same year, in favor of England, had stirred the most violent controversy. Turner and Palgrave had steadfastly supported the French claim, and by the time Britton was writing this was generally accepted in England, though well-informed and respected scholars such as John Carter had continued to fight a rearguard action and their influence was still felt. Britton preferred not to take up a position. To determine, he wrote, when "the pointed order of architecture" first appeared in Normandy, or anywhere else, "would require more space than can be allotted in this essay."

Surprisingly, Britton much admired the early Norman style that William Gunn, translating from the French, had in 1819 categorized as "Romanesque." "In the eleventh century," he wrote, "a new and most interesting era in the history of architecture commenced, for in it the Norman style may be said to have attained nearly its pinnacle of grandeur." Oddly, he thought to discern an Egyptian influence here. He was more responsive, however, to Gothic, though somewhat equivocal in his assessment of the architecture, even more so of scholarly attitudes: "With the gradual decline of the massy Norman, rose the beautiful pointed style, a description of architecture less understood by the French than by the English antiquaries, and of which Normandy presents some good specimens, though far inferior in the taste and execution of the detail." What he liked best, as one might expect, was St. Ouen, at Rouen. Later Gothic, especially of the secular sort, was not to his taste: "In the middle of the fifteenth century, and at the commencement of the following, an admixture of the Italian styles with that of the florid produced an inconsistent and inharmonious species of building, which Mr. Dawson

Turner has designated by the appellation of Burgundian."

There is more of this history, revealing of the tastes and scholarship of the period, but the major part of Britton's text was devoted to descriptions of seven buildings at Caen and the surrounding area (the Abbaye aux Dames and the Abbaye aux Hommes; the church of St. Nicholas and the tower of St. Peter's; St. Michael at Vaucelles, the church of Than, and the Château Fontaine Le Henri), eleven in Rouen (St. Ouen, St. Vincent, the nunnery of St. Clair, the fountain of La Croix de Pierre, the Palais de Justice, the Hôtel de Bourgtheroulde, the Abbaye St. Amand, the cathedral and archbishop's palace, St. Maclou, and, nearby, the church of Caudbec), and the cathedral and tower of St. Loup Bayeux.

When the first sheaf of plates, twenty in all, was issued in July 1825, it was reviewed in *The Gentleman's Magazine*, for September. The title was recorded as *Engraved Specimens of the Architectural Antiquities of Normandy. By John and Henry Le Keux, after Drawings by Augustus Pugin, Architect.* W. H. Leeds had already remarked on the anomaly of the title; writing to Turner on 30 July 1825, he noted:

> You have doubtless seen the first No. of Pugin's Normandy—Did not the title appear to you rather singularly worded?—The Architectural Antiquities of Normandy by John and Henry Le Keux etc.—since the work was published some of Pugin's friends have told him that he ought to insist upon the title being altered and having his name stand first as that of the party who is chiefly concerned with it, and he has accordingly written to Mr. Britton—and from what I understand neither is willing to concede the point, so that how they will adjust it remains to be seen.

Pugin resorted to law. The terms of his settlement with Britton have not yet come to light. But when the plate volume was completed in 1827, the title page (engraved in February 1827) read *Pugin and Le Keux's Specimens of the Architectural Antiquities of Normandy.* Pugin and Britton entered into no new agreements thereafter, and when the second edition of work was issued in 1833, the publisher was M. A. Nattali of Covent Garden, who was responsible also for subsequent editions in 1841 and 1847. The French edition, of 1855, was published by E. Noblet, the second, of 1863, by J. Baudry. Nattali was, perhaps, Pugin's nominee; together they had published a collection of plates as early as 1823, *Modern Furniture; Consisting of Forty-four Coloured Engravings from Designs by A. Pugin, J. Stafford of Bath and Others with Descriptive Letter-Press.* Though Pugin had done little work for Ackermann between 1817 and 1822, the book must have been issued with his fullest cooperation, for all the plates carry the imprint of the *Repository of Arts*, in some instances with dates of publication, though no more than ten had in fact appeared in that collection. The plates are unsigned, but there can be little doubt that the majority were by Pugin. The second edition of *Specimens of Gothic Architecture*, of 1825, was published by Taylor, Pugin, and Britton, though publication of subsequent editions was to be taken over by Nattali, who purchased the copyright and stock at an auction of Taylor's assets in April 1835.

The plates of the *Specimens of the Architectural Antiquities of Normandy* were issued in four parts, twenty numbers to each; the first section being published on 1 July 1825, the second on 1 April 1826, the third on 1 March 1827, the fourth on 1 October 1827. The plates were numbered in short series for each of the buildings illustrated, but the numbering is haphazard and dis-

Augustus Charles Pugin. *Historical and Descriptive Essays.* Plates VI–VII. Bayeaux Cathedral, section of choir. NGA Lib. Rare Book: N44P9788A351833

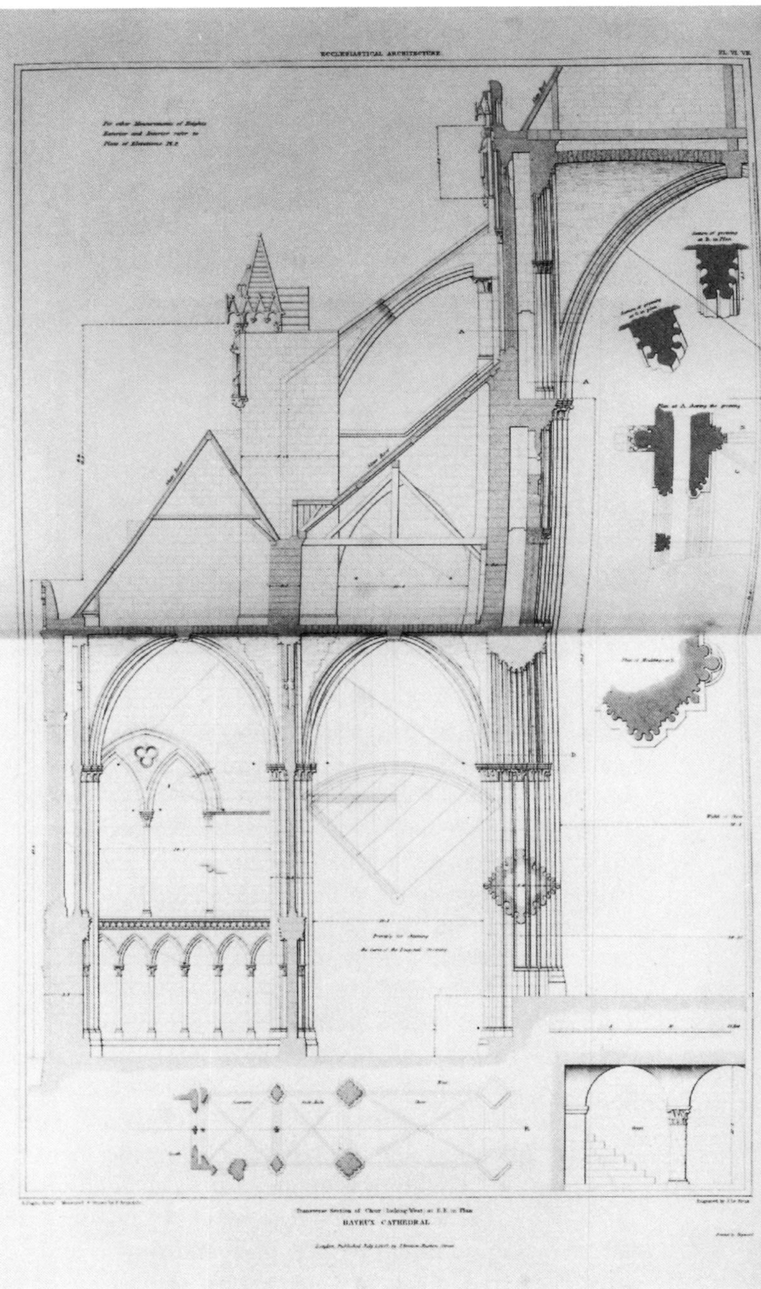

ordered and the plates were to be bound, in the end, in accord with their listing in the table of contents, arranged in something of chronological order.

The table of contents lists eighty plates, including the title page, six plates with double numbering and the two final plates of stained glass in both colored and uncolored format, for a total of seventy-two separate plates. Fifty of these were drawn by Pugin alone, one by George Belton Moore alone (engraved August 1827); twenty-one were done by Pugin's assistants or pupils under his direction: F. Arundale, eight (drawing dated on one only, 1825, engraving of all dated between 1 February and October 1827); T. T. Bury, Moore, and Willis, three each (Bury's drawings undated, engraving dated between 1 July and 1 September 1827; Moore's drawings undated, the engraving dated 1 February, 1 March, and July 1827; one of Willis' drawings is undated, two are dated 1824, their engraving is dated 1 and 15 June 1825); G. W. Shaw, two (both drawn 1824, engraved 1 June 1825); and Benjamin Ferrey and Thomas Kearnan, one each (their drawings undated; Ferrey's engraved August 1827, Kearnan's 25 June 1825). All the plates were engraved by the brothers John and Henry Le Keux, both trained by James Basire.

The plates focused on buildings in Caen, Bayeux, and Rouen. The chief buildings illustrated in Caen were the Abbaye aux Dames (five plates), the Abbaye aux Hommes (ten plates, one of them double), the church of St. Nicholas (two plates) and that at Than nearby (three plates), the ducal palace (one plate) and the tower of St. Peter's (one plate), and details from St. Michael's at Vaucelles (one plate). Bayeux was represented by the cathedral (seven plates, four of them double) and the tower of St. Loup (one plate). At Rouen the emphasis was on St. Ouen (six plates) and the Palais de Justice (seven plates), the porch of St. Vincent (two plates), the gateway of the nunnery of St. Clair (one plate), with details from the cathedral of Notre Dame (four plates), the Abbaye St. Armand (two plates), St. Andre (one plate), St. Maclou (one plate), the archbishop's palace (one plate), the Hôtel de Bourgtheroulde (two plates) and the Fountaine de la Croix (one plate), and, outside, the church of Caudebec (two plates), a doorway from St. Jacques at Dieppe (one plate), and the Château Fontaine Le Henri (three plates).

In the advertisement for the work it was noted that Pugin "conceives that the engravings will be very serviceable to artists in making new designs, and to artizans in the practical execution of new buildings." Almost all the plates were thus of measured plans, sections, elevations, and details, including two plates of stained glass (repeated in color), though seven sharp perspective views were included: the nave of the Abbaye aux Dames, drawn by Pugin (engraved 1 February 1827); the exterior and interior of the Abbaye aux Hommes, drawn by Moore (engraved 1 February 1827) and Arundale (engraved 1 March 1827) under Pugin's direction; the interior of Bayeux cathedral and the exterior of St. Ouen drawn by Moore, the first unaided (engraved August 1827), the second under Pugin's direction (engraved July 1827); and the exteriors of the Palais de Justice at Rouen (drawn 1825, engraved 1 April 1826) and the Château Fountaine Le Henri (engraved 1 February 1827), both drawn by Arundale under Pugin's direction.

Britton was later to suggest, somewhat maliciously, that Pugin was wont to take over the work of his students as his own, but he seems, on the contrary, to have been scrupulous in crediting their contributions.

When the book of plates was reviewed, complete, in *The Athenaeum* of January 1828, the spirit, accuracy, and delicacy of Pugin's drawings were praised in exalted terms: "Both the amateur and the student of Gothic Architecture are under infinite obligations to Mr. Pugin. He has done more toward making its merits understood and appreciated than any other, antiquary, or artist, who have ever yet treated on the subject. He is the Stuart and Revett of the Style."

By then Pugin had already determined to embark on his last, most scholarly, and precise publication of Gothic architecture, the *Examples of Gothic Architecture*, with an introduction and other text by E. J. Willson, the first volume of which, with seventy-one plates illustrating English examples alone, was completed in 1831. This was an independent endeavor, though John Le Keux did much of the engraving. The title page bears the words "Printed for the Author, Augustus Pugin." When he died, on 19 December 1832, Pugin left the completion of the second volume to his son, Augustus Welby Pugin, who was no more than twenty at the time. This task he completed only in 1836, constantly frustrated by Willson's procrastinations. R. M.

Bibliography

Stanton, P. *A. C. and A. W. N. Pugin*. New Haven, forthcoming

60

Augustus Welby Northmore Pugin (1812–1852)

designs for Iron & Brass work in the style of the xv and xvi centuries drawn and etched by A W N Pugin

London: Ackermann & Co., Feb[y]. 1st., 1836

NGA Lib. Rare Book: N44P979A33

Quarto: 295 × 235 (11 5/8 × 9 1/4)

Pagination 27 etched plates

Edition First edition

Illustrations Etched title plate with lettering in red (plate 1), and 26 etched plates numbered 2–27, with captions, printed in this copy in various shades of sanguine and sepia. All plates signed with Pugin's monogram and Ackermann's imprint, dated 1 February 1836

Binding Publisher's embossed tan cloth, copy of title page pasted on upper cover

Provenance Engraved armorial bookplate of William Arthur, 6th duke of Portland, signed "Inv. W. P. B. 1900"

References Belcher A5.1; Fowler 263

Augustus Welby Northmore Pugin. *designs for Iron & Brass work.* Plate 27. NGA Lib. Rare Book: N44P979A33

Augustus Welby Pugin was trained to draw and understand architecture by his father, Augustus Charles Pugin, but he had no professional education on which to rely. His early tastes were for medieval architecture of the elaborate kind, and he liked best the ornamentation and decorative detail. By June 1827, when he was fifteen, he was already working on designs for furniture in the Gothic style for Carlton House and Windsor Castle, alongside the young Frenchman, Louis-Auguste Boileau, also fifteen. Two years later he was designing furniture for Murthly Castle, for the architect James Gillespie Graham, and, thus encouraged, decided in November of that year to set up "business for myself," designing and making furniture. He produced a catalogue of designs and was commissioned by Mrs. Gough of Perry Hall, Birmingham, to make a set of dining room furniture. In the following year, 1831, he was listed in directories as "carver and cabinet maker, 12 Hart Street, Covent Garden." But his estimates of the cost of manufacture were awry; his enterprise failed in this same year and he was declared bankrupt. He returned to theatrical work, designing sets for Covent Garden for Messrs. Grieve, with whom he had first become involved two years earlier, and in assisting his father in the publication of the most serious of his Gothic enterprises, the *Examples of Gothic Architecture*, the text by the Lincoln antiquary E. J. Willson, the first volume of which was issued in parts, between January 1828 and May 1831. The elder Pugin had been forced to sell off much of his stock of books and prints, on 11 February 1831, to finance the publication. The young Pugin made no direct contribution to the work. But three of the plates in the first parts of the second volume, issued in 1832, while his father was still alive, are signed by him.

This was a period of rapid change in the family's affairs. In 1831 Augustus Welby Pugin had married Sarah Ann Garnet, a grandniece of the painter Edward Dayes; she died on 27 May 1832, giving birth to their daughter Ann. Pugin senior died on 19 December 1832, his wife followed a few months later, in April 1833, and before the middle of the next June Pugin junior had married again, Louisa Barton; their first child, Edward Welby, being born on 11 March 1834. By that date Pugin had decided to give up his father's book and print business, selling off all the remaining stock on 4 June 1833, and had moved from the family house in Great Russell Street, London, to Ramsgate, where his only amiable relative, his aunt Selina Welby, lived. She died on 4 September 1834. Pugin determined then to move once more and to become a Roman Catholic, a step he seems to have contemplated for two or three years, at least. By November he was buying ground at Salisbury for his new house, in the early sixteenth-century style, St. Marie's Grange, which, complete with a private chapel, was ready to receive him and his family in May 1835.

Whatever the family upheavals in these years, Pugin continued to work incessantly. He continued, as his father had wished, with the *Examples of Gothic Architecture*, publishing the last of the plates of the second volume in July 1834 with Thomas Larkin Walker, though Willson's text was to be issued only in 1836. The first twenty-five plates for the third volume, published by T. L. Walker, illustrating the Vicar's Close at Wells, which had been the subject of Pugin's father's last drawing expedition, were issued in June 1836. The book was taken over by Walker and completed, without any text from Willson, in April 1838.

More representative though of Pugin's imaginative enterprise at this period are his sketchbooks, the earliest dating from 1831 and 1832. One of his drawings illustrates contrasted house facades, of 1470, 1532, and 1832, an arrangement that seems to have been inspired by an example in James Peller Malcolm's *Anecdotes of the Manners and Customs of London during the Eighteenth Century* of 1808—though Malcolm, unlike Pugin, preferred the new to the old. Pugin was to develop the idea further. He did a series of imaginative compositions, freely improvising on the Gothic style, most of which were bound as books, the first, of 1831, was *A Catholic Chapel*, followed in 1832 by *The Chest* and *The Shrine*, then, in 1833, by *Le Chasteau*, *St. Margaret's Chapel*, the *Hospital of Saynt John*, *The Parish Church*, and, most significant of all, *Contrasts Designed and Executed by A.W. Pugin* MDCCCXXXIII, the first essay for his most influential book, to be greatly revised, and published only in 1836. From 1833 also dates the most coherent of Pugin's imaginary projects, *The Deanery*, which demonstrates at once how far beyond his father he had advanced in conjuring up interiors in the Gothic manner. The last of these exercises was *St. Marie's College*, of 1834, in which the architecture emerges, for the first time, more strongly than the decorative detailing.

The publisher who had most steadfastly supported A. C. Pugin throughout his career, Rudolph Ackermann, died in 1834, and the business was taken over then by his two sons. They agreed to publish a series of books on medieval decorative arts by Pugin. The first of these—twenty-five plates in all, the title page colored—was issued on 1 April 1835: *Gothic Furniture in the Style of the 15th Century*. This was the younger generation's

Augustus Welby Northmore Pugin. *designs for Iron & Brass work.* Plate 25. Lectorium. NGA Lib. Rare Book: N44P979A33

response to the elder Pugin's *Gothic Furniture*, of 1828, made up from plates published between 1825 and 1827 in the elder Ackermann's *Repository of Arts*. A. W. Pugin aimed at something of authenticity. But his response was conditioned also by the latest surveys of Gothic decorative arts, in particular the publications of Henry Shaw, which had transformed the field. Shaw's folio on the chapel at Luton Park, of 1829, had been a revelation of precise and colorful recording. The first parts of his *Illuminated Ornaments, Selected from Manuscripts and Early Printed Books, from the 6 to the 17th Centuries*, published by William Pickering, began to appear in 1830, to be completed in 1833, while his *Specimens of Ancient Furniture drawn from Existing Authorities*, of 1833 to 1836, published also by Pickering, served as a direct inspiration to Pugin, though not all of Shaw's examples were Gothic. Many were brilliantly colored. In comparison, Pugin might be judged to have failed. For whereas

Shaw was intent to name the source of his illustrations and to date them approximately, Pugin improvised freely, altogether imaginatively, in his depiction of furnishings and decorative ornamentation in the medieval style. His taste, moreover, veered still towards the intricate, richly embellished forms that he had encountered particularly on an extended tour he made of the Low Countries and Germany, from May to mid-August 1834. Nuremberg, which he visited for the first time, was his particular delight on this trip. His drawings for *Gothic Furniture*, now in the Victoria and Albert Museum in London, were made promptly after this expedition. His book, he informed Willson on 9 January 1835, was due to appear on 1 February. But there was to be a two-month delay. Already, however, on 12 February, Pugin noted in his diary, he had begun the drawings for *Designs for Iron and Brass Work*. Within twelve days he had finished them; today they are all, the "lectorium" apart, in the Steedman Collection in the St. Louis Public Library. By 12 March, he recorded, he had "finished work on plate." It was Pugin's practice, as it had been that of his father, to transfer his drawings to the plate and etch them lightly before sending them on to the engraver to work them over with the burin. On 17 June Pugin recorded again that he "began etching work of iron-work." Three days later he "sent 5 plates to Bury." That is Talbot Bury, the architect and engraver, who had trained with A. C. Pugin, and whom Pugin must have known from 1825, at least. Seven plates were sent to Bury on 26 June, with more to follow on July 4 and 9. But the book was not to be issued for a further six months.

Pugin's designs for window frames, rails and finials, hinges and bolts, handles and knockers, escutcheons and keys, lamps and fire irons, coffers and a lectern, are all of the intricate, richly embellished and linear kind that he was to continue to produce to the end of his life. Neither at this stage nor later did he share his father's taste for early Norman architecture, though his tastes did, in time, become less florid.

The title page, an echo of that his father had done for *Specimens of the Architectural Antiquities of Normandy*, consisted of an elaborate late Gothic frame, festooned with scrolls with the words "etched and drawn" and "by A. W. N. Pugin," and shields bearing the initials "A" and "P." Ackermann's name was on a scroll beneath. But it was on the final plate that Pugin most determinedly expressed something of himself. This too represents a carved late Gothic frame, above it Pugin's arms and motto, on either side scrolls with the words "avant" and shields with Pugin's initials; below is another scroll with the words "tout vient de dieu" (which is also carved on the top of the frame), and suspended beneath more shields with the symbols of his devotion, a palette and brushes, a compass and set-square, and a figure of the Virgin and Child. Within the frame Christ is depicted on the cross, Augustine of Canterbury on the left, Pugin, kneeling, on the right, with interwoven scrolls invoking the blessings of St. Augustine and salvation through Christ. The image is a very personal statement. Pugin's conversion to Catholicism took place on 7 June 1835, when the plates for his book were being engraved. (This one might well have been a last minute addition.) The book was published on 1 February 1836. A French edition of this work, together with that of *Gothic Furniture*, was published by Varin, in Paris, in 1844, another in 1849. There was also an edition by Noblet of Paris, perhaps earlier, and by Baudry of Liège, undated.

The years 1835 and 1836 were ones of feverish activity for Pugin. He began the drawings for the third of the Ackermann's volumes, *Designs for Gold and Silversmiths*, in March or April 1835, soon after the completion of the drawings for *Designs for Iron and Brass Work*, but he was forced to set them aside. From 28 April through to July (during which time he moved from Ramsgate to Salisbury), he was employed by Charles Barry on the detailing of the Edward VI Free Grammar School in Birmingham. In mid-July he left for a study tour in France, returning to London on 3 August. Both Barry and Graham were waiting for him, requiring his assistance on their competition drawings for the Houses of Parliament. Pugin spent twelve days in London, not only drawing incessantly but writing his response to A. W. Hakewill's pamphlet rejecting Gothic as suitable for the style of the new Houses of Parliament, before returning to Salisbury. It was during this interlude that he took up *Contrasts* again; on 16 August he wrote to Willson "I am beginning my work on Contrasts." But this too had, for the moment, to be set aside. He was at work again on Barry and Graham's competition drawings. Finally, on 11 December, after eleven days of strenuous work in London, they were complete. But even before this, on 8 December, he had begun work again on the *Designs for Gold and Silversmiths*; his diary reads, "began silver work." By 13 January 1836 the drawings, most of which are now in the Victoria and Albert Museum, London, and the lightly etched plates were complete and dispatched to Bury for engraving. With them Pugin sent a text recalling the glories of ecclesiastical plate in medieval times. His conversion to Catholicism had given him the strength and boldness to take every opportunity to preach of the wonders of Catholic times past. The book was published on 4 April 1836, without any letterpress. But this scarcely mattered; the images themselves conveyed the lost magnificence of thuribles and pyxes, reliquaries and monstrances.

Between 23 February and 5 March 1836 Pugin worked, as in a delirium, preparing the drawings and plates for the revised *Contrasts*. He thought the plates then done, but on 20 April more were dispatched to Bury. By 2 May the plates were completed. In a letter to Willson, of 6 May, Pugin triumphantly declared the text complete too, but he was still working at it. He left Salisbury on 20 June for London, and Dover on 1 July for France, to gather material for the fourth of his books for the Ackermanns, *Details of Ancient Timber Houses of the 15th and 16th Centuries.* He returned to London on 22 July. *Contrasts* was published on 4 August, from St. Marie's Grange. Pugin was at once caught up in the reaction to this work, but he was taken up also, in the final months of 1836 and in the beginning of 1837, with the revision of Barry's drawings for the Houses of Parliament. Though he had begun the drawings for the *Details of Ancient Timber Houses* immediately after his return from France, he could not work seriously at them until December. He noted on 16 January 1837 that they were finished. The title page is dated 1836, but the twenty-one plates are dated 20 February 1837. They cannot be accounted a success. The details illustrated were all continental examples, taken out of all context, even that of the facades of which they were a part. Though the final plate, showing, alongside houses dated 1835 and 1836, a medieval house being demolished and its carved timber details being burned, does give evidence of the fire and purpose in Pugin at this period.

Pugin determined on a grained, green cloth binding for the four related books—a technique introduced about 1823 by the Clerkenwell binder Archibald Leighton. By 1832 Leighton had perfected a technique for gold-blocking motifs on the cloth by machine—a technique Pugin was later to employ—but for the Ackermann series he chose rather the cheaper expedient of pasting a copy of the title page, printed in black with red overlay, on the front cover so that the cloth formed a frame. Different printings had different colors.

A fifth book intended for the series—"examples of internal fittings and decorations"—was abandoned. Pugin had by then found his voice with *Contrasts*; he no longer wished to provide exemplars for imitation, he wanted to pursue a crusade. R. M.

Bibliography

Stanton, P. *A. C. and A. W. N. Pugin.* New Haven, forthcoming

Wedgwood, A. *Catalogues of Architectural Drawings in the Victoria and Albert Museum. A. W. N. Pugin and the Pugin Family.* London, 1985

Augustus Welby Northmore Pugin. *designs for Iron & Brass work.* Plate 12. Keys. NGA Lib. Rare Book: N44P979A33

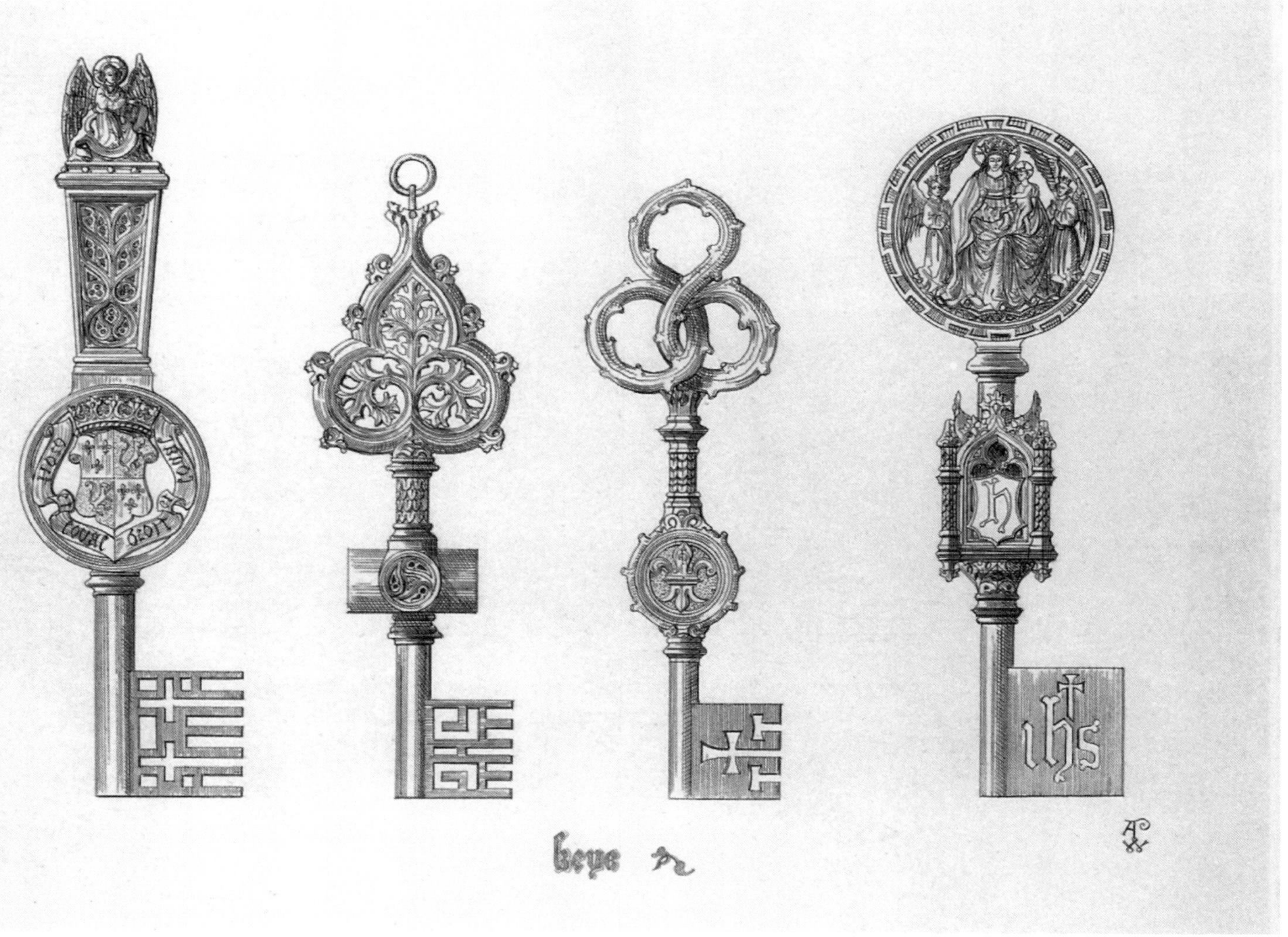

61

Augustus Welby Northmore Pugin (1812–1852)

The True Principles Of Pointed or Christian Architecture: Set Forth In Two Lectures Delivered At St. Marie's, Oscott, By A. Welby Pugin, Architect . . .

London: John Weale, 1841

NGA Lib. Rare Book: N44P979A5

Quarto: 255 × 202 (10 × 8)

Pagination [iv], 67, [1] pp., etched frontispiece, 9 etched plates

Edition First edition

Text pp. [i] title page, printed in red, with vignettes; [ii] printer's imprint; [iii] list of plates (verso blank); [1]–67 text; [68] John Weale's device, printed in red and black

Illustrations Etched frontispiece of a medieval architect in his study, incorporating a short title and signed with Pugin's monogram, with red hand-coloring; plus 9 etched plates numbered I–IX, all with Pugin's monogram. Pugin's woodcut armorial device on title page; woodcut initial printed in red, p. [1]. There are also numerous in-text woodcut or wood-engraved illustrations, many with Pugin's monogram and 2 on p. 26 printed in red and yellow (Pugin's own list of plates describes 47 "woodcuts" and 31 "vignettes")

Binding Publisher's dark green cloth, green morocco spine, Pugin's device stamped in gilt on upper cover, text edges gilt

Provenance Contemporary ownership inscription "Rev[d]. W. C. Lukis. Bradford. W."

References Belcher A29.1; Fowler 266

PUGIN FIRST revealed himself as a polemicist on 18 August 1835, when he published *A Letter to A. W. Hakewill, Architect, in Answer to His Reflections on the Style for Rebuilding the Houses of Parliament*. Hakewill thought Gothic "sullen" and "peculiarly monotonous," and, having been rid of the style for two centuries, there was no need now to attempt to perpetuate it. For Pugin Gothic was both a structural and decorative triumph, and a proper reflection of English life in an era of faith. But the work in which Pugin first gave forceful and effective expression to his beliefs was *Contrasts; or, A Parallel Between the Noble Edifices of the Fourteenth and Fifteenth Centuries, and Similar Buildings of the Present Day; shewing the Present Decay of Taste: accompanied by appropriate Text*, published on 4 August 1836. Pugin was then twenty-four. His ideas might not have been without precedent, but the wit and vigor with which he presented them both in his drawings and his text established him at once as the sharpest and most intolerant of architectural—and also social—critics in Europe. He was identified, in particular, with the notion that the life and architecture of the centuries preceding the Reformation were as one, and were glorious, and should be revived as the only possible solution to present ills. On 19 August 1836 Pugin received a letter of congratulation from Alton Towers, the home of John Talbot, sixteenth earl of Shrewsbury, who was to become his greatest patron. But the work being praised was the *Designs for Gold and Silversmiths*, published on 4 April 1836. The author of the letter was Daniel Rock, the chaplain. *Contrasts* had not yet been seen at Alton Towers. Within two months it had been perused. But Pugin's first visit to Alton Towers was made only on 1 September 1837. In the following month *Contrasts* was endorsed in the *Dublin Review* by Dr. Nicholas Wiseman himself. Pugin was soon established as the chosen architect not only of the earl of Shrewsbury, but other such eminent Catholics as Ambrose Phillips de Lisle, Bishop Thomas Walsh, and Father George Spencer, men who were all sympathetic to Wiseman's militant Catholicism.

In 1835 Walsh, as vicar-apostolic of the Midland District, and Henry Weedall, president of Oscott College, near Birmingham, decided—emboldened rather by Emancipation—to enlarge the college and develop it as an institution for the instruction of the Roman Catholic clergy. The earl of Shrewsbury gave financial support. The first architect they employed was a local man, Joseph Potter, who had completed the new building by the end of 1836. The chapel, however, was not yet decorated. Pugin paid his first visit to Oscott on 27 and 28 March 1837, perhaps at the instigation of the earl of Shrewsbury. He returned in April, May, and June, for he had accepted a commission to decorate the chapel, which was consecrated with rich ceremony, on 29 May 1838. He had also begun to teach at Oscott and to put together a collection of medieval objects to serve as demonstrations of his beliefs. He was named professor of ecclesiastical antiquities. He delivered five lectures at the college, on 17 November 1837; 23 February, 19 September, and 26 November 1838; and 23 March 1839. These five lectures might have been repeated, for Pugin visited Oscott at least thirty-three times between 1839 and 1845, and they were to form the basis of his instruction.

The first three lectures—on the nature of architecture as an expression of life and faith, in particular as revealed in the form and in the interior of the medieval church; on the history of the Gothic style, from its emergence in Germany in the thirteenth century to the "heretical novelties" of the sixteenth century and beyond; and on the history of stained glass and its symbolical role in architecture, both secular and ecclesiastic, from the thirteenth century to its destruction by the Protestants—were all published in the *Catholic Magazine* of April and June 1838, and January and February 1839. The fourth and fifth lectures were not to be published there, perhaps because the editor, John Smith, was unable to contain Pugin's intemperance. But the theme of the fourth and fifth lectures, concerning the honest expression of forms and materials, in relation to use and construction in Gothic architecture, as opposed to the deceptions of the classical and "Anglo-pagan" styles, was taken up a few months later and repeated in a speech Pugin made at the banquet following the blessing and laying of the foundation stone of his first large church, St. Chad, in Birmingham, on 29 October 1839. Walsh had officiated at the ceremony and Wiseman had preached. At the banquet, over which Wiseman presided, Spencer, Walsh, and Weedall had all spoken. Pugin's speech was published in the *London and Dublin Orthodox Journal* for 9 November 1839. This was the first public presentation, albeit in much reduced form, of the two Oscott lectures that were to be published in July 1841, by John Weale, as *The True Principles of Pointed or Christian Architecture: Set Forth in Two Lectures Delivered at St. Marie's, Oscott.*

The publication of *Contrasts* in 1836 had brought immediate recognition and success. Pugin's independent career as an architect followed, and it was at once extensive and intensive. But he was still desperately concerned in these early years to publicize his ideas. He agreed in 1840 to write three articles for *The Dublin Review* to promote the revival of Gothic as the Catholic style. In this same year, and in the early months of that following, he also rewrote the last two Oscott lectures, and took up *Contrasts* again, revising the text extensively, rejecting the plate in which he had pilloried Soane's house and adding five new plates, contrasted doors, altars and monuments, and, the most famous images of all, the contrasted towns of 1440 and 1840 and contrasted residences for the poor. These seem to have been last-minute additions, conceived, Phoebe Stanton has suggested, after reading Frederick Oakeley's article on "Ancient and Modern Charity," in *The British Critic* for 1 February 1841.

Pugin completed the draft for the first of *The Dublin Review* articles on 12 January 1841; it was published in May. This was later to become the first part of *The Present State of Ecclesiastical Architecture in England*, issued in 1843 by Charles Dolman. On 26 January 1841 Weale purchased the text and drawings of the *True Principles*. Three days later Pugin sent him an outline for the prospectus, the frontispiece, and a proposal for a final plate, which seems to have come to nothing. The prospectus, the text and drawings, and Pugin's correspondence with Weale between 29 January and 21 July are all in the collections of the Metropolitan Museum, New York. During this period Pugin was still busy revising *Contrasts*; this text was completed on 8 February, the revised plates the day after, but he was to revert to them again in August, after his annual summer expedition. *True Principles* was published on 3 July; *Contrasts*, perhaps in parts, probably completed in November 1841. The publisher for this last was Dolman.

Pugin's prospectus provides a fair summary of *True Principles*:

> The following important facts are fully explained in this work. 1. that all the ornaments of true pointed edifices were merely introduced as decoration to the essential construction of these buildings 2. that the construction of pointed architecture was varied to accord with *the properties of the various materials employed* shown by antient examples of stone, timber and metal constructions 3. that no features were introduced in the antient pointed edifices which were not essential either for convenience or propriety 4. that the pointed arch is most consistent as it decorates the useful portions of buildings instead of disguising them 5. that the defects of modern architecture are principally owing to the departure from antient consistent principles.

In the text of the book itself Pugin begins with two principles: "*1st, that there should be no features about a building which are not necessary for convenience, construction, or propriety; 2nd, that all good ornament should consist of enrichment of the essential construction of the building*." Lest there should be any doubt that these principles are seen to be embodied in Gothic architecture alone, Pugin makes clear, "it is in pointed architecture alone that these great principles have been carried out." He then surveys the application of these principles in relation to stone and metal in the first lecture, and in relation to timber construction in the second. Brusquely, he rejects classical architecture because it is a clumsy translation into timber of a stone system of construction, and also, no less important, because it is based on temples that were erected for an idolatrous worship. At some length he attempts to demonstrate how the forms of Gothic architecture, the piers and vaults, the buttresses and pinnacles, are a faithful expression of structural requirements. He deals at even greater length with the function of moldings in protecting structures from the rain. Though Pugin was clearly inspired by French rationalist theorists of the eighteenth century—by the Abbé Laugier no less than the great academic teacher Jacques-François Blondel, who in his *Cours d'architecture* laid as much stress on the finesse of Gothic construction as on its appropriateness to Catholic worship—it is equally clear that he saw architecture, ultimately, not in terms of structural expression, but in terms of its decorative overlay.

In considering metal construction he found no objection, in principle, to the use of iron, though if rationally used, members in iron were to his eyes "painfully thin and devoid of shadow," and were thus to be avoided. He chose to stress rather the metal work of hinges and bolts, locks and nails, and also of chalices and chests, crosses and shrines—"Their construction and execution is decidedly of a *metallic character*. The ornament is produced by *piercing, chasing, engraving, and enamel*." Craftsmanship of an old-fashioned kind was all important in the revival of the architecture and the decorative arts that he had in mind: "Mechanics' institutes," he wrote, "are a mere device of the day to poison the minds of the operatives with infidel and radical doctrines; the Church is the true mechanics' institute, the oldest and the best. *She was the great and never failing school in which all the great artists of the days of faith were formed*."

There are, as might be imagined, inconsistencies throughout Pugin's text. He disliked the painting of ironwork, he was not at all opposed to the painting of timber, indeed he much approved the patterning and coloring of all interior surfaces, provided always that the pattern be flat, with no perspective involved. But there were also firm convictions and consistencies conditioning his tastes. In the second lecture he put forward another principle, that of propriety: "what I mean by propriety is this, *that the external and internal appearance of an edifice should be illustrative of, and in accordance with, the purpose for which it is destined*." What he intended, as the illustrations he offered of a parish church, an old English manor, and a collegiate complex make clear, is that the function and role of the individual parts of each

Augustus Welby Northmore Pugin. *The True Principles of Pointed or Christian Architecture*. Page 60. Old English mansion. NGA Lib. Rare Book: N44P979A5

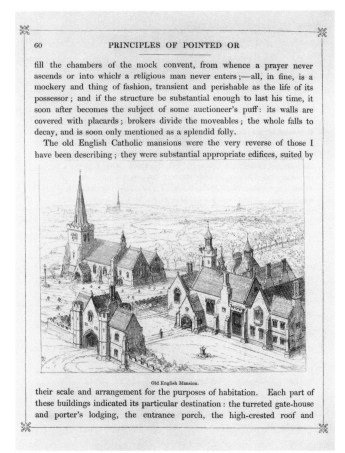

60 PRINCIPLES OF POINTED OR

fill the chambers of the mock convent, from whence a prayer never ascends or into which a religious man never enters;—all, in fine, is a mockery and thing of fashion, transient and perishable as the life of its possessor; and if the structure be substantial enough to last his time, it soon after becomes the subject of some auctioneer's puff: its walls are covered with placards; brokers divide the moveables; the whole falls to decay, and is soon only mentioned as a splendid folly.

The old English Catholic mansions were the very reverse of those I have been describing; they were substantial appropriate edifices, suited by

Old English Mansion.

their scale and arrangement for the purposes of habitation. Each part of these buildings indicated its particular destination: the turreted gate-house and porter's lodging, the entrance porch, the high-crested roof and

building should be at once evident in the forms of the architecture, but that the whole should be coherent and equally expressive of its purpose. Without qualm, Pugin wrote "Catholic England was merry England, at least for the humbler classes," and he argued again and again for a reversion to Gothic architecture of the pre-Reformation period, but he despised the unthinking imitation of Gothic forms, the greatest absurdity in this respect he considered to be the castellated style, his illustration for which he took from the first sketchbook he had done for his *Contrasts*, in 1833. He conjured up something of his larger aims in a moving description of a medieval town that should, perhaps, have formed part of the text of *Contrasts*, where his famous view of the medieval town is without any descriptive text:

It must have been an edifying sight to have overlooked some ancient city raised when religion formed a leading impulse in the mind of man, and when the honour and worship of the Author of all good was considered of greater importance than the achievement of the most lucrative commercial speculation. There stood the mother church, the great cathedral, vast in height, rising above all the towers of the parochial churches which surrounded her; next in scale and grandeur might have been discerned the abbatial and collegiate churches with their vast and solemn buildings; each street had its temple raised for the true worship of God, *variously beautiful in design, but each a fine example of Christian art*. Even the bridges and approaches were not destitute of religious buildings, and many a beautiful chapel and oratory was corbelled out on massive piers over the stream that flowed beneath.

There is much sharp criticism of contemporary architecture and practice, much condemnation and invective—Joshua Reynolds and James Wyatt are named as destroyers—but a sharp critical appraisal is offered also of his own performance, an admission of having perpetrated enormities in designing furniture for Windsor Castle in his early youth, and a recognition that his tastes in architecture were perhaps too much influenced by continental examples.

Thinking perhaps of St. Chad's, he wrote:

I once stood on the very edge of a precipice in this respect from which I was rescued by the advice and arguments of my respected and revered friend Dr. Rock, to whose learned researches and observations on Christian antiquities I am highly indebted, and to whom I feel it a bounden duty to make this public acknowledgement of the great benefit I have received from his advice. Captivated by the beauties of foreign pointed architecture, I was on the verge of departing from the severity of our English style, and engrafting portions of foreign detail and arrangement. This I feel convinced would have been a failure; for although the great principles of Christian architecture were everywhere the same, each country had some peculiar manner of developing them, and we should continue working in the same parallel lines, all contributing to the grand whole of Catholic art, but by the very variety increasing its beauties and its interest.

Most of the plates bear Pugin's monogram, but not

Augustus Welby Northmore Pugin. *The True Principles of Pointed or Christian Architecture.* Frontispiece. NGA Lib. Rare Book: N44P979A5

all, though he was certainly responsible for all the drawings. His letters to Weale reveal that he was much irritated to learn that Weale had entered into an agreement with Orlando Jewitt to prepare the illustrations for printing. Pugin feared that his style might be compromised and offered to prepare the plates himself for 110 pounds. However, Weale refused to change his agreement, and one must assume that Pugin was not altogether dissatisfied with the results, because he worked a few years later with Jewitt again on the plates for *An Apology for the Revival of Christian Architecture* and the *Glossary of Ecclesiastical Ornament and Costume.* Talbot Bury was also involved on the plates for *True Principles*, almost certainly on the title page, and the frontispiece, in which a Christian architect sits at work in his study, in a view reminiscent of a Dürer engraving (and also of an earlier, more richly detailed version of the theme that Pugin had included in the second volume of *Examples*, though he seems in this instance to have been inspired rather by a plate issued in 1827, as part of N. X. Willemin's *Monuments Français Inédits pour servir à l'Histoire des Arts*, based on a portrait of the chronicler Monstrelet in a manuscript in the Bibliothèque Nationale, Paris), and on the bird's-eye view of Magdalen College, Oxford, inspired by a view by Loggan. On the border of the frontispiece Pugin set the names of men of the Middle Ages who had sponsored buildings, William of Wykeham, Thomas Chillenden, William Bolton, William Waynflete, Richard Poore, William Orchyarde, Thomas of Canterbury, Alan de Walsingham, and Thomas Ickam, names he culled from the appendix of the fifth volume of *Britton's Chronological Architecture* of 1826. At the bottom were the names of St. George, with his badge, and Edward the Confessor with his arms.

For the binding Pugin once again selected a green cloth, a quatrefoil containing his motto and initials blocked in gold in the center, blind-stamped Gothic foliage in each of the corners. The spine was of leather with the title tooled in gold.

Pugin's book, rank with bigotry and intolerance, was nevertheless dazzling and persuasive. He laid down clearly and precisely some basic principles for the making of buildings, and these were to be repeated, again and again, entirely divorced from Pugin's religious contexts, through to the middle of the twentieth century. Absolutely, he had made his mark. R. M.

Bibliography

Stanton, P. *A. C. and A. W. N. Pugin*. New Haven, forthcoming

Wainwright, C. "Book Design and Production." In *Pugin: A Gothic Passion*. Eds. P. Atterbury and C. Wainwright. London, 1994

Wedgwood, A. *Catalogues of Architectural Drawings in the Victoria and Albert Museum. A. W. N. Pugin and the Pugin Family*. London, 1985

62

Augustus Welby Northmore Pugin (1812–1852)

An Apology For The Revival of Christian Architecture in England. By A. Welby Pugin . . .

London: John Weale, 1843

NGA Lib. Rare Book: N44P979A26

Quarto: 258 × 209 (10 1/8 × 8 1/4)

Pagination [viii], 51, [1] pp., 10 etched plates

Edition First edition

Text pp. [i] half-title; [ii] printer's imprint; [iii] title page printed in red and black (verso blank); [v] dedication, printed in red and black (verso blank); [vii] list of plates; [viii] "References to the Frontispiece" (list of churches represented in the frontispiece); [1]–51 text; [52] description of plate x

Illustrations Etched frontispiece (plate 1) and 9 etched plates numbered II–X, all signed with Pugin's monogram and dated. Title page with Pugin's woodcut armorial device; dedication page with large woodcut pictorial initial printed in red; p. [1] with woodcut ornamental initial, printed in red

Binding Publisher's dark green cloth, blind-stamped ornamental center panels, gilt title on cover

Provenance Ownership inscription "R. Cam . . . Ballantyne" on front endpaper

References Belcher A7; Fowler 268

WRITING TO THE Reverend John Rouse Bloxam of Magdalen College, Oxford, on 7 February 1843, Pugin noted that his latest book, *An Apology for the Revival of Christian Architecture*, would be out in a few weeks, and he enclosed a prospectus. The book, the fourth Pugin had written—or rewritten—and illustrated within three years, was published in April. The themes he explored, the examples to which he referred, appeared in more than one of these books, but despite all repetition, each is distinct and marked by a particular thrust. *An Apology* is even sharper and more intemperate than usual in its critique of contemporary architecture and design, but it is far more easily written and much more enjoyable to read. It also hints at the possibility of compromise between Catholics and Protestants, though the ostentatious dedication to the earl of Shrewsbury, as the chief reviver of the ancient glories of the English Church, made Pugin's ultimate hopes quite clear.

The thrust of Pugin's argument concerned the degenerated state of architecture in the nineteenth century—"Styles are now *adopted* instead of *generated*, and ornament and design *adapted to*, instead of *originated by*, the edifices themselves." The result was a carnival of styles: "its professors appear tricked out in the guises of all centuries and all nations; the Turk and the Christian, the Egyptian and the Greek, the Swiss and the Hindoo, march side by side, and mingle together; and some of these gentlemen, not satisfied with perpetrating one character, appear in two or three costumes in the same evening."

Pugin's condemnation was not just general, however; he focused his rage on particular buildings and architects. He attacked the new St. Paul's School, the new building of Christ's Hospital, the Guildhall and the Royal Exchange, Hardwick's arch at Euston Station, John Soane's Bank of England, and especially Charles Rennie Cockerell's new works at Cambridge and Oxford. The library at Cambridge was described as "a monstrous erection of mongrel Italian, a heavy, vulgar, unsightly mass, which already obscures from some points the lateral elevation of Kings' Chapel, and which it is impossible to pass without a depression of spirits and feelings of disgust." The Ashmolean Museum at Oxford was rejected equally rudely as "another unsightly pile of pagan details, stuck together to make up a show, for the university galleries immediately facing the venerable front of St. John's, and utterly destroying this beautiful entrance to the most Catholic-looking city in England."

The attack on Cockerell was motivated not by his architecture alone, but also his instruction as professor of architecture at the Royal Academy: "It is a perfect disgrace to the Royal Academy, that its Professor of Architecture should be permitted to poison the minds of the students of that establishment by propagating his erroneous opinions of Christian architecture." When he dealt later with what he considered to be the proper education of architects, Pugin derided the operations of this institution again as, "Pagan lectures, pagan designs, pagan casts and models, pagan medals, and, as a reward for proficiency in these matters, a pagan journey."

Pugin's arguments might have been unsound and his reasoning false, but he was at least honest enough to make clear his aims—"The object of this tract is, therefore, to place Christian architecture in its true position,—to exhibit the claims it possesses on our veneration and obedience, as the only correct expression of the faith, wants, and climate of our country." By Christian, Pugin meant Gothic. The problem was that even among those who admired Gothic there was little understanding of the true nature of that architecture. He himself, he acknowledged, had perpetrated abominations before understanding dawned. Among the countless opportunities offered in recent years, amid the many attempts to simulate the style, only one example of a public nature could be singled out—"the erection of the Parliament Houses in the national style is by far the greatest advance that had yet been gained in the right

Augustus Welby Northmore Pugin. *An Apology for the Revival of Christian Architecture.* Frontispiece. NGA Lib. Rare Book: N44P979A26

direction." But even then Pugin caviled—"The long lines of fronts and excessive repetition are certainly not in accordance with the ancient spirit of civil architecture, but the detail is most consoling." The detail, of course, was his own. The aim was not a revival of the Gothic style, but a revival of the true principles—"*we do not wish to produce mere servile imitators of former excellence of any kind, but men imbued with the consistent spirit of the antient architects, who would work on their principles, and carry them out as the old men would have done, had they been placed in similar circumstances, and with similar wants to ourselves.*"

Pugin was, once again, honest enough to broach, if he did not resolve, the consequences of such beliefs. He was forced to approve iron as a structural material, though he felt free to denounce it "as the meagre substitute for masons' skill." He could applaud the introduction of the steam engine as a source of power for lifting or moving things. He could even conceive that railway architecture might be impressive. "The railways," he wrote, "had they been naturally treated, afforded a fine scope for grand massive architecture. Little more was required than buttresses, weathering, and segmental arches, resistance to *lateral* and *perpendicular pressure.*"

But he found little to admire in what he saw. He concluded his assessment of the modern condition, nonetheless, with two simple and surprising statements—"Any modern invention which conduces to comfort, cleanliness, or durability, should be adopted by the consistent architect; *to copy a thing merely because it is old, is just as absurd as the imitations of the modern pagans,*" and "There is no reason in the world why noble cities, combining all possible convenience of drainage, water-closets, and conveyance of gas may not be erected in the most consistent and yet Christian character. *Every building that is treated naturally, without disguise or concealment, cannot fail to look well.*"

Pugin noted that it was his intention to write a treatise on natural architecture. Here, one might imagine, he thought to move beyond the restricting influence of Gothic architecture. It is clear from the context however, that he was thinking not of an architecture divorced from historical precedent, but of vernacular forms and common sense craftsmanship:

. . . the best gate must be the *strongest framed*; the sharp edges must be taken off the stiles and rails without weakening the joints and shoulders; they are chamfered and stinted, and the gate must and will look admirably well, and, of course, be in character with a pointed building, because a pointed building is a *natural building. In matters of ordinary use, a man must go out of his way to make a bad thing:* hence, in some of the rural districts, where workmen had not been poisoned by modern ideas; barns, sheds, &c., were built and framed, till very lately, on the true old principles, with braces, knees, and the high pitch.

Whatever hints Pugin might have held out for future theorists of architecture, the emphasis in *An Apology* remained the matter of the revival of Gothic for ecclesiastical buildings: "in the English Catholic body, any departure from Catholic architecture is utterly inexcusable." Churches must have a traditional plan, towers and spires, chancels, and screens, altars and fonts, stained glass and all manner of symbolical decoration. He referred once again to J. B. Mozley's articles on these subjects in *The British Critic*. Pugin was in a conciliatory mood. His recommendations might be applied equally well to Anglican churches. And when he was considering the details of this revival of ancient arts, sepulchral memorials, paintings and statuary, he was prepared even to consider John Flaxman as a possible contributor to the new harmony: "Had Flaxman lived a few years later he would have been a great Christian artist." Pugin's image of Flaxman was, clearly, not our own.

"In conclusion," Pugin wrote:

it must appear evident that the present revival of ancient architecture in this country is based on the soundest and most consistent principles. It is warranted by religion, government, climate and the wants of society. It is a perfect expression of all we should hold sacred, honourable, and national, and connected with the holiest and dearest associations; nor is there in the whole world a country which is better calculated for the revival of the ancient excellence and solemnity than England. We have immense power, vast wealth, and great though often misdirected zeal. Sounder views and opinions are daily gaining ground,—feelings of reverence for the past increasing in an extraordinary degree; and, with all her faults, we must remember that England, while she was the last to abandon Christian architecture, has been the foremost in hailing and aiding its revival.

Pugin illustrated his text with ten plates, the engraver of which is not known, though Orlando Jewitt is known to have done the initial letter for the dedication to the earl of Shrewsbury. Some of the plates are employed in the manner of *Contrasts*, to deride contemporary architecture—those of the railways and modern cemeteries—though more often, in key with the more positive tone of the book, the plates are merely illustrative of sepulchral memorials or religious sculpture and painting. One plate strikes a positive note for the future, namely, the adaptation of the principles of Gothic architecture to modern domestic requirements, illustrated in two designs for street facades. But two plates, the first and the last, give even further expression to the revival of Gothic that lay in Pugin's heart. The first, a response to Cockerell's famous "Tribute to the Memory of Sir Christopher Wren," a panorama of sixty-two of Wren's buildings, exhibited at the Royal Academy in 1838, engraved in 1842 and illustrated also in *The Civil Engineer and Architect's Journal* of October of that year, provided a comparable gathering of twenty-five of Pugin's own churches and ecclesiastical buildings, all complete or under construction. The last plate, also devoted to Pugin's works, presents a collection of all the church furnishings that he, together with John Hardman, was manufacturing in Birmingham. These furnishings, in essence, formed the subject of his next book, on which he was already hard at work, *The Glossary of Ecclesiastical Ornament*, published in 1844 by H. G. Bohn.

When *An Apology* was reviewed in *The Art-Union*, in June 1843, it was reviewed together with John Ruskin's *Modern Painters*. Both books were judged to be unacceptable; their authors indulged in too much ridicule and scurrilous comment. R. M.

Bibliography

Stanton, P. *A. C. and A. W. N. Pugin*. New Haven, forthcoming

Augustus Welby Northmore Pugin. *An Apology for the Revival of Christian Architecture*. Plate 10. Church furniture revived at Birmingham. NGA Lib. Rare Book: N44P979A26

63

Augustus Welby Northmore Pugin (1812–1852)

The Present State Of Ecclesiastical Architecture In England. By A. Welby Pugin, Architect. With Thirty-six Illustrations. Republished From The Dublin Review

London: Charles Dolman, 1843

NGA Lib. Rare Book: N44P979A47

Octavo: 221 × 141 (8¾ × 5 7/16)

Pagination 158, [2] pp., 16 wood-engraved plates, 17 [i.e., 16] etched plates (2 double-page)

Edition First edition, second impression

(*Note*: This copy conforms to the Fowler copy, there described as the "First edition, second issue," but actually a later, corrected impression, probably from stereotypes. Fowler describes the earlier impression from a copy at the Library of Congress, and this was also reprinted in facsimile with a new index [Oxford: St. Barnabas Press, 1969]. Belcher notes the facsimile but not the first impression from which it was derived)

Text pp. [1] title page; [2] imprint of Richards, printer; [3] divisional title page "On The Present State . . . Article The First. From the Dublin Review, No. XX. May 1841" (verso blank); [5]–52 text of Article 1; [53] divisional title page "On The Present State . . . Article The Second. From the Dublin Review, No. XXIII. February 1842" (verso blank); [55]–158 text of Article 2; [159] printer's imprint (verso blank)

Illustrations In addition to several wood-engraved illustrations in the text, there are 16 wood-engraved plates to Article 1 numbered I–XVI (plates XIII, XVI signed "Kirchner Sc."); and 16 etched plates to Article 2 numbered 1–17 (plate 16 omitted in numbering), most signed by Pugin with his monogram and plates 5 and 13 dated 1842

Binding Publisher's dark green cloth, lettered in gilt on spine (damaged). 5 of Dolman's trade catalogues, or sections thereof, bound in at the end

Provenance Ownership inscriptions "Thomas Ward Feb. 1879" and "WHW by C. F. Soames / 87"; stamps of "G. H. & G. P. Grima, A/ARIBA Dipl. Arch. . . ."

References Belcher A28.3; Fowler 267

In 1840 Pugin agreed to write three articles for the most militant of Catholic journals, *The Dublin Review*. The first was to be on the building of the parish church; the second on the cathedral, convents, and colleges; the third on ornament and vestments. The first article, "Elevation of the Cathedral Church of St. Chad, Birmingham," was completed in draft on 12 January 1841. By that time Pugin had prepared the twenty illustrations, woodcuts, and etchings that were to accompany it.

The article, published in May, was unsigned—though it was clear to all that it was by Pugin—and addressed directly to Catholics. The aim was to demonstrate how both the ancient forms and liturgy of the Roman Catholic faith of the pre-Reformation era might be revived in the nineteenth century. The tone was unusual. One could not hope, at the present time, to revive the glories of the great cathedrals and abbatical churches of the past, but one could begin to build parish churches:

> It is, in fact, by parish churches, that the faith of a nation is to be sustained and nourished; in them souls are engrafted to the Church by the waters of baptism; they are the tribunals of penance, and the seats of mercy and forgiveness. In them is the holy Eucharistic sacrifice continually offered up, and the sacred body of our Lord received by the faithful; there the holy books are read, and the people instructed; they become the seat and centre of every pious thought and deed; the pavement is studded with sepulchral memorials, and hundreds of departed faithful repose beneath the turf of the consecrated enclosures in which they stand.

Pugin took as his ostensible model St. Chad's, in Birmingham, which was dedicated on 21 June 1841 (though this was to serve as a cathedral church). But he described in detail an ideal parish church, the arrangement of forms and their meaning, the proper use of the ground in which the church was set, its orientation, its plan, the elements of which it was composed, and their proper relation one to another. He dealt with towers and spires and their placement, porches and stoops, fonts and rood screens, sepulchers, and sedilia. The first rood screen to be erected since the Reformation, he noted, was that put up in Ambrose Phillips de Lisle's chapel at Grace Dieu. He referred to no less than thirty-three old churches in England, more than once to the church of Holy Trinity, Long Melford, Suffolk, and also to eleven in France and Germany, but the churches he offered as exemplars and illustrated were all his own—St. Mary's, Stockton-on-Tees; St. Mary's, Warwick Bridge; St. Mary's, Dudley; St. Mary's, Derby; St. Giles', Cheadle; St. George's, London; St. Wilfrid's, Hulme; St. Oswald's, Liverpool; St. Anne's, Keighley; St. Mary's, Southport; St. Alban's, Macclesfield; and St. Mary's, Uttoxeter, all of which were complete or building. The authorities he referred to in support of his arguments as to correct forms and ritual were mainly traditional, though he found much also in the writings of the sixteenth-century theologians Pierre Le Brun and, especially, J. B. Thiers, and in De Moleon's *Voyage liturgique* of 1757. The only contemporary author he cited, though he did not mention him by name, was J. B. Mozley, J. H. Newman's brother-in-law, who was for a short time editor of *The British Critic*, and who had written some notable articles in that journal, much appreciated by Pugin—in particular those on "Internal Decoration of English Churches" published in April 1839, and "New Churches," published in October 1839 and October 1840. Clearly, Pugin hoped at this time that the Oxford Movement might lead to the reunification of the Church in England.

Although he admired Mozley's views on church architecture and decoration, Pugin was irritated by his criticism of the orientation of St. Mary's, Derby, which Mozley had delivered in his second article on "New Churches." Pugin defended himself at some length. Before Pugin's reply was published he had had a memorable meeting with both Mozley and Newman at Oxford, on 20 and 21 February, and Mozley had exonerated himself thereafter, praising the interior of the church in an article on "Open Roofs," published in April 1841. But Pugin let his angry reply stand, and left it still when the article was republished in book form.

Despite the high, even sanctimonious tone of the article, Pugin's anger surfaced again and again. Nor did he spare fellow Catholics; he castigated a chapel recently erected in Yorkshire in the Italianate style—"Alas! Catholic England, how art thou fallen, when thine own children forget the land of their fathers, and leave thy most beauteous works unnoticed and despised, to catch at foreign ideas, unsuited to their country, and jarring with its national traditions." He noted that the maintenance of a private chapel was regarded now by Catholics as something of merit, rather than a privilege:

> a man is not accounted liberal who keeps a cook to administer to his appetite, a butler to provide him drink, and, in fine, a vast number of persons to attend and supply all he requires; this all passes by, nor is it of course considered any way meritorious; but to support a chaplain to administer the sacraments—without which all food, all raiment, all wealth, all state, is utterly dead and unprofitable—is thought in these days something very great and praiseworthy. Out on such contradiction!

Even to the end, he chided:

> Everything Catholic in England is at so low an ebb at present, that it is folly to boast. All we contend for is, that Catholicism in this country possesses sufficient internal strength to revive its ancient glory; while the Establishment, however willing some of its members may be to produce such a result, cannot, under its present system, achieve it. And why is this? It is not from any want of piety, zeal, learning, disinterestedness, or holiness of life,—for all these requisites are possessed in a high degree by many among them; it is simply for want of a really Catholic foundation.

Pugin's second article for *The Dublin Review*, published in February 1842, was a review of a handful of publications by the Cambridge Camden Society and *Two Lectures on the Structure and Decorations of Churches*, which the society approved, by the Reverend G. A. Poole, perpetual curate at St. James', Leeds.

Pugin thought now, as he had earlier in surveying the writings of Mozley, that he had found new allies for his cause. He found praise for almost all the recommendations of the society, from the general arrangement of churches, asymmetrical rather than regular, to the introduction of stained glass and tiles, fonts and rood screens, and vestments. He upheld with the society the absolute inadmissability of pews and galleries. He demonstrated his agreement in three plates of his church of St. Barnabas, Nottingham, and one of the rood screen of St. Chad's, Birmingham, and he further described and illustrated in nine plates seven more of his buildings, some already under construction, some newly designed: St. John's hospital, Alton; Mount St. Bernard's

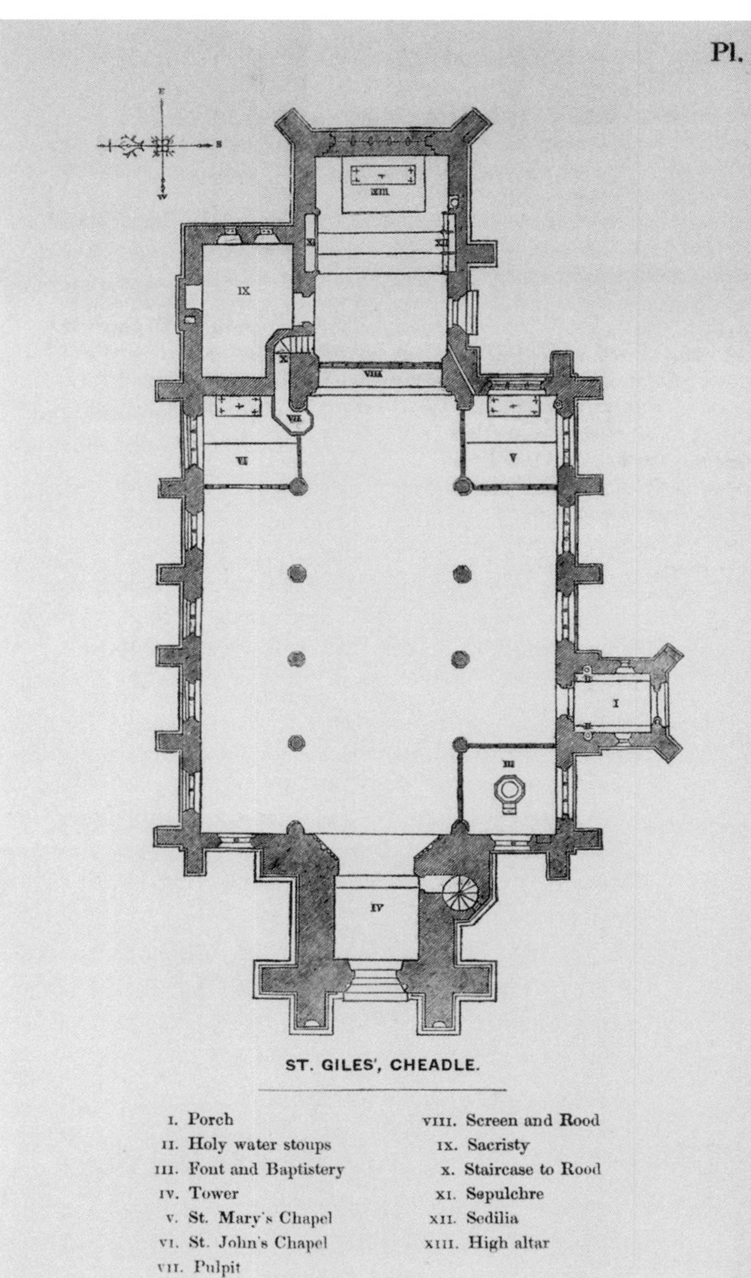

Augustus Welby Northmore Pugin. *The Present State of Ecclesiastical Architecture in England.* Plate 1. Plan of St. Giles, Cheadle. NGA Lib. Rare Book: N44P979A47

Augustus Welby Northmore Pugin. *The Present State of Ecclesiastical Architecture in England.* Plate XIII. Interior view of St. Giles, Cheadle. NGA Lib. Rare Book: N44P979A47

monastery in Leicestershire; the Jesus chapel, near Pomfret (in fact, the private chapel built for the Tempests, hard by Ackworth Grange, near Pontefract, Yorkshire); the Bishop's house, Birmingham; the convents of the Sisters of Mercy at Birmingham and Liverpool; and St. Gregory's Priory, at Downside. In addition, Pugin gave his approval of, and illustrated, the church of St. Bede's, Masbro, by Matthew Hadfield (whom Pugin names Hatfield).

But all was not well. The church of St. John, Duncan Terrace, Islington, by J. J. Scoles, which Pugin illustrated in two plates, was vilified: "This church, so far from exhibiting the adoption of true Catholic principles, which we have had so much pleasure in describing at Masbro, is certainly the most original combination of modern deformity that has been erected for some time past for the sacred purpose of a Catholic church."

Pugin raged also against *An Essay on Architectural Practice*, of 1841, by T. L. Walker (the elder Pugin's literary executor), who was then building the church of St. Philip, at Bethnal Green. "*The style* of the building," Pugin wrote, "is what, in the classification of competition drawings, would be termed *Norman*—that is to say, the arches are not pointed; but in other respects, it bears no greater resemblance to the architecture of the tenth century, than it has in common with ordinary cellars, the Greenwich railway, or any round arched buildings." He had more to say. But Pugin's real spleen was reserved for the end of his article, to which he appended a detailed and circumstantial history of the destruction of altars and rood screens, intent to prove that the real villains were not the Puritans, despicable though they might have been, but "*the leading schismatics during the reigns of Henry the Eighth, Edward the Sixth, and Elizabeth*." He singled out in particular, "that *arch apostate, the father of Puritans and modern Anglicans, Cranmer and his Zuinglian associates, whom he introduced and fostered to blaspheme and profane the saintly ecclesiastics and churches of our land*."

The section on the destruction of altars and rood screens might have seemed to many a mere addendum to Pugin's article, but he was carried along by the theme; in the end he subverted all the accommodation that he had sought at first with the Camden Society:

> the present system is too rotten and decayed to work upon; and patching up Protestantism with copes and candles, would be no better than whitening a sepulchre: for chairs, chancels, altars, and roods, have no part in modern Liturgies and Calvanised rubrics; either the things or the system must be abandoned: the glories of pointed architecture, if viewed *distinct from their Catholic origin, and as symbols of the true and ancient faith*, lose at once their greatest claim to our veneration; and far better would it be to see the churches left ruined as they are, than revived as a mere disguise for Protestantism.

Augustus Welby Northmore Pugin. *The Present State of Ecclesiastical Architecture in England.* No. 13. Benedictine Priory of St. Gregory's, Downside. NGA Lib. Rare Book: N44P979A47

When Pugin visited Cambridge in May 1842, three months after his article appeared, he spent a day in Ely with members of the society; it was not until the following year, when his two articles, unaltered, were published by Charles Dolman as *The Present State of Ecclesiastical Architecture in England* that John Mason Neale and Benjamin Webb felt impelled to open their attack on Pugin, and reject him forcibly as an ally. In their preface, dated Michaelmas 1842, to *The Symbolism of Churches and Church Ornaments*, they accused him, oddly and somewhat spitefully, of having no understanding of church symbolism. Catholics who had been called degenerate were no better pleased by Pugin's strictures. R. M.

Bibliography

Stanton, P. *A. C. and A. W. N. Pugin*. New Haven, forthcoming

64

Thomas Rawlins (c. 1727–1789)

Familiar Architecture; Or, Original Designs Of Houses, For Gentlemen And Tradesmen, Parsonages, Summer Retreats, Banqueting-Rooms, And Churches; With Plans, Sections, &c. To Which Is Added, The Masonry of Semicircular and Elliptical Arches; With Practical Remarks. By Thomas Rawlins, Architect. On Fifty-One Copper-Plates. A New Edition

London: printed for I. and J. Taylor, 1795

NGA Lib. Rare Book: N44R267A331795 fol.

Large quarto: 325 × 248 (12 ¾ × 9 ¾)

Pagination 26 pp., 51 engraved plates

Edition Second edition

Text pp. [1] title page (verso blank); [3] publisher's note (verso blank); 5–14 text; 15–26 explanation of the plates

Illustrations 51 engraved plates, all signed by Rawlins as designer and draftsman and T. Miller as engraver

Binding Recent three-quarter calf, marbled-paper boards. With an undated edition of I. and J. Taylor's 4-page *Catalogue of Books on Architecture* bound at end

References ESTC n18686; Fowler 275 (1st ed.); Harris 732

I. AND J. TAYLOR's opening remarks in this new edition elegantly summarize the purpose of this work:

> The publishers of *Mr. Rawlins's Familiar Architecture*, embrace this opportunity of returning their thanks to a generous public, whose approbation has made a new edition of the work necessary. It may be proper here to say, the work exhibits a great variety of plans and elevations of various dimensions, elegance, and degrees of accommodations, serving as hints to gentlemen who wish to obtain information on a subject so very interesting, as a comfortable dwelling, convenient in the plan, and handsome in the appearance: it will also serve as a guide to persons who, from situation, &c. are deprived of the assistance of professional men; in such circumstances, gentlemen, with a little attention, may proceed to execute these designs, with confidence of completing a structure, which shall be convenient and ornamental (advertisement [3]).

By presenting *Familiar Architecture* as a pattern book for modest family dwellings (the meaning of the title), the Taylors were retaining its most essential aspect as originally published by the author a generation before, in 1768; and the last phrase of the advertisement echoes the title of their most successful work in this genre, John Crunden's *Convenient and Ornamental Architecture*. They have, however, silently deleted from their edition the much more truculent preface Thomas Rawlins originally wrote, which not only deplored the lack of such pattern books but also included a rudimentary critique of architectural education: "The lofty and extensive ideas of our great authors, being solely confin'd to stateliness and splendor, rise to so superb a strain, that they can be of little assistance to the studies of the young architect. For before he can be made acquainted with the necessary conveniences of a building for a small family, he is hurried imperceptibly away with extatic views of becoming great at once" (1768, iii). Rawlins thought that architects should work from small houses up to bigger ones, an idea completely alien to contemporary practice. Furthermore, he saw no reason why an architect had to travel to see classical architecture when he could study it at home. Instead "my opinion is, that the seeds of genius are sown in the mind at our first formation in the womb, which may be term'd innate ideas, or such as nature has implanted in us. And if this natural genius be cherished, improved, and refin'd by proper methods of study and a close application, it gradually grows to maturity" (p. vii).

From this and other parts of the original introduction it is clear that Rawlins had a philosophical bent, taking as his starting point Robert Morris' *Rural Architecture* (1750) and developing his own ideas under the influence, perhaps, of writers such as Henry Home, Lord Kames, whose *Elements of Criticism* had appeared in 1762. The designs themselves do not make any radical departures from the Palladian norm, although his concern with the views from his country houses leads him to incorporate *bombé*-style rooms in about half of them; and he includes a triangular house "designed to command three Vistos" as a theoretical exercise in distribution. (Another triangular villa, supposedly built for John Maynard of Devizes, Wiltshire, was designed by T. C. Overton and illustrated in *The Temple Builder's Most Useful Companion*, 1766.) In his notes to the plates Rawlins is often very specific about his intentions, and he takes care to include offices for tradesmen and large cellars for wine merchants. Plate VIII is so specific it seems unlikely it was produced without reference to an actual project: "A plan and elevation of a building . . . designed for a gentleman who is centr'd in a row of houses two stories high, being his own estate. But his adjoining neighbours may retain shops in front, tho' it should so happen that he is in want of additional rooms, in order as little as possible to lessen the value of his rentals . . ." (p. 20). Plate XLVI shows his unexecuted design for the Dissenters' Octagon Chapel at Norwich, 1753.

The final three plates illustrate a critique by Rawlins of the sections on bridge building in William Emerson's *Principles of Mechanics* and John Muller's *Treatise on Practical Fortifications*; of an article by "Mr. Marter" in the *London Magazine* (March, 1760); and of designs for the two most recent London bridges, Westminster and Blackfriars. Rawlins preferred semicircular arches to catenarian or elliptical designs. The Taylors wisely added a disclaimer to their advertisement: "The *Practical Observations on Arches* are fully retained in this edition, though the subject, and the cause which gave rise to them have long abated of their novelty; but as they are the result of principles founded on the best theory, they may still be of important use."

The first edition was privately published by the author with an impressive list of 152 subscribers, including architects, surveyors, carpenters, bricklayers, plumbers, masons, sculptors, and cabinetmakers. Two booksellers also figure: Henry Webley (subscribing to twenty copies) and Francis Newberry (six copies), and at the foot of the list they are credited as London co-distributors along with the sculptor Abraham Webber. Despite his success at attracting subscribers, however, *Familiar Architecture* must have sold slowly, because in 1789 the Taylors reissued the bulk of the original letterpress with a new title leaf. Stock advertisements issued by the new publishers at around this time attribute it to "the late" Mr. Rawlins; the price was a guinea. Nine plates of uninspired chimneypiece designs were omitted (pls. XLVIIII–LVII). The Canadian Centre for Architecture's copy of this issue retains the chimneypieces, but the title page announces the work to be "On fifty-one copper plates," and it must be assumed they were intended to be suppressed. They may have migrated to another title in the Taylors' large stock of pattern books. Also omitted was the list of subscribers and a single leaf with "References to the Apparatus." The latter related to plate LX, but its presence in the first edition was in any case mysterious, since the same references are found on page 30 of the main text. Only for the present "new" edition was the text actually reprinted, in the abridged form described, twenty-seven years after Rawlins' first and only venture into professional promotion through print. G. B.

Bibliography

Colvin, H. *A Biographical Dictionary of British Architects 1600–1840*. 3d ed. New Haven and London, 1995: 793

Harris, E., and N. Savage. *British Architectural Books and Writers 1556–1785*. Cambridge, 1990

Thomas Rawlins. *Familiar Architecture; or, Original Designs of Houses.* Plate XXXVIII. Design for a triangular house. NGA Lib. Rare Book: N44R267A331795 fol.

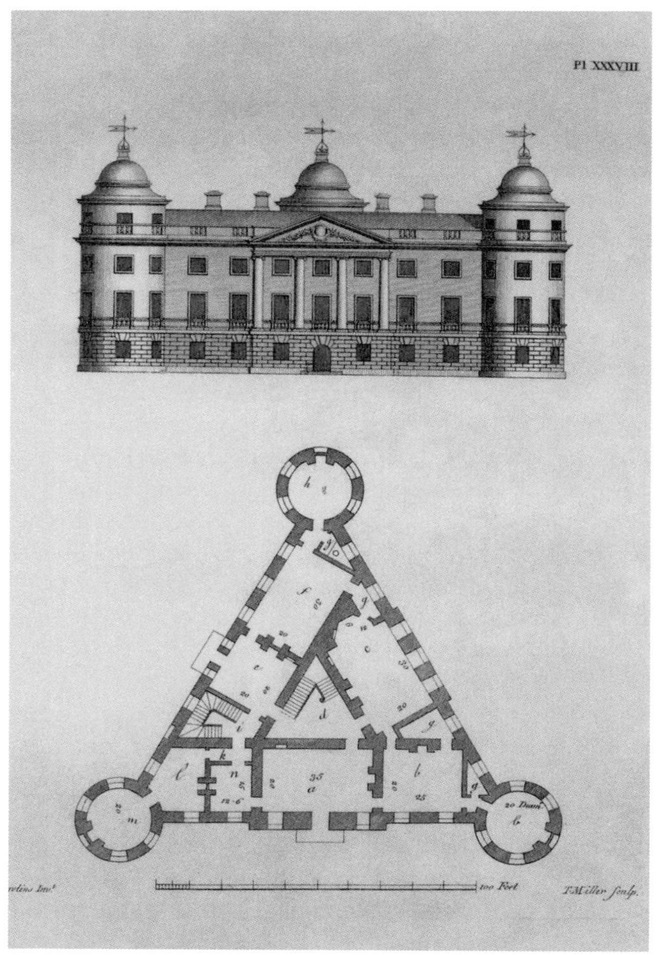

Thomas Rawlins. *Familiar Architecture; or, Original Designs of Houses.* Plate XLVI. Design for an octagonal chapel. NGA Lib. Rare Book: N44R267A331795 fol.

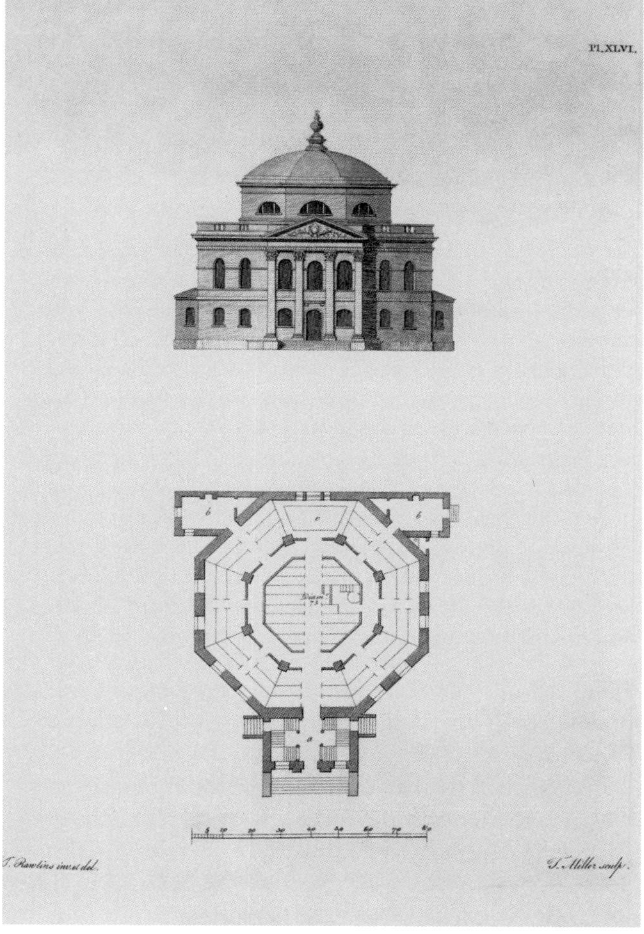

65

Humphry Repton (1752–1818)

Observations On The Theory And Practice Of Landscape Gardening. Including Some Remarks On Grecian And Gothic Architecture, Collected From Various Manuscripts, In The Possession Of The Different Noblemen And Gentlemen, For Whose Use They Were Originally Written; The Whole Tending To Establish Fixed Principles In The Respective Arts. By H. Repton, Esq.

London: printed by T. Bensley, for J. Taylor, 1805

1985.61.2642

Quarto: 334 × 275 (13 1/8 × 10 7/8)

Pagination 16, 222, [2] pp., aquatint portrait frontispiece, [27] engraved or aquatint plates (1 double-page, 1 folding)

Edition Second edition

Text pp. [1] title page (verso blank); [3] dedication to the king, dated 31 Dec. 1802 (verso blank); [5]–8 "Advertisement Explaining The Nature Of This Work"; [9]–14 preface; [15]–16 "List Of The Places Referred To As Examples"; [1]–222 text; [223–224] index followed by list of plates (including aquatint vignettes), printer's imprint at end

Illustrations An uncolored aquatint portrait of the author by William Holl (the elder) after Samuel Shelley is bound as a frontispiece. There are 12 hand-colored aquatint plates (facing pp. 9, 15, 34, 40, 64, 102, 106, 133, 162, 192, 202, 208, the last of these folding and all with overlays except those facing pp. 102, 106, 162, 192, 202); 10 uncolored aquatints (facing pp. 28 [x 2], 48, 51, 94, 112, 171, 179, 186, 200, the last double-page, those facing pp. 51 and 179 with overlays, and those facing pp. 28 [x 2] and 200 tinted); and 5 uncolored engraved plates (facing pp. 67, 182, 188, 209, 212, the first "Engraved by S. Porter" and the last "J. [i.e., John] Adey Repton inv. et delin^t.," "S. Porter Sculp^t."). In addition, there are 11 aquatint vignettes in the text on pp. [1] ("Pickett sc."), 44, 116, 144 (x 2), [145] (with overlay), [149], [151], [153], [155] (with overlay), [157]; and 19 wood-engraved diagrams or vignettes, the 1 on p. 219 hand-colored and included in the letterpress list of plates

Binding Twentieth-century quarter cloth, earlier marbled boards, text edges gilt. Binder's stamp on pastedown "Roger De Coverly"

References Abbey, *Scenery*, 390 (1st ed.); Berlin Cat. 3431 (1st ed.)

Humphry Repton came late to landscape gardening, but he at once thought of himself as its leading practitioner (he, in fact, coined the term) and principal theorist. And he wished to be remembered as such: "It is rather upon my opinion in writing," he wrote in the preface to his *Theory and Practice*, "than on the partial and imperfect manner in which my plans have sometimes been executed that I wish my fame to be established."

Repton was born in April 1752, at Bury St. Edmunds, in Suffolk, the son of an excise officer. His mother was the daughter of John Fitch of Moor Hall, also in Suffolk. At the age of twelve he was sent to Holland for two years to learn Dutch, in preparation for an apprenticeship to a textile manufacturer. He married in May 1773 and was given sufficient capital by his father to set up business, but he disliked trading in textiles and was not an efficient speculator. When his father died he gave up his business and settled, in 1778, at Old Hall, Sustead, in Norfolk, to lead the life of a country gentleman. He took an active interest in local affairs. He read and he sketched. He became friendly with the local lord of the manor, William Windham, a retiring intellectual who felt it incumbent upon him to take an interest in politics. He stood, with Repton's assistance, as a candidate for Norwich in 1780, but was unsuccessful. When the duke of Portland became prime minister in 1783, he appointed Lord Northington as lord lieutenant of Ireland, and he chose Windham as his chief secretary. Windham asked Repton to act as his private secretary. They left together, on 29 May, for Dublin. Windham resigned two months later, leaving Repton to tidy up his affairs. Repton had little taste for politicking, but he was impressed by the connections he made. He entered the political arena as an active support to Windham when he again stood, and was returned, as candidate for Norwich, in 1784. Windham was closely allied to the duke of Portland, and it was through this powerful Whig connection that Repton found his first clients, when, almost without preparation, he decided to earn a living as a landscape gardener. Repton's declaration took the form of a circular letter addressed to friends and acquaintances—only one of which, dated 26 August 1788, addressed to the Reverend Norton Nicholls, is known to survive—in which he solicited work. He also had a trade card printed, with a view over a lake, and the words "H. Repton, Landscape Gardener, Hare Street, near Romford, Essex." In 1786 he had moved from Sustead to Hare Street, where he was to reside until his death. His first commissions seem all to have come through Windham. Repton's first client was Jeremiah Ives, mayor of Norwich; his second was none other than Thomas Coke, of Holkham Hall, Norfolk, the focus of Whig politics in the country. Coke, however, did not engage Repton to carry out the work, but rather John Webb.

Whatever disinclination Repton might have had for politics, he continued to be actively involved. In 1790 he acted both as agent for Windham, when he stood again, and as electioneer for Sir Gerard Vanneck of Heveningham Hall, in Suffolk. The Whig connection was vital to Repton's career. In this same year he did his first designs for the duke of Portland's Nottinghamshire estate, Welbeck. Other commissions in the area followed. Later in his career, as Stephen Daniels has shown, Repton was as willing to work for Tories as for Whigs. He was not really concerned with party politics; he preferred only that his clients be old, landed gentry, rather than newcomers. He was extremely snobbish, but he was also a man of some honor and humanity, and his political concerns were not necessarily altogether opportunistic.

Within six years of his decision to become a landscape gardener, Repton had firmly established himself as a worthy successor to Capability Brown (who had died in 1783) and as the leader in the field. By then he had worked at more than fifty country houses. From the start he had recorded his ideas and his proposals for each estate in the form of a Red Book, illustrated with delicate watercolors, complete with slides or overlays, that showed the transformations Repton had in mind. The first of his Red Books was done for his fourth client, Lady Salusbury, of Brandsbury, to whom he submitted his bill for ten guineas on 13 March 1789. His next Red Book was done for Thomas Coke, dated 30 October 1789. Hundreds more were to follow—by 1792 he claimed to have done a hundred already. His first attempt at assembling his ideas and observations together in the form of a published book was made in 1794, when he wrote his *Sketches and Hints on Landscape Gardening*. The elaboration of Repton's aquatints and overlays occasioned some delay in the publication. The book, expected in the summer of 1794, was still not published in February 1795. Repton took advantage of this delay to reply to two altogether unexpected—and altogether hurtful—attacks that were delivered against him in 1794 by the two most prominent connoisseurs of the picturesque, Richard Payne Knight and Uvedale Price. Knight's elegant plea for the picturesque, *The Landscape, a Didactic Poem addressed to Uvedale Price*, was out before the end of April, Price's lengthier *Essay on the Picturesque* by the end of May. Knight certainly liked a shaggier landscape than Repton, but his particular jibes were addressed to Repton's presumption in attempting not only to appropriate distant prospects in his landscapes, but to pepper adjacent properties with marks of his clients' ownership, in the form of coats of arms on monuments and even stones. Price was intent to establish the picturesque as an independent aesthetic category distinct from the beautiful and the sublime as defined by Edmund Burke; its qualities were identified as sudden

Humphry Repton. *Observations on the Theory and Practice of Landscape Gardening*. Michel Grove, Sussex (slide open). 1985.61.2642

variation, irregularity, and roughness. And these were qualities, he thought, that had first been distinguished by painters. Brown was derided by both Knight and Price. Repton, though he might have agreed that Brown's landscapes were sometimes too bland and consistent, felt bound to defend him—the very profession of the landscape gardener was at stake. Repton also felt that his own work had been traduced. He thought that Price, even, had taken over some of his ideas. He added an extra chapter, "Concerning approaches . . . ," to the *Sketches and Hints* in reply to Knight, and a separately printed letter, dated 1 July 1794, in reply to Price, that was to be added to the book in the form of an appendix—whatever Repton's aspirations as a writer, much of this seems to have been written by William Combe, a literary hack, who was later to achieve something of fame with his hilarious satire of William Gilpin, *The Tour of Doctor Syntax in Search of the Picturesque*, of 1812. The controversy continued, Price producing *A Letter to H. Repton Esq.* in the following year that was about eight times the length of Repton's missive, and Knight responding in his wonderfully sharp and entertaining *An Analytical Inquiry into the Principles of Taste*, of 1805, which was more a response to Price than to Repton, for the two connoisseurs were by then themselves engaged in battle. In the end, Repton was forgotten, for he lacked the spleen for such sport. Whatever Repton's pretensions, he was looked down upon by the arrogant proselytes of the picturesque. He was not one of the landed gentry. He was not of an intellectual cast of mind; he was a practical man who illustrated each of his ideas with reference to one of his works. He was never to produce a theory of landscape gardening.

But he tried, once again with the help of Combe. Six years after the *Sketches and Hints* he issued a prospectus for *Observations on the Theory and Practice of Landscape Gardening*, announcing publication "In the course of the year 1802. . . ." Subscribers were to pay four guineas, the price after publication would be five guineas. The book, dedicated to the king, was published in 1803 by Josiah Taylor and reprinted, unaltered, in 1805. Altogether 750 copies were printed. The frontispiece, a portrait of Repton, was drawn by S. Shelley and engraved by W. Holl. The aquatint plates, both colored and uncolored, many with slides, are unattributed—although in his preface Repton remarks that the names of the various artists involved were affixed. Repton's eldest son John Adey had joined his father in 1800, and may have assisted him. Repton himself notes only in the book—"the art of colouring plates in imitation of drawings has so far improved of late that I have pleasure in recording obligations to Mr. Clarke under whose direction a

Humphry Repton. *Observations on the Theory and Practice of Landscape Gardening.* Michel Grove, Sussex (slide in place). 1985.61.2642

number of children have been employed to enrich this volume." Four of the engraved plates are signed by Adey, all five were engraved by S. Porter. One of the aquatint vignettes was engraved by Pickett.

Repton's book, whatever his intention, is not a theoretical treatise. He lacked the cast of mind for that. He offers instead a guide to his approach to landscape design, with explanations of his aims and his methods of achieving them in specific instances. The book is a compilation of texts from a number of the Red Books he had composed since his last publication, many of them now lost—those for Balstrode, Corsham, Gayhurst, Shardeloes, and West Wycombe. Several are now in American collections—those for Armley, Brandesbury, Culford, Ferney, the Royal Fort, Bristol, and Stonelands. Repton's *Observations* is, in effect, a handbook of tricks of the trade, or rather profession, for, unlike Brown, who had usually contracted himself for work, Repton acted only as a consultant and overseer.

"Seven years have now elapsed," he writes in the advertisement, "since the publication of my 'Sketches and Hints on Landscape Gardening,' during which, by the continued duties of my profession, it is reasonable to suppose much experience has been gained and many principles established. Yet so difficult is the application of any rules of Art to the works of Nature, that I do not presume to give this Book any higher title than 'Observations tending to establish fixed Principles in the Art of Landscape Gardening.'" He admitted in all frank-ness that he was unable to arrange the matter systematically—"In every other polite Art, there are certain established rules or general principles, to which the professor may appeal in support of his opinions, but in Landscape Gardening everyone delivers his sentiments, or displays his taste, as whim or caprice may dictate, without having studied the subject, or even thought it capable of being reduced to any fixed rules."

Theories of landscape gardening, he wrote, with obvious reference to Price, were made up of objections rather than positive propositions. He listed ten of these objections—that no error was more frequent in modern gardening than taking away hedges; that boldness and nakedness around a house was a part of this same mistaken system; that an approach which did not evidently lead to the house or which did not take the shortest course, could not be right; and so forth.

Repton's chapter headings alone convey his inability to himself produce a coherent theory or even a system-

Humphry Repton. *Observations on the Theory and Practice of Landscape Gardening.* Water at Wentworth, Yorkshire (slide in place). 1985.61.2642

atic guide to operation. The arrangement of his material seems arbitrary:

Chapter I. Introduction—General Principles—Utility—Scale—Various Examples of Comparative Proportion—Use of Perspective—Example from the FORT—Ground—Several Examples of removing Earth—The great Hill at WENTWORTH.

Chapter II. Optics or vision—At what Distance Objects appear largest—Axis of Vision—quantity or Field of Vision—Ground apparently altered by the Situation of the Spectator—Reflections from the Surface of Water explained and applied—Different Effects of Light on different Objects—Example.

Chapter III. Water—it may be too naked or too much clothed—Example from WEST WYCOMBE—Digression concerning the Approach—Motion of Water—Example at ADLESTROP—Art must deceive to imitate Nature—Cascade at THORESBY—The Rivulet—Water at WENTWORTH described—A River easier to imitate than a Lake—A bubbling Spring may be imitated—a Ferry Boat at HOLKHAM—A rocky Channel at HAREWOOD.

Chapter IV. Of PLANTING for immediate and for future Effect—Clumps—Groups—Masses—New Mode of planting Wastes and Commons—the Browsing Line described—Example MILTON ABBEY—Combination of Masses to produce great Woods—Example COOMBE LODGE—Character and Shape of Ground to be studied—Outline of new Plantations.

And thus he continues through fourteen chapters—on Woods, Fences, the Ferme Ornée, Pleasure Grounds, a Defence of the Art (a further response to Price and Knight), Of ancient and modern Gardening (Le Notre vs. Capability Brown), Miscellaneous, Architecture and Gardening inseparable, Ancient Mansions, Gardening and Architecture united in the Formation of a new Place—finished off with a section on color, "Theory of Colours and Shadows," especially commissioned from the scientist, the Reverend Isaac Milner.

There is, inevitably, much of interest in all this to historians of landscape gardening, much revealing of Repton's tastes and methods of operation; most interesting, in view of his later plea for the adoption of the Indian style for the Pavilion at Brighton, in preference to both the classical and Gothic styles, is the excerpt from the Red Book for Magdalen College, Oxford, in chapter thirteen, on the suitability of these last for contemporary architecture. The classical architecture of Greece and Rome, which finds its ultimate expression in the temple form, is rejected as unsuited to the English climate and to the requirements of most modern buildings, certainly those of the domestic kind. Even in its reduced form—what Repton refers to as "modern Italian"—the classical style remains unacceptable, for though it might be better adapted to useful purposes, it has been divested of almost all character. The Gothic, which Repton classes under three heads—castle Gothic, church Gothic, and house Gothic ("Elizabeth's Gothic corrupted by bad taste")—is viewed in an altogether different light.

"And although Grecian architecture may be more regular, there is a stateliness and grandeur in the lofty towers, the rich and splendid assemblage of turrets, battlements, and pinnacles, the bold depth of shadow produced by projecting buttresses, and the irregularity of outline in a large Gothic building, unknown to the most perfect Grecian edifice."

Repton lists, in his customary manner, the five "leading principles" of Gothic.

1. The *Uses* of a building were considered before its *Ornaments*. [He adds a note here suggestive of a knowledge of French structural theory—"Small turrets and pinnacles, or fineals, will be considered only as ornaments by the careless observer, but the mathematician discovers that such projections above the roof, form part of its construction because they add weight and solidity to those abutments which support the Gothic arch."]
2. The ornaments prevailed where they would be most conspicuous.
3. The several principal parts of the building were marked by some conspicuous and distinguished character.
4. Some degree of symmetry, or correspondence of parts, was preserved, without actually confining the design to such regularity as involved unnecessary or useless buildings.
5. This degree of irregularity seems often to have been studied in order to produce increased grandeur by an intricacy and variety of the parts.

And lastly, the effect of perspective, and of viewing the parts of a building in succession, was either studied, or chance has given it a degree of interest, that makes it worthy to be studied.

In thus approving Gothic as the most suitable style for contemporary buildings—and, inevitably, for Magdalen College—it is surprising to find that interiors, the hall and main corridors apart, were to remain in the "Grecian" mode. This, of course, was a matter of propriety. R. M.

Bibliography

Carter, G., P. Goode, and K. Laurie. *Humphry Repton Landscape Gardener 1752–1818*. Norwich and London, 1982

Robinson, J. M. Introduction to reprint of Repton's *Observations on the Theory and Practice of Landscape Gardening*. Oxford, 1980

Stroud, D. *Humphry Repton*. London, 1962

66

Humphry Repton (1752–1818)

Designs For The Pavillon At Brighton. Humbly Inscribed To His Royal Highness The Prince Of Wales. By H. Repton, Esq. With The Assistance Of His Sons, John Adey Repton, F. S. A. & G. S. Repton, Architects

London: printed for J. C. Stadler; and sold by Boydell and Co.; Longman, Hurst, Rees, and Orme; White; Cadell and Davies; Payne and Mackinlay; Payne; Miller; and Taylor. Printed by Howlett and Brimmer, Columbian Press, [c. 1822]

1985.61.2643

Large folio: 540 × 365 (21¼ × 14 5/16)

Pagination [4], x, 41, [1] pp., aquatint frontispiece, [9] aquatint plates (1 double-page, 1 folding)

(*Note*: Undated edition, paper with watermark dates of 1821 or 1822. The Berlin (1977) copy has paper with a watermark "1825," and the Canadian Centre for Architecture copy has an inscription dated 1828)

Edition Second edition

Text pp. [1] title page (verso blank); [3] Repton's dedication to the prince of Wales, dated February 1806 (verso blank); [i]–x "Prefatory Observations"; [1]–11 text; [12] blank; [13] divisional title page "An Inquiry Into The Changes In Architecture, As It Relates To Palaces and Houses in England. Including The Castle And Abbey Gothic, The Mixed Style Of Gothic, The Grecian And Modern Styles; With Some Remarks On The Introduction Of Indian Architecture" (verso blank); [15]–41 text of same; [42] blank

(*Note*: The following text pages are blank: [6], [8], [10], [12], [14], [16], [18], [26], [32], [36], [40], [42])

Illustrations 10 *hors texte* aquatint plates as follows:

[1] Frontispiece of "Flora Cherishing Winter" with a quotation from Burke, *On the Sublime*

[2] "General Ground Plan," following p. 4

[3–4] "View From The Dome," the first plate representing an archway through which the second is viewed, following p. [12]

[5] "West-Front of the Pavillon," following p. [32]

[6] "The General View from the Pavillon," double-page with 2 overlays, following p. 39

[7] "Design for an Orangerie," 2 figures on 1 plate, the upper with 2 overlays, following p. 39

[8] "The Pheasantry," following p. 39

[9] "West Front Of The Pavillon Towards The Garden," with overlay, following p. [42]

[10] "North Front towards the Parade," folding, with 2 overlays, following p. [42]

All the above are hand-colored except plates [3] and [5], which are tinted, and all are signed as engraved by J. C. Stadler after Humphry Repton, with Stadler's imprint dated 1 May 1808, except plates [2–3]. In addition, the text contains 11 aquatint plates, most uncolored and unsigned, on pp. [7] (colored, signed by Repton and Stadler), [13] (signed by Repton), [23], 24, 25, 28, 31, [35] (tinted, signed by Repton and Stadler), [38], [39] (colored, signed by Repton and Stadler), and [41] (colored, signed by Repton and Stadler, with overlay)

Binding Twentieth-century three-quarter green morocco, green buckram slipcase. Binder's stamp on front free endpaper "Bound By Zaehnsdorf, London, England"

References Abbey, *Scenery*, 55 (1st ed.) and 57; Berlin (1977) OS 2318[P]

Humphry Repton was already thirty-six when, in 1788, he embarked on the career of landscape gardener. But he soon built up an extensive practice, almost as extensive as that of his mentor Lancelot Brown. His style, however, was more varied than Brown's, less self-consciously Arcadian, richer in incident, and more diverse in the juxtaposition of elements, including flowerbeds, arbors and terraces. Like Brown, Repton was often consulted on matters of architecture. He became quite adept at producing architectural designs related to his landscapes, though he worked as a rule with established architects, notably John Nash. Nash trained his eldest son, John Adey Repton, who left Nash's employ in 1800 and worked thereafter with his father. Repton's youngest son, George Stanley, trained also with Nash, before joining his father. The most ambitious of Repton's architectural projects, Magdalen College, Oxford, of Gothic inspiration, and the Pavilion at Brighton, of Indian, were produced in collaboration with his sons. The design for Magdalen is more typical of Repton's work. He liked best the Gothic style, especially as an expression of irregular planning, though he was altogether competent in the handling of what he regarded as the Grecian or Modern style. He designed a succession of neat, classical villas. But though he had essayed the Chinese style in the pavilions for Woburn Abbey in 1804, he gave little early evidence of a taste for anything exotic—indeed, it is evident from his writings that he somewhat disapproved experiments of this sort.

The first knowledge we have of Repton's acquaintance with Indian art is a record in his "Memoir" of a visit to the Reverend Jolland's curious Hermitage at Louth, in 1790. A series of rooms there were decked with bamboo and Indian objects as a memorial to Jolland's brother, who had died in India. Repton was much impressed by

Humphry Repton. *Designs for the Pavillon at Brighton.* "West-front of the pavillon" (slide open). 1985.61.2643

this "original specimen of eccentric taste," but made no immediate attempt to emulate it. About 1804, however, he was called in by Sir Charles Cockerell, recently returned from India, who wished to record something of his experience there in the building and gardens of the estate he had purchased at Sezincote, Gloucestershire. The architect in charge was Sir Charles' younger brother, Samuel Pepys Cockerell; Repton was presumably expected to advise on no more than the gardens. However, he was shown some of Thomas and William Daniell's stunning aquatints of scenes and buildings in India, published between 1795 and 1808, in series, as *Oriental Scenery*, and features from these were eventually to appear in the garden. The only drawing by Repton to survive shows a flowerbed, in no sense Indian. Later, in the *Designs for the Pavillon at Brighton*, Repton wrote:

> I confess, the subject was then entirely new to me; but from his long residence in the interior of that country, and from the good taste and accuracy with which he had observed and pointed out to me the various forms of ancient Hindu architecture, a new field opened itself: and as I became more acquainted with them, through the accurate Sketches and Drawings made on the spot by my ingenious friend Mr T Daniell, I was pleased at having discovered new sources of beauty and variety which might gratify that thirst for novelty, so dangerous to good taste in any system long established. . . .

Repton had first been summoned to Brighton by the prince of Wales in 1797. Payments were made to him over the next five years for works in the garden of the prince's still modest marine villa. He must also, at this period, have introduced Nash to the prince, for in 1802 Nash added a conservatory or music room to the south side of the pavilion, the first of his many significant commissions for the prince. But he was not yet the favorite. From 1803 to 1805 William Porden erected the stables and riding school to the northwest of the pavilion, in the form of a great rotunda, known as the Dome, decorated in a "Saracenic" style. Porden was a pupil of Cockerell. Then, in October 1805, Repton was requested to attend on the prince in Brighton. Repton thought best to visit Craven Cottage, the bizarrely decorated house that Thomas Hopper had built for Mr. Walsh Porter at Fulham, much admired by the prince, before traveling to Brighton. The prince and Repton met only on 24 November. By 12 December Repton had returned

DINING ROOM.

In a Dining Room, as the number of guests may be different at different times, some provision should be made for either enlarging it by Recesses at the end, or on the side; and these Recesses might occasionally be detached from the large room, for a small or select party.

In this sketch some Ornaments are introduced to enrich the Ceiling, which from their novelty may appear too fanciful; but the difficulty of reconciling the mind to new forms will operate at first against every attempt to introduce them. These Ornaments of the Ceiling may be subservient to the framing of the roof, and may also supply expedients for ventilating the upper part of the room, which is apt, in Dining Rooms especially, to retain the rarefied air and vapour that cannot descend to the common apertures of doors, windows, or fire-places.

Humphry Repton. *Designs for the Pavillon at Brighton.* View of dining room. 1985.61.2643

to Brighton with a sheaf of drawings showing possible improvements, employing "my usual method of slides." The prince was intrigued and asked for a design for an entirely new house. Repton presented his scheme in February 1806 in the form of one of his folio Red Books, now in the Royal Library at Windsor Castle, to be published in 1808 as *Designs for the Pavillon at Brighton*. By then the prince's initial enthusiasm had dulled; he was beset with financial difficulties and had laid aside all elaborate schemes for the enlargement of the pavilion. Four years later James Wyatt was working on a scheme in the Gothic style, but this was interrupted by his sudden death in 1813. Nash was to be the architect of the marvelous extravaganza that was begun there in March 1815. "So ended my Royal Hopes!" Repton wrote in his "Memoir," "from which I had proudly prognosticated a new species of architecture more applicable to this country than either Grecian or Gothic."

Repton's Indian design was certainly striking, and must have inspired Nash in his triumph, but it was rather too lightweight and elegant, rather too painstakingly assembled by the direct transposition of details from the Daniells' prints to be considered a success. And whatever claims Repton might have made in the *Designs* to have fostered a new species of architecture, it is clear that he was doing no more than pandering to the prince's whims.

"As many parts of this volume," he writes in the preface to the *Designs*, "may appear to recommend a degree of novelty, to which I have frequently objected in former publications, it will perhaps subject me to some severity of criticism. I must therefore plead for candid and indulgent hearing, while I explain the origin of the following work, and endeavour to justify its intentions."

Repton's justification relates first to the site and the nature of the commission. Reverting to his larger theories of landscape design, he defines once more the three basic "distances"—"in forest scenery we trace the sketches of SALVATOR and of RIDINGER; in park scenery we may realize the landscapes of CLAUDE and POUSSIN: but, in garden scenery, we delight in the rich embellishments; the blended graces of WATTEAU, where nature is dressed, but not disfigured, by art; and where the artificial decorations of architecture and sculpture are softened down by natural accompaniments of vegetation." This last, the garden, Repton thought, was the only "distance" that might possibly be imposed on the site, given its limited extent. So restricted was it, moreover, that it would have to be opened up to its surroundings, without screens or hedges. Nor would there be any conflict in such a solution, for what was required by the prince was a pleasure garden.

Repton had clearly announced this realm of illusion, intricate and small of scale, in his elaborate frontispiece, which shows Flora triumphing over Winter through the artifice of the heated conservatory, and includes two inscriptions: "Gardens are works of art rather than of nature," and, from Edmund Burke, "Designs that are vast only by their dimensions, are always the sign of a common and low imagination; no work of art can be great but as it deceives, to be otherwise is the prerogative of nature only." This had the added twist of serving as a response to those critics of Repton who complained that his method of presentation with slides was, essentially, deceiving.

Repton's justification of his elaborate, exotic architecture is contained within "An Enquiry into the changes in architecture, as it relates to palaces and houses in England, including the castle and abbey gothic, the mixed style of gothic, the Grecian and Modern styles; with some remarks on the introduction of Indian architecture," which is presented, almost, as a book within a book. This is decorated with a vignette illustrating the various styles of buildings described, set under Time's scythe and the motto "Tempus omnia mutans." Repton's arguments may be summarily dealt with, because they are so specious. The ranges of Gothic styles are rejected first—the castle character because it requires massive walls, the abbey character because it requires large and lofty openings, which leaves only the "Mixed Style" of "Queen Elizabeth's Gothic," but this, because it is mixed, is necessarily imperfect. Similarly with the Grecian style—the model for the antique form is the temple, which, though suitable perhaps for churches and public buildings, is ill adapted to palaces and houses. The modern form of the Grecian style is, equally, unacceptable as it is, in effect, without character, "this consists of a plain building, with rows of square windows at equal distances." To further reinforce his arguments Repton analyzes the various styles from a structural point of view. Grecian, being a translation of timber forms into stone, requires massive blocks for its spans, which are not readily available. Gothic, involving lateral thrusts, requires a great deal of buttressing, which is unsuitable in domestic architecture. Indian architecture, however, with which Repton included "Hindûstan, Gentoo, Chinese, or Turkish; which latter is a mixture of the other three," was found to depend on a much sounder structural principle, the corbeled arch. The style could, moreover, be interpreted also in the modern material, cast iron. Altogether the Indian emerges as the most suitable style for the new pavilion, having far more variety of form than anything yet taken up.

Repton, perhaps, reveals more than he intends when he suggests that his choice was motivated by a desire to preserve the classical and Gothic styles from abuse—"It is not therefore," he explains in his preface, "with a view to supersede the known styles, that I am become an advocate for a new one, but to preserve their long established proportions pure and unmixed by fanciful innovations." Not surprisingly, after the Brighton indulgence, Repton made no further attempts to promote the Indian style. It is not upheld in the last of his publications, *Fragments on the Theory and Practice of Landscape Gardening* of 1816, though the *Designs for the Pavillon at Brighton* was reprinted—the frontispiece colored, the text unchanged, but reset—around 1822, after Repton's death, to coincide, one must assume, with Nash's completion of the pavilion. Both editions were dedicated to the prince of Wales.

The *Designs* as published on 1 May 1808 was based directly on the original Red Book, which was sent to the publisher and engraver, J. C. Stadler, of 15 Villiers St., Strand. There were no more than minor changes to the text, the omission of a section on the effects of purple glass windows apart. The drawings, by Repton and his sons, were sumptuously reproduced in aquatint, mostly in color, complete with their overslips and slides. Stadler himself took on the financial responsibilities. The book sold for six guineas. R. M.

Bibliography

Carter, G., P. Goode, and K. Laurie. *Humphry Repton Landscape Gardener 1752–1818*. Norwich, 1982

Connor, P. "Unexecuted Designs for the Royal Pavilion at Brighton." *Apollo* (March 1978): 192–199

Stroud, D. *Humphry Repton*. London, 1962

67

George Richardson (d. 1813)

A New Collection Of Chimney Pieces, Ornamented in the Style of the Etruscan, Greek, and Roman Architecture; Containing Thirty Six Designs, Suitable to the most elegant Range of Apartments; With Descriptions of the Plates in English and French. Composed, Etched and Engraved in Aquatinta By George Richardson, Architect. . . . [same in French] . . .

London: printed for the author, 1781

1985.61.2645

Folio: 503 × 325 (19 13/16 × 12 13/16)

Pagination [ii], 16 pp., 36 aquatint plates

Edition First edition

Text (parallel English and French) pp. [i] title (verso blank); [1] dedication to Sir Laurence Dundas, in English (verso blank); [3]–10 introduction; [11]–16 description of the plates

Illustrations 36 full-page aquatint plates numbered I–XXXVI, all after plate V signed "G. Richardson Arch^{t}."

Binding Recent quarter calf, marbled boards, red morocco label

Provenance Illegible ownership inscription on plate I, "Giorge Luis[?]"

References Berlin Cat. 3830; ESTC t90836; Harris and Savage 740

George Richardson was an obscure satellite in the Adam family constellation—his dates are unknown, his ascertained built works few, and his published designs and theories derivative—yet he played an interesting part in the development of architectural publication, notably through his use of aquatint illustration. Born in the second half of the 1730s and therefore several years younger than the Adam brothers, he was an apprentice in Edinburgh, quite possibly to John Adam, the eldest, in 1759. In 1760 he accompanied James Adam as a draftsman on his Grand Tour of Italy, and on their return to London in 1763 he entered the Adams' London office. According to a Mr. Lumley (*Gentleman's Magazine*, March 1814), perhaps the carpenter William Lumley who subscribed to *New Designs in Architecture*, Richardson was clerk of works to the Adams during the erection of the Adelphi buildings, but at some point in the late 1760s or early 1770s he left for independent practice. The collapse of the Adelphi scheme in 1772 may have precipitated his departure; at any rate, his services were not used on the plates for the *Works in Architecture of Robert and James Adam*, which the brothers published in 1773 as a response to their financial difficulties. Relations between them had, in any case, been based on mutual advantage rather than respect since at least 1758, when Robert wrote to James "if I could do without such a wretch you may be sure I would never hear of him again, but he knows my manner of drawing and I have nobody to supply his place." Richardson, for his part, complained from Italy in 1762 that James "has none other attention for me than merely for his own ends & purposes," but acknowledged "I cannot entertain the smallest thoughts of doing without him or his brothers, well knowing my own incapacity, small fortune, want of books and little hope of interest."

His change of heart on the latter point, with or without the Adelphi debacle, may have been prompted by a realization that Robert Adam's costive attitude to publication was leaving a gap in the market. Robert discouraged his brother from "throwing your most precious works into the public's hands" or indeed the hands of "every dirty artist" to criticize and copy, and when he did publish it was only under financial duress and as a record of built works discreetly advertising his taste and connections rather than anything resembling a pattern book. But at the same time, as the acclaim which greeted James Wyatt's Adamesque interior of the Pantheon in Oxford Street in 1772 demonstrated, there was a market for the style, one which George Richardson's first publication, *A Book of Ceilings* (1776), among others, sought to address. Richardson borrowed from the Adams' *Works in Architecture* the large format, the bilingual text, and the option of hand-coloring for the plates, and by acting as his own publisher he maintained the standards of presentation on which his artistic reputation would rest; but at the same time he aimed at wider sales. His designs are candidly offered for imitation and adaptation, his prices were kept down by the twin strategies of engraving his own plates and part-publishing, and he was remarkable successful in attracting subscriptions.

In *A New Collection of Chimney Pieces*, Richardson distances himself from the string of practical pocket-books that had appeared on the subject, such as Abraham Swan's *Designs for Chimnies* or Crunden and Baldwin's *Chimneypiece Maker's Daily Assistant*, both by the scale and artistry of his production and by the scholarship that he is at pains to display. He acknowledges not only his former masters the Adam brothers but also Vitruvius, Pliny, Chambers, and finally Piranesi, author of *Diversi Maniere d'Adornare i Cammini* in 1769. Perhaps Piranesi and Du Perron, whose *New Book of Chimney Pieces* appeared in the 1750s with six plates in a rococo-gothic style, were in Richardson's mind when he praised British chimneypiece design over that of the "whimsical and extravagant" Italians and French; the Adams certainly were when he wrote "the following designs are composed in the style of the present improved taste of finishing of rooms, which now reigns with success and eclat through these kingdoms." Richardson's selection of decorative motifs and subjects from antiquity may be compared with his own published version (1779) of Cesare Ripa's famous *Iconology*.

In *Ceilings*, Richardson had endearingly confessed "I never attempted to etch before this Publication, and hope to improve in this Respect, in proceeding with the other Numbers." *Chimney Pieces*, by contrast, is state of the art in having plates "Composed, etched and engraved in Aquatinta"; the first book in Britain to use the technique had been published only in 1775, by Paul Sandby, brother of Thomas Sandby, one of the subscribers to *Ceilings*. Richardson's text restates the principle of variety that he absorbed from the Adams: "it has also been studied to diversify the designs so far as is consistent with beauty, elegance, harmony and effect, and at the same time to make the whole produce a pleasing variety without deviating from propriety and the rules of architecture." This principle is then ingeniously carried through into the illustrations: each plate illustrates a chimneypiece design in two alternative finishes. The etched lines of the design are constant, but the plate is printed first with one aquatint treatment, then subjected to further aquatinting to produce a second, darker finish. Thus the variety of optional finishes to the chimneypieces, plain stone or painted wood, on the one hand, and textured marble or scagliola, on the other, is imitated by flat or mottled aquatint shading. In some plates the alternative finishes relate to the suggestions in Richardson's text: for example, he writes that the design in plate XXII might have the ornaments of frieze and pilasters painted in etruscan colors (second version) or done in scagliola on a white ground (first version); the correspondence is not, however, consistent. J. F.

George Richardson. *A New Collection of Chimney Pieces*. Plate v. Chimneypiece with alternative finishes. 1985.61.2645

68

George Richardson (d. 1813)

A Treatise On The Five Orders Of Architecture, In Which The Principles Of That Art Are Illustrated By Elegant And Correct Examples, Representing The Most Approved Forms, Proportions, And Decorations, Peculiar To The Several Orders; As Exhibited In The Remains Of The Beautiful Edifices Of Antiquity; Composed In The Style Most Consonant To The Orders That Adorn The Magnificent Temples, Baths, Theatres, Amphitheatres, Basilicas, Triumphal Arches, And Other Ancient Buildings . . . With complete Explanations in English and French, accompanied with Observations made on several of the Antiquities at Rome, and various Parts of Italy, at Pola in Istria, and the southern Provinces of France, in the Years 1760, 1761, 1762, and 1763; By George Richardson, Architect . . . [same in French] . . .

London: printed for the author, and sold by Mr. George Nicol, 1787

1985.61.2646

Folio: 511 × 329 ($20\frac{1}{8}$ × 13)

Pagination x, 32, [2] pp., XXII aquatint plates

Edition First edition

Text (parallel English and French) pp. [i] title page (verso blank); [iii] dedication to Thomas Sandby (verso blank); [v–vi] list of subscribers; [vii]–x preface; [1]–32 explanation of the plates; [33–34] advertisement, dated 15 May 1787

Illustrations 22 full-page aquatint plates numbered I–XXII, all signed "Drawn & engraved by G. Richardson & Son"

Binding Recent half calf, contemporary red morocco label. Bound with the Rev. Cooper Willyams, *The History of Sudeley Castle, in Gloucestershire*, 1791

References Berlin Cat. 2297; Berlin (1977) OS 2297; ESTC t90832; Harris and Savage 744

ANOTHER COPY

1985.61.2647

Folio: 510 × 363 ($20\frac{5}{16}$ × $14\frac{5}{16}$)

Binding Recent red half morocco, marbled boards, green label

A Treatise on the Five Orders is dedicated to Thomas Sandby, and the list of subscribers includes not only the usual grandees such as His Majesty's Library, but also the names of Robert and James Adam. The *Treatise* was the only one of Richardson's publications to elicit a subscription from his former employees, doubtless because the theoretical subject matter trespassed less than his previous works upon their sense of their own aesthetic integrity and was understood as marking the author's professional coming of age. Richardson explicitly aims the book at the world of "Polite Education," of architecture schools, students, and connoisseurs, thus establishing his independent credentials as a man of taste and scholarship with firsthand experience of classical antiquity. As such the book was conceived as an introductory volume to his *New Designs in Architecture*, in contrast to the Adamesque *Ceilings* and *Chimney Pieces* that had preceded it. Nevertheless, one wonders how James Adam reacted to the title page with its

George Richardson. *A Treatise on the Five Orders of Architecture.* Plate x. Ionic volute. 1985.61.2646

expansive references to the author's journeys to Rome, Italy, Istria, and southern France between 1760 and 1763. The reality is apparent from one of Richardson's letters dated 1762 from Rome: "during our stay abroad I have now got together several rough sketches of antiquities which will be very useful for my own study if I get them home concealed from Mr Adam's sight, for I know if he were to see them I would run the risk of his everlasting displeasure, though I do them in my by-hours and even when I should sleep."

John Harris has noted that Richardson's representation of the orders as all the same height derives from Chambers' *Treatise on Civil Architecture* of 1759, which had a second edition in 1768; in fact, Richardson borrows not only the idea itself but Chambers' text explaining it, almost verbatim: "the Orders are all represented of the same height, to render the Comparison between them more easy and distinct, and to give a more striking Idea of their different properties, by which means the gradual increase of delicacy and richness is easily perceivable." Similar plagiarism of Chambers occurs in Richardson's account "Of Caryatides and Persians," which accompanies no plates and therefore sits oddly in the work. Richardson parts company with Chambers, however, in his Graecising tendencies: he refers more than once to Stuart's *Antiquities of Athens* as the source for his favored version of the orders, most notably in the Ionic capital that he represents with a curving inferior fillet between the volutes: "this form of the capital produces an agreeable effect, and appears much more graceful than the Roman Ionic, exemplified in all other Works treating on this subject." Richardson, in any case, leans toward the decorative in his illustrations, showing the Doric column fluted, for example: but he does note that "the Examples in general . . . are fully enriched, for the purpose of shewing what ornaments may be introduced in the Frizes and Mouldings of elegant and rich Designs, . . . but not with an intention of recommending a profusion of Ornaments on every occasion." This decorative tendency nevertheless gives ample scope to the fine aquatinting, vastly superior to the crude aquatints contained in Isaac Landmann's comparable *Course of the Five Orders of Civil Architecture* of 1785. Richardson's title page announces the plates "engraved in Aquatinta, producing the Spirit and Effect of finished Drawings in Indian Ink," and in the preface he pursues this theme, pointing out that the plates are therefore ideal for copying by architectural students as "suitable patterns for drawing and shadowing [the orders] with propriety and effect." J. F.

69

George Richardson (d. 1813)

New Designs In Architecture, Consisting Of Plans, Elevations, And Sections For Various Buildings, Comprised In XLIV Folio Plates; Designed And Engraved By George Richardson, Architect. . . . [same in French] . . .

London: printed for the author, 1792

1985.61.2644

Folio: 401 × 326 (19 3/4 × 12 13/16)

Pagination ii, 40 pp., aquatint title plate, aquatint dedication, 44 aquatint plates

(*Note*: This pagination does not include a single-leaf list of subscribers, lacking in this copy)

Edition First edition

Text (parallel English and French) pp. [i]–ii introduction; [1]–40 text, description of the plates

Illustrations The aquatint title plate has English and French titles each in a framed rectangle, set together in a large neoclassical frame with heads and rosettes in small roundels. In addition to an aquatint dedication to Henry, earl of Gainsborough, there are 44 full-page aquatint plates numbered I–XLIV, all "Design'd & Engrav'd by G. Richardson & Son"

Binding Recent half calf, marbled boards

Provenance Partially legible ownership inscription (Giorge Luis?) on upper right corner of several plates

References ESTC t90835; Harris and Savage 741

THE DESIGNS range from modest cottages priced at 100 pounds, with alternative treatments of thatch and diamond-paned leaded lights or roofing in slates and tiles with sash windows, to country seats and town mansions at 13,700 pounds. The practice of including estimates had been introduced by Daniel Garrett in his *Designs and Estimates of Farm-Houses, etc*, of 1747, and popularized by William Halfpenny. Richardson aims at "not only . . . an agreeable and diversified contour on the plans but also a variety of light and shade in the elevations, which give beauty, spirit, and effect to the whole compositions. This movement of design adds much to the picturesque appearance of a building, and in some degree may be compared to the effect that hill and dale, foreground and distance have in landscape."

An advertisement for the book had appeared in some copies of *A Treatise on the Five Orders*, which was intended as an introduction to the later work, describing it as "to be adorned with figures in painting and sculpture by Mr W. Hamilton." Nothing came of this projected collaboration with the painter and royal academician, and instead Richardson was assisted in the production of the plates by his own son William.

New Designs carries an advertisement for the author's services in "Engraving of Architecture in Aquatinta executed in the manner of finished drawings," and aquatint is again employed tastefully for the title page and curiously (since it consists of mere unornamented lettering) for the dedication. But by this stage a new trend in architectural illustration had manifested itself. In 1785 John Plaw published his *Rural Architecture*. Where Richardson used aquatint to indicate simple shading and texture, Plaw exploited its true potential as an imitation of watercolor to present architecture picturesquely within a landscape. The influence of Plaw's book, to which Richardson subscribed, is visible in *New Designs*, which was published in six numbers between 1788 and 1792. It contains two plates showing four views of small cottages and country houses for which nonpicturesque plans and elevations were also included. The views are set in a Plaw-like landscape with staffage, but differ in being perspective views of the buildings themselves

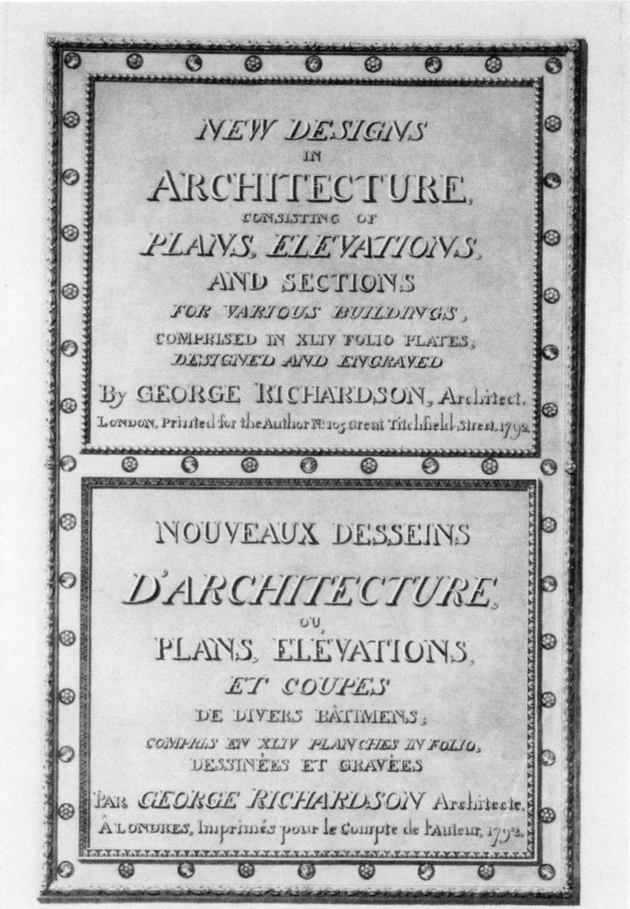
NEW DESIGNS IN ARCHITECTURE, CONSISTING OF PLANS, ELEVATIONS, AND SECTIONS FOR VARIOUS BUILDINGS, COMPRISED IN XLIV FOLIO PLATES; DESIGNED AND ENGRAVED By GEORGE RICHARDSON, Architect. LONDON, Printed for the Author No. 105 Great Titchfield Street, 1792.

NOUVEAUX DESSEINS D'ARCHITECTURE, OU PLANS, ELEVATIONS, ET COUPES DE DIVERS BÂTIMENS; COMPRIS EN XLIV PLANCHES IN FOLIO, DESSINÉES ET GRAVÉES PAR GEORGE RICHARDSON Architecte. À LONDRES, Imprimés pour le Compte de l'Auteur, 1792.

George Richardson. *New Designs in Architecture.* Title page. 1985.61.2644

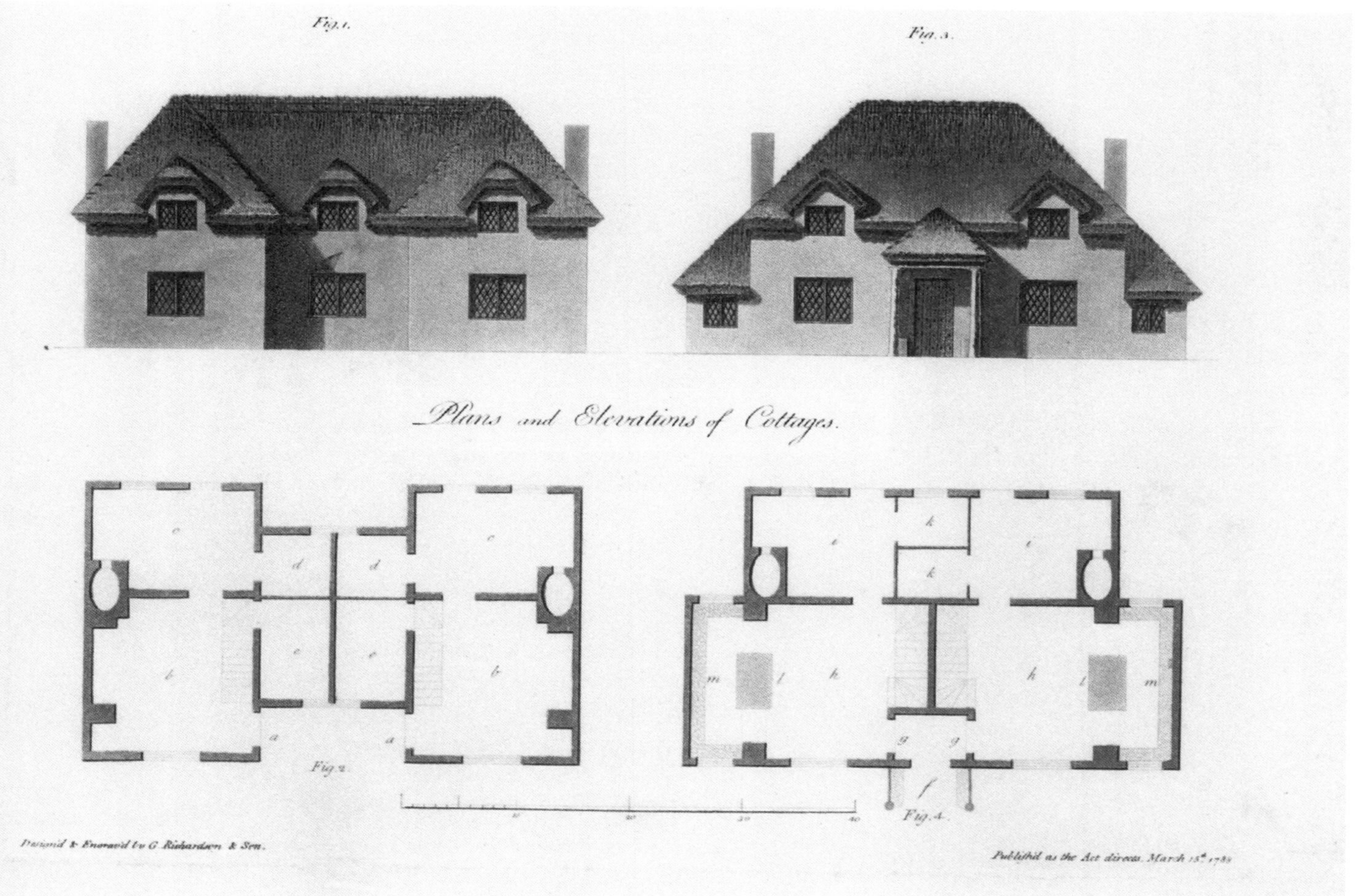

George Richardson. *New Designs in Architecture.* Plate 11. Perspective view of the cottage for two families. 1985.61.2644

rather than the flat elevations that Plaw provided. The publication history of *New Designs* is complex, but while these two plates are dated April 1788 and thus may have been issued with the first part of the publication, they must also be the illustrations referred to in the text: "the manner of engraving is well adapted for works in architecture, and gives the prints a close resemblance to drawings, executed with spirit and effect, especially those towards the conclusion of the book." Whether Richardson originally intended to provide picturesque views of other designs in the book is unclear.

New Designs also advertises hand-colored copies of *Ceilings* priced at an astronomical forty-eight guineas, but neither publishing nor architecture saved Richardson from a straitened old age. Dependent on charity from the Royal Academy and the sculptor Nollekens, he died in 1813. Shortly thereafter, in the *Gentleman's Magazine* for April 1814, a correspondent A. B. wrote:

> . . . the pretentions of Aquatinta to be classed as a style of Engraving are but moderate, being originally intended as an imitation of drawings in one simple primary colour, commonly Indian ink or bistre; and this end it fully answers, representing such drawings with an accuracy and effect, when successfully accomplished, that must be admired. I am, however, rather inclined to believe that its principal use consists in its adaptation to large Architectural subjects, where its great Utility is obvious, and where none can call it misapplied: such subjects, indeed, seem particularly within the reach of Aquatinta: and it would be well for Art in general had its views been confined to objects within its reach, for out of this style arose that most vitiated and monstrous taste for Coloured Engravings. J. F.

Bibliography

Brown, I. G. "The Fittest Place in Europe for Our Profession: George Richardson in Rome." *Architectural Heritage: The Journal of the Architectural Heritage Society of Scotland* 2 (1991): 29–40

Fleming, J. *Robert Adam and His Circle in Edinburgh and Rome.* London, 1962

Harris, E., and N. Savage. *British Architectural Books and Writers 1556–1785.* Cambridge, 1990

Harris, J. *Sir William Chambers.* London, 1970

70

George Richardson (d. 1813)

The New Vitruvius Britannicus; Consisting Of Plans And Elevations Of Modern Buildings, Public And Private, Erected In Great Britain By The Most Celebrated Architects. Engraved On LXXII. Plates, From Original Drawings (Engraved On LXX Plates, From Original Drawings. Volume II). By George Richardson, Architect. . . . [same in French] . . .

London: printed by W. Bulmer (T. Bensley), for the author; and sold by J. Taylor, 1802–1808

1985.61.2802–2803

Folio: 550 × 390 (21 5/8 × 15 5/16)

Pagination Vol. 1: [2], iv, 20 pp., 72 [i.e., 62] aquatint plates (10 double-page)

Vol. 2: [iv], 10 pp., 70 [i.e., 53] aquatint plates (17 double-page)

Edition First edition

Text (parallel English and French) *vol. I*: pp. [1] title page (verso blank); [i–ii] list of subscribers; [iii]–iv introduction, dated 1802; [1]–20 explanations of the plates (p. [16] blank); *vol. II*: [i] title page (verso blank); [iii] list of contents of vol. 1; [iv] list of contents of vol. 2; 1–10 explanations of the plates

Illustrations Vol. 1 contains 62 aquatint plates numbered I–LXXII, 10 double-page plates bearing 2 numbers each

George Richardson. *The New Vitruvius Britannicus*. Vol. 1, plate XLIX/L. Robert Adam. Gosford House, East Lothian. West elevation. 1985.61.2802

All have Richardson's signature or imprint ("Engraved & Published" by G. Richardson or G. Richardson and Son) and dates from 4 June 1796 to 26 Dec. 1801. Vol. 2 contains 53 aquatint plates numbered I–LXX, 17 double-page plates bearing 2 numbers each. Richardson's signature or imprint is followed by dates from 10 Nov. 1802 to 1 July 1807

Binding Late nineteenth-century three-quarter red morocco, red buckram boards, bound uniform as vols. 6–7 of S. D. Button's copy of *Vitruvius Britannicus* (for vols. 1–3, see under Colen Campbell; for vols. 4–5, see under John Woolfe). Vol. 1, pp. 9–10 taken from another, smaller copy. Extra-illustrated with an etched plate from another work bound in at end, a "Plan and Section of a Sluice or Flood Gate on the Grand Canal of China . . . ," numbered 34, "Engrav'd by Jos[h]. Baker, Islington" and "Published April 10th 1706 [?] by George Nicol"

Provenance Title page inscription "Presented to the Phila. Chapter of Architects By S D Button Arch.," with Button's ownership inscription and bookplate of the Philadelphia Chapter of the American Institute of Architects in both volumes

References Berlin (1977) OS 2342[P]

AT A MEETING on 12 August 1797, the council of the Royal Academy of Arts in London resolved "that Mess[rs]. Richardson's Two Books, sent to the President & Council, viz: A Series of Original Designs of Country Seats, &c. And, New Designs of Vases & Tripods, &c. be purchased for the use of the Academy; And also, that the Academy do subscribe for his new Work, in Architecture" (RA Council Minutes, 2: 329). The first two parts of the latter book (i.e., *The New Vitruvius Britannicus*), each containing seven plates and a single leaf of letterpress description, had appeared in the summer of 1796 and spring of 1797, respectively, with printed part wrappers entitling the work as "A Collection of

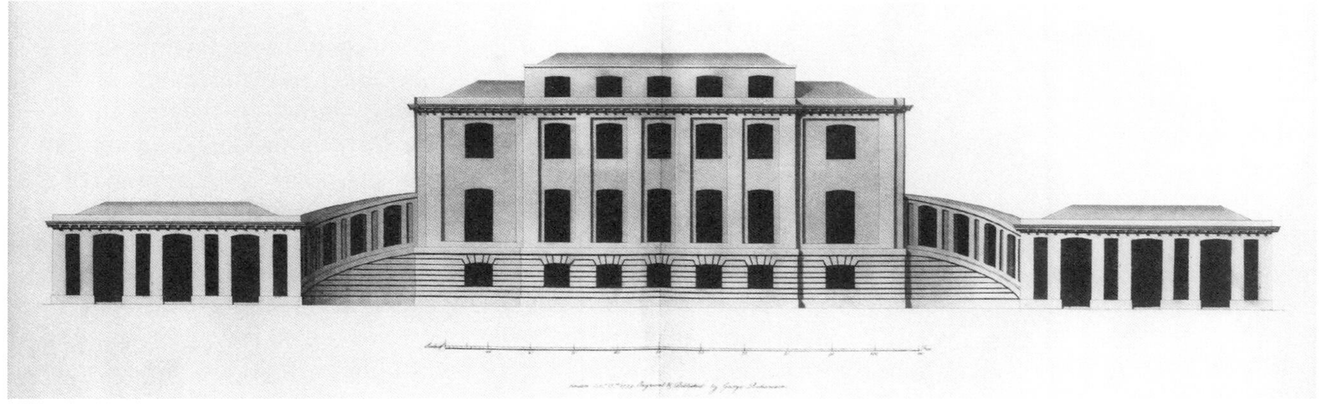

George Richardson. *The New Vitruvius Britannicus.* Vol. 1, plate XLI/XLII. Joseph Bonomi. Eastwell Park, Kent. South elevation. 1985.61.2802

George Richardson. *The New Vitruvius Britannicus.* Vol. 1, plate XXX. John Nash. Southgate Grove, Middlesex. North front. 1985.61.2802

Plans and Elevations of Modern Buildings, Public and Private; erected in Great Britain, by the most celebrated Architects . . ." (for a description of an incomplete copy in parts, see ESTC t150889). The academicians' support for George Richardson's latest and, as it turned out, last and most ambitious publication, is an important measure of their high regard for him, not as a practicing architect, but as an architectural author, draftsman, engraver, and publisher. Over the previous twenty years Richardson had produced, either single-handedly or in collaboration with his son William, a succession of handsome architectural books that evinced both a refined "modern" (i.e., neoclassical) taste, and a grasp of what was of practical benefit to artists and architects working in Britain in the last quarter of the eighteenth century. Richardson was also an astute promoter, not of his faltering career as an architect and designer, but of his success as an enterprising author of books on designing and composing domestic buildings with appropriate interiors in the latest and most approved manner. (It is not for nothing that so many of his books include the word "new" in their title.) Both his long experience as an independent publisher and the fact that he launched his *New Vitruvius Britannicus* toward the end of his independent career meant that Richardson was, in many ways, better qualified for the task than the overly ambitious Colen Campbell or naively optimistic John Woolfe and James Gandon had ever been.

Richardson's experienced hand as a publisher is evident in the careful marketing strategy that he devised for his latest venture. Although the idea of continuing where Woolfe and Gandon had left off was present from the start (the part wrappers state that the new "work will be comprised in ten numbers, and will form a proper supplement to the Vitruvius Britannicus and its continuation"), this intention was not reflected in any advertised title until the appearance, at the end of December 1801, of the tenth and final part. This comprised, in addition to the last seven plates and their descriptive text, a definitive title page bearing the new title, the author's "Introduction" postdated to 1802, a list of 170 subscribers (for 184 copies), and two plates more than the seventy originally promised. In this form the book was issued as a single-volume "Imperial Folio," complete in itself and half-bound, for £5 15s 6d (see Josiah Taylor's booksellers' catalogue dated 2 January 1802 in BAL Early Imprints Collection, RIBA, London). No mention was made of continuing the work further—a wise precaution, not only because it allowed Richardson to abstain from making a commitment that he couldn't fulfill, but also because it helped maximize the sale of the unsubscribed portion of the edition, as buyers could be certain that they were getting a complete book rather than a halfway stage toward something else. With only 184 copies subscribed for it was clearly essential to enlist the expertise of the book trade. Once again Richardson displayed acumen in his choice of Josiah Taylor as his distributing agent, since by the late 1790s Taylor's "Architectural Library" in Holborn had easily become the most important specialist architectural publishing and bookselling firm in the country. Taylor, however, did not underwrite any of the financial risks; the expression "sold by" in the imprint meant that he distributed the book for the author within the trade, almost certainly on a straightforward sale or return basis.

Richardson's caution in not advertising his "new work in architecture" as a continuation of *Vitruvius Britannicus* made good marketing sense, since it enabled him to appeal to those who did not own the original volumes and might well have no interest in acquiring them (this was a trap that Woolfe and Gandon had fallen into by numbering their volumes in Campbell's sequence). For these people what mattered was the contemporaneity of the new collection, not the updating of an existing historical survey of British architectural achievement. After twenty years of publishing his own books, Richardson had built up a formidable "mailing list" of potential subscribers, particularly among artists and architects. He also well understood how to promote a new book in such a way as to attract different sectors of the market at different stages of its evolution. By the time his subscription list closed he had effectively covered the "professional" sector—hence the astounding total of forty-nine architects and twenty others from the building trades, compared to a mere thirty-four members of the aristocracy. Armed with a new title and Taylor's expertise, the book could now be pitched to "the Amateur [who] . . . will be gratified by comparing the progressive improvements that Architecture has experienced in this country during the eighteenth century" (Introduction, iv). This strategy seems to have been effective enough to encourage Richardson to embark on his second volume before the end of 1802—so quickly, in fact, that he must have started gathering the material well in advance of advertising his decision to proceed. Increased confidence in sales based on the performance of the first volume was also probably responsible for the decision to issue the second volume in five "double" parts, each containing fourteen plates and (rather oddly) still only a single leaf of letterpress, thus severely curtailing the sometimes quite lengthy topographical guidebook-style descriptions of gentlemen's seats that had featured in the first volume. (This reduction in the amount of descriptive text may have been in response to adverse market reaction—Richardson was no master of English prose—but it is also possible that it was simply an economy

George Richardson. *The New Vitruvius Britannicus.* Vol. 2, plate LVIII. John Soane. Pitshanger Manor, Ealing, Middlesex. Principal elevation. 1985.61.2803

George Richardson. *The New Vitruvius Britannicus.* Vol. 2, plate 11/12. John Carr. Town Hall and Assembly Rooms, Newark, Nottinghamshire. Principal elevation. 1985.61.2803

measure.) The second volume, the fifth and final part of which appeared in the summer of 1807, was published in approximately the same span of time as that of the first—about five years—the parts appearing more or less annually rather than every six months or so. Such slow progress was the consequence, not of any difficulty in obtaining drawings to engrave, but of the need to spread production costs over the maximum period that subscribers would allow. Even so, taking eleven years to produce 115 plates was risking a falling off of interest in the latter stages, since it involved purchasers in a much more protracted wait than for any of his previous books, most of which had taken only about two to three years to complete. Richardson's excessively cautious pace also compared rather unfavorably with Woolfe and Gandon's, who had managed to produce their two-volume continuation of *Vitruvius Britannicus* at the more reassuring intervals of monthly parts, taking only six years to publish 155 plates. In spite of its protracted span, however, Richardson managed to keep to his original schedule. He was too experienced to be unaware of the danger of slippage and the consequent risk of lost sales from subscribers failing to complete their copies. Somewhat ironically, the copy in the Academy's library demonstrates this point because whether through impatience or incompetence, the librarian at the time, Edward Burch, had the second volume bound up without the fifth and final part.

On 11 July 1807, at the recommendation of the president Benjamin West, George Richardson was awarded a donation of thirty guineas and placed on the list of artists in regular receipt of the Academy's Charitable Fund. The Academy's final payment to him of twenty-one guineas was made on 9 July 1813, which is the last recorded date of Richardson's life. To qualify for the Academy's assistance he would have had to show that he had been professionally active as an artist or architect, and that he had no other recourse for improving his straitened circumstances. It is therefore odd that he was able to keep his outright ownership of the plates, copyrights, and unsold stock of all his books, not to mention his collection of prints and drawings, which was sufficiently important to be reported in the *Gentleman's Magazine* for March 1814 as having been sold on 29 November 1813 sometime after his death. Taylor continued to offer the two volumes of Richardson's *The New Vitruvius Britannicus* at an undiscounted price of eleven and a half guineas as late as 1814, when dropping the price before then could well have encouraged sufficient sales to improve the author's finances. It is also odd that in 1810 Richardson was apparently able to pay the printer Thomas Bensley for a reprint of the letterpress (if not also a reimpression of the plates) of the first volume of *The New Vitruvius Britannicus.* By 1792 Richardson was offering all five of his books to date at a wide range of prices, none of them discounted, the cheapest being an ordinary copy of his *Treatise on the Five Orders of Architecture* selling at £1 11s 6d and the most expensive a fully colored copy of his *Book of Ceilings* for which he asked the huge sum of forty-eight guineas (i.e., one guinea per plate). Such a range of stock and sales options should have offered plenty of scope for selling the copyright and plates of these books to an enterprising bookseller for republishing at reduced rates or in some other revamped form (rather as William Pain had done toward the end of his life with his popular *Carpenter's and Joiner's Assistant*, *British Palladio*, and *Practical House Carpenter*, fresh editions of which were issued by these works' new proprietors, I. & J. Taylor, in 1787, 1788, and 1792, respectively—see Harris and Savage 1990, 629, 634, 652). Richardson's obvious reluctance to adopt this course is perfectly understandable on a personal level—these books were quite literally his life's work—but this alone is unlikely to have carried much weight with the academicians when deciding his case for financial assistance. Clearly there was another factor working in his favor, and to understand what this was it is necessary to recall one of the still-not-quite forgotten ideals of the Society of Artists, namely, artistic independence. Implicit in the Academy's support of Richardson, both through the purchase of his publications and by charitable donations toward the end of his life, is the recognition of the importance of preserving the means of his independence as an architect/author who should be free to produce books of the highest merit and benefit to the profession without having to compromise artistic standards for the commercial gain of publishers and booksellers. This harks back, of course, to Campbell's pioneering stake in *Vitruvius Britannicus*, and on through to Woolfe and Gandon's "discovery" of serial publication as a means of enabling architects to publish their own books on the grandest scale without losing editorial and artistic control. It was precisely this control that Richardson's former employers, Robert and James Adam, had turned to maximum advantage when they decided to issue their *Works in Architecture* (1773–1779) themselves in carefully fashioned, semiautonomous fascicles. Richardson used serial publication in a less self-conscious way for the books he published himself, and this alone would make him a natural heir and successor to Woolfe and Gandon, even if he hadn't taken up the challenge of continuing their *Vitruvius Britannicus*. The importance that the Academy attached to "artistic independence" is neatly revealed in Richardson's case, since the only books by him that were *not* acquired for its library—*Capitals of Columns and Friezes* (1793) and *A New Book of Ornaments in the Antique Style* (1796)—were precisely the ones that he did *not* publish himself, these having been produced on commission for commercial publishers (see Harris and Savage 1990, 737 and 738).

The Academy's alleviation of Richardson's financial difficulties toward the end of his life was the last, rather sad chapter in an almost forty-year association with the institution, beginning in 1774, the year in which he launched his first book and exhibited for the first time "with the academicians" (to use the contemporary expression), having previously always shown his work

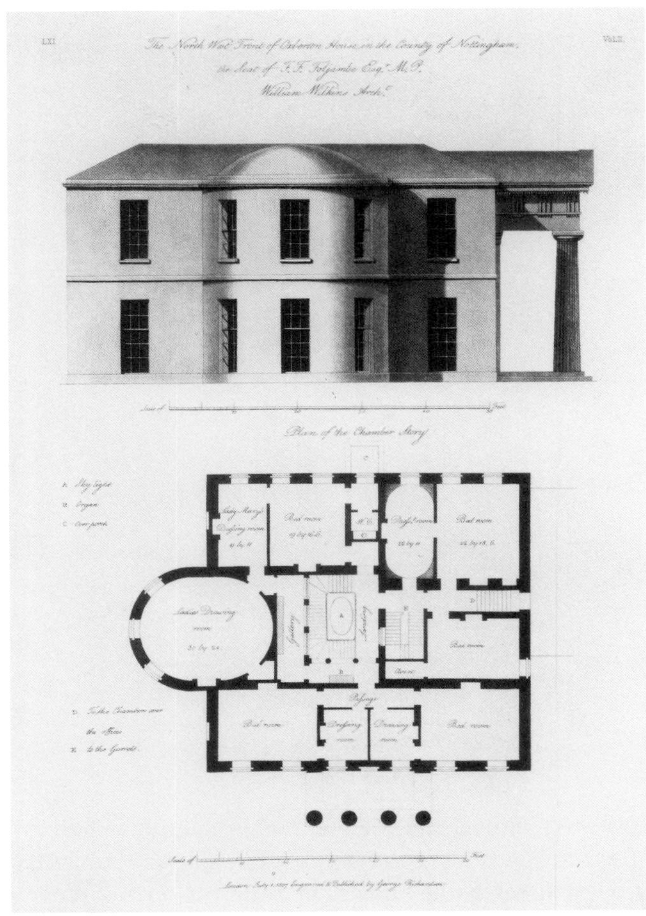

George Richardson. *The New Vitruvius Britannicus.* Vol. 2, plate LXI. William Wilkins the younger. Oxberton Hall, Nottinghamshire. Northwest front. 1985.61.2803

at the Society of Artists, to which he had been elected a Fellow on 6 October 1766. One might have thought that as an arch opponent of the Adam brothers and their attenuated "misuse" of antique ornament, William Chambers would have heartily disapproved of Richardson's *A Book of Ceilings composed in the Style of the Antique Grotesque* ([1774]–1776) and used his considerable influence to ensure that it was not given shelf space in the Academy's library, in the formation of which he was actively concerned. However, the reverse of this was true. Indeed, Richardson's *Ceilings* has the distinction of being one of the very first books to be subscribed for by the Academy as an institution (sixteen shillings was paid for the first number on 26 March 1774; it was apparently preceded only by subscriptions to Peter Brown's *New Illustrations of Zoology*, 1776, and Thomas Malton's *A Compleat Treatise on Perspective*, 1776–1783—see "RA Cash Book 1765–95," entries for December 1773). Perhaps there was an element of malicious pleasure on Chambers' part in pointedly not proposing the purchase of the first number of the Adams' *Works in Architecture* (which had appeared on 24 July 1773), and recommending instead that the institution subscribe to the work of their former assistant. The splendid effect of Richardson's hand-colored plates sufficiently rattled the Adams into including in the next part of their *Works* (published 14 May 1774) a design for a ceiling that could be had at extra cost with the backgrounds colored under their supervision (see *Works*, 1.2: pl. VII). It would be unfair, however, both to Richardson and to Chambers, to suggest that the only reason for the Academy's subscription to Richardson's *Ceilings* was Chambers' desire to snub his professional rivals. If this had been the case he would hardly have bothered to subscribe for his own copy, nor are the other architect members on Richardson's list, such as George Dance the younger, James Wyatt, and Thomas Sandby, the Academy's professor of architecture, likely to have subscribed as individuals had there not also been general agreement among them about the book's merits. A further sign of nonfactional support for Richardson's work within the Academy is the presence on his list of William Hunter, the Academy's professor of anatomy; the sculptor Joseph Nollekens, who later became a friend and benefactor; and the young painter William Hamilton, who, like Richardson, began exhibiting at the Academy in 1774 and was to collaborate with him on his next book, an English version of Cesare Ripa's *Iconologia* (1593). Richardson's *Iconology, or A Collection of Emblematical Figures* (1778–1779), a substantial two-volume folio work dedicated to the king, which he published himself in parts between November 1776 and April 1779, did nothing to advance hopes he may have had of establishing himself as an architect. It was, however, the ideal vehicle for advertising his awareness of the practical requirements of the latest fashion for figurative ornament, particularly among painters and sculptors who needed convenient source material for composing iconographically appropriate paintings and bas-reliefs for neoclassical interiors. Indeed, the obvious usefulness of this work to artists of all kinds would have undoubtedly helped to broaden Richardson's contacts within the Academy: not only did the library subscribe once again, so did the president, Sir Joshua Reynolds; the history painter Benjamin West; the Academy's professor of painting, Edward Penny; the specialist decorative painters G. B. Cipriani, Biagio Rebecca, and Antonio Zucchi; the coach painter Charles Catton; the gem engraver Edward Burch; the watercolor artist and printmaker Paul Sandby; and others.

The presence of Paul Sandby in the list is of some significance. Richardson's next book, *A New Collection of Chimney Pieces* ([1778]–1781), the first architectural book to be illustrated by aquatint engravings, was launched in May 1778, less than three years after Sandby's pioneering collection of *Twelve Views in Aquatinta from Drawings taken on the spot in South Wales* (September 1775), the first sustained use of the new medium in Britain. So novel were the techniques of aquatint that it is practically certain Richardson learned of them directly from Sandby. From now on Richardson invariably employed this new method of representing tone in intaglio prints, but in a manner diametrically opposed to Sandby's, since his interest stemmed solely from its capacity to reproduce the effect of a conventional monochrome pen and wash architectural drawing, in which different tones of wash are used merely to denote the advance and recession of architectural forms under an ideal light. Unlike picturesque specialists such as John Plaw and James Malton, who by 1800 had thoroughly exploited aquatint as a means of imitating full-blown landscape watercolor drawings in books of architectural designs, Richardson adhered to the old tradition of orthogonal projection for the representation of architecture. It was this tradition that Woolfe and Gandon had been concerned to maintain when they revived *Vitruvius Britannicus* without perspectives, in order to harness its nationalistic associations specifically for the promotion of the professional British architect's claim to public notice. This does not mean that the use of the orthogonal tradition for the representation of modern buildings continued untouched by the pressure for more naturalistic forms of depiction. These increased quite markedly in the mid-1780s, when an initial prejudice against exhibiting perspectives of architectural designs at the Academy began to break down following Thomas Sandby's exhibition in 1781 of his design for a "Bridge of Magnificence" over the Thames, and Joseph Bonomi's interior perspective of a "Design for a Drawing Room" at Mrs. Montagu's house in Portman Square, London (RIBA, London; probably exhibited RA 1783). The tension that was noted in Woolfe and Gandon's plates between their need for orthogonal clarity and precision, and their engravers' desire to emphasize chiaroscuro effects, becomes, as a result, particularly intense in Richardson's work. Reginald Blomfield's criticism of "geometrical drawings . . . in which the shadows are greatly exaggerated and the window-openings shown black, with the result that the design loses its breadth" (R. Blomfield, *Architectural Drawing and Draughtsmen*, 1912, 78), was leveled in particular at some of Woolfe and Gandon's elevations, and in general at "the later publications of the eighteenth century." Even allowing for Blomfield's neobaroque predilections, this is an acute observation of the essentially antipicturesque mode in which Richardson worked, in spite of his having introduced into architectural engraving a technical innovation that was to prove so well adapted to the growing requirement for picturesque representations in printed books. On only one occasion did Richardson succumb to the temptation of following the picturesque trend when, in some copies of the first part of his *New Designs in Architecture* ([1788]–1792), published in April 1788, he seems to have issued alternative versions of two plates in which the pairs of cottages and farmhouses shown in plates two and three are presented in perspective views instead of simply plan and elevation. The fact that these alternative plates are numbered one and two probably indicates an abandoned trial issue, while their rarity (they are known only from a copy in the British Library—see Harris and Savage 1990, 741, notes) suggests that Richardson must have suppressed them almost immediately after publication began.

Richardson published both the *New Collection of Chimney Pieces* ([1778]–1781) and his later *Series of Original Designs for Country Seats or Villas* ([1794]–1795) without a list of subscribers, so they are of no help in assessing his reputation within the Academy at the time of their publication. Only eight members of the Academy subscribed to his *New Designs in Architecture* ([1788]–1792), whereas twenty had put their names down for copies of the *Treatise on the Five Orders* (1787), encouraged no doubt by their professor of architecture, Thomas Sandby, to whom Richardson dedicated the latter work. The difference in the level of "Academic" support for these two books is revealing of how Richardson's talents could be seen to be of service to a teaching institution without this recognition necessarily involving any very high opinion of his abilities as a designer in his own right. Richardson must have been well aware of this limitation of his standing since, unlike the architectural draftsman Thomas Malton junior, whose ambitions of joining the Academy as an architect member were repeatedly rebuffed between 1790 and 1795, he never made the mistake of attempting to put himself forward as a candidate for associateship. When, therefore, Richardson claimed in his Introduction that "by an attentive consideration" of the plans and elevations in his *New Vitruvius Britannicus* "the Student may gain many hints and precepts, which must be useful to him in his future studies, and beneficial to his employer" (p. iv), he was proposing something that was not only absent from former conceptions of "Vitruvius Britannicus," but was also precisely calculated to meet a present need within the Royal Academy as the only public institution at that time in Britain concerned with the education and training of architects.

In addition to appealing to the Academy's sense of responsibility for nurturing native talent, Richardson was able to play another, more fundamental card in the timing of his approach to the president and council in August 1797. Rather like Campbell's original work of 1715–1717, Woolfe and Gandon's revival of *Vitruvius Britannicus* in the mid-1760s had followed on the heels of a series of resounding military and diplomatic triumphs over England's historic enemy France. This had generated an atmosphere of national euphoria when it seemed that the latter's cultural hegemony in Europe might for the first time begin to be realistically challenged by artists working in Britain. However, when Richardson approached the Academy with his project thirty years later, it would have been difficult to imagine a starker contrast to this happy time. In the spring and summer of 1797, with no allies left on the Continent, Britain was enduring one of the darkest hours in its history, facing imminent invasion and catastrophic defeat by Napoleon Bonaparte's unstoppable armies. The nation's sole remaining defense, the navy, had mutinied in April and June that year; prices had soared, the Bank of England had suspended cash payments, the whole country was on the verge of complete financial and political collapse. In a situation as extreme as this it is not unreasonable to detect a streak of defiance in Richardson's plowing on with a plan "to enlarge the continuation of a work so useful and much approved of [as *Vitruvius Britannicus*] . . . in order to display the taste and science of the English nation in its style of Architecture at the close of the eighteenth century . . ." (Introduction, iii). Such a reaction may be compared with that of an equally dark hour in 1940–1941, when the "Recording Britain" scheme dispatched artists all over the country to draw and paint the nation's most characteristic and best loved buildings in case they should be destroyed by future enemy bombardment or invasion. Of course, by the time Richardson wrote his introduction, the military situation had improved considerably thanks to Nelson's naval victories, resulting in the signing of the short-lived Peace of Amiens on 1 October 1801. Back in August 1797, however, when the civilized world must have seemed about to vanish with the expiring century, the Royal Academicians serving on the council (among whom was numbered Richardson's old friend and collaborator William Hamilton) had been stirred into supporting a book that, despite its infancy, they knew would reflect nothing but credit on the nation's artists at this testing moment in its history. Their sanction was in no way lightly bestowed, since it was based on a longstanding knowledge of and regard for the abilities of the book's author and publisher, and represented precisely the kind of authoritative support for the achievements of contemporary British architects that Woolfe and Gandon had failed to derive from the hopelessly divided Society of Artists thirty years earlier. N. S.

Bibliography

A Catalogue of the Library in the Royal Academy, London. London, 1802

Colvin, H. *A Biographical Dictionary of British Architects 1600–1840*. 3d ed. New Haven and London, 1995

Life in England in Aquatint and Lithography 1770–1860 . . . from the Library of J. R. Abbey: A Bibliographical Catalogue. London, 1954. Reprint, London, 1972; San Francisco, Calif., 1991

"Royal Academy Cash Book 1769–1795." RA Archives

Royal Academy Council Minutes, vol. II, 1785–1798." RA Archives

71

William Roy (1726–1790)

The Military Antiquities Of The Romans in Britain. By The Late William Roy . . . Published By The Order, And At The Expence Of, The Society Of Antiquaries Of London

London: printed by W. Bulmer and Co., and sold at the appartments of the Society; and by Messrs. White, Robson, Nicol, Leigh and Sotheby, Brown, and Egerton, 1793

NGA Lib. Rare Book: DA145R87 large fol.

Folio: 543 × 360 (21 3/8 × 14 1/8)

Pagination [10], xvi, 206, [6] pp., [1] table, [50] etched and engraved plates (6 double-page, 1 folding)

Edition First edition

Text pp. [1] title page (verso blank); [3] additional title page with extended title but without imprint (verso blank); [5] 2 resolutions by the Society of Antiquaries concerning publication (verso blank); [7–10] table of contents; [i]–xvi "Prefatory Introduction"; [1]–206 text in 4 books and an appendix, each with divisional title page; [207–208] list of plates; [209–212] list of members of the Society of Antiquaries

Illustrations A printed table is numbered XLIII as part of the plate sequence. There are 50 etched and engraved plates, all but 4 maps or plans, numbered regularly I–XLII, XLIV–LI (plates I–III, XII, XVIII, XL double-page; XXXV folding). Plate I is signed "J. Cheevers Sculp[t].," the remainder "Basire Sc." or "J. Basire Sc." (probably all James Basire senior). Plate XXXVII, a view, is also signed "J. [i.e., Joseph] Farington R.A. del."

Binding Contemporary dark blue full straight-grained morocco, elaborately gilt in the Pompeiian style

References Brunet 4: 1432

Not strictly an architectural book, Major General William Roy's archaeological treatise nevertheless finds its place in the Millard collection as a counterweight to the more important British studies of classical sites abroad. The Society of Antiquaries, appropriately concerned to document its activities for its membership and for posterity, added a preliminary page that explains how it came to be published:

> At a Council of the Society of Antiquaries of London, held April 11th, 1791. It was Resolved, "That the work of the late Major General Roy, entitled The Military Antiquities of the Romans in Britain, which was lately presented to this Society by his executors, be published at the expence of this Society; and that a Committee be appointed to direct and superintend the engraving of the plates, and printing of the letter-press of the said work.
>
> That the said Committee shall consist of the Earl of Leicester, President, Sir Henry C. Englefield, Baronet, Vice President, John Topham, Esquire, Treasurer, Thomas Astle, Esquire, Frederick Barnard, Esquire, and the Reverend Thomas William Wrighte, Secretary."
>
> February 23d, 1793, the Committee reported to the Council, "That in the execution of the charge instructed to them, the most minute and accurate comparison had been made between the drawings of the late Major General Roy, which were presented to the Society, and the copies thereof preserved in his Majesty's library, and the smallest variations noticed. That the two manuscript copies of the work had been likewise attentively collated; and the sheets of the letter press, and the impressions of the plates, had been carefully corrected and revised, so as to render the work as perfect and complete as possible: and that it had been judged proper to publish the work from the manuscript, without any commentary, or deviation from the style and orthography of the original."

Three months later, in May 1793, the book was issued, with an appendix dated 23 April listing the members of the society (founded in 1707, granted a royal charter in 1751). A copy was distributed free to every Fellow. Readings from the manuscript had been a substantial part of most of the society's meetings between January and April 1791, so there is no doubt the decision to publish was a considered one. Even so, the society probably recognized it was taking a financial risk by committing itself to a handsome folio on such a specialized subject. It lost a lot of money on the venture, and 146 copies were still unsold as late as 1846. In that year, unable to dispose of them even at half price to members, the finance committee recommended that they be remaindered; and in March 1849 the whole stock duly formed part of an unprofitable sale of society publications to the bookseller Edward Lumley. It is, however, still one of the period's best examples of book production, printed by William Bulmer in a clear type with generous margins on fine wove paper, and with fifty large plates, all but one of which were executed by the society's favorite engraver, the elder James Basire. Its quality reflects confidence at a time when membership was growing; and pride in a subject whose devotees were steadily progressing from amateur speculation toward professional discipline.

Roy's position was somewhere between these two poles, as he applied his military training in engineering and surveying to what remained a strictly leisure pursuit. He was a superb draftsman, whose first major achievement was a large-scale map of the Scottish mainland prepared for the duke of Cumberland when the latter was subjecting the clans to English rule. He saw active military service on the Continent but, apart from the present work, is now best remembered for his geodetical surveys made for the Royal Society, the basis for the later and definitive ordnance surveys. His surveying skills are evident on nearly all of the plates in the *Military Antiquities*, which is concerned primarily with surviving traces of Roman earthwork encampments rather than actual buildings. The text is divided into four sections: a summary of the Roman campaigns in Britain; an account of the ancient system of castrametation; a reconstruction of Agricola's campaign; and a study of the ancient topography of North Britain, with miscellaneous appendices. The whole represented a much-needed advance on the work of Alexander Gordon, whose *Itinerarium Septentrionale* (1726) had covered similar ground. Roy's reconstruction of a famous Roman sacellum, the so-called Arthur's O'on near Stonehouse in Scotland, was based on Gordon's work, which, in turn, had been inspired by one of the most famous and well-respected members of the Society of Antiquaries, Dr. William Stukeley. Stukeley had published a paper on the subject more than seventy years earlier (*An Account of a Roman Temple and other Antiquities near Graham's Dike in Scotland*, 1720). Sadly, his influence on Roy's treatise was in other respects very damaging to its long-term scholarly value. Erudite but gullible, Stukeley had fallen victim to a famous fraud perpetrated by Charles Bertram who, writing from Copenhagen, persuaded him to study what purported to be a map and manuscript account of Roman antiquities compiled by a fourteenth-century monk, Richard of Cirencester. Stukeley accepted its authenticity as early as 1747, and both he and Bertram published an edition of the text. It was this, a complete fiction, that stimulated Roy to do fieldwork on the same subject, and his research was seriously contaminated as a result. The forgery was not conclusively exposed until the 1860s.

The Millard copy of *Military Antiquities* is probably not one of those remaindered in 1849; its exceptionally fine binding, reminiscent of the work of German immigrant binders such as Samuel Kalthoeber, reflects a taste that flourished earlier. Roman antiquities in Britain were, of course, unable to supply its motifs, which derive from Pompeii. Similarly, British architects continued to study the classical archaeology of continental Europe far more than that of their native land. G. B.

Bibliography

DNB 49: 371–373

Evans, J. *A History of the Society of Antiquaries*. Oxford, 1956

William Roy. *The Military Antiquities of the Romans in Britain.* Plate XXXVI. Reconstruction of "Arthur's Oon." NGA Lib. Rare Book: DA145R87 large fol.

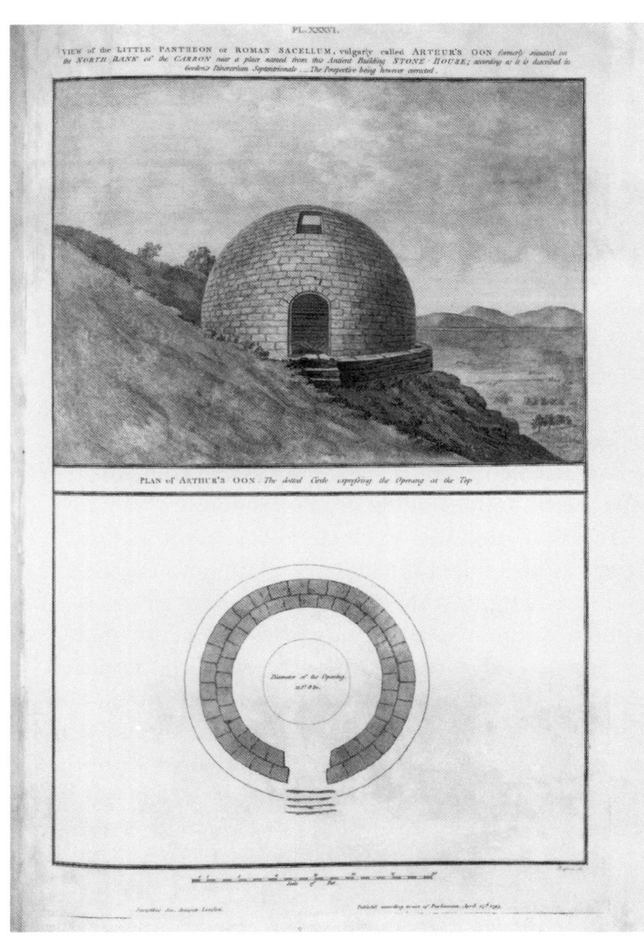

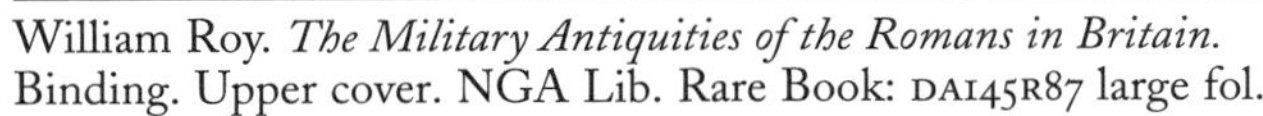

William Roy. *The Military Antiquities of the Romans in Britain.* Binding. Upper cover. NGA Lib. Rare Book: DA145R87 large fol.

72

John Rutter (1796–1851)

Delineations Of Fonthill And Its Abbey. By John Rutter, Shaftesbury

Shaftesbury: published by the author. London: by Charles Knight and Co.; Longman, Hurst, and Co.; Hurst, Robinson, and Co.; John and Arthur Arch, 1823

1985.61.2659

Quarto: 340 × 281 ($13\frac{3}{8} \times 11\frac{1}{16}$); large paper copy

Pagination xxvi, 127, [1] pp., 13 [i.e., 14] plates (1 folding)

Edition First edition

Text pp. [i] half-title (verso blank); [iii] title page (verso blank); [v] dedication (verso blank); [vii]–xi preface; [xii] blank; [xiii]–xvi contents; [xvii]–xxvi "Description Of The Embellishments"; [1]–100 text; [101] half-title "Appendix" (verso blank); [103]–107 Appendix A; [108]–112 Appendix B; [113] Appendix C (verso blank); [115] Table I; [116–117] Table II; [118] Table III; [119]–127 list of subscribers; [128] Rutter's wood-engraved armorial device

Illustrations 14 plates including a frontispiece (pl. 7) and added title plate "An Illustrated History and Description of Fonthill Abbey" (pl. 8). 13 are numbered and called for in the list of embellishments; the final plate, "South West View of Fonthill Abbey," is not. Plates 6–8 are hand-colored aquatints and the rest etchings or engravings except for a folding lithograph map. Plates are signed as drawn by C. F. Porden (pls. 3, 6, 8, 9); George Cattermole (pls. 4, 13); John Rutter (pls. 2, 10); W. Finley (pl. 7); [Thomas] Stedman Whitwell, architect (pl. 5); and Thomas Higham (unnumbered plate). The engravers are John Cleghorn (pls. 2, 3, 5, 7, 9, 10), Thomas Higham (pls. 11–13, unnumbered plate), Robert Havell and Son (pls. 6, 8), and J. C. Varrall (pl. 4). Plate 7 is also signed "Aquatinted by D[ean] Wolstenholme Jun."; the map was "Drawn on Stone by B. R. Baker" and "Printed by I. Boosey & Co." There are also 14 wood-engraved head- and tailpieces in the text and a wood-engraved title-page vignette of Beckford's coat of arms, all as listed. The credited draftsmen are Thomas Higham (4), John Rutter (3), and A. Harrison (1); 3 pieces have the initials "WS." 10 were engraved by W. Hughes and 1 by Higham. Rutter's own coat of arms on the final page is unsigned

Binding Recent three-quarter tan morocco, white buckram boards, gilt-lettered on spine

References Abbey, *Scenery*, 418

THE FASHION for country-house visiting reached a high point in Britain in the late eighteenth century, accompanied by a flow of guidebooks. Most were ephemeral: John Rutter's *Delineations of Fonthill*, like most things concerning William Beckford and his extraordinary Gothic abbey, was an exception. Since 1794 Fonthill itself had been closed to the would-be visiting public: a twenty-four-page guidebook by James Storer had been published in 1812, probably without the sanction of the abbey's reclusive owner. But in 1822 financial losses compelled Beckford to open the gates and admit floods of potential buyers (as well as the merely curious) at a huge sale announced by Christie's for 17 September. "Fonthill fever" swept the nation: the sale catalogue sold more than 7,200 copies at a guinea each, and Christie's astutely postponed the sale to 8 October. Several guidebooks, including one by Rutter, were rushed off the presses. On 26 September, a prospectus appeared for a weightier publication, *An Historical and Descriptive Account of Fonthill Abbey*, by the antiquarian John Britton, which was then "Preparing for Publication." But two days before its date the sale was abruptly canceled, a private buyer having emerged to acquire the abbey and its entire contents. Public interest was revived, however, in the following year when the new owner, John Farquhar, instructed the auctioneer Phillips to hold a sale of the contents only. In 1823, Britton's *Graphical and Literary Illustrations of Fonthill* appeared, as did Rutter's *Delineations of Fonthill*. Rutter's 1822 guidebook had "succeeded beyond the author's hopes" over six editions. Two years

John Rutter. *Delineations of Fonthill and its Abbey.* A view of the scenery of the American plantations. 1985.61.2659

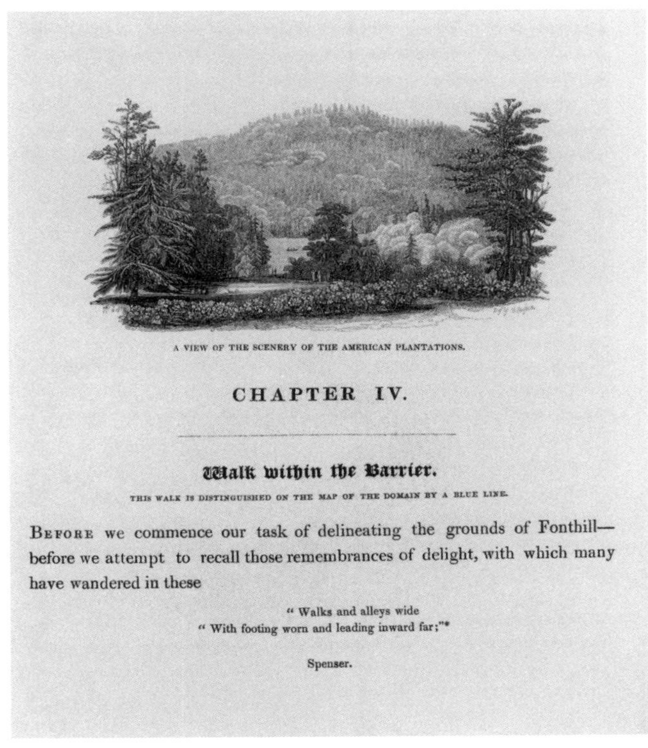

A VIEW OF THE SCENERY OF THE AMERICAN PLANTATIONS.

CHAPTER IV.

Walk within the Barrier.

THIS WALK IS DISTINGUISHED ON THE MAP OF THE DOMAIN BY A BLUE LINE.

BEFORE we commence our task of delineating the grounds of Fonthill—before we attempt to recall those remembrances of delight, with which many have wandered in these

"Walks and alleys wide
"With footing worn and leading inward far;"*

Spenser.

FONTHILL ABBEY.

INTERIOR OF ST MICHAELS GALLERY,

Looking across the Octagon into King Edwards Gallery.

later the abbey's gimcrack main tower collapsed and Farquhar died of apoplexy. The story was over.

Rutter's *Delineations* cannot be considered in isolation from Britton's *Graphical and Literary Illustrations*: as J. B. Nichols, borrowing Rutter's plates and Britton's descriptions for his 1836 publication on Fonthill, wrote: "No cost was spared in the production of these two rival works; and they certainly rank among the most successful specimens of embellished topography." In fact, Rutter's volume is superior: nearly twice as long, with many more illustrations but fewer dull genealogical tables; more detailed and without Britton's egocentric digressions; and it probably appeared first (all the plates were ready by 1 July: Britton's work came out in August). Britton's *Autobiography* implied that Rutter had more help from Beckford and his entourage, but this is contradicted by a comparison of the acknowledgments in the rival works: both mention Beckford himself, Chevalier Franchi, and Abbé Macquin, who showed Britton around the abbey in 1817, quite possibly before Rutter had even settled in Shaftesbury. The acknowledgments differ markedly, however, thereafter. Rutter writes "after the Abbey had changed possessors, the same advantage of free access, and warm interest in the success of his projected work . . . was uninterruptedly continued to him," whereas Britton admits "it would afford me much gratification to express thankfulness to other persons from whom I had a right to expect friendly and useful cooperation; but, as I cannot award praise, I forbear to censure." Clearly, from the references to professional rivalry, these remarks are directed at Rutter (no names are mentioned), and Rutter had, in Britton's view, contrived to deny him the access to Fonthill necessary to complete his book under the new ownership of Farquhar. When one realizes that Britton, who regarded Wiltshire as his home territory, had issued the prospectus for his book just days before Farquhar's purchase, his frustration becomes understandable, though he could not express it directly in his book without betraying the fact that his text was based on incomplete research. Instead he confines himself to berating the "deleterious effects of calumny" and defending his decision to exceed the print run originally promised to subscribers.

Born in 1796 in Bristol and raised a Quaker, Rutter settled as a bookseller and printer in Shaftesbury around 1818. His purpose for *Delineations* was threefold: as guidebook for visitors, souvenir, and information source for those who could not visit. His 1822 guidebook, available through agents in Amsterdam, Brussels, and Paris, had already evinced this concern for "the more distant Enquirer." For the visitor who toured the abbey with book in hand, the text is explicitly arranged as a processional narrative, orchestrated toward "a climax of agreeable and lofty sensations," and peppered with references to the sublime, quotations from Spenser, Tasso, Milton, and Chaucer, with visual highlights listed under the categories of furniture, architecture, paintings, and heraldry. All this constituted a "more perfect record" than the earlier guidebook made "amidst the hurry of the view." The text does not eschew earlier criticism, however, specifically of the accommodation afforded by the imposing abbey (only five usable bedrooms, none with dressing room) and the southwest front ("the composition as a work of art is exceedingly faulty"). But while Rutter notes the substitution of cement for stone in some of the external sculpture, and the replacement of parts of the abbey previously built of temporary materials, he omits the building's most glaring fault, its structural unsoundness. Even if he was unaware of it, the professional architect acknowledged as a source for his text, Whitwell, can hardly have been so, as it was evident to Charles Porden who provided three of Rutter's illustrations and remarked prophetically: "Would to God that it was more substantially built! But as it is, its ruins will tell a tale of wonder." Presumably it was thought impolitic to mention, and the abbey's "unfinished" state was taken to imply the eventual replacement of cement with stone.

The Millard copy is an example of the large-paper edition of *Delineations* and includes a list of subscribers, who were also offered an edition with proofs and etchings on India paper. For the "Embellishments," Rutter produced drawings for two plates and several wood engravings himself, and assembled the rest from various artists: Thomas Stedman Whitwell also contributed architectural insights to Rutter's text and designed the Gothic entrance ticket to the 1823 Phillips sale; Porden had connections with the family of Fonthill's architect, James Wyatt; George Cattermole and Thomas Higham also worked for Rutter's rival, Britton. Most of the plates are dated 2 June 1823; Higham's "South West View of Fonthill," dated 1 July, which is unnumbered and absent from the list of "Embellishments," may have been an afterthought or a late arrival. J. F.

Bibliography

Britton, J. *Graphical and Literary Illustrations of Fonthill Abbey, Wiltshire*. London, 1823

Harris, J. "English Country House Guides 1740–1840." In *Concerning Architecture: Essays on Architectural Writers and Writing Presented to Nikolaus Pevsner*. Ed. J. Summerson. London, 1968

John Rutter. *Delineations of Fonthill and its Abbey*. St. Michael's Gallery. 1985.61.2659

73

Vincenzo Scamozzi (1552–1616)

The Mirror of Architecture: Or The Ground-Rules Of The Art of Building, Exactly laid down by Vincent Scamozzi Master-Builder of Venice. Reviewed and inlarged with the Addition of a Diagonal Scale . . . By Joachim Schuym of Amsterdam. Translated out of Dutch by W. F. Hereunto is added the Description and Use of an Ordinary Joynt-Rule . . . By John Browne. The third Edition, with Addition of Stair-Cases and Chimney-Pieces

London: printed for W. Fisher, and E. Hurlock, 1676

1983.49.101

Quarto: 192 × 150 (7 9/16 × 5 7/8)

Pagination [viii], 23, [3], 29, [1], 22 pp., added title plate, [51] engraved plates (1 folding)

Edition Third edition

Text pp. [i] title page (verso blank); [iii–vi] preface; [vii–viii] description of Schuym's scale; 1–23 text, Scamozzi's *The Mirror of Architecture*; [24] blank; [i] divisional title page to John Browne's *The Description and Use of an Ordinary Joynt-Rule*, dated 1675 (verso blank); 1–29 text of same; [30] blank; [1] divisional title page to Henry Wotton's *The Ground-Rules of Architecture*, dated 1676 (verso blank); 3–22 text of same

Illustrations A total of 52 engraved plates, including an added title plate with a bust of Scamozzi on a pedestal inscribed "The Booke of Architecture by Vincent Scamozzi M^r. Builder of Venice [imprint] London Printed for W^m. Fisher and [blank]." In addition, there are 40 numbered plates belonging to Scamozzi's *Mirror*; a plate with figs. 1–3 illustrating the use of Schuym's scale; a folding plate with 5 figs. (4 numbered) illustrating Browne's joint rule; and 9 unnumbered plates of chimneypieces, staircases, and capitals. The folding plate is usually found cut up and bound as 5 separate plates. In the Millard copy it has been replaced by a photocopy on old paper

Binding Contemporary blind-ruled sheep, rebacked, with the plates relating to Scamozzi's *Mirror* and Schuym's scale bound at end

Provenance Late seventeenth or early eighteenth-century ownership inscription "Will: Felton" on front endpaper, with price (£0 1s 6d). Engraved library bookplate "E Bib. S^i. F^i. X^ii. Hereford:"

References ESTC r10290; Fowler 297 (1st ed.); Harris and Savage 803; Wing s810

Despite the prominence given to Vincenzo Scamozzi's name, *The Mirror of Architecture* is a pocket book compiled for builders, and therefore a far cry from *Dell'idea della architettura universale* (1615). A plan to publish the whole of the treatise did exist in England in the 1660s: John Leeke claimed the copyright by entering it in the Stationers' Register on 4 August 1664. Nothing, however, seems to have come of this, except perhaps an undated and otherwise inexplicable small folio edition of a few of Scamozzi's designs published as *XXX. Pieces of Architecture, taken out of the famous author Vincent Scamozze. and others*, with a parallel title and text in French (Harris and Savage 1990, no. 812).

The present work was less ambitious and more successful. Its publisher, William Fisher, enjoyed a long bookselling career on Tower Hill, lasting from about 1657 to 1690. He specialized in nautical books, but after the Great Fire of 1666 the dramatic increase in building work around the capital led him to develop a small sideline in builders' manuals. His first attempt in this direction was to produce, with the publisher and printseller John Overton, a new edition of the popular English translation of Hans Blum's *Quinque columnarum* (1550), now entitled *A Description of the Five Orders of Columnes and Tearms of Architecture* (1668). The first edition of *The Mirror* followed in 1669. Although only Fisher is named in the letterpress imprint, the title plate states it was "Printed for Wm. Fisher and Peter Parker" (see Fowler copy). Parker's name was later deleted (see Millard copy, and Harris and Savage 1990, 409), but Fisher found a new partner in Benjamin Hurlock when he reprinted the work in 1671. After Hurlock's death in 1673, his business was continued by his widow, Elizabeth, so her name joins Fisher's for the present third edition. Like most booksellers with premises on London Bridge, the Hurlocks carried mostly popular literature to catch the passing trade. However, they too specialized in nautical literature, and their customers would therefore have included those skilled craftsmen for whom *The Mirror* was intended.

The core of the work is Fisher's translation of a Dutch abridgment of book six of the *Idea*, on the orders. In the seventeenth century, it was not at all unusual for Italian architectural books to reach England via the Netherlands—another example is provided by Robert Peake's edition of Serlio—and the plethora of Dutch editions of Scamozzi that had appeared by the end of the 1660s were sure to attract attention on the other side of the channel. Fisher's source was apparently Joachim Schuym's *De grondt-regulen der bouw-konst* (Amsterdam, 1662), an abridgment based on a folio edition of Scamozzi's sixth book published by Justus Danckerts the previous year as part of a program to deliver the whole of Scamozzi's treatise. Judging by the English version, Schuym paid considerable attention to presenting the pedestals, bases, imposts, and cornices of each order in a new way, as they are as different from the original woodcuts as the other plates of the orders are similar

Vincenzo Scamozzi. *The Mirror of Architecture.* Added title plate. 1983.49.101

(see English edition, pls. 6–7, 12–13, 18–19, 24–25, 30–31, and 40). Schuym also copied two of Scamozzi's chimneypiece designs, ingeniously halving them and fitting them onto his smaller plate without losing scale (pl. 36). He similarly halved the section and elevation of Scamozzi's Palazzo Strozzi which, together with the plan, had mysteriously been transferred to book six in Danckerts' edition from its place in chapter seven of book three. This may have been a mere bibliographical accident, or a conscientious desire to exemplify the use of the orders, or an attempt to outshine the other books on Scamozzi's orders that were on the Dutch market. Whatever the case, Fisher dutifully followed his copy (pls. 37–39), and also included the scale devised by Schuym for calculating the measurements of each order.

A more original contribution was provided by the mathematical instrument maker John Browne, whose *Description and Use of an Ordinary Joynt-Rule* is an integral part of the present work. Fisher had already published or co-published the first three editions of another work by the same author, his *Description and Use of the Carpenter's Rule* (1656, 1662, 1667). The last of the twenty uses listed by Browne for his joint-rule is the most directly relevant: "The use of the scales to lay down or measure out on paper, or board, the members and parts of the five columns, and their ornaments, with their names and measures, digested into a table, for the more ease and use of workmen." Browne evidently wrote this specifically for *The Mirror*, since the table only demonstrates the Tuscan order and refers to "the figures in the book" for the others. The scales on the rule were logarithmic, and although neither Scamozzi nor Browne invented them, they became known as "Scamozzi's Lines" simply by association with the larger work.

No copy of the 1671 edition of *The Mirror* has been seen, but it is recorded as "The second edition, with addition of stair-cases and chimney-pieces" (Harris and Savage 1990, no. 803). These additions were presumably the nine unnumbered plates found also in the third edition, consisting of two capitals derived from Scamozzi; three chimneypieces from Jean Barbet's *Livre d'architecture* (1633); a double spiral staircase from Hendrik Hondius' *Institutio artis perspectivae* (1622); and three other staircases from Samuel Marolois' *Perspective* (1614). They were either taken from their original sources or English copies already circulating in pattern books. The subjects may seem random but they probably give a good indication of the specific problems that were troubling builders at the time: the relationship between booksellers like Fisher and his customers would have been very direct. It is interesting to see Barbet's designs in circulation both here and in Robert Pricke's *Booke of Architecture* (1670?), especially since Inigo Jones had frequently turned to them as a source for his own chimneypieces.

According to Harris and Savage, the abridgment of Henry Wotton's *Elements of Architecture* (1624) was also added to the second edition. The nine extra plates may even have been intended to illustrate Wotton's comments. An editor has deleted the discursive sections and focused on Wotton's practical advice, some of it quite loose and anecdotal. Retitled *The Ground-Rules of Architecture*, this abridgment typifies the seventeenth-century English book trade's impatience with the theory, as opposed to the practice, of architecture.

It is not surprising that Fisher felt compelled to enhance his book in these ways, since—although they mostly fell outside Mr. Millard's collecting policy, and therefore do not appear in this catalogue—there were already several rivals in the field. By 1676, *The Mirror* was in more or less direct competition with two versions of Giacomo Barozzi da Vignola (by Joseph Moxon and John Leeke), the third edition of Godfrey Richards' *First Book of Architecture, by Andrea Palladio* (1676), and Robert Pricke's version of Julien Mauclerc's *Traitté de l'architecture suivant Vitruve*, retitled *A New Treatise of Architecture* (1669). To a lesser extent, Pricke's *The Architect's Store-House* (1674) and John Evelyn's 1664 translation of Roland Fréart's *Parallèle* had also to be considered. The immediate impulse behind the present printing may have been the appearance of an even closer rival, Pricke's translation of Simon Bosboom's Scamozzi-derived *Cort onderwys vende vyf colommen*, as *A Brief and Plain Description of the Five Orders of Columns of Architecture* (1676). In the event, the latter was never reprinted, whereas in 1687 Fisher published with his new partner, Richard Mount, a fourth edition of *The Mirror of Architecture*. After a reissue of these sheets in 1693, it was again enlarged and survived to four more editions dated 1700, 1708, 1734, and 1752. G. B.

Bibliography

Harris, E., and N. Savage. *British Architectural Books and Writers 1556–1785*. Cambridge, 1990

Plomer, H. R., et al. *Dictionaries of the Printers and Booksellers who were at work in England, Scotland and Ireland 1557–1775*. London, 1977

74

Sebastiano Serlio (1475–1554)

The first (-fift) Booke of Architecture, made by Sebastian Serly, entreating of Geometrie. Translated out of Italian into Dutch, and out of Dutch into English

London: printed for Robert Peake, 1611

1983.49.112

Folio: 360 × 251 (14 1/8 × 9 7/8)

Foliation [iii], 13; [i], 26, [1]; [i], 73; 71, [1]; 16 leaves

Edition First English edition

Text *Book 1*: f. [i] title to book 1, as above (verso blank); [ii] Robert Peake's dedication to Henry, prince of Wales (verso blank); [iii] preface (verso blank); [1]–13 text; *Book 2*: f. [i], 1–26 title and text of book 2 ("The second Booke of Architecture . . . entreating of Perspective . . ."); [27] blank; *Book 3*: f. [i], [1]–73 title, preface, text, and colophon of book 3 ("The third Booke, Intreating of all kind of excellent Antiquities . . ."); *Book 4*: f. [1]–71, [72] title, [Pieter Coecke's] preface, Serlio's general preface and preface to this book, text to book 4 ("The fourth Booke. Rules for Masontry [sic], or Building with Stone or Bricke, made after the fiue maners or orders of Building . . ."); *Book 5*: f. [1]–16 title and text ("The fift Booke of Architecture . . . wherein there are set downe certayne formes of Temples . . ."), colophon at end "Printed at London, by Simon Stafford. 1611. B.W.," final page blank

Illustrations Books 1 and 2 have Serlian scrollwork woodcut title-page borders (repeated for books 5 and 4, respectively), and book 3 has the title printed in a cartouche supported by putti above a landscape of architectural ruins and fragments. Each book has numerous woodcut diagrams and illustrations, many full page. A large ornamental scrollwork cartouche with olive branches encloses the colophon of the final page of book 3, and there are various woodcut and typographic headpieces, tailpieces, and initials throughout

Binding Recent old-style calf

References ESTC S117091; Fowler 331; Harris and Savage 817; STC 22235

HENRY VIII OF ENGLAND was one of several potential patrons Sebastiano Serlio approached in the late 1530s, looking for employment and a subvention that would enable him to continue the architectural treatise he intended to write in seven books (Dinsmoor 1943, 67). The approach came to nothing, but Serlio's influence on British architecture can be traced long before the publication of this, until recently the only English edition of books one through five of his treatise. The earliest sign that he was known in England may be the geometrical pattern on the Chapel Royal's ceiling in St. James' Palace, London, said to have been built in 1540 and sometimes attributed to Holbein. This survives, and its octagonal, cross-shape, and lozenge panels match one of the ancient ceiling designs appended by Serlio to his book four, which was the first to be printed (as *Regole generali di architettura*, Venice, 1537). It is not an original design, and could have come to England by another route. But if, as Sir John Summerson has suggested, the chapel ceiling is derived directly from Serlio, it demonstrates the remarkable speed with which his work was adopted (Summerson 1983, 567, note 7).

Even if the chapel ceiling was not taken from Serlio, its design shows Henry VIII's desire to import the new Renaissance style from its native Italy. Henry had earlier employed Italian artists for his father's tomb in Westminster Abbey; and the screen and stalls of King's College Chapel, Cambridge, which he paid for, were probably designed by the same group (1533–1535). Craftsmen working in the office of the King's Works were also beginning to be conscious of developments in France, where Francis I was busy persuading many Italians to try their chances at his court. Since Serlio was one of those he attracted, English architecture was soon able to come under his influence via this route too. In 1540 he dedicated the second of his books to be published (i.e., *Il Terzo Libro*) to Francis, and left Venice the following year to advise the French king on Fontainebleau and other royal projects. When he published books one and two simultaneously in 1545, and book five in 1547, he did so from Paris with parallel Italian and French translations. He also issued a *Libro Estraordinario* (Lyons, 1551), and book seven appeared posthumously (Frankfurt, 1575), but these were not included in the English version, and the manuscript for book six was only published in the twentieth century.

Frequently reprinted, pirated, translated, and epitomized, the influence of Serlio's treatise on the second half of the sixteenth century was virtually inescapable, and the few significant architectural treatises published in England before Robert Peake's edition all mirrored and multiplied elements from it. The reason was simple enough: Serlio was seen as the best modern interpreter of Vitruvius, as well as being the most accessible, and authors and architects who copied his work did so because they believed it was an accurate reflection of ancient Roman practice. John Shute stated openly that

> I have for the first parte taken for my author chieflye to be followed the noble and excellent writer Vitruvius, one of the most parfaicte of all the Antiques; and for that neither any one man in what arte so ever it be is so absolute, and that other singuler men of the Antiques and he in many poinctes do disagre and differ (which Sebastianus Serlius, a mervelous conning artificer in our time in many places of his workes

learnedly doth declare), I have added unto him upon whatsoever in any thing semed nedfull the opinion and meaning of the sayde experte writer Sebastianus (*The First and Chief Groundes of Architecture*, 1563, preface, punctuation modified).

Similarly, Richard Haydocke's *Tracte Containing the Artes of Curiouse Painting Carvinge & Buildinge* (Oxford, 1598), a translation of Giovanni Paolo Lomazzo's *Trattato dell'Arte delle Pittura Scultura et Architettura* (Milan, 1584), contains plates with details taken from Serlio, used to illustrate the orders according to Vitruvius. Another translation (by John Thorne?), Hans Blum's *The Booke of Five Collumnes of Architecture* (1601), offered a highly successful simplification of Serlio's system of the orders—again, as a gloss on Vitruvius.

More importantly, details copied from Serlio's books survive on numerous Elizabethan houses built for the nobility—and many Serlian features on more modest buildings must have since been destroyed, or remain unrecognized. Sir John Thynne certainly used him for some of the details at Somerset House (1547–1552), and Robert Smythson did the same when working for Thynne at Longleat (1570 onward). Later, for the plan of Sir Francis Willoughby's Wollaton Hall (1580–1588), Smythson simply took one of Serlio's designs in book three and expanded it. Serlian features can also be traced at Hardwick Hall (1590–1597) and numerous less famous houses such as Kirby Hall (1570–1575), Holdenby (1574), and Wardour House (1578).

From 1610 the beginning of a new direction in British architecture may be observed, but Serlio's place in it was by no means lost. The change was symbolized by that year's Twelfth Night (6 January) masque, *Prince Henry's Barriers*, performed at the royal court. This masque was written by Ben Jonson and designed by Inigo Jones under the direction of King James' eldest son, Henry. It has been called "both in text and design a statement of the Prince's desire to reform architecture" (Strong 1986, 171). Jones' stage scenery transferred elements from the buildings of imperial Rome to a mythical ancient Britain, and thereby made manifest the synthesis of classical and vernacular traditions to which the court was aspiring. In June of the same year Henry was invested as prince of Wales, and was soon planning improvements to his palace and gardens at Richmond.

Any excitement stirred up by the young prince's evident desire for a cultural reformation must have included a strong element of fear for those artists dependent on royal patronage. Would they be displaced by a new influx of foreigners? Jones and Jonson excelled themselves with their masque for 1611, *Oberon, or The Fairy Prince*, which featured a stage setting drawn from an eclectic range of sources, including woodcuts in Serlio's book four. But the arrival that June of the Medici court painter and architect Constantino de Servi seems to have prompted at least two artists to resolve to raise their profile or risk falling out of favor. One, the Frenchman Salomon de Caus, who had taught Henry the principles of perspective several years earlier, chose to dedicate to the latter an original treatise, *La Perspective avec la Raison* (London and Frankfurt, 1612). The other, Peake, published the present translation, also dedicated to Henry. It was registered with the Stationers' Company on 14 December 1611, two months after the date of De Caus' dedication.

Peake was probably born about 1551, apprenticed to Laurence Woodham in 1565, and purchased his freedom from the Goldsmiths' Company in 1576. He was employed by the Office of the Revels between 1576 and 1579. He later established himself as a popular and prolific portrait artist, who from 1607 held the title of serjeant painter, as did John de Critz. He was Prince Henry's official painter, and must have found De Servi

The second Booke. The third Chapter. Fol. 26.

The Satiricall Scenes are to represent Satirs, wherein you must place all those things that bee rude and rusticall, as in ancient Satirs they were made plaine without any respect, whereby men might vnderstand, that such things were referred to Rusticall people, which set all things out rudely and plainely: for which cause Vitruuius speaking of Scenes, saith, they should be made with Trees, Rootes, Herbs, Hils and Flowres, and with some countrey houses, as you see them here set downe. And for that in our dayes these things were made in Winter, when there were but fewe greene Trees, Herbs and Flowres to be found; then you must make these things of Silke, which will be more commendable then the naturall things themselues: and as in other Scenes for Comedies or Tragedies, the houses or other artificiall things are painted, so you must make Trees, Hearbs, and other things in these; & the more such things cost, the more they are esteemed, for they are things which stately and great persons doe, which are enemies to nigardlinesse. This haue I seene in some Scenes made by Ieronimo Genga, for the pleasure and delight of his lord and patron Francisco Maria, Duke of Vrbin: wherein I saw so great liberalitie vsed by the Prince, and so good a conceit in the workeman, and so good Art and proportion in things therein represented, as euer I saw in all my life before. Oh good Lord, what magnificence was there to be seene, for the great number of Trees and Fruits, with sundry Herbes and Flowres, all made of fine Silke of diuers collors. The water courses being adorned with Frogs, Snailes, Tortuses, Toads, Adders, Snakes, and other beasts: Rotes of Corrale, mother of Pearle, and other shels layd and thrust through betweene the stones, with so many seuerall and faire things, that if I should declare them all, I should not haue time enough. I speake not of Satirs, Nimphes, Mermaids, diuers monsters, and other strange beastes, made so cunningly, that they seemed in shew as if they went and stirred, according to their manner. And if I were not desirous to be briefe, I would speake of the costly apparel of some Shepheards made of cloth of gold, and of Silke, cunningly mingled with Imbrotherie: I would also speake of some Fishermen, which were no lesse richly apparelled then the others, hauing Nets and Angling-rods, all gilt: I should speake of some Countrey mayds and Nimphes carelesly apparelled without pride, but I leaue all these things to the discretion and consideration of the iudicious workeman; which shall make all such things as their patrons serue them, which they must worke after their owne deuises, and neuer take care what it shall cost.

Sebastiano Serlio. *The First (-fift) Booke of Architecture.* Book 2, f. 26 recto, Stage design for a Satire. 1983.49.112

a particularly unwelcome arrival, as within a month the Italian had himself produced a portrait of the prince. Nevertheless, Peake seems to have kept his reputation at court. Soon after Henry's tragic death in 1612 he was commissioned to paint the latter's younger brother, the future Charles I, for Cambridge University. A slightly later foreign invasion, this time of Dutch artists, might have put his Elizabethan-style "costume pieces" out of fashion toward the end of the decade; but in any case Peake is now known to have died in 1619.

He confessed that his part in the English Serlio was "but small, saving my great adventure in the charge, and my great good-will to doe good" (dedication). The charge he bore was presumably for printing it and for purchasing the woodblocks used as illustrations. These had a long and complicated history dating from the Antwerp publisher Pieter Coecke van Aelst's Flemish

Sebastiano Serlio. *The First (-fift) Booke of Architecture.* Book 4, f. 58 recto, Design for a chimneypiece using the Corinthian order. 1983.49.112

language editions of book four (1539) and book three (1546), and his widow's of books one, two, and five (1553). None of these editions was sanctioned by Serlio, and some incorporated changes, including slight alterations to the stage designs in book two; an addition of a woodcut of the Arco dei Borsari in book three (taken from Torello Sarayna's *De Origine et Amplitudine Civitatis Veronae*, Verona, 1540); and the replacement of Serlio's chapter on coats of arms by one on Roman capital letters in book four. But in other respects the illustrations were careful enough copies which, frequently reprinted, did much to spread Serlio's influence beyond France and Italy. Their last appearance before 1611 had been in a German language edition of books one through five published by Ludwig Königs in Basel, 1608–1609, by which time one of the blocks (a plan of a Venetian town house) had gone astray. Peake's printer had to ink the rest of the set quite heavily to conceal their wear, although their useful life was later extended to include at least one more Dutch edition (Amsterdam, 1616). Despite their age and dubious pedigree, it probably represented something of a minor coup for Peake to have obtained them. There was certainly no shame attached to what might now seem a lack of originality. Many similar cases might be cited, as when, later in the century, Roland Fréart was happy to use Palladio's eighty-year-old and thoroughly worm-eaten woodcuts for his translation of the *Quattro Libri* (Paris, 1650; see Millard catalogue, *French Books* 1993, no. 129).

The impressive physical appearance of the 1611 Serlio—in particular its careful marriage of text and illustration so that both could be consulted at once, even though this demanded extra expense on paper and composition—reflects Serlio's revolutionary approach to book design, as imitated by Coecke, rather than English inventiveness. It made the printer's job difficult, and he occasionally slipped up. Two cuts are printed upside down (book two, fol. 7 verso; book four, fol. 36 verso); and the elevation and section of the Pantheon (book three, fol. 2 verso and 3 recto), and the details of the Arches of Septimus Severus and Constantine (book three, fols. 52 and 56 rectos), have been transposed. But Serlio had similar problems when first printing book four alone, so with more than three hundred blocks to reproduce it is not surprising that a few errors were introduced. According to the colophon, Simon Stafford printed the book. Another printer, Thomas Snodham, registered it at the Stationers' Company on Peake's behalf.

The translator is unknown. He may be represented by the initials "B. W." beneath the colophon, or he may be one John Land, to whom Blum's *Collumnes* had been dedicated in 1601 as a "merchant, and true favourer of art" who "intended . . . to set forth the workes of Sebastian Serly, and Albert Duree, and other worthy authors." His copy was presumably Cornelis Claesz' edition of *Den Eersten (-Vijfsten) Boeck van Architecturen Sebastiani Serlii* (Amsterdam, 1606). The translation (at least as concerns book two) was later criticized by Joseph Moxon, who prefaced his *Practical Perspective* (1670) with the comment that

> as yet nothing of this nature had been published in English except Sebastian Serlio, who though he were a man of skill and fame, yet his book being originally written in Italian was first translated into Dutch and afterwards from Dutch into English; one of which translators (if not both) doubtless understood the language better than the Art; for therein (as the generallity of ingenuous artists do with me confess) the words are translated, but not the Science.

Peake would have been disappointed to learn the opinion of Moxon's interlocutors: his stated aim was to "convay unto my countrymen (especially architects and artificers of all sorts) these necessary, certaine, and most ready helpes of Geometrie: the ignorance and want whereof, in time past (in most parts of this kingdome) hath left us many lame workes, with shame of many workmen" (dedication). One difficulty was noted by Coecke in book four's address, here translated as "To the wel-willers of Architecture." The establishment of a modern technical vocabulary that could cope with Vitruvius' Latin and Greek terms was a constant preoccupation of Italian Renaissance architects. Translating their solutions into Dutch, or English, was the same problem again. The following quotation from the English version of Coecke's address stands as a notable witness to this difficulty, as well as a reminder that the perceived relationship between Serlio and Vitruvius was extremely close:

> And for that all those that love workmanship, understand not the Italians, therefore (in my opinion) I have translated the most certayne and best rules out of Italian into Dutch, and out of Dutch into English; onely [i.e., except] the names of all procels [!], bases, capitals, cornices, &c. which are not named in Dutch nor English, for that bastian [i.e., Serlio], by Vitruvius termes [i.e., as far as Vitruvian terminology was concerned], useth the common and moderne Italian words, which by some should be as hardly understood as the Latine. But I would commend him, that seeing we take upon us to follow Vitruvius writings, that we give him the name[s] of Vitruvius, that the learned might be understood of the workeman, and the workeman also understood of the learned.

This is immediately followed by an allusion to the politics of typography: "And for that the workeman might better read it, I have printed it in our ordinary Dutch letter." The bulk of the text is accordingly in a black letter that would have been friendlier to the eyes of most Englishmen than roman or italic, which is reserved, not entirely consistently, for the royal dedication, the prefaces, and one or two of Serlio's excursus. If Peake had actually expected the prince to read his offering, he would have changed this arrangement; something like De Caus' elegant roman and italic faces would have been more admired at court. Peake's desire was to impress the prince less directly, and more economically, by showing himself willing to help cultivate his country-

Sebastiano Serlio. *The First (-fift) Booke of Architecture.* Book 3, f. 41 recto, Ancient bridges in Rome. 1983.49.112

men. But architects such as Jones had no need for an English Serlio, being perfectly familiar with his work already and preferring the more complete Italian editions (of which Jones seems to have owned at least two, namely, the 1600 and 1619 Venice printings of *Tutte l'Opere d'Architettura et Prospetiva di Sebastiano Serlio*; Jones' copies of these are in the Canadian Centre for Architecture and the British Architectural Library, RIBA, respectively. Jones also owned a copy of books one to four and part of book five, published in Venice 1560–1562, now in Queen's College, Oxford). Lower-ranking builders may have found the translation useful, but whether Peake was successful in selling them his bulky folio remains in doubt. Admittedly, it is difficult to judge the impact of the book because English architecture was already so indebted to Serlio, but surviving copies seem to lack the sort of marginalia that indicate practical use. Peake sold the woodblocks back to the Dutch trade within five years, clearly not anticipating further demand; and when his son and grandson, William and Robert Peake, published an architectural book from the same address in 1635, it was a reprint of Blum's *Booke of Five Collumnes.*

Perhaps, then, the English Serlio was not an episode in British architectural publishing to which too much significance should be attached. Nevertheless, a part, at least, of the work had its life extended. In 1657, Thomas Jenner reprinted books one and two as, respectively, *A New-Naturalized Work of a Learned Stranger* and *A Book of Perspective & Geometry*, with reduced and reversed engraved copies of the woodcut illustrations; and in 1670 Robert Pricke published folio and quarto versions of book one only as *An Excellent Introduction to Architecture. Being a Book of Geometrical-Practice.* (The British Library has a folio copy of the latter with a canceled imprint dated 1679; the Canadian Centre for Architecture's copy is also a reissue, with the cancel imprint in a variant state dated "167 .") Both Jenner and Pricke were aiming at "masons, carpenters, joyners, glasiers, bricklayers, plaisterers, painters, and all that live by hammer and hand" (Jenner's title page to book one). Both took their texts word for word from Peake's edition. Serlio's name was evidently no longer a useful selling point: his authorship is mentioned only in passing by Jenner, and suppressed entirely by Pricke. Such reprintings are a credit to Serlio's simple and effective style, and might seem to belie Moxon's comment on the translation. But they also indicate how poorly native mathematicians were catering for the building trades. For a decline in Serlio's reputation had begun, and his two books on geometry and perspective were already well out-of-date. G. B.

Bibliography

Bury, J. B. "Serlio. Some Bibliographical Notes." In *Sebastiano Serlio: Sesto Seminario Internazionale di Storia dell'Architettura.* Ed. C. Thoenes. Milan, 1989: 92–101

Dinsmoor, W. B. "The Literary Remains of Sebastiano Serlio." *Art Bulletin* 24 (1943): 55–91, 115–154

Edmond, M. "Limners and Picturemakers." *Walpole Society* 47 (1980): 129–133

Edmond, M. "New Light on Jacobean Painters." *Burlington Magazine* 118 (1976): 74–83

Harris, E., and N. Savage. *British Architectural Books and Writers 1556–1785.* Cambridge, 1990

Hart, V., and P. Hicks. *Sebastiano Serlio on Architecture.* Vol. 1. New Haven, 1996: introduction

Newman, J. "Inigo Jones's Architectural Education before 1614." *Architectural History* 35 (1992): 18–50

The Renaissance Stage: Documents of Serlio, Sabbattini and Furttenbach. Ed. B. Hewitt. Miami, 1958

Santaniello, A. E. *The Book of Architecture by Sebastiano Serlio, London, 1611.* New York, 1970: introduction

Strong, R. *Henry, Prince of Wales and England's Lost Renaissance.* London, 1986

Summerson, J. *Architecture in Britain 1530–1830.* 7th ed. Harmondsworth, 1983

75

Thomas Sheraton (1751–1806)

The Cabinet-Maker And Upholsterer's Drawing-Book. In Three Parts. By Thomas Sheraton, Cabinet-Maker

London: printed for the author by T. Bensley; and sold by J. Mathews; G. Terry; J. S. Jordan, L. Wayland; and by the author (41, Davies Street, Grosvenor Square), 1793

Appendix To The Cabinet-Maker And Upholsterer's Drawing-Book. . . .

London: printed for the author by T. Bensley; and sold by J. Mathews; G. Terry; J. S. Jordan; L. Wayland; and by the author (106, Wardour Street, Soho), 1793

An Accompaniment To The Cabinet-Maker And Upholsterer's Drawing-Book. . . .

London: printed by T. Bensley, for the author (106, Wardour Street, Soho), [1794]

1985.61.2677

Quarto: 263 × 210 (10 5/16 × 8 1/4)

Pagination Drawing-Book: [2], xxxii, [3], 6–446, [2] pp., engraved frontispiece, 61 [i.e., 65] engraved plates (5 double-page, 5 folding)

(*Note*: In three parts. This copy is without the separate title leaves for each part)

Appendix: 54, [2] pp., 32 [i.e., 33] engraved plates (3 double-page, 1 folding)

Accompaniment: 27, [1] pp., 14 engraved plates (8 double-page)

Edition First editions of the 3 works

Text Drawing-Book: pp. [1] explanation of the frontispiece (verso blank); [i] title page (verso blank); [iii] summary list of contents of the 3 parts (verso blank); [v]–viii list of plates, with directions to binder; [ix]–xix detailed table of contents; [xx] blank; [xxi]–xxxii list of subscribers; [xxxiii] additional subscribers (verso blank); [5]–14 preface "To Cabinet-Makers And Upholsterers In General"; [15]–18 introduction; [19]–446 text, parts 1–3; [447] errata (verso blank); *Appendix*: pp. [1] title page (verso blank); [3]–54 text; [55] list of plates, with directions to binder; [56] list of additional subscribers; *Accompaniment*: pp. [1] title page (verso blank); [3]–27 text; [28] blank

Illustrations Drawing-Book: engraved allegorical frontispiece by Hawkins after Sheraton, plus 65 engraved plates numbered 1–61 with nos. 25, 26, 29, and 56 repeated (but see notes below). The second plate 26 is actually numbered "54," a mistake noted in the letterpress list. Plate 1 is unsigned but all the others are signed by Sheraton as draftsman, and the engravers comprise J. Barlow (24 plates), Garnet Terry (23), J. Cooke (6), J. Newton (5), Thornthwaite (3), G. Barrett (1), Towes (1), and G. Walker (1). Most of the plates have imprints dated 1791 or 1792 (1 dated 1793). *Appendix*: 33 engraved plates numbered 1–30, 30–32. All signed by Sheraton as draftsman, engraved by Garnet Terry (14), James Caldwall "Direx[t]." (13), or Barlow (6). Imprints dated 1793 *Accompaniment*: 14 engraved plates numbered 1–14, all signed by Sheraton as draftsman and J. Barlow as engraver except plate 1, which was engraved under the direction of James Caldwall. Imprints dated 1793 or 1794

Binding Bound as 1 volume. Nineteenth-century dark green straight-grain morocco, gilt. Signed binding by Roger de Coverly and Sons. Plates 40, 41, and 45 of *Drawing-Book* misbound between plates 31–32

References Berlin Cat. 1234 (3d ed.); ESTC t91107

Though celebrated as one of the greatest cabinet-makers of the eighteenth century, very little is known of Thomas Sheraton. He was born in 1751 in Stockton-on-Tees, the son of a schoolmaster. Nothing is known of his early training, though he was clearly well schooled in draftsmanship. He was also fired with something of a religious fervor, for he was a devout Baptist and published a number of religious tracts. He was married at Norton, in County Durham, on 8 February 1779. He seems to have established himself in London around 1790 and is recorded at different addresses there in the years that followed, all in the Mayfair or Soho areas, though in 1800 he returned briefly to County Durham, where he was ordained as a minister. He was buried in the churchyard of St. James' Piccadilly on 27 October 1806.

Adam Black, later a well-known publisher, worked briefly for Sheraton two years before his death, "trying," Black wrote, "to put his house in order, for which I was remunerated with half a guinea. Miserable as the pay was, I was half ashamed to take it from the poor man."

"He is," he wrote further, "a man of talents, and, I believe, of genuine piety. He understands the cabinet business—I believe was bred to it, he has been, or perhaps at present is, a preacher; he is a scholar, writes well; draws, in my opinion masterly; is an author, bookseller, stationer and teacher."

Though Sheraton described himself as a cabinet-maker in his publications, there is no evidence that he owned a workshop, and no piece of furniture can be ascribed to him. One piece, at least, he is known to have designed: a piano made by Messrs. Broadwoods in 1796 for Don Manuel de Godoy to present to Queen Maria Louisa of Spain, now at the Heritage Foundation, Deerfield, Massachusetts. On the wrappers of the first

Thomas Sheraton. *The Cabinet-Maker and Upholsterer's Drawing-Book*. Frontispiece. 1985.61.2677

FRONTISPIECE.

Time alters fashions and frequently obliterates the works of art and ingenuity; but that which is founded on Geometry & real Science, will remain unalterable.

four numbers of *The Cabinet-Maker and Upholsterer's Drawing-Book*, of 1791, he noted that the "author intends to open an EVENING SCHOOL for teaching the ART of DRAWING." He was then at 4 Hart Street, Grovesnor Square, Mayfair. On a trade card of about 1796, with the address 106 Wardour Street, Soho, he described his capacities, "Teaches Perspective, Architecture and Ornaments, makes Designs for Cabinet-makers, and sells all kinds of Drawing Books &c." He was, it is clear, a draftsman and designer, perhaps a journeyman cabinetmaker.

Sheraton's claim to fame is his three pattern books, the *Cabinet-Maker and Upholsterer's Drawing-Book* issued, by subscription, fortnightly, at one shilling each, between 1791 and 1793; The *Cabinet Dictionary*, of 1803, which provided "an explanation of all the terms used in the Cabinet, chair and upholstery branches," and *The Cabinet-Maker, Upholsterer, and General Artist's Encyclopedia*, which was to have been published in 125 numbers, by subscription, beginning in 1803, but only 30 of which, A–Capstan, had appeared by the time of his death in 1806. Of these, the *Drawing-Book* is the most extensive, grandest, and best known.

The prospectus for the *Drawing-Book*, inviting subscriptions, was probably issued late in 1791, as dated. The book was to be in three parts: the first, a handbook of instruction on drafting and geometrical representation, including the five orders and their proportions; the second, the principles of perspective drawing, with examples "together with a little of the THEORY for such as would know some of the reasons on which this useful art is founded"—with an added note "The Examples in Perspective are intended to exhibit the newest taste of various Pieces of Furniture, and likewise to show the necessary Lines for designing them"; the third, "a Repository of various Ornaments, consisting of Designs for Pediments, with Cornices, &c. drawn at large, their Springs shewn, and the proper gaging marked off to work the several Mouldings by.—To which are added, two methods of representing a Drawing-Room, with the proper Distribution of the Furniture."

The prospectus included ten pages of text "To Cabinet-Makers and upholsterers in general" and also the "Frontispiece explained," though the frontispiece itself was to be issued only with the fifth number. The frontispiece, an allegorical image, dated 20 November 1791, engraved by George Hawkins, depicts a room, with the figure of Geometry on the right, standing on a rock, giving instruction to the figure of Perspective. On the left is seated an Artist, designing, attended by the Genius of Drawing. To the rear, also seated (one might say slumped), is the figure of Architecture, measuring a Tuscan column. Beyond, glimpsed through an archway, is a circular Temple of Fame. Underneath, a caption gives the assurance "that which is founded on Geometry & real Science, will remain unalterable."

Subscriptions were to be obtained from the author, then at 4 Hart Street—though he was to move after the issue of the ninth number to 41 Davis Street, Grovesnor Square—and at various London booksellers: J. Mathews, G. Terry, J. S. Jordan, and L. Wayland. The printer was Thomas Bensley. The work was to be issued in thirty, fortnightly numbers, priced at one shilling each. A rare copy of the *Drawing Book* as issued, in thirty numbers, complete with wrappers (with the exception of that for number 1) survives at The Furniture Library, High Point, North Carolina. This makes evident the progress of the publication. Each number contains sixteen pages of text (though 29 has twelve pages and 30, twenty-four pages), together with two or three plates (29 is again an exception with four plates). The numbers seem to have been issued fortnightly, as planned, with "a little pause in the publication" after 20, occasioned, it was explained, by a depletion in the stock of paper for the letterpress. Subscribers were emphatically reassured, twice, that the engraving of the plates had nothing to do with the delay, and that the engraving would continue in the interim to allow, perhaps, a more rapid publication after 22. But the inability of the principal engravers J. Barlow and G. Terry, who were responsible for twenty-four and twenty-three plates respectively, to keep pace with publication seems in fact to have been the reason for the pause. It was precisely at this period that G. Barrett, G. Walker, and Towes were recruited to produce a single plate each—Barrett's, dated 28 June 1792, appeared in no. 18; Walker's and Towes', dated 16 July 1792 and 30 August, respectively, both appeared in no. 21. Thornthwaite, who contributed three plates—dated 7 January, 20 February, and 4 March 1792—seems to have been called upon earlier in much the same way to sustain the pace of publication. His plates were issued in nos. 8, 10, and 11. The period of publication was thus spread over fifteen or sixteen months, from November or December 1791 to about February 1793.

The book was evidently planned as a whole. And though the description of the three parts offered in the prospectus and on all the wrappers, from first to last, describes the third part as a survey of ornamental details rather than the full-scale survey of furniture that it emerged as, there is no evidence to suggest any basic change in the makeup of the contents once publication began. The text was issued sequentially in successive numbers. The plates, sixty-three of which are dated, from 27 August 1791 to 1 February 1793, were issued, very roughly, in a sequence corresponding to their dating. The issue of the plates was as follows: no. 1 pls. 1, 30 "A library table," the plan alone; no. 2 pls. 2 , 48; no. 3 pls. 3, 56 "Ornament for a Frieze or Tablet"; no. 4 pl. 31, "A Sofa Bed," the perspective construction and the view separately; no. 5 frontispiece, pl. 25 "The Universal Table"; no. 6 pls. 5, 8, 29, "A Sideboard Table"; no. 7 pls. 6, 9, 28; no. 8 pls. 10, 32; no. 9 pls. 7, 40; no. 10 pls. 11, 45; no. 11 pls. 13, 37; no. 12 pls. 29 "Doors for Bookcases," 46; no. 13 pls. 12, 50; no. 14 pls. 38, 49; no. 15 pls. 14, 34; no. 16 pls. 27, 51; no. 17 pls. 15, 18, 41; no. 18 pls.

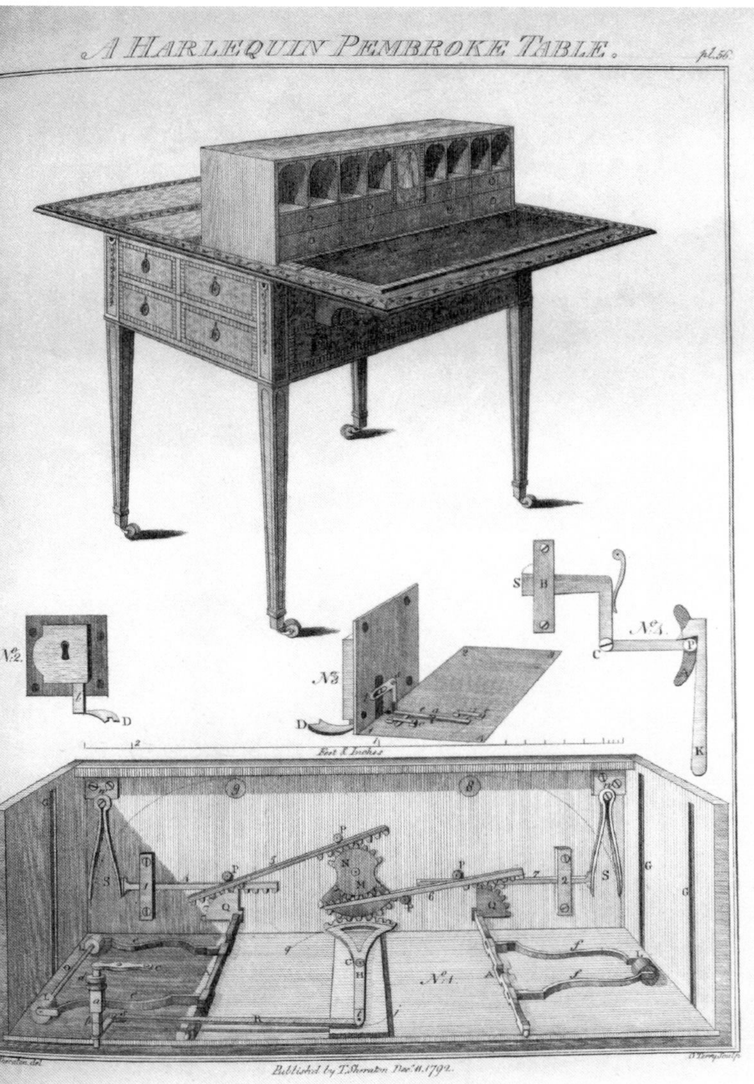

Thomas Sheraton. *The Cabinet-Maker and Upholsterer's Drawing-Book.* Plate 56. 1985.61.2677

17, 53; no. 19 pls. 16, 55; no. 20 pls. 24, 47; no. 21 pls. 35, 44; no. 22 pls. 36, 52; no. 23 pls. 33, 43; no. 24 pls. 25 "Tables in perspective," 26 "A Side Board," misnumbered 54; no. 25 pls. 19, 21, 58; no. 26 pls. 42, 54; no. 27 pls. 39, 59; no. 28 pls. 26 "How to put a Cylinder Desk and Bookcase in perspective . . .etc.," 56 "A Harlequin Pembroke Table"; no. 29 pls. 23, 30 "A Library Table," perspective only, 60, 61; no. 30 pls. 20, 22, 57.

The "DIRECTIONS for finding and binding in the PLATES" issued in 29 lists plates numbered from 1 to 61, but 25, 26, 29, and 56 each occur twice and plates 30 and 31, "A Library Table" and "A Sofa Bed," were issued in two separate parts, the plan of the desk, as noted above, in 1, the view in 29, the perspective construction and the view of the bed both in 4. The total number of plates, together with the frontispiece should thus, correctly, be sixty-eight. Sixty-five of these are signed.

The aim, in issuing the plates, seems to have been to have one plate from the first two parts of the book, on drafting techniques, and one from the third part, illustrating decorative details or furniture, in each of the numbers. This was no doubt seen as a means of sustaining interest. The six plates by J. Cooke, 2 to 7, dated 28 August 1791 to 10 December 1791, all concerned with setting out, were issued in numbers 2, 3, 4, 6, 7, and 9. In number 5 it was announced that the orders would be illustrated in five rather than on one plate (no doubt in emulation of Chippendale). These plates, 8 to 12, by J. Newton, dated 6 December 1791 to 17 March 1792, were issued in numbers 6, 7, 8, 10, and 13. Cooke's and Newton's plates were, invariably, issued alongside something more alluring in terms of design.

The book was aimed, primarily, at cabinetmakers and upholsterers, though on the wrappers of number 5 and onward, the attention of chairmakers, joiners, smiths, and carvers was also invited. Subscribers were coerced by all manner of means. The explanation to the frontispiece was included in the first number, but the frontispiece itself, as noted, was withheld. In 2 it was promised with 5, which is where it was issued. In 7 a note was inserted that "a very tasty ALCOVE BED" was to be included in number 8 or 9; it was issued in 9 as plate 40. Nonsubscribers were warned on the back of the wrapper of 5 that the price would shortly be raised to 1s 6d, and on the wrapper of 6 that the subscription list would close with 10 and the price be raised then. But on the wrapper of 11 this was put off to 12. The first list of subscribers was in fact issued in 12; there were 577, chiefly cabinetmakers, including one from abroad, "Stewart, Cabinet-maker, Bengal," with upholsterers to follow. Only two architects were listed, David Stevenson of Newcastle, and Woolley of Davies Street, London.

Despite all warnings, the price remained at 1s and the closing of the subscription list was put off yet again to 15. When this appeared it carried a note that the author "finds that he is now sufficiently supported, and will keep the subscription open till the end of the work, when a corrected list of subscribers will be published." The final list appeared with 30; the figure had risen by then to a surprising total of 717, with another cabinetmaker from abroad, "Dillon, Cabinet-maker, Russia," and another architect, England, of 21 South Street, London.

A preliminary title page, dated 1791, listing the contents of the three parts as described in the prospectus and on the wrappers, was issued with the first number; the final title page, dated 1793, without the description of the parts, with the words "Entered at Stationers Hall," was issued in number 29.

The introduction, addressed "To cabinet-makers and upholsterers in general," which had been part of the original prospectus, stressed Sheraton's particular abilities as a draftsman; comparing his work with those that had appeared in the preceding century, he noted, "none of these, as far as I know, profess to give any instructions relative to the art of making perspective drawings, or to treat of such geometrical lines as ought to be

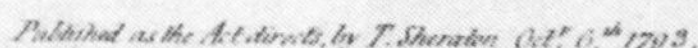

Thomas Sheraton. *The Cabinet-Maker and Upholsterer's Drawing-Book.* Plate 31. "A view of the south end of the Prince of Wales's Chinese drawing room." 1985.61.2677

known by persons of both professions." Reviewing his predecessors in detail, he was surprisingly sharp, in particular when reviewing the more famous names. He gave credit to Chippendale for including the five orders and some remarks on drawing, but "as for the designs themselves, they are now wholly antiquated and laid aside, though possessed of great merit, according to the times in which they were executed." He was even more dismissive of William Ince and John Mayhew's folio—"it may be said to have been a book of merit in its day, though inferior to Chippendale's, which was a real original, as well as more extensive and masterly in its designs." George Hepplewhite's work, of 1788, was, as before, acknowledged to have some merit, but "this work has already caught the decline."

Sheraton aimed himself to present "the newest taste," but it was, initially, it seems, to be represented by ornament rather than furniture—"With respect to mouldings and various ornaments, the subject of the third part, it is granted that these are of a changeable kind. Yet it is pretty evident that materials for proper ornaments are now brought to such perfection as will not, in the future, admit of much, if any, degree of improvement, though they may, by the skill and touch of the ingenious hand, be varied, *ad infinitum*, to suit any taste at any time."

Though the second part of the book included a number of examples of furniture associated with the name of Sheraton, it was the third part, as it emerged, that established his reputation as a designer of furniture and served as a model book for a century and more—"the design of this part of the book," he wrote, "is intended to exhibit the present state of furniture, and at the same time to give the workman some assistance in the manufacturing part of it." In forty-one plates, illustrating individual pieces of furniture for the most part, beginning with "The Universal Table," including a whole range of tables, beds, chairs, sofas, screens, and a great many small items, such as knife-cases and pot cupboards, Sheraton depicted the contemporary fashion in cabinetmaking. He described each item at some length, providing much useful information as to current practices. Though he laid much stress on practical knowledge and draftsmanship, much was in fact left for the interpretation of the individual craftsman, even the dimensioning. Plate 51, showing "Cornices, Curtains and Drapery for Drawing Room Windows," stands apart as something of an ensemble, as do the last plates, 60 and 61, which illustrate "A Dining Parlour in imitation of the Prince of Wales's" (at Carlton House), in perspective, and "A Plan & Section of a Drawing Room," which is directly comparable, and was no doubt intended as such, to Hepplewhite's final plates. Sheraton's exemplar is little different, if more intricate. "A drawing room," he noted, "is of that sort which admits of the highest taste and elegance; in furnishing of which, workmen in every nation exert the utmost efforts of their genius."

Even before the *Drawing-Book* was complete, Sheraton announced the publication, by subscription again, of an *Appendix to the Cabinet-Maker and Upholsterer's Drawing-Book*, the plates engraved by Terry, J. Caldwall, and Barlow, dated between 31 March and 1 November 1793, illustrating more items of furniture, more elaborated and decked with drapes than before (and also, to judge by the long description of "An English State Bed," more replete with symbolical meaning), ending, once again, with a decorative ensemble, two views of the Chinese drawing room at the prince of Wales' pavilion at Brighton—"the whole in effect, though it may appear extravagant to a vulgar eye, is but suitable to the dignity of the proprietor."

The *Appendix*, its title page dated 1793, was, as before, printed by Bensley for the author, then residing at 106 Wardour Street in Soho, and was available from the same booksellers as the previous work.

The success of the *Appendix* may be assumed to have prompted Sheraton to announce a final section of the work to subscribers, *An Accompaniment to the Cabinet-Maker and Upholsterer's Drawing-Book*, comprising fourteen plates, engraved in the main by Caldwall, with one by Barlow, dated between 4 July 1793 and 24 February 1794. This was devoted to "A variety of ornaments useful for learners to copy from, but particularly adapted to the cabinet and chair branches." This section, it seems, was a replacement for part three as originally proposed. This too was printed for the author—still at 106 Wardour Street—by Bensley. The *Drawing-Book*, separate, in forty-two numbers, was advertised on the title page as available for £2-3-6.

The *Drawing-Book* was astonishingly successful; a second edition, with seven additional plates to the *Appendix*, was issued in 1794, a third with minor alterations in 1802. A German edition was published in Leipzig in 1794. But its influence was in particular evidence in America, where Sheraton's designs were copied directly, memorably by Samuel McIntyre, of Salem, but less slavishly also by such famous craftsmen as Duncan Phyfe and Honoré Lannuier.

Josiah Taylor issued a collection of eighty-four of Sheraton's plates in 1812 as *Designs for Household Furniture by the Late Thomas Sheraton*, and in 1895 B. T. Batsford published a tidied up reprint of the *Drawing-Book*, stimulating the first revival of what was by then accepted as the Sheraton style. R. M.

Bibliography

Beard, G. and C. Gilbert. *Dictionary of English Furniture Makers 1660–1840*. Leeds, 1986

Sheraton, T. *The Cabinet-Maker and Upholsterer's Drawing-Book*. London, 1802. Reprint New York, 1970, with introductions by L. O. J. Boynton, W. P. Cole and C. F. Montgomery

76

Sir John Soane (1753–1837)

Designs In Architecture; Consisting Of Plans, Elevations, And Sections, For Temples, Baths, Cassines, Pavilions, Garden-Seats, Obelisks, and other Buildings; for decorating Pleasure-Ground, Parks, Forests, &c. &c. Engraved on 38 Copper-Plates. By John Soan

London: printed for I. Taylor, 1778

1985.61.2681

Quarto: 268 × 181 (10½ × 7¼)

Pagination [2] pp., 38 [i.e., 37] engraved plates

Edition First edition

Text pp. [1] title page (verso blank)

Illustrations 37 unsigned engraved plates numbered I–XXXVIII, the penultimate plate numbered XXXVI upper left and XXXVII upper right

Binding Contemporary half calf, marbled-paper boards, spine renewed

Provenance Title-page inscription "T. G. Barrymore from T. B. L. Ipswich 15/7/83"

References Berlin Cat. 2299 (1797 ed.); Berlin (1977) OS 2292[P] (1797 ed.); ESTC t82195; Harris and Savage 838

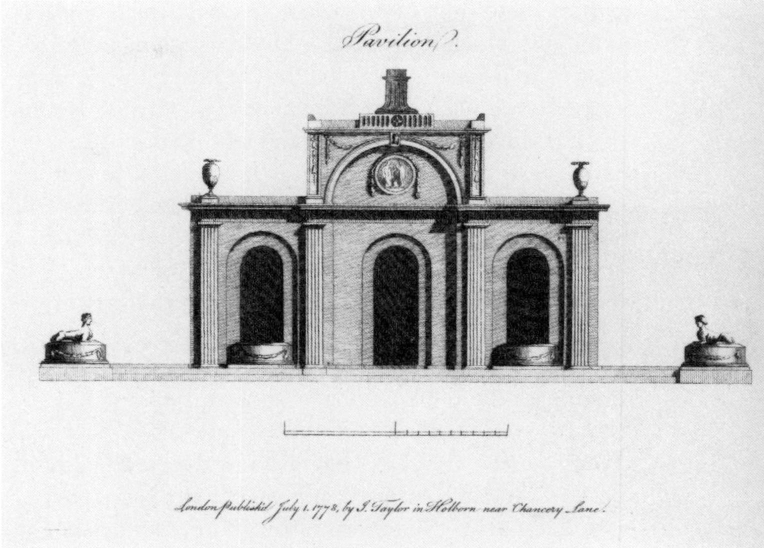

John Soane. *Designs in Architecture.* Plate XXII. "Pavilion." 1985.61.2681

JOHN SOAN (the "e" was added in 1783) was twenty-four when he published his first book of architecture in 1778. Although a slight, amateurish work, it was a considerable achievement.

Soan was born near Reading on 10 September 1753, the son of a bricklayer, with whom he no doubt worked. But he received some schooling at Reading and was spotted by a local resident, the surveyor James Peacock, who worked for George Dance. In 1768 Soan became a pupil of Dance, in London, and he remained in his office until 1772, when he moved to that of Henry Holland, where he worked until March 1778. During these years Soan had attended the schools of the Royal Academy of Arts, founded in 1768. He was formally admitted on 25 October 1771. The Academy was at that time installed in Old Somerset House. Soan was taught perspective drawing by Samuel Wale, and architectural history and theory by Thomas Sandby, all under the authority of William Chambers, who acted as treasurer of the Royal Academy. From the start Soan entered the school competitions and submitted drawings for the annual exhibitions. In 1772 he was awarded a silver medal for an elevation of the Banqueting House in Whitehall; in 1776 he received the gold medal for his design for a Triumphal Bridge, inspired both by Sandby's similar project and by the designs illustrated in Marie-Joseph Peyre's *Oeuvres d'architecture*, of 1765. This achievement was crowned in December 1777 with the award of a three-year traveling scholarship to Rome. In June of this same year he had submitted for the annual exhibition a grandiloquent design for a "Mausoleum to the Memory of James King, Esquire." King was a fellow student who had drowned in a boating accident on 9 June 1776, during an outing that would have included Soan had he not been completing his drawings of his Triumphal Bridge.

Soan set off on his Grand Tour only on 18 March 1778; during the waiting period he continued to work for Holland, but he also prepared designs, in May and June 1777, for St. Luke's hospital, and thereafter the thirty odd incidental garden structures that make up the *Designs in Architecture*—all of the plates for which are dated 1 July 1778. This surprising book seems to have been prompted by the award of the gold medal in 1776. Soan seems to have been approached soon after by the architectural publisher, Isaac Taylor. In March 1777 Soan submitted his first proposal for a book to Taylor—"A Work In Architecture To consist of designs for Public and Private Buildings with their internal decorations, to be comprized on 80 folio Copper plates"—the plates were to consist principally of designs for town and country houses, together with garden buildings, and details such as ceilings, chimneypieces and furnishings, with, in addition, designs for churches, mausolea, bridges, and a "British Senate House." Clearly this program was far too ambitious. Soan had taken as his model the first volume of James Paine's *Plans, Elevations and Sections of Noblemen and Gentlemen's Houses*, of 1767, in which Taylor had an interest, rather than the modest pattern books, such as T. C. Overton's *Original Designs for Temples*, of 1766, or William Wrighte's *Grotesque*

Architecture, of 1767, that Taylor had taken over from Henry Webley in 1767. Soan was required to produce something less pretentious.

In the end, the book, a quarto volume, sold at 6/-sewn, was made up of thirty designs for garden seats and pavilions, mostly in the classical style, though a Gothic summer house and a "moresque" dairy were included, together with two mausolea, one a revised version of that designed in memory of King. The small designs are neat and elegant, as one might expect from a pupil of Holland, though Pierre du Prey has detected the influence rather of Wrighte's *Grotesque Architecture* and John Carter's *Builder's Magazine*, of 1777, and, in particular, that of Chambers, who had taken up the fashionable interest of French pensionnaires in Rome in the early 1750s, and liked to set small garden pavilions and temples as design exercises for his pupils. "A Garden Building, Consisting of a Tea Room, Alcove, Bath, and Dressing Room to the Bath" that Soan exhibited at the Royal Academy in 1774 might, indeed, have been the outcome of such an exercise, and the forerunner of one of his projects for *Designs in Architecture*. Some of the original sketches for the engravings might be included among Thomas Webster's at the Canadian Centre for Architecture (DR 1980: 0042: 001–008). Though the designs are undeniably slight, they do give evidence of Soan's later ability to achieve effects with simple, pared down forms—with unmolded arched openings, for instance, set within an unmolded arched recess, such as he was to use soon enough in his Norfolk gate lodges, and later, far more convincingly, in series, in his buildings for Chelsea and Dulwich. Soan's design for the "moresque" dairy, though it might owe something to the mosque Chambers erected at Kew in 1761, and engraved two years after, is far more convincing and bolder than anything Chambers might have essayed in the unconventional mode—it is just possible even that the symbolical cow that stood atop the doorway was taken up by Robert Adam when he designed Oxenfoord. Soan's weakness is in evidence rather in the one large-scale design that was included in the book, the King mausoleum, which was a lumbering paraphrase of Chambers' design for a mausoleum for Frederick, prince of Wales, done in Rome in the early 1750s. Soan was never to be any good at the grand manner.

Though later critics and biographers have found *Designs in Architecture* something of an embarrassment, it was a publishing success, being reprinted in 1789, 1790, and 1797. When John Plaw took over one of Soan's plans, that for a hunting casino, for his *Rural Architecture*, in 1785, he, unusually, thought it necessary to acknowledge Soan. But then Taylor was his publisher, too. R. M.

Bibliography

Bolton, A. *The Portrait of Sir John Soane, R. A. (1753–1837) Set Forth in Letters from His Friends (1775–1837)*. London, 1927

Du Prey, P. *John Soane. The Making of an Architect*. Chicago, 1982

Harris, E., and N. Savage. *British Architectural Books and Writers 1556–1785*. Cambridge, 1990

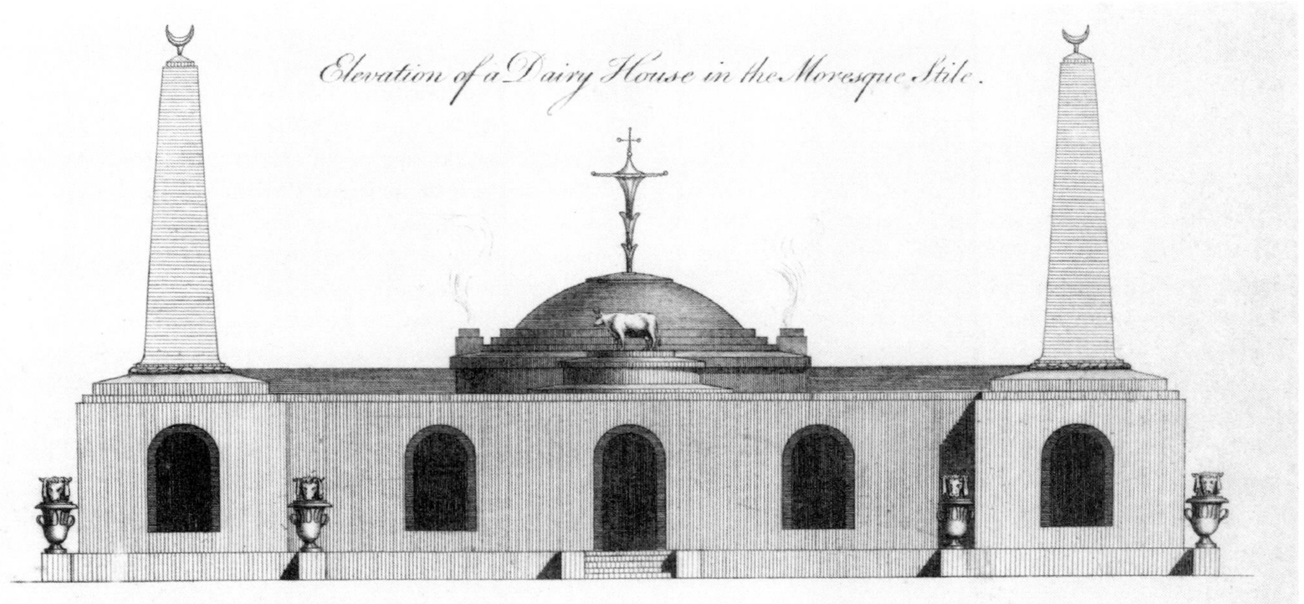

John Soane. *Designs in Architecture*. Plate XXXIII. "Elevation of a dairy house in the Moresque stile." 1985.61.2681

77

Sir John Soane (1753–1837)

Sketches In Architecture Containing Plans And Elevations Of Cottages Villas And Other Useful Buildings With Characteristic Scenery By John Soane . . .

London: published by Mess[rs] Taylor, 1793

George James Parkyns (1750–1820)

Six Designs For Improving And Embellishing Grounds. With Sections And Explanations. By G. J. Parkyns, Esq.

London: printed for I. and J. Taylor, 1793

1985.61.2682

Folio: 443 × 300 (17½ × 11⅞)

Pagination Sketches: [4], iv pp., 43 aquatint and engraved plates

Six Designs: iv, 20 pp., [11] etched and engraved plates

(*Note*: These 2 works were issued both separately and, as here, together)

Edition First editions

Text Sketches: pp. [1] title page (verso blank); [3] introduction (verso blank); [i]–iv explanations of the plates; *Six Designs*: pp. [i] title page (verso blank); [iii]–iv preface ("Advertisement"); [1]–20 "Descriptions, &c."

Illustrations Soane's *Sketches* contains 43 unsigned plates (i.e., 26 aquatint elevations and 17 engraved plans). Parkyns' *Six Designs* has 11 etched and engraved plates (i.e., 6 numbered 1–6 with plans for grounds of various residences; plus 5 unnumbered plates with "sectional geometrical views," bound to face the plans)

Binding Contemporary marbled boards, new calf spine, morocco label. Uncut. With 1 of I. and J. Taylor's undated 4-page catalogues, *A catalogue of modern books on architecture*, bound in at end, advertising on p. [1] "Sketches for Cottages, Villas, &c. with their Plans and appropriate Scenery, by John Soane; to which are added, Six Designs for improving and embellishing Grounds, with Explanations, by an Amateur, on 50 Plates, elegantly engraved in aqua-tinta, 2l. 12s. 6d. half bound"

Provenance From the library of the Bell family of Woolsington Hall, Northumberland, with its Woolsington bookplate

References Berlin Cat. 2304; Berlin (1977) 2304; ESTC t102002 and t102003; Harris and Savage 843

John Soane's third book of architecture, *Sketches in Architecture*, is a curious compilation, even more difficult to account for than his first book, *Designs in Architecture*.

In 1793, at the age of forty, Soane was established as architect to the Bank of England and had already completed the first of his Bank Stock Offices there. His mature style was in evidence also in the interior spaces of Tyringham House, in Buckinghamshire, and in Buckingham House in Pall Mall in London, both, admittedly, yet incomplete. His decision to publish a medley of designs, twenty-four in all, of miscellaneous cottages, villas, country houses, and garden buildings, to which he added a plan and perspective of the mausoleum for the earl of Chatham that he had designed in 1779, while yet a student in Rome, is almost incomprehensible and certainly not assuring of sound judgment.

The book was intended, he wrote in his introduction, as a sequel to his second book, the *Plans Elevations and Sections of Buildings Executed in the Counties of Norfolk, Suffolk . . . etc.*, that had appeared early in 1789—"another publication on the same subject but in a smaller scale, consisting of cottages for the laborious and industrious part of the community, and of other buildings generally calculated for the real uses and comforts of life, and such as are within the reach of moderate fortunes." But whereas the forty-seven plates of the *Plans* illustrated eighteen buildings by Soane, all but three of them were executed, thus constituting a record of a phase of his activity; the *Sketches in Architecture*, with forty-three plates, illustrated twenty-five designs, only six of which had been built—plates 11 and 12, a house for William Simonds at Reading, Berkshire; plates 15 and 16, a house for William Colhoun at Thetford, Norfolk; plates 17, 18, and 19, Chilton Lodge, for William Morland, near Hungerford, Berkshire; plates 36 and 37, alterations to Baron's Court, County Tyrone, for Charles Stewart, marquis of Abercorn; plate 41, a "Castello d'Acqua" for the earl of Hardwicke, at Wimpole Hall, Cambridgeshire—not one of them of any particular distinction, certainly less than any of his recently executed works. The assumption must be that Soane was persuaded to compile the book by Isaac Taylor, who had first approached him for *Designs in Architecture* and had later published the *Plans Elevations and Sections*.

Soane culled some of his introductory remarks from John Wood's *Series of Plans for Cottages or Habitations of the Labourer*, of 1792, another work published by Isaac Taylor and his son Josiah, but the seven cottage designs offered by Soane are not of the plain, undecorated kind. Soane was influenced rather by John Plaw's *Rural Architecture*, of 1785, also published by the Taylors, setting his buildings in "characteristic scenery," and representing them in aquatint. All Soane's elevations, like Plaw's, are strictly symmetrical. He had a limited interest, at this stage, in the picturesque—dormer windows he rejected as "always unsightly, and a sure indication of

John Soane. *Sketches in Architecture.* Plate XL. 1985.61.2682

a depraved taste." His plates are dated 1 January 1793, the introduction, March 1793.

Soane's work was available separately, but almost always is bound with *Six Designs for Improving and Embellishing Grounds* by George Isham Parkyns, a painter and engraver, born in 1750 in Nottingham who was later to command a company of Nottingham militia during the American War of Independence. America seems to have engaged him, for he was in New York in the early 1790s and in January 1796 exhibited a series of drawings there made in preparation for aquatinted views of the sights of the United States. However, he returned to London, where he continued to exhibit paintings until 1813. He died in 1820.

Parkyn's *Six Designs* illustrated six estates, in plan and section, on eleven plates, with short descriptions, indicating how they might be transformed into picturesque parks.

Soane's *Sketches in Architecture* was reissued in 1798, both with and without the Parkyns plates. On this occasion Parkyns' name was omitted; they were labeled as "By An Amateur." R. M.

Bibliography

Groce, G. C. and Wallace, D. H. *Dictionary of Artists in America 1546–1860*. New Haven, 1957

Harris, E., and N. Savage. *British Architectural Books and Writers 1556–1785*. Cambridge, 1990

Stroud, D. *Sir John Soane Architect*. London, 1984

John Soane. *Sketches in Architecture.* Plate XLI. 1985.61.2682

78

Sir John Soane (1753–1837)

Designs For Public And Private Buildings, By John Soane . . .

[London]: published by Priestley and Weale, Rodwell, Colnaghi & C°., and Ridgeway, 1828

1985.61.2680

Folio: 479 × 294 (18 7/8 × 11 5/8)

Pagination [iii]–vi, 36, [2] pp., etched title plate, 54 [i.e., 55] etched plates

Edition First edition with this title

Text pp. [iii] half-title; [iv] imprint of J. Moyes; [v]–vi introduction; [1]–34 text; 35–36 epitaphs, Moyes' colophon; [37–38] index to the plates

Illustrations Etched title plate, including vignettes of buildings and columns, with captions; plus 55 unsigned etched plates numbered 1–21, *21, 22–54

Binding Contemporary mottled paper boards, blue morocco corners, later cloth back, recent paper label on spine

Provenance Later bookplates of John Jay Ide and Pompeo Litta, Biumi Resta

References Fowler 338 (variant)

By 1826 the slow refashioning of the Bank of England was complete with the rebuilding of the last sections of the curtain wall; John Soane's assorted array of public buildings at Westminster were by then also more or less finished—the Houses of Parliament and the Law Courts, the Board of Trade and Privy Council Offices in Whitehall, and related works in Downing Street. Only the New State Paper Office, also in Westminster, was yet to come. Soane, at the age of seventy-three, might well have thought then to commemorate his final achievements in the form of a publication. His revered mentor, George Dance, had died in January 1825, and Soane must have been all too aware that there was no volume to record his works.

The first evidence of any such intention appears in *Bibliotheca architectonica*, a catalogue of books available from Messrs. Priestley and Weale, High Street, Bloomsbury, dated May 1825 (Soane Case 63). There, a book, "preparing for publication," is described at some length:

> Soane's . . . Whole Works: . . . a Series of Plans, Elevations, Sections, and Views of his Principal Architectural Works. This Work will consist of 100 Engravings, illustrative of the New Buildings of the Bank of England—those attached to the Houses of Parliament—the Law Courts—two or three Private Mansions—a Theatre—a Church—a Bridge—Galleries, & c. The work will be printed in quarto, and will include, besides explanations and descriptions of each separate Edifice, interesting historical facts and anecdotes of some Ancient Buildings which have been superseded by the New Works, or are immediately connected with them. The plates will be mostly engraved in outline by J. Le Keux, and other Architectural Engravers, from measured drawings made from the buildings, as executed. The work will form one large volume, and will be published in four separate parts, at 30s. each, small paper, and 2 guineas large paper (p. 91).

No evidence, however, for the preparation of a book of this size survives.

Soane was not really in a fit state to plan and supervise so ambitious a publication. Early in December 1824 he had been couched for a cataract operation, and though this was apparently successful, he continued to have severe eye trouble in the years that followed. In the summer of 1826 George Wightwick was hired as his guide and help, though he resigned soon enough, unwilling to endure the sharpness of Soane's comment.

Soane was in a bitter mood at the time. He was totally estranged from his eldest son George and his grandchildren, and his younger son John had died in 1823. More important, perhaps, was the humiliation he had endured at the hands of a Select Committee, headed by Henry Bankes, during the early months of 1824, when his Palladian elevation for the New Law Courts, alongside Westminster Hall, was vilified both in Parliament and the press, and he was instructed to demolish it and rebuild in a Gothic style. The public exposure was deeply wounding. Soane thought at first to resign, but that was not his way. He had fought too hard to establish his position. Instead, he determined, rightly, to defend himself. His proposed "Works" was clearly conceived with such an aim in view, as Weale gave evidence in a footnote to his catalogue, where he remarked that it would "serve as a refutation to his calumniators" (p. xiii). But Soane's defense was to take on another form.

The Court of King's Bench, the facade of which had been the subject of Bankes' attack, was opened on 31 January 1826, but other parts of the law courts were still being altered to suit new accommodations. Soane waited until all was finished. In September 1826 he traveled to Bath, Wightwick at hand, to take a "cure" and to compose his diatribe.

The archivist Susan Palmer has noted at least eight volumes of manuscript texts in the Soane Museum arising from this matter, in the hands of both Soane and Wightwick, written from 1826 onward (Soane Case 29, 30, 100, 101, 102, 103, 104, and 106). There are also between eleven and thirteen distinct printed folios, ranging from *A Brief Statement of the Proceedings Respecting the New Law Courts at Westminster and the New Entrance for His Majesty into the House of Lords*, of 1827, to the *Designs for Public and Private Buildings* of 1834.

These apparently separate works are closely interlinked

and cannot, properly, be considered in isolation. Their titles and their contents depend, in each instance, on Soane's motivating aim at the time of composition—whether to defend himself or whether to proclaim his abilities as a public architect and, eventually, as a private architect as well: what is offered here is a brief, but tentative history of these works. More research is required.

The first printed text of *A Brief Statement of the Proceedings Respecting the New Law Courts at Westminster* was more or less complete on 6 April 1827, when Soane was billed by James Moyes of Took's Court, Chancery Lane, for the printing of seventy-five copies. This consisted of a title page, a two-page introduction, and twenty-eight pages of text (twenty-three of them concerned with the proceedings of the Select Committee established on 23 March 1823), together with a petition presented by Soane on 21 May 1824 to rework the facade he had already erected alongside Westminster Hall in the Gothic style, and the subsequent history of its demolition and rebuilding; five of the pages concern the design of the Royal Entrance to the House of Lords, the demolition of the Prince's Chamber, and the alterations to the Painted Chamber (Soane Museum, Packet 6). Twenty illustrations were intended to accompany this text: fifteen devoted to the Law Courts; five to the Royal Entrance, the Scala Regia, and the Royal Gallery. Soane had begun the preparation of these plates in October 1826, assisted by his draftsman C. J. Richardson, who became his pupil in February 1824. Four bills in the Soane Museum from the engraver John Coney, dated between 25 October 1826 and 26 March 1827, indicate that at least six plates were prepared at this time: the site plan of the existing buildings at Westminster, plans of the New Law Courts, a plan and an interior of the King's Entrance, are listed. Other plates were in hand. But before this defense was finally assembled—there are gaps on the page proofs awaiting further insertions—reports of a parliamentary debate, once again involving Bankes, appeared in the *Morning Herald* of 11 May 1827, linking Soane's name with Nash's costly alterations to Buckingham House. He was outraged. He sought at once to disassociate himself and to put forward his own proposal for a new palace at the end of Constitution Hill, a design hinting at a fondness for Blenheim, exhibited first at the Royal Academy in 1821, though it harks back to projects done first as a student in Rome. He appended three additional pages of text and six more plates, once again by Coney, who billed him for them in May, illustrating not only a plan and a bird's-eye view of the Royal Palace, but also three views of the cluster of gates and screens that he had exhibited at the Academy in 1796, 1817, and 1826, that would not only form a forecourt to the palace, but also provide entries to London from the west and a gateway to St. James' Park. Two more plates illustrated a design for a triumphal arch between St. James' Park and Downing Place (now Downing Street), and a view of Downing Place, from Whitehall, with Soane's Board of Trade and Privy Council Offices duplicated on the opposite corner to create a grand unified setting. For what Soane was now putting forward, albeit summarily, was the idea of a ceremonial route, traversed by the king from Windsor Castle to his palace in London, and from thence, on the opening of Parliament, through St. James' Park, into Downing Place, along Whitehall, passing by the New Law Courts to the Royal Entrance to the House of Lords. The route was to be further adorned with a mausoleum in St. James' Park, set opposite the Horse Guards, dedicated to the duke of York. This last, designed in 1827, the year of the duke's death, and exhibited at the Royal Academy in 1828, was not to be illustrated; it is not included in the "Description of plates."

The title page of this version of *A Brief Statement of the Proceedings Respecting the New Law Courts at Westminster*, printed by James Moyes in 1827, states clearly that the work was not to be published, but was intended for circulation to members of both Houses of Parliament, officials of the treasury, judges, and officials of the courts. But though the text was largely complete in page proof and though the twenty-six plates must have been finished or in hand at the time, Soane set the project aside—for the moment. The three-page addendum had stirred his larger aims: his ambition to be recognized as a public architect was still rampant.

From his earliest years Soane had desperately desired to succeed as an architect in the grand, circumstantial manner. He yearned to build on the larger scale. His abilities, however, were of another kind. He failed signally in all attempts to compose a building in the academic manner. Yet his growing concern, evinced in particular in his last lectures for the Academy, to prove himself in this respect and also to produce a public architecture for England that might rival that of France, determined the form of his new enterprise, the *Designs for Public Improvements in London and Westminster* (Soane Case 89). This too was printed by Moyes late in September 1827. Only twenty-five copies were distributed to selected individuals, starting with the king, to whom the book was dedicated. The text, twenty-one pages in all, consisted largely of descriptive notes to the plates, thirty-four in all (though thirty-three only are listed), arranged to conjure up the route traversed by the sovereign at the opening of Parliament. The architecture of the triumphal arches that were to form the western entrances to London was, somewhat oddly, described as a combination of Grecian simplicity, Roman magnificence, and "the rich and playful effects so strongly marked in our ancient Ecclesiastical Structures, particularly in our Cathedrals,—those superb Monuments of National Glory,—Temples worthy of the Divinity" (p. 2). These, even more curiously, were upheld with reference to the works of "a celebrated French Writer on Architecture," from whom Soane quoted at some length:

Entrons dans quelqu'une de nos belles Eglises Gothiques:—plaçons nous au centre de la croisée:—écartons en imagination tous les empéchemens qui gênent la vue:—Que verrons-nous? une distribution charmante, où l'oeil plonge délicieusement à travers plusiers enfoncemens, dont les vitraux répandent la lumière avec profusion et inégalité; un chevet en polygone où ces aspects se multiplient, se diversifient encore davantage; un mélange, un mouvement, un tumulte de percés et de massifs, qui jouent, qui contrastent, et dout l'effet entier est ravissant.

The "French Writer" was, of course, Abbé Laugier; the source of the quotation—deliberately inaccurate—was his *Observations sur l'architecture*, of 1765 (p. 130), a work from which Soane was to draw more than once.

Some of the text concerning the Law Courts and the Royal Entrance was incorporated from *A Brief Statement* . . . , as, it would seem, were almost all the initial plates. The new plates in the folio, all, it seems, by Coney, who engraved them between 2 July and 4 September 1827, comprised a design for a British Senate House, from Soane's Roman years; an alternative design for a royal palace, triangular in plan, of the same period; the National Debt Redemption Office, near the Bank of England; a sepulchral chapel conceived for Mrs. Praed at Tyringham; two of his London churches; and the Royal Hospital at Chelsea. Soane was presenting himself as a public architect.

In January of the following year, 1828, a "Second Impression" of this work was printed, once again by Moyes, "with such additional Designs and Illustrations as a revision of the Subject suggested" (Soane Case 90). This involved a revision and expansion of the text (a two-page dedication to the king, a two-page introduction, with thirty-six pages of descriptive notes to the plates—the notes on the New Law Courts, including more of the text from the initial *Brief Statement* . . . now taking up nine full pages), and the addition of twenty-one plates bringing the total to fifty-five, numbered 1 to 54, with a 31 bis. Only fifty-one of the plates, however, were listed in the "Index of Plates." Eighteen, at least, of these plates had been prepared for the *Brief Statement*. . . . The new plates, still by Coney, though the lettering was engraved by W. Kersting, comprised a view of the mausoleum to Frederick Augustus, duke of York, intended to commemorate the victories of Trafalgar and Waterloo, done in 1827 (this had been described only as a feature of the ceremonial route outlined in the earlier works), together with the third of Soane's London churches, Holy Trinity Church at Marylebone; a smattering of domestic designs; Soane's competition entries of 1780 for male and female penitentiaries, including that for Norwich Castle jail; the Picture Gallery and Mausoleum at Dulwich; the Bank of England; the stables of the Royal Hospital at Chelsea; Soane's own house at 13 Lincoln's Inn Fields, including a plate of the Belzoni sarcophagus that he purchased in 1824; and, right at the end, the Soane family tomb in Old St. Giles' Burial Ground, St. Pancras. The plates were printed by Barnett and Son, Copper Plate Printers, to whom Moyes supplied paper.

The whole makes for an odd and very uneven assemblage. The buildings were haphazardly illustrated, often with no more than crabbed and ungainly elevations and views. Even the best of the plates, some based on drawings by J. M. Gandy, traced, like others, by Richardson, and supplied thus to Coney, are engraved in an unusual manner, intended to preserve something of the spontaneity of the sketch, but instead appearing as loose and coarse. Coney was being forced to work not only with inadequate drawings but at extraordinary speed, which might explain something of the slapdash quality. There can be no doubt though that the plates were approved by Soane. But, not altogether surprisingly, he was dissatisfied with the book.

Already on 24 January 1828 Soane had entered into a contract with the leading publishers of architectural books, Priestley and Weale, for a new edition of the *Designs for Public Improvements*, retitled *Designs for Public and Private Buildings*. This was to contain fifty-four plates, supplied by Soane (some to be used for a revised version of the *Brief Statement* . . . that Soane was already contemplating). Twenty-five copies of the book were to be printed on India paper and sold at five guineas each; regular copies, half-bound in morocco, were to be sold at three guineas. Priestley and Weale undertook to print a prospectus, advertise the work in a wide range of papers (the *Times*, *Herald*, *Morning Chronicle*, *John Bull*, *Sunday Times*, *Examiner*, *Literary Gazette*, and *Athenaeum*), and to distribute copies, specifically in Edinburgh, Paris, and New York. Soane, in return, was to receive five copies of the India-paper edition and books to the value of one hundred guineas.

The book, printed by Moyes, seems to have been published in late February or early March 1828. The publishers listed on the title page included not only Priestley and Weale, but also Rodwell, Colnaghi and Co., and Ridgeway (Soane Case 130).

Though George IV did not die until June 1830, *Designs* . . . was no longer dedicated to the king. However, a new and elaborate title page was provided, a perspective view of the Chatham mausoleum that Soane had designed as a student in Rome, in 1778, at the top; a view of the Triumphal Bridge with which he had won the Royal Academy gold medal and traveling scholarship, in 1776, at the bottom; with orders from the Whitehall government offices and the Bank of England flanking the letterpress. The design was Soane's own, six variations of the preliminary layouts in his hand surviving at the Soane Museum, the final version dated 17 January 1828 (SM vol. 60 fols. 75–77, recto and verso). To this he added Horace's ironical tag concerning the need for genius to be sustained by experience, "Mihi turpe relinqui est . . ." (It would be dreadful if I fell behind . . .), *Ars poetica* 417. The contents of the book were close to those of the "Second Impression" of 1828. The number of plates was the same, fifty-five in all. The numbering

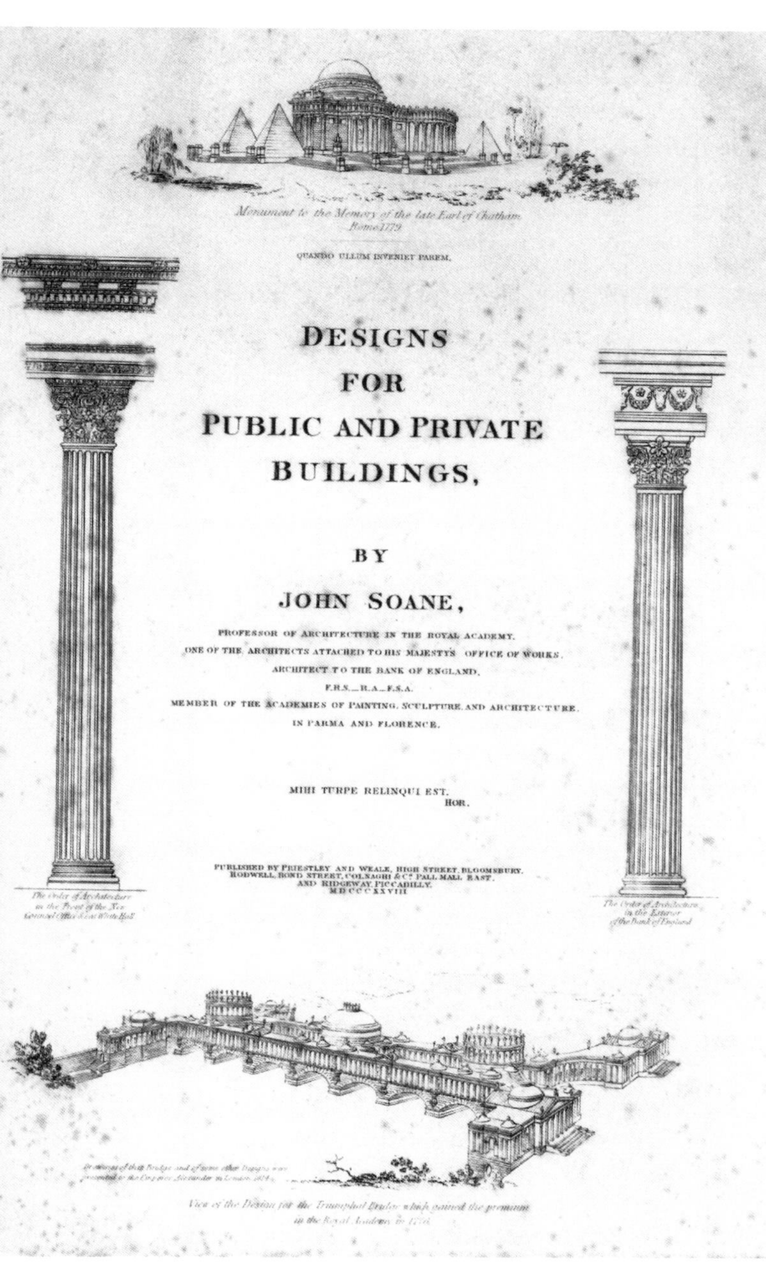
Monument to the Memory of the late Earl of Chatham. Rome 1779

QUANDO ULLUM INVENIET PAREM.

DESIGNS
FOR
PUBLIC AND PRIVATE
BUILDINGS,

BY

JOHN SOANE,

PROFESSOR OF ARCHITECTURE IN THE ROYAL ACADEMY.
ONE OF THE ARCHITECTS ATTACHED TO HIS MAJESTYS OFFICE OF WORKS.
ARCHITECT TO THE BANK OF ENGLAND.
F.R.S._R.A._F.S.A.
MEMBER OF THE ACADEMIES OF PAINTING, SCULPTURE AND ARCHITECTURE,
IN PARMA AND FLORENCE.

MIHI TURPE RELINQUI EST.
HOR.

PUBLISHED BY PRIESTLEY AND WEALE, HIGH STREET, BLOOMSBURY.
RODWELL, BOND STREET, COLNAGHI & Cº PALL MALL EAST.
AND RIDGEWAY, PICCADILLY.
MDCCCXXVIII.

John Soane. *Designs for Public and Private Buildings.* Frontispiece. 1985.61.2680

on all but two of the plates was also retained, but these two plates were rearranged, renumbered, and repositioned. The large perspective view of a gallery in the House of Lords that had formed the top part of plate 31, page 23 bis in the Moyes edition of 1828, was reengraved in a smaller format to match two views of similar galleries that were included on plate 31 of the same edition, and inserted between them in place of a site plan that had, rather oddly, been set there. The reformed plate became 21, page 19 in the Priestley and Weale edition, though it is sometimes bound between plates 24 and 25. The layout, plans, and elevations of the Scala Regia that had been included at the bottom of plate 31, page 23 (additional plate) of the 1828 Moyes edition, were discarded. The site plan that had been included on plate 31, page 23 of the Moyes edition, was reused in the Priestley and Weale edition to form the bottom half of a new plate, misnumbered 6 instead of 21, with two new alternative views of the exterior of the House of Lords entrance above. The introduction and the thirty-six pages of descriptive notes remained much as before. The plates were now interleaved in the text. The index to the plates was revised, but only fifty-four were listed.

There is an extraordinary copy of this work, apparently dating also from early in 1828, in the Soane Museum (Soane Case 119), without the publishers' names, but with an additional text "Explanatory illustrations, etc. of the Designs for Public Improvements in London and Westminster," numbered consecutively with the earlier text, pages 37 to 75, and a "Conclusion," numbered pages 76 and 77. On pages 49 to 51 is the first version of Soane's famous defense of the classical tradition, "Observations and Remarks on the State of Architecture in England in the Nineteenth Century," presented as a parody of the five orders of architecture, "The Five Orders of Architects." These are described, from the lowest to the highest, as "The Heaven-Born Architect" or "The Pictorial Architect, or the Architect a-la Mode," "The Chinese Architect," "The Middle Ages Architect," "The Dilettante Architect," and "The Classical Architect." This last is the only one worthy of emulation:

> Professional Architects of the Old School—men who, having devoted, with unceasing ardour, their lives to the study of Architecture, endeavouring to combine in their Works, the solemn, grand, and terrific character of the Egyptian—the elegant refinements of the Grecian—the vastness and magnificence of the Romans, with the fanciful variety and picturesque effects of the best Works of the Middle Ages,—have now the mortification to see the degraded style of their Art, and to lament the preference given to the Works of barbarous ages: they, however, indulge the fond and pleasing hope that some Bruneleschi will arise, by whom, under the auspices of His Majesty, Architecture will be restored to its ancient glory and importance, and make London and Westminster worthy to be compared to Athens in the time of Pericles, and Rome in the time of Augustus. . . .

Two months after his first agreement with Priestley and Weale, on 27 March 1828, Soane entered into another agreement with them to publish a revised version of *A Brief Statement*. . . . The publishers undertook, as before, to advertise the work and to distribute it—to Edinburgh, Dublin, and Paris in this instance. Soane was to receive five copies on India paper, five on plain, with five copies of the plates, together with the sum of fifty pounds.

A note appended to the memorandum acknowledged Soane's right to determine the date of advertising and publication, which, it was foreseen, might be withheld to 5 May. In the event, publication was further delayed.

In both the *Times* and the *Morning Chronicle* of 13 May 1828 strong criticism was made of Soane's Law Courts; the attorney general himself, it was noted, had complained that he was required to fight his way into court "with the mob." Soane determined once more to defend himself. He at once took up the page proofs of *A Brief Statement* . . . of 1827, revised them to suit the occasion, removing the addendum relating to the Royal Entrance, the Prince's Chamber, the Painted Chamber, and the ceremonial route that led to them, and rushed the pages to Moyes for resetting. By 21 May he had received his new galleys and had further corrections in hand. Two days later the galleys he had forwarded to the lord chancellor for his approval had been returned. The whole—a folio consisting of a title page, a one-page introduction, a one-page address to the chief justice of the court of king's bench, sixteen pages of text, and fourteen plates—was not to be published, but was printed and distributed to members of the bar, and others, before the end of May. The proof copy (Soane Case 112) and four bound versions of the work are to be found in the Soane Museum (Soane Case 108, 109, 110, 111), one of them, that sent by Soane to the lord chief justice, Lord Wynford, having been spotted and purchased by Weale from a bookseller, Sitchell of King Street, and returned to Soane on 25 June 1830.

This abbreviated version of *A Brief Statement* . . . was overtaken later in the year by the publication of *A Brief Statement of the Proceedings Respecting the New Law courts at Westminster, the Board of Trade, and the New Privy Council Offices* . . . , printed by Moyes, for distribution, in accord with Soane's contract of 27 March 1828, by Priestley and Weale, and also Rodwell and Colnaghi and Son. This folio consisted of a four-page introduction; a list of contents; thirty pages of text and explanatory notes, including the "Observations and Remarks on the State of Architecture in England in the Nineteenth Century"; and twenty-five plates. (There is a copy in the Canadian Centre for Architecture in Montreal.) But this was almost at once superseded by a revised version, held in the Soane Museum (Soane Case 113) and elsewhere, with a twelve-page introduction; a three-page address to the chief justice of the king's bench; thirty pages of text and explanatory notes, as before; followed by an "Abrégé of the proceedings respecting the new buildings at Whitehall," numbered pages 31 and 32; and thirty-two plates. The "Abrégé" had been set in type first, on 30 April 1828, by Moyes, as a separate publication. Soane was billed for the printing of one hundred copies on 10 May 1828. Whether these were distributed separately or incorporated into the revised *Brief Statement* . . . is uncertain. A note on the revised "Table of Contents," on page vii, set after "Conclusion as intended p. 30," reads "Subsequent events have made it desireable to give an Abrégé of the Proceedings respecting the New Buildings at Whitehall, and also a design for completing those buildings; together with new offices for the State Papers and Record Offices:—the present Home Office to be added to the Treasury Chambers, and a new building to be erected for the Home Department p. 31, 32."

The text of *A Brief Statement* . . . includes not only all of Soane's tortuous and somewhat confused history of the building of the Law Courts, but also his account of the building of the Royal Entrance, together with the demolition of the Prince's Chamber and the transformation of the Painted Chamber, and the designs for the new Houses of Parliament. His proposals for the royal route are also included, along with a description of the Board of Trade Offices and the Privy Council. At the end, the new designs for the State Paper Office are discussed, though not illustrated. Soane made all too clear now his contempt for the "committee of taste." The text of the "Five Orders of Architects," at the end, is much the same as that in the extraordinary copy of the *Designs for Public and Private Buildings*, though it is reset. How-ever, he now added some interesting remarks on the proper manner of designing of the Classical Architect: "he must have been convinced that a facade, although beautiful in its parts,—replete in movement and rich in variety,—with all the attractions of symmetry and harmony, is only a body without a mind, when unaccompanied with a picturesque, convenient, and well-balanced Plan."

He concluded his text with a long quotation, in French, to further reinforce the significance of planning, from Abbé Laugier's *Observations sur l'Architecture* of 1765: "S'il y a quelque chose qui soit de l'invention de l'Architecte, c'est le plan de l'édifice. C'est-là qu'il peut manifester un génie créateur, par des combinaisons toujours nouvelles et toujours également justes . . ." (p. 152), and so on. The *Observations* was a book Soane knew well; there were three copies in his library. He had translated sections from it in March 1807, August 1813, and July and August 1816, in preparing his Academy lectures, and he so much approved of Laugier's remarks on planning that he was to repeat them again, in 1830, in his *Description of the House and Museum on the North Side of Lincoln's Inn Fields*, where they appear in the appendix on page 45. Yet in the *Brief Statement* . . . he, unaccountably, credited the quotation not to Laugier, but to "Journals printed at Amsterdam, Nov. 1765." Soane's whole discussion of the "Five Orders of Architects" was to be repeated, in 1835, in the *Memoirs of the Professional Life of an Architect*.

Neither the new edition of the *Brief Statement* . . . nor the *Designs for Public and Private Buildings* was a success. Before the year was out Soane was assembling yet another variant, *Civil Architecture. Designs for Completing Some of the Public Buildings in Westminster, and for Correcting Defects in Others* (Soane Case 92). Moyes billed Soane for 175 copies of the text on 30 December 1828. The contents pages were printed on 10 January 1829. The folio, as issued in this year, and "humbly submitted to the consideration of His Majesty," consisted of an engraved frontispiece, twelve pages of text, and seven plates interleaved (five of them illustrating the New Law

John Soane. *Designs for Public and Private Buildings.* Plate 10. "Interior of the Privy Council Chamber." 1985.61.2680

Courts). There were also a handful of vignettes of the Law Courts arrayed on an extra plate at the end, designed as a title page for "A Brief Statement of the Proceedings Respecting the New Law Courts at Westminster. . . ."

Soane received warm enough thanks from the host of friends and acquaintances to whom he forwarded copies of his new works, both in 1828 and the following year. But John Britton, more honest than most, gave voice to his reservations in a letter of 27 March 1828: "There are certainly some defects in literary construction and arrangement," he wrote of the *Designs* . . . , "at least according to *my fastidious* notions, the plates are certainly coarse, ragged and executed in slovenly style, which to an eye accustomed to the beauty, clearness and accuracy of Le Keux's work appear the worse by comparison." The work he referred to was the *Illustrations of the Public Buildings of London*, one of his own publications, composed with the elder Pugin, largely engraved by John Le Keux. The two volumes were issued between 1823 and 1828. Several of Soane's buildings were included in these: his house in the first volume; the Law Courts, Royal Entrance, Privy Council Offices, and the Bank of England in the second. They were indeed better engraved there, though at a much reduced scale. But what would most have appealed to Soane was W. H. Leeds' essay on the Bank of England, which he praised with stirring enthusiasm. No other contemporary building, he wrote, was "so fraught with what may be considered the *poetry* of the art, and so striking an example of what it is capable of achieving in the hands of a master." Britton was to repeat his criticism of Soane's plates in his *Brief Memoir of Sir John Soane*, of 1834, remarking that his Brief Statement, of 1828, had "twenty-five etchings by Coney, in a loose, ragged style" (p. 9).

Soane soon fell out with Weale. Soane had advanced one hundred pounds toward the cost of printing the *Brief Statement* . . . , which he regarded as no more than a loan; Weale, whatever the nature of their agreement, conceived of it rather as a subsidy. He might, moreover, have considered Soane's distribution of an abbreviated version of the work as a form of undercutting. He put off the repayment. On 6 August 1829 he wrote in response to Soane's request for repayment, describing his own financial difficulties and suggesting that he be allowed more time. Two months later, on 23 October, by way of mollification, he proposed that the supplementary volume to the *Antiquities of Athens*, to be published in 1830, be dedicated to Soane. Soane accepted. On 7 February 1830 Weale suggested that he be allowed to repay the money in four installments by the following 1 October. No money, however, was forthcoming. On 27 June 1830, in response to a firm demand from Soane, he promised to pay on the morrow, but again failed to do so. The correspondence continued. Soane, in the end, got his money, but on 27 February 1832 he received a letter from John Britton.

> Dear Sir John,
>
> Weale writes me word that he intends to sell the remaining copies and coppers of the two works of yours, and that he has an offer of 140 pounds for the whole, but wants *at least* 150 pounds.
>
> The stock consists of the coppers and 73 letter press of "Public etc. Buildings," and 140 copies "Law Courts," making 213 sets of the letter press. Altho' I feel some reluctance in *troubling* you again about this subject, yet it would mortify me to see your books scattered about the town, and sold for little more than waste paper. If I could spare the money I would purchase the works.

Inevitably, Soane purchased the coppers and stock from Weale and began to compose yet another variant of the work. Three variants of the final versions of the *Designs for Public and Private Buildings* exist in the Soane Museum (Soane Case, "rough copy" 125, 123, 124/1, 124/2), though all are based on the same revised letterpress, and a similar collection of plates. To the earlier collection of fifty-five plates Soane added an engraved frontispiece, based on the portrait bust Sir Francis Chantrey had done of him between 1827 and 1829. This was also published separately in January 1832. Soane experimented with both a letterpress title page and a lithographic version of the decorated title page of 1828, redrawn by Richardson, the lithography by Charles Hullmandel. Soane commissioned an additional twenty-two lithographic plates—once again based on drawings by Richardson with the lithography by Hullmandel—five of which are no more than repetitions of previously engraved views (the Hyde Park gateways, the two versions of the Royal Palace, the York and Praed Mausolea, and the National Debt Redemption Office); seventeen of which illustrate additional designs, dating both from his earliest years (the Castello d'Acqua proposed by the Parma Academy in 1779, the Canine Residence and the Dining Room drawn in the same years for the bishop of Derry) and from his latest production (the Freemasons' Hall, Great Queen Street, London, of 1828 to 1831; the State Paper Office, overlooking St. James' Park, of 1829 to 1831; the refacing of the Banqueting House in Whitehall, of 1829 to 1832; and the anteroom to Sir Francis Chantrey's sculpture gallery at 30 Belgrave Place, London, of 1830 to 1831). A range of other works was also included: Holwood House, Kent, of 1797; Pellwall House, Staffordshire, of 1822–1828; two ideal country houses; a detailed study of the Whitehall elevation of the Board of Trade Offices; proposals for widening the roads around the Bank of England and the New Bank Buildings on Prince's Street, of 1807 (the plates for this are in two versions, showing the elevation both incomplete and complete); together with some large but dull projects, the National Bank of Ireland, Dublin, of 1799, Brasenose College, Oxford, of 1806, and the Belfast Academical Institution, of 1808.

Whatever semblance of coherence the first editions of the book might have possessed was now lost. The lithographic plates were even less attractive than the earlier engravings.

The descriptive text was, inevitably, enlarged to accommodate the additional items, but the stress, as from the first, was on the matter of the Law Courts. Most of the *Brief Statement* . . . was now incorporated, together with the title page of that publication.

The three variants of the book in the Soane Museum have a dedication to William IV, but this does not always appear in the copies printed and made up by James Moyes for Soane in 1832 and sent to selected individuals. A note in the flyleaf to Richardson's copy, now in the Victoria and Albert Museum, records:

> This work is a reprint of one published by Mr. Weale about eight years before Sir John Soane's death. Sir John having quarrelled with Weale collected together what plates he had by him and adding to them, a collection of shaded lithographs, made up about 16 copies. He gave these to different Sovereigns of Europe and to his private friends, this copy was given by him to his pupil Mr. Richardson, who has illustrated it with 423 drawings of his old master's works.

More than the sixteen copies noted by Richardson were probably made up by Soane. Moyes sent a bill on 22 March 1832 for printing twenty-two extra sheets for seventy-three copies of the book, presumably to be added to the letterpress for seventy-three copies of the 1828 edition that Soane had purchased from Weale. In April 1832 Soane was having individual copies bound by Edwin Hutchinson. There are other related bills, both in this and subsequent years. The figures in the engraved view of the Court of Chancery were removed after 1832. The lithograph of the Princes' Street buildings, as noted, was redone to show the entire elevation. Some of the lithographs are dated July 1834, but although a bound copy of the ultimate version of the *Designs* . . . , of this same year, is to be found in the Soane Museum, none seems to have been distributed.

The urgent need to provide a record of his work had passed. The Private Act for preserving his house and its contents as a museum was given royal assent on 20 April 1833. Soane turned then to his *Professional Life* and a revised *Description of the House*.

There are fourteen unbound copies of the 1832 version of the *Designs* . . . in the Soane Museum and twenty-one copies of the letterpress complete, together with a number of assorted plates. As Soane used the same letterpress for the 1832 and 1834 versions of the book, as many as thirty-eight copies might thus have been made up and dispatched—though more work needs to be done on these last two compilations before any firm pronouncement can be made. And account will have to be taken also of other related publications of these last years: *Observations Respecting a Royal Palace*, for which Soane was billed by Moyes for twenty-five copies on 22 March 1832; and the *Description of Three Designs for the Two Houses of Parliament, made in 1779, 1794 and 1796 . . . Extracted from a Work Now in Progress*, a quarto, of 1835, copies of which are in the British Library and the Soane Museum R. M.

Bibliography

Bolton, A. T. *The Portrait of Sir John Soane, R.A. (1753–1837) Set Forth in Letters from His Friends (1775–1837)*. London, 1927

Colvin, H. M., ed. *The History of the King's Works*, vol. 6 (1782–1851). London, 1973

du Prey, P. de la Ruffiniére. *Catalogue of Architectural Drawings in the Victoria and Albert Museum. Sir John Soane*. London, 1985

79

Society of Dilettanti

The Unedited Antiquities Of Attica; Comprising The Architectural Remains Of Eleusis, Rhamnus, Sunium, And Thoricus. By The Society Of Dilettanti

London: printed by W. Bulmer and Co. Published by Longman, Hurst, Rees, Orme, and Brown; and John Murray, 1817

1985.61.2684

Large folio: 552 × 366 (21⅝ × 14 7/16)

Pagination [viii], 59, [1] pp., [78] etched plates

Edition First edition

Text pp. [i] half-title (verso blank); [iii] title page (verso blank); [v] list of members of the Society of Dilettanti, dated 1 March 1817 (verso blank); [vii] table of contents (verso blank); [1]–59 text, chapters 1–9, Bulmer's imprint at end (W. Bulmer and Co., Shakespeare Press); [60] blank

Illustrations A total of 78 etched plates, numbered by sequence within each chapter, as follows. *Chapter 1*: 8 plates (i.e., 2 maps, the first signed as engraved by James Walker and the second by James Walker, Jr., after measurements and drawings by Sir William Gell; a plan engraved by S. Porter after John P. Gandy; and 5 views numbered 4–8, etched by George Cooke after Gell). *Chapter 2*: 16 plates numbered 1–16 etched by John Roffe (9) or S. Porter (7) after Francis Bedford. *Chapter 3*: 8 plates numbered 1–8 etched by Cosmo Armstrong (6) or Roffe (2) after Francis Bedford. *Chapter 4*: 7 plates numbered 1–7 etched by Roffe (6) or Armstrong (1) after Gandy. *Chapter 5*: 8 plates numbered 1–8 by Roffe (5) or Porter (3) after Gandy. *Chapter 6*: 13 plates numbered 1–13 by Porter (7), Roffe (5), or Armstrong (1) after Gandy. *Chapter 7*: 5 plates numbered 1–5 by Porter (3) or Roffe (2) after Gandy. *Chapter 8*: 10 plates numbered 1–10, of which 4 are by Roffe after Bedford, 2 by Roffe after James Walker, 3 signed only as etched by James Newton (2) or Porter (1), and 1 unsigned. *Chapter 9*: 3 plates numbered 1–3 by Roffe after Bedford

Binding Recent blue-green quarter morocco, maroon cloth boards, white vellum corners. Uncut

The Society of Dilettanti, which still exists, was founded as a social dining club by a small group of British aristocrats and gentlemen, probably in December 1732. One of its toasts gives an indication of the spirit in which it was formed: "Viva la Virtù, Grecian Taste, and Roman Spirit." Although its earliest connections were with Italy, its most important contribution to European culture was to be its support of archaeological surveys in Greece and Asia Minor. Leaving aside early and unsponsored tours by Robert Wood and the earls of Moira, Sandwich, and Charlemont, the germ of this involvement can be traced in James Stuart and Nicholas Revett's historic first expedition to Athens. Two months after Stuart and Revett embarked at Venice, in March 1751, both were elected as members of the Society at the recommendation of Sir James Gray, and they were admitted to meetings as soon as they returned to England in 1755. The subsequent encouragement and financial assistance provided by the Society to the publication of *Antiquities of Athens* is noted in Harris and Savage's article on Stuart and Revett, reprinted in the present catalogue.

The first expedition to Greece and Asia Minor wholly financed by the Society was undertaken between June 1764 and November 1766 by the classical scholar Dr. Richard Chandler, with Revett and the painter William Pars in attendance. Again, the circumstances surrounding it, and the subsequent publication in 1769 and 1797 of two volumes of the *Antiquities of Ionia*, have been described by Harris and Savage (Harris and Savage 1990, 431–437). Chandler also published a volume of inscriptions and two journals of the expedition (i.e., *Inscriptiones antiquae, pleraeque nondum editae; in Asia Minori et Graecia, praesertim Athenis collectae*, 1774; *Travels in Asia Minor*, 1775; and *Travels in Greece*, 1776). The *Unedited Antiquities of Attica* (1817) and a new edition of the first volume of *Antiquities of Ionia* (1821) are both products of a second expedition, undertaken between November 1811 and the summer of 1813. The follow-ing account of it is largely based on available printed sources.

Lionel Cust identified a critical change in the membership and aspirations of the Society between the dates of the first and second expeditions:

> The first Dilettanti had been a company of gay and brilliant carousers, animated both by the passion and the fashion for art, but professing no special knowledge of their own. They wrote no essays and delivered no oracular opinions upon the subjects in which they took a common interest. What they did was to select the best men they could to carry out the work they desired to see accomplished, and in most instances to testify to their sense of the workers' merits by electing them in due course members of the Society—a highly coveted social distinction. The work done, they presented it to the world at large in as handsome and complete a form as they could, displaying thereby not only their true enthusiasm for the subject, but a generous and honourable public spirit. But from the beginning of the period on which we are now entering (about 1780–1820) the guiding spirits of the Society were chiefly drawn from the special group of cultivated amateurs whose accession to the ranks has just been mentioned. Some of these gentlemen were not content to be merely patrons and collectors, but must needs take the tone of *savants* and professors. To their minds the pursuit of antiquarian knowledge was a perquisite of wealth and influential position, and under their

guidance the Society was sometimes induced to pose as the oracle and arbiter of taste and learning, pronouncing judgement with dogmatic authority, and not always according to wisdom (Cust 1898, 111–112).

In the early part of the nineteenth century, the most notorious case in which the Society attempted to arbitrate in this manner was over the Elgin marbles, which, following the opinion of Richard Payne Knight, were at first foolishly declared to be Roman copies dating from the time of Hadrian. But the changing nature of the Society also had its positive aspect. Two of the more rigorous classicists to be granted membership were George Hamilton Gordon, 4th earl of Aberdeen (1805), and his friend the architect William Wilkins (1809). Both were Cambridge University graduates who had visited Greece a few years before and developed an intensely romantic attachment to ancient Greek civilization in general and its buildings in particular. They collaborated on an abridged edition of Vitruvius, also in the Millard collection. On 2 June 1811, they were appointed members of a special Ionian committee set up by the Society to arrange the new expedition. This committee was formed by combining the members of the committees of painting and of publication. According to minutes dated 5 January 1812, it first "made enquiry relative to some gentlemen [presumably Charles Cockerell's party] already in the Turkish Dominions, and employed in architectural pursuits, whose cooperation with the views of the Society it was hoped might have been obtained; but their enquiries in this line proved fruitless" (Cust 1898, 149). At the beginning of August, therefore, one of the committee members, another Cambridge graduate, William Gell, declared himself willing to head an expedition. Two young architects were also enlisted: John Peter Gandy and Francis Bedford. The committee rapidly agreed to Gell's proposition and Aberdeen was made responsible for drawing up instructions, dated 15 September 1811, for which he consulted Wilkins on the choice of monuments to be inspected.

Gell is now better known for his later works on the topography of Rome and the ruins of Pompeii, but in his late twenties he had traveled widely in Greece and Asia Minor, and by 1811 he was already the author of *The Topography of Troy* (1804), *The Geography and Antiquities of Ithaca* (1807), and *The Itinerary of Greece, with a Commentary on Pausanias and Strabo, and an Account of the Monuments of Antiquity at Present Existing in that Country* (1810). He narrowly escaped being the butt of one of Lord Byron's jibes in *English Bards and Scotch Reviewers* (1809). One of Byron's couplets originally read "Of Dardan tours let dilettanti tell, / I leave topography to coxcomb Gell." As the poem was in press Byron met Gell, liked him, and altered "coxcomb" to "classic." This, in turn, was altered to "rapid" for the fifth edition, after Byron visited Troy, the poet adding a note that Gell was "Rapid indeed! He topographised and typographised king Priam's dominions in three days" (quoted, DNB 7: 995).

Gell's architect companions were a few years younger, chosen for their skill as draftsmen. Francis Bedford, twenty-seven, may have been a pupil of William Porden, and was yet to start an independent practice. J. P. Gandy (later Deering), twenty-four, was the younger of three brothers who were all pupils of James Wyatt. He had been a Royal Academy student, and in 1810 produced a winning but unexecuted design for the new Bethlehem Hospital in London. Both Gandy and Bedford achieved modest success in their careers after the expedition, although Gandy's was curtailed by the inheritance of a friend's estate, allowing him to retire in 1828.

Aberdeen's instructions, based on those given to the earlier team led by Chandler, were as follows:

1. You are forthwith to embark on board such ship as may be found most eligible for your purpose, and to proceed to Smyrna. Our principal object at present is, that fixing upon Smyrna as your head-quarters, you do from thence make excursions to the several remains of antiquity in that neighbourhood, at such different times and in such manner as you shall, from the information collected on the spot, judge most safe and convenient; and that you do procure the exactest plans and measures possible of the buildings you shall find, making accurate drawings of the bas-reliefs and ornaments, and taking such views as you shall judge proper, copying all the inscriptions you shall meet with, and remarking such circumstances as may contribute towards giving the best idea of the ancient and present state of those places.

2. As circumstances, best learnt upon the spot, must decide the order in which you shall proceed in the execution of the foregoing article, we shall not confine you in that respect, but shall only enumerate, for your information, the principal objects of your research in the order in which they are most interesting to the Society:—Samos, Sardes, Aphrodisias, Hierapolis, Tralles, Laodicaea, Telmessus, Pata, Cnidus.

3. We cannot too strongly urge you to exercise the utmost accuracy of detail in your architectural measurements; recollecting always that it is the chief object of the Society to promote the progress of architecture by affording practical assistance to the architects of this country, as well as to gratify a general curiosity respecting the interesting monuments of antiquity still remaining in those parts.

4. You are hereby requested to correspond with the Secretary of the Society, stating at length, from time to time, your own proceedings; and although the principal view of the Society is directed towards the ancient state of those countries, it is not intended to confine you to that province; on the contrary, it is expected that you transmit, together with such drawings as you shall have made (all of which shall be considered as the property of the Society), a full narrative of occurrences, with all the information you may be able to obtain, accompanied by such observations as you may consider to be worthy the perusal of the Society.

5. Having entire confidence in the knowledge and zeal of Mr. Gell, we hereby declare that the direction of the whole of the expedition is intrusted to his care, and state implicitly, that it is our intention he should be vested with the sole management of the undertaking, as well in the necessary expenses to be incurred as in the manner and time of carrying into effect the general objects of the Society.

6. In addition to the expenses of the undertaking (the ac-

counts of which Mr. Gell will from time to time transmit to the Secretary), the Society engages to pay to Mr. Gell the sum of £50 per month, which, in case of his decease, shall be paid up to the time of his death to such person or persons as he may appoint to receive it. The Society further engages to pay both Mr. Gandy and to Mr. Bedford the sum of £200 per annum, on condition that they shall accompany Mr. Gell, and follow his directions and instructions relative to the objects of the mission (Hamilton 1855, 47–48).

The first step in meeting these conditions was made when Gell, Gandy, and Bedford embarked on the Turkish frigate *Africa*, which after six weeks delay set sail from Portsmouth on 20 November 1811. Keppell Craven, Gell's closest companion and eventually his executor, was also on board, accompanying them at his own expense.

No fixed amount of money was allotted for the expedition. Happily, a fair amount was available, since, despite the costs of various other publications, the Society had accumulated eleven thousand pounds in three percent stocks. By October 1814, the cost of the venture had reduced this sum to three thousand pounds. The Society's first historian, W. R. Hamilton, points out in mitigation that "the price of stocks at this period was varying from £62 to £66, and the exchange with foreign countries very much against the drawer upon the English banker" (Hamilton 1855, 49). In his manuscript notes, he added that "this sudden drain on finances was not, however, the signal of despondency, the spirit of our predecessors still lived on" (quoted, *Antiquities* 1915, 3). A large number of bills for equipment and supplies have survived, ranging from a fifty-five pounds gold repeater watch for Gell to one pound eighteen shillings worth of pencils. Before leaving England, Gell also purchased

an assortment of such articles as would be acceptable to the men in authority in the countries they were about to visit. Bacchish under different names has a great degree of influence in every country yet known, but in the East it is indispensable, as it would be an actual affront to appear before a superior empty handed. . . . Telescopes, pistol barrels and locks, some articles of cut glass, and some shawls of British manufacture, compose the assortment . . . (Ionian committee minutes, 5 January 1812, quoted in Cust 1898, 150–151).

The Society also obtained in advance the cooperation of British diplomats in the Levant, necessary even though Turkey was neutral in the Napoleonic Wars, and the local Pasha considered friendly to the English.

The expedition's progress is described in a "Short Narrative of the Voyage, reprinted from the Zante Gazettes," which appeared in a *Report* printed by the Ionian committee for the Society in 1814 (see Cust 1898, 158–162). Having disembarked at Zante, the team traveled to Athens where, "detained by the difficulty of procuring a safe passage to Smyrna" (*Report* 1814, 2), they began excavations at Eleusis. This chance delay resulted in their greatest achievement, documenting the Temple of Ceres (now called Demeter) and other buildings on the site of the famous Eleusinian mysteries. Eleusis is the subject of the first five chapters of the *Unedited Antiquities of Attica*. Eventually finding a passage to Asia Minor, the travelers were prevented by plague from examining the Temple of Artemis at Sardis and therefore spent June 1812 at Samos, first on the list of the Society's priorities. They then went to Didyma near Miletos, which Chandler's expedition had also visited, and on by way of Halicarnassus to Cnidus, Telmissus, Patara, Myra (in September), and Antiphellos in Lycia. The plague again blocked their way to the ruins of Laodicea and Hierapolis, but another *coup* was achieved when they discovered the Temple of Venus (Aphrodite) at Aphrodisias, along with a huge agora and "an entire volume of inscriptions" (*Report* 1814, 5). The Temple of Diana (Artemis) at Magnesia was next on the list, followed by the Temple of Minerva Polias (Athena) at Priene, another ruin already examined by Chandler. Returning to Athens, they were delayed again and spent the time excavating and measuring at Rhamnous (Temple of Nemesis, Temple of Themis), Sunium (Temple of Minerva, now called Poseidon), and nearby Thorikos. They returned to England in the summer of 1813.

During the expedition, Gell regularly reported back to the Society. Cust records that in 1812 one of his letters relating to the marbles discovered by Charles Cockerell and others at the Temple of Aegina was sent with some tracings to the British Museum, in the unrewarded hope that the British government would acquire the sculpture. In the same year, at Gell's request, the Society applied to the Admiralty for assistance against pirates in the seas near Asia Minor. The 1814 report lists a total of 274 architectural drawings and 209 views and maps made during the expedition. Unfortunately, much of this material has since disappeared. According to W. R. Lethaby's account in volume five of the *Antiquities of Ionia* (1915), William Leake was the culprit. On 12 August 1822, the latter signed a receipt from Sir Thomas Lawrence, secretary of the Society, for:

Three volumes bound in red leather of Sir W. Gell's Journal, 8 inches by 4. Three volumes in yellow paste-board of sketches and views, by Sir W. Gell, rather smaller. Two volumes in red leather of a large size (10 inches by 5) of views and drawings, by Sir W. Gell. Four volumes of drawings, chiefly architectural, by the architects of the Mission, of the same size as the two preceding (10 inches by 5); the leaves in one of these volumes are separated from the binding, in two others they are entirely loose and unsecured (*Antiquities* 1915, 6).

Lethaby all but accuses Leake of never returning the loan, selfishly guarding its evidence for his own series of publications about Greece and Asia Minor. There are, however, several mitigating factors. First, Leake would have needed the material on a long-term basis, since along with Wilkins he "had a large share in superintending the work" on volume three of *Antiquities of*

Society of Dilettanti. *The Unedited Antiquities of Attica.* Chapter 4, plate 7. Fragments found at Eleusis. 1985.61.2684

Ionia, which finally appeared in 1840 (Cust 1898, 168). Second, Leake probably deserves credit as the one responsible for passing a number of Gell's notes on inscriptions to the philologist August Böckh, who incorporated them in early volumes of the *Corpus inscriptionum Graecarum* (1828–). Last, it is unclear whether or not some of what Leake borrowed is among the expedition material known to have survived beyond his death in 1860. This material includes:

1. An album owned by the Society of Dilettanti in 1861, when its contents were listed by Sir Frederic Madden in volume three of his *Catalogue of the Manuscript Maps, Charts, and Plans, and of the Topographical Drawings in the British Museum* (1844, 1861). Madden describes this as "A collection of 41 views and plans of antiquities in Greece and the islands of the Grecian Archipelago; drawn, partly by Sir William Gell, partly by Francis Bedford, and partly by John P. Gandy Deering, forming the mission sent by the Society of Dilettanti to Greece and Asia Minor in 1811 and 1812. These drawings still remain in the possession of the Society of Dilettanti, but will be found described in their respective places in this catalogue" (British Museum 1861, 79). It contained, *inter alia*, drawings not exceeding ten inches in height or length of Eleusis (nos. 26–32, 34–36), Sunium (nos. 39–40), and Rhamnous (no. 41). Madden identifies those that were subsequently engraved for the *Unedited Antiquities of Attica*. Perhaps he anticipated they would soon be transferred to the British Museum, but this never happened and the volume is said to have been destroyed in a fire (see British School at Athens *Annual* 18: 273).

2. A journal consisting of brief notes in Gell's hand covering the period 30 April to 17 July 1812, bound in red leather ($4\frac{5}{8} \times 3\frac{1}{4}''$), presented by Thomas Ashby to the British School at Athens and edited by A. M. Woodward in the BSA's *Annual* for 1926–1927. Ashby acquired this and other Gell material—some perhaps also relating to the Dilettanti expedition—from a bookseller in Naples in 1923 (see British School at Athens *Annual* 27: 67–80; 28: 107–127).

3. Two volumes of a fuller version of Gell's journal reported to Woodward as still in the possession of the Society of Dilettanti. The period covered overlaps the BSA journal at both ends, and Woodward suggests the two-volume version was written up from the shorter diary. These volumes contain illustrative sketches and about 180 inscriptions in all (see British School at Athens *Annual* 28: 67).

4. Six sketchbooks and diaries compiled by Francis Bedford during the expedition, now in the British Architectural Library (RIBA) Drawings Collection (see RIBA, *Catalogue of the Drawings Collection*, B: 71, col. 1).

One of these, which Thomas Donaldson persuaded Bedford's son Edwin to donate in 1879, is actually a scrap album with material added later. The other five appear to have been given to the RIBA by the Society in 1912. At the same time, some related notes and lists and many finished drawings by Bedford and Gandy were presented, along with proof plates prepared by the Society between 1820 and 1840 for the *Unedited Antiquities of Attica*, for the second edition of volume one of the *Antiquities of Ionia*, and for volume three of the same. Some of the previously unpublished plates and drawings were then used by Lethaby for volume five of the *Antiquities* (see RIBA, *Catalogue of the Drawings Collection*, B: 61–71; S: 102–103).

In March 1853, thirteen of Gell's sketchbooks and a packet of about seventy views were presented by Craven to the British Museum in accordance with his late friend's wishes. There are a large number of views of Greece and Asia Minor among them, some not by Gell, as listed by Laurence Binyon, but most if not all of these date from Gell's earlier tours.

Francis and Edwin Bedford's scrap album includes transcripts of letters written during the expedition and subsequently published in *Extracts from the Journals and Correspondence of Miss [Mary] Berry from 1783 to 1852* (1865), such as this from Craven:

> . . . Gell is sitting on the floor making a map of this place and fighting the splashing of the rain that beats in upon his paper through the only window we can suffer to have open. I am sitting on the opposite side of the fire, on my own bed, my table consisting of a pair of blue trousers bundled up into an inclined plane, that I may catch the few rays of light that are to be had and at the same time the many fleas that may be inclined to read this letter. At my feet lies Mr. Bedford in one of those painful attitudes which makes one feel the cruel inconvenience of one's own legs. He is mending the fractures of broken columns, architraves, which are scattered in all directions about this village by drawing them in a perfect state such as you will see them in when published by the Soc. of Dilettanti. Then our other artist Mr. Gandy is in the distance trying in vain to make a large writing-desk lie flat and steady upon the top of a small round trunk. . . . The Albanian peasant to whom the mansion belongs occasionally comes in to see what he can steal under pretence of making up the fire, doing which generally involves us in a cloud of dust and smoke for some minutes. But think not it was always thus, for till this day the weather was so fine that I shaved every morning on the flat roof of our neighbour's house and we found it so warm on our perambulations that a sudden thought struck me and we spontaneously left off cravats. . . .

Another letter to Miss Berry, this time from Gell, shows that Bedford and Craven traveled to Myra alone, "whence they brought home the richest collection of tombs, good, bad, quizzickle and clockcasical ever seen which I hope we shall have published. . . ."

Publication was evidently an exciting prospect for the travelers. Even before their return, in January 1813, the Society began to place some of the drawings of Eleusis with the engravers (Cust 1898, 157). On 2 February 1814 the Ionian committee approved plates of the Temple which had been engraved under Wilkins' superintendence, and agreed that Wilkins and Sir Henry Englefield should continue a work that "as soon as completed shall be offered to the publick under the title of *Antiquities of Eleusis*" (Cust 1898, 160). Wilkins was to explain the illustrations, Knight to provide an account of the Eleusinian mysteries, and Gell to describe the mission. The 1814 *Report* was compiled to impress upon other members of the Society the value of this enterprise. The committee tabled two motions on or before 1 May. The first was proposed by Wilkins, stating that on the one hand "the elaborate and accurate drawings from the buildings of Attica alone, hitherto unknown . . . are abundantly sufficient to form a volume; which in point of interest, would be surpassed by no architectural publication extant, and equalled only by the second volume of the Antiquities of Athens"; but on the other hand "That the excavations . . . have afforded facilities of investigation to the travellers of every European nation; amongst whom some one might be found, who, jealous of the honour resulting to the English nation from the spirit and enterprise of the Society of Dilettanti, might endeavour to anticipate the appearance of the publication, already in progress, if it be not pursued with promptitude and vigour" (pp. 15–16). Englefield tabled the second motion, which required that each member "do annually subscribe ten guineas each for five years, for the purpose of promoting the publication of the drawings collected by the Ionian Mission, over and above the other payments made to the Society: and further, that any Member choosing to pay the whole fifty guineas at one payment, shall receive from the Society his copy of the works published, within the five years, with the plates taken off on India paper" (p. 18). Englefield concluded by announcing that "the first part of the Antiquities of Eleusis, containing general views and plans, and the details of the Temple of Diana Propylaea, are so far advanced, that they will be ready for delivery to the Members early in the next winter; and that the second part, which will give the details of the Doric and Ionic Propylaea, are in hand, and considerably advanced; and they [i.e., the committee] beg leave to observe, that it is important that the engravers engaged by them, should be as far as is possible, kept constantly employed, as otherwise they may be induced to seek other engagements, which may materially delay the publications" (p. 18).

Wilkins and Englefield's proposals were accepted by all twenty-six members present and eleven out of twelve votes made by letter or proxy. (Some of the subscription fees were later diverted to subsidize the second volume of the Society's *Select Specimens of Antient Sculpture*, 1835.) The work schedule was reorganized on 6 June: one volume was now to cover all the ruins of Attica,

Knight would draw up an abstract of the voyage, and Aberdeen would edit Gell's account of the so-called Sacred Way. Wilkins would continue to superintend the plates and obtain from the artists full accounts of the excavations (Cust 1898, 160). Both Gandy and Bedford had been given a twenty-five pound gift for their labors, to be spent on "a piece of Plate according to their own wishes, on which shall be engraven an inscription to be furnished to them by the Committee expressive of the satisfaction the Society feels at their successful and laborious exertions during their late voyage" (Cust 1898, 157–158). Now they were to spend at least three years producing finished drawings for the engravers. Knight's new role is odd and seems to reflect a situation where Gell was no longer available. Sir Thomas Lawrence's portrait of him, commissioned by the Society for its rooms on 6 February, was never executed. It may be relevant that Gell and Craven were both chamberlains to the prince regent's wife, Princess Caroline. When she decided to quit England for Italy later that year they left with her. Also, Gell's enthusiasm for Greece was dampened by getting to know the nation better, whereas his love of Italy grew to the extent that, after giving evidence at Caroline's somewhat scandalous trial in England in 1820, he spent the rest of his life in Rome and Naples. Unavailable, unwilling, or both as the case may be, Gell cannot safely be credited with much in the present volume even though those sections describing the monuments in their ruined state were presumably by him or taken from his journals. According to Cust, Aberdeen and Knight also failed to complete their tasks, leaving Wilkins to be the anonymous editor, responsible for the book in its final form. All the more credit goes to Wilkins since he was at the same time completing two other publishing projects, his edition of Vitruvius (1812–1817?) and *Atheniensia, or Remarks on the Topography and Buildings of Athens* (1816). Neither, incidentally, makes much use of Gell's discoveries. Most of the Vitruvius was already printed; and in the preface to *Atheniensia*, he claims his essay was inspired by observations made in Athens in 1802, and only published now because its length prevented it appearing in the Reverend Robert Walpole's long-delayed but forthcoming compilation, *Travels in Various Countries* (1820).

Wilkins did not allow his other commitments to interrupt publication of the expedition's findings in the area surrounding Athens, which he rightly saw as its main achievement even though they were not part of the original instructions and were, in fact, the fortuitous result of unanticipated delays. For several reasons, time was of the essence. With the nation's purchase of the Elgin marbles in 1816, British interest in Greek architecture had never been higher. Then there was the ever-present fear, expressed in the 1814 report quoted above, that foreigners would attempt to make a scoop, as Julien-David Leroy had by publishing *Ruines des plus beaux monumens de la Grèce* (Paris, 1758) before Stuart and Revett's first volume was ready. Archaeologists now knew the need to excavate—a laborious process that had given Gell all his most spectacular finds, but which left his discoveries available to anyone who took the time to make a site visit after his departure. The ruins around Athens were particularly vulnerable in this respect. Wilkins was also aware of the mistake Stuart had made in beginning his publishing program with relatively minor buildings. Eleusis was already under way and had to be published as soon as possible. By appending the work done at Rhamnous, Sunium, and Thorikos, Wilkins could claim that all the ancient buildings so far discovered in Attica outside Athens were present in the one volume.

These decisions were good, but they inevitably left an impact on the Society's earlier publications. Chandler's research at Eleusis had already appeared in volume two of *Antiquities of Ionia* (1797). This was superseded by Bedford's more accurate measurements and because "The subject of Grecian architecture was at that period quite new to European artists, and it happened, in consequence, that several peculiarities of the novel style of building were either overlooked or not sought after" (*The Unedited Antiquities of Attica* 1817, 9). Chandler had also visited Sunium, the southernmost part of Attica, and in this case Wilkins decided to combine the evidence of the two expeditions. Bedford's drawings of the propylaea (ch. 8, pls. 1–4) were added to six plates of the Temple that were either reprinted (pls. 5–6, 9) or reengraved (pls. 7–8, 10) from the 1797 volume. As a result, both the Eleusis and Sunium sections of *Antiquities of Ionia* would have had to be suppressed from a new edition of volume two, had this part of Wilkins' editorial program been carried out (see notes to *Antiquities of Ionia*).

On 8 March 1816 Wilkins was able to report that the engravings were ready for publication. There was, however, a problem: no bookseller would agree to take the work on. The Society decided to publish it themselves, using William Bulmer to print the text and Edward Cox the plates. Three hundred copies would be printed, including one hundred on India paper for the use of the Society. A printed label dated March 1816 and pasted on the Canadian Centre for Architecture's copy of the *Report* states that "A volume containing the unedited Antiquities of Attica will be published early in May.—200 copies only will be taken off for sale." But circumstances must have altered these arrangements, since when the book was finally announced as ready on 13 April 1817, there were no India paper copies and Longman and Co. and John Murray are both named as publishers on the title page. Copies were presented to the prince regent, the duke of Somerset—who had donated fifty guineas even before the resolution concerning subscriptions—and to the heirs of three deceased members (Cust 1898, 163–164). On 25 April 1819 it was further resolved "That every member of the present Society who has been admitted since the publication of the

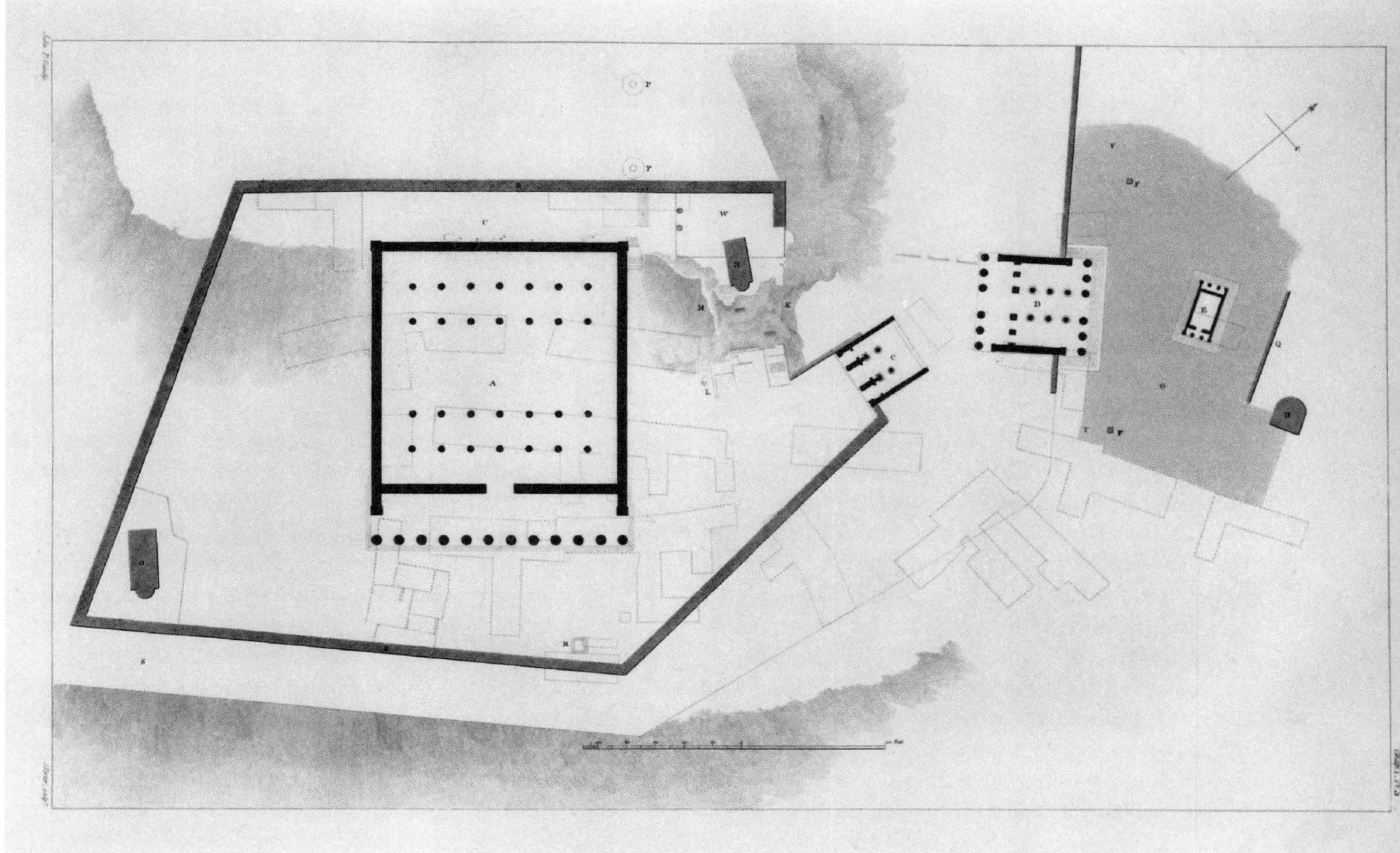

Society of Dilettanti. *The Unedited Antiquities of Attica.* Chapter 1, plate 3. General plan of the buildings at Eleusis. 1985.61.2684

second volume of the Ionian Antiquities, or since that of the Antiquities of Attica, be presented with a copy of either or both works, on payment of all arrears due to the Society, provided he has not already received them" (Cust 1898, 167). In May 1824 the Society accepted an offer from the publishers Priestley and Weale to buy the remaining copies of *Unedited Antiquities* for seven pounds each. Priestley and Weale were therefore able to sell it alongside their new four-volume edition of Stuart and Revett's *Antiquities of Athens* (1825–1830).

Knowing that the *Unedited Antiquities* was prepared in sections and under time pressure partly explains the lack of a preface giving proper acknowledgment to the expedition members, and why five of Gell's views were etched by Cooke for chapter one but none thereafter (ch. 1, pls. 4–8). The decision to exclude views also reflects Wilkins' overriding interest in the architectural significance of the voyage, rather than any lingering sense of picturesque adventure other Dilettanti may have had. It marks a turning point in the history of archaeological publications, differentiating this work from the more eclectic tradition described by Kaufman. Gell also provided two maps of Eleusis (ch. 1, pls. 1–2). These are followed by a plan of the site by Gandy that acts as a key to the text (ch. 1, pls. 1–3). Chapters two through five are arranged in a sequence that first follows the Sacred Way from "Propylaea" (marked D on the plan) to "Inner Vestibules" (C) to "Temple of Ceres" (A), before returning to the outlying "Temple of Diana" (E). Since Knight's account of the Eleusinian mysteries never materialized, a partial reprint of Chandler's account of the drugged initiates' ordeal is given—an account that would not have looked out of place in a contemporary Gothic novel ("Lamentations and strange noises were heard. It thundered. Flashes of light and of fire rendered the deep succeeding darkness more terrible. They were beaten, and perceived not the hand. They beheld frightful apparitions, monsters, and phantoms of a canine form . . . ," 28–29). The texts for Rhamnous, Sunium, and Thorikos are comparatively brief, those for the last two amounting to little more than a description of the plates, confirming Wilkins' increasingly solitary role as chief compiler.

It is beyond the scope of this essay to deal with the reception awarded to the *Unedited Antiquities*, but one of the most valuable critiques is to be found among the papers given by the Society of Dilettanti to the RIBA in 1912 (see RIBA, *Catalogue of the Drawings Collection*, B: 70, col. 3). It is in a small folded notebook containing nine pages of detailed comments evidently written by one or other member of the expedition, probably Bedford. The manuscript refers by page and line number to the first two chapters of the published text. Its tone is critical with the sure knowledge of one who had been on the spot. For example, where the published text describes the height of the Propylaea columns at Eleusis as unascertainable because they were inaccessible (p. 10), the manuscript notes that "It was not the difficulty of gaining access to the fragments that prevented the heights of the columns from being ascertained but that the pieces which formed the shaft varied in their heights in the different columns and as they were heaped confoundly [sic] together, it was impossible to ascertain with certainty to which column any particular piece belonged. . . ." Other comments are simple glosses, as when the author explains the curiously large epistylia of the Propylaea's Ionic columns as "made of this unusual size in order that they might possess sufficient strength to support the immense beams of the ceiling, one of which rested over the centre of each epistylium—for the same reason they were made in single blocks instead of being in two thicknesses, as was the usual practice of the Greeks." These corrections and additions show that the official account of the expedition did not make a triumphant progress into print without provoking a private critique from at least one member of the team.

Nevertheless, publication of the *Unedited Antiquities of Attica* represents one of the Society of Dilettanti's finest achievements. Under Wilkins' editorship, the book was not the miscellaneous collection of leftovers that its unprepossessing title might suggest, but part of a conscious effort to supplement the *Antiquities of Athens* by extending its geographical coverage. And this was how it was received, at least on the Continent. Leopoldo Cicognara refers to it as a sort of fifth volume of the *Antiquities* (Cicognara, no. 2713); Jacques-Charles Brunet as a continuation (Brunet 5, col. 570). Jakob Hittorff even edited a French translation so that it was "en tout conforme à celle des *Antiquités d'Athènes*, publiée par C. Landon, et continuée par Bance ainé" (*Les Antiquités inédites de l'Attique*, Paris, 1832, viii). The French edition was preceded by a German translation published by C. W. Leske as *Alterthümer von Attika* (Darmstadt, 1829). In 1833 a second edition of the English version was issued by Priestley and Weale. G. B.

Bibliography

Binyon, L. *Catalogue of Drawings by British Artists and Artists of Foreign Origin working in Great Britain, Preserved in the Department of Prints and Drawings in the British Museum*. Vol. 2. London, 1900

British Museum. *Catalogue of the Manuscript Maps, Charts, and Plans, and of the Topographical Drawings in the British Museum*. Ed. F. Madden. Vol. 3. London, 1861. Reprint London, 1962

Crook, J. Mordaunt. *The Greek Revival* (RIBA Drawings Series). Feltham, 1968

Crook, J. Mordaunt. *The Greek Revival: Neo-Classical Attitudes in British Architecture 1760–1870*. London, 1972

Cust, L. *History of the Society of Dilettanti*. Ed. S. Colvin. London, 1898

Hamilton, W. R. *Historical Notices of the Society of Dilettanti*. London, 1855

Harris, E., and N. Savage. *British Architectural Books and Writers 1556–1785*. Cambridge, 1990

Kaufman, E. "Architecture and Travel in the Age of British Eclecticism." In *Architecture and Its Image: Four Centuries of Architectural Representation*. Ed. E. Blau and E. Kaufman. Montreal, 1989: 58–85

Lethaby, W. R. "The First and Second Ionian Missions of the Society of Dilettanti." In Society of Dilettanti. *Antiquities of Ionia. Part the Fifth*. Ed. W. R. Lethaby. London, 1915: 1–9

Liscombe, R. W. *William Wilkins 1778–1839*. Cambridge, 1980

The Princeton Encyclopedia of Classical Sites. Ed. R. Stillwell. Princeton, 1976

Society of Dilettanti. *Report of the Committee of the Society of Dilettanti, appointed by the Society to Superintend the Expedition lately sent by them to Greece and Ionia; containing an Abstract of the Voyage of the Mission, a List of the Materials collected by them, and a Plan to Facilitate the Publication of those Materials*. London, 1814

Woodward, A. M. "The Note-Books of Sir William Gell." In *The Annual of the British School of Athens*, 27 (1925–1926): 67–80 and 28 (1926–1927): 107–127

80

Society of Dilettanti

Antiquities Of Ionia, Published By The Society Of Dilettanti. Part The First (Second)

[vol. 1] London: printed by W. Bulmer and W. Nicol. Sold by G. and W. Nicol; Payne and Foss; Longman and Co.; and Rodwell and Martin, 1821

[vol. 2] London: printed by W. Bulmer and Co. for George Nicol, 1797

1985.61.2700–2701

Vol. 1: large folio: 570 × 386 (22 7/16 × 15 5/16)

Vol. 2: large folio: 580 × 395 (22 3/4 × 15 1/2)

Pagination Vol. 1: [6], xiv, [2], 68 [i.e., 66] pp., [43] etched and engraved plates

(*Note*: Pages 65–66 misnumbered 67–68)

Vol. 2: [4], 43, [3] pp., [63] etched plates (1 folding)

Edition Second edition of vol. 1; first edition of vol. 2

Text vol. 1: pp. [1] title page (verso blank); [3] list of members of the Society of Dilettanti in 1769, in order of seniority (verso blank); [5] second list of members of the society, dated 1 June 1821 (verso blank); [i]–iv preface to the first edition, 1769; [v]–xiv introduction (i.e., preface to new edition); [xv] table of contents (verso blank); [1]–66 text, chapters 1–5; *vol. 2*: pp. [1] title page (verso blank); [3] list of members of the society, dated 1797 (verso blank); [i]–xiv preface; [15]–43 text, chapters 5–7; [44] blank; [45] table of contents to vols. 1–2 (verso blank)

Illustrations vol. 1: a total of 43 etched or engraved plates, numbered by sequence within each chapter, as follows. *Chapter 1*: 3 plates numbered I–III engraved by T. Miller (1), James Basire (1), or unsigned (1). *Chapter 2*: 18 plates numbered I–XVIII, namely, 2 maps engraved by James Walker after Sir William Gell; 7 by S. Porter after Francis Bedford; 2 by John Roffe after Bedford; and 7 signed only as etched or engraved by John Roffe (1), T. Miller (2), Thomas White (2), J. [i.e., John?] Gwyn (1), and G. Sherlock (1). *Chapter 3*: 9 plates numbered I–VIII (2 plates numbered II), namely, 1 map by Walker after Gell; 1 plate by Porter after John P. Gandy; 1 by Roffe after Bedford; and 5 signed as etched or engraved by Basire (2), White (2), and Byrne (1). *Chapter 4*: 5 plates numbered I–V, namely, 1 by William Byrne after William Pars and 4 signed as engraved by James Newton. *Chapter 5*: 8 plates numbered I–VIII (plate III misnumbered II, corrected in MS), namely, 1 map by Walker after Gell; 4 plates by Roffe after Bedford; 2 by Roffe after Gandy; and 1 unsigned. Additionally, there is an engraved title-page vignette signed "F"; an etched headpiece to the preface; an engraved pictorial headpiece to the introduction (signed "[William] Woollett & J. [i.e., James] Basire sculp."); and engraved pictorial headpieces to each chapter (4 drawn by J. P. Gandy, 1 engraved by E. J. Roberts, 1 signed as title-page vignette)

Vol. 2: a total of 63 etched plates numbered I–LIX, I–IV, of which 44 are signed solely by James Newton as etcher. Chapter 7 gives additional information regarding the sources of the illustrations: "The Society are indebted to Sir Robert Ainslie for the two views of the Theatre of Patara [plates LVI, LVII], that of Castell Rosso [plate LVIII], and of Macri or Temessus [plate LIX], which are taken from drawings by Mr. Mÿers, in his possession, and finished under his inspection. The rest of the views have been engraved from drawings of the late Mr. [William] Pars, belonging to the Society. The architectural designs from those of Mr. [Nicholas] Revett." 11 are signed by Pars as draftsman, 9 with Byrne and 2 with James Newton as etcher. Plates LXVI–LXIX are signed as drawn by Luigi Mayer after Byrne (2), James Newton, or Samuel Middiman, and the additional plates numbered I–IV are also signed by Mayer as draftsman ("Mÿers delin^t."), all etched by Byrne. These last are slightly smaller in format compared to the other views in the work (300 × 480 mm rather than 313 × 494 mm). They show the harbor and citadel of Halicarnassus and 2 views of the Island of Tortosa. Additionally, an etched title-page vignette is signed "F" (repeated from vol. 1) and there are 8 etched vignettes of antiquities as head- and tailpieces, 6 signed by James Newton as draftsman and/or etcher, 1 signed "F" and 1 unsigned

Binding Contemporary gray paper boards, new cloth spines, original printed tickets

Provenance Early nineteenth-century bookplates of James Whatman

References Brunet 1: p. 1782n; Cicognara 2658 (1st ed. of both vols.); ESTC t104764 (vol. 2); Fowler 276 (1st ed. of vol. 1); Harris and Savage 847–850 (1st ed. of both vols.)

A COMPLETE SET of the Society of Dilettanti's *Antiquities of Ionia* would consist of six volumes published over 136 years. Volume one, relating to Richard Chandler's expedition of 1764–1766, was published in 1769 as *Ionian Antiquities*; a chapter on the Temple at Jackly (i.e., Labranda) was added to a reissue in 1785. Volume two, also the fruit of Chandler's trip, was delayed until 1798 (dated 1797). A second edition of volume one, extensively revised according to the findings of William Gell's expedition of 1811–1813, appeared in 1821. More of Gell's findings were used for volume three (1840). Volume four (1881) was the product of R. P. Pullan's excavations at Teos, Priene, and Smintheion in the 1860s. Finally, in a largely antiquarian exercise, proof plates and finished drawings prepared long before by the Society for another volume relating to Gell's expedition were edited by W. R. Lethaby and published as volume five in 1915.

The Millard collection contains the second edition of volume one and the first edition of volume two, which is all that would have been available between 1821 and 1840. This copy's bookplates are those of James Whatman (1777–1843), son of the more famous paper manufacturer of the same name. The fine wove paper used for volume two was produced at the father's mill in the year he sold out and retired, 1794. The discrepancy in the chapter numbers of volume two (i.e., chs. 5–7 following chs. 1–5) would have been rectified if a second edition of volume two had appeared. But there was little new matter to add and what there was had been transferred to a separate work, *The Unedited Antiquities of Attica* (1817). Furthermore, copies of the first edition were still available for sale, making any revision an unrewarding task. An edition of volume two dated 1820 is mentioned by Lethaby (*Antiquities* 1915, 5: 6), but this seems to be an error.

Society of Dilettanti. *Antiquities of Ionia.* Vol. 1, page v. "Capital of one of the Antae at Didyme." 1985.61.2700

INTRODUCTION.

THE Society of Dilettanti being convinced by a former survey of the shores of Asia Minor made, at their expense, with the view of searching for the remains of ancient architecture, that much of that interesting quarter of the globe contained monuments of antiquity hitherto unnoticed or imperfectly described, had long contemplated a second mission, provided with more ample means and more extensive powers. Accordingly, in October of the year 1812, Mr., now Sir William, Gell, accompanied by two architects, Mr. John Peter Gandy and Mr. Francis Bedford, embarked for the Mediterranean, having received the necessary instructions for the mode of their proceeding.

The result of their researches in Attica has been made known by the splendid work which was published from the drawings transmitted to the Society. In the present work, and in another now in progress, it is proposed to give to the

Since the genesis of the first editions of both volumes has been dealt with by Harris and Savage, the present note is confined to a summary of the revisions made to volume one (see Harris and Savage 1990, 431–437). These are anonymous and may have been a collaborative effort, but the chief editor was undoubtedly William Wilkins, continuing a task that had already resulted in the publication of Gell's discoveries in Attica as the *Unedited Antiquities.* He might have been tempted to publish another new title, leaving the *Antiquities of Ionia* as the relic of a previous generation. Instead, he chose to blend Gell's research with Chandler's, overlaying them both with his own theories about ancient Greek architecture and thereby producing what now seems a curiously hybrid volume, but one which reflects his genuine desire to summarize the significance of all five sites covered: Teos (Temple of Bacchus, now called Dionysos Setaneios), Priene (Temple of Minerva Polias, i.e., Athena), Didyma (Temple of Apollo), Labranda (Temple of Zeus Stratios), and Samos (Temple of Juno, i.e., Hera). He gives his rationale in the introduction:

> At the period when the first work of the Society appeared, Grecian architecture was very little understood; for, although the first volume of the Antiquities of Athens had been seven years before the public, yet this portion of this justly celebrated work referred only to buildings of little note, compared with the nobler productions of the Athenians, and those of very simple construction.
>
> Many of the architectural details of the buildings selected for publication in the first volume of Ionian Antiquities, where they differed from the better known specimens of Roman art, were disregarded by the artists attached to the first mission; and several omissions, the consequence of their more limited means of excavation and inspection, necessarily occurred.
>
> The attention of the later mission was, in the first instance, directed to the correction of the errors which had arisen from the imperfect knowledge of Grecian architecture; and to examine with greater minuteness, by means of excavations made within and around the buildings, the plans and mode of construction observed in the edifices which formed the subject of the first volume of Ionian Antiquities.
>
> The researches for this purpose, which were conducted with great science and ability, have put the Society in possession of more ample documents, both in general and in detail, relating to the buildings in question; and have enabled them to re-publish the first volume of the Antiquities of Ionia, which has been long out of print, corrected and considerably augmented (pp. v–vi).

Most of the rest of the introduction is taken up by Wilkins' theory that Greek temples typically had no openings in their roofs to admit light. This section was reprinted much later in Wilkins' *Prolusiones Architec-*

Society of Dilettanti. *Antiquities of Ionia.* Vol. I, chapter 2, plate III. Ruins of the Temple of Minerva Polias. 1985.61.2700

tonicae; or, Essays on Subjects connected with Grecian and Roman Architecture (1837). A footnote was added to the reprint at the last moment, stating that he was in the process of revising the essay, perhaps no more than a strategy to forestall criticism.

Wilkins' recasting of chapter one of *Ionian Antiquities* introduces his new and more rigorous standards. For the first edition, Nicholas Revett had drawn a reconstruction of the so-called Temple of Bacchus at Teos that was based far more on Vitruvius' description of it, and of other Greek temples, than on the ruin itself, of which Revett freely admitted "The disorder, in which [it] lies, is so great, that no fragment of a column, or portion of the cell, is found unmoved from its original place. No vestige of the plan could be discovered, much less could the aspect or the species of the temple be determined, from its present state" (*Antiquities* 1769, I: 6). Gell's expedition never visited the site, but even so Wilkins was unable to leave Revett's conclusions unchallenged. He suppressed the latter's elevation (pl. II), and although he preserved two outline engravings of details (pls. III, V, renumbered II–III) he rejected the plates that showed these details "restored and shaded, in order to give a more complete idea of the effect" (pls. IV, VI; see *Antiquities* 1769, I: 10). The wisdom of Wilkins' decision was proved by Pullan's excavations at Teos in the 1860s, which revealed that the temple described by Chandler and Revett was not the one referred to by Vitruvius after all (*Antiquities* 1881, 4: 38–39). Wilkins also replaced Robert Wood's charming but architecturally irrelevant view of the bay of Segigeck by an unsigned view of the temple ruins (pl. I).

The situation was reversed for chapter two: Revett had not dared to offer a restoration of the Temple of Minerva Polias at Priene, but Francis Bedford of Gell's party had brought back a wealth of new information and Wilkins was able to add seven new plates offering a complete reconstruction (pls. II–I7). Shaded details were again deleted. Wilkins also includes a map and plan of the area measured by Gell (pls. I–2), but characteristically ignores all the views of Priene brought back by the expedition and listed in the Society of Dilettanti's 1814 *Report*. Instead, he re-uses the first edition's view of the ruins, etched by G. Sherlock (pl. 3). Curiously, the area of sky on the original copperplate was first ruled over and the left-hand border brought in a few centimeters. The view of the Temple of Apollo at Didyma is treated in similar fashion, in this case the curtailment of the right-hand border removing John Miller's signature (ch. 3, pl. 2).

In chapter three, Wilkins retained the engravings of details with shading in preference to the more informative outline versions, perhaps because one of the outline engravings included an extremely dubious reconstruction of the Temple of Apollo's Ionic volute, based on

Palladio (see *Antiquities* 1769, 1: pls. V–VI). He again added a map by Gell and a plan and elevation of the temple, based on the work of Bedford and John Peter Gandy (later Deering). Chapter four, on the temple at Jackly, here called Labranda, is left virtually untouched.

The final chapter of the second edition is entirely new:

> The island of Samos, notwithstanding its magnitude and importance, has been little visited by modern travellers, and its geography is in consequence so little understood, that, in the year 1820, a map of its ancient capital was engraved at Paris, which represented the Heraeum as situated within the walls of the city; while the English charts published previously to the Dilettanti mission were so faulty, that it was found impossible to correct them. The present survey of the ancient Samos, contains only that part of the island immediately connected with the ancient city and the Heraeum (p. 59).

To improve on the information supplied by earlier visitors (notably Joseph Pitton de Tournefort, Richard Pococke, Marie Gabriel Choiseul-Gouffier, and the Reverend James Dallaway), Samos had been a top priority on the list prepared by Wilkins and George Gordon, 4th earl of Aberdeen, for Gell and his team before they set out (see notes to *The Unedited Antiquities of Attica*, 1817). They reached it in June 1812, but their research was limited because

Society of Dilettanti. *Antiquities of Ionia*. Vol. 1, chapter 2, plate V. Elevation of the Temple of Minerva Polias. 1985.61.2700

> By the contrivance of Pisani, the interpreter at Constantinople, the island of Samos was not mentioned in the firhman, but the names of Aleppo and Diarbekir substituted. The consequence was, that the archons of the island prohibited people from working at the excavations, and the gentlemen of the mission were obliged, in the month of June, to work themselves with spades and axes, while the interpreter was employed in drawing off the inhabitants from the spot, by telling them amusing stories, and the practice of several ridiculous mummeries (p. 62).

Wilkins' text is illustrated by a map by Gell (pl. 1), an unsigned view of the remains (pl. 2), and six plates of details and fragments engraved by John Roffe after Bedford and Gandy (pls. 3–8). Reuther gives an excellent summary of the significance of this part of the Dilettanti expedition (Reuther 1957, 12–14).

The British Architectural Library (RIBA) Drawings Collection has thirteen original drawings prepared for the second edition of volume one of the *Antiquities of Ionia* (see RIBA, *Catalogue of the Drawings Collection*, B: 66–67). Most of these are finished drawings prepared for the engraver and duly included in the book. More interesting are a sketch plan and a rejected finished plan of the temple at Samos, the latter signed as measured and drawn by Bedford. This was presumably omitted because Wilkins wisely decided that there was not enough evidence to warrant Bedford's hypothetical reconstruction. G. B.

Bibliography

Balston, T. *James Whatman Father and Son*. London, 1957. Reprint, 1979

Cust, L. *History of the Society of Dilettanti*. Ed. S. Colvin. London, 1898

Liscombe, R. W. *William Wilkins 1778–1839*. Cambridge, 1980

The Princeton Encyclopedia of Classical Sites. Ed. R. Stillwell. Princeton, 1976

Reuther, O. *Der Heratempel von Samos: der Bau seit der Zeit des Polykrates*. Berlin, 1957

Society of Dilettanti. *Report of the Committee of the Society of Dilettanti, appointed by the Society to Superintend the Expedition lately sent by them to Greece and Ionia; containing an Abstract of the Voyage of the Mission, a List of the Materials collected by them, and a Plan to Facilitate the Publication of those Materials*. London, 1814

81

James Stuart (1713–1788) and Nicholas Revett (1720–1804)

The Antiquities Of Athens Measured And Delineated By James Stuart F.R.S. And F.S.A. And Nicholas Revett Painters And Architects. Volume The First (–Third).

[vol. 1] London: printed by John Haberkorn, 1762

[vols. 2–3] London: printed by John Nichols, 1787–1794

1985.61.2690–2692

Folio: 531 × 365 (20 7/8 × 14 3/8)

Pagination Vol. 1: [10], x, 52 pp., etched portrait frontispiece, [71] etched and engraved plates (2 folding)

(*Note*: With list of errata pasted on preliminary p. [10])

Vol. 2: [2], iv, viii, 46 pp., [73] etched and engraved plates (2 folding)

Vol. 3: xviii, xxv, [1], 64 [i.e., 58], [2] pp., [4] etched maps (3 folding), [82] etched and engraved plates (1 folding, 1 double-page)

(*Note*: Vol. 3, pp. 31–34, 45–46 omitted)

Edition First edition

Text vol. 1: pp. [1] title page (verso blank); [3–4] dedication to the king; [5–9] list of subscribers (corresponding to the Fowler rather than the John Hopkins copy; see Fowler, p. 273); [10] blank (errata pasted on sheet); [i]–viii preface; ix–x description of the general view of Athens; [1]–52 text, chapters 1–5; *vol. 2*: pp. [1] title page (verso blank); i preface "To The Publick" by Elizabeth Stuart, James Stuart's widow (verso blank); iii–iv introduction; [i] half-title, vol. 2; [ii] note to the reader "Advertisement," by James Stuart; iii–iv explanation of the view of the Acropolis; v–viii explanation of the plan of same; 1–42 text, chapters 1–5; 43–46 explanation of the vignettes; *vol. 3*: pp. [i] title page (verso blank); iii–xviii preface, signed Willey Reveley, September, 1794; [i]–vi explanation of the plan of Athens; vii–xxv explanation of the map of Attica; [xxvi] blank; 1–64 text, chapters 1–12; [65] errata and additional observations (verso blank)

Illustrations Vol. 1: a medallion portrait of James Stuart, a soft-ground etching "Drawn & Engraved by C. [i.e., Charles] Knight" and dated 1789, is sometimes found in vol. 2 but here inserted as a frontispiece to vol. 1. There are 71 other plates (i.e., an unnumbered folding view of Athens bound between p. viii and p. ix, and 70 plates numbered according to their chapters 1: I–VI, 2: I–VIII, 3: I–XIX, 4: I–XXVI, and 5: I–XI). The plates are signed as engraved by James Basire (41 plates), Edward Rooker (13), Anthony Walker (6), Sir Robert Strange (2), P. Fourdrinier (1), and Charles Grignion (1), with 7 unsigned. There are 10 etched vignettes as head- and tailpieces to each chapter (8 engraved by Basire, 2 by J. Couse), plus engraved title page and dedication vignettes by Basire, a headpiece to the preface by Couse, and a tailpiece by I. Green

Vol. 2: 2 unsigned folding plates plus 71 etched and engraved plates numbered according to their chapters 1: I–XXXI (i.e., 30: plate XXIX omitted from numbering), 2: I–XX, 3: I–II, 4: I–VI, and 5: I–XIII. 12 plates are signed as etched by James Newton, 2 by William Sharp after William Pars, 2 by Samuel Smith, and 1 by F. G. Aliamet. There are also 10 engraved vignettes as chapter head- and tailpieces, including 1 signed "[William] Skelton Sculp." and 1 by J. Hall after C. R. Ryley; plus a title-page vignette engraved by Thornthwaite, and another, unsigned, tailpiece

Vol. 3: 4 etched maps plus 82 etched plates numbered according to their chapters 1: I–XXIV, 2: I–III, 3: I–X, 4: I–IV, 5: I–XI, 6: I–IV, 7: I–III, 8: I, 9: I–XIII, 10: I–VI, 11: I–II, and 12: I. The maps are [1] folding, hand-colored in this copy, map of "Greece, Archipelago And Part Of Anadoli. By L.S. De La Rochette, MDCCXC. London, Published for Willm. Faden . . . January 1st. 1791," engraved by William Palmer (title within emblematic cartouche signed "C. [i.e., Conrad Martin?] Metz fec"); [2] folding map "Attica from an Actual Survey by M^r. Stuart," engraved by James Walker after Aaron Arrowsmith; [3] folding map "Plan of the Antiquities of Athens as Surveyed by J. Stuart. 1752"; and [4] full-page map without title, including the Bay of Phalerus, signed as engraved by T. Foot after Aaron Arrowsmith. The plates to the chapters are signed as engraved or etched by William Skelton (13), the poet William Blake (chap. 1, plates XXI–XXIV), Wilson Lowry (5), Thomas Medland (1), John Record (3), Daniel Lerpinière (1), John Landseer "direxit" (1), J. Hall (4), and James Newton (1). The named draftsmen include William Pars (18), Nicholas Revett (23), William Reveley (6), and James Stuart (15). In addition, there is an etched title-page vignette, and 24 etched vignettes as head- and tailpieces to the preface and chapters 1–11, unsigned except for the tailpiece to chapter 1, which is by Hall after Stuart

Binding Early nineteenth-century diced calf, blind-tooled Greek key borders, rebacked

Provenance Inscribed "Presented to the Phila[delphia] Chapter of Architects By S.D. Button Arch^t"

References Cicognara 2713 (vols. 1–4); ESTC t22194; Fowler 340 (vols. 1–3); Harris and Savage 857 (vols. 1–4)

JAMES STUART, Nicholas Revett, and Gavin Hamilton had been studying painting in Rome for six or seven years when, late in 1748, they hit upon the idea of visiting and drawing the antiquities of Athens.[1] Which one of them originated the plan is not known and is not particularly important.[2] Much more significant is what precipitated it.

In the spring of 1748 the three artists made a walking tour to Naples in the company of Matthew Brettingham junior, who had recently arrived in Rome to study architecture and to purchase sculpture for Lord Leicester of Holkham.[3] This excursion, doubtlessly taking in the excavations at Herculaneum and possibly those begun in 1748 at Pompeii, might well have stimulated a taste for adventure and for investigating the remains of antiquity in situ. Even more influential was the presence in Rome in the winter of 1748 of Lord Charlemont, who was planning an expedition to Greece and Asia Minor on which he embarked in April 1749.[4]

The fullest and most reliable account of the scheme formulated in 1748 was given by Revett in a letter to his father dated 6 January 1749.[5] This speaks of three volumes: "the first to contain fifty-three views of the country and its edifices"; the second, seventy-one plates of "plans, elevations and architectural details"; the third, "sixty-seven plates of sculpture." These 191 plates they intended to engrave themselves and, in their state of ecstatic optimism, estimated that the whole task, including one year in Greece, would only take four years to complete and would earn them a "neat profit . . . after paying every expense while thus employed" of at least ten thousand pounds and eventually three times that amount.

The ill-conceived idea of presenting the antiquities of Athens in separate volumes of views, sculpture, plans, and elevations betrays a lack of experience both of architecture and of publishing. It reflects a necessary division of labor that quite likely was made to accord with the differing interests and abilities of the three artists, Revett being distinctly more inclined than the others to the dry precision of architectural line drawing. Whatever part Hamilton was to have taken he abandoned sometime before the spring of 1750 and returned to England, where he practiced successfully as a portrait painter until 1756 when he returned to Rome to take up classical history painting, archaeology, and the art dealing for which he is best known.[6]

Having formulated their plan, Stuart and Revett had not only to learn as much as they could about the architecture, history, and topography of Greece and to perfect their knowledge of Greek and Latin (which Stuart evidently accomplished at the Collegio di Propaganda Fide),[7] but above all they had to find financial assistance to supplement Revett's private income. Stuart succeeded in distinguishing himself and gaining his first important patron by drawing and engraving in 1749 the obelisk found in the Campus Martius, and writing an account of it in the form of a letter addressed to Charles Wentworth, earl of Malton (later marquis of Rockingham) and dated April 1750. This was published at the expense of the pope as a separate piece and as part of A. M. Bandini's *De Obelisco* (1750) containing contributions by such esteemed scholars as Poleni, Scipione Maffei, Muratori, and Heinsius.

Their greatest good fortune at this juncture, however, was to meet the wealthy James Dawkins and his mentor Robert Wood, who had twice been to Greece in 1742 and 1743 and had an excellent reputation as a classical scholar. They, together with their colleague John Bouverie and draftsman G. B. Borra, were spending the winter of 1749 in Rome preparing for an expedition to the Levant in May 1750, which was unprecedented in its organization. This meeting had far-reaching consequences for Stuart and Revett's projected work, for not only did they receive financial support from Dawkins and learned and practical advice from Wood, but, equally important, a high standard of accuracy was set, most probably at Wood's insistence, for making and reporting their investigations.

About the same time that Wood and Dawkins set off on their expedition, Stuart and Revett went to Venice, intending to sail from there to Greece. Before doing so however they spent from July to November at Pola in Istria, measuring and drawing the antiquities there with an exactness and accuracy that revealed numerous mistakes in the depictions made by Palladio, Serlio, and Maffei, who, by contrast to them, "seem neither to have dug, nor to have raised the necessary scaffolds."[8] Their voyage to Pola certainly was "much to their advantage and instruction"; their thirty-four drawings of the Roman amphitheater, arch, and temple proved, as Thomas Hollis reported, that they were "in all respects equal" to their Grecian undertaking and brought them promises of subscriptions from Englishmen passing through Venice and distinguished Italians.[9]

The British consul in Venice, James Smith, and the resident, Sir James Gray, "both of them ingenious and learned Gentlemen," gave them "recommendatory letters to all the principal persons of the places where they [were] to go" and were instrumental in getting Sir James Porter, our ambassador in Constantinople, to obtain the "Grand Signor's Firmin."[10] Gray secured further important encouragement for them by arranging their membership in the Society of Dilettanti in March 1751 and was "the first to set on foot a subscription for [their] intended work."[11]

The earliest surviving "Proposals for publishing a new and accurate Description of the Antiquities &c. in the Province of Attica" were drawn up in the interval between their return from Pola in November 1750 and their departure for Greece on 19 January 1751 and circulated in manuscript.[12] This contains a provisional "catalogue" of the monuments they intended to include, which they made after consulting the works of Jacob Spon and Sir George Wheler,[13] and "conversing with several gentlemen who have visited Greece," as well as with Wood, Charlemont, and his draftsman Richard Dalton, who had returned in 1750. The arrangement of the plates in three volumes was to be exactly as that described by Revett in 1749, though their number was increased to 235.[14]

It did not take Stuart and Revett long after their arrival at Athens on 18 March 1751 to recognize that their original plan needed recasting. New proposals were made that were privately printed in London in 1752—first by Colonel George Gray (brother of the resident), then by their friend Samuel Ball and again by Wood and Dawkins, who had joined them in Athens in May 1751 before returning to England.[15] For all this, however, these proposals are known only from the version published by Stuart in volume one of the *Antiquities of Athens* (1762).[16]

While no changes were made to the contents of the catalogue, the architecture, sculpture, and views of each building were sensibly to be grouped together and distributed in the three volumes according to their location: those on the Acropolis in volume one, in the city of Athens in volume two, and in the surrounding areas in volume three. The number of plates was again increased. There were to be 233 in the first two volumes alone and thus above 300 in all.[17]

By 30 September 1752 Stuart and Revett had procured three hundred subscriptions; yet they wanted further encouragement from the public to enable them to complete the entire work. A description of their proposed publication and a copy of the catalogue were sent with a covering letter to the editor of the *Journal Britannique* in Amsterdam, M. Maty, who published it in full in January–February 1753.[18] While the catalogue of volumes one and two remained essentially the same, that of volume three was expanded to include a map of Attica, several antiquities found in different parts of Greece, and, subject to the approval of the subscribers, the thirty-four plates of antiquities at Pola.

Though more than half the task of measuring and drawing was said to be finished, the price of subscription (mentioned here for the first time) was not yet possible to fix, but was estimated at ten to twelve pounds per set of three volumes, depending upon the final number of plates, each costing nine pence. Most likely it was this latest state of the proposals that was printed at Venice in 1753 and "dispersed in various parts of Europe by Consul Smith."[19]

The plans for the *Antiquities of Athens*, so carefully formulated by Stuart and Revett and so widely broadcast, had no effect upon the procedure of their investigations. What they did not foresee (and indeed no one has fully realized) was that the reverse would happen, that their procedure would come to undo their plans. To do them justice, their movements were not in their control but were dictated to a great extent by the location of a Turkish garrison on the southern ridge of the Acropolis.[20]

Thus, instead of starting with the buildings on the Acropolis, which by virtue of their importance were intended for the first volume, they left them and other ruins in the southern part of the city until last and began in the northern part, where there were numerous monuments of lesser importance and of a later date (Hellenistic and Roman) and where they were relatively free to work as they pleased. This freedom, however, was a mixed blessing. The thoroughness with which they were able at the outset to examine the Tower of the Winds set a standard requiring them to devote considerably more time to the task than the eight to twelve months they had originally estimated.[21]

In the summer of 1753—when they had been in Athens for just over two years and were at last measuring and drawing the buildings on the Acropolis and the Temple of Jupiter (the Olympieion) and the Arch of Hadrian in the southwestern part of the city—political disturbances arose that made their work in this area more difficult and dangerous than ever. To make matters worse, Stuart was "provoked" to knock down the British consul, a Greek who was also their landlord, thereby causing a minor diplomatic crisis requiring both parties to present their case to the ambassador in Constantinople. Stuart departed from Athens on 20 September 1753 leaving Revett behind to continue working as best he could. This he did until January 1754 when he left to join Stuart in Salonica.[22]

Ill luck continued to pursue them. An outbreak of plague prevented them from returning to Athens to finish measuring and drawing the Propylea and parts of the Parthenon, the Arch of Hadrian, and the Temple of Jupiter. Rather than risk all the work they had accomplished, they decided to go back to England, recognizing that by so doing they would be unable to fulfill their promise to publish the Acropolis in their first volume. In May 1754 they wrote from Negrepont, probably to Sir James Porter in Constantinople, that "it was at that time their intention to publish only the Lanthorn of Demosthenes and the Tower of the Winds in the first volume and then to return to Athens to complete their admeasurements previous to any further publication."[23]

True to their word, shortly after arriving in England on 27 October 1754, they dispatched some of their finished drawings of these two buildings to James Basire to engrave as specimens to accompany new proposals that they published in January 1755.[24]

The work was to consist of four volumes, "The two first of which comprehend all the Antiquities of the City; as the third will those of the Acropolis; and the Fourth all the remains scattered in different Parts of the Athenian Territory."[25] In addition to the Lantern of Demosthenes and Tower of the Winds, the first volume was to contain "I. The Corinthian Colonnade supposed by Wheler to be the remains of the Temple of Jupiter Olympius. II. A Doric portico supposed by Wheler to be the front of a Temple dedicated to Rome and Augustus. III. A Temple of the Ionic Order supposed to have been dedicated to the Celebration of the Lesser Mysteries."[26] With these additions they had at least exhibited "specimens of the several kinds of columns in use among the ancient Greeks,"[27] and may even be said to have fulfilled one important part of their original promise, which was to supply Desgodets' "very great deficiency . . . in what regards the Doric and Ionic Orders."[28]

The hope was that the publication of these five buildings, all in the northern part of Athens, would bring enough encouragement in the way of subscription (fixed now at four guineas, two on subscribing and two on receiving the book, taken in by the authors and at White's coffee house) to enable them to return to Athens to finish their work in the southern part of the city and on the Acropolis for volumes two and three.[29]

As they already had more than three hundred promises, their prospects were excellent. Their specimen plates, which were circulated on the Continent as well as in this country, were a great success; indeed, so much so that the *Antiquities of Athens* achieved international fame for its Grecian taste, its accuracy and exactness long before it was published. Abbé Barthélemy had heard it so well spoken of in Italy that he advised Count Caylus in December 1755 to delay publication of Le Roy's book until after the English one appeared, for "if it should chance to be better than Mr. Leroi's, that lofty nation would exult. . . ."[30]

They had their measurements and drawings, money to pay for engraving them once they were worked up, ample encouragement to proceed with the work, and fame as well. What they did not have, however, was an explanatory text to accompany their plates, which was "chiefly to consist in pointing out their conformity to the Doctrine of Vitruvius and the description of Strabo, Pausanias, &c."[31] This, along with the views and bas-reliefs, was Stuart's responsibility[32]—Revett's being wholly confined to the architectural parts—and Stuart was not only notoriously dilatory but also deflected by the opportunities for quite a successful career as an architect which were presented to him at his time.[33]

Though the work involved in preparing the book for the press was not inconsiderable, it should have been fairly far advanced by 1756 and perfectly possible to publish a year or two later, before Le Roy could bring out his rival publication, *Les Ruines des plus beaux Monuments de la Grèce*, for which proposals were printed in March 1756.[34] It seems clear however that very little progress had been made since January 1755 and work only started in earnest after the appearance of Le Roy's proposals.

There must have been sufficient evidence of advance by March 1757 to convince the Society of Dilettanti to "present the Authors of the *Antiquities of Athens* the sum of Twenty Guineas for their first volume and for the further Encouragement of so great and useful a work do intend the same sum for each volume as they shall be published."[35] A year later, on 21 February 1758, Thomas Gray reported hearing that "Stuart's Attica will be out this spring."[36] In August, just when it was on the verge of completion, Le Roy's *Ruines* was published.

Stuart, as Abbé Barthélemy had predicted, found the book full of errors and was determined to triumph over it. Instead of doing so in a review in a journal, he decided to revise his text which he had been so long in writing, and on 13 January 1759 gave notice in the press that the *Antiquities of Athens* would speedily be published showing "many of the mistakes and misrepresentations of Mons. Le Roy. . . ."[37]

Revett's experience would certainly have told him that this decision was bound to delay the appearance of the book for several more years and further diminish their chances of a return to visit Greece, which he was freer and keener than Stuart to undertake and which depended for support on something to show for the first visit.[38] It was almost certainly over the "further prosecution" of the first volume (as Lesley Lewis concluded),[39] rather than the second (as Joseph Woods supposed),[40] that differences arose between Stuart and Revett, "which were terminated by [Stuart's] purchasing all Mr. Revett's property in the work, and all the materials which related to it . . . ," and continuing it "in his own way" and in his own time. Four more years elapsed before the *Antiquities of Athens* was published in January 1763.[41]

Stuart's "way" was to employ the greater part of his text to detecting and exposing Le Roy's errors, a task that he considered a righteous obligation, "advantageous to the Art" and "instructive to the Reader," for which the "the excellent Desgodetz" furnished "sufficient authority" in his book correcting the errors of such approved authors as Palladio, Serlio, and Labacco.[42] While some degree of artistic license was admissible in the views, in the architectural plates "any omission of inaccuracy . . . is censurable as it frustrates the chief End which Books of this sort propose to answer. Accuracy is the principal and almost the only merit they can have."[43]

His demolition of Le Roy is systematic and thorough, even savage at times, demonstrating firstly that Le Roy took the idea of going to Greece from their proposals, and secondly that in his haste to forestall them he did not carefully examine the monuments or faithfully depict what he saw but rather repeated the mistakes of Spon and Wheler, adding some of his own.

Stuart, until the last moment, had also been following Spon and Wheeler. But while revising his text he discovered, in a recent English translation of Thucydides, that the generally accepted text contained an error which had misled Spon and Wheler and other authors, himself included, to identify the Corinthian colonnade in the northern area of Athens as part of the remains of the Temple of Jupiter Olympius, when that temple was, in fact, to the south on the site of what was vulgarly known as the Columns of Adrian.[44]

This discovery required him to rewrite his description of the colonnade, which was to have had pride of place in the first chapter, reflecting the importance of the Olympieion as one of the four sacred edifices most celebrated for their beauty and magnificence.[45] Though it contributed to a further delay in the publication of the

Antiquities of Athens, bringing despair to subscribers and a lampoon from Hogarth, it was Stuart's most powerful weapon against Le Roy and he was not going to hesitate to use it finally to demolish him.[46]

His attack upon Le Roy for wrongly locating the Temple of Jupiter within the Corinthian stoa, and even worse for giving a reconstruction of it despite the absence of any vestiges of a temple on that site, is absolutely devastating.[47] Foolishly, however, he let the excessive strength of it drive him off his proper subject, which was the identification of the stoa (now known as the library of Hadrian), on to hasty and pompous statements regarding the "particulars" of the Olympieion which, it must be remembered, he had not carefully examined before leaving Athens, though he was in possession of the drawings made by Revett after his departure.

With the same knowing air that he so resented in Le Roy, he stated that besides their site, the stately columns of Adrian "agree in so many other particulars" with the description of the Temple of Jupiter given by the ancients that "it is not easy to conceive how any other building could ever be mistaken for it."[48] He then cited Vitruvius' description of the Temple of Jupiter at Athens as a dipteral octastyle, that is, a temple with two rows of eight columns in front and no more than seventeen on its sides. Yet Revett's measurements showed that Le Roy, guided by Spon and Wheler, was correct in describing Hadrian's columns as part of a building with two rows of twenty columns on the flanks, which, by Vitruvius rule, had to be decastyle not octastyle.[49] This opinion was generally accepted until excavations by Francis Penrose in 1886 proved it to be an exceptional octastyle, as Vitruvius said.[50]

Le Roy, replying to Stuart's criticism, first in a pamphlet, *Observations sur les Edifices* (1767)[51] and again in 1770 in the second edition of *Les Ruines*,[52] noted this discrepancy and therefore rejected Stuart's identification of Hadrian's columns as the remains of the Olympieion, though he no longer insisted that the stoa was the site of that temple. The controversy was an important one, not just because it concerned the Olympieion but, as Willey Reveley said, "on account of the discussions to which it leads, on the length and breadth of temples in general. . . ."[53]

In 1771 William Newton's English edition of Vitruvius appeared, giving Stuart a respectable way out of the corner in which Le Roy had put him. Newton, following Galiani's Latin and Italian edition of 1758 found an ampersand in the relevant passage, which had escaped Philander and all subsequent editors of Vitruvius, and which altered its meaning from "an octastyle at Athens, in the Temple of Jupiter" to "an octastyle at Athens *and* in the Olympian Temple,"[54] making the octastyle and the Olympieion different buildings. In his notes Newton discussed the implications of his translation upon the controversy between Stuart and Le Roy, concluding that Stuart, "notwithstanding the answer of Le Roy, has given sufficient reason to believe [the columns of Hadrian] are the remains of the Temple of Jupiter Olympius," but that "this temple must have had twenty columns in flank," as the disposition of the seventeen remaining ones proved, and therefore "the front must certainly have had ten columns."[55]

Stuart was able to correct his error by putting the blame on "the conjectural emendations of Philander and those who followed him," but he adamantly refused to concede even the smallest shred of veracity to Le Roy by admitting that the building had twenty columns on the flank, despite the fact that he had Revett's measured drawing confirming this. Sticking to Vitruvian rule, he insisted that, in accordance with Greek custom, there were twenty-one columns.

"From the whole of his memorandum on the subject," Willey Reveley found that Stuart "considered this rule as so general that it did not even admit of a more particular enquiry." He also found among Stuart's papers "the plan of the temple, drawn in ink with twenty columns by Mr. Revett, . . . to which Mr. Stuart has, with red chalk added a row of columns."[56] This plan, including the different profiles of the bases of the inner and outer columns drawn by Revett, was engraved and published in the second volume with an accompanying text attempting to prove geometrically that the isolated column of the northwest or back portico was not in the outer row (as its base proved it was) but "had another row of Columns standing before it."[57]

A plan and one page of text appended to a chapter on the Parthenon was scarcely adequate treatment for this celebrated Grecian temple. Stuart had, in fact, begun writing a chapter on the Olympieion but decided to suppress it, not just because it was extremely short, as Reveley concluded, but also because he had no other illustrations, for the views made by William Pars for the Society of Dilettanti were "missing according to Mr. Revett's Recollections."[58]

All of this was put right by Reveley in the third volume. A chapter on the Olympieion, without which *The Antiquities of Athens* would look ridiculous, was a priority. On 10 May 1790 application was made and granted by the Dilettanti for the loan of the now rediscovered views.[59] One of these together with Revett's plan redrawn in its original correct form and the details removed to a third plate (to which Reveley added his own drawings made on a visit to Greece in 1785) comprised the illustrations. A text was made up of the short piece left by Stuart, in which he confused matters more by suggesting that the octastyle hypaethros dedicated to Jupiter was not in Athens but in Elis, and of Reveley's descriptions of the capitals and columns.[60] Mrs. Stuart cannot have been very pleased with Reveley's revelations

James Stuart and Nicholas Revett. *The Antiquities of Athens.* Vol. 2, chapter 2, plate XVII. Caryatid from the Temple of Erechtheum. 1985.61.2692

Vol. II. Chap. II. Pl. XVII.
Fig. 1.
Fig. 2.

regarding her husband's distortion of the facts; but at least Revett was exonerated since he had given over his material and resigned his interest in the publication before the first volume appeared.

In 1764 Revett, apparently more captivated by archaeology than architecture, accepted an appointment "to take charge of the province of architecture" on an expedition to Asia Minor, financed by the Society of Dilettanti. Here was a substitute for his abandoned Grecian interest. But as chance would have it plague forced the party (himself, Dr. Richard Chandler, a classical scholar, and William Pars, the painter) to leave Smyrna for Athens, where they spent ten months completing work that Stuart and Revett had had to abandon a decade earlier, chiefly on the Acropolis.

The Grecian drawings belonging to the Society of Dilettanti were exhibited to members, of whom Stuart was one, in 1766.[61] Did he regard these drawings, which were made to the same high standard of accuracy that had been set in 1749 with Robert Wood for *The Antiquities of Athens*, as a dangerous threat to his unfinished project or as a potential blessing containing the means to complete it and to save face in the eyes of his encouragers? The latter is much more likely the case, as by now it was out of the question for him to return to Greece to obtain this material himself, without Revett's assistance.

According to the 1755 proposals the second volume was to contain the remaining monuments in the city of Athens, but whether, or when, after volume one was finally published he intended to proceed with this plan, we do not know. Evidently he was in no hurry and is not known to have given much thought to the work until after the publication of Le Roy's *Observations* in 1767 and the second edition of his *Ruines* in 1770.

At about this time the Society of Dilettanti began to think of publishing their Grecian drawings and money was advanced to Revett to prepare his material for engraving, which he was expected to pay for himself out of the profits he earned from sales of the first volume of *Ionian Antiquities* (1769). However, by his own misjudgment Revett had made a serious loss rather than a profit and was unable to afford the cost of engraving.

In 1776 the Grecian drawings still being unpublished, it was suggested that Pars' views be given to Paul Sandby to engrave at his own expense and within "a certain moderate period" and that on the same conditions Stuart be granted use of "some of the drawings which related to the work which he is now employed on."[62] The "list of Drawings, measurements and Bas Reliefs wanted by Stuart to complete the volume of the Acropolis in Athens, a part of which he has received from the Society" included views of the Erechtheum and the Parthenon, which, along with those of the Temple of Jupiter Olympius, were reported missing by Revett (probably being with Pars in Rome), the Parthenon sculpture, including "42 drawings of the Bas Relief round the cell given to Mr. Pars for publication," and thirty drawings of the Propylea, one of which was the view that had already been given to Sandby.[63]

While Sandby's request was promptly granted, Stuart's was not. On 2 March 1777 the Society ordered that Revett appear with all the drawings and a committee be appointed to "take into consideration whether Mr. Stuart is to be permitted to have any of them for his use."[64] Stuart's request, though reduced to "1 view, 10 architecture and 4 bas reliefs of the Propylea,"[65] was referred by the committee to Sir William Hamilton, who was to meet Stuart and Revett at the latter's house on 29 March. As this meeting produced no results, another was arranged on 26 April at George Stanhope's, who with Hamilton was "to take into consideration the final determination of the parties."[66]

What had to be considered was not just Revett's claim on the drawings, which the society had put at his disposal to publish for his sole benefit, but more immediately a proposal which he presented to the committee for "forming the materials intended to be published into two volumes," the second of which was to be devoted to the ruins of Greece and to contain the Propylea and the Arch of Hadrian wanted by Stuart.[67] Revett's argument was that the society's Grecian and Ionic material ought to be published in a "regular, uniform and complete" way and not be dismembered by giving views to Sandby and architectural drawings to Stuart.

In 1779, after mature consideration of the risks of publishing an entire volume at once, Revett came up with a proposal to spread the work (and the costs) over a period of time by publishing it in four numbers.[68] This "perfectly satisfied" Stuart, and Revett agreed to his request for "a plan of the Propylea to complete his General plan of the Acropolis &c. with whatever drawings are in Mr. Revett's possession that may relate to other buildings in the Acropolis."

Revett's plan almost certainly was to pass material to Stuart *after* he had published it in a "number"; to give it to Stuart first, as he and the society knew from experience, was bound to result in years of delay. Having made this concession to Stuart, who it must be remembered had no claims to the drawings, Revett was forced by his desperate financial situation to admit that without assistance from the society he could not undertake any form of publication. The society decided that the best course was to pay off Revett and retrieve the drawings.

On 27 April 1782 they decided to lend Stuart the drawings he desired on condition that "the said Mr. Stuart agree to return the same into the hands of the Secretary within twelve months from the Day when they shall be delivered to him and to publish engravings of each and every one of them in the second vol. of his work entitled Antiquities of Athens within eighteen months from the said day on which they shall be delivered by hand, or present to the Society finished proofs of all of them under Penalty of 20 guineas to be paid by the said Mr. Stuart and applied to the General Fund."[69]

They might as well have asked a pig to fly.

Stuart, who was sixty-nine years old, ill and infirm, had more than he could handle in the rebuilding of the Chapel at Greenwich Hospital. On 13 March 1785, after three years had elapsed with no sign or proofs of the second volume, the society instructed its committee of publication (of which ironically Stuart was a member) "to assist Mr. Stuart immediately and effectively towards the publication," but also to be "answerable to the Society for the Property of the Plates engraved at their expense untill the Publication of the second volume of the said Antiquities of Athens be actually effected."[70] A year later the drawings were still in Stuart's possession and not yet engraved. Although many plates and a title page were completed in 1787, the work was evidently far from finished when Stuart died on 2 February 1788.

The society renewed its earlier (13 March 1785) promise to pay for the engraving of their drawings, generously estimating that three hundred pounds would fully answer the purpose.[71] Most of the outstanding plates were given to James Newton to engrave. His brother William, who had been Stuart's clerk of the works at Greenwich, took responsibility for completing the volume. The "great confusion and disorder" in which he found Stuart's papers, with "many incomplete and several missing," delayed publication for almost two years, until January 1790.[72] Strained by overwork, Newton was unable to see the second volume of his translation of Vitruvius to press before he died in July 1790.

Newton's place was filled by Willey Reveley, who, though he had an even more difficult task, at least had the advantage of having been to Athens and the good sense to draw on Revett's expertise too. The doubts he cast upon Stuart's concern for truth and accuracy may seem out of place in *The Antiquities of Athens*, but they are nothing compared to the sarcasm he hurled at Sir William Chambers for censuring the *gusto greco* in the third edition of his *Treatise* (1791). The gist of his argument, conducted with remarkable wit, is the reasonable one that Greek architecture deserves as much attention as Roman if true excellence is to be attained, and that firsthand observation is essential if the profession is not to be too circumscribed by rules.

With the publication of the third volume in 1795 *The Antiquities of Athens* could be regarded as finished, nearly fifty years after it was conceived. The fourth volume was a different venture, a wholly commercial one by the publisher Josiah Taylor, who in c. 1809 acquired all Stuart's papers and employed the architect, scholar, and writer Joseph Woods to edit them. The result is a gathering of leftovers, including the Pola drawings, which was made very topical by the presence of a large number of plates of the Parthenon sculpture sold to the nation in 1816, the year the volume was published.

The Antiquities of Athens did not live up to expectations. The long-awaited first volume, instead of presenting examples of Greek architecture at its finest, contained insignificant buildings of the Hellenistic and Roman periods, for which it was frowned upon by Winckelmann.[73] The fault was caused, as we have seen, by the necessity of an early departure from Greece before investigations were finished and by Stuart's headstrong decision to use the first volume to put down the rival work of Le Roy, thereby greatly delaying his own work and causing him to forgo his planned return to Athens.

Whether publishing the buildings on the Acropolis in the first volume would have resulted in a revival of Greek architecture is doubtful. Nor is there any evidence that Stuart and Revett intended to promote such a revival. Their principal purpose was to add, to the existing stock of Roman examples, Greek ones as dependable as those depicted by Desgodets, and thus to enable a truer judgment of ancient architecture to be formed. E. H.

Notes

1. *Antiquities of Athens*, 1: v; 4: xxii.

2. Papers given to Joseph Woods, editor of volume four, by the Revett family in c. 1810, claimed that the design originated with Revett and Hamilton, who persuaded Stuart to join them, knowing his "temper, talents, acquirements and reputation." Woods thought it probable that the design originated with Hamilton because of the "speculative turn of [his] mind, as shown in the whole of his conduct through life," referring, presumably, to his art dealing for which he was principally known in the 1770s. *Antiquities of Athens*, 4: xxii. This was rejected by Stuart's posthumous son, Lieut. James Stuart, RN, in a memoir on his father, written in 1856. BM Add. MS 27, 576, fols. 96–97.

3. Brettingham's possible contribution deserves further exploration. He was one of several friends who received and distributed proposals sent by Stuart and Revett from Athens. BM Add. MS 6210, fols. 139–140. Woods' list of the vast quantity of Stuart papers acquired c. 1809 by the publisher Josiah Taylor includes "Letters to Stuart during his excursion, the most important are from Brettingham," *Antiquities of Athens*, 4: ii. These are presumed lost.

4. The Treaty of Aix-la-Chapelle in October 1748, ending the War of Austrian Succession, may have helped somewhat to facilitate the upsurge of interest at this date in travel to the Levant.

5. This is summarized in *Antiquities of Athens*, 4: xxiv–xxv; also D. Wiebenson, *Sources of Greek Revival Architecture* (1969), 75, but is now lost. The account given by Stuart in *Antiquities of Athens* 1: v–vi, is misleading. He purposely made the contents of his 1751 proposals read as the 1748 plan in order to prove that Le Roy, who was in Rome in 1748, got the idea of going to Athens from their proposals of that date, which were not published but were circulated in manuscript and much discussed.

6. E. Waterhouse, *Dictionary of British 18th-Century*

Painters (1981), 155–156.

7. *Antiquities of Athens*, 4: xxvii.

8. Proposals 1751, BM Add. MS 6210, fol. 96; Wiebenson 1969, 81.

9. Thomas Hollis to John Ward, 26 Feb. 1751, BM Add. MS 6210, fol. 96, and Wiebenson 1969, 76–77. The impression given by Stuart in his 1751 proposals that the voyage to Pola was an unplanned venture to employ their time usefully while waiting for a passage to Greece is not convincing. Wiebenson 1969, 80. *De Obelisco* alone was scarcely sufficient evidence of their ability to execute their proposed work to the standard they knew Wood and Dawkins would maintain.

10. Wiebenson 1969, 76–77.

11. *Antiquities of Athens* 1: v.

12. A copy was sent by Thomas Hollis to John Ward, Gresham Professor and Fellow of the Royal Society. BM Add. MS 6210, fol. 96. Wiebenson 1969, 76–82.

13. J. Spon, *Voyage d'Italie de Dalmatie, de Grèce et du Levant* (Lyons, 1678) and Sir George Wheler, *A Journey into Greece* (London, 1682).

14. It also includes a list of the finished Pola drawings, apparently only as an example of Stuart and Revett's thoroughness, with no mention of publication.

15. In January 1752 Wood and Dawkins issued proposals for publishing their own work, the *Ruins of Palmyra*—see *General Advertiser*, 16 January 1752.

16. *Antiquities of Athens*, 1: v–vi. Wiebenson 1969, 82–83.

17. These proposals remained fundamentally unchanged until their return to England. The "new" proposals sent by Matthew Brettingham junior from Rome to Thomas Hollis in Genoa in December 1752 were "effectively the same as the first," meaning, no doubt, the proposals drafted just before Stuart and Revett went to Greece, which were the first Hollis had. These new ones, as he said, were "somewhat more methodized." The seven or eight proposals listed by Wiebenson are in fact repetitions and minor variations upon four or at most five proposals, i.e., 1748, 1750–1751, 1751, September 1752, January 1755.

18. *Journal Britannique* (1753), 165–172; Wiebenson 1969, 84–85.

19. *Antiquities of Athens*, 1: v.

20. The front scene of what they thought was the Theater of Bacchus formed part of the outwork of the fortress and was directly underneath its only entrance. Hence they were only allowed to measure and dig a bit behind the scene. *Antiquities of Athens*, 2: 23. This monument is, in fact, the Roman Odeum of Herodes Atticus. The true Theater of Bacchus (Dionysus) on the southern slope of the Acropolis they mistook for the Odeum of Pericles, which had entirely disappeared. J. Landy, "Stuart and Revett: Pioneer Archaeologists," *Archaeology* 9 (December 1956), 259.

21. Not only did they undertake some excavations, they also managed to persuade a resident to pull down his house just for them to see the bas-reliefs. *Antiquities of Athens*, 1: 17. They were the first to publish the building adequately, Landy 1956, 258.

22. *Antiquities of Athens*, 4: xi; 2: 37; 3: 14.

23. Ibid., 4: xvii.

24. Wiebenson 1969, 109, no. 90. See also G. Jackson-Stops, *West Wycombe Park*, National Trust Guide Book (1981), 27, discussing the copy of the Temple of the Winds executed in 1756 in the garden for Sir Francis Dashwood (afterwards Lord Le Despenser).

25. Bodleian Library, Oxford. John Johnson Collection, J. Pros. 125.

26. Seventy plates were promised: a general view of Athens, particular views of the five monuments, 38 "architectonic prints," 25 "basso relievos." Presumably the general view was counted as two, making seventy.

27. *Antiquities of Athens*, 2: Stuart's "Advertisement."

28. Wiebenson 1969, 81.

29. The ambiguous statement in Stuart's "Advertisement," volume two, that when they returned and took subscriptions for volume one they were "uncertain whether [they] should be encouraged to proceed further with this work" can be understood to mean to "proceed" to return to Athens.

30. Abbé Barthélemy, *Travels in Italy* (1802), letter eight from Naples, p. 47. Letter ten, 20 December 1755, p. 58, reported seeing the "first proofs of the ruins of Athens. . . . They appear to be very well executed, and confirm me in my sentiments, which I imparted to you formerly." Thomas Gray to William Mason, 8 June 1756, "I rejoice to hear the Prints succeed so well & am impatient for the Work. . . ." Robert Adam, apropos the taste and accuracy of Wood's *Palmyra* and *Balbec*, which he did not like, wrote to James Adam, 1 November 1757: "we all know how much the fame of it [Stuart's proposed work] has blasted the Reputation of these Works of P——a & B——k." Quoted by Wiebenson 1969, 96, no. 28; 97, no. 29; 108, nos. 85 and 87.

31. 1755 proposals, Bodleian, John Johnson, op. cit. See also 1751 proposals, *Antiquities of Athens*, 1: v–vi, and Wiebenson 1969, 80.

32. *Antiquities of Athens*, 1: vii–viii.

33. As painter to the Society of Dilettanti he was ordered in 1763 to produce two portraits of James and Henry Dawkins. Despite repeated reminders he had done nothing by 1768 and was replaced by Reynolds. Society of Dilettanti, minutes, 1 May 1763, April 1766, January 1768. See also committee book, 17 March 1782, for reference to his "usual delay." Lesley Lewis (née Lawrence), "Stuart and Revett: Their Literary and Architectural Careers," *Journal of the Warburg and Courtauld Institutes* 11 (1938–1939), 138 ff. In September 1755 Stuart was working for the 2d marquis of Rockingham at Wentworth Woodhouse, Yorkshire; in 1757 he was making designs for Kedleston; in 1758 he was appointed surveyor of Greenwich Hospital and was employed at Hagley Park, Worcestershire, by the 1st

Lord Lyttleton and at Wimbledon by the 1st Earl Spencer.

34. Wiebenson 1969, 85–87. These appeared in full in *Année Littéraire*, March 1756, and in *Mercure de France*, April 1756, and cannot conceivably have escaped Stuart and Revett's notice.

35. Society of Dilettanti, minute book 2, March 1757.

36. Wiebenson 1969, 108, no. 89, letter from Gray to Thomas Wharton.

37. *Public Advertiser*, 13 January 1759.

38. Revett was not the only one to despair of ever seeing anything published. Robert Adam wrote from London to James in Rome, 24 July 1760, "Stuart you will see will never Publish More. Le Roy has done no justice. . . ." On 16 November 1760 James reported to his sister that even in Rome "they begin to think they are never to see the English Athens." The rumor that Stuart was correcting his own plates, commented upon by James Adam (17 September 1760), cannot be corroborated and was not the cause of the delay. See Wiebenson 1969, 109, nos. 93, 94, 95.

39. Lewis 1938–1939, 131.

40. *Antiquities of Athens*, 4: xxiv.

41. The title page is dated 1762. However, the thanks returned to Stuart by the Society of Dilettanti on 23 January 1763, minute book 3, for presenting them with a copy, the review in the *Annual Register* (1763), 6: 247–249, and the *Monthly Review* (April 1763), 302–308, all suggest publication in January 1763.

42. *Antiquities of Athens*, 1: 52.

43. Ibid., 5.

44. W. Smith, *The History of the Peloponesian Wars*, 2 vols. (London, 1753). *Antiquities of Athens*, 4: 21. Had Stuart made this important discovery earlier, one can be certain he would have drawn attention to it in his notice in the press in January 1759.

45. Vitruvius, book 3, proem.

46. Hogarth's "Five Orders of Perriwigs . . . In about Seventeen Years will be compleated, in Six Volumes folio, price Fifteen Guineas, the exact measurements of the Perriwigs of the ancients . . . Octr 15, 1761."

47. *Antiquities of Athens*, 3: 14. This information was given by Revett to the editor, Willey Reveley.

48. *Antiquities of Athens*, 1: 38.

49. Wheler 1682, 372, found it hard to determine whether the temple of Jupiter Olympius was here [on the site of the columns of Adrian] or not. The temple was "promiscuously" mentioned by Pausanias. On the evidence of 120 columns and the passage in Thucydides erroneously locating it in the northern part of the city, he was convinced that the remains were part of Hadrian's palace.

50. L. Bevier, "The Olympieion at Athens," *Papers of The American School of Classical Studies at Athens* (1882–1883), 1: 183–212. F. C. Penrose, *An Investigation of The Principals of Athenian Architecture* (London, 1888), 74–87.

51. J. D. Le Roy, *Observations sur les Edifices* (1767), 35–36.

52. J. D. Le Roy, *Les Ruines des Plus Beaux Monumens de la Grèce* (1770), 21.

53. *Antiquities of Athens*, 3: v.

54. Ibid, 2: 6. W. Newton's Vitruvius (1771), 1: 49. The earlier reading is now, in fact, accepted as correct, cf. T. Granger, *Vitruvius on Architecture* (London, 1931), 1: 171. A. Choisy, *Vitruve texte et traduction* (Paris, 1909), 2: 133, however, followed Galiani.

55. Yet Newton, following Galiani's plates, illustrated a decastyle temple with nineteen columns on the flank, for according to Vitruvian rule the number of the flank must be one less than double the front by Roman custom and one more by Greek custom, i.e., 19 or 21. See Newton's Vitruvius (1771), 1: fig. XXI.

56. *Antiquities of Athens*, 3: 14.

57. Ibid., 2: pl. XXXI.

58. Landy 1956, 239. *Antiquities of Athens*, 3: v. Society of Dilettanti, letter book 1, fol. 227. Stuart may well have had this information personally from Revett, which would explain the absence of these views from the lists of drawings he requested from the society c. 1776 to complete the second volume.

59. Society of Dilettanti, minute book 3. L. Cust, *History of the Society of Dilettanti* (1898), 102.

60. *Antiquities of Athens*, 3: ch. 2, 11.

61. They were sent back to London and exhibited at the Star and Garter in Pall Mall in February 1766. Cust 1898, 89. They were shown to the Society again when the party returned in December 1766.

62. Society of Dilettanti, letter book 1, fols. 121–123.

63. Ibid., fol. 223, c. 1776. He had received from Revett measurements of details of the portico of Minerva Pollias.

64. Minutes. Cust 1898, 97.

65. Letter book 1, fol. 233.

66. Committee book.

67. Letter book 1, fols. 225–226, March or April 1777, following Charles Greville's receipt 3 March 1777 of the views for Sandby.

68. Letter book 1, fol. 237.

69. Cust 1898, 99.

70. Minutes.

71. Cust 1898, 102. The final cost was £247 16s. Letter book 1, fol. 379.

72. Reviewed in *Gents Magazine* (February 1790), 141–142; *Monthly Review* (July 1790), 316.

73. Wiebenson 1969, 113. J. J. Winckelmann to H. Fuseli, 22 September 1764, *Briefe* (Berlin, 1952–1957), 3: 57.

82

Abraham Swan

A Collection Of Designs In Architecture, Containing New Plans and Elevations of Houses, For General Use. With A great Variety of Sections of Rooms; from a common Room, to the most grand and magnificent. Their Decorations, viz. Bases, Surbases, Architraves, Freezes, and Cornices, properly inriched with Foliages, Frets and Flowers, in a New and Grand Taste. With Margins and Mouldings for the Panelling. All large enough for Practice. (Vol. II: With Margents and Mouldings for the Penelling; with some rich Sections to a larger Scale for proportioning the Architraves, Freezes and Cornices to the Heighth of the Rooms. To Which Are Added . . .) To which are added, Curious Designs of Stone and Timber Bridges, Extending from Twenty Feet to Two Hundred and Twenty, in One Arch. Likewise some Screens and Pavilions. In Two Volumes. Each containing Sixty Plates, curiously engraved on Copper. By Abraham Swan, Architect. Vol. I. (Vol. II.)

London: printed for and sold by the author; by Mr. Meadows; Messrs. Hitch and Hawes; H. Piers and Partner, 1757

1985.61.2698–2699

Folio: 400 × 260 (15¾ × 10¼)

Pagination Vol. 1: vi, 8 pp., 60 engraved plates

Vol. 2: iv, 12 pp., 60 engraved plates

Edition First edition, first issue

Text vol. 1: pp. [i] title page (verso blank); [iii]–vi preface; [1]–8 explanation of the plates; *vol. 2*: pp. [i] title page (verso blank); [iii]–iv preface; [1]–12 explanation of the plates

Illustrations Vol. 1: 60 engraved plates signed "Ab. Swan Archt.," most engraved by James Addison but 7 by Swan himself, 2 by Francis Patton, and 9 unsigned. Most of the plates have imprints dated January 1757; 1 plate is dated in error 18 Jan. 1756, and the last 3 are dated July 1757. *Vol. 2*: 60 engraved plates, all signed as drawn by Swan, most as engraved by James Addison but with 11 engraved by "Tho. Miller" or similar (probably Tobias Miller, formerly Müller), and 8 engraved by Swan himself. Imprints dated January, July, and 28 November 1757. In a second issue of the first edition, 5 additional plates dated Jan. 1758 and numbered 61–65 were added to vol. 2 (see Harris)

Binding Recent mottled light brown quarter morocco, brown and yellow marbled boards

Provenance Some plates annotated, apparently by a contemporary architect applying the designs in practice (e.g., for "Mr. Harvys Great Room")

References Berlin Cat. 2285 (1st ed., 2d issue); Berlin (1977) OS 2285 (mixed set); ESTC t101999; Harris and Savage 867

Abraham Swan. *A Collection of Designs in Architecture.* Vol. 1, plate 58, Architrave, Frieze and Cornice. Designed and engraved by Abraham Swan. 1985.61.2698

LITTLE IS KNOWN of the author's life and career as carpenter, joiner, and self-styled architect. Perhaps he followed in his father's footsteps: an Abraham Swan was registered as apprentice at the Worshipful Company of Carpenters on 2 May 1682 (*Records* 1913, 1: 166). He may have worked at Mereworth Castle, Kent (see next entry), and he is probably "Swan the carver," who was paid in 1732–1733 "for travelling to Houghton & return on Acc[oun]t of the Dining Room chimneypiece," that is, to oversee the replacement of an earlier chimneypiece in the Marble Parlour at Houghton Hall (*Houghton Hall* 1996, 27). In about 1750, "Abraham Swan and Co. joiners" fitted the interiors at Edgcote House in Northamptonshire, and the present work includes staircase and bridge designs for the duke of Atholl at Blair Castle, Perthshire. Its preface also claims "more than thirty years application to, and experience in, the theory and practice of architecture." In 1760, when Robert Adam replaced James Paine as the architect at Kedleston in Derbyshire, he wrote that "Mr. Swan the great is dismissed and Mr. Wyatt the carpenter now fills his place" (Fleming 1962, 368). Apart from his books, which give an address in Portland Street, Cavendish Square, he is otherwise untraced. Harris and Savage point out that he was probably a Freemason and died between 1765 and 1768 (Harris and Savage 1990, 450–451).

Adam's sarcastic juxtaposition of "Mr. Swan the great" with "Mr. Wyatt the carpenter" shows he thought the former had pretensions above his station. Swan's books would have confirmed the prejudice. *The British Architect*, issued as a thirteen-shilling folio with sixty plates in 1745 and later destined to be the first architectural book published in America, was the most important of these. On its title page, Swan describes himself as a carpenter. But by 1757, when the present work appeared, he was "Abraham Swan, architect," a title he retained for two later pattern books, *Designs in Carpentry* (1759) and *Designs for Chimnies* (1765). As Yeomans has noted, the three main areas in which a carpenter might need instruction were elementary geometry, the framing of structural carpentry such as roofs and floors, and how to execute decorative details (Yeomans 1986, 17). Swan's efforts were largely directed to providing the latter; only *Designs in Carpentry* can be considered as a treatise on the technical aspects of his trade. Adam's resentment of a craftsmen who encroached on the architect's domain is entirely in character.

A Collection of Designs in Architecture was Swan's attempt to provide an inexpensive pattern book of inexpensive designs. Quantity, rather than quality, was his boast in the preface to volume two:

> I hope that whatever defects may be observed in any of them will be candidly excused, considering what a number of designs are contained in these two volumes, and that they are all of my own contriving and drawing. Such a number without faults would be next to impossible, and indeed we find with the most careful and deliberate inspection there will still remain some room for improvements; and indeed it cannot be supposed that so much time and care has been laid out on every one of these as if I had published a quarter of the number.

Volume one begins with the plans and elevations of twenty-three Palladian-style houses with between four and seven rooms on each floor. These are followed by thirty-seven plates of details, first of bases and surbases

Abraham Swan. *A Collection of Designs in Architecture.* Vol. 2, plate 46. Design for a Bridge over the River Tay. 1985.61.2699

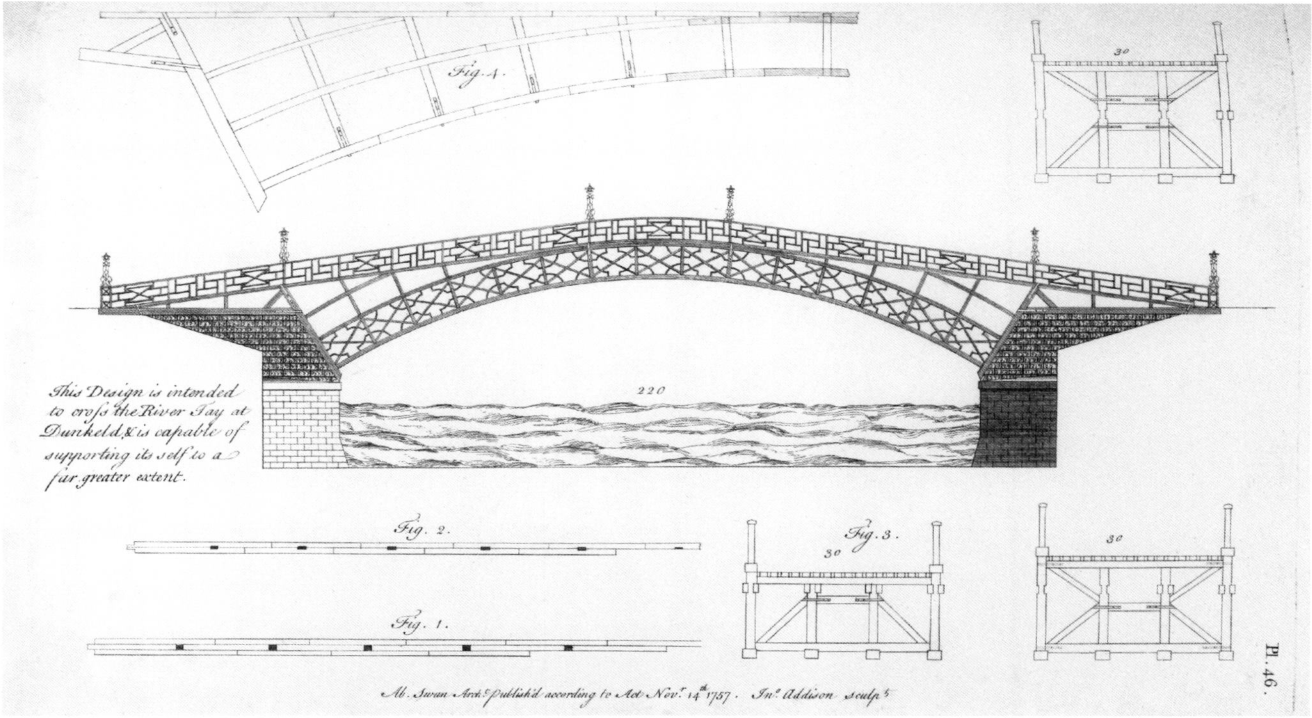

(pls. 24–43) and then of cornices (pls. 44–60). The accompanying text is minimal. The only novelty is his belief that egg and anchor ornament was a debased form of a "nuts and husks" decoration that he hoped would be reinstated in its place, since "I have known some gentlemen forbid it their houses, being displeased with its name, and supposing it to represent an unnatural mixture or combination of things which have no relation to one another" (1: v). This preference for naturalistic over artificial ornament is a distinguishing feature throughout.

In volume two Swan extends his range of house plans and elevations up to ten rooms per floor. As they grow in size, bombé room shapes appear, roof balustrades become more common, and on the last three plates in the series domes are introduced (pls. 18–20). They are followed by interior walls. At first either three or four sides of any one room are given, but, after four plates of the staircase at Blair Castle (i.e., pls. 29–32), Swan seems to have paused. As if thinking aloud, he inscribes on plate 33 his opinion that "After having so many whole sides of rooms, I suppose the centres or middles, will be sufficient to compleat any of the following designs." Accordingly, he proceeds with ten plates of panels drawn on a larger scale in the fashionable rococo style. Then come nineteen designs for Chinese-style bridges in wood (one "intended to cross the river Tay at Dunkeld") and Palladian-style bridges in stone (pls. 43–50), followed by practical advice on the "margents and mouldings" mentioned in the title page and a second series of cornices.

In January 1768 Swan offered a supplement to this work of five more plates of cornice and frieze designs for an extra shilling (pls. 61–65). No accompanying text was ever issued, but they were included in two undated reprints probably published in 1765 and 1768 (Harris and Savage 1990, nos. 869–870). Proposals for an American edition were issued with John Norman's edition of *The British Architect* (Philadelphia, 1775). This was to be paid for by subscription in monthly fascicles, but only the first number seems to have appeared, with a dedication to the merchant politician John Hancock, eight pages of text, and ten plates (copy at the New York Public Library). G. B.

Bibliography

Colvin, H. *A Biographical Dictionary of British Architects 1600–1840*. 3d ed. New Haven and London, 1995

Harris, E., and N. Savage. *British Architectural Books and Writers 1556–1785*. Cambridge, 1990

Houghton Hall: The Prime Minister, the Empress and the Heritage. Ed. A. Moore. London, 1996

Records of the Worshipful Company of Carpenters. Vol. 1: Apprentices' Entry Books 1654–1694. Ed. B. Marsh. Oxford, 1913

Yeomans, D. T. "Early Carpenters' Manuals 1592–1820." *Construction History* 2 (1986): 13–33

83

Abraham Swan

Designs In Carpentry, Containing Domes, Trussed Roofs, Flooring, Trussing of Beams, Angle-Brackets, and Cornices. By Abraham Swan

London: printed for, and sold by, the author; Mr. Meadows; and H. Piers and Partner, 1759

1985.61.2683

Quarto: 263 × 221 (10 3/8 × 7 5/16)

Pagination 8 pp., 55 engraved plates

Edition First edition

Text pp. [1] title page (verso blank); [3]–8 explanation of the plates

Illustrations 55 plates numbered 1–55, all except plates 1 and 50 with imprint line "Ab. Swan Arch[t] publish'd according to Act Nov. (8 Nov.) 1758"

Binding Contemporary sprinkled sheep

References ESTC n6536; Harris and Savage 874

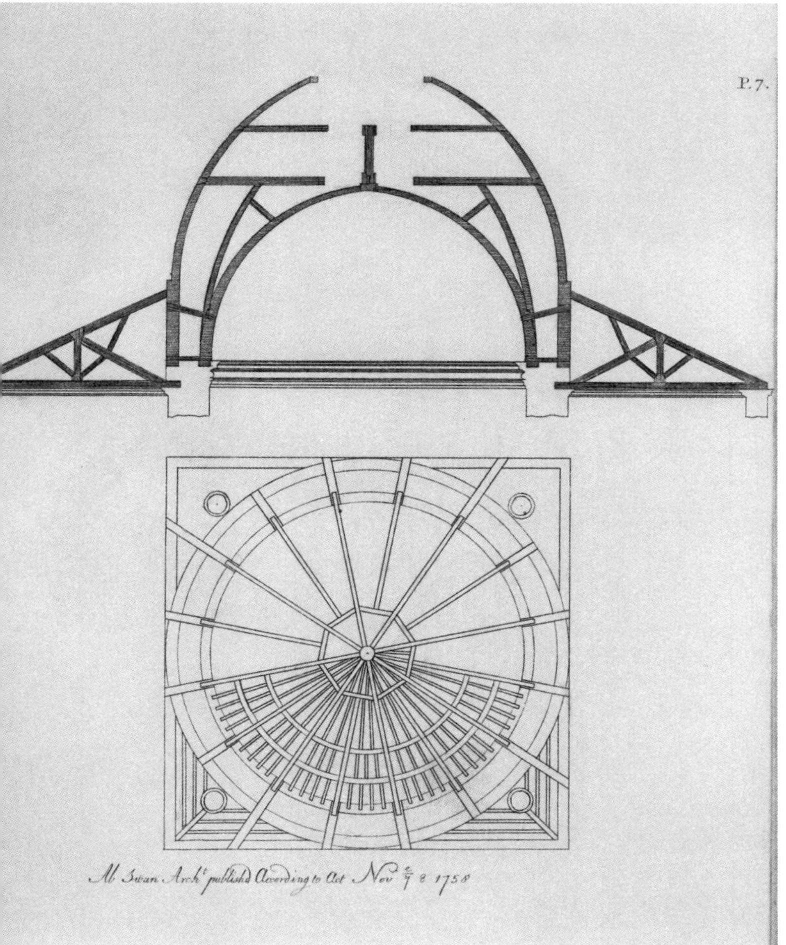

UNLIKE SWAN'S other books, *Designs in Carpentry* is a trade manual for carpenters that offers structural information rather than patterns for ornament. Its quarto format matches that of its main rival, Francis Price's *The British Carpenter*, first published as *A Treatise on Carpentry* in 1733 and in its fourth edition by 1759. The text consists only of brief captions to the plates, most of which illustrate roofs. Swan also added another nine wooden bridges to those he published in *A Collection of Designs* (1757), and the last five plates introduce practical geometry as applied to joinery and cornice design. It was not a particularly successful book, although when Robert Sayer acquired Swan's copyright he reprinted or reissued it with a new title, *The Carpenters Complete Instructor* (1768).

Most of Swan's designs are either theoretical or anonymous, but the exceptions are interesting. Two cornices on plate 53 are "traced from Palladio's wooden cuts" (i.e., from an early edition of Andrea Palladio's *Quattro Libri*). Plate 1 is a relatively elaborate engraving of the section of the dome of St. Paul's Cathedral. Swan emphasizes that he has used it "only to shew the carpentry work by which it is supported," clearly not wishing to enter the contemporary debate about the completion of Sir James Thornhill's interiors. His source was a much larger engraving by Edward Rooker after a drawing by John Gwynn, which showed the dome painted according to the designs of Gwynn's friend Samuel Wale (the original plate is credited "J. Gwyn Architecturam Delineavit. S. Wale Decorabit. Edwardus Rooker Sculpsit"). This had been published in 1755, dedicated to the prince of Wales as a "Section of S[t]. Paul's Cathedral decorated according to the original Intention of S[r]. Christopher Wren" (reproduced in *The Fourteenth Volume of the Wren Society* 1937, pl. XLV; for its exhibition by the Society of Artists, see the entry for John Woolfe and James Gandon's *Vitruvius Britannicus*, 1767–1771). Its incidental detail of the dome's structure naturally attracted Swan, who had earlier used Rooker to engrave nearly all the plates in *The British Architect* (1747). Nevertheless, carpenters probably found Swan's reversed copy of it less informative than Price's plate of the same subject, as published in *The British Carpenter*.

Plates 6 and 7 are also derived from an actual building. They give two dome sections and a plan of the rafters "at Lord Westmoreland's house in Kent," Mereworth Castle, built about 1720–1725 by Colen Campbell for John Fane, later 7th earl of Westmorland. These are not copied from Campbell's illustrations of the house in volume three of *Vitruvius Britannicus* (1725), which include a less detailed section of the whole building (pl. 38). Swan's plates of Mereworth might indicate personal involvement on the project, preceding his first known work at Houghton Hall. It is, however, also possible that Campbell's ingenious chimney design aroused his curiosity after its

Abraham Swan. *Designs in Carpentry.* Plate 7. Mereworth Castle. Section of the dome and plan of the rafters. 1985.61.2683 completion. Campbell was particularly pleased with the dome, contrasting it at some length with Palladio's at the Villa Rotonda, and unconsciously providing a better gloss on Swan's illustrations than Swan himself (see *Vitruvius Britannicus* 1715–1725, 3: 4). G. B.

Bibliography

The Fourteenth Volume of the Wren Society. Ed. Wren Society. Oxford, 1937

Harris, E., and N. Savage. *British Architectural Books and Writers 1556–1785*. Cambridge, 1990

Abraham Swan. *Designs in Carpentry*. Plate 1. St. Paul's Cathedral, London. Section of the dome. 1985.61.2683

84

William Thomas (d. 1800)

Original Designs In Architecture, By William Thomas, M.S.A. Architect and Surveyor: Consisting Of Twenty-seven Copper-Plates, in Folio; Which Contain Plans, Elevations, Sections, Cielings, and Chimney Pieces, for Villas and Town Houses; Designs for Temples, Grottos, Sepulchres, Bridges, &c. in the most approved Taste. To Which Are Prefixed, A Suitable Introduction, And a Description, explaining the Several Designs

London: printed for the author, 1783

1985.61.2702

Folio: 551 × 372 (21 11/16 × 14 7/8)

Pagination 12 pp., 27 engraved plates

Text pp. [1] title page (verso blank); [3] preface; 4–5 introduction; [6] blank; 7–10 explanation of the plates; 11–12 list of subscribers

Illustrations 27 engraved plates numbered I–XXVII, of which plates V and XIV are hand-colored in the Millard copy. All of the plates are signed by Thomas as architect, engraved by Edward Malpas (9), William Thomas (9, including 1 with Roberts), John Roberts (8, including 1 with Thomas), or T. [i.e., Tobias?] Miller (2)

Binding Contemporary half calf, marbled boards

References Berlin Cat. 2294; Berlin (1977) OS 2294; ESTC t101998; Harris and Savage 878

WILLIAM THOMAS is remembered for a handful of neoclassical buildings and for the present collection of designs, inspired by Robert and James Adam's *Works in Architecture* (issued in parts between 1773 and 1779).

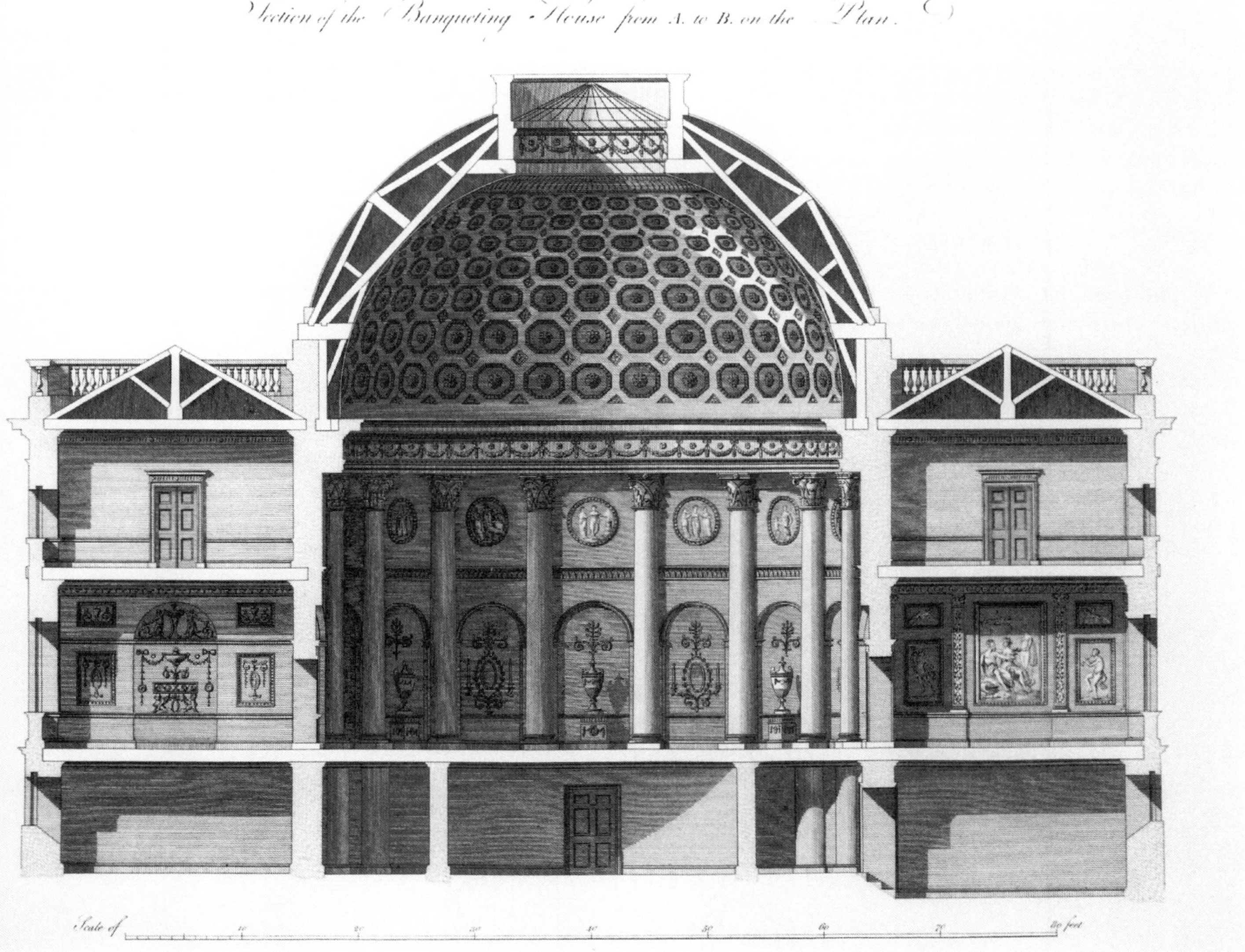
Section of the Banqueting House from A. to B. on the Plan.

William Thomas. *Original Designs in Architecture.* Plate X. "Section of the Banqueting House from A to B on the Plan." 1985.61.2702

Thomas was born in Pembrokeshire, the son of William Thomas senior (1711?–1800), and although the date of his birth is not known, it is probable that he began his career as an architect and surveyor in the late 1770s. Before 1780 he moved to London, and in this year began to prepare engravings of his designs and to exhibit his drawings at the Royal Academy. The first engravings to be completed (pls. I–XIV) show unexecuted designs for a villa, mausoleum, "Banqueting House," and "Casino," and various interior decorations, all very much in the Adam style. These plates are dated between 1780 and 1782, and it is probable that Thomas had a few copies of each printed and circulated privately as advertisements for his talents. (There is no evidence that *Original Designs* was formally issued in parts, as the Adams' work had been, although this may have been Thomas' original intention.) With plate XV comes the first mention of a patron, in this case Lord Shelburne, for whom Thomas designed a "Garden Temple," attesting to the growth of his business and reputation. Thereafter the plates consist of a mixture of executed designs—the Surrey Chapel in Southwark (destroyed by bombing in 1940), Brownslade House in Pembrokeshire, and probably the offices at Stackpole Court, also in Pembrokeshire—and speculative designs for various patrons. Among the latter are his "Design for the Garden Front of the West Wing of Stackpole Court . . ." (pl. XVIII) and designs for a "Hunting Seat" (pls. XXIV, XXV). The series of engravings ends with a group of ornamental mirror frames and a sideboard, all executed for various patrons. At least two of his designs had also been exhibited at the Royal Academy.

Original Designs was completed and issued in 1783, with a brief preface and introduction describing the architect's philosophy. Here Thomas says that "Architecture, properly defined, is partly an Art, and partly a Science: It is not founded wholly on a System of Problems and Deductions, but requires a peculiar Turn of Mind; and as it thus depends in a great measure on the Imagination, the Object will continually admit of farther Appropriation to its important Ends, so that it may be enlarged on *ad infinitum*" (p. 3). It is, he says, his belief in this tenet, his love of the subject, and "the urgent Importunity of several respectable Friends, rather than any motives of a pecuniary Nature" that inspired him to publish these designs, "the Intent of which is to present such a Variety of Subjects as, by an Adherence to Simplicity of Design . . . may contribute to render Convenience compatible with Permanence, and Elegance with Oeconomy" (p. 3). After a breakneck history of architecture, Thomas concludes by commenting that "a certain *Movement* in the design . . . [is] required to produce the Sensation which arises in the Mind, from the view of a beautiful Building," this beauty being derived from "the Assemblage of the Parts, the Agreeableness of the Modification, which regulate the Dimensions of the Parts of a Building, with regard to themselves and to the Whole" (p. 5). "In Conclusion," he says, "it appears that the Orders Alone are determined by the fixed Rules of Architecture; the Art of Designing is scarcely to be reduced to any fixed Precepts; as the Knowledge of what Part any Arch or Column may have, in producing the general Effect . . . has never yet been demonstrated by any invariable Geometrical Rules, but still remains a *Desideratum*: Genius considers it in *Theory*; in Practice it can only be the Fruit of Judgment, matured by Habit and constant Application" (p. 5).

Thomas' theories, and the innate ability that he regarded as vital, led his book to become a moderate success. Some 175 subscribers are listed on pages 11 and 12, including a number of noble patrons and many of the leading architects of the day (Robert Adam, William Chambers, S. P. Cockerell, Dance, Henry Holland, Marquand, Mylne, James Stuart, James Wyatt, and others). Some of the plates, particularly the earlier examples, were engraved by Thomas himself and show considerable skill in the technique. He also employed three of the same engravers who had worked on the Adam brothers' *Works in Architecture*—Tobias Miller, John Roberts, and Edward Malpas—with similarly fine results. The work no doubt played a part in encouraging later commissions, and between 1783 and 1799 Thomas was patronized by the duke of Clarence, Sir Richard Arkwright, and Sir John Danvers. Between 1786 and 1789 he was responsible for remodeling Grosvenor House in the Adam manner. Throughout this period his business was clearly successful, and in 1793 he took on Thomas Downes Wilmot Dearn (1777–1853) as an apprentice (in 1806 Dearn described himself as "Architect To His Royal Highness The Duke of Clarence," thus assuming a title formerly held by his teacher). Thomas' architectural drawings continued to be exhibited at the Royal Academy until 1799, when what was probably his last project, "Plans and elevations of a naval obelisk, intended to be erected on Portsdown Hill, near Portsmouth," was shown. He died on 25 October 1800, in the same year as his father, and his library and drawings were sold at auction in February of the following year. P. W. N.

85

John Vardy (1718–1765)

Some Designs Of M[r]. Inigo Jones and M[r]. W[m]. Kent. Published by John Vardy according to Act of Parliam[t]

[London]: John Vardy, 1744

1985.61.2731

Folio: 410 × 257 (16 7/16 × 10 1/8)

Pagination Etched and engraved title plate, [55] engraved plates

Edition First edition

John Vardy. *Some Designs of Mr. Inigo Jones and Mr. Wm. Kent.* Plate 4. 1985.61.2731

Illustrations The engraved title is set within an etched ornamental cartouche designed by William Kent. An engraved list of plates extends over 2 more unnumbered plates and is followed by plates 1–53, all full-page except for 2 smaller prints making up plate 25. All except plate 33 (unsigned) are signed by Vardy as draftsman and engraver/etcher, plates 1–17 being based on designs attributed to Inigo Jones and the remainder on designs by William Kent

Binding Contemporary mottled calf, rebacked

References Berlin Cat. 2279; Berlin (1977) OS 2279; ESTC t116216; Harris and Savage 881

Almost nothing is known of John Vardy's early life; he was born in Durham in February 1718, the son of a laborer, but made his career in London. He is remembered chiefly as the architect of Spencer House, Green Park, built for the 1st Earl Spencer between 1756 and 1765. This reveals him as a faithful follower of William

John Vardy. *Some Designs of Mr. Inigo Jones and Mr. Wm. Kent.* Plate 27. 1985.61.2731

Kent. Kent was his senior colleague in the Office of Works, and this was the focus of Vardy's career. He began in May 1736 as clerk of works at the Queen's House, Greenwich, moving in 1745 to Hampton Court; in 1746 to Whitehall, Westminster, and St. James'; and in 1754 to Kensington. From 1756 he served, in addition, as clerk of works at Chelsea Hospital. He died at the age of forty-seven in May 1765.

As clerk of works to Whitehall, he was placed in charge, together with William Robinson, of the building of the Horse Guards, after Kent's death in 1748. Between 1751 and 1753 Vardy published plans and elevations of this. But he had long before established his association with Kent, engraving plans and elevations of Esher, his pulpit at York, and then, in 1744, publishing *Some Designs of Mr. Inigo Jones and Mr. Wm. Kent.* This followed hard on the second edition of Isaac Ware's *Designs of Inigo Jones* of 1743. Vardy's book is a wonderfully lively compilation, with a title page designed by Kent, followed by a table of contents and fifty-three plates (though only fifty are called for in the table of contents), mostly drawn and engraved by Vardy. The first seventeen plates are devoted to designs by Inigo Jones—or rather purported designs by Jones—twelve of them for chimneypieces (drawings for six of which are in the Burlington-Devonshire Collection). The chimneypieces for Northumberland House (pl. 9) and Wimborne St. Giles (pl. 16) are now considered no more than attributions, the former being credited to Webb. Kent's designs are mainly for decorative features and furnishings, plate covers, urns and candlesticks, an epergne and a standish, chair and tables, an organ case and a pulpit, but also small garden buildings, such as Merlin's Cave at Richmond, and the screens in the Gothic style that Kent erected in Westminster Hall, for the Court of King's Bench, in 1739, and at Gloucester Cathedral, in 1741. The last two plates illustrate details of the Royal Barge. Kent's inventiveness, range, and flexibility are marvelously described. R. M.

Bibliography

Harris, E., and N. Savage. *British Architectural Books and Writers 1556–1785*. Cambridge, 1990

White, R. "John Vardy, 1718–65. Palladian into Rococo." In *The Architectural Outsiders*. Ed. R. Brown. London, 1985: 63–81

John Vardy. *Some Designs of Mr. Inigo Jones and Mr. Wm. Kent.* Plate 48. "The Court of King's Bench in Westminster Hall." 1985.61.2731

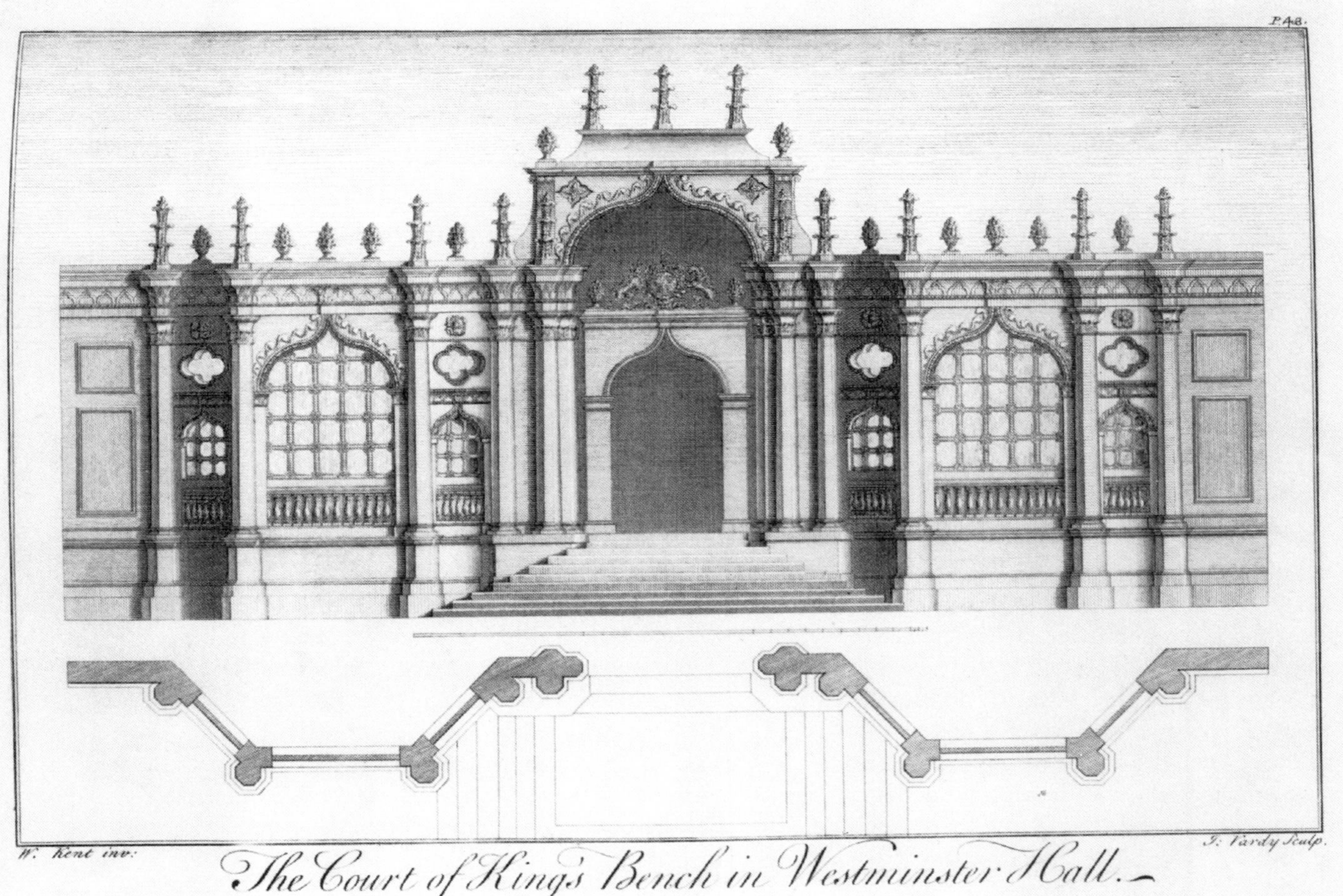

86

Marcus Vitruvius Pollio

The Civil Architecture of Vitruvius. Comprising Those Books Of The Author Which Relate To The Public and Private Edifices of the Ancients. Translated by William Wilkins . . . With An Introduction, Containing An Historical View Of The Rise And Progress Of Architecture Amongst The Greeks

London: printed by Thomas Davison, for Longman, Hurst, Rees, Orme, and Brown, 1812 [i.e., 1813–1817?]

1983.49.144–145

Large quarto: 351 × 272 (13 7/8 × 10 3/4)

Pagination [8], lxxvi, 282, [2] pp., [41] engraved plates

Edition First edition

Text pp. [1] title page (verso blank); [3–4] dedication, dated 31 Dec. 1812; [5–7] preface "Advertisement"; [8] errata; [i]–lxxvi introduction; [1]–29 section 1; [30] blank; [31]–52 explanation of the plates, section 1; [53]–93 section 2; [94] blank; [95]–120 explanation of the plates, section 2; [121]–172 section 3; [173]–196 explanation of the plates, section 3; [197]–236 section 4; [237]–260 explanation of the plates, section 4; [261]–282 glossary; [283] blank; [284] printer's imprint

Illustrations 41 engraved plates numbered 1–14, 1–13, 1–9, and 1–5 within sections 1–4. All are signed by Wilson Lowry as engraver except 4 by S. Porter, with imprints from February 1813 to 1817

Binding Bound as 2 vols. Contemporary three-quarter green morocco, green and pink marbled boards, spines gilt in neoclassical style, red morocco labels

Provenance Nineteenth-century engraved armorial bookplates of George Hutton Wilkinson, Harperley Park, County Durham

References Cicognara 744; Fowler 429

R. W. Liscombe's biography of William Wilkins, which includes a detailed study of this work, reveals that Longman and Co. commissioned *The Civil Architecture of Vitruvius* on 27 June 1808, and that although it is dated 1812 on the title page, with a dedication dated 31 December the same year, even the first part was actually published later (Liscombe 1980, 255). According to the Longman Archive at Reading University library, part one was issued on 9 June 1813. This probably consisted of the title page, dedication, Lord Aberdeen's introduction, and the first section of the translation, with the accompanying plates. These last have credit lines dated 1813, usually 25 February, whereas most of the plates to sections two through four are dated 1814 (sometimes 25 February 1814, altered from 1813), and two as late as 1817 (section 3, pl. 2; section 4, pl. 1). All this accords with the publisher's record that "Part II" was entered at Stationer's Hall on 10 September 1817, but whether even this signaled completion of the work remains in doubt. The text to part two was issued before the illustrations, as Leopoldo Cicognara's note reveals ("Non sono di quest'opera pubblicate che due sezioni, con 14 tavole della maggior nitidezza ed eleganza nella prima, e non ancora le tavole, ma il solo testo nella seconda"). A payment for engraving the plates was made as late as 14 January 1818 (£600 to Wilson Lowry, of which Wilkins paid a third), and notices of the finished book did not appear in the *Edinburgh* and *Quarterly* reviews until the following year (1: 507; 21: 25–40, respectively).

It is a pity Cicognara could not comment on the finished work, for he clearly enjoyed listing his great collection of Vitruvius editions, and described William Newton's earlier complete translation, the first into English (1771–1791), as an "opera prodotta con tutto il lusso, e l'eleganze delle edizioni moderne Inglesi" (Cicognara, no. 736). Wilkins' abridgment deserved similar praise, the clarity of its text and illustrations demonstrating the heights to which British book production rose shortly before the machine-press period. It also answered Cicognara's criticism of the last major edition, J. G. Schneider's immensely erudite but unillustrated recension of 1807–1808, which was not intended for architects, "che bramano giugnere diritto allo scopo" (Cicognara, no. 743). The present work was equally scholarly, but was written by an architect with contemporary architecture very much in mind.

Archaeological tours of ancient Greece had already led to a new interest in Vitruvius in Britain and across Europe, some four centuries after Renaissance scholars began studying him in the context of ancient Rome. Wilkins' edition was a product of this revived interest. He confined himself to a translation of books three through six, that is, those most concerned with building design rather than materials, inventions, etc., and omitted the short introductions to each. In this way Wilkins became the first editor to focus exclusively on Vitruvius in his role as historian of Greek architecture. By comparing the text with surviving remains, he hoped to disseminate a better understanding of both, and consolidate his position as a leading British protagonist of the Greek Revival. During the work's long gestation, he remodeled two country houses in this style (Osberton House and Grange Park) and designed two colleges (Haileybury and Downing), besides accepting other commissions that sometimes led him into the less congenial but more fashionable Tudor Gothic mode. Lasting fame was secured later, for the National Gallery in Trafalgar Square (1834–1838).

Wilkins was the eldest son of an architect, also called William (1751–1815). Even as a mathematics undergrad-

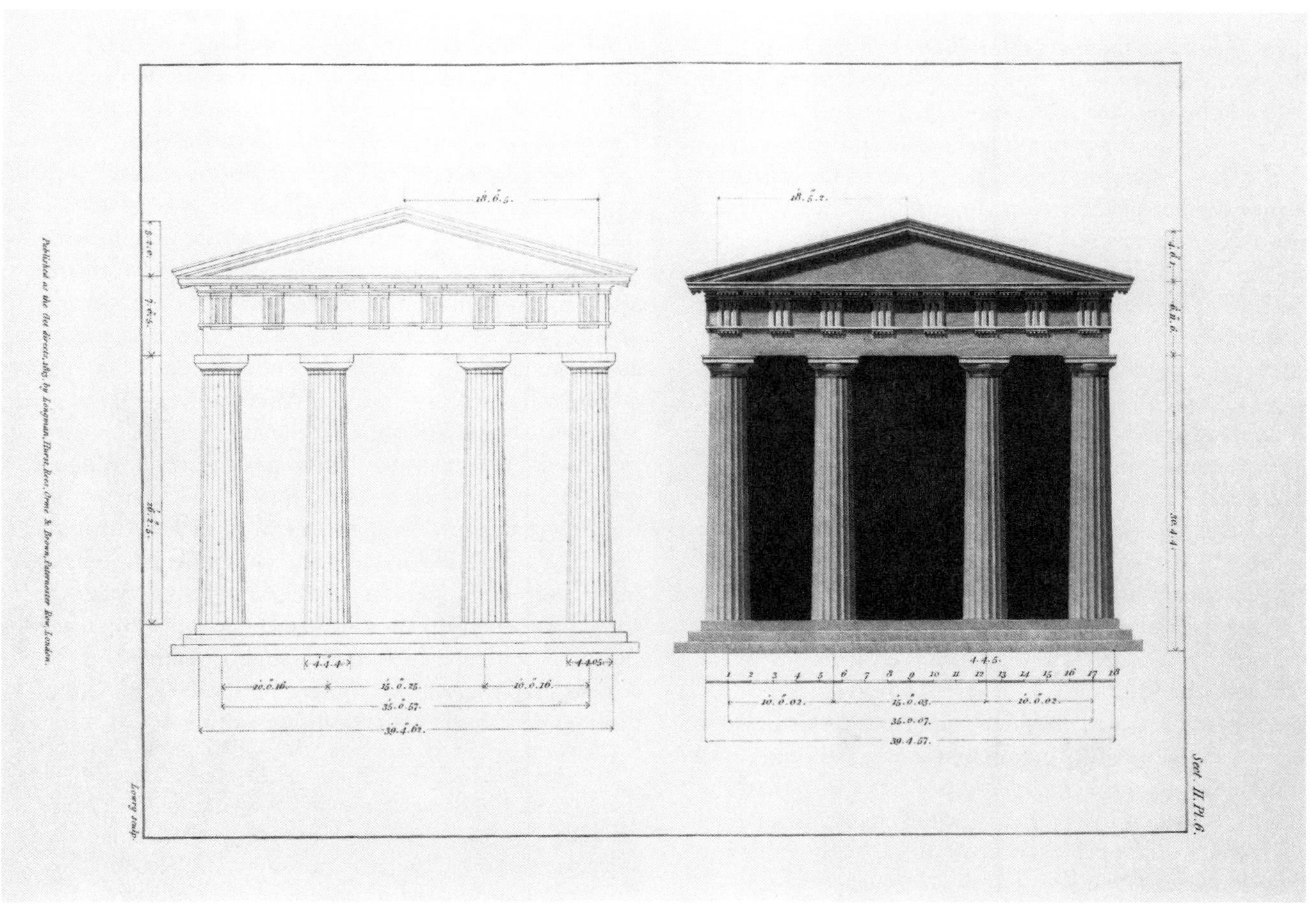

Marcus Vitruvius Pollio. *The Civil Architecture of Vitruvius.* Section 2, plate 6. A parallel between the tetrastyle monotriglyph front of Vitruvius, and a tetrastyle front, having the proportions of the gate of the Agora at Athens. 1983.49.144

uate at Cambridge, he spent a part of his time taking measured drawings of King's College Chapel and preparing architectural views for exhibition at the Royal Academy. After graduating, he was awarded a traveling scholarship and spent four years in Greece, Asia Minor, and Italy, one result of which was his first book, *The Antiquities of Magna Graecia* (1807), written while he was establishing his professional practice in Cambridge. The subject of this expensive folio is the form of the Greek temple, as revealed by examples remaining at Syracuse, Girgenti, Selinus, Segesta, and Paestum. It is easy to see the germ of the present work in it, for Wilkins uses many of his observations to diminish the credibility of Vitruvius, who, as he notes at the beginning of the introduction, "has undertaken to explain the rules which the Ancients followed in rearing their various edifices," but from whom "it appears that the principles, by which the Romans were guided in constructing temples . . . will by no means generally apply, when referred to the temples of the Grecians" (*Antiquities* 1807, [i]–ii). His agreement the following year to produce a critical edition was therefore a natural step.

In his advertisement, Wilkins justifies his effort as the first to recognize that the architecture of Vitruvius must be compared to Greek, rather than Roman, remains; and the first translation to be based on the authority of early manuscripts rather than printed editions. As for the latter claim, he never identifies the manuscripts he used, but at one point states he has compared the readings of five (p. 9n). The British Museum's Harleian collection alone contained this many, including the oldest and most important (Harleian, no. 2767), and it is significant that the great philologist T. H. Horne was cataloguing the collection at precisely the same time (1808–1812). Horne's new and more scientific approach to the study of early manuscripts might have appealed to Wilkins. The museum also possessed a tenth- or eleventh-century text in the Cotton collection, and Lord Arundel's fifteenth-century version was at the Royal Society, so Wilkins need not have gone beyond London to do his research. Had he done so, Sir Henry Wotton's copy was available at Eton and Archbishop Laud's in St. John's College, Oxford.

Armed with his new readings, Wilkins provides a largely uncluttered translation of each book, although some of his most important interpretations, such as that for *scamilli impares*—wedge-shaped plinths of various sizes, used to make stylobates rise slightly in the middle—are given in footnotes (see 1: 21–22). His comparison of Vitruvius with Greek remains is left to the two series of plates and their accompanying explanations. It is here that his academic training, archaeological fieldwork, and practical experience combine to greatest effect. Many of the plates present elevations, details, etc., according to Vitruvius, along with or immediately followed by the same elements based on archaeological evidence. This comparative technique is further refined by the use of shading to add substance to the Vitruvian versions, whereas their companions are only engraved in line—a subtle reversal that gives more concrete expression to Vitruvius than to the monuments themselves. Even shading, however, hardly relieves the strict purity of Lowry's precise engravings.

There is no doubt that due to the attention he and other Grecophiles had given to public architecture, Wilkins was able to give an unprecedentedly learned and coherent explanation of books three through five of *De architectura*. Book six was more of a challenge, because he felt obliged to illustrate a Greek private house while having little evidence on which to base it. He was forced to work backwards, so to speak, from a reconstruction of the Roman equivalent, and then append a final plate, the "Supposed ichnography of the Palace of the Odyssey." This last is a brave attempt to match Vitruvius with Homer's description of the Palace of Ulysses, supposedly justified because "although, in the interval between the age of Homer and the date of the houses described by Vitruvius, some change in manners might have taken place, yet they must at that time have been so far established as to render the supposition of any important revolution inadmissible" (pp. 249–250). The plan is in fact a result of the sort of ingenious but unwarranted speculation Wilkins would have been quick to condemn in other editors, being partly based on how far away a cry might be heard, or a sneeze might echo, or how many suitors could fit into one room (see pp. 248–260 and section 4, pl. 5). However, it must have passed muster with Wilkins' friend and collaborator Lord Aberdeen, because they had been in correspondence about this and other parts of the translation since at least 1809; and a large part of Aberdeen's anonymous introduction is concerned with a literary evocation of the same subject.

George Hamilton Gordon, 4th earl of Aberdeen, was another, slightly younger, Cambridge graduate and Grecophile. Mainly remembered as a politician, he also founded the Athenian Society in 1805 and became president of the Society of Antiquaries in 1812. He wrote little on architecture besides the present treatise and the preface and notes to G. D. Whittington's *Historical Survey of the Ecclesiastical Antiquities of France* (1809), but his deep interest in the subject was well known, and his introduction to *The Civil Architecture* was "selected from materials for a much more extensive work, which the author has wanted leisure to arrange and complete" (advertisement). It is a substantial essay. Correspondence with Wilkins, written while Wilkins was redecorating Aberdeen's London house, shows a close cooperation between the two, although the revisions to a surviving set of the printed proofs are apparently all in Aberdeen's hand (see Paul Breman's sale catalogue *Vitruviana*, cat. 167, Oct. 1995). His theme is described by the essay's later title, *An Inquiry into the Principles of Beauty in Grecian Architecture; with an Historical View of the Rise and Progress of the Art in Greece*. It begins with a rejection of Edmund Burke's aesthetic theory, and ends with a discussion of the invention of arch construction, which Aberdeen dates to the time of Alexander the Great or after, and laments because it led to "a greater corruption of style, and a more truly vitiated taste, than would probably have been witnessed had it never existed" (p. lxxvi).

The influence of Aberdeen's essay was at least as great as Wilkins' translation and commentary. The abovementioned title was attached to a separate, considerably revised edition of it published by John Murray in 1822, the first to acknowledge Aberdeen as author. Around the same time, Wilkins sold the copyright and remaining copies of *The Civil Architecture* to John Weale. Weale reports this in his advertisement to a popular edition of Aberdeen's essay that he published in 1860. The advertisement gives clues to the publication history of both works, and is worth quoting in full:

> Thirty-five years ago I purchased of the late William Wilkins, Esq., the copyright and copies of his translation of the four books of Vitruvius's Civil Architecture, to which is attached an Inquiry into the Principles of Beauty in Grecian Architecture, written for this work by the Right Hon. the Earl of Aberdeen. This introduction was printed and published separately through another publisher, and although this separate publication was at that time injurious to my interest, yet I did not complain, knowing the great value of the Inquiry to the public as a work of art, and its issue being made in a convenient form for the use of those admiring classic art.
>
> The publication of this separate inquiry being seven shillings, much too high in price for purchase by the numerous students desirous of the study of it, I have been induced to add it to my series in a shilling volume, first apprising the noble author of my intention of doing so, and asking for any suggestion his Lordship might be disposed to make; but receiving no reply, it is presumed that none can be made; and as I have had it carefully read in its passing through the press, it is anticipated that it will be found correct, and that it will moreover, from its very convenient size and price, be well received by all admirers of Grecian architecture.

What Weale is doing, of course, is excusing himself for breaching Murray's copyright on Aberdeen's revised version by politely claiming tit-for-tat. Weale probably knew that by 1860, the year of Aberdeen's death, he was too ill to want to undertake a further revision. His note that he applied for one, like the note on his careful proofreading, is merely an attempt to distance himself from less scrupulous pirates.

As a result of Weale's decision to reprint the *Inquiry*, it became one of the standard works available to architectural students, and even reappeared as the introduction to an undated edition of Joseph Gwilt's translation of Vitruvius, published by Crosby, Lockwood & Co. in about 1893. This fate would have pleased neither Aberdeen nor Wilkins. The first edition of Gwilt's Vitruvius, dated 1826, had superseded their own in most architects' offices simply because it was complete and relatively cheap—all the more irritating because Gwilt refused to follow Wilkins' text, or scarcely even to mention it. Gwilt's imminent appearance on the market was probably what prompted Wilkins (and/or Longman and Co.) to sell *The Civil Architecture* to Weale. Or perhaps Weale made a preemptive purchase to avoid competition, since he and Priestley were the publishers of the new translation. They were then in the position of owning Gwilt's only possible rival and, not surprisingly, chose not to reprint it.

Despite the fact that he had lost control of the copyright, there is evidence that Wilkins was unhappy to leave the field entirely to Gwilt, who became one of his most vociferous critics in the following decade. In 1833, Wilkins' friend T. L. Donaldson published a book on the design of ancient doorways which included a translation of Vitruvius' chapter on the subject from book four. Donaldson frequently quotes from an essay by Wilkins "On certain passages in the fourth and fifth books of the Architecture of Vitruvius," supposedly published in the third number of the Cambridge journal *The Philological Museum* (see *A Collection of the Most Approved Examples of Doorways, from Ancient Buildings in Greece and Italy* 1833, 19n, passim). However, only two volumes of *The Philological Museum*, for 1832 and 1833, are usually recorded. As the article is not included in Wilkins' *Prolusiones architectonicae* (1837), nor in Liscombe's bibliography, it seems likely that Donaldson was using an unpublished draft, now perhaps lost along with most of his other papers. Its existence adds credence to the idea that Wilkins was seriously intent on producing a revised version of at least part of *The Civil Architecture*—an intention otherwise known only from an advertisement that appeared in the *Architectural Magazine* for 1834, stating that he was preparing a new edition of two of the "principal" books (Liscombe 1980, 255–256).

Both projects indicate how important his work on Vitruvius was to Wilkins. Admittedly, he had published an angry letter the previous year declaring that Vitruvius was "A man of moderate qualifications, envious and jealous of his contemporaries, vain and a plagiarist"; and that "It would have been better for modern architecture that the work of Vitruvius had never reached us; the errors it has propagated are numerous, and so rooted, that it will require the greatest efforts to eradicate them" (*Athenaeum*, 16 February 1833). This, however, is not the only case of an editor temporarily wishing his text had never existed. Two weeks later he was in a more sober mood, writing that "Far from propagating the errors of Vitruvius, the aim of my translation is to separate them from such parts of his system as are in conformity with Grecian principles" (*Athenaeum*, 3 March 1833). No second edition ever appeared, but the footnotes and digressions on Vitruvius that litter his later books act as constant reminders that the present work only represented one phase in his long pursuit of this aim. G. B.

Bibliography

Colvin, H. *A Biographical Dictionary of British Architects 1600–1840*. 3d ed. New Haven and London, 1995

Liscombe, R. W. *William Wilkins 1778–1839*. Cambridge, 1980

87

Isaac Ware (1704–1766)

A Complete Body Of Architecture. Adorned With Plans and Elevations, From Original Designs. By Isaac Ware . . . In which are interspersed Some Designs of Inigo Jones, never before published

London: printed for T. Osborne and J. Shipton; J. Hodges; L. Davis; J. Ward; and R. Baldwin, 1756 [i.e., 1755–1757]

1985.61.2752

Folio: 440 × 272 (17¼ × 10¾)

Pagination [xviii], 748 [i.e., 754], [4] pp., engraved frontispiece, [114] engraved plates (14 folding)

(*Note*: 3 unnumbered leaves follow pp. 96, 116, and 120)

Edition First edition

Text pp. [i] title page, printed in red and black (verso blank); [iii–vii] preface; [viii–x] table of plates, errata; [xi–xvii] table of contents; [xviii] blank; [1]–748 text, books 1–10; [749–752] index

Illustrations In addition to the allegorical frontispiece by Henry Roberts after Samuel Wale, and a title-page vignette of the Pantheon and headpiece to the preface also engraved by Roberts, there are 114 engraved plates, irregularly numbered both in the "Table of Plates" and on the plates themselves. The last numbered plate in the Millard copy is 113; in other copies, the 9 plates that follow it are numbered 114–122 (see Fowler). The plates are engraved by Henry Roberts (23), P. Fourdrinier (14), William Proud (12), J. Couse (9), Isaac Ware (9), [Samuel?] Boyce (8), [Charles] Grignion (4), R. Benning (3), Butler Clowes (3), James Noval (3), [George] Edwards with [Matthias] Darly (2), J. Mynde (2), Francis Patton (2), Benjamin Cole (1), J. Hill (1), and G. L. Smith (1)

Binding Recent half calf, marbled boards. Uncut. With page references added to the "Table of Plates" in a contemporary hand

References Berlin Cat. 2283; Berlin (1977) os 2283; Fowler 436; Harris 906

Isaac Ware. *A Complete Body of Architecture.* Frontispiece. 1985.61.2752

A Complete Body of Architecture was issued in eighty parts from 29 November 1755 to 3 September 1757. Samuel Wale's frontispiece was issued with the first part, and its allegorical transparency must have reassured those subscribers for whom architecture was a new subject. Athena holds up a tablet illustrating the orders for a novice who leans on his set square, flanked by Geometry and Masonry. The background to the site indicates he is part of the fifth great age of building; the previous four appear behind him as a Palladian house, a Roman amphitheater, a Greek temple, and an Egyptian pyramid. The other plate issued in the first number (pl. 1) was similarly straightforward, an elevation and plan illustrating some technical terms; the accompanying three sheets of letterpress (pp. 1–12) were also confined to definitions. This, clearly, was to be a beginner's guide to the art and science of architecture.

Many of Ware's contemporaries would have known as much just by reading the title. A similar work on a different subject, *A Complete Body of Husbandry*, had been appearing in weekly numbers, courtesy of the same publishers, since June of the same year. It was advertised as being "from the original papers of the late Thomas Hale, Esq." Nothing appears to be known of Hale, who may have been a pure fiction created to conceal the true origin of the *Husbandry* text. By comparison, Isaac Ware's name was a familiar one, Ware being not only "Of His Majesty's Board of Works," as the title page notes, but also editor of *Designs of Inigo Jones and Others* [1731]; *Plans . . . of Houghton* (1735); *The Four Books of Architecture of Andrea Palladio* (1738); and, most recently,

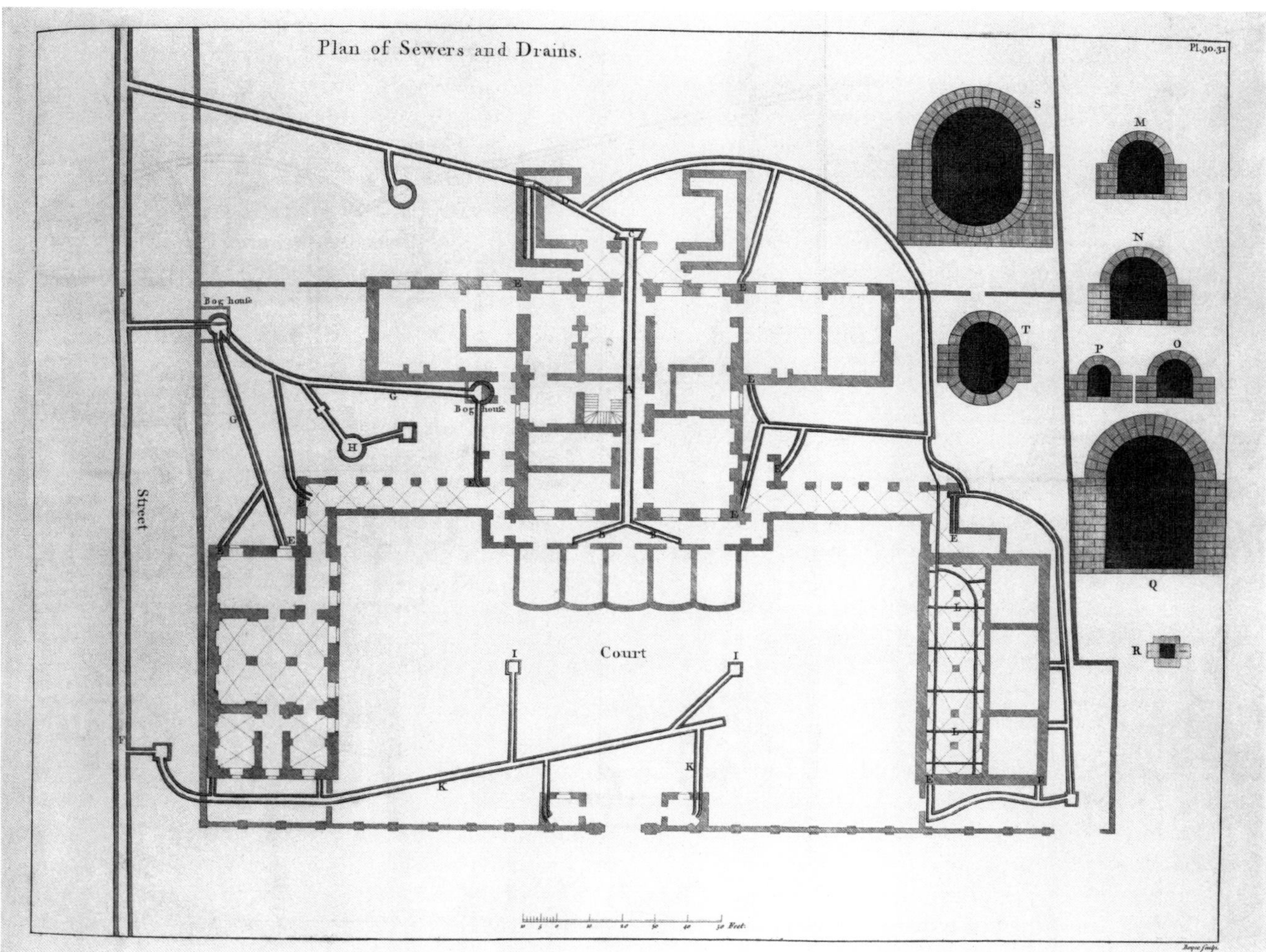

Isaac Ware. *A Complete Body of Architecture.* Plate 30/31. Plan of sewers and drains. 1985.61.2752

The Practice of Perspective, from the Original Italian of Lorenzo Sirigatti (1756). His association with the late Lord Burlington and his followers would have been well-known in architectural circles, as would his prominence in the influential group of artists called the St. Martin's Lane Academy. He was also an architect in his own right, and had recently designed and built for himself Westbourne House in London, later to be occupied by another architect, S. P. Cockerell. All in all, his sudden decision, at around fifty, to provide text and drawings for a work intended for the lower end of the market raises the suspicion that he was inspired more by financial need than pedagogical zeal. But if so, his achievement in bringing such a project to completion within two years is all the more remarkable, especially as it has far more originality than such works typically possessed; and for historians it will always remain "a massive work of 748 folio pages, providing a comprehensive statement of Georgian architectural theory and practice" (Colvin 1978, 865).

Like Vitruvius and Alberti before him, Ware arranged his treatise in ten books. Having defined the most commonly used architectural terms, he devotes the rest of book one to a discussion of materials. Book two is divided into five sections: the first on location; the second on the functional parts of a building; and the third, fourth, and fifth on the orders. Book three begins the practical advice on house construction. Books four, five, and six deal with doors, windows, and interior ornament, book seven with exterior ornament and garden buildings, book eight with bridges. Book nine consists of an interesting return to what Ware calls "the construction of elevations upon the true principles of architecture," presented as if in response to those who found the precepts earlier in the treatise too hard to apply. It is in the nature of an appendix to the whole, and allows Ware to write cuttingly of modern practices. Book ten is a brief introduction to mathematics and mensuration, left to the end to avoid "the tediousness and disgust that must have arisen to many from giving courses of those several sciences in the first sheets of our publication" (preface).

Throughout the book, Ware takes every opportunity to reiterate his architectural principles. As Wolfgang Herrmann has noted, these may be reduced to a notion of "classical freedom" that significantly differs from Claude Perrault's antiacademic stance, even though large sections of the *Complete Body* are little more than paraphrases of the latter's *Ordonnance des Cinq Especes de Colonnes* of 1683 (English trans. 1708). Others are the product of a close reading of Marc-Antoine Laugier's revolutionary *Essai sur l'architecture* of 1753 (English trans. 1755). Ware's most reiterated view is that Vitruvius and Palladio are unquestionably the two great authorities to which all disputes may be referred, but neither are infallible. Vitruvius needs to be studied in the light of Antoine Desgodetz; Palladio in the light of his own practice; and both in the light of common sense. Ware is most fond of the mean, or middle way, perhaps best expressed in his conclusion to book two where the student is recommended to Palladio with a caution:

> Let him not be captivated with the name of this author, or over awed by his reputation: but examine what he proposes as freely as if it came from another. If he find it better than this medium which he had drawn from the various excesses of others, let him prefer it in practice; if otherwise let him consider whether the exact medium, or some measure near it, be most excellent, and having found what is best, let him not be afraid to use it.
>
> We have shewn him Palladio can do wrong, and that may be an answer to such, as, being bigotted to his opinion, would give it their voice against truth. Palladio is oftener right than any man, and let that be esteemed sufficient praise: no man is always.

It may at first seem surprising to find such critical distance in the work of a man whose English translation of *I Quattro Libri* was so painstakingly accurate. But the number of times this attitude is expressed might indicate how very much Ware, after the death of his patron Lord Burlington, wished to redefine his position in relation to English Palladianism. Certainly there are passages in *A Complete Body of Architecture* that show Ware struggling between a mandate to provide a simple, practical guide to the art of sound building, and a desire to fix his own philosophy in print. Read as the work of a man required to produce a certain quantity of text every week to satisfy subscribers, it is even possible to see a very British drama being played out in Ware's mind during the course of publication. The question to be settled was how British architectural theory could advance beyond Burlington's so-called Rule of Taste and the inspirations behind it. It is easy enough now to see that two answers were soon to be found: in the renewed exploration of classical sites, as undertaken by Robert Wood, James Stuart and Nicholas Revett, Robert Adam, and others; and in the elevation of the architect's own powers of judgment, as expressed in William Chambers' *Treatise on Civil Architecture*, published just two years after the *Complete Body* was finished. Ware's philosophy of architecture can be seen as an anticipation of both answers, but he lacked the authority that would have given his ideas a lasting influence.

One reason for this was social: Ware's origins were probably too humble for him to have been allowed to set a new course for British architecture. (He was actually the son of a London cordwainer, respectably apprenticed to the architect Thomas Ripley; but stories of his early life as a chimney-sweeper's boy were better known to his contemporaries.) Furthermore, he had already made enemies. Anything he wrote was certain to draw a hostile response from Joshua Kirby, with whom he had clashed over the objectives of the St. Martin's Lane Academy, and over his translation and publication of Sirigatti's *La Pratica di Prospettiva*. Soon after the *Complete Body* was finished, it was subjected to a withering critique by Kirby, who mocked Ware's attempt to be "the correcting genius of the age" and likened him to a builder of the Tower of Babel (*Critical Review*, November 1757, 427). This attack must have damaged sales of the book, and limited the influence of Ware's opinions among the more important arbiters of taste.

The practical value of the treatise was unaffected by such criticism. In this respect, Chambers' treatise provided no competition, and Ware's willingness to deal at length with the lower elements of the art must have been invaluable to estate managers and would-be architects. He nowhere follows the rigid division between architecture and engineering that his contemporaries were so carefully and successfully establishing. This is graphically demonstrated by his plate illustrating the drains of a town house with its offices, garden, and court (plate "30.31"). The plan of the house is here presented as subordinate to the more heavily shaded sewer channels. Alternative designs for the latter are illustrated on the same plate, grotesque equivalents of the elaborate and fluid vignettes commonly found surrounding maps and plans of the period. No engraving recording such mean necessities had covered a double-page plate in a British architectural treatise before. The many illustrations of by now all-too-familiar Palladian doors and windows, Jonesian chimneys and ceilings, etc., seem uninteresting by comparison. The dullness of these designs is compounded by the publishers' use of low-grade reproductive engravers such as Henry Roberts and W. Proud, although some of the more decorative pieces are signed by P. Fourdrinier or Charles Grignion. Ware was perfectly capable of doing a better job himself, but only nine are credited to him.

At various points throughout the treatise Ware introduces his own designs. These include the plan, elevation, ceilings, and chimneys of Chesterfield House in London, demolished in 1937, the interior decoration of which, in French rococo style, must have provided a welcome surprise to visitors after the pedestrian Palladian frontispiece (pls. 60–61, 81–83, 85, and 88). Also featured, but not always named, are Amisfield House (pls. 39, 45), Clifton Hill farmhouse (pl. 40), Oxford Town Hall (pls. 48–49), Wrotham Park (pls. 52–53), and Eythrop House (pls. 104–105, 107), besides numerous chimneypieces for London town houses. Designs by Sir Thomas Robinson for Rokeby Park in Yorkshire, and an unexecuted parsonage nearby, could be included because Ware had been Robinson's draftsman and amanuensis on the project. Not all, if any, of the "designs of

Inigo Jones, never before published," advertised on the title page and doubtless a major selling point for the volume, can now be reliably attributed to Jones.

Despite the appearance of Chambers' more critically acclaimed *Treatise on Civil Architecture* (1759), Ware's work certainly found a place in the market. On 2 June 1760, the bookbinders of London and Westminster published a new list of prices for their work, arranging titles by format and size of paper (see Mirjam M. Foot, "Some Bookbinders' Price Lists," in *Studies in the History of Bookbinding*, Aldershot, 1993). As the list was intended to serve as a general guide, only popular titles were included. "Ware's Architecture" was sufficiently well known to be in a group of fifteen demy folios, costing 6s 9d to bind in calf, lettering on the spine included. The only other architectural treatises listed are two imperial folios, namely, Wood's *Palmyra* and *Balbec*; and two royal folios, James Gibb's *Book of Architecture* and Colen Campbell's *Vitruvius Britannicus*. Not too much should be made of the fact that some of the original sheets were still available when the *Complete Body* was reprinted and published a decade later (1767–1768). For such a publication, this is more likely to indicate a large initial print run than disappointing sales. The second edition, postdating the deaths of the author and the original copyright holder, Thomas Osborne, was again issued in parts, with minor amendments. G. B.

Bibliography

Colvin, H. *A Biographical Dictionary of British Architects 1600–1840*. 3d ed. New Haven and London, 1995: 1020–1022

Harris, E., and N. Savage. *British Architectural Books and Writers 1556–1785*. Cambridge, 1990

Herrmann, W. *Laugier and 18th Century French Theory*. London, 1962

Herrmann, W. *The Theory of Claude Perrault*. London, 1973

88

Isaac Ware (1704–1766)

The Plans, Elevations, And Sections; Chimney-Pieces, and Cielings of Houghton in Norfolk: Built by the R[t]. Honourable S[r]. Robert Walpole; First Lord Commissioner of the Treasury, Chancellor of the Exchequer, and Kn[t]. of the Most Noble Order of the Garter. Who was for his great Merit created Earl of Orford &c. The whole Designed by Thomas Ripley Esq[r]. Delinated [sic] by Isaac Ware and William Kent Esq[rs]. And most elegantly engrav'd by the Ingenious M[r]. Fourdrinier. With a Description of the House and of the Elegant Collection of Pictures

London: sold by C. Fourdrinier, M[r]. Lewis, Mess[rs]. Piers & Webley, 1760

1985.61.2753

Folio: 583 × 420 (22¾ × 16½)

Pagination 10 pp., engraved title plate, 35 [i.e., 28] etched and engraved plates (9 double-page)

Edition Third edition

Text pp. [1]–10 text "A Description Of the most Magnificent Seat of Houghton-Hall, in Norfolk, Built By Sir Robert Walpole, Earl of Orford; Designed by Thomas Ripley, Esq; With a Description of the Elegant Collection of Pictures, and the Measures of them."

Illustrations Engraved title plate, unnumbered double-page engraved "Geometrical Plan of the Garden, Park, and Plantation of Houghton," and 27 etched and engraved plates numbered 1–35, including 8 double-page plates given 2 numbers each. All but the unnumbered plan are signed by Ware as draftsman, engraved by P. Fourdrinier (24, including plan) or Ware (4). 12 plates are also signed by Thomas Ripley as architect, and 13 by William Kent as designer

Binding Recent three-quarter calf, marbled boards. Uncut

References Berlin Cat. 2331 (1st ed.); Berlin (1977) os 2331[a]; Harris and Savage 912

Houghton Hall, near King's Lynn in Norfolk, was built between 1722 and 1735 for Sir Robert Walpole, Britain's first prime minister, on land occupied by his ancestors for six centuries. It replaced a more modest house that his grandfather, Sir Edward Walpole, had built about 1660—"Could those virtuous men your father and grandfather arise from yonder church," wrote Horace Walpole later to his father, "How would they be amazed to see this noble edifice and spacious plantations, where once stood their plain homely dwelling!" (*Aedes Walpolianae* 1747, v). Having inherited it in 1700, Sir Robert made at least two attempts to improve the old house, in 1707 and 1716, before deciding around 1720 to start anew. Houghton was built largely with profits made from the sale of his South Sea Company stock, purchased while he was chancellor of the exchequer. Christopher Hussey neatly summarizes its significance as one of the three outstanding monuments to Whig genius: "The landscapes of Stowe display most completely its ideals, Holkham its taste, and Houghton the political oligarchy's conception of the good life" (Hussey 1965, 72).

The complicated history of Houghton's design and construction has received so much attention recently, culminating in a 1996 monograph published to accompany an exhibition, that only the briefest recapitulation is necessary here (see bibliography, and especially the articles by John Harris and others in *Houghton Hall* 1996). Henry Bell, a gentleman-architect from King's Lynn, supplied Walpole with some early designs. The first architect positively recorded as working in connection with the new building is Thomas Ripley, a protege of Walpole who began his career combining carpentry with running a coffee shop. After marrying one of Sir Robert's servants, he was awarded numerous official appointments and sinecures even though he was regarded with utter contempt by abler architects such as Lord Burlington and Sir John Vanbrugh (to whose position as comptroller of the works he succeeded in 1726). Before the first of these appointments, in 1720, Walpole gave him the job of supervising construction of his new house. In June 1721 he was viewing timber and in August he was arranging the supply of facing stone from Whitby in Yorkshire. He appears to have continued as supervisor from the laying of the foundation stone on 24 May 1722 to Houghton's completion more than a decade later. But despite the attribution on the title and half the plates of the present work, he was not its principal architect. Ripley's credit for the Houghton exterior must be divided with at least three more prestigious names: Colen Campbell, James Gibbs, and William Kent. The relative contribution of each is still in doubt. Campbell had dedicated a design for a large Palladian house to Walpole in volume two of *Vitruvius Britannicus* (1717). Although this was ignored or rejected, a series of plates in volume three (1725) and a group of drawings by Campbell now in the British Architectural Library (RIBA) Drawings Collection are explicitly related to Houghton. Together, these show that he drafted more than one version of the house between 1723 and 1725, and was still producing designs for the offices in 1726. Evidence for Gibbs' involvement is equally conclusive, consisting of two designs in his hand for elevations of the portico and side front, found among the Campbell drawings; a preliminary plan for the *piano nobile*, now

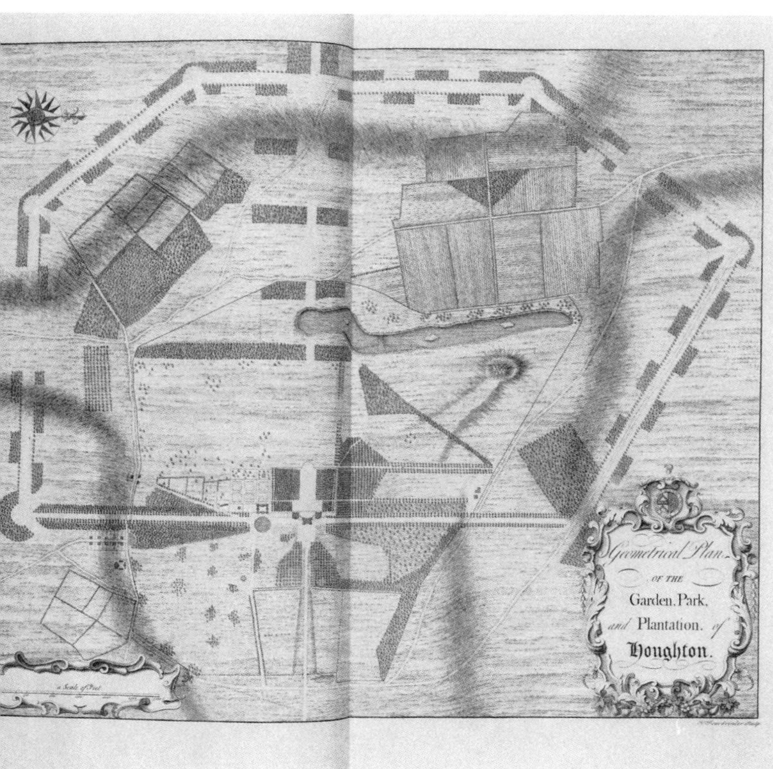

Isaac Ware. *The Plans...of Houghton.* Unnumbered preliminary plate. "Geometrical Plan of the Garden, Park, and Plantation of Houghton." 1985.61.2753

attributed to Gibbs by John Harris; and a comment made by Gibbs' patron Lord Harley in 1732 that the Houghton roofs "were altered by Mr. Gibbs from the first design. The house as it is now is a composition of the greatest blockheads and the most ignorant fellows in architecture that are. I think Gibbs was to blame to alter any of their designs or mend their blunders" (quoted in *Houghton Hall* 1996, 23). This evidence has led John Harris to suggest that Gibbs' designs for Houghton pre-date Campbell's, who adapted them after becoming involved in 1723. Gibbs may also have been used a second time, after Campbell's departure in about 1726. Furthermore, Harris attributes the design for the entrance to the *piano nobile* on the east front to William Kent, executed in 1727 at the latest. Kent may have designed the stables as well, built between 1733 and 1735 and replacing those of 1719–1721 illustrated on Campbell's plan of Houghton in volume three of *Vitruvius Britannicus*. Meanwhile, a series of extensive alterations to the gardens and plantations was also being made before and during construction, apparently using designs prepared by Charles Bridgeman.

Whatever claims might be made on behalf of Ripley, Campbell, Gibbs, and Kent, there is little doubt that Walpole would have enjoyed dictating to all of them. In 1731, for example, Lord Hervey told the prince of Wales that the cupolas on the main house were "obstinately raised by the master, and covered with stones in defiance of all the virtuosi who ever gave their opinions about it" (quoted in Friedman 1984, 107). Responsibility for most of the interior decoration lies more clearly with Kent, who made designs for the saloon as early as 1725. The stuccoist Giuseppe Artari, the sculptor John Michael Rysbrack, and the furniture carver James Richards were also among the host of artists and craftsmen employed.

The present folio was originally published in 1735 with a slightly different title: *The Plans, Elevations, and Sections; Chimney-Pieces, and Cielings of Houghton in Norfolk; The Seat of the R^{t}. Honourable S^{r}. Robert Walpole; First Lord Commissioner of the Treasury, Chancellor of the Exchequer, and Kn^{t}. of the Most Noble Order of the Garter. MDCCXXXV.* As John Harris has noted, it was the first monograph devoted to the architecture of a British country house (*Houghton Hall* 1996, 24). The imprint, engraved in a vignette on a separate copper printed between title and date, read simply "Published by I: Ware." The suite was wholly engraved and consisted of title plate, preface, and twenty-eight single- and double-page plates of designs numbered 1–35. Plates 29–32 were probably late additions, since in early states the plan and two elevations of the stables that follow them are given these numbers as well (copy at Canadian Centre for Architecture; pl. 31 [recto 34] is also signed "I. Ware, Delin^{t}." in the earlier state instead of "I. Ware Delin^{t}. et sculp").

The draftsman and publisher, Isaac Ware, had been apprenticed to Ripley for seven years in August 1721, just as preparations for Houghton were beginning in earnest. His celebration of its completion fourteen years later was a collaboration with his former master, and the credit lines on the plans, elevations, and sections give the false impression that Ripley was sole architect of the exterior. Campbell had died in 1729, and Gibbs may not have wanted to be associated with Harley's "ignorant blockheads," so their roles were probably easily suppressed. But in this context, the attribution here of the stables to Ripley can be taken as a small piece of evidence against the argument that Kent designed them. Ware would not have wished to offend Kent, who is properly credited on the plates of ceilings and fireplaces. Their association had begun at least four years earlier, when Ware published in octavo his first suite of architectural engravings, *Designs of Inigo Jones and Others*. It included several after Kent, one a rejected design for the west wall of the Marble Parlour (pl. 35), for which the original drawing still exists, marked on the verso "for your great dining room at Houghton WK 1728" (*Houghton Hall* 1996, no. 58). Another was an early version of the chimneypiece design illustrated on plate 27 of the *Plans* (pl. 51). Ware may have simply found these drawings lying around at Houghton, but it is much more likely that Kent approved of and arranged for their publication as advertisements of his skill. Lord Burlington's favorite engraver, Fourdrinier, also worked on both suites. The loss of his and Ware's time might have been a reason for the poor progress of Burlington's pet project,

Isaac Ware. *The Plans...of Houghton.* Plate 1/2. "West Front of Houghton in Norfolk." 1985.61.2753

the *Fabbriche antiche*, dated 1730 but not issued until about a decade later.

The unsigned Latin preface that followed the title in the 1735 edition is not very informative. Perhaps Sir Robert's eighteen-year-old son Horace Walpole was behind it; he compiled his first manuscript catalogue of the pictures at Houghton the following year. Horace later owned Ware's finished drawings for the plates, and had them bound up in an autograph manuscript copy of his own book, *Aedes Walpolianae*, now at the Metropolitan Museum of Art, New York (see Harris 1971, 265). In the second impression of the *Plans*, this engraved preface was replaced by an identically worded letterpress version. Still dated 1735, the later impression is also distinguished by the different paper used and an additional imprint engraved on the title plate beneath Ware's vignette, "and Sold by P. Fourdrinier at the Corner of Cragg's Court Charing Cross" (copy at Canadian Centre for Architecture). The present impression, dated 1760, with the revised title as above, is therefore the third. Fourdrinier's initial in the imprint has been changed to that of his son, Charles, and the names and addresses of his co-publishers added beneath. The Millard copy is without the preface, which would make sense if the original copper had disappeared along with any motivation for resetting it in type.

The first, unnumbered, plate in the Millard edition is therefore the "geometrical" plan of the estate, one of several Houghton plans extant from the period. It is the only plate to have been significantly revised: by 1760 a cutting excavated in the 1740s to improve the view from the east of the house has been shaded in toward the bottom margin. It is followed by a boldly original plate of the garden or west front, which, besides showing one solution to the problem of depicting a long low building on a double sheet, introduces what amounts to a series of visual puns on methods of architectural representation. Ware has divided the picture area into two halves and, taking the north wall of the south court as his vanishing point and the tops of the main building's cupolas as his horizon line, has projected a perspective elevation onto the upper half and a perspective plan onto the lower. The latter is completely subordinate to the former, severely limited on an informational level and visually austere, but intellectually harmonious. Only the title cartouche invades this lower space. The size and position of the cartouche demands attention, but its orthodox perspective actually sets it apart from both halves even as it links them, and highlights the artful mathematics of the main design. In the lower corners of the top half of the plate, two compositions of stone fragments from ancient Rome allude to Houghton's classical design and to Britain's imperial aspirations—Walpole, incidentally, having commissioned a bust from Rysbrack portraying himself as a Roman senator. Stylistically, Fourdrinier's treatment of the house and gardens is reminiscent of Johannes Kip's engravings of Leonard Knyff's bird's-eye views of country houses, collected in *Britannia Illustrata* (1707–1731). As for other precedents, perspectives linking plan and elevation can be found in the French tradition of Jacques Androuet Ducerceau's

Leçons du Perspective positive (Paris, 1576) and Jean Marot's suites of engravings. This tradition was adopted in Britain by Henry Aldrich for his *Elementorum Architecturae Pars Prima* (Oxford, c. 1708) and two spectacular views of Peckwater Quad, Oxford (included in the second volume of *Britannia Illustrata*, 1715). Nevertheless, the design of the Houghton plate is novel, and although the cartouche and staffage looks Kentian, Ware deserves credit for the composition. His interest in perspective later led him to translate and publish an edition of the first book of Lorenzo Sirigatti's *La Prattica di Prospettiva* (Venice, 1596).

The remaining plates are in keeping with the style established by earlier Palladian publications. The ground and first floor plans (pl. 3–5) have had room names added to them since the 1735 edition. They are followed by three elevations (pl. 6–10), five sections (pl. 11–18), seven ceilings (pl. 19–25), ten chimneypieces (pl. 26–31), and the plan and elevations of the stables (pl. 32–35). The text makes no reference to any of the illustrations, being a catalogue of the paintings. It is an unacknowledged abridgment of Horace Walpole's *Aedes Walpolianae*, first published with reduced copies of Fourdrinier's plans and elevations in 1748 (but dated 1747), reprinted with corrections in 1752 and 1767 (see Hazen 1948, 26–32). The two most important early descriptions of Houghton are therefore united, probably without permission. The abridgment omits Walpole's sermon on painting and John Whaley's poem about a journey to Houghton, and curtails the longer catalogue entries.

Sometime between 1760 and 1784, the plates of *Plans* were acquired by John Boydell, who renumbered them 1–28, added his imprint, and put them as a preface to his great series of reproductive engravings, eventually given the title *A Set of Prints Engraved After the Most Capital Paintings in the Collection of Her Imperial Majesty, the Empress of Russia, lately in the Possession of the Earl of Orford at Houghton in Norfolk: with Plans, Elevations, Sections, Chimney-Pieces & Ceilings* (1774–1788; see *Houghton Hall* 1996, 65–73). This suite was a printed memorial to the splendors of Houghton before 1779, when the debt-ridden 3d earl felt compelled to sell its art collection to the empress Catherine for thirty-six thousand pounds. G. B.

Bibliography

Colvin, H. *A Biographical Dictionary of British Architects 1600–1840*. 3d ed. New Haven and London, 1995

Cornforth, J. "Houghton Hall, Norfolk." *Country Life* 181, no. 18 (30 April 1987): 124–129; no. 19 (7 May 1987): 104–108

Cornforth, J. "The Growth of an Idea: The Making of Houghton's Landscape." *Country Life* 181, no. 20 (14 May 1987): 162–168

Friedman, T. *James Gibbs*. New Haven, 1984

Harris, E., and N. Savage. *British Architectural Books and Writers 1556–1785*. Cambridge, 1990

Harris, J. *Catalogue of British Drawings for Architecture, Decoration, Sculpture and Landscape Gardening 1550–1900 in American Collections*. Upper Saddle River, N. J., 1971

Harris, J. *A Catalogue of the Drawings Collection of the Royal Institute of British Architects: Colen Campbell*. London, 1973

Harris, J. "John Talman's Design for his Wunderkammern." *Furniture History* 21 (1985): 211–217

Harris, J. "Who Designed Houghton?" *Country Life* 183, no. 9 (2 March 1989): 92–94

Harris, J. "James Gibbs, Eminence Grise at Houghton." In *New Light on Palladianism* (Papers given at the Georgian Group Symposium 1988). Ed. C. Hind. London, 1990: 5–9

Hazen, A. T. *A Bibliography of Horace Walpole*. New Haven, 1948. Reprint, 1973

Houghton Hall: The Prime Minister, the Empress and the Heritage. Ed. A. Moore. London, 1996

Hussey, C. *English Country Houses: Early Georgian 1715–1760*. Rev. ed. London, 1965: 72–86

Mittmann, I. S. "Houghton Hall: Studien zum Neopalladianismus am Beispiel eines Englischen Landsitzes aus dem 18. Jahrhundert." Inaugural Diss. Freiburg, 1982

The Treasure Houses of Britain: Five Hundred Years of Private Patronage and Art Collecting. Ed. G. Jackson-Stops. Washington, 1985: especially cats. 153, 154, 349, and 363

Worsley, G. "Houghton Hall, Norfolk: A Seat of the Marquess of Cholmondeley." *Country Life* 187, no. 9 (4 March 1993): 50–53

Worsley, G. "Riding on Status: The Stables at Houghton." *Country Life* 184, no. 39 (27 Sept. 1990): 108–111

89

William Watts (1752–1851)

The Seats of the Nobility and Gentry In a Collection of the most interesting & Picturesque Views. Engraved by W. Watts From Drawings by the most Eminent Artists

London: published by John & Josiah Boydell [c. 1818]

1985.61.2755

Oblong quarto: 206 × 262 ($8\frac{1}{8} \times 10\frac{5}{16}$)

Pagination [170] pp., engraved title plate, [84] engraved plates

Edition Late, undated edition, with the title plate imprint altered from "Publish'd by W. Watts, Kemp's Row, Chelsea, January 1st. 1779.," and credit "H. [i.e., Henry] Shepherd sculp." removed. Text printed on paper with watermark "1814"; plates printed on paper with watermark "1818"

Text pp. [1–168] single leaf of descriptive text for each interleaved plate, most versos blank; [169] "An Alphabetical Index of the Names or Titles of Possessors of Seats contained in this Work" (verso blank)

Illustrations In addition to the engraved title plate, there are 84 engraved views of country houses numbered in their accompanying descriptions 1–84, all signed by William Watts as engraver and 24 by him as draftsman. The other credited artists and/or draftsmen are George Barret (plates 6, 12, 16, 22, 24, 31); William Beilby (plates 58, 77); Mr. Brooks (plate 37); [Adam] Callander (plates 65, 69, 73); Lord Viscount Carlow (plate 33); J. [i.e., John?] Carter (plate 19); Richard Carter (plate 45); Thomas Chubbard (plate 76); D. Dalby (plate 23); Anthony Devis (plates 14, 21, 41); W. Donn (plate 26); [John] Feary (plate 74); Rev. Gooch (plate 32); J. A. Gresse (plate 40); Thomas Hearne (plates 8, 32, 43–45, 55, 75); William Hodges (plate 10); James Luttrell (plate 4); Thomas Malton, Jr. (plates 13, 20, 29, 51, 66, 84); C. [i.e., Conrad Martin?] Metz (plate 11); Claude Nattes (plates 79–80); George Perceval (plate 54); Ensign Plumridge (plate 31); Frederick Ponsonby, Lord Duncannon, later 3d earl of Bessborough (plates 57, 61, 71); Humphry Repton (plates 36, 44, 59); J. Richards (plate 15); Robertson (plate 62); M. A. Rooker (plate 7); Paul Sandby (plates 1–3, 9, 81); Thomas Sandby (plates 5, 18, 42); Mr. Stewart (plates 65, 69, 73); Samuel Stringer (plate 64); William Tomkins (plate 83); and Richard Wilson (plate 82)

Binding Nineteenth-century straight-grain green morocco, elaborate gilt and blind borders, gilt spine

References ESTC t145839

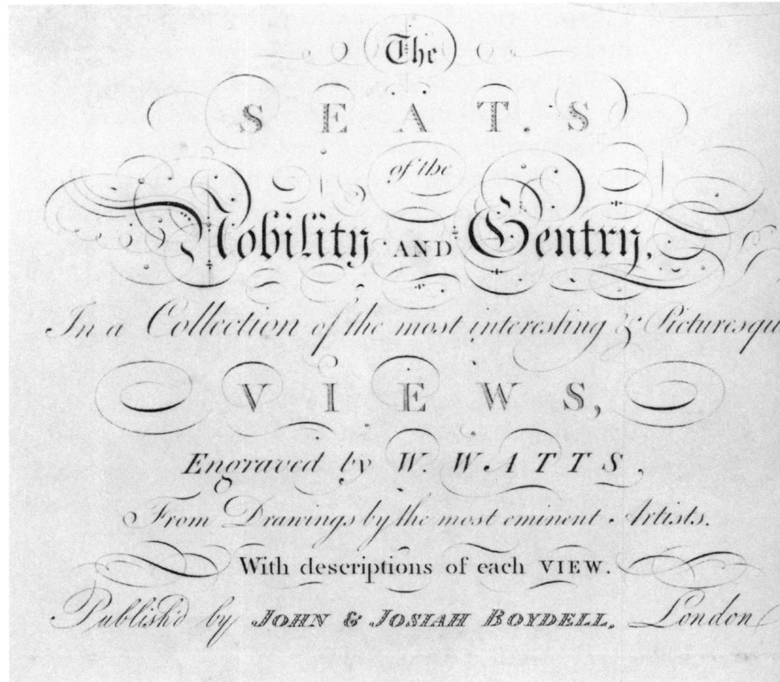

The SEATS of the Nobility AND Gentry, In a Collection of the most interesting & Picturesque VIEWS, Engraved by W. WATTS, From Drawings by the most eminent Artists. With descriptions of each VIEW. Publish'd by JOHN & JOSIAH BOYDELL, London

William Watts. *The Seats of the Nobility and Gentry.* Title plate. 1985.61.2755

WILLIAM WATTS' *Seats of the Nobility and Gentry* is one of a group of books and periodicals that was published in the 1770s as a result of a new middle-class market for inexpensive British landscape views. A subset of this group was devoted to country-house views. Despite similarities of subject matter and geographical coverage, it had little in common with either of the earlier traditions established by *Britannia illustrata* (1707–c. 1731) and *Vitruvius Britannicus* (1715–1771). Both of these were large folio collections of country houses aimed primarily at the landowning classes and the architects and landscape gardeners who hoped to serve them. They were, therefore, intent on supplying accurate graphic representations to a select and critical audience. The new type, represented in the Millard collection by the present work and William Angus' sequel, was more modest in size, price, and objective. As the preface to one of them explained, they were "cheap and rational amusements" offering young gentlemen "a beautiful addition . . . to the furniture of their apartments for less than the value of a masquerade ticket" (*The Virtuosi's Museum*, preface, quoted in Yale 1985, 104).

The reasons for a rise in popularity of British landscape painting of all kinds in the 1770s have been discussed by Herrmann (1973). For present purposes, one event is particularly relevant: the exhibition of a 952–piece dinner service commissioned by the anglophile empress Catherine of Russia from Josiah Wedgwood. Completed in 1774, the dinner service had, according to Wedgwood's partner Thomas Bentley, no less than 1,244 views of Great Britain, and a large proportion of these were views of country houses and their gardens. Only a few were specially commissioned drawings; shortage of time forced the firm to poach most of their illustrations from guidebooks, county histories, and architectural monographs such as William Chambers' *Plans . . . of the Gardens and Buildings at Kew* (1763). Nevertheless, the search for suitable subjects must have alerted artists all over the country, and before shipping it to Russia, Wedgwood exhibited the set in his new premises at 12/13 Greek Street, Soho, London, where it attracted great publicity. It is no coincidence that the month after the show closed, in August 1774, George Kearsley began publishing British landscape views in a new periodical, *The Copperplate Magazine.* Paul Sandby, already the best-known British topographical artist, was able to supply Kearsley with all the views he needed, and his work must have been the major attraction for subscribers. When Kearsley ended the magazine in January 1778, he immediately started a more specialized series, *The Virtuosi's Museum*, which ran for another three years. Every month, this contained three views of scenery in Great Britain and Ireland, again mostly by Sandby. The preface, already quoted from above, gives the fashionable justification for the new craze:

> In the choice of our subjects . . . we follow an illustrious example. The renowned Empress of Russia . . . has paid the highest compliment to the genius and taste of this country; by procuring, at an immense expence, views of all the noblemen and gentlemen's seats, and of every delightful spot throughout the kingdom, drawn on the spot, and painted upon setts of china dishes and plates. If these views appear so enchanting in the eyes of this Princess, surely it must afford the highest satisfaction to Britons themselves, to have in their possession complete representations of them on a better plan for preservation, and on much easier terms (*The Virtuosi's Museum*, preface, quoted in Herrmann 1973, 43).

It was just as the first year of *The Virtuosi's Museum* was coming to a successful close that Watts, one of Kearsley's engravers, copied the idea and issued the first number of *The Seats of the Nobility and Gentry*, devoted to views of country houses. Watts had been born near Moorfields in 1752, the son of a master silk-weaver, and began his artistic education as an apprentice to Sandby and Edward Rooker. In November 1774, after the latter's death, he had taken over Rooker's work of engraving views for *The Copperplate Magazine*; and in 1777 Kearsley had published *A Collection of Landscapes, Drawn by P. Sandby . . . and engraved by Mr. Rooker, and Mr. Watts.* He was, therefore, a young man with all the right contacts and business experience for such a venture. The initial financial risk would have been low, since he could abort the series as soon as it proved unprofitable. But as sole proprietor of the new title, and able to execute the engravings himself, his chances of keeping it afloat were better than most, particularly as there now seemed to be plenty of amateur artists willing to turn their oil paintings, their watercolors, and their sketches over to the print trade. As for the professionals, even as distinguished a figure as Sir Joshua Reynolds had long recognized that the market for reproductions of an artist's work could not only bring immediate profit by a sale, but also increase the fame and prestige of the originals.

Judging by its longevity, and the fact that Angus continued it after the author's departure, Watts' *Seats* was a success. The plate publication lines show that it was issued in twenty-one installments, each with four plates and four accompanying letterpress leaves, over a period of seven and a half years (i.e., January, April, and August 1779; January, May, and September 1780; January, May, and September 1781; January, May, and September/October 1782; January/February, June, and November 1783; June and November 1784; April and September 1785; January and 20 May 1786). This was a leisurely pace: subscribers could at first expect an installment every four months, and later twice yearly. A fine calligraphic title plate by Henry Shepherd was issued with the first part, and an alphabetical index to the house owners came at the end.

Every view is the same size and at first glance the completed work presents itself as a remarkably homogenous series, almost monotonous in its display of one country house after another in an idyllic landscape, ornamented by strolling figures or domesticated animals beneath a cloudy summer sky. No effort was made to publish the houses in order of age, style, location, or grandeur. Despite this, and the lack of any preface or other address to the reader, a closer examination allows clues to the priorities of Watts and his audience to emerge. First came the skill and reputation of the artist providing the view. A desire to make a splash with the opening number led Watts to include three Sandby views (of a total of five). Plate I shows Westcombe House, Blackheath, rebuilt in about 1730 to the designs of Roger Morris and its owner, Henry Herbert, earl of Pembroke. This was a house many subscribers would know well, both because of its location near London and because Sandby had already provided an engraving of it in *The Copperplate Magazine.* It is followed by Picton Castle in Wales (worked up by Sandby from a sketch by Charles Greville) and a historically important view of Sheffield Place, showing the house "in the best Gothic Taste," as it appeared between James Wyatt's successive remodelings for John Baker Holroyd (c. 1775–1777; c. 1780–1790). Watts used another Sandby view to open the third number (Drumlanrig Castle, pl. IX), and his only other contribution is the first plate in the last installment, a magnificent view of Chatsworth's newly landscaped grounds.

Like Sandby, George Barret (frequently spelled Barrett) was a founder member of the Royal Academy. Watts engraved two paintings and four drawings by him. The only other credited academicians are "J. Richards, Esq." (sometimes identified with John Inigo Richards) and Sandby's brother Thomas, professor of architecture. Other well-known artists included Edward Rooker's son, Michael Angelo Rooker; Anthony Devis; and Thomas Hearne, who in collaboration with William Byrne was publishing a major survey of Britain's medieval remains, *Antiquities of Great Britain* (1777–1807). It is also appropriate that Watts included one painting by the first true master of the genre, Richard Wilson, who really belongs to the generation before. His evocative view of Wilton House from across the lake, with the artist himself shown sketching in the foreground, is an outstanding example of what Ruskin called Wilson's "sincere landscape art founded on a meditative love of nature" (quoted in Waterhouse 1981, 416). It is the most famous of a series of five Wilson paintings of the same subject, painted c. 1758–1759 (see Harris 1985, 250, 276–277). Views by capable young artists like Thomas Malton, Jr., and Frederick Ponsonby, Lord Viscount Duncannon, seem routine by comparison—though often more useful to the architectural historian.

Many of the paintings and drawings used by Watts can be traced to the major annual exhibitions in London, either at the Royal Academy or the Society of Artists of Great Britain. Barret, for example, exhibited a view of Burton Constable at the Academy in the same year Watts published one (pl. XII); William Hodges' view of Sandbeck had been at the Society of Artists a decade earlier (pl. X); and J. Richards' oil painting of Halswell was an old view, having appeared at the Society of Artists in 1764 (pl. XV). Watts probably never had to commission any of his material, though he may have bought for his own collection. There was in any case no need for the trouble and expense of getting someone else to do what he could do himself. From the fifth installment onward he regularly credits himself as draftsman, and while he evidently considered the Home Counties his natural territory, he also made trips to Cornwall and Norfolk.

Despite exceptions, and although a few of his sources were not up to date, Watts seems to have had a general preference for relatively modern estates (which had been eschewed by Wedgwood and Bentley as "unpicturesque"). In the second installment, for example, Wentworth House, Claremont, Harewood, and Ranston had all been either built, rebuilt, or remodeled within the last fifty years. An emphasis on the latest improvements, with its concomitant delight in landscapes by Lancelot "Capability" Brown or his followers, continues throughout the work—three of the best landscape views are from drawings by Brown's most famous successor, Humphry Repton. The architect James Paine is particularly well represented. The second volume of his *Plans . . . of Noblemen and Gentlemen's Houses* (1783) is anticipated twice, by views of Worksop Manor (pl. XIII) and Thorndon Hall (pl. XVII), and Axwell Park also appears (pl. LXXVII). Thorndon, completed in 1770, is the first in the series to be drawn by Watts himself.

The text accompanying each plate is always brief, usually sycophantic, and often derivative. Occasionally, however, Watts lets slip a useful fact for the historian. For example, whereas the owner of Harewood House (pl. VII), Edwin Lascelles, "has politely fixed every Saturday as a public viewing day," the duke of Devonshire gets a strongly worded paragraph—the only one in the whole book—for his absentee arrangements at Chiswick (pl. XXX):

> It is somewhat remarkable that no persons are admitted to see this place without tickets for that purpose, a ceremony, we believe, not observed at any other seat in the kingdom; and that upon admission you are prohibited from making any drawings. The author of this publication, unacquainted with these particulars, met with very disagreeable treatment, in consequence of having taken some sketches of the building. This illiberal injunction is the more extraordinary, as plans and elevations of the house have been published many years since by Kent.

In the first golden age of country-house tourism, the duke's desire to control the crowds was evidently an unwelcome novelty. The reference at the end to William Kent's *The Designs of Inigo Jones* (1727) is one of several clues to Watts' familiarity with the major British architectural books of the century.

Although the progressively slow pace of the series might imply falling profits, Watts' decision to end the *Seats* after the twenty-first installment probably sprung from a general desire to change his circumstances. Having issued the last number in May 1786, he sold all his furniture and his substantial art collection and took to Italy, reaching Naples in September. On his return a year later, he remained unsettled, living in quick succession in Sunbury, Carmaerthon, Bristol, and Bath. With the outbreak of the French Revolution, he declared himself an enthusiastic supporter by traveling to Paris and losing all his savings, including a substantial inheritance from his father, in the French public funds. Although some of his money was returned after 1815, he was meanwhile compelled to return to his trade, and his name appears in various topographical books until his retirement in 1814. A few landscape paintings attributed to him, including one at the Metropolitan Museum of Art and one at the Louvre, are in the style of John Constable. His sight failing, he was ninety-nine when he died in 1851. Lowndes records the subsequent sale of Watts' personal copy of the *Seats*, morocco bound and extra-illustrated with eighteen drawings by the publisher and thirteen other plates mounted on tinted paper (Lowndes 1864, 2859).

The title plate of the Millard copy of this work is in its later, more common, state, with an undated Boydell imprint instead of the original, "Publish'd by W. Watts, Kemp's Row, Chelsea, January 1st. 1779." The title-plate credit "H. Shepherd sculp." has also been removed. The views themselves appear to be unaltered reprints, and the text is unchanged from the first edition, except for the correction of a few errata noted on the verso of the

R. Wilson pinx.t
W. Watts, Sculp.
Wilton in Wiltshire, the Seat of the Earl of Pembroke.
Published as the Act directs May 20th 1786, by W. Watts, Chelsea.

William Watts. *The Seats of the Nobility and Gentry.* Plate LXXXII. "Wilton in Wiltshire, the Seat of the Earl of Pembroke." 1985.61.2755

original list of owners. As John Boydell died in 1804, after which his nephew Josiah continued the business alone, the firm must have bought the plates and begun republishing them long before the present printing, which, as the watermarks show, appeared no earlier than 1818. G. B.

Bibliography

Colvin, H. *A Biographical Dictionary of British Architects 1600–1840*. 3d ed. New Haven and London, 1995

Graves, A. *The Royal Academy of Arts: A Complete Dictionary*. London, 1905. Reprint, 1970

Graves, A. *The Society of Artists of Great Britain 1760–1791, the Free Society of Artists 1761–1783: A Complete Dictionary*. London, 1907. Reprint, 1969

Harris, J. *The Artist and the Country House*. Rev. ed. London, 1985

Herrmann, L. *British Landscape Painting of the Eighteenth Century*. London, 1973

Herrmann, L. *Paul and Thomas Sandby*. London, 1986

Kelly, A. "Wedgwood's Catherine Services." *Burlington Magazine* 122 (1980): 554–561

Lowndes, W. T. *The Bibliographer's Manual of English Literature*. New ed. London, 1864. Reprint, 1967

Maxted, I. *The London Book Trades 1775–1800*. Folkestone, 1977

Redgrave, S. *A Dictionary of Artists of the English School*. London, 1878. Reprint Amsterdam, 1970

Thieme-Becker 35: 201–202

Waterhouse, E. *The Dictionary of British 18th Century Painters in Oils and Crayons*. Woodbridge, 1981

Yale Center for British Art. *The Art of Paul Sandby*. New Haven, 1985

90

Rev. Cooper Willyams (1762–1816)

The History Of Sudeley Castle, In Gloucestershire, By The Rev. Cooper Willyams, Vicar Of Ixning, In Suffolk

London: printed for J. Robson, 1791

1985.61.2646

Folio: 510 × 329 (20 1/16 × 13)

Pagination [12] pp., aquatint frontispiece

Edition First edition

Text pp. [1] title page (verso blank); [3–12] text

Illustrations Etched and aquatint frontispiece dedicated by Cooper Willyams to Samuel Egerton Brydges, printed in sepia

Binding Bound after a copy of George Richardson, *A Treatise on the Five Orders*, 1787 (q.v.)

References ESTC t95162; Upcott 272

To SAMUEL EGERTON BRYDGES,

Masquerading as a disinterested account of Sudeley Castle, this short book actually has a genealogical axe to grind for Samuel Egerton Brydges, lifelong friend of the author and dedicatee of the aquatint view of the castle. In 1789, on the death without heirs of the 3d duke of Chandos, Brydges persuaded his elder brother to claim the title of Baron Chandos of Sudeley. The book was evidently published in support of this claim, and was perhaps even underwritten by Brydges himself. Willyams claims that he has no "material original matter to communicate," which is certainly true from an architectural viewpoint: he devotes only a few sentences to the physical description of the castle, then in ruins. But he digresses, with half-hearted apologies ("The gross mistakes of the peerages have led me rather unwillingly into this length of note"), into long genealogical asides. Eventually the reader learns that John Bridges, 1st Baron Chandos of Sudeley, who was given the castle by Queen Mary in 1553, had no remaining heirs in the main line except through his third son Anthony, whose descendants "settled in Kent, and are now remaining there." Samuel Egerton Brydges lived in Kent. The elder Brydges' claim was finally thrown out by the House of Lords in 1803, to the undying chagrin of his younger brother.

Cooper Willyams was born in 1762, a contemporary of Samuel Egerton Brydges at King's School, Canterbury. In 1788 he became vicar of Exning, in Suffolk, as he is described on the title page of his *Sudeley*, and he published an antiquarian account of Exning in *The Topographer* in September 1790. By 1791, Sudeley Castle had been a ruin for a century and a half, having been besieged and slighted during the civil war. Ralph Boteler, Lord Sudeley, erected the main structure of two quadrangles in the mid-fifteenth century, but the property was forfeited to the Crown in 1469. It passed through the hands of Richard III, both when duke of Gloucester and subsequently as king; Willyams shows no awareness of this connection, in spite of his own professed desire to bring the ruins to life with an account of notable previous occupants and the fact that Horace Walpole's *Historic Doubts* of 1768 had propelled Richard into the limelight among the antiquarians. Instead he offers a sympathetic account of Katherine Parr, last queen of Henry VIII, whose burial site in the chapel at Sudeley was overrun, to Willyam's pious dismay, with rabbits.

Rev. Cooper Willyams. *The History of Sudeley Castle, in Gloucestershire.* View of the ruins of Sudeley Castle in Gloucestershire. 1985.61.2646

He also, along with other authors, repeats the observation of John Leland, visiting the site in the 1530s or 1540s, that the windows had formerly been magnificently glazed with beryl. In 1837 the ruins were restored as a residence for the Dent brothers by Sir George Gilbert Scott.

The English Short Title Catalogue refers to British Library copies of the book as "wanting all the plates but the frontispiece," implying that the book should have more than the one plate present in the Millard copy; this does not appear to be correct, however. Willyam's own text refers to "the print that accompanies this account" in the singular, and other bibliographical sources corroborate this; an extra-illustrated copy may have given rise to the confusion. The plate was absent from an octavo reprint of 1803 by S. Harward of Cheltenham. By this date Willyams had begun and partly published his voyages as a naval chaplain in the West Indies and the Mediterranean. In 1806 his old friend and patron Brydges appointed him rector of Kingston near Canterbury, Kent; he died in 1816. J. F.

Bibliography

DNB (under Brydges, Willyams)

91

John Wood (1704–1754)

The Origin Of Building: Or, The Plagiarism Of The Heathens Detected. In Five Books. By John Wood, Architect

Bath: printed by S. and F. Farley, and sold by J. Leake: M. Lewis, Bristol: W. Innys; C. Hitch; R. Dodsley; J. Pine; and J. Brindley, London, 1741

NGA Lib. Rare Book: NA2111W8 fol.

Folio: 388 × 250 (15 1/4 × 9 13/16)

Pagination [vi], 235, [3] pp., 36 [i.e., 25] engraved plates (11 double-page)

Edition First edition

Text pp. [i] title page (verso blank); [iii–vi] table of contents, directions to the binder; [1]–235 text, books 1–5, each with a divisional title page; [236] blank; [237] errata (verso blank)

Illustrations 25 unsigned engraved plates numbered 1–36 (11 double-page with 2 numbers each)

Binding Recent quarter calf, marbled boards, red morocco label

References Berlin (1977) OS 2276[m]; ESTC t65432; Fowler 441; Harris and Savage 929

JOHN WOOD was born in Bath in 1704, the son of a local builder. He attended school there, but by 1725 was established in London, in Oxford Street, where he remained for at least two years, involved in speculative building in Oxford Street and in Cavendish Square. He worked both for Lord Bingley (who employed him also on his country seat, Bramham Park, in Yorkshire) and Edward Harley, 2d earl of Oxford, whom he was to regard, through life, as his patron. Harley seems to have stirred his interests in historical study, and it was Harley who, in 1740, stimulated him to investigate Stonehenge and Stanton Drew and to prepare measured drawings of these monuments.

Though still involved with building in London and Yorkshire, Wood had taken up residence in Bath by May 1721 and had begun to refashion that town. Work on Queen Square began the following year, while the Circus, though conceived early enough, was not begun until February 1754, three months before his death. He was succeeded in his enterprise by his son.

Wood's fame rests on his activity as an architect and builder, but he was also the author of five books, the most curious of which was *The Origin of Building: Or, The Plagiarism Of The Heathens Detected*, published in Bristol and London in 1741. Two manuscripts of this survive, one in Sir John Soane's Museum, London, written, for the most part, in 1737 and early 1738, and the other in the Bath Reference Library, a fair copy of the first, with alterations and additions, probably written in 1739, certainly before May 1740. Wood's aim was to prove that all order and beauty in architecture was a reflection of divine wisdom, as the wonder and splendor of architecture had been revealed by God to Moses, who had first given form to these revelations in the Tabernacle built in the desert, later to be interpreted in permanent materials by Solomon in the Temple of Jerusalem. The classical architecture of the Greeks and

John Wood. *The Origin of Building*. Plates 2–3. Plan of a tabernacle. NGA Lib. Rare Book: NA2111W8 fol.

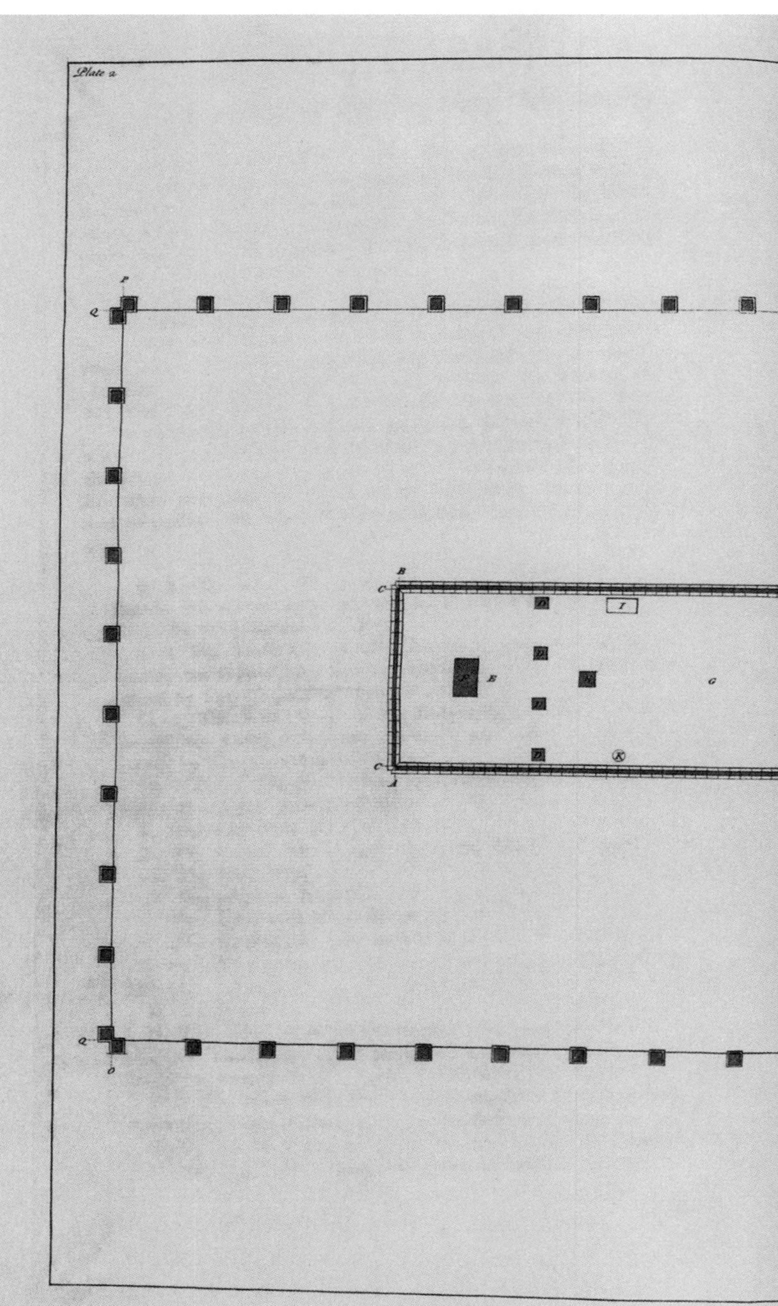

the Romans was thus no more than an imitation of that of the Hebrews:

the *Knowledge* our Ancestors first had in Arts and Sciences, *was given them immediately By* GOD; we propose, in the following Sheets, not only to weigh and consider, the Origin, Progress, and Perfection of Building, so as to make an Account thereof consistent with Sacred History, with the Confession of the Antients, with the Course of great Events in all Parts of the World and with itself; but, from Time to Time, to point out the *Plagiarism* of the *Heathens*; and then, to shew, that the *Dignity* to which *Architecture* was rais'd by the Grandeur of the Egyptian, the Assyrian, the *Median*, the *Babylonian*, the *Persian*, the *Grecian*, and the Roman Empires, was not comparable to the Lustre with which it first shined in the Sacred Works of the Jews.

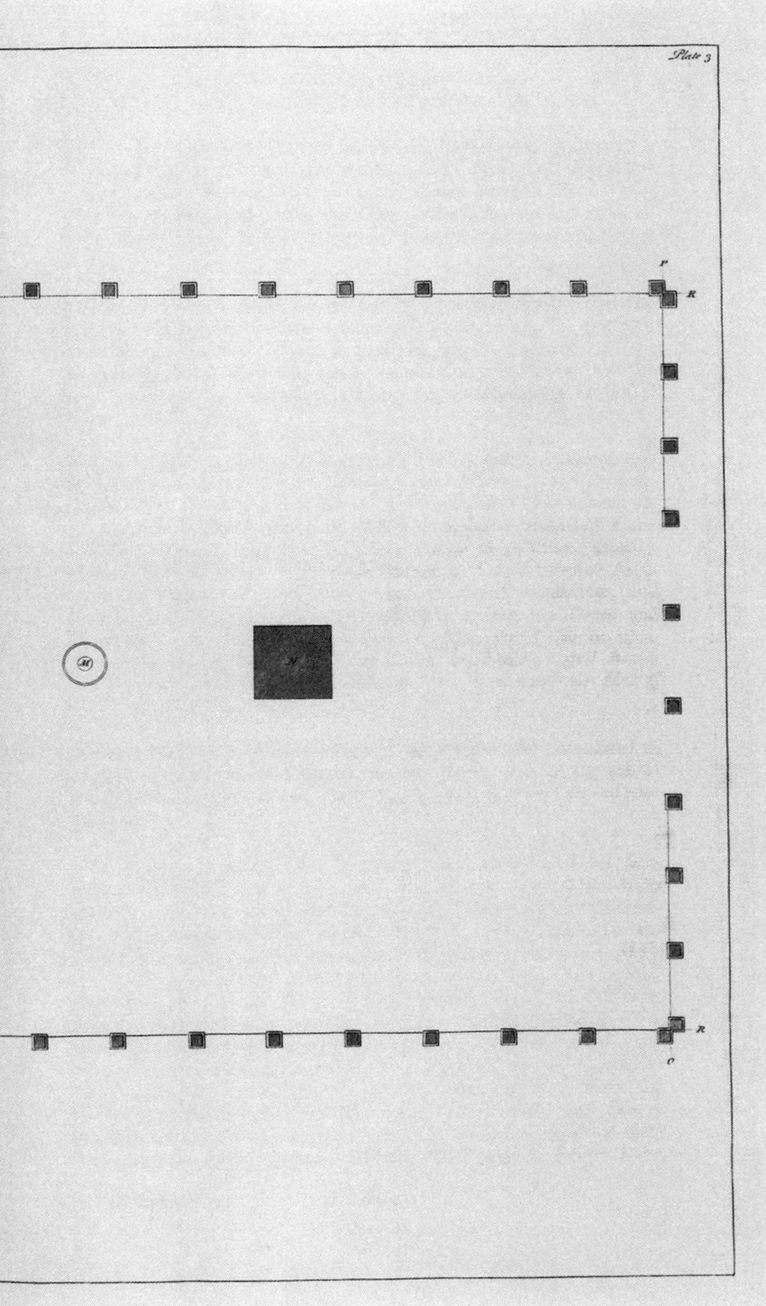

Wood's book is divided into five sections, the first a history of architecture from Cain's early imitation of the nests of the birds, to the building of the Tabernacle. All "facts" are culled from the Bible. Architecture, for Wood, was essentially a symbolic representation of aims and beliefs. The first tentative expressions in architecture emerge thus from five significant causes: shame, fear, piety, gratitude, and fidelity. The first two, shame for the loss of paradise and fear for the murder committed by Cain, give rise to the principles of convenience and strength. The third cause, piety, which is close to idolatry, leads to confusion. The fourth and fifth causes, gratitude for God's providence and fidelity, lead to the building of the first altars and thus to God's revelation to Moses of beauty to be embodied in the Tabernacle. Before that there was no real architecture; even the pharaohs of Egypt knew nothing of splendor—"In short, a room to eat in, and another to sleep in, made a nobleman's apartment; Beauty and Grandeur in building, being as yet imperceptible in the best of edifices."

The second part, "A Description of Speculative architecture, of Proportion, of Order, of Beauty, and of the various Parts of the Tabernacle," outlines the next phase of history, in which Wood demonstrates how the first three orders took form in the Tabernacle, giving rise to principles of order, proportion, and beauty. Numbers are a very important aspect of Wood's system of belief, transmitted later through Pythagoras to the Western world.

Thus the history of architecture continues. In the final part the architecture of classical antiquity is surveyed. The Romans are condemned for their effrontery and extravagance in adding two orders to those revealed by God. Likewise, though much in Vitruvius is shown to be derived from the tradition of divine revelation, he is condemned for his distortion and falsification of history in upholding the Romans as architectural creators.

Through an adherence to numerical systems, Wood was able to interpret Stonehenge, Gothic architecture (in particular Llandaff cathedral), the work of Palladio, and all his own buildings as derivations of the architecture of the Tabernacle. What he condemned was any attempt to break the system of mathematics and rule that he recognized, to indulge in individual inventions. His despised example of such self-aggrandizement in architecture was Federico Zuccari's house in Florence, illustrated in 1724 in F. Ruggieri's *Studio d'Architettura Civile* (which seems to have been noticed by Soane, for he too viewed the house thus, and prepared no less than two illustrations of it for his Academy lectures). There is a great deal more requiring comment in Wood's book, much of it fantastical, though his wilder flights of fancy were to be contained in his *Essay Towards a Description of the City of Bath*, of 1742 and 1743, and in *Choir Gaure: Vulgarly called Stonehenge*, of 1747: the mythical Bladud, ninth king of Britain, is upheld as a priest of Apollo, who had traveled to Greece and studied under Pythagoras; in Greece he was known by the names of Abaris and Aithrobatus, a figure identified a few years earlier by the Reverend Henry Rowland as a Welsh Druid. Bladud, Wood claimed, was the founder of Bath. He was also the founder of a Druid university at Stanton Drew, the layout of which was modeled on the planetary system, the forerunner of that at Stonehenge. All could be related, through numbers, to Solomon's Temple, the Tabernacle, and thus to God.

This extraordinary search for origins is a legacy of seventeenth-century thought, evident even in the writings of earlier architects. John Webb, for example, was much concerned to determine the origin of language. In *An Historical Essay Endeavoring a Probability that the Language of the Empire of China is the Primitive Language*, first published in 1669, he argued, his Bible to hand, that Chinese was the original language. Noah, he claimed, was none other than the Chinese emperor Jaus, the Ark had been constructed in China, and the Chinese, not being present at Babel, had escaped the Confusion of Tongues—"the language of the Empire of China," he confidently concluded, "is the PRIMITIVE language." Nor was his claim considered outlandish. Webb's book was reissued, its title slightly changed, in 1678. Scholars such as William Whiston, Isaac Newton's renegade disciple, continued to claim in *A New Theory of the Earth*, of 1696, that China was inhabited by Noah's descendants. And even into the eighteenth century, Samuel Shuckford, in the *Sacred and Profane History of the World*, of 1731 to 1737, still upheld the connection between Noah, China, and the primitive language. All this is germane to Wood's investigations, for he made it quite clear that he followed the methods and drew his ideas from men such as Whiston, Shuckford, and, also, Dean Humphrey Prideaux.

The notion that the forms and measures of classical architecture were first revealed by God was first argued at length in a three-volume commentary on the book of the prophet Ezekiel, *In Ezechielem Explanationes*, by G. B Villalpando and H. Prado, published in Rome between 1596 and 1604. Villalpando was making his assertions within the context of the pious court of

John Wood. *The Origin of Building*. Plates 12–13. The camp of the Israelites. NGA Lib. Rare Book: NA211W8 fol.

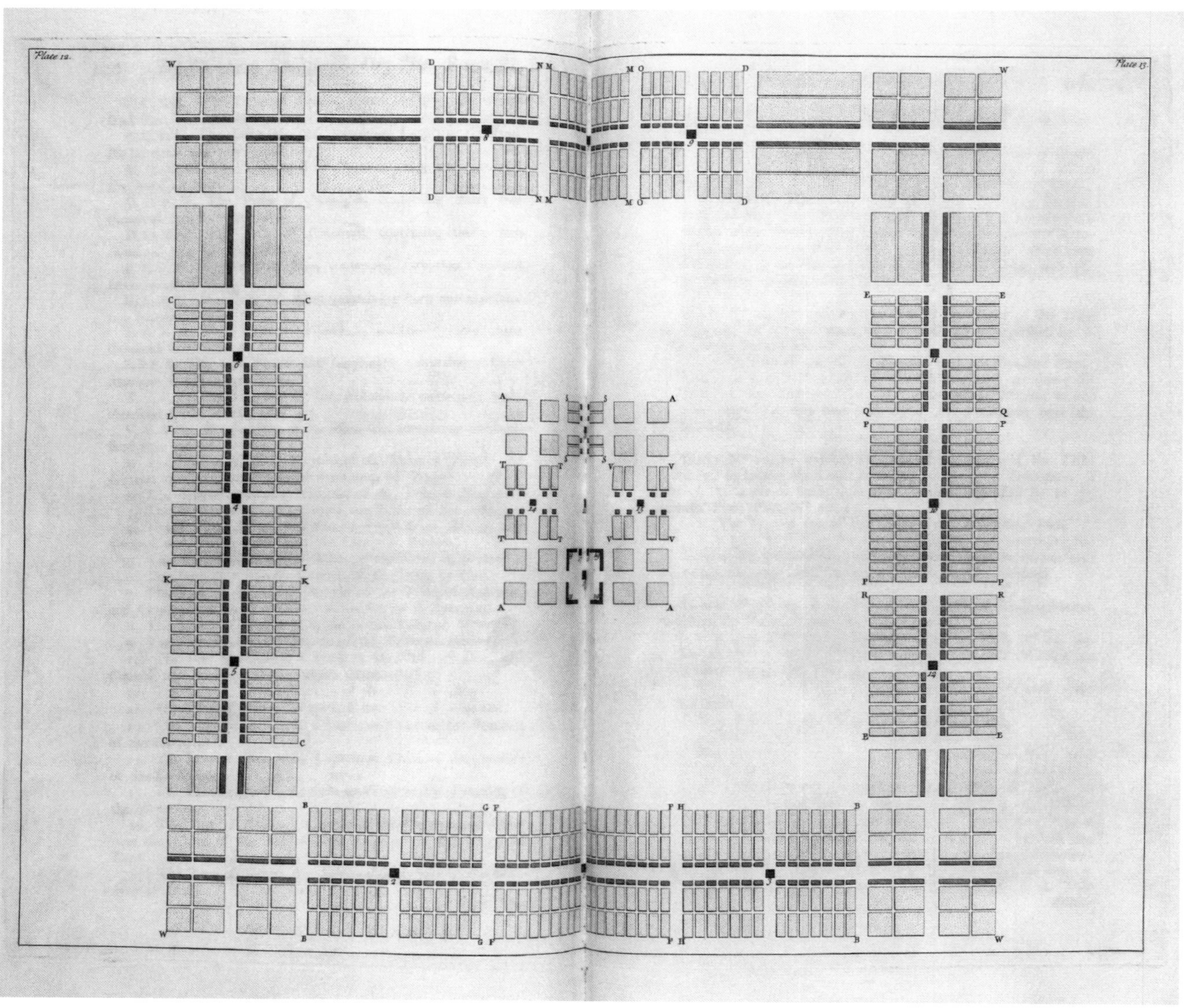

Philip II of Spain. But his idea that the divine knowledge of architecture was first revealed to Ezekiel and then, as described by Josephus Flavius, embodied in the Temple of Solomon, thus providing a biblical model for architecture, was clearly appreciated throughout Europe, even in anti–papist circles in England. Bishop Brian Walton's *Biblia polyglotta*, of 1657, included plates, engraved by Wenceslas Hollar, illustrating Villalpando's reconstruction of the Temple of Solomon, and these were used again in John Ogilby's Bible, published in 1660. The frontispiece to the *Biblia polyglotta* was designed by Webb. There can thus be little doubt that Villalpando's designs became an accepted part of architectural knowledge.

In 1724 and 1725 large wooden models of both the Tabernacle and the Temple, constructed by Johann Jacob Erasmus of Hamburg, were exhibited in London, and a pamphlet was issued—*The Temple of Solomon . . . As Also the Tabernacle of Moses . . . Erected in a Proper Model and Material Representations.* This was no doubt known to Wood, as he was in London in those years. Even before the appearance of the model in London, the matter of the Temple was a topic of earnest speculation. Both Newton and William Stukeley had been drawing up possible plans from 1721 onward. Newton's disciple Whiston was so roused by what he regarded as the errors in Erasmus' reconstruction after Villalpando that he commissioned new models of the Tabernacle and the Temple, in 1726, and exhibited and described them in lectures in London, Bristol, Bath, and Tonbridge Wells. Two or three years after, having consulted further with Newton, he finalized his reconstructions and outlined them in a pamphlet, a copy of which is inserted in Josephus Flavius' *Genuine Works*, of 1737, in the British Library. Whiston's reconstruction was certainly known to Wood. Shuckford himself, in the *Sacred and Profane History of the World*, of 1728, accepted without question the idea that the Tabernacle and the Temple were the issue of divine revelation and the basis of all true architecture.

Though Wood was much stimulated by these scholars, and might himself have possessed a copy of Villalpando's commentary (a copy is listed in the sale of his son's books in 1795), he did not imitate their reconstructions, but considered the matter, himself, anew. And, like Newton, he aimed to illustrate no more than a plan of the Temple; an elevation, he thought, might serve as an invitation to idolatry.

Wood's ideas were influenced also, as Tim Mowl and Brian Earnshaw have shown, by masonic teachings, though these relate to his subsequent interpretations of history resulting from his detailed study of Stanton Drew and Stonehenge. Mowl and Earnshaw quote a passage from *The Constitutions of the Free Masons*, by James Anderson, published in 1723, that would seem to summarize Wood's notions of the transposition of knowledge:

> Pythagoras travell'd into Egypt the year that Thales dy'd, and living there among the Priests twenty-two Years, became expert in Geometry, and in all the Egyptian learning, until he was captivated by Cambyses King of Persia, and sent to Babylon, where he was much conversant with the Chaldean MAGI and the learned Babylonish JEWS, from whom he borrow'd great knowledge, that rendered him very famous in Greece and Italy; where afterwards he flourish'd and dy'd when Mordecai was prime Minister of State to Ahasuerus King of Persia, and ten years after Zerubbabel's TEMPLE was finish'd. AM 3498, 506 Ante Ch.

The Circus at Bath, it is proposed, was conceived in the form of Zerubbabel's Second Temple.

This, however, is an aspect of Wood's later endeavors, once again linked to the earlier activities of Webb who, adapting Jones' "few indigested notes," had published *The Most Notable Antiquity of Great Britain, Vulgarly called Stone-Heng* in 1655, claiming Stonehenge as a Tuscan temple, dedicated to Coelus, the god of heaven, erected during the late Roman occupation, the plan based on four intersecting equilateral triangles inscribed in a circle (a pattern Vitruvius had proposed for the layout of a theater). Webb's book, together with Dr. William Charleton's refutation of it, in favor of a Danish origin, *Chorea Gigantum*, of 1663, and Webb's lengthy reply, *A Vindication of Stone Heng Restored*, of 1665, were published in a single book in 1725. All were thus readily accessible to Wood to stoke his historical passions. As also was Stukeley's slightly more prosaic study—though it, too, was based on a Mosaic interpretation of the Tabernacle—*Stonehenge, A Temple Restored to the Druids*, of 1740.

The key, however, to all Wood's attempts to equate scriptural accounts and historical knowledge was Newton's *Chronology of the Ancient Kingdoms Amended*, of 1728, which enabled Wood to reduce drastically the chronology of Egyptian history in relation to that of the Israelites. This source, acknowledged on the title page of his manuscript version of *The Origins of Building*, was not made overt in the final publication; nor did he publish the preface he had written explaining the use he had made of scriptural detail, making interpretation of his book a far more tedious and complex matter than it need have been. R. M.

Bibliography

Bold, J. *John Webb. Architectural Theory and Practice in the Seventeenth Century*. Oxford, 1989

Colvin, H. *A Biographical Dictionary of British Architects, 1660–1840*. London, 1978

Harris, E., and N. Savage. *British Architectural Books and Writers 1556–1785*. Cambridge, 1990

Mowl, T. and B. Earnshaw. *John Wood, Architect of Obsession*. Bath, 1988

Reuther, H. "Das Modell des Salomischen Temples im Museum für Hamburgische Geschichte." *Niederdeutsche Beiträge zur Kunstgeschichte* 19 (1980): 161–195

92

Robert Wood (1717–1771)

The Ruins Of Palmyra, Otherwise Tedmore, In The Desart

London, 1753

1985.61.2767

Folio: 552 × 367 (21¾ × 14 7/16)

Pagination [vi], 50 pp., 57 [i.e., 59] engraved plates

Edition First edition

Text pp. [i] title page (verso blank); [iii–vi] "The Publisher To The Reader," signed by Wood; [1]–23 text, "An Enquiry Into The Antient State Of Palmyra"; [24]–32 text, "The Inscriptions"; [33]–35 text, "A Journey Through The Desart"; [36]–50 explanation of plates, ending with errata

(*Note*: In a variant state, the first erratum on p. 50 reads, "Page 7. l. 28. for Herencanius, read Herenianus." This has been corrected in press in the present copy, and the first erratum is instead "Page 9. l. 26. for emperor's, read emperors")

Illustrations 3 full-page plates of inscriptions in the text, engraved by J. Gibson; plus 59 engraved plates numbered I–LVII (plate I extending over 3 leaves, here bound as 3 separate plates but sometimes bound as 1 long folding plate). Most of the plates are signed as drawn by G. B. Borra and engraved by P. Fourdrinier (plates III–X, XII–XVI, XVIII–XIX, XXII–XXV, XXVIII–XXX, XXXII–XXXIV, XLI–XLII, XLIV, XLVII–LI, LIV–LVI), J. S. Müller, i.e., Miller (plates XXI, XXVI, XXXV, XXXVIII, XLIII), or T. M. Müller, junior (plate XL). Some plates are only signed by the engraver, i.e., T. M. Müller, junior (plates XI, XX, XXXVII, XXXIX, XLV, LIII, LVII) or Thomas Major (plates I–II, XXVII). Plates XVII and XXXVI unsigned

Binding Contemporary calf, gilt borders, gilt corner ornaments, rebacked

References Berlin Cat. 1884; Cicognara 2722; ESTC t137526; Fowler 443; Harris and Savage 939

ROBERT WOOD was born near Trim in County Meath, Ireland, in 1717. He was neither an architect nor a draftsman, but a classical scholar trained in law at Glasgow and later admitted to the Middle Temple. In 1756 he was appointed undersecretary of state in William Pitt's administration and held high public office until his death in 1771. But in his youth he acted as a traveling tutor. He was taken to Greece, Syria, Egypt, and Mesopotamia in 1742 and 1743. In Rome, in 1749, he encountered—probably for the first time—two Oxford graduates, James Dawkins and John Bouverie, both well off (Dawkins had inherited a Jamaica fortune in 1744) and well connected in Jacobite circles. They had been traveling in Europe for four years at least, at first with Richard Phelps as their guide. Bouverie had already formed a collection of drawings and coins that established him as something of a connoisseur, but they were looking for larger adventure and larger objects of antiquity on which to focus their attention. They thought to travel to the Levant and invited Robert Wood to join them.

In the preface to *The Ruins of Palmyra*, he wrote:

> As I had already seen most of the places they intended to visit, they did me the honour of communicating to me their thoughts upon that head, and I with great pleasure accepted their kind invitation to be of so agreeable a party.
>
> The knowledge I had of those gentlemen, in different tours through France and Italy, promised all the success we could wish from such a voyage; their strict friendship for one another, their love of antiquities and the fine arts, and their being well accustomed for several years to travelling, were circumstances very requisite to our scheme, but rarely to be met with in two persons, who with taste and leisure for such enquiries, are equal both to the expence and fatigue of them.

Also in Rome that year was Lord Charlemont, who was planning an expedition to the Levant. He had selected as his draftsman Giovanni Battista Borra, a pupil of Vittone, from Turin, whom he had no doubt encountered while attending the Academy there in 1747 and 1748. But Borra declined at the last moment, and Charlemont instead invited Richard Dalton, another traveling tutor who happened to be in Italy, to take his place. Charlemont and Dalton embarked on their journey in April 1749. Before his departure, Charlemont had encouraged James Stuart, Nicholas Revett, and Gavin Hamilton, who had been studying painting in Rome for six or seven years, but late in 1748 had been struck by the idea of venturing to Athens and recording the antiquities there. Hamilton was to abandon the enterprise, returning to England in the spring of 1750. Stuart and Revett were more determined; they remained in Rome, studying and looking for support. Stuart thought he had found a patron in Charles Wentworth, earl of Malton, in 1749, but nothing came of this connection. Luckily, at this point, they met Dawkins and Bouverie, who were planning their expedition with Wood. Whether or not Stuart and Revett received financial support from them at this period, they certainly found inspiration and guidance, both in his depth of classical scholarship and his practical knowledge of travel in the East. Dawkins, Bouverie, and Wood spared no pains or expense in the planning of their expedition and were deeply involved through the winter of 1749. By then—probably as early as March or April—they had induced Borra to accompany them as their draftsman. The following spring they moved south to Naples to begin their journey; Stuart and Revett moved north to Venice to begin theirs. Dawkins, Bouverie, Wood, and Borra sailed from Naples on 5 May 1750 in the *Matilda*, a ship chartered in London, equipped with a library of travel literature and Greek classics, measuring and excavating gear, and supplies. They sailed direct to Smyrna (Izmir), where they landed on 18 May, and from there ventured inland to Pergamon and Sardis, embarking on 9 June for Constantinople, where they dropped anchor on 16 June. They required permissions for their explorations and were forced to spend some time in the city and its surrounds. Surprisingly, they were not much impressed by Santa Sophia, which they were allowed to view from the gallery—"I can't say the Inside does dedommage the Trouble and Expense of most Visitors," Dawkins noted in his record of their travels, "& I firmly believe that if St. Sophia was in Rome that no Traveller except a German would ever enter It."

Robert Wood. *The Ruins of Palmyra.* Tab. XXXV. 1985.61.2767

They left Constantinople on 10 July, sailing west through the Sea of Marmora. Their first concern was to explore the Troad, the site of Homer's Troy, and to understand Homer, Wood fervently believed—and this was to be his special contribution to Homeric studies, outlined first in 1767 in *A Comparative View of the Antient and Present State of the Troade. To which is prefixed an Essay on the Original Genius of Homer*—it was necessary to walk the land and to view the sky that Homer had seen, and to experience the manners and customs, even as they survived, that he had known. They rode the Trojan plain, they crossed the Scamander, but found little enough. They moved south then, down the Turkish coast, stopping off on the mainland and the islands on the way. On Samos they transferred to a Greek boat to make a jaunt up the Meander River, into Caria, to explore the sites of Miletus, Priene, Magnesia, and others. Here disaster struck. Bouverie died on 19 September, near Magnesia (from pleurisy), and his body was shipped to Smyrna for burial. But the expedition continued. Bouverie was regarded as the archaeologist; he was to have been responsible for the description of monuments. Wood, who concentrated on the topography of sites and inscriptions, and Dawkins, whose interest was local customs, flora and fauna, were now forced to share Bouverie's task. They rejoined their boat at Bodrum on 10 October and, moving south, reached

Alexandria in Egypt on 4 November 1750. Six weeks were spent in the region of Cairo, measuring the pyramids for publication. They thought then to travel to Athens. However, rough weather forced them to run for Haifa. From there they decided to venture inland, and after an inevitable delay in obtaining permissions, traveled to Damascus, arriving there on 1 March 1751. Only at this period, it seems, did they determine on the visit to Palmyra and Baalbek. They reached Palmyra on 14 March and Baalbek on 1 April. How long they stayed at each of these sites is uncertain; most of their diaries for this period are lost. In their subsequent publication Wood claimed that fifteen days were spent in Palmyra, but this is not borne out by the surviving diaries (along with Borra's drawings in the collections of the Royal Hellenic Society). No more than five full days seem to have been spent at Palmyra, eight at Baalbek, though after five days there they complained that their work was done—they must all have worked with a rare intensity. Their personal servants must have been coerced to help with the measuring—Dawkins and Bouverie had started with three servants, Wood had one. Rejoining their ship at Tripoli, they sailed on 9 April for Cyprus. They traveled then, more or less direct, for Greece, stopping only at Stanchio (Kos) before making a final jaunt to the mouth of the Meander to visit the temple of Didymi, and also Delos, dropping anchor on 8 May at Porto Raphte, where they were met by Stuart, who conducted them that evening to Athens.

"When we arrived at Athens," Wood wrote in his preface to *Palmyra*, "we found Mr. *Stewart* and Mr. *Revet*, two English painters, successfully employed in taking measures of all the architecture there, and making drawings of all the bas reliefs, with a view to publish them, according to a scheme they had communicated to us at Rome."

The explorers are recorded together, inspecting the Monument to Philopappos in Athens, in a magnificent plate, drawn by Revett, published only in 1795 in the third volume of the *Antiquities of Athens*, Stuart and Revett in local costume, Wood and Dawkins sprucely attired as gentlemen. It was Dawkins' liberality that enabled Stuart and Revett to stay on in Athens, quietly measuring the ruins. Publication of their work was a protracted affair: the first volume of the *Antiquities of Athens* appeared only in 1762.

Wood and Dawkins left Athens for home on 7 June 1751; by the end of the year, traveling though the Straits of Gibraltar, they were back in London. Borra was still with them. By that time Dalton, ignoring any claims Charlemont might have had, had begun to publish the record of his travels. On 15 April 1751 "Twenty-one Prints of the Antiquities of Athens, Mount Aetna in Sicily and Pompey's Pillar at Alexandria" were announced, to be followed on 20 February 1752 by twenty more views and antiquities of Greece and Egypt. But no more were published until 1781. Subscriptions for *The Ruins of Palmyra* were announced in the *General Advertiser* of 16 January 1752. The volume was to contain sixty plates, the first of which could be viewed at Wood's house in Lancaster Court, London. The cost would be three guineas, half of this to be paid in advance. Most of the plates (only fifty-seven in the event) were engraved by P. Fourdrinier, though the plan and the panoramic view of the site, this last on three copperplates, were by Thomas Major, with the six other views by J. S. Müller (J. S. Miller) and T. M. Müller, Jr. The inscriptions were engraved by J. Gibson. Borra was scrupulously credited on each of the plates for which he was responsible. Subscriptions continued to be taken until March 1753, the intended date of publication. But this was delayed, perhaps because Wood had left England early in 1753 to conduct the young duke of Bridgewater to France and Italy. The book appeared, according to the *Public Advertiser*, on 23 November 1753, in both French and English editions.

The Ruins of Palmyra was something of a revelation, more so even than *The Ruins of Balbec* that was to follow in 1767. Palmyra was rediscovered for Europe in 1678 by a party of English merchants from Aleppo, led by a Dr. Huntington. Another such expedition visited the site in 1691, led on this occasion by William Halifax of Oxford, who published an account of the journey illustrated with a crude, but striking panorama of the site in the *Philosophical Transactions of the Royal Society* of October, November, and December 1695. Another such panorama was included in the *Reizen . . . door de vermaardste deelen van Kleinasia, die Eylanden Scio, Rhodus, Cyprus, Metelino, Stanchio, &c., mitsgaders de voornaamste Steden van Aegypten, Syrien en Palestina*, by the Dutch painter Cornelis de Bruyn, who spent the years from 1678 to 1685 in the Levant; it was first issued in Delft in 1698, and in Paris in 1700 as the *Voyage au Levant*. A third panorama was produced in 1711 by Cornelius Loos, an engineer in the train of Charles XII of Sweden, then beleaguered in Bender. Johann Fischer von Erlach took up this view for his panorama of Palmyra included in the first version of his *Entwurff einer historischen Architectur* of 1712. The first published edition appeared in 1721 with more to follow; the book was available in English by 1730. But Palmyra remained little known.

Baalbek had been visited first in 1647 by Balthasar de Monconys, in 1660 by Laurent d'Arvieux, in 1668 by De Monceaux, and in 1688 by Jean de la Roque, each of whom had published accounts of the experience, though the buildings there were to be revealed to the world in the seventeen fine engravings of the temples published around 1670 by Daniel Marot (probably on the basis of De Monceaux's observations). Some of these were copied by Bernard de Montfaucon for his *Antiquité expliquée*, issued in fifteen folio volumes between 1719 and 1724. The English translation, much reduced, appeared between 1721 and 1725. The buildings of Baalbek were lavishly illustrated again in Richard Pococke's *Descrip-*

tion of the East and Some Other Countries, of 1743–1745.

Though Palmyra and Baalbek were to be the subjects of Wood and Dawkins' major publications, it must be evident that they were not intended, at first, to be the focus of their studies. Wood and Dawkins, like their contemporaries, were inspired to tour the Levant by such books as Jacob Spon's *Voyage d'Italie, de Dalmatie, de Grèce et du Levant*, of 1676, a plagiarized version of which was published in English in 1682 by his companion George Wheler, and by the works of De Bruyn and Pococke. This last, without doubt, was the book that had stirred so much interest in the sites of the eastern Mediterranean in the late 1740s. It was a discursive travel book in three volumes. The views of buildings were clumsy and inaccurate, but Pococke made evident at once the richness and variety of sites demanding to be explored.

Robert Wood. *The Ruins of Palmyra.* Tab. LVI. 1985.61.2767

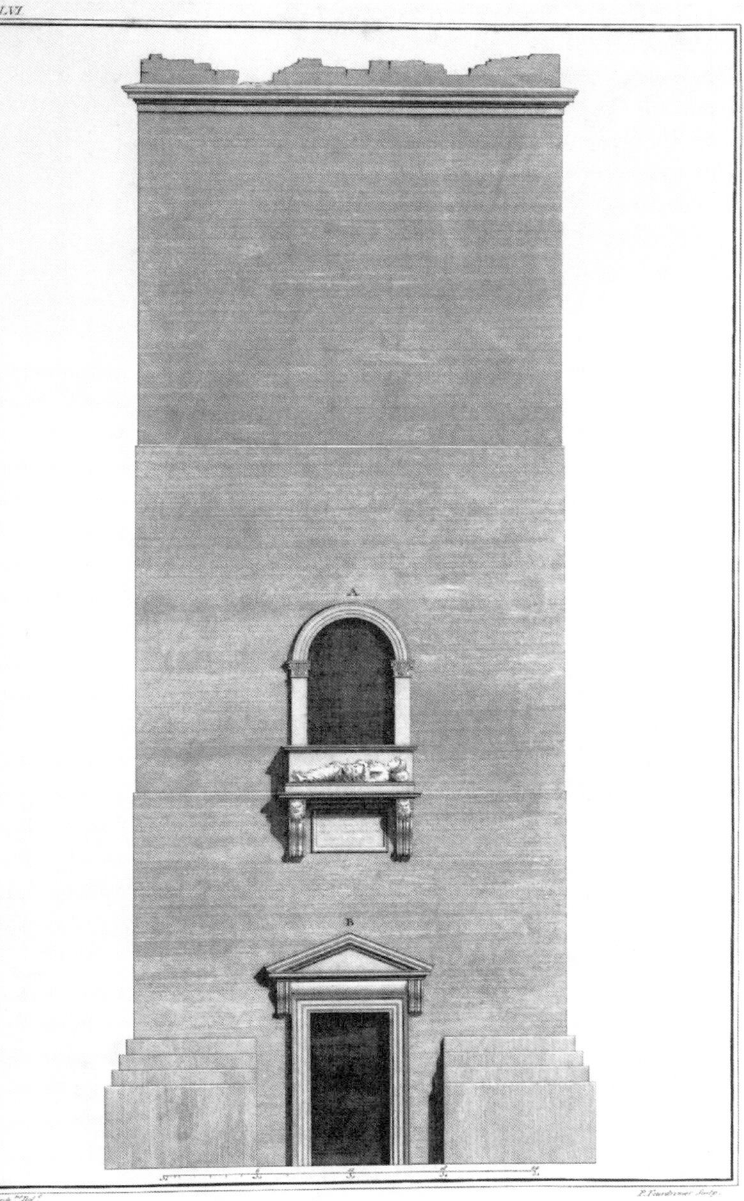

Wood and Dawkins were attentive throughout their journey to Pococke's remarks and observations, mainly, it must be admitted, to refute them. But he remained their basic reference. For the most part they visited only sites that he had visited, though he did not travel to Palmyra. This they knew from De Bruyn and Fischer von Erlach. De Bruyn, of course, did not visit Baalbek. But neither Palmyra nor Baalbek seems at first to have been intended as a particular goal. Wood and Dawkins traveled there, almost inadvertently, when their ship was forced to make port in Haifa, en route to Athens.

The preface that Wood composed for *The Ruins of Palmyra* opens with the statement: "As the principle merit of works of this kind is truth, it may not be amiss to prefix to this, such an account of the manner in which it was undertaken, and executed, as will give the publick an opportunity of judging what credit it deserves."

The aim was to provide as dispassionate an account as may be of their adventure and of their findings. Wood offered the first synthetic history of Palmyra, based on antique sources, also an account of their journey, "A journey through the Desart" (not altogether accurate), and an analysis of the inscriptions they found. But the focus of attention was the architecture, and this was presented essentially in the form of illustrations—a site plan, an overall view, with views of individual buildings or features followed by measured plans, elevations, and details. The emphasis was on the details, restored. Very little comment was made on the architecture itself; references to it were in the nature of reporting; though there are hints that it was not altogether to their taste: "There is a greater sameness in the architecture of Palmyra, than we observed at Rome, Athens, and other great cities, whose ruins evidently point out different ages, as much from the variety of their manner, as their different stages of decay."

Their model in the care of measuring and representation was Antoine Desgodetz's *Les Edifices Antiques de Rome*, first published in 1682. This had established a new standard for archaeological reporting and was a byword of meticulous surveying.

"Architecture," Wood wrote, "took up our chief attention; and in the enquiry our expectations were more fully satisfied. All lovers of that art must be sensible that the measures of the antient buildings of Rome, by Monsieur Desgodetz, have been of the greatest use: We imagined that by attempting to follow the same method in those countries where architecture had its origin, or at least arrived at the highest degree of perfection it had ever attained, we might do service."

Given the speed of their surveying, the accuracy of their representations are amazing. And they were recognized at once as authoritative. An early review of the work appeared in the *Journal Brittanique* in September–October 1753, another in the *Monthly Review* of December 1753—"this beautiful and elegant work." In the same month Horace Walpole wrote to R. Bentley—

"Palmyra is come forth, and is a noble work; the prints finely engraved, and an admirable dissertation before it." There were other encomiums. Even in France the book was appreciated. Charles-Joseph Natoire, writing to the marquis de Marigny on 24 December 1754, described it as "un beaux livre." Jacques-François Blondel made mention of it in several anonymous reviews, and extolled it, at even greater length, in the fourth volume of his *Architecture françoise* of 1756 (p. 40). But there was also some criticism. Robert Adam, writing to his brother James from London on 1 November 1759, noted ". . . I am not for praising the Taste of W. ds work, the greatest connoisseurs here, are of my own private opinion that Taste & Truth, or as W. terms it, Accuracy, are not the Characteristicks or Qualifications of these Works. They are as hard as Iron, & as false as Hell . . ." (SRO GD 18/4843). Adam, nonetheless, upheld the book as a model when he came to write the introduction to his own *Ruins of the Palace of the Emperor Diocletian at Spalatro* of 1764.

The influence of *The Ruins of Palmyra* was considerable. Elements of the soffit of the Temple of the Sun can be discerned in ceilings by Adam at Osterley, Syon, Bowood, and Compton Verney; by Borra at Stowe and Norfolk House, St. James' Square, London; and by Henry Flitcroft at Woburn. There are more such transpositions, including some in Turin and Piedmont, to which Borra later returned. But it was not as a source for the imitation of details that the book was valued, rather as a dispassionate and accurate survey of the architecture of antiquity; it wrested the lead in such matters from the French, and initiated a series of archaeological works that came to characterize the activities of both connoisseurs and architects in England in the second half of the eighteenth century. R. M.

Bibliography

Constantine, D. *Early Greek Travellers and the Hellenic Ideal.*

Harris, E., and N. Savage. *British Architectural Books and Writers 1556–1785.* Cambridge, 1990

Hewlings, R. "A Palmyra Ceiling in Lincoln." *Architectural History* 31 (1988): 166–170

Hutton, C. A. "The Travels of 'Palmyra' Wood in 1750–51." *The Journal of Hellenic Studies* 47 (1927): 102–128

Kunoth, G. *Die Historische Architektur Fischers von Erlach.* Düsseldorf, 1956

Wiebenson, D. *Sources of Greek Revival Architecture.* London, 1969

Zoller, O. "Der Architekt und der Ingenieur Giovanni Battista Borra (1713–1770)." Ph.D. dissertation, University of Bonn, 1993

93

Robert Wood (1717–1771)

Les Ruines De Balbec, Autrement Dite Heliopolis Dans La Coelosyrie

A Londres, 1757

1985.61.2768

Folio: 551 × 363 (21 5/8 × 14 1/4)

Pagination [2], 28 pp., 46 [i.e., 47] engraved plates (9 folding, 2 double-page)

Edition First edition of French translation

Robert Wood. *Les Ruines de Balbec*. Tab. XXXII. 1985.61.2768

Text pp. [i] title page (verso blank); [1]–16 text; 17–28 explanation of the plates

Illustrations 47 engraved plates numbered I–XLVI (plate III bound as 2 double-page plates; plates II, V, VI, IX–XII, XIV, XXI folding). All of the plates are signed as engraved by P. Fourdrinier or Thomas Major after drawings by G. B. Borra

Binding Contemporary mottled calf, gilt borders with corner ornaments, gilt spine, red morocco label

Provenance The Liechtenstein copy, with armorial bookplate

References ESTC t219382; Fowler 444 (English ed.); Berlin Cat. 1887; Cicognara 2723; Harris and Savage 937

The acclaim with which *The Ruins of Palmyra* was greeted prompted James Dawkins and Robert Wood to proceed with the sequel—indeed with more than one sequel. Drawings by Giovanni Battista Borra, complete with plate numbers, at the Yale Center for British Art (ninety-eight) and in the collection of E. Neville-Rolfe of Tisbury (seven), attest to plans to publish other volumes surveying the sites they had visited. Proposals for publishing *The Ruins of Balbec*, once again by subscription, were announced in the *Public Advertiser* on 26 July 1754. By then the work was "already in great forwardness," and some of the plates could be viewed at A. Millar's, in the Strand. But publication was delayed for some years; Borra was by then working on Norfolk House in St. James' Square and at Stowe, and, presumably, could not devote too much time to the drawings required for engraving. Wood was traveling again. In 1755 he was in Rome, then in 1756 he was appointed William Pitt's undersecretary of state. The book was published only on 21 April 1757, in both English and French editions. It was noticed in the *Critical Review* for July of that year.

> The *classical* part of their travels, with the illustration of *antient fable*, will be a valuable acquisition to the learned world. . . . the ruins of Balbec will afford the lover of art and *virtù* the highest satisfaction, as they will exhibit to him the finest remains of antient architecture perhaps now in the world. . . . Mr. Wood . . . informs us, that Mr. Dawkins, with the same generous spirit which had so indefatigably surmounted the various obstacles of their voyage, continued, during Mr. Wood's unavoidable absence, to protect the fruits of those labours which he had so chearfully shared; and that he not only attended to the accuracy of the work, by having finished drawings made under his own eye by their draughtsman, from the sketches and measures he had taken on the spot, but had the engravings so far advanced as to be now ready for the public under their joint inspection.

There were fulsome reviews also in the *Journal Brittanique* for November–December 1757 and the *Journal encyclopédique* of 15 May 1758, though a warning was issued in the *Anné littéraire*, on 8 November 1758, that the rich array of details offered in the *Balbec* volume might tempt architects to imitation rather than understanding:

Tab. XLIII.
B
A
A
A
B
C
D
Borra Arch. Del.
P. Fourdrinier Sculp.

"[les bâtiments de l'antiquité] sont nos modèles sans doute, mais pour être leurs imitatieurs, non leurs plagiaires; c'est l'esprit de leurs ouvrages & de leurs leçons qu'il faut saisir." Here is the exact note struck by J.-D. Leroy in his later dispute with James Stuart and Nicholas Revett, marking the essential difference between the French and the English approaches to archaeology in the second half of the eighteenth century.

The text of *The Ruins of Balbec* was written by Wood, with a history of the site, an account of the "Journey from Palmyra to Balbec," and an analysis of the inscriptions found. The tone was as before: "It shall also, in this, as in the former volume, be our principal care to produce things as we found them, leaving reflections and reasonings upon them to others. This last rule we shall scrupulously observe in describing the Buildings; where all criticism on the beauties and faults of the Architecture is left entirely to the reader."

There were fifty-seven plates to illustrate the site and the architecture, with five of the perspective views engraved by Thomas Major, and the plans, sections, and details of the buildings by P. Fourdrinier, though on this occasion he was entrusted also with the two views of the [Temple of Bacchus] and the three of "The circular temple."

The volume was, in many ways, even more appreciated than the first, and more influential. Daniel Marot's engravings were revealed as no more than approximations of the architecture; his restorations were demonstrably unsound. Many of the details of the temples at Baalbek were taken up by English architects; the "Circular Temple" was twice imitated, by William Chambers at Kew, in 1761, and Henry Flitcroft, a few years after, at Stourhead. But it was the example of archaeological objectivity that was set by this and the previous work that was to be valued above all else. Horace Walpole, in his *Anecdotes of Painting*, of 1762, gave the surest estimate:

> But of all the works that distinguish this age, none perhaps excel those beautiful editions of Balbec and Palmyra—not published at the command of a Louis quatorze, or at the expense of a cardinal nephew, but undertaken by private curiosity and good sense, and trusted to the taste of a polished nation. When I endeavour to do justice to the editions of Palmyra and Balbec, I would not confine the encomium to the sculptures; the books have far higher merit. The modest descriptions prefixed are standards of writing: The exact measure of what should and what should not be said, and of what was necessary to be known, was never comprehended in more clear diction, or more elegant stile. The pomp of the buildings had not a nobler air than the simplicity of the narration. . . .

The French translations, one might note, were not so sound. *Les Ruines de Palmyre* was issued again, in Paris, in 1819, and yet again in 1829. A combined edition of the books, *The Ruins of Palmyra and Balbec*, was still deemed necessary in 1827. R. M.

Bibliography

Constantine, D. *Early Greek Travellers and the Hellenic Ideal*. Cambridge, 1984

Harris, E., and N. Savage. *British Architectural Books and Writers 1556–1785*. Cambridge, 1990

Wiebenson, D. *Sources of Greek Revival Architecture*. London, 1969

Zoller, O. "Der Architekt und der Ingenieur Giovanni Battista Borra (1713–1770)." Ph.D. dissertation, University of Bonn, 1993

Robert Wood. *Les Ruines de Balbec*. Plate XLIII. 1985.61.2768

94

John Woolfe (d. 1793) and James Gandon (1742–1823)

Vitruvius Britannicus, Or The British Architect; Containing Plans, Elevations, And Sections; Of The Regular Buildings Both Public And Private, In Great Britain. Comprised In One Hundred Folio Plates, Engrav'd By The Best Hands; Taken From The Buildings, Or Original Designs By Woolfe And Gandon Architects. Vol. IV. (V.) . . . [same in French]

[London], 1767–1771

1985.61.442–443

Folio: 572 × 380 (22½ × 15)

Pagination Vol. 4: 12 pp., engraved title plate, engraved dedication, [79] engraved plates (19 double-page)

Vol. 5: 10 pp., engraved title plate, engraved dedication, [75] engraved plates (23 double-page)

Edition First editions

Text (parallel English and French) *vol. 4*: pp. 1–2 introduction; 3–10 explanations of the plates; 11–12 list of subscribers; *vol. 5*: pp. 1–2 list of subscribers; 3–10 explanations of the plates

Illustrations *Vol. 4*: engraved title plate, engraved dedication and 79 engraved plates numbered 1–98 (19 double-page plates given 2 numbers each). Woolfe and Gandon sign themselves as draftsmen and the engravers include Matthias Darly (41), Thomas White (22), James Gandon (9), Tobias Miller (3), Anthony Walker (2), Marley (1), and [John] Roberts (1). Many of the plates also bear the names of the architect of the design, signed lower left, including Roger Morris (8, 3 with Stephen Wright); William Chambers (7); John Sanderson (7, 3 with [William] Smith); Giacomo Leoni (6, some signed "B. Leoni"); Robert Adam, John James, James Paine (5 each); Henry Flitcroft (4); Matthew Brettingham ("Brickingham"), Lord Burlington, George Dance, John Vardy, John Wood (3 each); William Kent, Isaac Ware, Thomas Wright (2 each); Giovanni Niccolo Servandoni, Robert Taylor (1 each). *Vol. 5*: engraved title plate, engraved dedication, and 75 engraved plates numbered 3–100 (23 double-page given 2 numbers each). The draftsmen were Woolfe, Gandon, and J. Milton ("mensur. et del. 1766," 3), and the engravers were Thomas White (63), H. Mackworth (4), Christopher Ebdon (3), Tobias Miller (2), James Gandon (1), and [John] Roberts (1). Architects credited include John Carr of York (12, 1 signed "R. Carr"), Robert Adam (7), Roger Morris (7, 2 with Lord Burlington), William Hiorne (4), William Chambers, John Donowell, Sir James Thornhill, James Gandon, Joseph Pickford, John Wood (3 each); Lancelot Brown, Kenton Couse, Inigo Jones, Stiff Leadbetter, and Isaac Ware (2 each)

Binding Early nineteenth-century marbled boards, spines and corners renewed. With 1 of I. and J. Taylor's 4-page catalogues, *A Catalogue of Modern Books on Architecture*, printed on blue paper and bound at the end of vol. 4. Uncut copy

Provenance Ownership inscriptions "J. Daniell [?]" in both volumes

References Berlin Cat. 2329 (vols. 1–5); Berlin (1977) os 2329 (vols. 1–5); ESTC t60851; Fowler 76 (vols. 1–4); Harris and Savage 945

ANOTHER COPY

1985.61.447–448

Folio: 550 × 385 (21⅝ × 15³⁄₁₆)

Binding Late nineteenth-century three-quarter red morocco, dark green buckram boards, bound uniform as vols. 4–5 of S. D. Button's copy of *Vitruvius Britannicus* (for vols. 1–3, see under Colen Campbell; for vols. 6–7, see under George Richardson). With an early nineteenth-century? 12–page MS "Catalogue of the Pictures, Statues &c. at Kedleston With some Account of the Architecture" bound between plates 75 and 76 in vol. 4

Provenance Presented by S. D. Button to the Philadelphia Chapter of the American Institute of Architects

"WE HAVE throughout this production considered Mr. Campbell as our leader; and have, therefore, no way deviated from his plan, that this might be a proper supplement to his work, forming a fourth Volume of Vitruvius Britannicus" (Introduction, p. 2). This declaration at the opening of John Woolfe and James Gandon's revival of *Vitruvius Britannicus* seems clear enough: since they intended, above all, to appeal to owners of Campbell's book, it was incumbent upon them to match it as closely as possible in form and content. As is often the case with sequels, however, the real interest of Woolfe and Gandon's book lies in the particular ways in which it differs from Campbell's. Indeed, by focusing on these differences it may be possible to suggest why Woolfe and Gandon undertook a project that on the face of it seems little more rewarding than hack work, and also to detect the influence of some significant changes that had taken place in the social and artistic milieu of the "British architect" since Campbell's time.

So why did two unknown but professionally well-connected young architects—one a "labourer in trust" in the Office of Works who had worked under James Paine, the other a brilliant but as yet unproven pupil of William Chambers—decide that a sequel to a book begun half a century earlier was the best way to launch an independent career? Was the conservative character of this enterprise merely a corollary of their need to find a commercially safe vehicle in which to advertise their abilities and knowledge as architects? Or did its adherence to an old model convey, with what Gandon's recent biographer Edward McParland has called "an element of assertive insularity," a message as pointed in its time as Campbell's championing of Inigo Jones had been fifty years earlier? Does their gathering up of some of the Palladian movement's most distinctive achievements, such as William Kent's Horse Guards, Whitehall (5: pls. 3–8; built 1750–1759) and Holkham Hall, Norfolk (5: pls. 64–69; built 1734–1765), Lord Burlington's Assembly Rooms in York (4: pls. 78–81; built 1731–1732), and Roger Morris' White Lodge, Richmond Park (4: pls. 1–4; built 1727–1728) and Combe Bank, Kent (4: pls. 75–77; built c. 1725), mean that Woolfe and Gandon are concerned to counter fashionable brands of imported neoclassicism with a celebration of British Palladian heroes of the past?—a conclusion that might sit uncomfortably with James Gandon's subsequent career as one of the most advanced and original neoclassical architects in the last quarter of the eighteenth century. Or is their "assertive insularity" an architectural equivalent of Hogarth's patriotic self-reliance, the father of the British School's old battle-cry against the dilettanti and connoisseurs of antique bric-à-brac and fake old masters finding a renewed echo here in an explicit call for the solid achievements of the British architect—"Vitruvius Britannicus" himself—to be given due recognition on the world stage? (Hogarth had died on 25 or 26 October

John Woolfe and James Gandon. *Vitruvius Britannicus.* Vol. 4, plate 79. Richard Boyle, 3d earl of Burlington. The Assembly Rooms, York. Elevation. 1985.61.447

Elevation of the Assembly Room at York.

Elevation de la Maison d'Assemblée a York.

J. Gandon del.

1764, only five months before Woolfe and Gandon's book began to appear.) And could this perhaps be related to the start of a gradual shift in the status of the architect, in which the creation of good architecture begins to be seen no longer primarily as an expression of the refined taste and connoisseurship of the patron who commissions it, but rather as the product of the professional skills, experienced judgment, and "genius" of the architect he employs? It is clearly impossible to address all these questions here—they are put forward simply to suggest that the normative character of Woolfe and Gandon's book offers rich territory for an analysis of the underlying conventions governing a certain type of architectural publication in the third quarter of the eighteenth century.

After Campbell's trenchant preface, carefully weighted commentary, and the pointed juxtapositioning of his plates (so that the design of each successive building is implicitly judged against that of its neighbors), however, Woolfe and Gandon's assertion of the superiority of British architecture seems merely routine, their avoidance of issues of relative architectural merit bland, and their uniformly "technical" presentation cold and impersonal. Moreover, their sequel has none of the comparative structure that gives Campbell's first two volumes their punch, and their text is scarcely more architecturally informative than an estate agent's patter. However, none of this implies that they had no other concern than to satisfy an "obvious" captive market among existing owners of Campbell's book. Paradoxically, while Campbell's *Vitruvius Britannicus* appears to be an independent creation serving Campbell's private ambitions, but is, in fact, the product of close collaboration with his publishers, Woolfe and Gandon's continuation appears to be a booksellers' confection, but is rather the independent creation of two young architect/authors acting as their own publishers. The limitations of their undertaking were essentially self-imposed since, unlike Campbell, they were at liberty to please no one but themselves and their subscribers. This fact alone should be enough to signal the possibility that their conservatism arose from deliberate choice rather than expediency, and may indeed have had a distinct resonance in the context of the cultural politics of Britain in the mid-1760s.

Probably the most important difference between Campbell's book and Woolfe and Gandon's sequel is the way in which they were published. Campbell's role as architect/author had been a fundamentally negotiated intervention in a major publishing venture, while his successors assumed complete editorial control from the outset. The initial publication of Woolfe and Gandon's book in parts, which began on 27 March 1765, greatly reduced the amount of start-up capital required to cover production costs, as it was not necessary to complete the work before beginning publication. Whereas the team of book- and printsellers that published volumes one and two of *Vitruvius Britannicus* had to raise sufficient funds to engrave and print a hundred folio plates before seeing a return on their investment, Woolfe and Gandon risked no more than the cost of issuing a single monthly part of six plates at a time, proceeds from the sale of which, at four shillings in ordinary printer's (i.e., black) ink or five shillings for impressions in "Italian Brown," could be used to finance the production of each succeeding part. Serial publication became so normal a means of producing "plate books" in the last quarter of the eighteenth century that it is difficult to realize just what a novel step Woolfe and Gandon were taking in using it here for the first time in Britain to spread the initial costs of producing a large and expensive folio of architectural engravings. Until then, initial publication of such books had nearly always depended upon advance payments made by subscribers acting as sponsors. The only real exceptions to this are the very few architectural books that were wholly paid for by an institution, such as the Society of Antiquaries' *Vetusta Monumenta*, 5 vols. (1747–1838), or by a single patron, such as Joshua Kirby's *The Perspective of Architecture* (1761), which was funded by George III, and Matthew Brettingham's *Plans, Elevations and Sections of Holkham* (1761), which was probably financed by the family of the recently deceased 1st earl of Leicester.

Though Woolfe and Gandon had no previous experience of publishing, they may have been familiar with the use of part publication in the 1730s and 1750s as a method of republishing or repackaging existing architectural books and engravings as economically as possible for purchase by ordinary builders and craftsmen who, though unable to afford the three or four guineas needed to buy Leoni's translations of Alberti and Palladio when they first appeared, might be willing to spend sixpence every week to acquire a cheaper edition or version of them in parts or "numbers." However, this marketing technique, well proven for recycling previously published or purely derivative architectural books, had never before been used to launch the type of grand, predominately engraved architectural folio of which, in England at least, Campbell's *Vitruvius Britannicus* was the epitome. Thus Woolfe and Gandon's insistence that they have followed Campbell in every respect serves also as a reassurance of its respectability in spite of the down-market methods they had used to publish it. It is clear also from the price Woolfe and Gandon asked for each part that they had no intention of attracting a wider market than that established fifty years earlier by Campbell. Their appeal to exclusivity and connoisseurship was further reinforced by the option they gave of buying more expensive copies with the plates printed in "Italian Brown" ink to give a closer facsimile of original drawings (such as Lord Burlington had stipulated for his private printing of Palladio's *Fabbriche antiche*, 1730 [recte c. 1736], and as had also probably been the case for Brettingham's *Plans . . . of Holkham*, 1761, nearly all copies of the first edition of which were printed in sepia).

All of this suggests that Woolfe and Gandon saw advantages to serial publication that had little to do with its potential for broadening the market for their book, a factor that had been paramount in the distribution of Batty Langley's huge compendium, *Ancient Masonry* (1733–1736), and in the publication of Isaac Ware's *A Complete Body of Architecture* (1755–1757). Rather, what seems to have been important for them was the ability it gave them to spread their production costs, to reduce the advance commitment needed from subscribers, and to maintain their independence from both middlemen who would want a percentage of their profits, and powerful sponsors who might expect to influence the content of their book in return for their support. Leaving aside the fact that neither of them were well off—both were without independent means, Woolfe's salary as the holder of a minor post in the Office of Works was no doubt meager, and Gandon was on the point of having to make a living after completing his apprenticeship under Chambers—the extreme riskiness of their enterprise can hardly have escaped their notice. The sales pitch concocted by John Wilcox, George Foster, and Henry Chapelle to market their combined backlist of topographical prints as *Vitruvius Britannicus, volume the fourth* (1739), enjoyed so little success that, to judge from the extreme rarity of their collection today, it is possible Woolfe and Gandon were not even aware of its existence. The same could be true of William Adam's ill-fated *Vitruvius Scoticus*, begun in 1727 and still unpublished forty years later, although in this case it is more likely that they had heard rumors of its vicissitudes, perhaps through one of the four London engravers hired by John Adam to produce nine new plates for the work between c. 1758 and March 1764. And finally, less than three years before the earliest date Woolfe and Gandon are known to have been at work on their book (September 1764), another architect as unknown and no doubt as desirous of fame as themselves, had failed with a proposal for publishing almost precisely the same book as they were now undertaking. So similar, in fact, is Thomas Milton's unsuccessful project, and so close in time (subscription proposals had appeared in the *Public Advertiser* on 5 October 1761), that Eileen Harris has speculated that it might have had some connection with Woolfe and Gandon's venture. Whether or not this is the case, it is inconceivable that they were not at least aware of their predecessor's attempt to carry off essentially the same idea—an idea that, insofar as it constituted a retrospective celebration of British architecture under George II, had clearly been timed to coincide with customary optimism over the possibility of improved state patronage of the arts in Britain under a new monarch. Four years into George III's reign, however, the first flush of this optimism must have faded, and certainly could no longer be counted on to give immediate buoyancy to Woolfe and Gandon's relaunch of *Vitruvius Britannicus*. That no publisher had previously come forward to underwrite an updating of Campbell's book is a clear sign that it was not the obvious commercial opportunity it appears to be in hindsight. Indeed, had it been, it would be difficult to understand why the fourteen booksellers who financed the reprinting of volumes one through three of *Vitruvius Britannicus* (probably in 1751) never tried to maximize their investment by commissioning just such a continuation as Woolfe and Gandon now had the audacity to undertake independently.

It is also probable that from very early on (if not from the beginning) the two architects had the benefit of advice and help from Matthias Darly (fl. 1750–1780), an enterprising engraver-printseller of some acumen who not only engraved nearly half the plates for their first volume, but may well have come up with the idea of serial publication as a way of publishing their work independently. As a printseller and publisher Darly would have been quite accustomed to "packaging" plates in suites that could then be combined more or less to individual order, that might well suggest the idea of publishing a preconceived collection of engravings in parts. Darly had been responsible not merely for engraving the plates for William Ince and John Mayhew's *Universal System of Household Furniture* ([1759]–1762), but also for handling subscriptions for its original appearance in weekly shilling parts. As a precedent for Darly's involvement with Woolfe and Gandon, this earlier publishing exercise is instructive as much for its differences as its similarities. In both instances Darly seems to have been a silent, subordinate partner, contributing publishing expertise alongside his skills as an engraver, probably in return for some share in the profits. This point of similarity, however, makes all the more striking the contrast between Ince and Mayhew's desire to disseminate their furniture designs to as wide an audience as possible, and Woolfe and Gandon's decision to play for the exclusivity of the "Vitruvius Britannicus" market. It also suggests that it is unlikely that Darly was in any sense "behind" the original idea of continuing *Vitruvius Britannicus*. Unlike Joseph Smith's influence upon the original concept of *Vitruvius Britannicus*, Darly's involvement appears to have had little or no effect upon the shape and content of Woolfe and Gandon's continuation. Had it done so, he certainly would have tried to broaden its appeal by introducing pattern-book elements of use to craftsmen, such as he was able to provide subsequently in the fortnightly two-shilling parts of his *The Ornamental Architect* [1770–1771]. However, such a use of their book was so far from Woolfe and Gandon's intention that they did not even bother to invoke copyright protection for their plates by including the requisite imprint lines and, apart from the years of completion, gave no publishing information, not even the place of publication, in either volume. Such reticence also suggests that they were uncomfortable about appearing before the public as publishers/printsellers (i.e., tradesmen), believing that this would detract from the image they needed to project in this context as professional architects. Darly's role, therefore, had to be suppressed if it was not to appear to be greater than it really was. Indeed, Darly's contribution beyond that of engraving plates is known only because he is identified as both "Engraver and Publisher" in press advertisements for the work while it was in progress (see *Public Advertiser*, 26 November 1766 and 26 January 1768).

As a jobbing engraver of caricatures and ornament, who in 1771 parodied his occupation as that of a "Political Designer of Pots, Pans and Pipkins," Darly can have felt no sensitivities on his own account that might have made him want to conceal his part in publishing and distributing a continuation of *Vitruvius Britannicus*. Not only was he happy to take in subscriptions and display specimens of the plates, probably in the window of his fashionable print shop in Castle Street, Leicester Fields (later removed to No. 39, The Strand), he also elected to demonstrate his skill as an engraver by exhibiting, for three years in succession, proofs of plates he had engraved for Woolfe and Gandon's book at the Society of Artists' annual exhibitions between 1765 and 1767: the section of G. N. Servandoni's spectacular sculpture gallery at Brandenburg House, Hammersmith, for George Bubb Dodington (4: pls. 28–29, exhibited 1765, cat. 207); the elevation and section of George Dance the elder's Mansion House, London (4: pls. 41–42, 43–44, exhibited 1766, cats. 241, 242); and the elevation of the principal front of John Sanderson's Stratton Park, Hampshire, for the 3d duke of Bedford (4: pls. 53–54, exhibited 1767, cat. 232). Interestingly, both Tobias Miller and Thomas White (who was to succeed Darly as the principal engraver of the work, contributing in the end well over half the plates), both followed Darly's example in 1767: White by exhibiting his superb engraving after Gandon of the section of Robert Adam's design for Kedleston Hall, Derbyshire (4: pl. 51, exhibited 1767, cat. 281), and Miller by showing a proof of his engraving of the front of Longford Castle, Wiltshire (5: pls. 95–96, exhibited 1767, cat. 255). Although Miller did not again choose to exhibit plates from *Vitruvius Britannicus*, White included two more examples of his work for the book among his exhibits in 1771, the east front of Adam's Shelburne (i.e., Lansdowne) House, Berkeley Square (5: pl. 10, exhibited 1771, cat. 300), and the section of Gandon's "intended" (but unexecuted) design for Nottingham County Hall (5: pls. 76–77, exhibited 1771, cat. 299). Unlike the numerous "specimens of the unpublished part" of *Antiquities of Athens* that James Stuart exhibited at the Free Society of Artists in 1773 and 1774, or the "proof prints of ancient Thermae" that Charles Cameron also exhibited there in 1767 as "intended for the work which is now publishing" (i.e., his *Baths of the Romans Explained*, 1772), Darly, Miller, and White exhibited these plates not so much as an advertisement for the book or its authors, but as a public demonstration of their professional skills as engravers and artists in their own right. Although the phrase "Engrav'd by the Best Hands," like virtually the whole of Woolfe and Gandon's title, is a verbatim repetition of the original, it is worth remarking how much more prepared they were to allow engravers to take credit for their work than Campbell had been, who published his first volume without a single engraver's name appearing on any of the plates.

What is new here is a spirit of common artistic endeavor, a community of interests that gives equal credit within their own spheres to architects, draftsmen, and engravers. The only people excluded from this circle are the "absentee" publishers, the middlemen who had been so powerful and essential an influence in the making of the original book. This is one reason why Woolfe and Gandon's sequel reveals no trace of professional competitiveness, nor the implicit weighing up of each architect's work in parallel with that of a great national master (i.e., Inigo Jones, Britain's own Vitruvius), which is such a hallmark of Campbell's book.

The source of this new sense of the common interests of artists is not hard to discover. As Eileen Harris has noted, the launch of Woolfe and Gandon's continuation of *Vitruvius Britannicus* followed only two months after a significant change in the status of the Incorporated Society of Artists of Great Britain, by virtue of the grant of its royal charter of incorporation on 26 January 1765. This established the governance of the society in the hands of twenty-four annually elected directors, including a president, vice president, treasurer, and secretary, all of whom were to "be either painters, sculptors, architects, or engravers by profession." It also confirmed a triumvirate of James Paine, William Chambers, and John Gwynn as the three directors of the society responsible for architecture, a role they had undertaken since November 1761 as the three architect-members elected to serve on the Society's committee "for arranging the public exhibition." In spite—or perhaps because—of this powerful connection, both Gandon and Edward Stevens, his fellow pupil in Chambers' office at this time, began their exhibiting careers in 1763–1764 at the Free Society of Artists, their subordinate position as apprentices making it perhaps impossible to appear before the public in the same exhibition as their master. If this was indeed the case, it was only one of a number of difficulties that young architects faced in trying to advertise their abilities in the context of a public art exhibition. Indeed, the powerful position occupied by both Chambers and Paine in the affairs of the Society of Artists—Chambers had been from the start a key figure in its formation, and Paine was to serve for several years as its president following the debacle of the directors' secession in November 1768—seems to have positively discouraged other architects from exhibiting with them. Thus architecture made only a very faltering appearance in the early exhibitions: on average only six architects per year exhibited with the Society of Artists between 1760 and 1778, and

Elevation of the Design intended for the County Hall at, Nottingham
Elevation de la Façade destinée pour la Hale de Nottingham.

John Woolfe and James Gandon. *Vitruvius Britannicus.* Vol. 5, plate 74/75. James Gandon. Nottingham County Hall. Elevation of the "intended" design not executed. 1985.61.448

not until after its move to New Somerset House in 1780 did the Royal Academy's exhibition do much better. It is not surprising, therefore, that of the twenty-two architects represented in Woolfe and Gandon's book who were alive in 1765, only five (Chambers, Paine, Dance the elder, Vardy, and John Donowell) had previously exhibited at the Society of Artists.

One of the reasons for the reluctance of architects to use the early exhibitions to promote themselves was the disadvantage they had in competing for the attention of visitors who had naturally come to see finished works of art, not geometrical diagrams. Although it was important that exhibited designs retained an orthogonal character that enabled them to be readily distinguished from topographical drawings (with which they were invariably hung both at the Society of Artists, and later at the Royal Academy until 1792), nonetheless, the exhibition arena put great pressure on architects to render their drawings in a picturesque manner. This can be seen in the exhibited work of Chambers and, more especially, in that of his slightly later pupil John Yenn, who followed Chambers' lead by setting elevations in naturalistic landscape, presenting elaborate sections that revealed precise details of interior decoration, and introducing various atmospheric and pictorial effects (such as weathered masonry, smoking urns, stormy or benign skies, &c.), all by means of an exquisite handling of watercolor tints and, on occasion, bodycolor. Unfortunately, none of Gandon's early exhibition drawings survive, so it is not known how far he adopted Chambers' manner in this respect. He cannot, however, have been unaware of it, or of the way in which it distracted the public from a proper appreciation of the architectural as opposed to pictorial qualities of a design.

Another, related problem with the exhibition forum, from the architect's point of view, was that the presence of architectural prints and drawings, in which it was the skill of the engraver and/or draftsman that was intended to be admired as much as the beauty or propriety of the architecture, inevitably subtracted from the public credit given to the role of the architect responsible for the design, execution, or restoration of the buildings shown. In the very first Society of Artists exhibition in 1760, the specialist architectural engraver Edward Rooker, who was a member of the exhibition organizing committee, exhibited his famous engraving of John Gwynn and Samuel Wale's "Transverse Section of St. Paul's Cathedral, decorated according to the original intention of Sir Christopher Wren" (1755). Had this same work been exhibited by Gwynn himself, attention would have been drawn to his contribution—namely, the proposed decorations; similarly, if it had been exhibited by Wale, it would have the latter's superb draftsmanship that was on view, rather than Rooker's translation of it into another medium. Gwynn and Wale both exhibited other works in the same exhibition and they probably viewed the inclusion of Rooker's print as useful, if somewhat indirect, publicity for their own talents. However, it is worth noting that Gwynn subsequently reiterated his responsibility for proposing that Wren's decorative scheme for the interior of St. Paul's be carried out by exhibiting further drawings to that effect in the 1764 and 1766 exhibitions. The titles of Rooker's other exhibits in 1760 are given in the catalogue as "Three Antiquities of Athens" and "Section of a Temple." It is practically certain that these were either proof plates from Stuart and Revett's forthcoming volume (not published until January 1763), or, alternatively, were from the unauthorized English edition of Le Roy's rival work, which had been published on 2 June 1759 by the printseller Robert Sayer with unsigned engravings (the latter alternative is perhaps more likely since the reference to "Three Antiquities" seems more applicable to the Sayer volume's capriccio presentation, which is certainly up to Rooker's high standard). Whichever the case, their presence could well explain why Stuart was never to have any truck with the Society of Artists (even after Chambers and his allies had seceded to found the Royal Academy), but always exhibited instead at the Free Society where, practically every year from 1765 to 1783, he showed a huge quantity of drawings, proof engravings, models, medal designs, paintings, and architecture. The same problem—or at least awkwardness—would have been brought home to Chambers himself when he exhibited for the first time the following year (i.e., 1761). Once again Rooker exhibited architectural engravings, this time proof plates of the temples of Victory and of Pan from Chambers' forthcoming book on Kew Gardens (*Plans, Elevations, Sections and Perspective Views of the Gardens and Buildings at Kew* [1763]) and, for good measure, the engraving he had also done of the Triumphal Arch at Wilton for Chambers' *Treatise on Civil Architecture* (1759). It is difficult to believe that Chambers can have been pleased to discover the latter engraving hanging in the same exhibition as his own beautiful watercolor presentation drawing of the Wilton Arch as executed for the 10th earl of Pembroke (BAL Drawings Collection, RIBA, London; J4/22). Gandon was working in Chambers' office during this period—he had also labored (and been credited) as Chambers' draftsman on six plates of the orders in the latter's *Treatise*—so it is reasonable to conclude that he would have been quite aware of the issues that these exhibits raised, especially since two more engravings from the Kew book were included by Rooker in the next year's exhibition (i.e., 1762).

This then was the context in which Woolfe and Gandon sought to find a way of launching independent careers as architects by means of a timely reassertion of the proper responsibilities and achievements of their profession. Although public art exhibitions formed a clear stimulus to this endeavor, the unsatisfactory environment they provided for a proper appreciation of architecture pointed up the virtues of the old-fashioned, purely technical presentation of plans, elevations, and sections that Campbell had pioneered in Britain fifty years earlier. It must have seemed clear to them that the Society of Artists' theoretical championing of the common interests of all artists could be given more effective expression, for architects at least, within the pages of a revived *Vitruvius Britannicus* than on the walls of the Society's exhibition room in Spring Garden. At the same time they must have hoped that, by performing such a necessary service to the cause of promoting the reputation of British architecture at home and abroad, they could establish their own reputations as knowledgeable and responsible professionals at the disposal of the public. In this latter expectation, however, they were to be sorely disappointed. In sharp contrast to the immediate and dramatic boost that *Vitruvius Britannicus* gave to Campbell's career, Woolfe and Gandon's unexecuted joint project to add flanking wings to Duff House, Banffshire, for the earl of Fife (5: pls. 58–60), seems to have been the only commission to arise directly out their book, despite newspaper announcements of each number that had advertised their availability to undertake "Designs in Architecture, Surveying and Measuring Buildings."

One reason for this lack of response is that despite Walpole's praise of it as more worthy of its title than its predecessor (*Anecdotes of Painting in England*, ed. R. N. Wornum (1862), 2: 696), Woolfe and Gandon's book failed to create the stir that Campbell's had done. This can be seen quite clearly by comparing the numbers of subscribers they managed to attract: it took 28 months for 213 people to put their names down for 227 copies of Woolfe and Gandon's publication, and only ten months for 303 people to come forward as subscribers for 370 copies of Campbell's; in the two years between Campbell's first and second lists, he managed to find an additional 155 subscribers for 175 more copies, but in the four years between Woolfe and Gandon's first and second volume only 74 new names came forward for 76 more copies. In spite of Woolfe and Gandon's best efforts to produce "a proper supplement" to Campbell's work, the descendants of the majority of Campbell's subscribers (or their social equivalents) were clearly unconvinced of the necessity of adding further volumes to their sets. More than half (i.e., 165) of the 303 names on Campbell's March 1715 subscription list were peers, knights, or baronets, or members of their families. Woolfe and Gandon, on the other hand, were only able to muster forty-two members of the aristocracy in their 1767 list, and although this figure rose to seventy-two by 1771 (probably thanks to canvassing by the earl of Radnor, whose active promotion of the book is acknowledged by the authors in the text of their second volume), it is quite apparent that their core support came from a completely different quarter. Thus, whereas Campbell's list had included a mere half-dozen named craftsmen, almost exactly a third (i.e., seventy-three) of Woolfe and Gandon's subscribers were connected with the building industry. (The breakdown is as follows: twenty-one architects; twenty-one carpenters/joiners; thirteen bricklayers; six plasterers; five masons; two surveyors; one carver; one sculptor; one paviour; one "upholdsterer," and one "engine-maker.") Clearly they had produced a far more specialist interest book than Campbell's, and this fact was recognized by purchasers in spite of its authors' determination that it should form "a fourth volume of *Vitruvius Britannicus*." Radnor's help had its price, namely, the acceptance of his gift of engravings of Coleshill, Berkshire (5: pls. 86–87; built c. 1650–1662), and of his lordship's seat at Longford Castle, Wiltshire (5: pls. 94–97–98; built 1591), neither of which were at all appropriate to a celebration of the past fifty years of architectural achievement in Britain.

Apart from its down-market method of publication, one of the factors influencing the perception of Woolfe and Gandon's sequel as more oriented to the interests of the architectural profession than its predecessor must have been its strict adherence to orthogonal projection (i.e., plans, elevations, and sections) to the exclusion of all other forms of representation. The presence of perspectives and bird's-eye views in the original *Vitruvius Britannicus* had undoubtedly helped to broaden its appeal, even though staffage and other topographical distractions were eliminated to focus on the design of existing buildings as distinct from their actual state. Woolfe and Gandon's concentration on architectural forms, though similar in intent to Campbell's, seems to project a more rigid assertion of the architect's domain. One of the reasons for this is that when a building is completely abstracted from its setting, so that it can be seen only as "pure" design, it is shorn of local, historical, and topographical associations. Instead of appearing as the seat of a particular nobleman, it becomes instead the product of the architect's drawingboard. Such a staking out of the architect's proper arena of professional responsibility and expertise lies at the heart of Woolfe and Gandon's project, which, unlike Campbell's, did not have to enter into compromises with a publisher concerned to maximize the return on his investment. In some respects Woolfe and Gandon's decision to limit themselves to the reproduction of architect's drawings—which led James Dallaway, the editor of the 1826–1828 edition of Walpole's *Anecdotes*, to dub them "scientific architects"—was a natural consequence of Campbell's success in pioneering this form of presentation in English architectural publishing. However, in comparison with books on "modern" extant British buildings by Campbell's neo-Palladian successors—Kent's *The Designs of Inigo Jones* (1727), Gibbs' *A Book of Architecture* (1728) and *Bibliotheca Radcliviana . . . containing its several Plans, Uprights, Sections, and Ornaments* (1747), Ware's *Plans, Elevations, and Sections, Chimney-pieces, and Ceilings of Houghton* (1735; 2d ed., 1760), Paine's *Plans, Elevations, Sections and other Ornaments of the Mansion-House . . . of Doncaster* (1751), Brettingham's *Plans, Elevations and Sections of Holkham* (1761), and Chambers' *Plans, Elevations, and Perspective Views of the Gardens and Buildings at Kew* (1763)—it is immediately apparent that each in its own way succeeds, either by combining orthogonal projections with perspectives or by introducing a wide spectrum of architectural and ornamental details, in creating a much more varied graphic image of their subject than Woolfe and Gandon could possibly achieve using Campbell's standard compression of a whole building onto two or three plates. Furthermore, this lack of variety in terms of presentation seems still more of a straitjacket in Woolfe and Gandon's case because of the great predominance in their collection of a single building type (i.e., the country house or villa).

Such a deliberate, self-imposed restriction of the means at their disposal may have contained an implied criticism of the more picturesque, nonarchitectural values encouraged by the exhibition environment. A small, but nonetheless revealing, indication of this issue can be detected in the order in which the plates relating to each house are given. In the first three numbers to be published (i.e., pls. 1–18 of vol. 4), the plate showing the elevation of a building is numbered *before* that showing its plan; from this point on, however, this order is reversed, so that the plan of a building is always given first and everything else follows *after* (and by implication from) that. Campbell had almost invariably adopted this latter order, which expresses the supremacy of the plan as the most complete and important notation of a design. Woolfe and Gandon's correction of this probably involuntary, minor deviation from their "leader" betrays on the one hand the pervasiveness of an attitude that naturally placed elevations before plans, and on the other their awareness of the need to redress this situation. A comparable correction of emphasis can also be seen in the fact that, apart from the rudimentary indication of the banks of the river Mimeren in Gandon's drawing of Chambers' bridge for Thomas Brand at The Hoo, Kimpton, Hertfordshire (4: pl. 18; built c. 1760–1764), the only plate in the entire two volumes

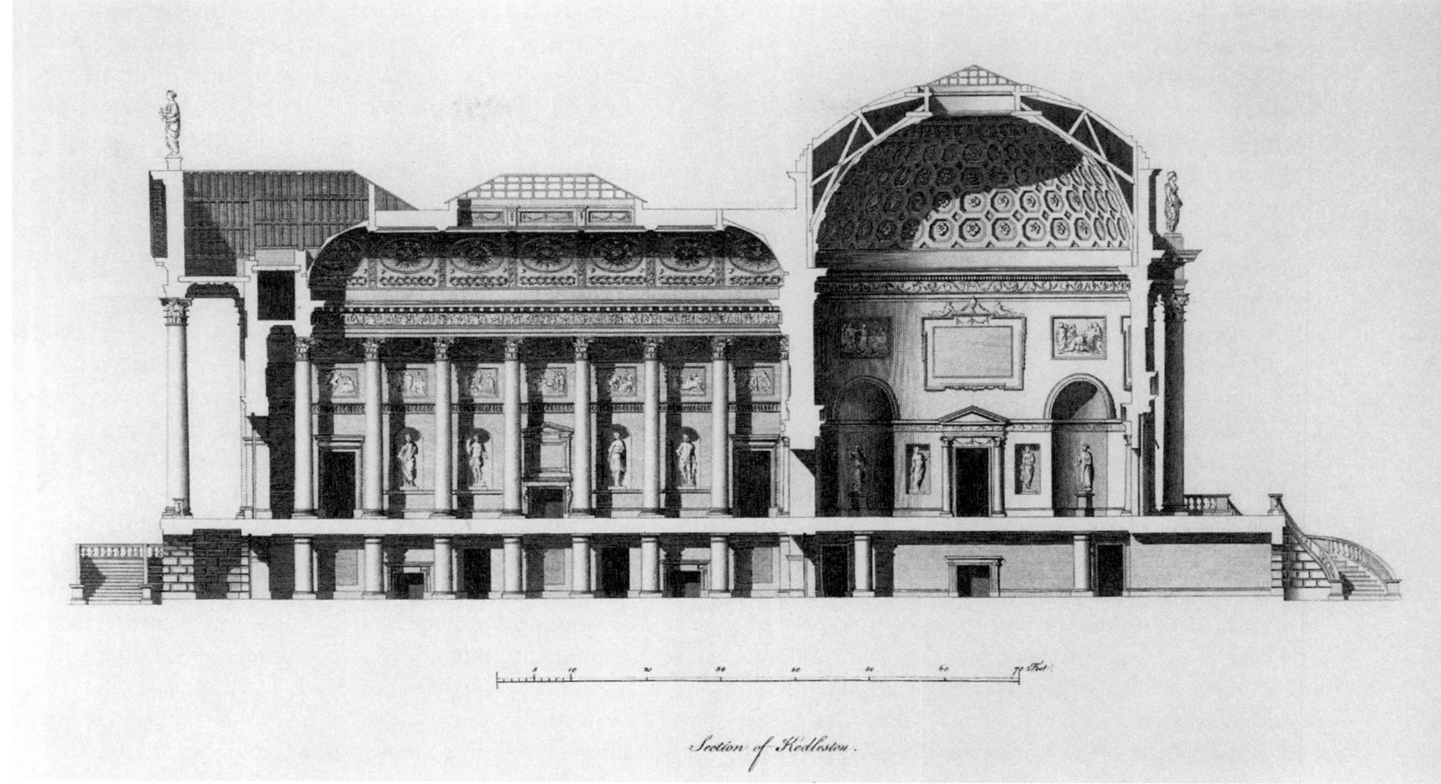

John Woolfe and James Gandon. *Vitruvius Britannicus.* Vol. 4, plate 51. Robert Adam. Kedleston Hall, Derbyshire. Section. 1985.61.447

to include any landscape is the very first, that is, the elevation of Morris' White Lodge, Richmond Park (4: pls. 1–2).

It would be wrong, however, to imagine that Woolfe and Gandon could remain altogether untouched by the pictorial considerations that they sought to resist, even though, as one would expect, the evidence for this is revealed in quite subtle ways. One of the most significant proofs of their susceptibility is the attention that they give to cross-sections. Not only are there more in number (eight in vol. 4 and two in vol. 5) but, more importantly, they are more elaborate and detailed than Campbell's, which were, by contrast, usually concerned to reveal structure rather than interior decorations and fittings (hence the latter's use of outline only in the sections of St. Peter's, Rome, the Banqueting House, St. Paul, Covent Garden, and Castle Howard). The greater provision of detail in Woolfe and Gandon's sections (especially those of York [i.e., Cumberland House, 86 Pall Mall], Foot's Cray, Kent, Mansion House, London, and, above all, Kedleston Hall, Derbyshire and Wricklemarsh, Blackheath—see 4: pls. 7, 9, 43–44, 51, and 64, respectively), is combined with a more precise attention to the shadows cast by the projection of the intersected walls, so as to establish the relative distances of various surfaces from the picture/sectional plane. In one sense this is more "realistic" in that it gives the section the appearance of a doll's house with the front removed; but in another sense it is more "artificial," in that it reveals the interiors of rooms in a literally impossible light, as they could never actually be seen except in the architect's mind. Such sections were undoubtedly popular as exhibition pieces. Both Chambers, who pioneered the genre by exhibiting in 1761 his extraordinary drawing of a design for York House as a Roman ruin, and Paine, who almost always included at least one section among his exhibited designs, as well as their pupils and followers, seem to have realized that here was one type of architectural representation that could exploit naturalistic devices and yet retain its essentially architectural character.

Another way in which the graphic means at Woolfe and Gandon's disposal were unavoidably affected by prevailing tastes was in the matter of engraving technique. It is worth noting that in the original announcement of their proposals in March 1765 Edward Rooker had been named as one of the three engravers involved in the project (the other two were Darly and Miller). Lauded by Walpole as the "Marc Antonio of architecture" (*A Catalogue of Engravers*, 2d ed. [1765], p. 140), Rooker was then undoubtedly at the height of his reputation as the leading architectural engraver of his generation, having contributed plates to virtually all the important architectural books published in England since the mid-1740s (e.g., Abraham Swan's *The British Architect*, 1745; Paine's *Plans . . . of the Mansion-House . . . of Doncaster*, 1751; Chambers' *Designs of Chinese Buildings*, 1757, and *Treatise on Civil Architecture*, 1759; Brettingham's *Plans . . . of Holkham*, 1761; Stuart and Revett's *Antiquities of Athens*, 1762; Chambers' *Plans . . . at Kew*, 1763; and Robert

Adam's *Ruins of the Palace . . . at Spalatro*, 1764). Although Rooker did not in the end engrave any plates for Woolfe and Gandon, his influence is evident in the style of engraving employed in their book, in particular by the engraver who effectively took Rooker's place, Thomas White, about whom very little is known except that he had assisted for a time the line- and stipple-engraver William Wynne Ryland (1738–1783). Ryland is credited with the introduction into England of the "dotted" or chalk manner of etching, and although Rooker's architectural etching technique is quite different from this, the latter was developed for much the same purpose, as a way of rendering tone in etching that was simpler and more effective than one based on an imitation of the traditional methods of a line engraving. The new technique, which is characteristic of Rooker's mature manner, is distinguished by its virtuoso deployment of vertical and horizontal etched lines that, through minute variations of thickness and spacing alone, can accurately reproduce the graduated tones of a pen-and-wash drawing. It represented a considerable advance on the "fixed value" method of rendering the succession of vertical planes in an elevation by means of a finite number of tonal differentiations, such as had been used by Hulsbergh in Campbell's original volumes and by Fourdrinier and others thereafter. (A typical set of such tonal differentiations would be plain white for smooth ashlar in sunlight; flecks for rough-dressed stone in sunlight; horizontal hatching for half-shading of ashlar; cross-hatching for voids; diagonal cross-hatching for cast shadows, &c.) The older method derived essentially from an imitation in etching of the "net" of intersecting, swelling, and diminishing engraved lines that had been developed in the seventeenth century as the standard graphic medium for the reproduction of oil paintings.

Rooker's method (he can perhaps be credited with its invention) offered both a more accurate means of reproducing architectural drawings and, because of its elimination of cross-hatching, provided a simpler and therefore clearer way of introducing shadows and shading without interfering with the essential lines of an architectural form.

In one way this improved clarity, which had for instance added sparkle to Stuart and Revett's plates of architectural details in their *Antiquities of Athens*, 1762, and was exactly what Woolfe and Gandon needed to focus attention on the architectural form of a building rather than its actuality. In another way, however, it opened up greater opportunity for expressing naturalistically the advance and recession of the elements of which an elevation was composed. This could now be done not only through careful rendering of the way forms are modeled by light and shade, but also through correct delineation of the shape and relative intensities of the shadows that these forms cast. On the one hand, therefore, this more refined etching style contributed to the "scientific" approach that Woolfe and Gandon needed to adopt, while on the other it encouraged engravers to pursue more dramatic chiaroscuro effects in the interests of greater naturalism. White's engraving of the section of Kedleston (4: pl. 51) is an example of the finesse that could be achieved by a skilled engraver using this technique: it is both a perfectly balanced composition in terms of light and shade and, in spite of including a wealth of finely etched detail, presents the essential form and structure of the architecture with clarity and drama. In the hands of a rather less sensitive engraver it could be much less successful, as, for instance, in Darly's elevation of The Mansion House (4: pls. 41–42), where, in striving for stronger chiaroscuro, he allows the shadows cast by the columns of the portico to obscure their true proportions, a mistake that Anthony Walker was careful to avoid in his fine engraving of the south front of Wricklemarsh, Blackheath (4: pl. 61).

John Woolfe and James Gandon. *Vitruvius Britannicus*. Vol. 4, plate 61. John James. Wricklemarsh, Blackheath, Kent. Elevation to the south. 1985.61.447

(Walker was an extremely distinguished engraver and artist in his own right who, had he not died suddenly on 9 May 1765, would have almost certainly contributed more plates than this one elevation and a "General Plan" of the house [4: pls. 58–59].)

It is instructive to compare Darly's engraving of the Green Park front of Vardy's Spencer House (4: pls. 39–40; built 1756–1765) with the watercolor Gandon made for the purpose (London Metropolitan Archive, GLC Gardner Collection II, lot 1103, Westminster DD5409). In the engraving the shadow cast by the rustication of the basement and ground floor stories is carefully shown in the reveal of each window opening, as are those cast by the mutules in the soffit of the cornice, and by the capitals of the Doric order in the *piano nobile*. In the drawing, however, none of these shadows is registered, and although Gandon employs watercolor over his ink drawing, he follows the earlier convention of "fixed value" tonal differentiations in a probably conscious approximation of Hulsbergh's *Vitruvius Britannicus* engraving style. Darly, on the other hand (perhaps unconsciously), translated Gandon's watercolor into the modern manner of architectural etching, thereby enabling him to introduce a concern for the enlivening effect of shadows that is quite absent in the original from which he was working. Another revealing comparison can be made between Darly's Spencer House engraving and the elevation of The Banqueting House, Whitehall (*Vitruvius Britannicus* I: pl. 13), one of the most highly finished of all Campbell's "geometrical" plates. In an effort to express some of the relief of Jones' facade, Campbell's engraver (presumably Hulsbergh) shows the dentils in the cornice of both orders in false perspective, receding obliquely in one direction only. While this kind of surreptitious intrusion of perspective into an orthogonal projection is rigorously avoided in Woolfe and Gandon's plates, the ability of their engravers to create the illusion of three-dimensionality through a realistic rendering of shade and shadow (rather than a graphic encodement into fixed tonal values) more than made up for the suppression of such "unscientific" draftsmanship.

The careful attention paid to "sciography" (the science of drawing shadows) in Woolfe and Gandon's plates is not simply an indication of advances in drawing techniques over the previous half century; it is a measure of a qualitative change in the way architecture could be visualized by the mid-1760s. Such change is not a matter of individual choice, but forms rather part of the "given" that Woolfe and Gandon had to work with and against which they were to some extent reacting. The pressure to employ naturalistic effects in architectural drawings was just one symptom of a more general tendency, usually referred to as the rise of a new, "picturesque" appreciation of British scenery dating from the 1750s, but probably more properly seen in the mid-1760s as part of that general groundswell of naturalism in the topographical depiction of British landscape (and the buildings within it), which was to lead eventually to the emergence of a distinctive school of watercolor painting by the end of the century. A key figure in this developing aesthetic was undoubtedly Paul Sandby, whose close friendship with Gandon (dating from about 1764) was instrumental in securing for the otherwise unknown young architect his first important commission, the new County Hall at Nottingham. It would be interesting, but in the present context inappropriate, to reflect further on the probably quite complex influence that Sandby as an artist had on Gandon as an architect seeking to establish an independent career. Nonetheless, that one of the two authors of the sequel to *Vitruvius Britannicus* moved in the most advanced artistic milieu of the day and was in a good position to react and respond in a well-informed way to the leading ideas of his fellow artists is a salient point.

But what of Woolfe? Although his date of birth is unknown it is practically certain that he was somewhat older than Gandon and that, as the primacy of his name on the title plate suggests, he was the senior partner in the enterprise. As Maurice Craig pointed out in the 1969 reprint of T. J. Mulvany's edition of the *Life of James Gandon* (1846, p. 18 n.), the claim made there that Woolfe undertook only a subsidiary role is belied by his credit as draftsman on eighty-four plates compared to Gandon's lesser contribution of fifty-seven as draftsman and ten as engraver. In the early stages of the book's publication, Gandon was involved in the mundane task of engraving some of the simpler plates. As it was no doubt through his connection with Chambers that some of the first drawings to be obtained were of the earl of Bessborough's new villa at Roehampton (i.e., Parksted, now known as Manresa House, built 1760–1768) and the 8th earl of Abercorn's new seat at Duddingston House (built 1763–1768), it is perhaps not surprising that he should have undertaken to save costs by engraving several of these himself. All might have been well had Gandon stuck to engraving plans only, as with The White Lodge, Richmond New Park (4: pls. 3 and 4) and Foots Cray, Kent (4: pl. 10; built c. 1754 for Bouchier Cleeve, possibly to his own design or that of Isaac Ware), but faced with the classic problem of how to produce a convincing elevation of the perron entrance to Bessborough's villa (4: pl. 11), the result would have hardly impressed his former master. Although he escaped mishap in his engraving of the simpler forms of the service block at Duddingston (4: pls. 16–17), his limitations became all too apparent in the hard and mechanical plate of the front of Giacomo Leoni's Moulsham Hall, Essex (4: pl. 31; built 1728–1745 for 1st Earl Fitzwalter). The contrast provided by Darly's lively rendition of G. N. Servandoni's sculpture gallery at Brandenburg House, Hammersmith (4: pls. 28–29), which may well have been issued in the same number as Gandon's plate, could not be more marked. Whether by his own choice, or because he was asked to do no more,

John Woolfe and James Gandon. *Vitruvius Britannicus.* Vol. 4, plate 39/40. John Vardy. Spencer House, Green Park, London. Elevation to St. James's Park. 1985.61.447

Gandon engraved only one other plate in the book after that, namely, the ground plan of his own Nottingham County Hall as executed in 1770–1772 (5: pl. 72).

While it would be unwise to attempt to be more precise about Woolfe and Gandon's respective roles than the above comments suggest, there are some other, circumstantial grounds for locating Woolfe at the center rather than the periphery of the book's planning and direction. The most important evidence for this is the closeness with which James Paine, Woolfe's particular associate, followed the revived *Vitruvius Britannicus* model when putting together his own book of *Plans, Elevations, and Sections of Noblemen and Gentlemen's Houses*, part I (1767). Woolfe's connection with Paine dated from the 1750s when he was employed as his clerk, and it may well have been through Paine's influence that he had secured his post in the Office of Works. The association between the two men was probably still very much alive at the time the *Vitruvius Britannicus* sequel got under way, since Woolfe went on to help raise subscriptions for and distribute copies of Paine's book, the proposals for which were announced in the *Public Advertiser* on 20 January 1767. Each subscribed to the other's work and there is some evidence to indicate that the genesis of their two ventures might have occurred if not simultaneously, at least concurrently. Paine managed to produce his book within a year after its initial announcement, suggesting that he had begun work on it considerably earlier, as is borne out by the probability that the "Section from west to east, through the center of the stables at Chatsworth" exhibited by Tobias Miller at the Society of Artists in 1765 (cat. 225) was a proof of his plate published two years later in Paine's *Plans* (pt. I: pls. VI–VII). In addition, the similarities of Paine's work to Woolfe and Gandon's in terms of formal characteristics are quite marked, partly because four people worked on both books—Miller, White, and H. Mackworth as engravers, and Christopher Ebdon (who was apprenticed to Paine in 1761) as draftsman in the former and engraver in the latter. More significant, however, is the way both books employ exclusively the classic Renaissance formula for representing architecture—plans, elevations, and sections of complete buildings—which, ever since Raphael's famous letter to Leo X canonizing orthogonal drawings as the proper medium for this purpose, had been one of the principal hallmarks of the architect's claim to a higher intellectual status than that accorded to builders and craftsmen. Paine was the first British architect to publish a collection of his executed works in this "scientific" way since Giacomo Leoni, whose "Some Designs for Buildings both Publick and Private" supplementing the third volume of his translation of Alberti (1726–1729/1730?) had been separately reissued as recently as 1758. Could perhaps some realization of this fact had been the catalyst for reviving *Vitruvius Britannicus*?

In his introduction Paine gives two principal reasons for venturing into print at this particular moment, which are equally applicable to the rationale of Woolfe and Gandon's endeavor. The first is "that as a competitor for public favor, he may receive whatever share of applause the public shall be inclined to confer on him" (*Plans*, pt. I: iv). Paine's exposure of his work to public scrutiny in this way recalls the function of the exhibition forum, which was a similarly important factor in shaping Woolfe and Gandon's project. In the preface to the Society of Artists' 1762 catalogue, Dr. Johnson characterizes the desire to gain public esteem in the exhibition as "not only innocent but virtuous, while it is undebased by artifice and unpolluted by envy," as it certainly is, claims the doctor, when "men . . . who, already enjoying all the honours and profits of their profession, are content to stand candidates for public notice, with genius yet unexperienced, and diligence yet unrewarded." Paine's hope of receiving a due share of public approbation through the publication of his work stems from the same root as Woolfe and Gandon's hope of heightening public appreciation of British architects' achievements generally. Both, in effect, appropriate Johnson's argument that their purpose (like that of the exhibition) "is not to enrich the Artists, but to advance the Art; the eminent are not flatter'd with preference, nor the obscure insulted with contempt; whoever hopes to deserve public favor is here invited to display his merit."

Paine's second hope was that by "producing a collection of designs which have actually been put in execution . . . [and] have been approved by, and rendered useful to individuals of the greatest rank and taste, he may, in some degree, become serviceable to his country in general." Like Woolfe and Gandon, by limiting his book to executed buildings, Paine was effectively attempting to mobilize the legitimizing power of his past patrons in support of the practice of architecture by professionals such as himself, hence the elimination of ideal designs looking for a builder and his notorious attack on Capability Brown and other "surprizing genius's . . . who are *born architects*" (*Plans*, pt. 1: ii). The problem, however, with total reliance on the opinion of one's patrons was that it invested the authority one was seeking not in the intrinsic qualities of one's work as judged by one's peers, but rather in the approval of those who could well be ignorant, misinformed, or misguided. This made it impossible for the architect to receive that credit which Paine on his own behalf, and Woolfe and Gandon on the behalf of others, considered his due. Although Paine may not have been aware of it, the tension caused by this underlying contradiction in the rationale of his book fueled the frustration he felt at the way recent archaeological publications by "laborious and ingenious gentlemen" (such as those by Robert Wood, Stuart and Revett, and Robert Adam) were currently misleading the public (i.e., the public to which his own book is now addressed) into sacrificing "convenience and propriety" in architecture "to the modes of the most despicable ruins of ancient Greece" (*Plans*, pt. 1: ii). But however useless and pernicious such studies were in Paine's view, in the context of his book all that could count against them was the example that his patrons set by following his advice and building to the designs that he gave. Paine's failure to recognize this limitation led him not only to overstate his case against the validity of "modern travelling knowledge" in the education of the architect (a heresy that may well have contributed to his displacement at Kedleston by Robert Adam in 1760), but to go so far as to complain openly of "the most hurtful consequences" that arise when a patron fails to follow the advice of his architect who, nonetheless, "stands accountable for absurdities, in the designing of which, he had not any share whatever" (*Plans*, pt. 1: 16). In the long account he gives of his unfortunate professional experience at Axwell Park, Paine's attempt to reassert the authority of the architect over that of the patron breaches the tacit pact whereby the former is both literally and metaphorically permitted to "borrow back" his design from the latter in order to display it to the public for the mutual benefit of both parties.

Woolfe and Gandon's avoidance of value judgments in relation to architectural taste suggests that they understood the nature of this "pact" better than Paine did. Their tediously fulsome praise of the beautiful views and delightful situations enjoyed by every one of the houses they describe reads almost as a parody of the long English tradition of eulogistic country-house literature stemming from Ben Jonson's early seventeenth-century panegyric "To Penshurst." It also reflects in a generalized way the interest in locality and setting that their plates resolutely ignore. And it might even be argued that their frequent commendation of the judicious choices that have been made of propitious sites and sound and appropriate building materials is not solely intended to flatter the owners of the houses concerned, but is also meant to suggest that the judgment of the architect in these matters is a more reliable measure of his professional standing than the refinement or sophistication of his taste could ever be. Whether or not such an implied critique was ever intended or read as such, to be effective it had to remain unstated. This presented little difficulty so long as Woolfe and Gandon's own credit as architects was not directly at stake. The test came, however, when, in their second volume, they quite exceptionally included two of their own designs. The first—their joint project to add wings to Duff House (5: pls. 58–60)—was unexecuted and therefore formed no basis for asserting any professional status as architects. The second—Gandon's Nottingham County Hall (5: pls. 72–77)—was a different matter. Gandon's juxtapositioning of his preferred design ("being of opinion it would the best have answered the intended purpose") with the one chosen by the commissioners simply on the grounds of "it being the least expensive," is not unlike Campbell's inclusion of variant designs for Wanstead in the first volume of *Vitruvius Britannicus*. Bearing in mind that both architects were publishing the breakthrough commission of their careers to date, it is remarkable how very differently they reacted to the realities of architectural patronage: Campbell by deferentially conceding the inferiority of the design that was not chosen (*Vitruvius Britannicus*, 1: pls. 21–22); and Gandon by airily complaining of the provincial parsimony of Nottinghamshire worthies.

More than anything else, perhaps, the eruption of this "incident" in the otherwise unruffled equanimity of Woolfe and Gandon's sequel to Campbell's work high-

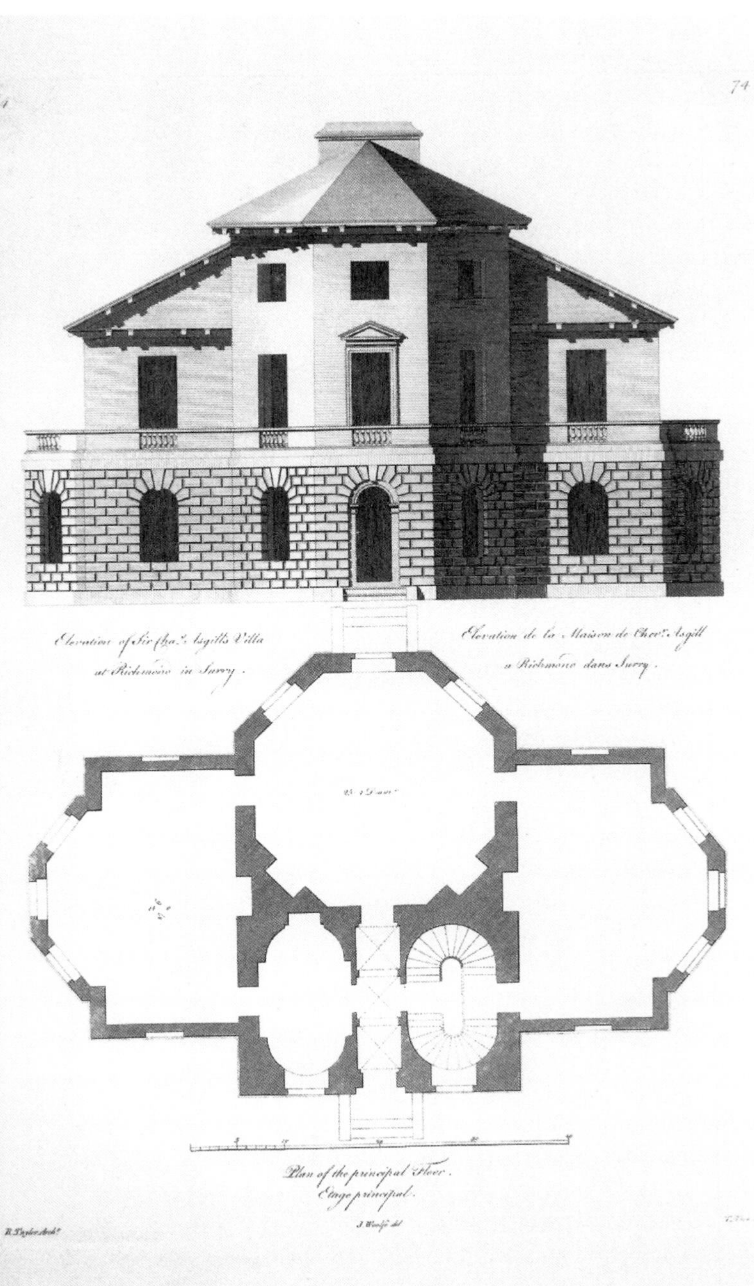

John Woolfe and James Gandon. *Vitruvius Britannicus.* Vol. 4, plate 74. Sir Robert Taylor. Asgill House, Richmond, Surrey. Elevation and plan of principal floor. 1985.61.447

lights the changes that had occurred in the architect's social and artistic milieu since the second decade of the eighteenth century. Although Gandon's stand at Nottingham is mild indeed in comparison with Paine's at Axwell Park, it brings him and his collaborator firmly in line with the tragically flawed attempt of the Society of Artists to establish itself as a self-sufficient source of artistic authority without any dependence upon the influence of collectors, critics, connoisseurs, and all other nonpractitioners of the arts. Unlike Paine, however, Gandon was astute enough to keep his options open by enrolling on 7 October 1769 as one of the first students in the Royal Academy Schools, in spite of having been a Fellow of the Society of Artists since 1 September 1767. In fact, he continued to sit on the fence by accepting election as a director of the society on 18 October 1771, having earlier that year exhibited with them what was almost certainly his R.A. Gold Medal-winning "Design for a Triumphal Arch" (cat. 243). It is probably significant also to an assessment of Paine's influence that it was not until after Paine had extricated himself from further involvement in the society's affairs in 1773 that Gandon finally "crossed the floor" and started to exhibit at the Royal Academy in 1774.

The dream of artistic independence, of a self-ratifying body of respected artists with the collective authority to establish themselves as arbiters of excellence in the arts they professed, was at last realized with the foundation of the Royal Academy of Arts by the direct command of George III on 10 December 1768. But the price of this new-found authority was that it should be perceived to be vested in the king himself and delegated by the crown to an exclusive oligarchy of forty Royal Academicians. The rise of the Royal Academy and concomitant collapse of the Society of Artists so altered the cultural scene that, in the space of a few years, the illusion of an egalitarian fraternity of artists that had been Hogarth's particular legacy to the new body formed in 1760 to organize annual art exhibitions, evaporated almost without trace. And with it disappeared the underlying concept of a community of British architects, each as entitled as the other to access to public credit, which had informed and, for a few years in the mid-1760s, been fostered by Woolfe and Gandon's revival of *Vitruvius Britannicus.* It is hardly surprising, therefore, that in this harsh new climate of competition between artists for royal favor, their sixth volume, though announced as "in great forwardness" (5: p. 2), never materialized. There was now no level ground, "undebased by artifice and unpolluted by envy," that could enable the least known to stand alongside the best known and receive their due share of the fair repute owed in common to "Vitruvius Britannicus." N. S.

Bibliography

Graves, A. *The Society of Artists of Great Britain 1760–1791; The Free Society of Artists 1761–1783: A Complete Dictionary of Contributors.* London, 1907

Harris, E., and N. Savage. *British Architectural Books and Writers 1556–1785.* Cambridge, 1991.

McParland, E. *James Gandon: Vitruvius Hibernicus.* London, 1985

Mulvany, T. J., ed. *The Life of James Gandon, From Materials Collected by His Son.* Dublin, 1846. Reprint, London, 1969

95

Sir Henry Wotton (1568–1639)

The Elements Of Architecture, Collected by Henry Wotton Knight, from the best Authors and Examples

London: printed by John Bill, 1624

NGA Lib. Rare Book: NA2515W68

Small quarto: 179 × 140 ($7\frac{1}{16} \times 5\frac{1}{2}$)

Pagination [xii], 123, [1] pp.

(*Note*: In this copy, f. B4 [pp. 15–16] is a cancel. See Fowler 445)

Edition First edition

Text pp. [i–ii] blank; [iii] title page (verso blank); [v–xii] preface; 1–123 text, ending with errata; [124] blank

Binding Contemporary limp vellum, lacking ties, lettered in ink on spine "Ellements of Architecture" and in a later hand "Wotton" and "1624." Unidentified crest stamped on both covers (horse's head with sword in mouth, chain and halter). Lower cover inscribed "This is a curious Performance of as fine a Genius as any of his Time." Preserved in cloth slipcase

Provenance Early ownership inscription on rear pastedown "Sum ex libris Josephi Davie"; and a later inscription, "James Davies," on final blank page. Recent ownership signature of Holbrook Jackson. Contemporary marginal annotation (by Wotton?) "NB Look at the Errata in y[e] last Page of this Book," p. 88

References ESTC S120324; Fowler 445; Harris and Savage 948; STC 26011

Henry Wotton's *Elements of Architecture* was the first significant British contribution to architectural theory. When he wrote it, the author had just returned from a diplomatic career spent mainly in the service of James I at Venice, and was again looking to be appointed provost of Eton College, having been turned down twenty years earlier. The appointment was more or less in the hands of the king's first minister, George Villiers, duke of Buckingham, to whom Wotton wrote a characteristically witty begging letter, observing that "after seventeen years of foreign service, in continual employment, either ordinary or extraordinary, I am left utterly destitute of all possibility to subsist at home; much like those seal-fishes, which sometimes, as they say, oversleeping themselves in an ebbing-water, feel nothing about them but a dry shore when they awake" (Smith 1966, 2: 284). There were, however, other strong contenders for the post: Sir Dudley Carleton, son-in-law of the last but one provost; Sir William Beecher, clerk of the Privy Council; Sir Ralph Freeman, master of requests; Sir Robert Ayton, the queen's private secretary; Sir Albertus Morton, Wotton's own nephew; and most formidable of all, Sir Francis Bacon, whose early interest is shown by a letter to the secretary of state, dated 23 March 1623, baldly stating that "Mr. Thomas Murray, Provost of Eton (whom I love very much) is like to die. It were a pretty cell for my fortune. The college and school I do not doubt but I shall make to flourish. . . . This is a thing somebody must have and costs His Majesty nothing" (Hard 1968, xliv).

Faced with such competition, Wotton could not afford to be a passive spectator of the decision-making process. So why, after arriving back in London at the end of 1623, did he promptly leave the city and finish a treatise which, on the face of it, had nothing to do with either his former career or his future prospects? One reason given out was poor health: John Chamberlain wrote to Carlton on 31 January 1624 that "Sir Henry Wotton hath been sick, poor man, since his coming home, and I hear is now retiring to some corner in the country to finish a work he is setting out of the mathematics or perhaps building of castles in the air" (Hard 1968, xlv). In a dedication of the finished work to Charles, prince of Wales, Wotton himself was more specific, referring to "a miserable stopping in my breast and defluxion from my head," meaning perhaps a cold that had gone to his chest. In the same dedication, Wotton describes his "pamphlet" as a mere "diversion of my mind from my infirmity." In this, however, as so often, he was being disingenuous, since he continues: "It was printed sheet by sheet, as fast as it was born, and it was born as soon as it was conceived; so as it must needs have the imperfections and deformities of an immature birth, besides the weakness of the parent" (Smith 1966, 2: 284). The only possible reason for the rush was to have it published before a decision on the provostship was made. On 24 January 1624 it was duly entered in the Stationers' Company Register and was on sale by 10 April, when Chamberlain again wrote to Carlton that Wotton had "set out lately a book on architecture which I have not leisure to read, but hear it reasonably commended, though at first I thought he had busied himself to little purpose" (Smith 1966, 1: 199). In addition to Prince Charles, Wotton also sent copies to the king, the lord treasurer, the archbishop of Canterbury, the scholar and diplomat William Boswell and, no doubt, the duke of Buckingham and others. He arranged for some copies to be bound in gilt vellum, and corrected their errata in his own hand. On 9 April 1624 Murray died. On 19 July Wotton was appointed provost of Eton College in his place.

It is not of course known how much Wotton's election really depended on *The Elements of Architecture*, rather than his other merits, or the considerable debt of honor owed to him by both the king and Buckingham. But Wotton knew that Buckingham was an enthusiastic patron of architecture and the arts, sure to agree with the well-known opening lines of the preface: "I shall not neede (like the most part of writers) to celebrate the subject which I deliver. In that point I am at ease. For architecture, can want no commendation, where there are noble men, or noble mindes." This alone represents a great advance on previous architectural writers, from Alberti onward, who had invariably felt compelled to justify the subject whenever addressing (as Wotton is doing) an audience of patrons and scholars. His boldness is continued in the treatise itself. This opens with a superbly dramatic generalization ("In architecture as in all other operative arts, the end must direct the operation"), followed immediately by a first principle ("The end is to build well"); a Vitruvian classification ("Well building hath three conditions. Commoditie, firmenes, and delight"); and an early warning of the author's critical distance from his "principall master" ("A common division among the deliverers of this art, though I know not how, some what misplaced by Vitruvius himselfe lib. 1. cap. 3. whom I shalbe willinger to follow, as a master of proportion, then of methode"). These first sentences were clearly intended to be memorable whether or not the reader got beyond them. They exemplify a literary strategy that Wotton has borrowed from the essay-writing tradition of Montaigne and Bacon, not

Henry Wotton. *The Elements of Architecture.* Title page. NGA Lib. Rare Book: NA2515W68

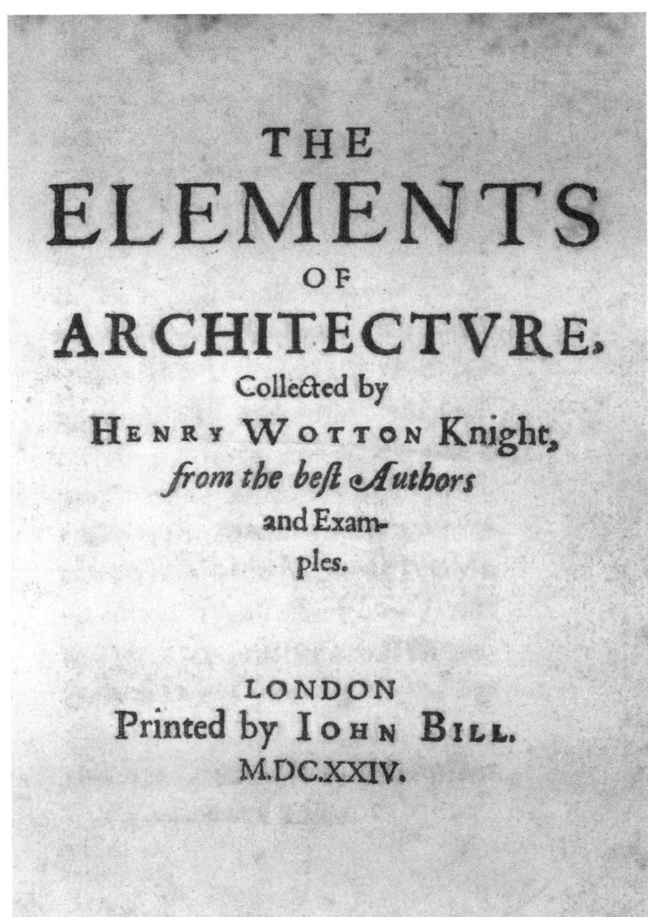

THE
ELEMENTS
OF
ARCHITECTVRE.
Collected by
HENRY WOTTON Knight,
from the best Authors
and Examples.

LONDON
Printed by IOHN BILL.
M.DC.XXIV.

from the much bulkier treatises that were his main sources. One of Wotton's achievements was his skillful removal of serious theoretical discourse about architecture away from illustrated folios, requiring long hours in a library, and into a slim quarto pamphlet that could be carried in the pocket and read almost anywhere.

This can only be achieved if the reader has confidence in the writer's learning. Even by listing those sources directly invoked, Wotton's long study of his subject is obvious. Besides Vitruvius, he had consulted one or other edition of the major Vitruvian commentaries by Guillaume Philandrier, Walther Ryff, and Daniele Barbaro; Alberti's *De re aedificatoria*; Philibert de l'Orme's *Premier tome de l'architecture*; Vasari's *Vite*; Vignola's *Regole delle cinque ordini*; and Palladio's *Quattro libri.* He also refers to Dürer on arch construction (p. 50) and Bernardino Baldi (pp. 49, 79), besides nonarchitectural writers such as Johan van Herne (p. 5), Nicholas of Cusa (p. 88), and Tycho Brahe (p. 113). Classical quotations are drawn from Aristotle, Homer, Pliny the Younger, and Quintilian. The omission of any reference to Serlio's treatise is not surprising, since it was more about practice than theory; but his failure to comment on Vincenzo Scamozzi's *Dell' idea della architettura universale*, published in Venice nine years before, is definitely odd. He also makes no specific references to the drawings by Palladio that he owned, although these presumably influenced his high opinion of the latter. One of his citations, to a treatise on fish ponds by John of Salisbury (p. 114), is mysterious unless, as Hard suggests, Wotton was mistakenly referring to *De piscinis* by Jan Dubravius, bishop of Olomouc.

The recent discovery of Wotton's own copy of Philibert de l'Orme's *Premier tome de l'architecture*, in a 1603 reissue of the sheets of the first edition (1567), gives some important clues to his working methods. In particular, Herbert Mitchell's detailed description of the book suggests an answer to one simple question hitherto avoided by historians, namely, how did Wotton manage to write his treatise so quickly? By his own account, he had not begun it before returning to England on 24 November 1623; yet it was surely complete by the time it was registered with the Stationers' Company exactly two months later. It now seems likely that he had already made extensive notes on his reading, and that he used these, directly or indirectly, when compiling *The Elements.* Besides numerous underlinings, there are twenty-eight short notes in the margins of his copy of De l'Orme, of which five are paraphrases or translations from the French that reappear, modified, in *The Elements.* A sixth (the phrase "The preparation of the materials," from the heading of book one, chap. 13) is reused exactly but in a new context (p. 10). The variety of handwriting styles identified by Mitchell indicates that the marginalia were written at different times and under different circumstances. Considering twenty-two of them were not reused, and that the one lengthy borrowing, on chimneys, is unmarked in this copy, it is unlikely that many of them were made while Wotton was actually compiling his treatise. If, on the other hand, these (and perhaps similar ones in other, untraced, books) were earlier notes to which he was now able to turn, the speed with which he wrote begins to seem more plausible.

Despite the above, Wotton's treatise is far from a mere bookish compilation, and he frequently adds his own observations on building practices in Italy, Germany, and England. Italian buildings to which he specifically refers include S. Giustina, Padua (p. 12); Sanmicheli's Palazzo Grimani, Venice, and Palazzo Bevilacqua, Verona (pp. 42, 119–120); and Palladio's colonnade in the S. Carità, Venice, and Villa Maser (pp. 43–44, 70). These he probably knew firsthand, whereas he may have known Vignola's Palazzo Farnese at Caprarola only by the drawings that he later sent Albertus Morton to show Buckingham. Buckingham's curiosity had evidently been piqued, as Wotton advised Morton that "Upon the design you must play the mountebank. And tell the Duke, that the one paper containeth the plant or ground-lines, the other, the reared work, in perspective with all the dimensions so exactly, as if it please him, he may easily have a model made thereof in pasteboard" (Smith 1966, 2: 286–287). Wotton's own opinion of Caprarola was guarded, noting that "the architect did ingeniously wrestle with divers inconveniences in disposing of the lights, and in saving the vacuities. But as designes of such nature doe ayme at rarity, then commoditie: so for my part I had rather admire them, then commend them" (p. 19). His general admiration for the north Italian Renaissance is also tempered by knowledge of the different requirements and materials in his own country, as when he prefers De l'Orme's above-mentioned advice on chimneys because Italians make only "very frugall fires" (pp. 59–63).

Discussing gardens, Sir Henry Fanshawe's Ware Park receives high praise, and Wotton seems to have known Salomon de Caus' work in Richmond as well as Heidelberg (pp. 110–112), but in general he is carefully nonspecific about English architectural practice, wishing perhaps to avoid charges of partisanship. His principles point to his admiration of Inigo Jones, probably the only contemporary Englishman who could reasonably claim to have studied Italian architecture with as much attention.

English frequently left Wotton with no word for the technical terms used by Vitruvius or later writers, and Latin and Italian borrowings abound. Wotton comments on the problem, familiar to the translator of Robert Peake's Serlio thirteen years before, in his preface—"languages, for the most part in tearmes of art and erudition, retayning their original povertie, and rather growing rich and abundant, in complementall phrases and such froth." When describing the dentils and modillions of the Corinthian order, he knew enough about common usage to add that "our artizans call them teeth and cartouzes" (p. 37). More often he provides his own approximate definitions for foreign words, without reference to the terms used by the trade. Semantics were so important to the study of Vitruvius throughout the Renaissance that it might be interesting to study the effects of the reverse translation process, that is, when, after Wotton's death, the English of *The Elements* was turned into Latin for Johannes de Laet's Vitruvius compendium (*M. Vitruvii Pollionis De architectura libri decem. Cum notis* . . . , Amsterdam, 1649). Wotton's "commoditie, firmenes, and delight," for example, are his equivalents of Vitruvius' *utilitas*, *firmitas*, and *venustas*. In other contexts, the adjective "venust" (and perhaps the noun "venustity") had been used by several earlier English writers to express the last of these words. Wotton may have been intentionally changing the sense of the original from beauty to delight. But if he was simply avoiding an awkward Latinism, the 1649 retranslation of "delight" as "delectationem" probably went beyond his purpose.

It seems to have been this Latin version that was translated into Spanish as *Elementos de Architectura, recogidos de los authores, y exemplares mas aprobados* in 1698 (see Zamora Lucas and Freyre, *Bibliografía Española de Arquitectura [1526–1850]*, Madrid, 1947, no. 75); and the *Elementa architecturae* was also included in Giovanni Poleni and Simone Stratico's Vitruvius anthology (*M. Vitruvii Pollionis Architectura, textu ex recensione codicum emendato, cum exercitationibus* . . . , 1825–1830). No other early architectural book by an Englishman achieved such honors on the Continent. In England, the original text was disseminated in the seventeenth century through the author's collected works (*Reliquiae Wottonianae*, 1651, 1654, 1672, and 1685) and by being abridged for the second and subsequent editions of William Fisher's building manual, *The Mirror of Architecture* (see entry under Scamozzi). In the eighteenth century, the full text was revived and added to Roland Fréart's *Parallel* (1722 and later editions) and Edward Oakley's *Magazine of Architecture* (1730 and later), then anthologized in William Somers' *Second Collection of Scarce and Valuable Tracts* (1750). Appropriately enough, it was therefore readily available throughout the period when interest in Inigo Jones was at its height. G. B.

Bibliography

The Elements of Architecture by Sir Henry Wotton: A Facsimile Reprint. Ed. Frederick Hard. Charlottesville, 1968

Harris, E., and N. Savage. *British Architectural Books and Writers 1556–1785*. Cambridge, 1990

Mitchell, H. "An Unrecorded Issue of Philibert Delorme's *Le premier tome de l'architecture*, Annotated by Sir Henry Wotton." *Journal of the Society of Architectural Historians* 53, no. 1 (March 1994): 20–29

Smith, L. Pearsall. *The Life and Letters of Sir Henry Wotton*. Oxford, 1966

96

Sir Christopher Wren (1632–1723)

A Catalogue of the Churches of the City of London; Royal Palaces; Hospitals; and Publick Edifices; Built by Sr. Christopher Wren . . .

[London]: printed for Sam. Harding, Dan. Browne, & Wm. Bathoe, [1749?]

1985.61.2769

Large folio: 617 × 470 ($24\frac{5}{16} \times 18\frac{1}{2}$)

Pagination 15 engraved plates (7 double-page)

Edition First edition

Christopher Wren. *A Catalogue of the Churches of the City of London.* Tab. 1. Title plate (later state). 1985.61.2769

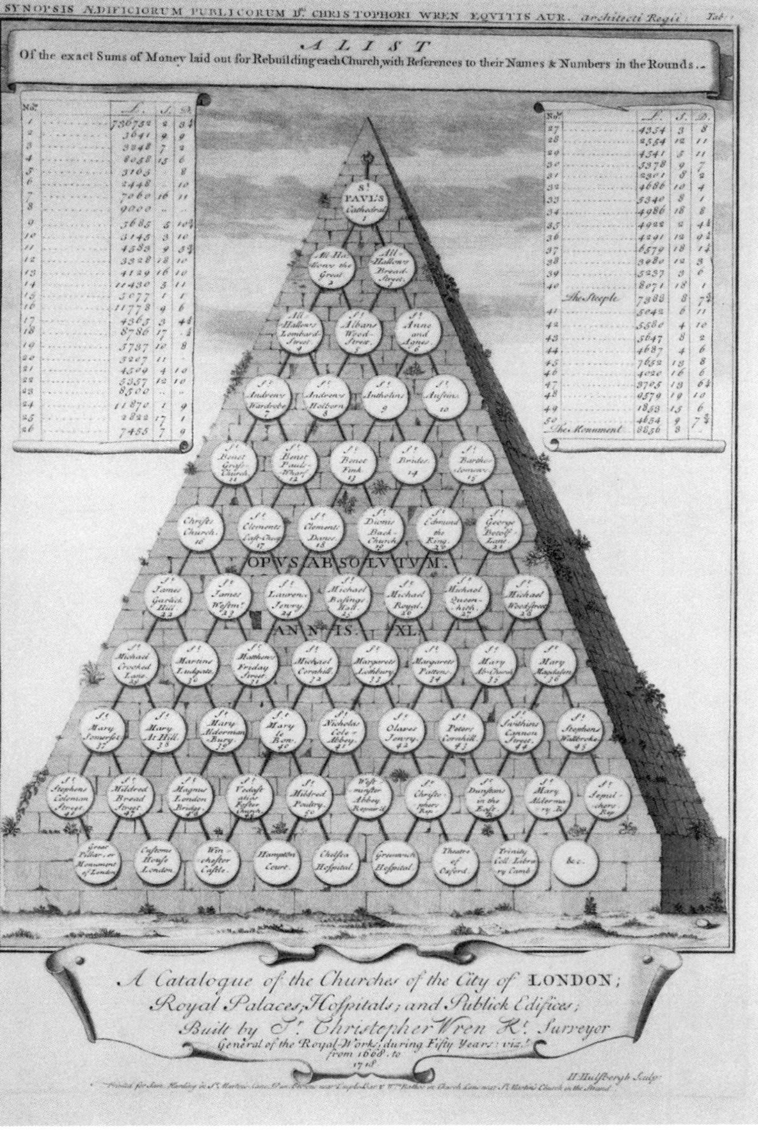

Illustrations 15 engraved plates numbered 1–15, varying widely in size, with captions in Latin and English. Plate 2 consists of 2 plate impressions on 1 leaf, the second used for explanatory text. The title of the whole work is taken from the caption to plate 1, given in Latin as "Synopsis Ædificorum Publicorum Dni. Christopheri Wren. . . ." 3 plates are signed by Nicholas Hawksmoor as draftsman (plates 4, 14, 15), and the credited engravers are Henry Hulsbergh (plates 1–4, 6–7, 9, 14–15), Benjamin Cole (plate 5), Jacob Schijnvoet (plate 8), and Simon Gribelin (plate 11). Plates 10, 12–13 are unsigned. The Millard copy is extra-illustrated with a second impression of plate 1 on a slightly smaller sheet of paper and in a later state (see notes)

Binding Contemporary gray paper boards, recent calf spine and corners

Provenance Engraved bookplate of William Chadwell Mylne (1781–1863), second son of the architect and engineer Robert Mylne (1733–1811)

References Harris and Savage 950

This work is the only published part of a much grander idea which, like the closely related project that became *Parentalia*, was conceived in the 1720s. It would have stood as a proper memorial to Wren's architectural career, and might well have significantly extended his influence, though perhaps not so much within Britain as beyond it. In particular, it might have had a similar effect on North America as Gibbs' *Book of Architecture* (1728), and would certainly have found admirers on the Continent. But, instead, the fifteen plates that constitute this suite, and give such a partial record of Wren's work, were not publicly available for more than twenty years after their completion, and were hardly published in any proper sense even then.

The sad and complex tale of what happened has been pieced together by Eileen Harris (Harris and Savage 1990, 503–508). Sir Christopher Wren's son, also called Christopher, began preparing a volume of designs, from the very substantial archive he had inherited, soon after his father's death on 23 February 1723. The first part was to be called *A Specimen of the Works in Architecture of Sir Christopher Wren.* A start was made on engraving the plates, and at some stage Wren junior felt justified in drafting "Proposals for Publishing by Subscription," though these were apparently never printed. The proposals describe the plates as "near finished," to be issued to subscribers for a guinea. This publication was to be a separate step toward the more ambitious plan, a complete description of Wren's major works, "The Plates to be in a like Scale with those in Fontana's History of the Vatican Church of St. Peter in Rome," followed by his unexecuted designs, and lastly his historical and theoretical essays.

Wren's copy of the book to which the proposals refer, Carlo Fontana's *Templum Vaticanum* (Rome, 1694), is now in the British Architectural Library (RIBA). It is a thick folio with a substantial text and large plates. It may have seemed natural to allude to a book on St. Peter's when proposing a monograph on the architect of St. Paul's; and the studious evasion of any comparison with the native books of the Palladians, so hostile to Wren's memory, is understandable. But whereas Gibbs, a student of Fontana, was able to push his own collection of designs into the marketplace in spite of Lord Burlington's so-called Rule of Taste, Wren junior, who subscribed to Gibbs' book, evidently found himself unable to do the same for his late father. Years passed, and not even the *Specimen* materialized. As late as December 1739 Wren junior was writing to a cousin, James Hodgson, that the three proofs from "large copper plates" he had sent him were not to be allowed "away out of your possession because not publish'd." In early 1741 John Ward ended a brief account of Wren's architectural career with the comment:

> I have indeed been shorter in this part of his character, as I understand that province is intrusted in the hands of a very ingenious and learned gentleman; who, it is hoped, will in due time oblige the public with a full account of the just debt due to his memory for adorning his country with so many of its finest buildings. Several of which have been already ingraven for that purpose; tho with less art and care than they deserve, for want of proper artists in designs of architecture (*Lives of the Professors of Gresham College* 1740 [i.e., 1741], 105).

Since Ward had corresponded with Wren junior when preparing his book, it is reasonable to assume that he introduced this information by consent, and therefore that one cause of delay may have been a dissatisfaction with the plates hitherto prepared, which may of course have included some subsequently suppressed. However, just by mentioning it in print, Ward implies that the project had still not been abandoned, and he evidently saw it as a part of what became *Parentalia*.

The next reference to it is more final, and comes in the same month as Wren junior's death. George Vertue, jotting down whatever he knew or had heard about that interested him, recorded in his notebook entry for August 1747 that "at Hampton Court near the Palace livd Mr Christp^hr Wren son of S^r. Chris Wren the famous architect, this Gent had great Collections of his Fathers—and was inclind once to publish much of them but some disgust happend tho many plates of Architecture & buildings—were already done. yet that work never came to light—he was well striken in years—and grew weak and feeble before he died—aged about 70—he left a Son" (Vertue, *Note Books* 3, in *Walpole Society* 22 [1934], 136). The historian is left to speculate whether the "disgust" that "happened" related to the quality of the plates, or Wren's unpopularity during the Palladian revival, or both. Had his son pursued the project with less ambition and more energy, it is hard to imagine that either of these obstacles could not have been overcome.

It may be significant that the little we know about his efforts does not include any negotiations with the printsellers and publishers on whom its success or failure would largely depend.

Those copperplates that were already engraved passed to the architect's grandson, Stephen. He sold them, probably, along with other parts of his inheritance, at Abraham Langford's auction on 4–6 April 1749. Vertue noted that a volume of bills and accounts relating to Wren's churches "was sold in Mr Wrens sale & bought with all the Copper Engraved plates—by M^r. Harding & Batho" (Vertue, *Note Books* 6, in *Walpole Society* 30 [1955], 149). These might have been the *Specimen* engravings, as might have been lot 44 on 5 April, described as "Fourteen Copper Plates of Antiquities, Architecture, &c." In any case, three printsellers, Samuel Harding, Daniel Browne, and William Bathoe, acquired them and the present suite finally made its appearance sometime afterward. It is usually dated 1749, following a note by the historian Richard Gough (*British Topography*, 1780, 1: 611). Gough, however, is not always reliable, and it seems unlikely John Gwynn would have troubled to publish Wren's plan of London in October 1749 if Hulsbergh's version of the same was already available (see pl. 2, described below), so 1750 or even later is just as likely. It was probably the new owners who numbered the plates, adding their imprint at the same time. Remarkably, as will be seen, they were also prepared to invest time and money into improving one of the plates; but there would have been no question of commissioning further designs to complete the series. In February 1750, Harding was among the booksellers who were exhibiting *Parentalia*, and the disappointing response to this would only have confirmed his decision not to expend much time or labor on what was now a separate and far less finished work.

The plates as published have been listed and illustrated in two volumes of the series published by the Wren Society, using the Soane Museum library copy (see 14: xii–xiii, pls. I–V, IX, XI, and XXII; 18: 189 ff, pls. XVI–XXI). All have parallel Latin and English captions. The Latin caption to plate I reads "SYNOPSIS ÆDIFICORUM PUBLICORUM D^ni. CHRISTOPHERI WREN EQVITIS AUR. Architecti Regii:," and this, or the English version given above, is the title by which the collection is now generally known. In fact both captions refer only to plate I, and were not intended to describe any of the other fourteen. The "Catalogue" is presented as a series of linked medals on a pyramid, the inscriptions naming fifty of Wren's churches (more or less alphabetically, but with St. Paul's at the top), five that he repaired, his eight most important secular commissions, and a final et cetera. The pyramid itself carries the legend "OPVS. ABSOLVTVM. ANNIS. XL." Like eight others in the series, it is signed as engraved by Henry Hulsbergh, who died in 1729. The design is ingenious, even if it ignores the laws of perspective.

Christopher Wren. *A Catalogue of the Churches of the City of London*. Tab. 8. View of the wooden model of St. Paul's Cathedral, "according to the first design of the architect." 1985.61.2769

Ward used a proof copy of this plate for his list of Wren's works in the appendix to the above-mentioned book, noting some additions and adding that "besides these, several other designs of buildings were drawn by him in pursuance of the royal commands, that were not put in execution, but are yet in the hands of his son" (appendix, 37). The plate Ward saw could not have included the banner heading and two scrolls that give "A List Of the exact Sums of Money laid out for Re-building each Church, with References to their Names & Numbers in the Rounds." For these were added by Harding, Browne, and Bathoe after they acquired the suite: the Millard copy has the plate in both states, both carrying their imprint. Clearly, the new owners wished not only to exploit the copperplates they had acquired, but the bills and accounts that Vertue had noted as well. These accounts now form part of the Rawlinson collection at the Bodleian Library. A careful hand must have copied the figures over to the illustration: most of the totals match perfectly, and for St. Mary Somerset there is only a farthing—one quarter of one penny—difference (see the "Table of the fifty-four churches with trades and costs from the official building accounts," Wren Society 10: [45]–53). The most interesting figures are for St. Mary-le-Bow, which differs by a few pounds from the Wren Society tabulation, and for four churches whose accounts are left blank by the society, described as missing: St. Andrew's, Holborn (£9,000), St. Clement Dane's (£8,786 17s ½d), St. James, Piccadilly (£8,500), and St. Mary, Aldermanbury (£5,237 3s 6d). St. Paul's is costed at £736,752 2s 3¼d, and the monument commemorating the Great Fire at £8,856 8s 0d.

Plate 2, dedicated to Thomas, earl of Pembroke, and dated 1724, shows Wren's plan for rebuilding London after the Great Fire of 1666, engraved after the drawing now at All Souls College, Oxford (see Wren Society 12: pl. xxv). The area burned down was supposed to be colored by hand. A second plate has been used to add an explanation extracted from the "Proposals for rebuilding the City of London . . ." given in part two, section two of *Parentalia* (268–269). John Gwynn published a version of this plan in October 1749 to demonstrate how "narrow spirited contests about identical property" had thwarted a great idea (see Harris and Savage 1990, 214–215). Plate three is Wren's first approved design for the monument. This dramatic design is topped by a phoenix and has flames up and around the pillar (for the original drawing, see Wren Society 5: pl. xxxv). Inset views of Roman columns have been added, as classical justifications for the design. Plate 4 shows the very different monument that was actually built, in an elaborately didactic engraving by Hulsbergh after a 1723 drawing by Wren's former assistant Nicholas Hawksmoor.

The next nine plates all relate to St. Paul's, comprising a plan, elevation, section and view of the so-called Great Model Design (pls. 5–8); a plan of the cathedral as built (pl. 9); a section "Wherein the Dome is represented according to a Former Design" (pl. 10); a section of the transverse aisle (pl. 11); and elevations of the east and west ends (pls. 12–13). This group includes plates engraved by Benjamin Cole, Jacob Schijnvoet, and Simon Gribelin. The Great Model engravings form a coherent unit, but the cathedral as built is woefully underrepresented, and had been treated better by other engravers, notably William Emmett in a suite published by Thomas Bowles nearly fifty years before. The final two plates illustrate St. Mary-le-Bow, Cheapside. Both are engraved by Hulsbergh after Hawksmoor, the first with a dedication by Wren junior to the memory of his father, dated 1726. A preparatory drawing for this plate is at All Souls, and a proof engraving, before the addition of the explanatory cartouches, is in the British Library (Sloane Add. MS 5238, no. 68; see Wren Society 9: pls. 25–26).

Not surprisingly, the suite was never reprinted and is now rarely found complete. The copy in the Millard collection was owned by the architect and engineer Robert Mylne (1733–1811); like many of his books it contains the bookplate of his second son, William Chadwell Mylne (1781–1863). This is an interesting, almost poignant, association, for Robert was an admirer of Wren and for many years the surveyor in charge of St. Paul's. Near the end of his career his thoughts turned toward his great predecessor, and in 1807 he erected a long overdue monument to him in St. Paul's crypt, where he was buried, and next to which Mylne himself would soon be buried, too. The crypt being a relatively obscure place for visitors to pay homage, he also copied Wren's epitaph onto a conspicuous brass plaque in the cathedral itself. Here anyone following the advice of its famous final lines—"Lector, si monumentum requiris, circumspice"—would be rewarded with a proper view of Wren's greatest triumph. Such acts were part of the huge salvaging operation performed on Wren's reputation that gained momentum in the early part of the nineteenth century, and has continued ever since. G. B.

Bibliography

Colvin, H. *A Biographical Dictionary of British Architects 1600–1840*. 3d ed. New Haven and London, 1995

Downes, K. *Christopher Wren*. London, 1971

The First (–Twentieth) Volume of the Wren Society. Ed. Wren Society. Oxford, 1924–1943. Especially vols. 5, 9, 10, 12, 14, and 18.

Harris, E., and N. Savage. *British Architectural Books and Writers 1556–1785*. Cambridge, 1990

Little, B. *Sir Christopher Wren: A Historical Biography*. London, 1975

Whinney, M. *Wren*. London, 1971

97

Sir Christopher Wren (1632–1723)

Parentalia: Or, Memoirs Of The Family of the Wrens; Viz. Of Mathew Bishop of Ely, Christopher Dean of Windsor, &c. But Chiefly Of Sir Christopher Wren, Late Surveyor-General of the Royal Buildings, President of the Royal Society, &c. &c. In which is contained, besides his Works, A great Number of Original Papers and Records; On Religion, Politicks, Anatomy, Mathematicks, Architecture, Antiquities; and most Branches of Polite Literature. Compiled, by his Son Christopher; Now published by his Grandson, Stephen Wren, Esq; With the Care of Joseph Ames, F.R.S. and Secretary to the Society of Antiquaries, London

London: printed for T. Osborn; and R. Dodsley, 1750

NGA Lib. Rare Book: N44W948W73 fol.

Folio: 348 × 200 (13 11/16 × 8 11/16)

Pagination [2], xii, [4], 120, 125–159, [1], 181–368, [4] pp., mezzotint frontispiece portrait, [11] engraved plates

Edition First edition

Text pp. [1] title page, printed in red and black (verso blank); i–ii list of subscribers; [iii]–vi editor's preface; [vii]–xii introduction; [xiii–xvi] table of contents; [1]–368 text; [369–371] names index; [372] directions to the binder

Illustrations A mezzotint portrait of Christopher Wren, Jr., engraved by John Faber, is bound as a frontispiece. In addition there are 11 engraved plates consisting of a dedication with armorial headpiece, engraved by E. Thorowgood; a portrait of Matthew Wren engraved by Gerard van der Gucht; a portrait of Christopher Wren, dean of Windsor, also by Van der Gucht; a portrait of Sir Christopher Wren "Engraved from a Bust by S. Coignand [i.e., Coignard]"; and 7 diagrams engraved by J. Mynde (3) or by Van der Gucht after Henry Flitcroft (4)

Binding Early nineteenth-century paneled and blind-stamped russia, spine with gilt ornaments and devices in blind-tooled compartments separated by pairs of false raised bands, gilt title and date, marbled gilt edges

Provenance The William Beckford and Earl of Rosebery copy. With a note on the verso of the first endpaper "Beckford Sale 1883. / lot 596," a page of Beckford's notes on the third endpaper, and the engraved armorial bookplate of Archibald Philip, earl of Rosebery

References ESTC t145737; Harris and Savage 949

THE HISTORY of Christopher Wren junior's *Parentalia* shares much in common with the compilation of his father's architectural designs, *A Catalogue of the Churches* . . . , and had an equally slow progress toward publication. There are three surviving manuscript versions, of which the earliest can be dated to about 1719, well before the architect's death in 1723 (British Library Add. MS 25,071; see Harris and Savage 1990, 507, n 12 for details). Most of the work on two later manuscripts, both fair copies, was completed by 1728, although extracts from later books by other authors were occasionally added. In early 1741 Wren junior sent information to John Ward, and in his *Lives of the Professors of Gresham College*, 1740 [i.e., 1741], Ward looked forward to the son's biography of his father. But by then the son in his turn had grown old, and weak, and had lost interest. The project was not brought forward, the manuscript remained unaltered, and it duly passed to the architect's grandson, Stephen Wren, after Christopher's death on 24 August 1747. Stephen sent a lot of his inheritance to auction, but delivered *Parentalia* to Joseph Ames, fellow of the Royal Society and secretary of the Society of Antiquaries, for him to organize its publication. On 3 February 1750 the book was said to be "in the press" when proposals for printing it by subscription appeared in the *General Advertiser*. The printers—apparently John Hart and Henry Woodfall—worked directly from Christopher's manuscript. The book, probably ready late in 1750, was announced as published on 15 January 1751.

So, finally, the famous architect had some sort of memorial in print. Despite its lengthy gestation, *Parentalia* still ranks as the first published biography of an English architect, excluding the brief memoir of Inigo Jones' life added to the second edition of his description of Stonehenge (1725). But although *Parentalia* has therefore been described as "the father of English architectural history" (Harris and Savage 1990, 506), it was not conceived, executed, or marketed as an architectural book. Half of it is devoted to Matthew Wren, bishop of Ely (1585–1667), and to the architect's father, Matthew's younger brother, Christopher Wren, dean of Windsor (1589–1658). The memoir of the architect is divided into two parts, the first further subdivided to itemize his considerable achievements in mathematics, anatomy, astronomy, and other sciences. Only the second part (pp. 263–368) is given over to his architecture. It is more a miscellaneous gathering of source material than a thoughtful, connected narrative.

A brief introduction ends with the guarded but accurate promise that "A view (however short and imperfect) of the Surveyor's proceedings . . . may be taken from the following sections, put together out of some scatter'd papers, and publick accounts, such as the collector hath hitherto met with" (p. 264). What follows immediately alerts the reader to Christopher junior's real interests, not entirely relevant to the task he has in hand, which may fairly be described as academic antiquarianism. For the architect's career must wait while his son first outlines the Anglo-Saxon origins of London, and quibbles over the inscription on a Roman tablet dug up after the Great Fire. Wren's "Proposals for rebuilding the City of London" are then transcribed, and a paragraph taken from James Ralph's *Critical Review of the Publick Buildings . . . in, and about London and Westminster* (1734). Ralph was probably the first to state that "The Fire of London, furnish'd the most perfect occasion that can ever happen in any city, to rebuild it with pomp and regularity" (p. 268), and that "the hurry of rebuilding, and the disputes about property" prevented Wren's "glorious scheme" from being executed. This version of events has since been shown to be partisan—the fact was that Wren's scheme, like others, was laid aside as unworkable. But as a critical commentary, it was surely more relevant than Wren junior's quotation from Seneca on the burning of ancient Lyon.

The history of St. Paul's Cathedral, which follows, is given in some detail. A description of the so-called Great Model includes the anecdote that "the Surveyor in private conversation, always seem'd to set a higher value on this design, than any he had made before or since" (p. 282). Here more than anywhere else the reader might regret the separation of the *Parentalia* from the plates commissioned by Wren junior, now owned by Harding, Browne, and Bathoe. For their appreciation of Wren's masterpiece, readers have to make do with one small, unsigned vignette of the west front as built (p. 283).

After Wren's description of his work on Westminster Abbey, both father and son's opinions of Gothic architecture are given in a section on repair work at Salisbury Cathedral. This, like the brief descriptions of Wren's fifty-four London churches, the account of the London monument, and the "catalogue" of Wren's other royal commissions that follow, is unillustrated. Wren's work for the universities is listed but only his first executed building, the Sheldonian Theatre in Oxford, is treated in any detail, focusing on the "geometrical flat-floor" from which its ceiling was hung. This celebrated innovation consisted of a complex system of wooden trusses made from interlocking scarf joints. It had already been illustrated and described (probably with Wren's cooperation) in Robert Plot's *Natural History of Oxfordshire* (1677; 2d ed., 1705). The four *Parentalia* illustrations were presumably copied from Plot, although the presentation is slightly different. They were engraved by Gerard van der Gucht after drawings by Henry Flitcroft. The latter's interest was natural: he was apprenticed as a joiner before being taken under Lord Burlington's wing and turned into a loyal Palladian. The Sheldonian's original beams have long since been replaced, but not before Wren's next biographer, James Elmes, had inspected them and confirmed the accuracy of Flitcroft's drawings.

Christopher junior ends his account with a rambling "Conclusion," quoting praise from his father's admirers

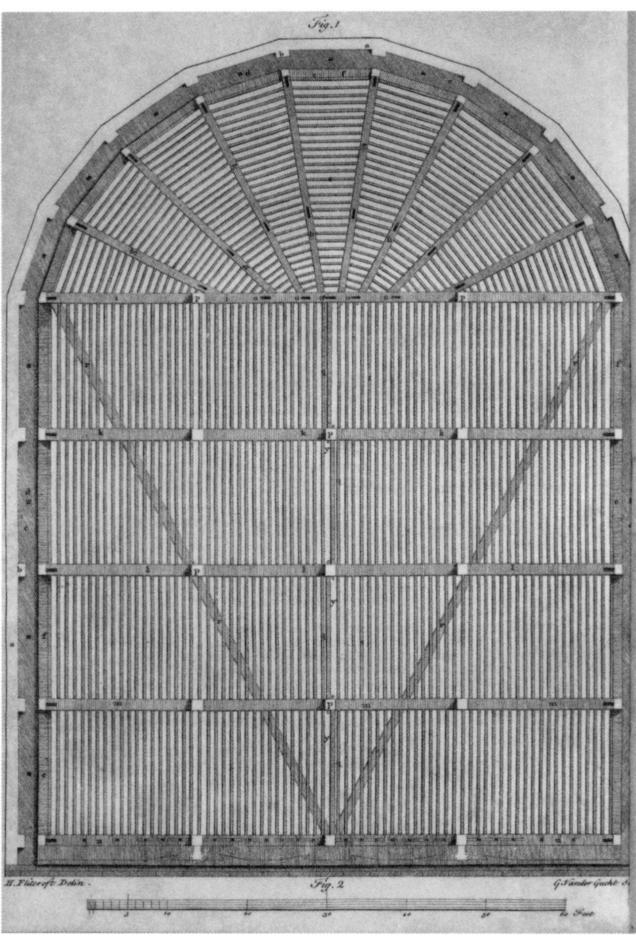

Christopher Wren. *Parentalia: or, Memoirs of the Family of the Wrens.* Section XII, fig. 1. Roof of the Sheldonian Theatre at Oxford. NGA Lib. Rare Book: N44W948W73 fol.

and sprinkling his asides with classical quotations. An appendix prints four of the architect's tracts "From some rough draughts, imperfect," which form the bulk of his theoretical legacy, although another tract on architecture survived unpublished. These have been analyzed in detail for the tantalizing glimpses they give of Wren's architectural philosophy. In doing so, caution has had to be exercised because the original manuscripts have been lost, and only Christopher junior's transcripts survive. They are illustrated by diagrams (tract two), and plans and elevations of the Temple of Diana at Ephesus and Mars Ultor at Rome (tract four). Stephen might have elected to add a biography of his father, to bring the family memoirs up to date, but provides only a brief note in the preface and, as a frontispiece, a fine mezzotint portrait of him by John Faber. The portrait of Sir Christopher himself, by contrast, is a crude reproduction of a bust by the little-known S. Coignard (or, as spelled on the plate, Coignand).

Stephen paid for the book's printing, and must have felt he had acquitted himself well enough, saying as much in his short preface and adding "that [financial] interest had so little share in this undertaking, that if the book clears its charges, my pecuniary views are gratified to their utmost extent." It is extremely unlikely that it did so. A mere forty-five people and one institution (the Mathematical Society at Wapping) subscribed to *Parentalia*, accounting for forty-seven copies in all—the physician Richard Mead ordered two. Only one architect appears on the list (Charles Labelye). This lack of interest on the part of the profession was perhaps natural, given that the book was not adapted to their use. Although it has been invaluable to later historians, the section on Wren's architecture must have seemed strange to many contemporary readers, edited a generation before from fragments written a generation before that.

In any case, architects were certainly not the son's, or the grandson's, target audience. Much more important was the approval of established institutions, and in particular the Royal Society, to whom Stephen presented the original manuscript on 22 February 1751. Another fifty copies of the printed work can be accounted for by reproducing his two presentation letters to the universities at Oxford and Cambridge. Both are signed and dated "Great Russell-street, April 1, 1751," and were first published by Elmes (who does not give the names of the addressees):

> Sir,
> My grandfather, Sir Christopher Wren, was so well known, and his memory is so much esteemed at Oxford, that the history of his life and works will not, I am convinced, be thought a disagreeable present. I have, therefore, sent thirty books by the waggon, and as I had the honour of being educated under the judicious Dr. Newton, have fixed upon that most worthy friend of mine to present every college and hall in the university with one of them. Desiring he would also do me the favour to accept the remaining copies, and distribute them among those he thinks most worthy. I shall make a tour into the country in a day or two, when I hope to have the pleasure of seeing you; but if the holidays prevent my having that pleasure, you will please to favour me with a line to let me know what reception the books met with. I am, Sir, &c.

> Sir,
> Mr. Ames acquainted me a few days ago that he had seen you, and that you had been so kind as to promise to present, in my name, one of my books of Parentalia to every college and hall in your university, for which I return you thanks. I have therefore sent twenty books; but as I am informed that exceeds the number of colleges, I desire you will accept of the remaining copies to be distributed among those you think most worthy; and I should be particularly obliged to you, if you would favour me with an answer, to let me know what reception the books met with. I am Sir, &c.

There is more than a hint in these letters that Stephen is offloading a surplus, just a few months after publication, albeit to suitably respectable venues. This is a common enough fate for privately published memoirs even today.

Christopher Wren. *Parentalia: or, Memoirs of the Family of the Wrens.* Part 1, section 1 [p. 180]. Portrait of Sir Christopher Wren. NGA Lib. Rare Book: N44W948W73 fol.

The history of another copy of the *Parentalia* should also be noted. In 1911, the Wren family's "heirloom" copy was presented to the Royal Institute of British Architects. Bound in with it are a large number of prints and manuscripts, all reproduced in a facsimile issued by the Gregg Press in 1965. G. B.

Bibliography

Colvin, H. *A Biographical Dictionary of British Architects 1600–1840*. 3d ed. New Haven and London, 1995

Downes, K. *Christopher Wren*. London, 1971

Elmes, J. *Memoirs of the Life and Works of Sir Christopher Wren*. London, 1823

The First (–Twentieth) Volume of the Wren Society. Ed. Wren Society. Oxford, 1924–1943. Especially vol. 19

Harris, E., and N. Savage. *British Architectural Books and Writers 1556–1785*. Cambridge, 1990

Reddaway, T. F. *The Rebuilding of London after the Great Fire*. London, 1940

Index

I. Persons, Institutions, and Books

This index covers personal names, names of institutions, and titles of books in the collection (their principal authors noted in capitals).

References are to pages except for boldface numbers, which indicate catalogue entries. These numbers follow titles of books in the collection, the names of those who participated in their production (authors, engravers, publishers, et al.), and the names of former owners.

Page numbers in italics indicate illustrations in this volume.

N.B. The qualifying term "as publisher" is here used in its broadest sense to include all names mentioned in the imprint except printers. The term "engraver" covers all intaglio processes.

C

D

H

I

J

K

L

M

Q

R

S

Y

Z

II. Buildings, Country Houses, and Classical Sites

Page numbers in italics indicate illustrations in this volume.